FOUNDATIONS of CLINICAL and COUNSELING PSYCHOLOGY

fourth edition

For information about this book, contact:
Waveland Press, Inc.
4180 IL Route 83, Suite 101
Long Grove, IL 60047-9580
(847) 634-0081
info@waveland.com
www.waveland.com

10-digit ISBN 1-57766-410-8
13-digit ISBN 978-1-57766-410-9

Printed in the United States of America

12 11 10 9 8

To Dan and Karen

CONTENTS

PART III PSYCHOTHERAPEUTIC APPROACHES 135

PART IV
CONTEMPORARY ISSUES 365

PREFACE

At the present time, the field of clinical psychology and psychotherapy continues to confront many challenges. In this, the fourth edition of our clinical and counseling psychology text, we focus on updating trends toward the future while retaining the coverage of the topics that have traditionally constituted the field of clinical psychology. Our original goal in writing the first edition was to design an introductory professional psychology text that emphasized psychotherapy while covering other important topics such as assessment, history, and professional, legal, and ethical issues. Our experience was that our students in introductory clinical psychology courses wanted more material on psychotherapy than other texts provided.

In this edition, we build on that foundation by updating and adding coverage of topics such as brief therapy, computerized treatment programs, Internet testing, online therapy, the development of treatment guidelines and the controversies associated with them, radical behavior therapies, the importance of cultural and gender issues, the expanding roles for psychologists in neuropsychology and primary health care, including the issue of prescription privileges, and developments in the fields of psychotherapy research and psychotherapy integration. We have added an instructor's manual and a Web site for instructors and students.

As in the previous editions, one of our goals has been to write a useful book. It is impossible to learn how to do therapy from a survey-type textbook (or from any book, for that matter). We have opted to focus on presenting a clear, understandable view of how each theoretical perspective regards the person, the person's problems, and how to help the person change. While we could not hope to teach counseling skills, we do hope to give students a "feel" for how therapists of differing persuasions see their clients and work with them. We believe that our book gets "inside" the differing perspectives better than any other book.

We also believe that a useful book should be flexible so that individual instructors and readers can use it differently to suit their needs. We wrote this book so that the chapters can be read in almost any order because of careful cross-referencing and a consistent, eclectic, integrative viewpoint that makes connections between topics.

Finally, a useful book should be readable and enjoyable. We have tried to write the text in an interesting, down-to-earth manner, using case material and everyday examples to flesh out the more abstract theoretical material. Because we like to laugh, we have included several items of humor, believing that humor can "help the medicine go down" and illustrate important points in a memorable manner.

The current edition emphasizes the extensive changes that are occurring in the helping professions. Major changes in how these services are paid for affect both how these services are provided and the nature of the services. The individual private practitioner who hangs out his or her "shingle" and works with clients for as long as he or she and the client deem necessary is an endangered species. Increasingly, psychologists and other types of counselors are working for health maintenance organizations or getting reimbursed through managed care companies that carefully monitor the length and kind of services provided in order to control and cut costs. As a result, psychotherapy is becoming briefer and more focused. At the same time, these changes in practice may lead to opportunities for psychologists to be increasingly responsible for health care in general.

Accompanying these changes is an increased pressure for accountability: Health care and governmental agencies want to know that what they are paying for is cost-effective. We cover the controversy in the American Psychological Association over "empirically validated or supported treatments" both in the chapter on psychotherapy research and in our concluding chapter on the future of professional psychology.

The research chapter is included because we believe it is important that students be aware of the great difficulties involved in sorting out belief and opinion from knowledge about psychotherapy. We are dismayed whenever a student is dogmatically sure that the behavioral approach or the humanistic approach or the systems approach is best. We hope that the research chapter will introduce students to the complexities of how one goes about truly *knowing* something, provide them with an overview of the current (but rapidly changing) state of knowledge, and increase their critical reasoning skills about research and the nature of knowledge.

Our text is written from an eclectic, integrative point of view. We do not believe that any one approach to psychotherapy or counseling can be said to be "the" correct one. Instead, we believe that the practitioner of the future will have theoretical and empirical knowledge of differing points of view and an ability to use "what works" with individual clients.

The psychotherapy integration chapter has been updated. When we were writing our first edition, the field of psychotherapy integration was young (and so were we!). The Society for the Exploration of Psychotherapy Integration was only a year or so old. Since then, the *Journal of Psychotherapy Integration* has been founded, and numerous books and articles have been published in which attempts are made to integrate various aspects of the differing approaches to psychotherapy. One of us (JT) would like to point out that the other of us (AB) has, since the first edition, become an internationally recognized expert and author in the field of psychotherapy theory integration. In addition to summarizing the work of others, the chapter on psychotherapy integration is based largely on Dr. Bohart's work and describes his theoretical framework for how differing approaches converge. Readers of the this edition will benefit from his latest thinking on this topic.

We believe this edition remains suitable for a one-semester course; however, it is designed so that instructors may assign selected chapters if they do not wish to use the whole text. Some might choose, for instance, to emphasize assessment and perhaps not assign all parts of all chapters on psychotherapy. Others might decide that psychotherapy integration or the history of clinical psychology are topics that need not be covered in their course. Generally, the chapters have been written so that they stand on their own. The psychotherapy integration chapter is the one exception; it depends on having read most of the earlier chapters on individual.

Although this book was originally written for use in upper-division clinical psychology courses, we have since learned that it has been used in a much wider range of contexts. We know of instructors who have used it as a text in graduate courses on personality theory in clinical psychology programs, in graduate courses on counseling theory in education programs, and in upper division counseling psychology classes. We also know of some practitioners in the United States and England who bought the book for their own review, and it would make an excellent reference for mental health professionals. The usefulness of our text in such different contexts is very gratifying.

Great appreciation goes to the reviewers of our various editions: Jim Archer, University of Florida, Gainesville; Lenore Defonso, Indiana University, Purdue; Gerald Mohatt, University of Alaska, Fairbanks; Dick Schmidt, California State University, Long Beach; Mary Anne Watson, University of Colorado, Denver; Leslie Greenberg, York University, Toronto; Beverly Palmer, California State University, Dominguez Hills; Susan Regas, California School of Professional Psychology, Los Angeles; Robert Rosenbaum, California Institute of Integral Studies, San Francisco; Jeremy Safran, Derner Institute at Adelphi University, New York; Franz R. Epting, University of Florida; Ruthellen Josselson, Towson State University; Joseph Lyons, University of California, Davis; Lyle Schmidt, The Ohio State University; T. Gale Thompson, Bethany College; Donald H. Voss, Slippery Rock College of Pennsylvania; Rudolph L. Zlody, College of the Holy Cross; and Fran Miller, California State University, Dominguez Hills; with special gratitude to proofreader extraordinaire, Hope Todd, and many thanks to the excellent editor of this edition, Jeni Ogilvie.

Judith Todd
Arthur C. Bohart

PART I

In the Beginning

Professional Psychology in Context

Frank S., age 38, unemployed engineer, sits at home most days, watching TV and drinking beer. He appears glum, says little, and reacts with irritation when his wife or children try to talk to him. While he dozes frequently during the day, he has difficulty sleeping at night; therefore, he is too tired to look for work. Frank's thoughts center on why he can't find work, and when drunk, he occasionally stands on the front porch accusing the neighbors of being "after" him, along with "the others." Mrs. S., who began to work as an office clerk when her husband was laid off his job, is beginning to lose patience with his depressed mood, confused thinking, erratic behavior, and constant drinking. She thinks he needs help. If she is correct, what sort of help does he need and who should provide it?

Clinical psychology and counseling psychology are helping professions. In the United States today many individuals, groups, and institutions offer to help people in many different ways. Schools and churches, for instance, attempt to help members of the community by teaching academic skills and moral behavior. Many groups, from weight clinics to seminars on how to become rich and famous, are in the business of changing the behavior of others. Although clinical psychology and counseling psychology exist in a social matrix with a variety of helping groups, nevertheless they can be distinguished from others in several important ways. Professional psychologists are just that—professional. They have attended recognized universities where they have received extensive postgraduate education and training in research, evaluation, and implementation of helping methods. They are licensed or certified by the state to engage in specific kinds of helping practices. They are guided by a professional code of ethics.

Educated in the graduate departments of universities and independent graduate schools, professional psychologists are unique in that there is emphasis on research in their training. Clinical psychology as a field was based on what is known as the scientist-practitioner model, a model that incorporates both academic research and applied helping skills as necessary for the profession. Clinical and counseling psychologists employ helping methods and theories that are more likely to have been subjected to empirical research than those of other helpers.

Although professional psychologists are trained to help people and to change behavior, each situation they encounter is unique and requires evaluation in order to determine the best plan of action. The questions of who needs professional help and what kind of help is needed may be answered differently by the various individuals involved. Take Frank S. as an example. His neighbors may regard him as dangerous, needing imprisonment; his minister may see him as weak, needing spiritual help; his wife may see him as sick, needing medical help; and Frank himself may deny that he needs help at all.

Helpers, too, may recommend different types of help, as even professional helpers may disagree on what is needed. A psychiatrist may believe Frank S. suffers from a disease, a literal "mental illness," requiring proper diagnosis and medication. A psychologist may see him as exhibiting emotional, cognitive, or behavioral disorders requiring psychological intervention. Even within the specialty of clinical psychology, a psychodynamic therapist may view Frank as having unconscious intrapsychic conflicts requiring individual psychotherapy; a cognitive-behavioral therapist may see him as living in an environment that reinforces his helpless behavior and hopeless cognitions and as needing modifications in his environment and thinking; a neuropsychologist would want to consider the possibility of brain damage; a family therapist might consider Frank's problem as a symptom of family dysfunction; and a community psychologist might regard Frank as reacting to social change and in need of a support group and a job. Decisions about what type of help best suits the needs of a particular individual will draw from different models and theories of disorder and treatment and may also reflect a level of competition between helping professions.

The question of who should receive professional help also reflects society's attitudes toward problem behavior. These attitudes change with time. In the eighteenth century in the United States, public drunkenness was considered normal, socially acceptable behavior; at that time, Frank's drinking behavior would not have been considered a problem. In the nineteenth century, excessive drinking came to be regarded as a sin, to be railed against by ministers and temperance workers. By the twentieth century, public drunkenness was a crime, to be controlled through laws and imprisonment. In recent decades, excessive drinking has been regarded as a disorder requiring professional help and as a disease requiring medical treatment and hospitalization.

When public drunkenness was socially accepted, it was not defined as a problem. Once excessive drinking came to be viewed as a problem of concern to the whole community, how best to prevent and control it raised the difficult issue of balancing traditional values of individual liberty with the need to control the behavior of certain individuals. Our society is comfortable dealing with individuals who engage in behaviors that have serious consequences for others, such as murder or assault, by depriving them of their liberty. Our society seems to prefer trying to use medical treatment or psychological help to control individuals who engage in behaviors with less serious or more ambiguous consequences. In fact, it has been argued that in the United States there is a tendency to medicalize social problems that have not been solved by other means. Furthermore, by medicalizing or psychologizing social problems, Americans can continue to regard them as problems of the individuals involved and thereby avoid community responsibility and the difficulties of social change. Clinical and counseling psychology allow us to treat social problems while preserving the value of individualism.

Because our society constantly redefines social problems and the types of behaviors that require professional help, the roles of clinical and counseling psychologists are constantly changing. Although these types of changes occur over time, it is important to define and describe the fields of clinical psychology, counseling psychology, and the other mental health professions as they exist in the United States today.

The Mental Health Professions

Besides clinical psychology and counseling psychology, there are several other mental health professions (MHPs) that help individuals whose thoughts, feelings, or behaviors are problematic to themselves or to others. The differences among these professions can be examined in terms of their areas of expertise, their education and training requirements, licensing and certification requirements, and even levels of pay and prestige. The type of education required for psychiatrists and psychologists is standard across the United States, but the requirements for the other professional groups vary from state to state. The professional duties of the different MHPs also vary, but in most cases, they overlap.

Clinical Psychology

The following definition appeared in a public information brochure published in 1992 by the Division of Clinical Psychology (Division 12) of the American Psychological Association (APA). It appears to cover every aspect of human life.

> The field of clinical psychology integrates science, theory, and practice to understand, predict, and alleviate maladjustment, disability, and discomfort as well as to promote human adaptation, adjustment, and personal development. Clinical psychology focuses on the intellectual, emotional, biological, psychological, social, and behavioral aspects of human functioning across the life span, in varying cultures, and at all socioeconomic levels.

Education and Training

According to the APA, the term *psychologist* should be used only for individuals with a doctoral degree in psychology. However, increasing numbers of people are earning master's degrees in psychology. What are they to be called? Master's-level psychologists almost always find appropriate employment, and even individuals with a bachelor's degree may hold jobs in agencies or companies that require performing some of the functions of a psychologist. However, their status remains an issue within the APA.

There are two educational models for the profession of clinical psychology. The first, established in 1949 when the APA held a conference in Boulder, Colorado, to formulate training requirements for psychology, is known as the ***scientist-practitioner model***, also called the ***Boulder model***. In this training model, clinical psychology requires both the academic research skills obtained by completing a research dissertation for the doctoral degree and the applied helping skills obtained by supervised internship experience (Shakow, 1949). Clinical psychologists trained according to the scientist-practitioner model are unique among mental health professionals in their knowledge of assessment, evaluation, and the empirical basis for their methods.

The second training model was established in 1973 at the APA training conference held in Vail, Colorado. Because of criticism that research training is irrelevant to the majority of professional practice, the ***professional model***, also known unsurprisingly as the ***Vail model***, still requires a doctoral degree, but eliminates the academic research requirement for clinical psychology. As a result of the development of this new training model, schools of professional psychology were established as institutions separate from universities, and these graduate schools emphasize clinical training, not research.

At present there are two types of doctoral degrees in clinical psychology, reflecting the two training models. The Ph.D., or Doctor of Philosophy, is awarded by academic departments of psychology in universities upon the completion of a research dissertation. For a Ph.D. in clinical psychology, a year of internship in an APA-approved clinical setting is required in addition to three years of related course work and the research dissertation, for a minimum total of five postgraduate years. A Ph.D. in other areas of psychology, such as social or experimental psychology, is supposed to require three years, since there is less course work and no clinical internship. In many cases doctoral degrees take longer than these minimums.

The Psy.D., or Doctor of Psychology, is offered at professional schools of psychology, and their programs take from four to six years after the bachelor's degree. Recently, some professional schools began offering the Ph.D. as well as the Psy.D., and thus they now require the research component in the form of the doctoral dissertation.

Training requirements for clinical psychology undergo constant evaluation and change as the nature of psychologists' work changes. The APA has held several conferences regarding training since the Vail Conference in 1973 to discuss such issues as the growth of specializations within psychology and the need for core curriculum requirements, but these conferences have not created a coherent new model to replace the scientist-practitioner and professional models (Bickman and Ellis, 1990; Ellis, 1992).

The increasing diversity of professional psychology means that individuals considering applying to graduate school must do a great deal of research in order to choose the appropriate one. There are reference books on graduate education to assist students in their search, including one published annually by the APA. As early as possible in their educational careers, students should write to the graduate schools that interest them and obtain a description of their programs and requirements. Once in graduate school, students are still responsible for seeing to it that they obtain training in the specializations they prefer.

Professional Ethics

The APA has established, and constantly evaluates and changes, a professional code of ethics for all its diverse members. All versions of the APA code of ethics contain general principles regarding competence, integrity, professional and scientific responsibility, respect for people's rights and dignity, concern for others' welfare, and social responsibility. In addition there are ethical standards that detail the implementation of the general principles in specific situations. These cover evaluation, assessment, and intervention; therapeutic relationships; privacy and ***confidentiality***; teaching, training, supervision, research, and publishing; resolving ethical issues; and other topics. The complete code of ethics for psychologists can be seen on the APA Web site (www.apa.org).

Licensing and Certification

At present, all states regulate the practice of clinical psychology through licensing, certification, and registration. Most laws regarding licensure were enacted in the 1950s and 1960s. Psychologists urged state governments to enact laws to license psychologists in order to protect the public and to gain professional status.

A ***license*** is issued to professionals who have demonstrated competence in their field, and it permits them to practice in the state. Regulations vary, but we can use California licensing law, which is similar to that of many states, as an example. California law requires 2,000 hours of supervised clinical practice in a multidisciplinary setting to be obtained within a 24-month period after acquiring a doctoral degree. After candidates apply for a license and verify their education and training, they must take a national multiple-choice examination relating to all areas of psychology, including statistics, research design, and clinical practice. If they pass the written exam, candidates must submit to a one-hour oral examination by two licensed psychologists, in which they are asked about ethics, the law, and clinical practice. After obtaining a license, psychologists retain it by taking mandatory continuing education courses each year. This procedure is supposed to ensure that only ethical, competent people are licensed as psychologists and allowed to offer psychological services to the public.

State ***certification*** is a weaker form of control than licensure. The state certifies that the person claiming to be a psychologist has indeed completed all the educational and training requirements for the profession, but issuing a certificate does not include evaluating the candidate for competence. Certificates in specialized areas, such as alcoholism counseling, are offered by many public and private educational institutions, and again, these certificates guarantee only that an individual has completed certain course requirements.

Registration is a still weaker form of state control. Practicing psychologists merely register their practice with the state. In California, registration is required for psychology trainees and psychological assistants working for agencies or psychologists in private practice. Employed psychologists who are not yet licensed may also be required to register with the state. In addition, there is the ***National Register of Health Service Providers in Psychology***, first published in 1975. Psychologists who are licensed or certified in their own states may submit their names for inclusion in the register (see www.nationalregister.com). It is easier for insurance companies to consult this national publication when deciding whose fees to reimburse than to check who is licensed in each state.

In addition to licensing or certification, experienced psychologists may seek to become diplomates of the ***American Board of Professional Psychology*** (see www.abpp.org). To qualify for this diploma, a psychologist must have five years of professional experience, be a member of the APA, hold a Ph.D. from an APA-approved program, submit copies of his or her work, see an unknown patient under observation, and pass an oral examination. Being an ABPP diplomate implies additional competence and professional status for the psychologist.

Employment

Clinical psychologists work in a wide variety of settings and engage in a wide variety of activities. In fact, one of the advantages of the profession is the flexibility to do so many different, interesting things. Employment may involve private practice, hospitals, public agencies, health maintenance organizations, businesses, universities, schools, or the military; professional duties range from teaching, research, assessment, psychotherapy, and mental health services to administration, consultation, and supervision. Professional psychologists assess and treat children, adolescents, adults, families, groups, businesspeople and workers, people with neurotic and psychotic disorders, people who abuse alcohol and drugs, smokers, overweight people, prisoners, people with mental retardation, and individuals with brain damage as a result of accidents, strokes, and the like. Clinical psychologists are the second most prestigious group of MHPs (the first being psychiatrists), and they command, on average, the second highest fees.

Counseling Psychology

Although similar in many ways to clinical psychology, counseling psychology is distinguished by requiring a doctoral degree in counseling psychology or counselor education, by stressing certain theories of therapy (such as client-centered therapy, discussed in chapter 8), and by working with a relatively nondisturbed clientele. Counseling psychologists may assess and counsel individuals or groups regarding their life problems, career plans, relationship issues, academic choices, and the like. They may teach in counseling psychology programs at universities and conduct research on communication, relationships, and the counseling process. They may also do counseling and therapy with the goals of helping people through the difficulties of life, preventing severe disturbance from developing, and improving personal functioning. Some counseling psychologists obtain the psychologist's license and work in private practice, while others work in clinics, hospitals, student counseling services, and business in as many diverse roles as clinical psychologists. Here is the official definition of counseling psychology from Division 17 of the APA:

> Counseling psychology as a psychological specialty facilitates personal and interpersonal functioning across the life span with a focus on emotional, social, vocational, educational, health-related, developmental, and organizational concerns. Through the integration of theory, research, and practice, and with a sensitivity to multicultural issues, this specialty encompasses a broad range of practices that help people improve their well-being, alleviate distress and maladjustment, resolve cri-

ses, and increase their ability to live more highly functioning lives. Counseling psychology is unique in its attention both to normal developmental issues and to problems associated with physical, emotional, and mental disorders.

Career Counseling

Once called vocational guidance, career counseling has grown in recent decades in response to an increasingly complex economy. Early "vocational aptitude" tests tried to determine what sort of job a particular individual was suited for in terms of skills and abilities. Present-day vocational assessment investigates interests and personality as well as skills, and its goal is to match career planning with an individual's interests, abilities, and temperamental suitability for certain jobs so that the person's happiness and personal growth will be enhanced. Career counseling takes a comprehensive, developmental approach to lifelong career planning, helping both individuals beginning to choose their careers and those who change careers later in life because of personal desire or economic need. Career counselors often work in educational settings, where career decisions may determine educational choices, and they may provide a variety of educational services, such as workshops on job searches and resume writing or training in the social skills needed to apply and interview for jobs.

Marriage and Family Counseling

Like clinical psychologists, counseling psychologists may work with couples (married or not), families, and children to assist them with the expected difficulties of close relationships, including communication, conflict resolution, issues of closeness and trust, and childrearing practices. The theories and intervention methods used in this type of counseling are described in chapter 13. Counseling psychologists working with couples, families, and children are to be distinguished from the person who obtains a license in Marriage and Family Therapy, a master's level mental health profession described later in the chapter.

Clinical Neuropsychology

Clinical neuropsychologists also call themselves neurocognitivists or neuroscientists, a labeling issue that reflects that this is a relatively new field and training has been diverse. Although some neuropsychologists began as clinical psychologists, many originally held doctorates in psychophysiology, comparative psychology, cognition, or medicine. Today it is possible to obtain a doctorate in clinical neuropsychology at some universities, and the training parallels that of clinical psychology. Students receive intensive academic education in the research on the relation between brain and behavior, they complete a research dissertation, and they serve in a supervised internship where they are trained to apply their academic knowledge in a work setting.

A large body of research in several disciplines analyzes the behavioral consequences of central nervous system damage. The development of quantitative and qualitative neuropsychological procedures has led to clinical applications of this knowledge to the assessment and treatment of a variety of brain and nervous system disorders. A description of neuropsychological assessment is presented in chapter 4.

In addition to careers in basic research on the brain and its relation to behavior, neuropsychologists find employment in hospitals, medical schools, and universities, and they may also work in private practice. They often engage in assessment, they make treatment recommendations, and they may be involved in rehabilitation. Their clients may be aphasics (people lacking speech), epileptics, children with learning difficulties, stroke victims, accident victims, or individuals with congenital brain abnormalities. It appears that clinical neuropsychology is a growing field, since advances in medical treatment now save the lives of many people who would have died in previous decades but who now survive with varying degrees of brain damage, such as extremely premature infants or people with head injuries from automobile accidents. Neuropsychology enjoys prestige and relatively high pay, partly because it fits in well with our society's current emphasis on biological causes of disorders.

Educational Psychology

Overlapping with clinical and counseling psychology is educational psychology, which requires an Ed.D., Doctor of Education, degree. There are also master's degrees in educational psychology and counselor education. Training in educational psychology is available from universities with a graduate school of education, department of educational psychology, or similar unit.

Educational psychologists stress research, assessment, and methods relevant to the educational process. They draw from psychology's scientific knowledge of assessment, learning and motivation, cognition, child development, computers and artificial intelligence, and other areas. They develop theories and methods aimed at improving the educational process, teacher effectiveness, and student learning and motivation, and they develop training programs to implement their methods in the schools. As with other psychological specialties, educational psychology often finds itself involved in conflicts about public policy. Which programs (such as Head Start) are effective and deserving of federal funds and whether simply setting and assessing high standards are effective in improving children's learning are important issues that educational psychologists can help address.

Educational psychologists often obtain the psychologist's license and work in schools, universities, private practice, or mental health agencies, in a variety of roles similar to those of clinical psychologists.

School Psychology

The requirements and roles of school psychologists vary from state to state and from school district to school district. Generally, school psychologists have had teaching experience and hold at least a master's degree in school psychology, pupil personnel, or other areas. As the name implies, they work in schools and participate in the evaluation of and intervention with individual pupils, groups of pupils, teachers, administrators, or the educational system itself. There may be much overlap with educational psychology.

Other Fields in Professional Psychology

As psychological research and social need lead psychologists to apply their skills to new problems, new specialties are developed. For example, the rapid development of the Internet has led to "e-therapy" (counseling by e-mail or over the Internet), and there are psychologists who specialize in the way people relate to and through the

Internet. Human factors psychologists help design industrial and office environments and machines so that humans can interact with them safely and effectively. Industrial and organizational psychologists consult with business, government, and organizations to help them function more effectively. Such psychologists may develop specializations to prevent or deal with terrorism. Although any list of specialties is soon incomplete, the following are some of the other special fields within psychology.

Rehabilitation Psychology

The field of rehabilitation psychology is relatively old, and some consider it a precursor to neuropsychology. Rehabilitation psychologists identify and remediate both individual and environmental factors that impede the disabled person's maximum participation in the "normal life" of the community.

Community Psychology

Also a relatively old specialty, community psychology was rather "in" during the 1960s, when there was both money available and optimism about social change. Community psychology differs from clinical psychology and most other specialties in two profound ways. First, it emphasizes the prevention of psychological disorders. Second, it views intervention to be most effective and necessary at the community level. Community psychologists emphasize holistic theories, such as systems theory, which analyzes community organization and how groups relate to each other, and the ecological approach, which analyzes the relationship between individuals and resources within the community. Community psychology interventions vary widely and may include crisis intervention, client advocacy, improving and integrating community services and support, and political activism.

Legal Psychology

Legal or forensic psychology involves the application of psychology to issues relating to law and the legal system. Legal psychologists may do psychological assessment for criminal court, as in determining competency to stand trial or assessing other psychological issues, and for dependency court, as in assessing parental suitability for child custody. They may give expert testimony in a wide variety of matters, such as children's memory in child abuse cases or the effects of posttraumatic stress syndrome in an assault case, but the admissibility of psychologists' testimony varies by judicial jurisdiction. They may prepare briefs for the court summarizing psychological knowledge on a certain issue, treat individuals under court jurisdiction, or conduct research on issues that affect the legal system, such as jury selection, factors influencing jury verdicts, witness memory, and the like. These are just a few of their roles.

Specialties Related to Health

With the increasing awareness of the intricate connection between psychological and behavioral variables and the physical body and brain, psychologists have become involved in treating disorders that traditionally were considered the province of physicians or part of "medicine." Some psychologists are working toward the day when psychology is regarded as a health profession, not a mental health profession. At present, psychologists work within the health care system in a variety of roles and with a focus on research and interventions that help people make behavior changes that will prevent disease or improve their health, such as quitting smoking, or that are necessary to treat their illnesses, such as modifying the eating habits of a person with high blood pressure or diabetes. As previously mentioned, clinical neuropsychology deals directly with the diagnosis and treatment of brain and nervous system disorders. As will be discussed in chapters 12 and 16, psychology's role in health care may grow to include the right to prescribe medication or to be the primary health care provider.

Specialties Involving Children

Although fields that deal with children overlap a great deal, clinical child psychology is mostly concerned with the assessment and treatment of psychologically disordered children, and pediatric psychology deals with problems presented by normal development or with children who are physically ill. The theories and intervention methods in clinical child psychology are similar to those in clinical psychology, with the additional consideration of the developmental stages of children. Pediatric psychologists may work with pediatricians and help them deal with such developmental issues as toilet training, sleep difficulties in young children, temper tantrums, separation anxiety, and the like. Others work with ill children and their families in pediatric or hospital settings. Children with catastrophic illnesses or injuries need assessment and interventions to help them deal with painful medical procedures, disfigurement, loss of previous abilities, fears of death, anger or depression over their fate, jealousy of healthy siblings, or a number of other difficult issues. Pediatric psychologists combine knowledge of child development, family functioning, and therapy theories and methods to intervene with the goal of improving the child's health or helping the child and family cope with an ongoing illness.

Psychiatry

Psychiatry is the most prestigious and powerful mental health profession. Psychiatrists are physicians who have specialized in psychiatry, and as physicians, they utilize the medical model. In the medical model, diagnosis is the crucial first step, for only by diagnosing what is wrong can one identify a specific disorder and then search for the underlying cause of it, the discovery of which leads to the development of prevention or cure. Thus, diagnosis is always required, because diagnosis determines the treatment, and treatment cannot begin without an accurate diagnosis. This model is logical and has been highly effective for physical diseases, but difficulties arise when it is applied to psychological, behavioral, and social problems. The medical model has been criticized as being incorrect, authoritarian, leading to labeling and stigmatization, focusing too much on pathologies and deficits, and biasing treatment policies toward psychiatry. While these issues are discussed in more detail in chapter 3, the point here is that belief in the medical model differentiates psychiatry and psychology and may explain some of the difficulties the two fields have with each other.

As implied, psychiatric training requires an M.D., or Medical Doctor, degree (or other medical degree) from an accredited medical school, followed by an internship and a three-year residency in psychiatry, during which residents provide psychiatric services under the supervision of one or more psychiatrists. Critics of this admittedly rigorous and demanding regimen complain that the majority of it is irrelevant to the practice of psychiatry. Others argue that because organic processes and physical diseases may be part of or must be distinguished from mental disorders, the extensive medical training is necessary. And some argue that all mental illness must ultimately have a biological basis such as a brain abnormality or a biochemical dysfunction and thus medical training is required to treat any psychological disorder.

Psychiatrists are licensed by state medical boards, and they are thus qualified to work in hospitals and agencies and to engage in private practice. Only psychiatrists may prescribe medications, including psychotropic drugs, although this situation is changing, since two states and one federal agency give prescription privileges to psychologists, as discussed in chapters 12 and 16. In most states, only psychiatrists may commit people to mental hospitals against their will. In California, a psychiatric nurse, clinical social worker, or psychologist on a hospital staff may sign commitment papers, but only with the additional signature of a psychiatrist.

Psychiatrists are by law permitted to engage in a variety of forms of psychotherapy, including individual, group, and family therapy. Because they tend to believe that psychological disorders are biologically based and because they have the power to prescribe medication, they may emphasize drug treatments. They may also prescribe electroconvulsive shock therapy, occupational therapy, art therapy, and other forms of treatment in hospitals or out.

Many psychiatrists work in private practice and are affiliated with a hospital; some work exclusively in mental hospitals and psychiatric wards. Psychiatrists also work in outpatient mental health clinics, and the director of such community facilities is often a psychiatrist.

Psychiatrists have the highest status and highest rate of pay of all the MHPs, although their status within the medical field may have slipped in recent years. The number of medical graduates pursuing psychiatric residencies has decreased, and compared to other medical specialties, the pay of psychiatrists is considered low.

Psychoanalysis

At the present time in the United States almost all psychoanalysts hold a medical degree and receive special psychoanalytic training at a psychoanalytic institute, including taking special courses, seeing patients under a training analyst, and undergoing a long and intensive analysis of their own with an experienced psychoanalyst. The psychoanalytic institutes are independent of medical schools. In the United States, social workers and psychologists may take analytic training at certain institutes, and they may engage in analytically oriented psychotherapy, although it remains controversial whether they may call themselves psychoanalysts. Since psychoanalysis is a long and expensive procedure, psychoanalysts almost always work in private practice. They may see patients individually several times a week for one to several years. Since most psychoanalysts hold medical degrees, they may prescribe drugs and hospitalize patients if necessary. Their fees are equivalent to those of psychiatrists.

Social Work

Social work is a fairly old mental health profession, older than professional psychology. The roots of social work can be traced back to the support and assistance people gave each other in small communities, but in the nineteenth century, such community volunteerism began to be delivered through organized charities. Although they often ran completely with volunteers, some charities hired people to do their work full time, and the field of social work began. In the early years of the profession, social workers provided direct services to the disadvantaged portions of the population through organized charities. They helped the needy obtain charitable services, find jobs, get training, get medical treatment, deal with crises, and the like. The practice of social work has changed in recent years, evolving to resemble clinical psychology.

There is a bachelor's degree in social work (B.S.W.) at some universities. The master's degree in social work, or M.S.W., requires two years of course work and supervised experience after the bachelor's degree. Licensing (for the LCSW, Licensed Clinical Social Worker) and certification requirements vary from state to state. In some states and in some jobs, social workers need only the bachelor's degree. Although the master's degree is considered the usual requirement for social work, some social workers, especially those working in universities, supervision, and training, obtain a doctoral degree, such as the D.S.W. (See www.naswdc.org for details.)

Like psychologists, social workers work in a variety of settings, including private practice and hospitals and agencies, and they provide several types of psychotherapy. Some decades ago many social workers became analysts, and many still remain psychodynamically oriented in theory and practice. Today most social workers do intake interviews, make treatment plans, conduct individual and group therapy and counseling, and manage cases.

Also like psychology, social work has developed a set of specialties. Social workers may specialize in child welfare, family services, protective services, victim assistance, mental health, medical social work, school social work, psychiatric social work, gerontology, and other fields. In addition to individual and group therapy, the interventions of social workers are more likely than those of psychologists to include providing concrete information and direct assistance to clients by, for example, helping them find child or elder care, apply for public assistance, develop a budget or go for debt counseling, search for jobs, enter an alcohol or drug rehabilitation program, obtain a place in sheltered housing, and similar services.

In terms of power, prestige, and pay, social workers generally rank somewhat lower than psychologists. However, fees for social workers in private practice vary greatly and may be as high as those of psychologists or psychiatrists.

Marriage and Family Therapy

Some states license or certify MHPs called marriage and family therapists (MFTs). In most states, an MFT license requires a master's degree, but some graduate schools now offer a doctoral degree in MFT. In California, for example, the MFT license requires 3,000 hours of supervised training and a master's degree in MFT or its equivalent. An equivalent degree is presently open to interpretation and controversy, so that people with master's degrees in several subjects, such as clinical psychology or pastoral counseling, may be allowed to take the MFT examination. The MFT examination has written and oral components that test for knowledge, ethics, and clinical competence.

MFTs are supposed to engage in marriage, family, and child counseling and therapy, according to their expertise. They work in a variety of settings, as well as in private practice. (See www.aamft.org for details and careers.)

Since most MFTs have less training and a lower-level degree, they are usually paid less than psychologists and often less than social workers. Some agencies prefer to hire MFTs as a way to cut costs. While MFT fees are usually lower than those of psychologists, some energetic and successful MFTs in private practice command higher fees.

Other Mental Health Professions

Psychological Assistants

Some states allow unlicensed persons to work under the supervision of licensed psychologists as psychological assistants, so they may gain necessary experience. A psychological assistant is employed by a licensed psychologist or psychiatrist to perform limited psychological functions with supervision. The assistant must be registered with the licensing board and be making progress toward an advanced degree in psychology. In other words, being a psychological assistant is not a long-term career.

Bachelor's-Level Professions

There are several bachelor's-level mental health professions that involve forms of counseling, such as human services. Students majoring in human services do course work in topics such as clinical psychology, psychopathology, social work, case management, agency administration, and counseling skills, and they do many hours of fieldwork in many different settings. Human services workers work in agencies providing services for children, the disabled, the elderly, and other disadvantaged portions of the population. They also work in law enforcement, probation, and the prisons. In many ways, the human services worker resembles the social worker of old. (See www.aphsa.org for more information on this field.)

Other bachelor's-level graduates work in hospitals, clinics, and community agencies under a variety of job titles: case manager, counselor, alcoholism counselor, intake worker, community worker, recreation leader, group leader, welfare officer, evaluation officer, drug rehabilitation leader, and many others. The job requirements, skill level, and services performed in these positions vary, but often resemble the work of psychologists and other therapists.

There are jobs in the mental health field for people without a bachelor's degree. For example, the position of psychiatric technician in a hospital requires two years of college. Psych techs, as they are called, usually perform protective or custodial services in hospital wards, but some engage in individual and group counseling with patients.

Counselors

Some states certify mental health counselors. These individuals may hold a bachelor's or master's degree and have various types of training and experience required for the certificate. They engage in group and individual counseling in various service settings. There are a number of certified counselor roles in the field of addictions, and the certificates do not require any degree at all, but rather special training. There are certified alcoholism counselors, certified chemical dependency counselors, and certified substance abuse counselors, among others. (See www.naadac.org for details.)

Peer counselors, also called paraprofessional or nonprofessional counselors, may have little formal education, but they receive special training in counseling skills to enhance their natural helping abilities. Paraprofessionals generally work in community agencies that treat special populations that are underserved by the usual mental health institutions. Often, a paraprofessional counselor is a member of the underserved group. For example, ex–drug addicts may assist drug abusers, and a minority group member may counsel minorities. The use of paraprofessional counselors was encouraged by research in the 1960s that showed that naturally helpful nonprofessionals were as effective as psychiatrists and psychologists in counseling certain groups.

Trainees and Volunteers

Many undergraduate and graduate students in psychology and related fields volunteer to work in mental health and community agencies in order to obtain training and experience in their chosen fields and to be of service to the community. If there are formal ties between the agencies accepting volunteers and the university sending out students, the volunteers may have a formal role with a title such as trainee or intern. In return for giving their time, the interns receive supervision and in-service training, which help the students obtain future employment, get into graduate school, and explore how well they like the mental health field. Trainees take part in many mental health services, including many activities similar to those undertaken by professional psychologists.

Professional Psychology in Practice

As all the mental health professions have grown, the overlap in functions and populations served and, to some degree, the competition among the professions have also grown. Clinical psychology is constantly expanding into new areas as research suggests new applications and as society comes to view psychological intervention as the solution to its problems, old and new. For example, the research discovery that people could learn to control their own brain waves and other autonomic responses thought to be outside of conscious control led to behavioral treatments for migraine headaches, high blood pressure, and other disorders. In the past, church and state failed to control problem drinking, and it became defined as a psychological or psychiatric disorder. Psychologists are now involved in addressing terrorism, from treating victims to identifying causes of terrorism.

Along with growth has come increased contact between professional psychology and the other mental health professions. Often this contact is cooperative and fruitful, but as has long been the case between psychiatry and clinical psychology, there may be competition and conflict over expertise, methods of treatment, and the right to treat certain groups. Some people, including many MHPs, have come to believe that a system that involves many specialist groups, each with its own methods, training, and regulations, has outlived its usefulness.

In actual practice, the similarities among the various MHPs appear to be greater than their differences, and cooperation among the different professions is common. A psychologist in private practice may work with a psychiatrist in order to obtain medication or hospitalization for clients when necessary. A psychiatrist may make referrals to a psychologist when patients need assessment or a special kind of treatment. Psychologists, social workers, and MFTs may refer clients to each other when the clients' problems are outside their areas of expertise or when clients are unable to afford their fees.

The licensing and certification laws of most states explicitly state what psychologists may do. The APA has developed a Model Act for State Licensure of Psychologists, which serves as a model for some state laws. This act's definition of the practice of psychology gives a fairly complete description of the roles of psychologists:

> The practice of psychology is defined as the observation, description, evaluation, interpretation, and modification of human behavior by the application of psychological principles, methods, and procedures, for the purpose of preventing or eliminating symptomatic, maladaptive, or undesired behavior and of enhancing interpersonal relationships, work and life adjustment, personal effectiveness, behavioral health, and mental health. The practice of psychology includes, but is not limited to, psychological testing and the evaluation or assessment of personal characteristics, such as intelligence, personality, abilities, interests, aptitudes, and neuropsychological functioning; counseling, psychoanalysis, psychotherapy, hypnosis, biofeedback, and behavior analysis and therapy; diagnosis and treatment of mental and emotional disorder or disability, alcoholism and substance abuse, disorders of habit or conduct, as well as of the psychological aspects of physical illness, accident, injury, or disability; and psychoeducational evaluation, therapy, remediation, and consultation. Psychological services may be rendered to individuals, families, groups, and the public. The practice of psychology shall be construed within the meaning of this definition without regard to whether payment is received for services rendered. (APA, 1987, p. 2)

The following sections attempt to give a brief synopsis of the possible components of the professional practice of psychology.

Psychotherapy and Counseling

In both private and institutional practice, psychologists engage in a variety of types of psychotherapy and counseling. In addition to individual, group, marriage, family and child therapy, the types of interventions clinicians may use include behavior modification, biofeedback, cognitive retraining and rehabilitation, environmental consultation and design, psychoanalysis, and hypnosis, according to their training and expertise. Short-term therapies are emphasized today, but long-term psychotherapy is still available, especially for those who can afford to pay for it themselves.

Assessment

In addition to doing psychotherapy and other interventions, clinical psychologists engage in assessment of the psychological factors associated with mental, physical, behavioral, and emotional disorders and of other aspects of human functioning. They utilize interviews, behavioral assessments, and observation, and they are qualified to administer, score, and interpret a variety of tests designed to assess psychopathology, personality development, aptitudes, and intellectual and cognitive functioning.

Teaching and Research

Some psychologists engage in university teaching and research, as well as or instead of assessment and treatment. Working in a university setting may involve teaching courses such as abnormal psychology, introduction to clinical psychology, counseling theory, and many other possibilities. Advising students regarding their course work and their careers, supervising students in fieldwork placements, and supervising student research are also involved. Although evaluation research is often conducted in clinical settings, most psychological research is conducted at universities. Research may require writing grant applications and even political lobbying in order to obtain funds necessary to carry out the research, as well as designing measurements and experiments. Some psychologists pursue research careers outside of universities; they direct and conduct research in a variety of government and business settings.

Consultation

Consultation may occasionally be done by professors or therapists or as a full-time private practice by other types of psychologists. By consulting with, advising, and teaching specific skills to such people as teachers or the police, psychologists can help them help many other people, more than a psychologist could help individually. Consultation may be used for mental health goals, as in teaching pediatricians how to recognize child abuse or teaching parents how to modify their children's negative behaviors. Consulting with industry may involve helping businesses organize themselves more effectively, working with management in order to improve company communication, or teaching ways to improve employee morale or reduce employee problems such as absenteeism or alcoholism.

Administration

All psychologists must engage, at least occasionally, in administration. Psychologists in private practice must keep case notes, write assessment reports, bill clients, bill insurance companies, obtain malpractice insurance, deal with the licensing board, and keep financial records. Those working for agencies may not have to do their own billing, but they will have to keep case notes and write a variety of reports to meet the requirements of the agency or its funding sources. Child abuse reporting laws, custody evaluations requiring court testimony, victim assistance laws, changes in Medicare regulations, and many other situations require administration and documentation. Psychologists who direct agencies will find themselves doing a great deal of paperwork in order to meet legal requirements and to obtain and retain grants and funds. They often find themselves embroiled in struggles with regulatory and funding agencies, and at times, in political lobbying in order to maintain government funding, which is constantly threatened with cuts. Research and university psychologists not only write grant applications; they must also administer them if they receive them. Documentation and careful records are crucial in research.

Administration is a part of the real world of the professional psychologist. Another, the ability to write well, is an advantage to all professional psychologists. Researchers must publish papers, clinicians must write assessment reports, therapists must write treatment notes, and so on. Perhaps even more important, obtaining funding requires writing grant applications both for research and for mental health clinics. Well-written grants are more likely to be funded, and well-written reports and articles reflect favorably on the profession.

Psychology in the Public Forum

One of the advantages of psychology as a career is the possibility to do one or several of many different, interesting activities, from teaching, research, and consultation to psychotherapy, assessment, and community work. Psychology has become highly involved in the public forum. Rather than emphasizing individual psychotherapy, professional psychology may help more people by educating the public regarding its research findings and its methods, by becoming involved in court proceedings that affect people's mental health, such as cases involving sexual harassment, and by lobbying the government to alter or enact laws that affect the public. As psychology develops a solid base of knowledge relevant to issues affecting the public's health and well-being, it has the responsibility to become involved in the public forum and to contribute to society's attempts to address social problems. For example, if neuropsychological work demonstrates links between neurological damage, behavior problems in children, and certain environmental pollutants, then psychology would have a moral obligation to educate the public of the dangers of pollution and to work on laws to get the environment cleaned up. As with administration, a possibly unanticipated task for professional psychologists is to keep up to date on a wide variety of legal developments and to be willing to engage in political action to change laws and court rulings that are detrimental to the public or the profession.

Psychotherapy Integration

At the same time as differing psychological theories and techniques are proliferating, there is a growing movement to integrate psychotherapy, to synthesize psychological knowledge instead of delineating it. There are three basic approaches to psychotherapy integration. One approach, the ***common factors approach***, is to search for the commonalities present in all the therapeutic approaches. For example, it has been suggested that all therapies instill hope, impart information, and model interpersonal skills, while research indicates that all good therapists share such characteristics as warmth and empathy. A second approach to psychotherapy integration, ***technical eclecticism***, involves pragmatically selecting techniques that work from all the different approaches, as exemplified by the "multimodal therapy" of Arnold Lazarus. The third approach, ***theoretical integration***, is to combine theories, exemplified by an early attempt by Dollard and Miller (1950) to recast psychoanalysis in learning theory terms. Some integrative theorists attempt the difficult task of developing a new, overarching theory that can account for the other psychotherapy theories and unify them all. In chapter 14 we make our contribution to the common factors and this last approach.

Briefly, we note that all psychotherapies face a common problem: psychological change is difficult. Of course, if it were easy, there would be no need for therapists! Despite saying they want to change and making great efforts to change, people constantly find that they cannot. One answer to this puzzle has been to consider the personality as composed of at least two parts: the part that wants to change and the part that doesn't.

All psychotherapy theories split the personality into parts. These parts are given different labels in different theories, such as id, ego, and superego in psychoanalysis or cognition, emotion, and behavior in cognitive-learning theory. Modern neuropsychology research suggests that the brain may be composed of a loosely connected set of modules, each with its own organization and way of behaving, so it is possible that these theoretical divisions of the personality have a basis in the physiology of the brain. The psychotherapy theories differ as to which parts of the personality are considered to be for or against change. For example, psychoanalysis considers the conscious personality to be the part that wants to change and conflicts in the unconscious part stand in the way of change. Other theories, such as client-centered therapy, consider the conscious personality to be the problem, while the individual's ignored or "unconscious" emotions lead to change.

Briefly, we theorize that all psychotherapy techniques are attempts to get around the part of the personality or situation that resists change and to access or get to the part of the personality that favors change. For example, the psychoanalytic technique of free association can be seen as an attempt to sneak around defenses and into the resistant unconscious and to make its contents conscious. Client-centered therapy's use of empathy can be seen as a way to focus on and empower the individual's ignored emotional side while avoiding the self-criticism of the person's conscious cognitions. Hypnosis may be viewed as a technique designed to confuse the logical mind so that suggestions can be given directly to other parts of the personality. These examples should become clear as we discuss the different theories in the following chapters.

We discuss psychotherapy integration in Chapter 14, but in the chapters before that, we encourage you to try to discover for yourself the similarities and commonalities in the different therapeutic approaches.

In Conclusion

We trust that by now you have a good idea of the scope of modern clinical and counseling psychology. We believe that professional psychology is an exciting field precisely because it is constantly changing in response to important social issues. It is part of the process by which we as a people at this point in history are determining the meaning and direction of our lives.

Historical Development of Professional Psychology

Henri D. was a 30-year-old, unmarried farmer who worked hard on his family's farm. During the previous year, he had gradually become more withdrawn and uncommunicative. Now he stayed in bed most days, face turned to the wall, unable to work, unwilling to talk. He had difficulty sleeping and paced the floors at night, occasionally wringing his hands and murmuring that he was damned. No one could determine what was bothering him, and his family and neighbors became quite anxious to have an explanation for his behavior.

In cases of melancholy . . . I conclude it is merely the work of the devil. Men are possessed by the devil in two ways; corporally or spiritually. Those whom he possesses corporally, as mad people, he has permission from God to vex and agitate, but he has no power over their souls.

—Martin Luther, *Colloquia Mensalia*

As is already clear from chapter 1, professional psychology currently exists in a complex social matrix, and it developed historically from a complex set of social forces. Examining the history of the field will help explain why the practice of professional psychology is organized the way it is and why certain issues are important and still problematic. Understanding the history of the field helps us predict and plan for the future.

Modern professional psychology evolved as the synthesis of two distinct trends in the history of Europe and the United States. One trend is the development of psychology as an independent academic discipline within universities. The other is the failure of other institutions and professions to deal adequately with deviant members of society. Its current theories and practices, its controversial issues, and its status as a field of endeavor can be more easily understood by examining these two historical forces, which came together in the individualistic, pragmatic United States of the twentieth century to develop a unique scientific and applied field, clinical psychology.

Academic Psychology

Modern academic psychology developed in Western Europe, and thus, this history will emphasize Europe and the United States. However, the kinds of questions that the academic discipline of psychology studies have interested individuals and scholars of all cultures since ancient times, and complex bodies of philosophy have been developed by other cultures to deal with what we label psychological issues. In Europe, the Middle Ages question of "What is the relation between the pure immortal soul and the corrupt mortal body?" became in recent centuries "What is the relation between the mind and the body?" and "How do the brain and behavior affect each other?" How does the mind work? What motivates people to behave the way they do? How can we explain deviant behavior? What can we do about it? How can we all get along together? These are ancient and universal questions.

Among some ancient peoples, gods and demons were believed to cause everything and provided the answers to the above questions. In the early Christian era, the conflict between God and Satan and the concept of sin provided answers. After universities were founded in Europe in the fifteenth and sixteenth centuries, secular scholars as well as priests began to study these ancient questions, and academic departments of philosophy were formed.

After the Renaissance, the world entered a period of rapid social change brought on by the expansion of knowledge, increases in the population, urbanization, and the Industrial Revolution. Religion no longer seemed adequate to provide the guideposts needed. Science emerged with what seemed to be more adequate explanations for many phenomena through the scientific method of empirical observation, measurement, and experimentation. There was hope that the method would eventually solve all the questions that have long perplexed humankind.

In the nineteenth century, these ancient questions were still in the province of philosophy departments of universities. In the last half of that century, a new discipline, psychology, broke away from philosophy to become a separate academic specialty. It charged itself with studying the same types of problems as philosophers, but by applying the new scientific method. Some scholars in the new field viewed humans as just another natural phenomenon, not special creations in God's image, and others saw them as machines, but all psychologists agreed that the nature of humanity and the nature of the mind could best be discovered through empirical measurement and experimentation, not through metaphysics or philosophical argument.

Psychology as an experimental science began in the mid-nineteenth century with the psychophysical experiments of Fechner and Helmholtz in Germany. However, the year 1879 is the generally accepted date for the birth of academic psychology. In that year, Wilhelm Wundt established the first independent psychology laboratory at the university in Leipzig, Germany. Wundt argued that the subject matter of psychology was experience, not the relation of the body and soul, and that the mind alone was a legitimate object of scientific study. While Wundt is considered the first "great mind" in psychology, other scholars at that time were also doing work that became part of psychology. In 1869, Francis Galton in England began his study and measurement of individual differences in attributes and abilities. And in 1875, William James, considered the first American psychologist, equipped part of a small laboratory at Harvard for the study of mental associations.

Even though James began his work before Wundt opened his laboratory, psychology became established as a separate academic discipline in the United States somewhat later than in Europe. Most early American psychologists traveled to Europe for graduate study in psychology. Nevertheless, psychological topics were taught in schools and universities in the United States throughout the nineteenth century under topics such as moral philosophy. For example, *Elements of the Philosophy of Mind, Applied to the Developement of Thought and Feeling* by Elizabeth Secord was published in 1840. However, the first full-scale psychology laboratory in the United States was established in 1883 by G. Stanley Hall at Johns Hopkins University. He also established the first psychology journal, the *American Journal of Psychology,* in 1887. In 1888, James M. Cattell at the University of Pennsylvania held the first professorship in psychology. In 1890, William James published the first book officially devoted to psychology, *The Principles of Psychology.* Hall founded the American Psychological Association (APA) in 1892, and by that time, American universities had established about 20 psychology laboratories or departments.

American psychology as an academic discipline has continued to emphasize the empiricism and experimentation of the scientific method that helped create it, but it has experienced several major shifts in the focus of its subject matter over the years. Early psychology was concerned with the structure and contents of the mind, a view called ***structuralism.*** Then the focus of psychology became ***functionalism***, the study of the functions of the mind, what it does and how.

In about 1913, the approach called ***behaviorism*** broke with previous positions. John B. Watson, a major proponent of this view, argued that the proper study of psychology was observable behavior, since the mind cannot be observed. Pavlov's studies in Russia on the conditioned reflex bolstered Watson's position. You may recall that Pavlov trained dogs to salivate at the sound of a bell by associating food with the bell. Like the nature of society in the United States at that time, behaviorism was mechanistic, materialistic, and positivistic. By the 1920s, behaviorism had largely replaced the study of the mind and individual experience in academic psychology in the United States. B. F. Skinner carried behaviorism further, from the 1940s into the 1980s, with his arguments for strict empiricism and the objective, atheoretical description of behavior without any reference to a mind.

Although it always emphasized experimental empiricism, academic psychology has had to deal with the fact that its graduates have continued since the beginning to find employment in the applications of psychology. Professors, researchers, and students interested in applied psychology were considered suspect, and distinctions in prestige and even promotion were made between the "hard" scientists involved in experimental psychology and the "soft" psychologists interested in practice. This

Unbeknownst to most historians, Pavlov got his first idea from Mrs. Pavlov.

attitude favoring hard science is still evident today, although the scientist-practitioner model described in chapter 1 and discussed later in this chapter helped legitimize the status of professional psychology.

In recent years, the mind has crept back into academic psychology. Albert Bandura, a prominent psychologist, developed social learning theory in the 1960s, which added the concept of imitation and the influence of other people to behavioristic learning theory. In the 1970s, Bandura began to write about possible internal, or cognitive, variables that affect behavior and learning. He contributed to the development of a currently important body of theory and research called cognitive behaviorism. Swiss biologist Jean Piaget's influential research on cognitive development in infants and children also contributed to the growing emphasis on cognition. The growth of psychotherapy also helped turn attention to the mind. The old conflict over whether the proper study of psychology is aimed at the mind or at behavior appears to be reaching a synthesis that includes both: cognition and behavior are related and affect each other.

Society's Treatment of Its Deviant Members

For far longer than academic departments of psychology have existed in universities, society has had to deal with its deviant members. People who do not conform to the behavior or beliefs of the majority of the members of society have always existed.

For the sake of discussion, let us divide such deviant or nonconforming members of society into two types, the disturbed and the disturbing. Disturbing people are bothersome to other people. They may hold politically radical views and foment revolution; they may get drunk and fail to work; they may steal. The way our society is organized in the United States today, extremely bothersome people are handled by the legal system. Laws are supposed to protect the life, well-being, and property of all the members of the community from the harmful acts of the criminal few. The most common method of social control of "disturbing" people is imprisonment as a form of punishment, isolation, or rehabilitation.

There are also disturbed people. Other people, or they themselves, think that there is "something wrong" with them, but no one is quite sure what it is. They suffer from uncontrollable urges to kill themselves; they are severely anxious for no reason; they see or hear things that others say are not real; they suffer paralysis or weakness when others say they are well; they are troubled by intrusive thoughts; they feel compelled to perform certain acts over and over. In the United States today, such individuals are viewed as being psychologically disordered and in need of treatment by various mental health professionals. In previous ages, disturbed people were sometimes tolerated or even venerated as "seers." They were also sometimes killed, tortured, and locked away, although many such individuals were protected and cared for by their families, just as many are today. Our present society has developed a number of ways of dealing with the disturbed, including voluntary or involuntary hospitalization, electroconvulsive shock treatments, group therapy, individual psychotherapy, cognitive-behavior modification, psychoanalysis, counseling, pastoral counseling, and medication that affects the brain.

Perhaps the most difficult cases for society are the disturbed disturbing people who don't do anything bad enough to merit prison and yet resist or seem unsuitable for psychological treatment. What of the schizophrenic who stands in the middle of the freeway trying to direct traffic because God told him to? What of the alcoholic executive who functions well in the morning but is drunk all evening? What of the psychopathic person who continually exploits, deceives, and abandons those who love him or her? How is society to help or control the behavior of such individuals, especially if they deny having any problems? As institutions such as the church, the school, the family, the workplace, and even the prison system fail to help or change these people, the community may turn to the mental health professions for solutions. In recent decades, it seems that such social control problems are increasingly defined as being suitable for treatment by the mental health professions.

The history of how society has arrived at ways of dealing with disturbed and disturbing people is fascinating. We can safely assume that what we call mental illness or emotional disturbance today has always existed. Although described in different terminology according to the times, examples of mentally disturbed individuals abound in history. King Saul of Israel suffered terrible bouts of depression and tried to kill his own son. The Roman emperor Caligula was grandiose and delusional, claimed to be a god, and slaughtered hundreds of people, including the beloved sister he married. King George III was depressed and manic in cycles, and his erratic behavior lost Britain the American colonies. Their behavior as described by their contemporaries would clearly be called symptomatic of mental disorder today.

From the Supernatural to the Medical Model

Demonology

Many early peoples, including the early Greeks and Romans, believed that disturbance was caused by the invasion of spirits, gods, or demons, and priests were viewed as the appropriate professionals to treat disturbed individuals. Hippocrates disagreed with the prevailing view and argued that disturbance was due to natural, not supernatural, causes. He believed that most disorders were due to brain pathology, while hysteria in women was due to the wandering of the womb to other parts of the body. He recommended humane treatment for the victims of brain pathology and marriage for the victims of wandering wombs.

Plato wrote that mental disturbance was partly organic, partly moral, and partly divine. Anticipating a modern idea, he believed that dreams represented denied desires. Aristotle raised the possibility that disturbance was due to purely psychological causes, but rejected this hypothesis in favor of organic causes. Galen believed that the causes of disturbance could be either physical or mental.

Although the belief in natural causes of mental disturbance persisted, many Europeans returned to the model of ***demonology*** in the Dark Ages. They believed that the causes of mental disturbance and some other forms of deviance were wickedness, possession by a devil, or witchcraft, and they returned such problems to the province of religious experts. In the early Middle Ages the clergy treated disturbed individuals by using prayer, the laying on of hands, and other relatively benign measures. The monasteries were refuges for the mentally ill, who were usually treated kindly. In the latter part of the Middle Ages, however, the treatment of disturbed people often involved cruelty, torture, and execution.

The end of the Middle Ages was a chaotic period in European history. Natural and manmade disasters abounded—war, plague, the breakup of the feudal system. People were confused and fearful, and they needed explanations for the distressing events around them. The Inquisition, witchcraft, and demonology at least provided explanations and guidelines for what to do. If members of the community were disturbed or disturbing, it was natural to suspect them of practicing witchcraft or of being victims of witchcraft. The suspected persons were then tortured until they confessed to whatever the community expected to hear, usually implicating other members of the community, who were then tortured and confessed, and so on.

Although not all of the victims of the Inquisition were mentally disturbed, some were, and we may wonder how anyone could conceive of torturing an unfortunate disturbed person (or anyone, for that matter). If it is unquestionably believed by the religious experts and all the members of the community that the disordered person is possessed by an evil demon, and if helpful and concerned people want to save that individual's immortal soul, then it becomes logical to make the body such an uncomfortable and miserable place that the demon will want to leave. The person was tortured for her own good. The disturbed individual may have welcomed the treatment, for it is common for some severely disturbed people to believe that they are guilty, worthless, and deserving of punishment. This historical example demonstrates the power of what people think, or cognition. It may also suggest the importance of scientific empiricism.

Nineteenth-Century Reform

From the sixteenth through the nineteenth centuries, the care of the mentally disturbed was transferred from the monasteries and dungeons to asylums run by charities and local governments. The conditions in the asylums were not much better than in the dungeons. Inmates were chained, poorly fed, exhibited to the public for a fee, and subjected to various "treatments" such as hot pokers, cold baths, and straitjackets. It seems that many asylum inmates were the poor, the violent, or the unwanted but undivorceable wives.

By the eighteenth century, some priests and scholars began to argue openly against the prevailing views and to advocate more humane treatment for disturbed persons. At the end of the eighteenth century, French physician Philippe Pinel was able to convince important people to allow him to try an experiment at the large asylum in Paris: to release the inmates from restraints and to treat them with kindness and provide them with decent food and conditions. These changes worked wonders, and most inmates improved dramatically. At the same time in England, William Tuke established a country house where disturbed individuals lived, worked, and rested in a kindly religious atmosphere. And in the United States, reformer Benjamin Rush (1745–1813) encouraged humane treatment of the mentally disordered.

By the nineteenth century, writers and intellectuals were proclaiming the dignity, worth, and equality of all men (only a few included women). The benefits of the scientific revolution were becoming observable in the form of new machines, better hygiene and health care, and improved living conditions for some. In short, the times were changing, and reform was in the air, from abolition to temperance and women's rights.

Dorothea Dix (1802–1887) was an important nineteenth-century American reformer. Through extensive traveling and zealous campaigning between 1841 and 1881, she improved conditions in prisons, almshouses, and asylums throughout the United States and Europe. Single-handedly, she convinced charities and state governments to build at least 32 new mental hospitals in the United States for the care of the retarded and disturbed. She was particularly interested in the care of the "deserving poor" and the indigent mentally ill, although the state hospital superintendents, then called alienists, were more interested in attracting affluent lunatics. Dorothea Dix was ahead of her time in giving legislatures detailed analyses of the hidden costs of failing to build hospitals and treat the needy.

Another contribution to efforts to reform asylums was made by Clifford Beers. Beers was forcibly hospitalized near the turn of the twentieth century, and in 1908 he published a book, *A Mind That Found Itself,* in which he described his terrible experiences. He helped form the National Committee for Mental Hygiene and served as its secretary for 30 years.

During the early and middle nineteenth century, "moral treatment" was used in some mental hospitals, led by the Reverend Dr. Woodward of Worcester State Hospital in Massachusetts. The advocates of moral treatment believed that the mentally disturbed were normal people with temporary problems who would benefit from a favorable environment, emotional support, and being involved in work. Recovery rates for moral treatment were reported to be between 70 and 90% in the early part of the century, although these figures were later considered inflated in order to obtain funding, a familiar modern problem.

In the latter part of the nineteenth century, the effectiveness of moral treatment and other treatments in mental hospitals declined because of a number of factors, including overcrowding, as funds were cut and large numbers of poor immigrants were consigned to the hospitals. The ineffectiveness of moral treatment and the mental hospitals set the stage for a new set of authorities to claim the ability to solve the problems of the disturbed, and the medical model of "mental illness" gained credence at the end of the nineteenth century.

The Medical Model

The model of scientific medicine appeared to be a useful way to define and discover solutions to the suffering of the disturbed. Some also saw it as a way to reduce the stigma attached to psychological disturbance. The medical model first takes note of symptoms, such as fever or red spots. The study of symptoms reveals that certain symptoms often appear together in syndromes, such as red spots appearing just after the onset of fever. The study of syndromes may reveal a specific disease process, such as measles. Once a disease can be diagnosed, then its cause, such as a measles virus, can be investigated and discovered. Only after the cause is known can a prevention or treatment, such as a measles vaccine, be developed. Accurate diagnosis must, in this logical system, precede treatment.

Physician Emil Kraepelin (1856–1926) developed the first diagnostic system for mental disorders at the turn of the century. Kraepelin believed that each type of mental illness was a separate and distinct disorder with an organic cause and that the course and outcome of each mental illness were as predetermined as those of measles. Using only his own keen powers of observation and organization, he developed a precise and comprehensive system of diagnostic categories that is still used with some modifications today.

The medical model of mental illness is probably the most widely accepted view of disturbed people today. Its wide acceptance is due to its great success with numerous diseases that have long plagued humankind and to the credibility and power of the medical profession. Because of the success and power of medicine, there is a tendency to define increasing numbers of human problems as medical disorders. To return to an earlier example, at various points in our history excessive drinking has been viewed as acceptable, a sin, a crime, and a disease. When moral exhortation and Prohibition failed to control excessive drinkers, people began to view alcoholism as a disease and to turn to the medical profession to control drinking through medical "treatment." In a similar manner, previous views of disturbed people were not successful in helping or changing them, and a disease model led to hopes for a "cure." Another explanation for the wide acceptance of the medical model of mental illness can be found in the tremendous influence of Sigmund Freud, who was a physician, although he himself believed that his form of psychotherapy should be practiced independently of medicine.

From the Medical to the Psychological Model: Sigmund Freud

Sigmund Freud (1856–1939) developed the first comprehensive theory of personality development and psychopathology. His influence on twentieth-century thinking has been equated with that of Karl Marx. The impact of Freud's ideas and extensive writings can be seen in the widespread acceptance of some of his ideas today, ideas that are almost taken for granted, such as that childhood experiences affect adult personality or that we defend ourselves against certain thoughts and feelings. He developed the theory and therapeutic techniques of ***classical psychoanalysis*** (described in chapter 6), a therapy that survives today in both its original form and in numerous variations (covered in chapter 7).

Early in his medical career, Freud intended to become a neurologist and pursue research. He went to Paris to study with the famous neurologist Jean Charcot and his student Pierre Janet. Charcot treated those with ***hysteria***, such as women with paralyzed healthy limbs or inexplicable yet disabling pains, through hypnosis and suggestion, with impressive success. Back in Vienna, Freud watched his friend and colleague Josef Breuer treat a patient diagnosed as a hysteric with daily sessions of talking and hypnosis, again with what he considered to be impressively successful results. After some time this patient, known as Anna O., began to talk of sexual fantasies regarding Dr. Breuer during her hypnotic trances. At this point, Breuer abruptly terminated treatment, which Freud thought was a mistake. Freud argued that the patient's expression of feelings for the doctor was a necessary part of psychotherapy. In 1895, Breuer and Freud published *Studies in Hysteria,* in which the concept of ***transference*** in the therapist–patient relationship was described.

Soon most of Freud's medical practice was composed of neurotic women seeking relief. He began by using hypnosis, but soon abandoned it in favor of having the patient simply talk while in a relaxed state on a couch. He directed patients to engage in ***free association***, that is, to say freely whatever entered their minds. He found that childhood memories and sexual thoughts were invariably reported. (The sexual content is perhaps unsurprising, given that his women clients were lying on a couch talking intimately to a man!) Freud discovered that when the patient could not free associate, some especially painful memory was later reported. He noticed that patients were helped to free associate and to uncover important material when they discussed their dreams. In 1900, he published his classic work, *The Interpretation of Dreams.* In this book, he presented his theory of neurosis, his concept of the unconscious, and his belief that dreams symbolize repressed desire—conclusions he had deduced from the data of his clinical cases. Although Freud was brilliant in synthesizing and applying these concepts, he did not simply invent them, for ideas about psychology, dreams, and the unconscious were being discussed by the European intellectuals of his day.

At first, Freud thought that neurosis was due to a genuine sexual trauma early in childhood, such as viewing the primal scene of parental intercourse or being sexually molested. These ideas met with considerable resistance and scorn from the medical community, and Freud himself was horrified by them. After a long period of self-analysis, he arrived at the insight that the sexual traumas and memories of his patients might be fantasies. Although somewhat relieved, he was distraught that his theory of neurosis was destroyed. However, he soon came to the conclusion that fantasy can have just as much impact, possibly more, on the small child's developing psyche as real events, and he elaborated his theory of neurosis to include the effect of unconscious conflicts as expressed in fantasies, dreams, and imaginary "screen memories." In recent years, some psychoanalytic writers and other scholars have gone back to Freud's original idea and believe that Freud's patients' difficulties were due to genuine sexual traumas. Particularly in the case of Anna O., many now believe that she was actually molested by her father (Masson, 1984).

In 1909, the ambitious American psychologist G. Stanley Hall daringly invited Freud to speak at Clark University in Massachusetts. He gave five highly influential lectures, now considered classics, which were published in 1910 in the *American Journal of Psychology.* In the United States at that time, only a few people in academic psychology were interested in Freud's ideas, while most psychologists and physicians ignored him or considered him a quack. However, the public found Freudian ideas fascinating, and by 1920, over 200 books on psychoanalysis had been published in the United States alone. In the two decades from 1919 until his death in London from cancer of the jaw in 1939, Freud's prominence increased, and there was widespread acceptance of psychoanalytic theory, both by the public and in the psychiatric community.

Academic psychology, on the other hand, continued to view psychoanalysis with even more suspicion than it did applied psychology. Some even considered it a cult to be eradicated. As a young science, psychology felt threatened by the greater prominence of psychoanalysis. Academic psychology and psychoanalysis developed during the same time, but they were unrelated in aims, methods, and subject matter. The aim of early academic psychology was the scientific study of the normal mind; that of psychoanalysis was the treatment of disturbed individuals. The method of psychology was scientific experimentation; that of psychoanalysis was observation of clinical cases. Academic psychology finally asserted itself as the true scientific authority by conducting experiments on psychoanalytic hypotheses, so as to have the ability to pass judgment on them. Eventually, just as professional psychology was accepted by academic psychology, psychoanalytic ideas were gradually incorporated into the field. Now there is even a Division of Psychoanalysis (39) in the American Psychological Association.

Psychoanalytic theory was a historical turning point from the late nineteenth-century medical view that the cause of disturbance was organic malfunction of the body to the twentieth-century psychological view that at least some of the causes were to be found in the mind. Once this view was widely accepted, the individualistic United States was ready for the development of clinical psychology. As the twentieth century neared its end, the acceptance of psychological causes of mental disturbance was waning, and the emphasis was shifting back to biological and medical models of psychological disorders.

The Psychological Model in the United States

Although psychology as an academic discipline began in Europe, psychology rapidly expanded in the United States while remaining a relatively minor area of study in

Europe. Clinical psychology developed in the United States, remained an American specialty for decades, and is now exported to Europe and other countries. The popularity of professional psychology in the United States is partly due to its ability to address certain social problems while preserving the American value of individualism and without necessitating social change.

Early Developments in Clinical Psychology

By the end of the nineteenth century the United States had experienced three decades of official peace after the Civil War. A rapid expansion of the population and a large influx of immigrants allowed the country to be settled from coast to coast. Urbanization and industrialization were underway in all sections of the country. Attempts at social reform that had begun with abolitionist, feminist, and temperance movements in the early part of the century had been blunted by the violence of the Civil War. Cultural values tended toward rugged individualism, competition, and individual achievement. Academic psychology and its scientific study of the individual fit the times well. It only remained for individualistic scientific psychology to be applied to help the casualties of the social forces of the era for clinical psychology to develop as a field.

In 1896, Lightner Witmer established the first psychological clinic at the University of Pennsylvania for the evaluation of children. The founding of this first clinic for psychological services in a university setting established the combined academic and applied approach that is characteristic of clinical psychology. In 1907, Witmer established and edited a journal called *Psychological Clinic.* The *Journal of Abnormal Psychology* also began in 1907, so applied psychologists had two journals for the communication of their ideas and research. About 20 psychological clinics had been established at American universities by 1915. Some included counseling services for students at the universities, but the emphasis was on services for children.

Although clinical psychology flourished in the United States, work in Europe influenced its practice. In 1904, Carl Jung in Switzerland was experimenting with a word association test for the assessment of personality. In 1905, Alfred Binet and Theodore Simon in Paris developed the first intelligence test for children. Swiss psychoanalyst Hermann Rorschach developed his famous inkblot test for the assessment of personality and psychopathology about the same time.

World War I provided a big opportunity for applied psychology to define and prove itself. The U.S. Army needed a way to predict which soldiers would do well and which would not, so that the costs of training and shipping a soldier who would fail could be saved. Psychologists developed the Army Alpha test, the first group test of intelligence. It did a fairly good job of screening recruits. The Army Beta was a nonverbal test for illiterates. At the same time, Robert Woodworth developed the Personal Data Sheet, a pencil-and-paper personality test also useful for screening recruits. By the end of the war, the statistical procedures and standards for establishing the ***norms***, ***reliability***, and ***validity*** of psychological tests had been formulated. And by the end of the war, clinical psychology was recognized as a discipline, as reflected in the formation of a clinical section within the American Psychological Association in 1919.

Between the wars, clinical psychology was dominated, as were all mental health professions, by psychoanalysis. The publication of *Counseling and Psychotherapy* by Carl Rogers in 1942 provided the first comprehensive psychological theory and treatment alternative to psychoanalysis and a framework for clinical psychology to move from assessment into treatment. World War II provided the demand in the form of thousands of returning disturbed soldiers needing treatment. The Veterans Administration and the Department of Defense funded clinical psychology.

The professional identity of clinical psychology was solidified in 1949 with the APA conference on graduate education in clinical psychology, held in Boulder, Colorado. Prior to World War II, most early applied psychologists held bachelor's or master's degrees. The Boulder conference determined that the degree for a clinical psychologist would be the Ph.D., with training in both science and practice. The scientist-practitioner model required competence in research, as well as assessment and psychotherapy.

Early Developments in Counseling Psychology

Counseling psychology shares many of the early roots of clinical psychology and has been subject to the same historical and social forces. The career counseling branch of the field developed in the United States in the late 1800s and early 1900s in response to increasing industrialization and its need for a skilled workforce. Frank Parsons is credited with founding the vocational guidance movement. He established the Vocation Bureau in Boston in 1908 and published a book, *Choosing a Profession,* in the same year, followed by *Choosing a Vocation* in 1909. The year 1913 saw the formation of the National Vocational Guidance Association, a precursor to the professional organization of counseling psychology. Parsons emphasized evaluation of individuals coupled with helping them with self-exploration and decision making. As psychological assessment developed through World War I, Parsons included the use of tests in vocational guidance. Partly because of the demand for vocational services created by the Depression, there was a testing boom between the world wars, and many group and individual tests of intelligence, achievement, aptitudes, interests, and personality were developed for use in education and industry.

Vocational guidance began its movement into counseling between the world wars (Super, 1955), and as with clinical psychology, World War II provided a major impetus for the growth of the field. In 1942 two books were published that greatly affected counseling psychology: Rogers's *Counseling and Psychotherapy* and *The Dynamics of Vocational Adjustment* by Donald Super. Rogers emphasized helping individuals realize their innate positive potential, and Super conceptualized vocational guidance as involving a developmental, life span process, rather than a single advising event. These works provided the theoretical framework for the application of psychological knowledge and interventions to problems and issues in normal life. World War II provided thousands of returning soldiers needing personal and career counseling, and the Veterans Administration provided training funds to develop needed staff.

The Society of Counseling Psychology (Division 17) within the APA was formed in 1946. Two conferences helped establish the professional identity of counseling psychology: the Northwestern Conference in 1951 and the Greystone Conference in 1954. These conferences adopted the term *counseling psychology* and developed standards for the training of counseling psychologists. Since then, counseling psychology has grown tremendously, and it shares theories, research, intervention methods, and values with clinical psychology. We will now turn to a detailed history of the two fields in the twentieth century.

Professional Psychology in the Twentieth Century

The first recognized applied profession in psychology—clinical psychology—was well established in the United States by the end of World War I. Other specialties in professional psychology shared these early roots. World War I provided the initial impetus for the development of professional psychology, but World War II ignited its phenomenal growth in the mid-twentieth century. Growth continued exponentially until the 1980s, when it slowed sharply. In that decade and after, professional psychology became embroiled in a series of interesting professional and social conflicts that presaged its role in the twenty-first century.

In order to examine these developments a review of the history of professional psychology will be divided into three topics: assessment, treatment and interventions, and professional organizations. A strictly chronological presentation of important historical events is presented in box 2.1.

Assessment

Psychology's first big public success was assessment. The role of assessment in World War I has already been described. In addition to the short group tests of intelligence and personality for screening soldiers, psychology gained public recognition for its individual intelligence tests for children. While the roots of testing individual differences go back to Galton's work in England in the 1870s, the work of Binet and Simon at the turn of the twentieth century in France marks the foundation of modern intellectual assessment.

Intellectual Assessment

In 1904, the Paris school commission asked Binet and his colleague to develop a test that would predict which children would do well in school and which would not, so that something could be done about the latter. They developed a test that sampled school-related skills in a standardized manner, and a child's score could be compared to the scores of other children. Binet's development of the concepts of norms and deviations from norms gave meaning to an individual's test score. Knowing that a child's score on a vocabulary test is 13, for example, does not tell you much, but knowing that the child scored one standard deviation above the mean for children of her or his age does. Binet contributed substantially to the field of intellectual assessment and thus to professional psychology.

English translations of the Binet-Simon test were used in the United States until Lewis Terman at Stanford University greatly modified it and standardized it with American children. The Stanford-Binet was published in 1916 and has been revised and updated several times since then. In 1928, Gessell published his developmental scales for use with babies and young children. In 1939, David Wechsler published the Wechsler-Bellevue, the first satisfactory individual test of adult intelligence. Several revisions of the Wechsler and the addition of versions for children in 1949 and for very young children in 1967 have helped make the Wechsler tests the most used individual intelligence tests today. Other intelligence tests are constantly being developed and marketed, such as the Kaufman Assessment Battery for Children, published in 1983.

Box 2.1 Important Historical Events in Professional Psychology in Chronological Order

1879 Wundt established first psychology laboratory
1883 Hall established first U.S. psychology laboratory
1887 First psychology journal, *American Journal of Psychology*, founded
1888 First professorship in psychology (Cattell)
1890 William James published *Principles of Psychology*
1892 Hall founded American Psychological Association
1895 Freud and Breuer published *Studies in Hysteria*
1896 Lightner Witmer established first psychological clinic
1900 Freud published *The Interpretation of Dreams*
1905 Binet and Simon published first intelligence test
1907 The *Journal of Abnormal Psychology* began publication
1908 Frank Parsons established the Vocation Bureau in Boston
1909 Freud delivered lectures on psychoanalysis in the United States
1916 Terman developed Stanford-Binet intelligence test
1917 Army Alpha test developed
1919 Clinical section (Division 12) formed within the APA
1920 Watson and Rayner applied learning theory to develop a phobia in Little Albert
1921 Rorschach inkblot test published
1935 Thematic Apperception Test published by Morgan and Murray
1938 Wechsler-Bellevue intelligence test for adults published; Bender-Motor-Gestalt Test published
1942 Carl Rogers published *Counseling and Psychotherapy*, which described client-centered therapy as first major alternative to psychoanalysis; Donald Super published *The Dynamics of Vocational Adjustment*
1943 Minnesota Multiphasic Personality Inventory published by Hathaway and McKinley
1944 APA reorganized into division system; Division of Clinical Psychology (12) formed
1946 Division of Counseling Psychology (17) formed
1949 Boulder Conference held; scientist-practitioner model of clinical psychology established; Halstead published first neuropsychological test battery
1951 Northwestern Conference held; term *counseling psychology* adopted
1954 Greystone Conference held; training requirements for counseling psychology established
1958 Wolpe published *Psychotherapy by Reciprocal Inhibition*
1963 Community Mental Health Act enacted
1973 Vail Conference held; professional model of clinical psychology established
1987 Practice and Science Directorates formed within the APA
1988 American Psychological Society formed

Personality Assessment

After psychology had demonstrated its power with intelligence testing, psychologists working in clinics and hospitals were asked to help with other problems besides school performance and mental retardation. Psychiatrists and social workers wanted help with differential diagnosis of psychopathology and with understanding personality dynamics. Professional psychology responded with two types of tests, projective and objective.

Projective Tests. Early word association tests were developed by Galton, Jung, and others in the nineteenth century, but the most successful projective test was the inkblot test developed by Hermann Rorschach and published in his *Psychodiagnostik* in 1921. The test consists of a series of inkblots, and individuals are asked to tell what the blots look like to them. While the title "projective technique" wasn't used until 1939, the assumption behind the Rorschach was that individuals would project their personalities and unconscious conflicts onto the ambiguous inkblots in order to make sense out of them.

In 1935, Christiana Morgan and Henry Murray published the Thematic Apperception Test (TAT), which consists of a series of drawings of people in a variety of situations. Individuals are asked to make up a story about what is going on in the pictures, and again, it is assumed that they must use their own personalities and experiences in order to do so.

In 1938, Lauretta Bender published the Bender-Motor-Gestalt Test, a series of geometric designs to be copied, which is used as a projective test of personality as well as a measure of brain damage. In 1949, Karen Machover published her description of the Draw-A-Person test. Individuals are simply asked to draw a person, and the way they do so is supposed to indicate how they perceive themselves and others.

Despite ongoing controversy over their validity, projective tests have enjoyed widespread acceptance. Developed before and between the world wars, they continue to be used today. Other projective tests have been developed, such as the House-Tree-Person drawing test, the Roberts Apperception Test for Children, and Sentence Completion tests.

Objective Tests. Empirical psychology would not let these psychoanalytically tinged projective measures hog the assessment show. Psychology took the measurement concepts of norms and deviations invented for intelligence tests, applied them to measuring personality, and developed the so-called objective tests. After Woodworth's Personal Data Sheet and his Psychoneurotic Inventory of World War I, the first major empirically derived, pencil-and-paper personality test, the Minnesota Multiphasic Personality Inventory (MMPI), was published by Hathaway and McKinley in 1943. Several scales were developed by giving hundreds of true-or-false statements to many "normal" people and to people who were known to belong to certain diagnostic groups, such as the depressed or the socially introverted; those statements that the diagnostic groups answered differently from the "normals" became the scales. The MMPI was a phenomenal success. It became and remains the personality test most often used in research and in clinical assessment in the world. Not until 1989 was a revision, the MMPI-2, published.

Other objective tests soon followed: the Edwards Personal Preference Schedule in 1954, the California Psychological Inventory in 1957, the Myers-Briggs in 1962, the

Beck Depression Inventory in 1972, and the Eysenck Personality Inventory in 1975, among others. New objective tests are constantly being developed and marketed for a wide variety of uses, from assessing childrearing practices to measuring management styles. A competitor for the MMPI, in terms of its use in assessing psychopathology, is the Millon Clinical Multiaxial Inventory, developed and constantly revised by Theodore Millon since the early 1980s and designed to give psychiatric diagnoses. Again, despite years of controversy over the reliability and validity of the objective personality tests, the MMPI remains widely accepted and used in a variety of settings today.

Other Forms of Assessment

With the success of intelligence tests, psychologists moved into many different types of assessment. As noted, achievement, vocational, aptitude, and interest tests were developed during the 1920s and 1930s by counseling, school, and educational psychologists to help advise students about their careers and to supplement the information gained from the ability tests.

Behavioral assessment was developed during the 1970s to be used with behavior therapy, which is based on learning theory. The techniques of behavioral assessment, such as naturalistic observation, self-monitoring, psychophysiological measures, and the like, are used to identify target behaviors to modify, to identify causal variables so interventions can be made at that point, and to evaluate and modify the interventions.

Neuropsychological assessment, which experienced an increase in use during the 1970s and 1980s, involves a set of procedures designed to detect the presence, extent, and type of organic brain damage or neurological impairment in individuals as well as the behavioral consequences of that damage. The oldest test of this type, the Bender-Motor-Gestalt (mentioned above) was published in 1939. Involving the copying of a few designs, it is short, quick, and easy to administer, but it merely suggests the presence or absence of organic impairment. Modern tests, though long, complex, and difficult to administer, give a complete picture of the nature of the impairment. The Halstead-Reitan Battery, originally developed in the 1960s, is constantly revised by Ralph Reitan and his colleagues. There are now several quantitative procedures available in neuropsychology, including the Luria-Nebraska Neuropsychological Battery, the Boston Diagnostic Aphasia Examination, and others. Research in neuropsychology is "in" at present, so it receives funding, and new findings will undoubtedly lead to new measures.

Treatment and Interventions

Psychological interventions for alleviating human misery have a long history. Shamanistic dances to drive evil spirits from the ill could be considered psychological interventions. In the early nineteenth century in Europe, Franz Anton Mesmer developed hypnotic techniques to treat a variety of problems, and mesmerism, as it was then called, was used in obstetrics as early as 1831 (Chertok, 1981). Later Charcot and Janet also used hypnosis, as did Freud at first. In the early nineteenth century in the United States, "moral treatment" incorporated group discussions and emotional support. For the most part, however, in the early years of professional psychology, the vast majority of psychologists were involved in assessment. Furthermore, a great deal of their work dealt with children or the so-called "feebleminded."

The first two psychology clinics focused on children. As mentioned previously, Lightner Witmer established the first one in 1896 at the University of Pennsylvania in order to help children who exhibited learning difficulties or disruptive classroom behavior. The second, William Healy's child guidance clinic in Chicago, was established in 1909 to deal with delinquents. Parsons's Vocation Bureau, established in 1908, dealt with guiding education and work. Thus, if professional psychologists were involved in treatment at all, it was generally limited to counseling children or youth or to vocational guidance. The child therapists of that day adopted the psychoanalytic model, especially the version developed by Alfred Adler and the play therapy developed by Anna Freud, Sigmund's daughter.

In terms of psychological treatment and interventions with adults, the dominant model in the mental health field at that time was psychoanalysis, and the dominant profession was psychiatry. Nevertheless, in 1920, John Watson demonstrated that a phobia could be learned (Watson & Rayner, 1920), but even though he clearly pointed out that phobias could be treated with behavioristic methods and Mary Cover Jones showed how in 1924 (Jones, 1924), it would be several decades before professional psychology developed behavioral interventions based on learning theory. In the late 1930s, Carl Rogers (1902–1987) developed his client-centered counseling theory and methods, but again, it would be several years before his ideas achieved prominence. Furthermore, Rogers made an important contribution to professional psychology by being the first to do systematic research on his therapy, examining both the theory behind his methods and the process of psychotherapy itself. As an interesting historical aside, at about the same time, and even for a time at the same university, psychiatrist Heinz Kohut was developing a new model of psychoanalysis called object relations theory, a model with striking parallels to the theory and methods developed by Rogers. Yet Rogers and Kohut never met (Rogers, personal communication, 1985).

World War II created an enormous demand for assessment, counseling, and psychotherapy services for hundreds of thousands of soldiers. There was so much business to go around that professional psychology was able to move rapidly into providing psychotherapy and counseling for adults, not just assessment and treatment for children, without encountering much resistance from medicine or other groups. In 1946, the Veterans Administration, the National Institute of Mental Health, and the U.S. Public Health Service began to fund training programs in clinical psychology and counseling psychology at universities. They supported training programs in order to produce more psychologists to provide the many services that the returning soldiers would require for years to come. This financial support contributed greatly to the expansion of psychology as a field.

The decade after World War II saw tremendous strides in professional psychology as it expanded into new and varied research and treatment areas. In 1947, the National Training Laboratory at Bethel, Maine, held its first summer workshop. This event saw the birth of T-groups, or sensitivity training groups, which were designed to help businesspeople improve their communication and productivity through meeting in and examining the process of small groups. In T-groups, as with vocational guidance, therapy-like services were offered to nondisturbed individuals. In 1949 Andrew Salter published *Conditioned Reflex Therapy,* and in 1958 Joseph Wolpe published *Psychotherapy by Reciprocal Inhibition,* both of which helped establish behavior therapy as a major alternative to the psychoanalytic view.

The 1960s saw an explosion of diverse theories and techniques. Important therapies at this time included client-centered, humanistic, Gestalt, and behavior therapy, all covered in detail in later chapters. Psychologists were conducting individual, group, marriage, and family therapy. They were involved in the human potential movement, which offered psychological services to nondisturbed people in order to help them reach their full potential. In short, many new ideas were tried. And, as is typical of psychology, many of these new ideas were subjected to research.

The tremendous postwar growth of psychology was due to several factors. The scientist-practitioner model bore fruit, for academic research frequently provided new applications of psychological principles and developed new techniques of behavior change. By the early 1960s, the majority of people in the United States were prosperous to a degree never before seen in history, and they could afford a sense of social responsibility for less fortunate individuals. The public turned to psychology for solutions to social problems, because psychology had proved so successful after the two world wars. Psychology also fit in with the still-treasured value of individualism. It was essentially a conservative approach in that problems were defined as being within individuals or, at most, their families, and solutions could be found that did not require change in anyone else, the community, or society; that is, social problems were addressed solely through the treatment of individuals.

In 1963, President Kennedy signed the Community Mental Health Act, which provided funding for many community-based mental health agencies. The goal of this act was to reduce the population warehoused in large mental hospitals and to allow the mentally disturbed to be treated in their own communities. Psychologists found extensive employment in the agencies and programs funded by the act. The federal government and the Veterans Administration continued to be generous with funds for training psychologists, and research was also liberally funded. This steady flow of money coupled with positive public attitudes contributed to the growth of professional psychology.

The years since this expansive period have been a mix of good and bad for psychology and society. Even during the height of 1960s prosperity, the poor were never provided with services adequate to help them. The community mental health agencies were also inadequately financed, yet the big state mental hospitals closed, forcing many disturbed people into prisons, cheap hotels, or onto the streets. There have been wars, assassinations, and recurring recessions. While the 1980s appeared to be another highly prosperous decade, it was so only for some people, and they did not appear to feel the earlier sense of social responsibility for the disadvantaged. In the 1980s, the Republican government chose to cut spending for mental health research and services, and the poor economy of the early 1990s meant it had to. The prosperity of the late 1990s allowed for welfare reform and improved services for the disadvantaged, but in the early twenty-first century tax cuts coupled with huge increases in defense spending again meant cuts in funding for social and psychological services.

Nevertheless, there were advances in research, theories, and methods of intervention during the late 1970s and 1980s. Examples include the development of cognitive-behavior therapy, strategic and paradoxical interventions, and family systems therapies, all covered in later chapters. Even before reduced government spending, psychologists were concerned that individual therapies were not a cost-effective way of reaching people and solving social problems. Some psychologists responded to the ineffectiveness of psychotherapy to address social problems by advocating social and political action. Others contributed to the development of community psychology in the 1970s. In this model, interventions are aimed at the prevention of psychological disorders through education, parent training, crisis intervention, or changing parts of the community. The 1980s saw the development of behavioral medicine, or health psychology, another preventive field, in which interventions are aimed at changing people's health-risking behaviors. The appeal of this field is that its interventions are cost-effective: early, relatively inexpensive behavioral treatment prevents the need for later, more costly medical interventions. Demonstrating the cost-effectiveness of its interventions is crucial for the future of professional psychology, and the need for cost-effective interventions may well lead to new treatment theories and methods and to new and varied roles for professional psychologists.

Professional Organizations

The development of the field of psychology has been inextricably linked with that of the American Psychological Association. Changes and struggles within that organization reflect both academic and professional developments, as well as changes in society at large. The size of the APA (150,000 members) suggests the importance of psychology in the United States today. All students of psychology should be familiar with their useful Web site, www.apa.org.

The division structure of the APA as of 2005 is shown in box 2.2. It is worth examining this box both for its history and to see that along with increasing numbers has come increasing diversity in the special interests of APA members. The higher the number of the division, the more recently it was added, so the types of roles for psychologists that have proliferated in recent years can be seen in the later divisions. With its many divisions, it is, in a way, amazing that the APA continues to function as one organization.

The Early Years

The key word in the APA is *American,* and the organization prospered by fitting in well with American society. In the nineteenth century, the rapidly developing sciences began to organize themselves into specialties. G. Stanley Hall invited several colleagues and friends to a meeting in 1892 in order to form a disciplinary society for psychology, the American Psychological Association. The organization held annual meetings for the presentation of papers, the election of officers (unsurprisingly, Hall was the first president), and the election of new members. Annual dues were a whopping three dollars (now about three hundred dollars, depending on the divisions a member joins and still a bargain considering inflation). Journals were published, research was encouraged, and ties were maintained with related disciplines. The APA functioned well to create an identity for scientific psychology.

Since the goals of the APA were scientific, it became involved in professional psychology almost against its will. A Committee on Physical and Mental Tests was formed in 1896, and a Committee on Measurements in 1906. By 1919, there were enough applied psychologists working in various settings that a Section of Clinical Psychology was created within the APA.

World War II

As described earlier, World War II profoundly affected the field of psychology. The APA was reorganized into the division system in 1944, and Division 12 became the Division of Clinical Psychology. As noted, in 1949, the APA Boulder Conference on graduate education in clinical psychology bridged the academic–applied schism in the field and determined the future of clinical psychology as a profession. The Boulder conference determined that the degree for an applied psychologist would be the Ph.D. with training in both science and practice. The scientist-practitioner model required competence in research, assessment, and psychotherapy. The inclusion of psychotherapy was a courageous stance for the APA, considering the opposition of

Box 2.2 Divisions of the American Psychological Association as of 2005

1. Society for General Psychology
2. Society for the Teaching of Psychology
3. Experimental Psychology

*

5. Evaluation, Measurement, and Statistics
6. Behavioral Neuroscience and Comparative Psychology
7. Developmental Psychology
8. Society for Personality and Social Psychology
9. Society for the Psychological Study of Social Issues (SPSSI)
10. Society for the Psychology of Aesthetics, Creativity and the Arts

*

12. Society of Clinical Psychology
13. Society of Consulting Psychology
14. Society for Industrial and Organizational Psychology
15. Educational Psychology
16. School Psychology
17. Society of Counseling Psychology
18. Psychologists in Public Service
19. Society for Military Psychology
20. Adult Development and Aging
21. Applied Experimental and Engineering Psychology
22. Rehabilitation Psychology
23. Society for Consumer Psychology
24. Society for Theoretical and Philosophical Psychology
25. Behavior Analysis
26. Society for the History of Psychology
27. Society for Community Research and Action: Division of Community Psychology
28. Psychopharmacology and Substance Abuse
29. Psychotherapy

psychiatry at the time. The later Northwestern and Greystone conferences established the training requirements for counseling psychology, as described previously. The Division of Counseling Psychology (17) was formed in 1946.

Other events also affected professional psychology. The first certification law for psychologists was passed in Connecticut in 1945. In 1946, the APA formed the American Board of Examiners in Professional Psychology (later ABPP, mentioned in chapter 1) to certify the competence of Ph.D. applied psychologists. In 1953, the APA published its first *Ethical Standards,* a code of ethics designed to protect the public and enhance the professionalism of applied psychology.

30. Society of Psychological Hypnosis
31. State Psychological Association Affairs
32. Humanistic Psychology
33. Mental Retardation and Developmental Disabilities
34. Population and Environmental Psychology
35. Society for the Psychology of Women
36. Psychology of Religion and Spirituality
37. Child, Youth, and Family Services
38. Health Psychology
39. Psychoanalysis
40. Clinical Neuropsychology
41. American Psychology-Law Society
42. Psychologists in Independent Practice
43. Family Psychology
44. Society for the Psychological Study of Lesbian, Gay, and Bisexual Issues
45. Society for the Psychological Study of Ethnic Minority Issues
46. Media Psychology
47. Exercise and Sport Psychology
48. Society for the Study of Peace, Conflict, and Violence: Peace Psychology Division
49. Group Psychology and Group Psychotherapy
50. Addictions
51. Society for the Psychological Study of Men and Masculinity
52. International Psychology
53. Society of Clinical Child and Adolescent Psychology
54. Society of Pediatric Psychology
55. American Society for the Advancement of Pharmacotherapy

* There is no Division 4 or Division 11. Division 4 was saved for the Psychometric Society, but they decided not to join the APA. Division 11 was Abnormal Psychology and Psychotherapy, but they combined with Division 12 when the APA reorganized in 1946.
Source: http://www.apa.org/about/division.html

Recent Decades

The incredibly rapid postwar growth of professional psychology, discussed earlier, led to further changes in the field and the APA. The 1973 APA conference on education and training in clinical psychology, held this time in Vail, Colorado, developed the professional model as an alternative to the scientist-practitioner model. The APA continues to hold conferences to discuss issues that arise in training as professional psychology changes.

The debate over academic versus applied psychology is far from over. Furthermore, the split between the two factions in the APA has widened. As suggested by box 2.2, the number of APA divisions that could be considered applied now outweighs the number of strictly scientific divisions. The majority of APA members are professional psychologists. By the 1980s, the scientists began to feel neglected. To scientists, it seemed that the APA was devoting all its energies to issues of importance to clinicians, such as licensing laws, hospital privileges, lawsuits over insurance reimbursement of psychologists' fees, and the like. The APA responded to these charges by assessing clinicians higher dues than scientists and then by forming the Practice Directorate and the Science Directorate in 1987.

A plan to reorganize the APA was voted down by the membership in 1988. As a result, the dissatisfied members left and in that year formed their own professional organization, the American Psychological Society (APS), dedicated to the advancement of scientific psychology. The first APS convention was held in 1988, and the APS now publishes newsletters and scientific journals. The formation of the APS may result in the APA's becoming a completely professional organization.

There are many who oppose this breakup of psychology. They believe that both sides benefit by one strong, unified organization. Furthermore, they argue, research and applied psychology should continue to inform each other and benefit from each other's input. Many fear that the splintering into special-interest groups predicts the disintegration of the discipline, and they contend that the goal of psychology should be the integration of theory and knowledge. At present, many psychologists belong to both the APA and the APS, a fact that suggests that psychology as a discipline may be able to both specialize and synthesize, as it has in the past.

In Conclusion

This brief history of professional psychology should set the following chapters in context. The majority of this book is devoted to the description, explanation, and analysis of the theories and methods of professional psychology, especially psychotherapy and counseling. As you read these chapters, remember that the theories and methods under discussion developed at a certain time and place as a result of certain social forces. Once you have gained a comprehensive understanding of the field of professional psychology by reading the following chapters, we will return in the last chapter to some of the same social and professional issues that appeared in this history. The meaning of the legal, ethical, professional, and social issues facing the field in the past will affect the future of professional psychology.

PART II

Assessment and Measurement

Issues in Psychological Assessment and Measurement

Several people are quietly riding the noon bus downtown when, suddenly, a middle-aged, well-dressed man stands up and begins to shout incomprehensibly and wave his arms about. Most passengers try to ignore him, but one asks him what is wrong and another mumbles at him to be quiet. He gives no reply, but sits back down for a few moments, quietly shaking. He stands again, staggers up and down the aisle twice, pointing his finger and glaring at a few passengers. This time, the passengers try different responses: glaring back, shaking their heads, cowering, and telling him to calm down. After sitting quietly for a few moments more, he stands, shouts, and seems to throw himself to the floor. What should the others do now?

As you read this description, you undoubtedly began thinking, "What is going on here? What is wrong with this man?" It seems obvious that something *is* wrong, but it is not clear what. Nevertheless, what the passengers will do depends on what they think is wrong. How can they assess this man's behavior and decide what to do? Most chose to observe him. One asked him to tell her what he thought was wrong, and others gave him orders to see if he could understand and would obey. Some may have concluded that he was a lost foreigner, others that he was drunk, crazy, or ill, and some may have wondered if he was a terrorist. Clearly, the results of these assessments lead to different behavior on the part of the assessors.

All people engage in assessment every day of their lives. A young woman meets a young man, looks him over, asks him a few questions about his zodiac sign and his interests, and observes his reactions to her. On the basis of this assessment procedure, she may diagnose him as a "nerd," a "hunk," or a "nice guy" and then try to predict whether she should go out with him. We all need to observe others, categorize them, and make predictions about their behavior so we can understand them and guide our behavior toward them.

In everyday life, the observations are informal and haphazard, the categories used contain value judgments (nerd), and the predictions may well be wrong. Assessment in psychology, on the other hand, is supposed to be systematic, objective, and accurate. Psychology has applied the scientific method of empirical observation and measurement to the very human activity of trying to assess and predict others' behavior. Psychologists use assessment and measurement in a variety of ways, in research, in clinical work and diagnosis, and in evaluation of the effects of interventions and programs.

A Review of Psychological Measurement

A review of test construction theory, scaling methods, and the rules of empirical verification is beyond the scope of this book. We assume that you have already studied research methods and measurement. However, certain measurement concepts should be reviewed, namely, types of scales, test standardization and norms, and test reliability and validity.

Scales of Measurement

All types of measurement, including psychological measurement, utilize scales. A *nominal scale* simply puts what is being measured into categories. Dividing eggs into white, brown, and speckled utilizes a nominal scale. Nominal scales may sound simplistic, but the complex process of diagnosis of mental disorders involves a nominal scale. An *ordinal scale* places what is being measured into an order. Movie ratings, with four checks indicating an excellent movie and one check a dud, are ordinal scales; from the rating one knows that one movie is judged to be better than another, but not how much better or in what way. A researcher studying the effects of anxiety may create an ordinal scale and order people based on their scores on an anxiety test, such as individuals scoring 20 points below the mean being considered low in anxiety, those scoring at the mean average in anxiety, and those scoring 20 points above the mean high in anxiety. An *interval scale* measures in equal units. A thermometer utilizes an interval scale. A *ratio scale* is similar, but it has an absolute zero. A yardstick is a ratio scale. Not only is the distance from 5 to 6 inches equal to the distance from 25 to 26 inches, but also 8 inches is twice as long as 4 inches.

It is difficult to develop a measurement that is an interval scale or a ratio scale in psychology. For example, is the difference in IQ from 95 to 100 equal to the difference between 120 and 125? It is unlikely, and it is clear that a person with an IQ of 120 is not merely twice as smart as one with an IQ of 60. The different types of scales become important in statistics, research, and interpretation of the meaning of scores. For the purposes of research and statistical analysis, psychological scales are often treated as if they are interval scales.

Norms and Standardization

In order to attach meaning to their measurements, many psychological assessment instruments are standardized and utilize the concept of norms. When a psychological test is constructed, it is given to a large number of representative people. The scores of this ***standardization group*** become the *test norms*, that is, how most people perform on the test. The score of a particular individual who later takes the test can be compared to the test norms, and her score is then set in a meaningful context.

To make scores even more meaningful, the scores of the representative or normative group are often subjected to a statistical transformation that sets the mean at a certain number and produces a specific standard deviation, a statistic that accounts for a set percentage of the normative group's scores. The most famous example of this type of score transformation is the so-called Intelligence Quotient, or IQ. The raw scores on the various test items are transformed through a statistical procedure so that the mean is 100. In this case, an individual who scores 100 on an IQ test has scored higher than 50% of the people in the normative sample. An individual who obtains an IQ of 115, when the standard deviation has been set at 15, has scored higher than 84% of the people in the normative sample.

Even with score transformation, the meaning of a specific individual's score requires interpretation. To know that Mr. Smith scored 32 on an anxiety test is basically meaningless. If we know that among a standardization group of 200 representative people the mean score on the anxiety test was 30, then we also know that Mr. Smith is probably average in the degree of anxiety he reports; if the normative group is assumed to be "normal" or typical of most people, then we may conclude that anxiety is not bothering Mr. Smith. Suppose he scored 40 on the anxiety test. If we also know that the standard deviation of the normative group's scores is 10, then we know that Mr. Smith scored higher than 84% of the representative group. Most people would agree that this is quite above average and probably problematic for Mr. Smith.

Reliability and Validity

Reliability and validity help psychologists know if their tests or measurements meet the criteria for scientific acceptability. ***Reliability*** refers to the "trustworthiness" or consistency of a measuring device; that is, is the same result obtained every time the measure is used, even when different people use it? If you use a yardstick to measure your desk and find that it is 38 inches wide, you will find that it is still 38 inches wide when you measure it the next day or if someone else measures it—the yardstick is therefore a very reliable measuring device. People trust it, and they will believe you when you tell them how wide your desk is.

Evaluating the reliability of a psychological measurement is more difficult. Several methods for determining test reliability have been developed. All of them involve a statistic called the correlation coefficient, r, which varies from 0 to 1.0. As the name implies, a correlation reveals to what degree two things vary together. If $r = 0$, the two variables are completely unrelated, or independent of each other. An r of 1.0 would mean the two behave identically. If you measure 10 objects with your yardstick and your friend measures the same 10 objects with her yardstick, you can subject your answers and her answers to a correlation and see if they vary in the same way. That is, if your yardstick says something is large and another thing is small, does her yardstick result in measures in the same direction? It is likely that the correlation between your measurements and your friend's will be about $r = .98$. It is unlikely that it would be a perfect 1.0, because small errors in measurement always occur.

There are several types of reliability, but we will cover *test-retest*, *internal consistency*, and *observer* reliability. In test-retest reliability, the question is, does the test give the same answer at different times? A large group of people is given a psychological test, and a month later the same people are given the test again. The correlation between their answers the first time and their answers the second is the test-retest reliability for that measure. With internal consistency, also called split-half reliability, the question is, do different parts of the test give the same results? A large group of people is given a psychological test at one time, and the test itself is split in half, often into odd-numbered and even-numbered test items. The correlation between the two halves of the test is the measure of the test's internal consistency. In observer reliability, also called interrater reliability, the question is, do different people using the same measuring device come up with similar answers? If two psychiatrists diagnose the same disordered person, do they agree? If two psychologists give the same individual the Rorschach inkblot test, do they come up with similar conclusions?

Validity refers not to the measuring system itself but to the appropriateness of the interpretation of the results of the measurements; that is, does the measuring device really measure what the person using it says it is measuring? What is really being measured with psychological tests is highly controversial. Validity refers to the meaning of the results of the measurement, that is, the appropriateness or accuracy of the interpretation of those results.

Several methods for evaluating validity have been developed, many of which also involve the correlation statistic. *Face validity* (which doesn't involve the correlation statistic), is an appealingly simple way of determining validity. Does the test look like it is measuring what its developer says it measures? For example, items such as "Do you feel worried at times?" on a test of anxiety make it appear to have face validity. *Predictive validity* addresses how well test scores predict the behavior that the test should predict if it is indeed measuring what it purports to measure. Do people who score high on an anxiety test later act worried and agitated under stress while those who score low remain calm? *Concurrent validity* can be determined by the correlation of a test's scores with those of another, better-known or already well-researched test. A group of people may be administered a new anxiety scale as well as the older, well-established Taylor Manifest Anxiety Scale (TMAS), and the correlation between the two sets of scores would indicate the concurrent validity of the new measure. *Construct validity* involves the relationship of a test to other test scores and behaviors that would be predicted by theory. For example, high anxiety is theoretically linked to poor performance under pressure, and if scores on a test of anxiety can be shown to be related to school grades in a theoretically predicted way, then construct validity may be demonstrated.

Most measurement experts agree that a test cannot be valid unless it is also reliable. It is, however, possible for a method of measurement to be reliable but not valid. For example, suppose that you measure your desk with a plastic tape measure that over years of use has stretched. When you or anyone else uses this tape to measure your desk several times, it gives consistent results—it is reliable. However, concluding that your desk is 38 inches wide is inappropriate, and other people using yardsticks to measure your desk will disagree with you.

As the next chapters show, a great deal of controversy is generated over the validity of psychological tests. A major reason for the controversy is that test results have consequences in the real world, in that decisions about people are made based on test scores. In fact, Messick (1995) proposed a concept of validity that included its consequential aspects. An important example is the use of intelligence tests, which are highly reliable, in the public schools. If a test purporting to measure intelligence is used to disproportionately assign minority children to special education classes, then people will argue that the test does not really measure intelligence but rather a set of skills that white children are taught by their families and culture but minority children are not.

Psychological tests in the hands of a professional psychologist may affect people's lives significantly and positively. However, psychological tests are used in many different contexts, often in ways that are inappropriate and therefore invalid. They are even used as entertainment. There are several Internet sites that allow you to take various tests, including tests that claim to measure your intelligence. You may want to find one of these sites to see what psychological tests are like, but please don't take your score very seriously.

Measurement and Assessment in Research

Assuming the reader already understands the concepts of *variables* (what the scientist is studying or measuring), *independent variable* (the one the scientist manipulates), and *dependent variable* (the one that changes as a result of changes in the independent variable), we wish to elaborate the important concept of the *operational definition* in experimental research. An operational definition of a variable involves a complete description of the operations or procedures that the scientist goes through to define or measure a variable, so other scientists can replicate or criticize the study. Operational definitions may be relatively simple in some research. A scientist studying the effect of children's height on self-confidence could operationally define height as measurement in eighths of an inch from the top of the head to the floor when a barefoot child stands as tall as possible against a wall, using a Smith-Harding measuring device (a ratio scale). A scientist could operationally define the manipulation of the independent variable of height by dividing children into groups of short (below 44 inches), medium (46 to 48 inches), and tall (50 inches or above), resulting in an ordinal scale. We'll leave you to imagine an operational definition of "self-confidence."

As you have probably guessed, operational definitions in psychological research are often complicated and subject to differing interpretation and controversy. Studying a supposed personality trait such as shyness would involve developing a measurement of shyness and demonstrating its reliability and validity, before the research could even be conducted. The measurement could be behavioral, such as number of comments a person makes in a five-minute conversation about politics among three peers, or test-based, such as the number of true responses to a set of true-false statements such as "I would rather watch TV than go to a party" or "I hate giving speeches in class." In the behavioral example, a shy person could be operationally defined as an individual who made 25 or fewer comments in that situation and an outgoing person as one who made 50 or more. Because shyness was operationally defined, other scientists can argue with the interpretation of the results of the study by saying, for example, that discussing politics may make a dissenter stay quiet because of tact not shyness. The arguments about interpretation of a variable operationally defined by a psychological test can be endless. The operational definition of intelligence, for example, remains controversial, as discussed in the next chapter.

Of interest to us is the use of measurement and assessment in research about psychotherapy. The research questions in this area can range from "Which is better—psychoanalysis, client-centered therapy, or behavior therapy?" or "Which interventions are most effective with a specific disorder?" to "What sort of therapist statement leads to what sort of client response?" among many others. The "which is better" question has a long history in professional psychology, as discussed in chapter 5. The obvious problem in this area is how the effectiveness of psychotherapy is defined and assessed.

Research on psychotherapy has tried to measure improvement in many ways. One way is to ask the client to rate himself, for example on the severity of his symptoms on a scale of 1 to 7, with 1 representing "no problem" and 7 representing "completely interferes with everyday functioning." Self-ratings could be collected at the beginning and end of 20 sessions of therapy. Besides the problem of even defining a symptom and the question of whether symptom reduction is the proper goal of therapy, self-ratings may show improvement for a number of reasons other than therapy, such as wanting to please the therapist or a reduction in environmental stress on the client. Researchers have used clinical tests, discussed next, to assess improvement. For example, a client could complete a depression questionnaire before and after therapy. The interpretation of the results of such a study would hinge on the previously demonstrated reliability and validity of the test.

Clinical Psychological Assessment

Although we have pointed out that all people try to assess others, we should also point out, before we begin to discuss the topic, that not all psychologists use or even believe in clinical psychological assessment. We can define clinical psychological assessment as the process of collecting information in a systematic, objective, empirical way about individuals' intellectual functioning, behavior, or personality so that predictions and decisions about them can be made.

The most common method of assessment, used by professional psychologists and everyone else, is the interview. It is possible to gather useful information and data by conversing with a person and asking pertinent questions. Because of their special training in science and experimentation, psychologists have developed additional methods of assessment, namely, tests. A psychological test is any procedure or method used to obtain information during the process of assessment. Often, tests are regarded as methods of collecting samples of behaviors under standardized conditions, and as such, the results are subject to methods of data analysis.

Psychological tests vary in how they are constructed, administered, scored, and interpreted and in what they are supposed to measure. There are group and individual intelligence tests, which may be short or long, with sections that test vocabulary, arithmetic, logical reasoning, and other abilities. Personality tests may involve true-or-false responses to a series of statements about life, or they may require making up stories about pictures or supplying the endings to incomplete sentences. Whatever their form, psychological assessment procedures have certain characteristics in common. They are designed to serve specific purposes and to measure specific aspects of people, they attempt to be as objective as possible, and they are subject to empirical verification.

The Clinical Assessment Process

Psychological tests and measurements are used for many different purposes: in research, for diagnostic purposes, to determine intellectual functioning, to design behavioral interventions, to evaluate psychotherapy outcomes, to screen candidates for jobs, to help individuals decide on a career, and more. The clinical assessment of individuals, however, is a complicated process, and psychological tests are only part of it. It is similar to the scientific process of formulating hypotheses, designing measures to test the hypotheses, collecting data, and interpreting the results. Psychological assessment involves framing a question about an individual, deciding how best to examine the possible explanations, collecting data through interviews and with appropriate psychological tests, analyzing the results of data collection, integrating and interpreting the results in terms of how they answer the original question, and making predictions and recommendations based on the analysis and interpretations.

The Referral Question

Individual psychological assessment is conducted only when someone needs to know something about a specific individual. While psychologists may occasionally decide to assess their own clients, in general, assessment is initiated by a referral question from other professionals. Teachers, physicians, social workers, psychiatrists, speech therapists, or others may ask psychologists for assistance in evaluating and understanding the difficulties of individuals with whom they are working. Individuals may request assessment of themselves or their children for a number of reasons.

It is important to obtain a clear understanding of the nature of the question from the referral source. Only with a clear, concrete, specific question can the assessment process begin. An important part of psychologists' expertise is knowing what tests to use for what purposes. Appropriate requests for assessment from psychiatrists, schools, or the courts should ask one or more questions about the client and leave the choice of assessment methods to the professional judgment of the psychologist.

Test Administration and Scoring (Collecting Data)

Once the psychologist has an appropriate referral question about an individual, the psychologist begins the process of collecting data, or gathering information. Psychologists frequently begin by interviewing the individual involved and possibly his or her family members. Information will be collected from other sources if possible, such as previous physical or psychiatric evaluations, school reports, and the like. If psychological tests are used, they are generally administered along with other relevant tests in a test battery. The test battery consists of all the tests that can help answer the referral question. After all, a single test result in isolation is meaningless, and only when it is substantiated by other results can a meaningful conclusion be drawn. For example, a single high score on the TMAS is not evidence of a disorder, but coupled with certain signs on the Rorschach inkblot test and elevated scores on certain Minnesota Multiphasic Personality Inventory (MMPI) scales, it can be seen as part of the evidence for a diagnosis of an anxiety disorder.

Psychologists are often requested to do intellectual assessments, usually of children who are having some kind of problem in school. The evaluation of a child having difficulty in school will include interviewing the child and the parents and collecting other available information, especially school reports. Children may do poorly in school because of neurological problems (such as difficulty with perceptual-motor coordination) or because of emotional problems, as well as because of low intelligence. A professional psychologist may decide to assess such a case with a test battery that might include a Wechsler intelligence test, an achievement test to assess current grade-level performance, a test to rule out organic causes, and one or more other tests, including personality tests to assess emotional factors.

Interpreting the Data

After administering and scoring psychological tests, the psychologist must interpret the test results and integrate the findings in order to develop a comprehensive picture of the psychological functioning of the individual and his or her difficulties and strengths. It has been said that interpretation is the clinician's most important skill. Unfortunately, while we will describe the major psychological tests and their uses in the next chapter, the procedures for scoring and interpreting the tests are beyond the scope of this book. Postgraduate course work and hundreds of hours of supervised experience are necessary to become competent in these tasks.

A psychologist's theoretical orientation will determine the types of interpretations made. Suppose, for example, a client says one of the Rorschach inkblots looks like a squashed witch. A clinician with a psychoanalytic orientation may say this response indicates the client's unconscious hostility toward her mother. Another clinician from a different theoretical perspective may regard this response as suggesting a lack of contact with reality, because the blot does not look anything like a squashed witch. A behavioristic psychologist may consider any response to the Rorschach to be irrelevant. Regardless of theoretical orientation, all psychologists must make inferences in order to move from their assessment data to predictions and recommendations.

The Psychological Assessment Report

After scoring the tests, making interpretations, and formulating predictions and recommendations, the psychologist must communicate the findings to others, particularly the referral source. This is generally done in the form of a psychological assessment or evaluation report (an example report is shown in box 4.5 in chapter 4). Most psychologists develop a standardized way of writing their assessment reports. Sometimes the agencies where they work require the report to be in a certain form. Psychological assessment reports vary greatly, according to the theoretical orientation of the writer, the needs of the client, the nature of the information sought, and the person who will read and use the report. As the final step in the assessment process, reports of the findings should be useful, understandable, and helpful.

Ethics in Assessment

Psychologists have certain ethical obligations when engaged in psychological assessment. As in all situations, including psychotherapy and teaching, psychologists must serve the best interests of the client. This ethical principle includes obtaining the individual's consent before assessment, fully explaining the nature and purposes of psychological assessment procedures to clients, and revealing the results of such assessments to them in a helpful way. In addition, clients should be informed of their right not to be tested or to discontinue testing at any time and of the limits to confidentiality.

Like all psychological information, the information obtained by psychological assessment must be protected and kept confidential, except under special circumstances such as when the client is a danger to others or when the testing is ordered by the court. The client owns the information, and it may be released to another professional, the courts, an agency, or a school only with the written consent of the client or the client's parent or guardian.

Controversial Issues in Psychological Assessment

Although an in-depth discussion of controversies about the proper way to construct a psychological test is beyond the scope of this book, some important issues in assessment must be addressed.

Patterns of Test Usage

Over the years, interviews and certain psychological tests have remained in consistent use. Lubin, Larsen, and Matarazzo (1984) surveyed over 200 clinical psychologists as to which psychological tests they used most frequently. Camera, Nathan, and Puente (2000) completed a similar survey with similar results, as shown in box 3.1. It

Box 3.1 Ten Most Frequently Used Individual Psychological Tests, 1982 and 2000

In 1982, Lubin, Larsen, and Matarazzo (1984) surveyed over 200 psychologists who worked in psychiatric hospitals, community mental health centers, schools for the mentally retarded, counseling centers, and Veterans Administration hospitals. The psychologists were asked to rank order the psychological tests most frequently used at their agencies. In 2000, Camera, Nathan, and Puente (2000) conducted a similar survey. The two lists are quite similar and several of the tests on them are old, facts which suggest that psychological test usage remains stable.

1982 Survey

1. Wechsler Adult Intelligence Scale
2. Minnesota Multiphasic Personality Inventory
3. Bender-Motor-Gestalt Test
4. Rorschach
5. Thematic Apperception Test
6. Wechsler Intelligence Scale for Children
7. Peabody Picture Vocabulary Test
8. Sentence Completion Tests
9. House-Tree-Person Drawing Test
10. Draw-A-Person Test

2000 Survey

1. Wechsler Adult Intelligence Scale—Revised
2. Minnesota Multiphasic Personality Inventory—I and II
3. Wechsler Intelligence Scale for Children
4. Rorschach
5. Bender-Motor-Gestalt Test
6. Thematic Apperception Test
7. Wide Range Achievement Test
8. House-Tree-Person Drawing Test
9. Wechsler Memory Scale—Revised
10. Beck Depression Inventory*
10. Millon Clinical Multiaxial Inventory*

*Last two tied for tenth rank

appears that psychological test usage remains quite consistent, perhaps even resistant to change, over the years.

Furthermore, several of the frequently used tests are quite old. The Rorschach was developed in the 1920s; the Thematic Apperception Test and the Bender-Motor-Gestalt Test in the 1930s; and the first Wechsler, the Minnesota Multiphasic Personality Inventory, and the Draw-A-Person in the 1940s. New psychological tests are constantly being developed and marketed. In fact, the market is so flooded with new tests that psychologists may feel unable to evaluate them adequately, and so they stick with the old standbys. They use these old tests despite continuing controversy over the reliability and validity of some of them.

The two lists presented in box 3.1 point out a discrepancy in belief between academic and applied psychologists regarding projective tests. Academic psychologists are quite critical of projective tests, citing research that shows poor reliability and validity of these tests. Nevertheless, half of the top 10 tests in actual use were projectives (Rorschach, Thematic Apperception Test, Sentence Completion Tests, House-Tree-Person, and Draw-A-Person) in 1982 and in 1995 (Watkins, Campbell, Nieberding, & Hallmark, 1995), and three of the top ten in 2000 were projectives, with three more in the top fifteen. Lubin, Larsen, and Matarazzo (1984) noted that

> psychological test usage shows only a modest relationship to test quality as judged by academic psychologists. . . . Despite the fact that surveys of university clinical faculty consistently show that the majority of them express negative attitudes toward the clinical value of projective techniques and recommend against increasing the amount of time devoted to teaching projectives at the university . . . , sev-

For diagnosis and assessment of pets.

> eral of these instruments . . . still rank among the top 10 in frequency of use in 1982. (p. 453)

This statement remains pertinent today.

Clinical versus Statistical Prediction

In the 1950s, Paul Meehl (Meehl, 1954, 1956) started a controversy that threatened to tear clinical psychology apart when he presented convincing evidence that statistical interpretation of test results is better than clinical interpretation. Clinical prediction refers to the complicated, deductive process by which professional psychologists use their extensive training and clinical experience to integrate and interpret the results of psychological tests. Statistical prediction refers to the application of empirically derived arithmetic rules or actuarial tables for the same purposes. According to Meehl, a statistical table—or today, a computer—can do the same thing as a trained clinical psychologist and do it better. If there is empirical evidence that certain test scores predict certain behaviors, then the "interpretation" of test results does not take any particular skill other than looking up in a table what a score means. Many clinicians find this idea unacceptable (Matarazzo, 1986, 1992).

Over the years there have been many studies to try to settle this controversy. A typical study gives a group of clinical psychologists some test results and asks them to make certain predictions about the individuals based on their clinical interpretation of the test results. The same set of results is subjected to statistical interpretation, predictions based on empirical data about what scores predict what behaviors. Then the two types of predictions are compared as to which is most accurate. After years of such studies (reviewed by Westen & Weinberger, 2004), Meehl's original conclusion still stands: Where appropriate statistical information exists, clinical interpretation cannot improve on it. The key phrase is "where appropriate statistical information exists," since statistical predictions will only be as good as the empirical evidence on which they are based. Meehl and others argue that psychologists' efforts should be directed toward collecting the empirical evidence necessary to create manuals or "cookbooks" for psychological tests so as to make good statistical interpretations and predictions. They claim that training in clinical interpretation should be dropped. It has been proposed that therapy also be done according to manuals, another proposal embroiled in controversy, as discussed in chapters 5 and 16.

Some critics argue that the whole statistical versus clinical prediction controversy is irrelevant because neither process is very accurate. They argue that the most accurate predictions can be made using only a person's past behavior as a basis. For example, an experimental study may demonstrate that several clinical psychologists can examine psychological test results of 100 prisoners and predict which ones will return to crime on release with about 30% accuracy. A statistical rule applied to the same test results may be able to hit about 40% accuracy. This finding may be interesting to academicians, but it is certainly not exciting when we realize that released prisoners return to crime about 60% to 80% of the time. Simply predicting that all prisoners will return to crime will result in an accuracy rate of 60%. And it is a lot cheaper and quicker than either clinical judgment or statistical methods.

However, accuracy of prediction is not the only important criterion in assessment. Ethics and the social consequences of certain decisions for specific individuals are often more important than an accurate prediction. Take suicide, for example. Only about 2% of callers to a suicide prevention hotline actually make a suicide attempt (Farberow & Schneidman, 1961). If all we were interested in was accurate prediction, we could simply predict that all callers would not attempt suicide and hang up on them. After all, we would be right 98% of the time, an incredibly high level of predictive validity. Obviously, though, the consequences of the 2% error are not acceptable in the case of suicide. Thus, questions and procedures have been developed to identify callers at high risk for suicide so preventive actions can be taken. This assessment procedure has poor accuracy; that is, it results in a high rate of errors by incorrectly identifying persons who would not attempt suicide as suicide attempters. This kind of error is morally more acceptable than the error of incorrectly identifying a person who ultimately attempts suicide as a nonattempter. Even though it is error ridden, we conclude that the assessment procedure in this case is valuable and even cost-effective.

The Use of Technology in Assessment

Like every other field, professional psychology makes increasing use of computers and other modern technology in its work. Probably the earliest use of computers or computer-like machines was scoring test answers, since machines can quickly scan answer sheets and print out scores. Now computer programs administer a variety of psychological tests. In a computerized administration, the directions for taking the test appear on the screen first; then, as each item appears, the client presses certain keys to respond.

Computer programs have been developed to interpret the results of tests as well. These programs are supposedly based on extensive research and use empirically derived rules to interpret individual test results. The evidence favoring statistical over clinical prediction suggests that computer interpretations of tests may be more accurate than those of individual psychologists, because computers can store and integrate far more empirical data than most people can learn and remember. Nevertheless, because clients are individuals and may exhibit exceptions to empirical rules, all ethical computerized reports carry the caution that they are only to be used by psychologists who know the client being evaluated and who have the expertise to evaluate the reported results. Computers are also used to compose and print psychological assessment reports. Some programs score the test, interpret the scores according to built-in empirical rules, and then compose and print out the report.

As already mentioned, many psychological tests are now published on the Internet. Professional psychologists are concerned that the confidentiality of test results may be compromised on the Internet and that tests may lose validity because people become familiar with them or practice with them. The possibility for the misuse and misinterpretation of tests would seem to be increased by their availability on the Internet.

Not everyone is enthusiastic about the increasing use of technology in psychology. Some critics fear that psychological "interpretations" printed out by a computer will appear to have greater "scientific value" than they truly have or that such printouts might be misused by nonprofessionals. Some believe that the computerized assessments have not been sufficiently validated (Matarazzo, 1986, 1992). At any rate, increasing use of technology in both assessment and therapy appears to be inevitable.

Criticisms of Clinical Psychological Assessment

Psychological tests and assessment procedures have been criticized for their reliability and validity since they were first developed. Other criticisms have long been made. For example, even if it is generally agreed that psychological tests are reliable and valid, they can still be criticized as not cost-effective if a simpler, less expensive way of doing the same thing exists. Many critics have argued that psychological tests are open to misuse. The most well-known controversy over the use of psychological tests has to do with intelligence tests. The alleged misuse of intelligence tests is directly related to issues of their validity. Intelligence tests have been used to place certain students in institutions or special education classes. If the tests do not appropriately and validly measure intelligence, then it is possible that at least some individuals so placed do not belong there. For example, if the tests in fact measure acquired knowledge or level of education or values particular to a certain culture, then the results of such a test taken by individuals who have not had the opportunity to acquire knowledge, reach a certain level of education, or participate in the culture upon which the test is based (in the U.S., these individuals are often members of minority groups) might result in discriminatory practices against these individuals or in their inappropriate placement. (See Helms [1997] for an excellent discussion of this issue.)

The controversy over the validity and misuse of intelligence tests has been brought into court. The California State Supreme Court in 1979 in the case of *Larry P. v. Wilson Riles and the Board of Education* ruled that intelligence tests were biased in favor of middle-class white children and against minority groups. ***Larry P.*** was an African American child assigned to special education classes on the basis of his score on an intelligence test. Special education classes contain far more minority group students than their proportion in the population. Larry P.'s parents argued that this disproportionate assignment of minority students to special education classes constituted discrimination and denied Larry P. an equal education. The California State Supreme Court agreed, determining that the scientific evidence for the validity of intelligence tests was inadequate and ruling that schools could no longer assign students to special education classes on the basis of their intelligence test scores alone, that they had to take into account other information as well. While the court and many others believe that Larry P.'s case represented a misuse of psychological tests, others such as Lambert (1981) believe that the court was wrong, and that intelligence tests are a valid way to make such educational decisions and less prejudicial than teachers' judgments and other methods. Interestingly enough, by the end of the 1980s, the use of IQ tests in determining special education placement had been almost entirely eliminated in California and other states, but the proportion of minority children in such classes was even greater than in the 1970s. In 1988, a group of African American parents went to court in order to *obtain* IQ testing for their children, arguing that *not* allowing the use of such tests was discriminatory, and in 1992, a federal judge in California lifted the ban on IQ testing of African American children.

The most frequently used personality test of all is the Minnesota Multiphasic Personality Inventory (MMPI), which was originally developed in order to diagnose mental disorders. Its very success and popularity may lead to its misuse, as people try to apply it in situations for which it was not designed; the MMPI was (and sometimes still is) used to make employment and personnel decisions, although adequate research to test its validity for those kinds of decisions does not exist. Individuals applying for jobs or promotions complain that they cannot see the relevance of MMPI test items to either the job they want or their competence to do it. Employers may respond that they do not want to hire and train a disturbed or unstable individual who will be unable to do the job properly or will quit or cause other problems.

In 1991, a California state appeals court in a class action suit against Target Stores (*Saroka v. Dayton Hudson Corporation, dba Target Stores*) prohibited Target from requiring job applicants to take the MMPI, because it contained certain questions about religion and sex that are not job related and violate the individual's constitutional right to privacy (Hager, 1991). This decision was appealed to the California Supreme Court, and the American Psychological Association filed an *amicus curiae,* friend-of-the-court, brief. The APA believed the court needed to be educated about how the MMPI was constructed (described in chapter 4), because the crucial point is that responses to groups of items, not specific items themselves, are related to job performance. However, in late 1993, the court prohibited Target from using the test for five years and awarded damages to those denied employment. The use of the MMPI or similar tests to deny employment or promotions would appear to be open to the criticism of misuse and to be an issue that will continue to appear in the courts.

Diagnosis

One of the traditional goals of psychological and psychiatric assessment is to reach a diagnosis of the patient's disorder. Diagnosis involves determining that a certain disorder is present or identifying a specific disorder that best matches an individual's symptoms. In ***differential diagnosis,*** the goal is to distinguish which of two or more possible diagnoses best matches the client's conflicting symptoms. In ***functional diagnosis,*** assessment focuses on the types and severity of specific deficits, as well as strengths, in order to design treatment interventions.

As discussed in earlier chapters, the medical model holds that the first step in dealing with a disordered individual is to make a diagnosis, so the cause of the problems can be discovered and a treatment can be scientifically developed. In this model, diagnosis determines the type of treatment prescribed, although this may not be what happens in actual practice. This emphasis on diagnosis as a logical first step may seem simplistic compared to professional psychology's complex process of assessment as a method for developing a comprehensive picture of the intellectual, personality, and behavioral functioning of an individual. Furthermore, some psychologists argue that diagnosis as practiced in the United States has no validity for other cultures, and some theoretical approaches reject diagnosis and assessment entirely. Nevertheless, because of the power of physicians and the prevalence of the medical model it is important for psychologists to understand diagnosis and to know the diagnostic categories commonly used by psychiatry.

The German physician Emil Kraepelin developed the first modern classification system for mental illnesses at the turn of the twentieth century. He carefully observed which symptoms tended to go together and gave a label to each set of symptoms. He believed that each disorder had a separate cause and a definite, predictable course and outcome. Kraepelin's original nosology, or system of classification, has held up well over time. The first *Diagnostic and Statistical Manual of Mental Disorders* (***DSM***), published by the American Psychiatric Association in 1952, was basically an expanded version of Kraepelin's categories, and even later revisions of the DSM retained many of these original categories. Psychiatry's diagnostic system has grown in complexity and numbers of categories and now includes such "disorders" as tobacco dependence, binge eating, sexual dysfunctions, and adjustment reactions. Albee (1985, p. 61) noted, "Clearly the more human problems that we label mental illnesses, the more people that we can say suffer from them. And, a cynic might add, the more conditions therapists can treat and collect health insurance payments for."

Reliability and Validity of Diagnosis

Diagnosis can be looked at as a nominal scale of measurement, that is, a measuring scale that names items or puts them into categories (sorting eggs into white, brown, and speckled categories is our previous example of a nominal scale). Thus, we can assess the reliability and validity of any system of diagnosis. There are serious problems with the reliability of diagnosis of mental disorders, especially with observer reliability. Many studies have documented that different diagnosticians often reach different diagnoses for the same patients (Nobins & Helzer, 1986). For one thing, the more categories there are, the more room for disagreement there is. For example, how does a diagnostician distinguish between agoraphobia with panic attacks, social phobia, panic disorder, and generalized anxiety disorder? Or between schizophreniform disorder and schizoaffective disorder? Agreement between diagnosticians tends to be higher for broad categories, such as neurosis versus psychosis or schizophrenia versus organic brain damage, than for narrow categories such as those just mentioned.

The validity of diagnosis may be even more controversial than reliability. The medical model implies that diagnosis is tapping "real" underlying organic disorders. But there has been a great deal of debate about the existence of "mental illnesses" at all (Szasz, 1961). Some argue that there is no such thing, that what are being labeled in diagnosis are problems in living, reactions to high levels of stress, poor social competence, faulty social learning, communication disorders, and the casualties of poor parenting, abuse, exploitation, and poverty. Albee (1985, p. 61) has noted that political ideology is implicated in this debate. As he said, "Conservatives strongly favor a constitutional-organic disease explanation, largely because no major social change is called for if the problems are all inside the skin." A "scientific" resolution to the debate over the validity of diagnosis and the medical model of mental illness is probably unlikely.

The Diagnostic and Statistical Manual

The first DSM was published by the American Psychiatric Association in 1952. It was next revised in 1968 as the DSM-II. Another revision, the DSM-III, was published in 1980, partly as an attempt to solve the problems with the reliability and validity of the DSM-II. An interim revision, the DSM-III-R, was published in 1987, and the DSM-IV was published in 1994.

A major change occurred between the DSM-II and the DSM-III. The DSM-II categories were short, vague, and contained much psychiatric and psychoanalytic jargon. They required a high degree of inference about the patient's internal state, as in this description of phobic neurosis: "Phobias are generally attributed to fears displaced to the phobic object or situation from some other object of which the patient is unaware" (American Psychiatric Association, 1968, p. 40). Because of the level of inference required, the reliability of the DSM-II was low. The DSM-III attempted to correct these defects by basing categories on "objective" criteria and observable behavior, so that all observers would be able to agree on whether a given person exhibited a specific behavior or not. A diagnosis is reached when a given person exhibits so many of the listed behaviors for a specific category. In this way, it was hoped, diagnosis would be more reliable.

In addition, the DSM-III tried to take into account the complexity of psychological disorders by including more variables in each diagnosis. It was based on what is called a ***multiaxial model,*** still used in the DSM-IV. Any single patient can be evaluated and categorized along five independent dimensions, or axes, which are summarized in box 3.2. Axis I contains the clinical syndromes, or typical diagnostic labels for mental disorders, such as adjustment reaction of adolescence, bipolar depression, and schizophrenia. Axis II deals with personality disorders, such as narcissistic and borderline personality disorder, and certain developmental disorders, such as mental retardation. Axis I diagnoses cover what are supposed to be relatively temporary disorders, while Axis II covers those that are present early and are relatively enduring characteristics that are more difficult to change. Axis III assesses physical disorders and conditions, such as injuries or chronic illnesses that may affect the course of a mental disorder. Axis IV is designed to measure the severity of psychosocial stressors, and Axis V estimates both the current and the highest level of adaptive functioning in the past year. Patients are categorized on all five axes, which are supposed to be independent of each other. (See box 3.2 for an example DSM diagnosis and a typical diagnostic decision tree.)

Work began on the DSM-IV in 1988 to prepare for its publication in 1994. The work was supposed to be scientific and empirical, but many criticized the revisions as being more political than scientific, as discussed in box 3.3. Furthermore, critics say the DSM revision process occurs so frequently that it disrupts research and does not allow sufficient empirical review of the diagnostic system to develop. The frequent changes without sufficient research increase the probability that theoretical and political biases will affect the development of diagnostic categories. Nevertheless, revisions continue, and by the time this book is published, there may be a DSM-V.

Box 3.2 Understanding the DSM

The Diagnostic and Statistical Manual of Mental Disorders (DSM) employs a multiaxial model. Each of the axes refers to a different class of information, and the resulting diagnosis is supposed to be quite complete. The multiaxial system is supposed to ensure that certain types of disorders, aspects of the environment, and areas of functioning that might otherwise be overlooked are considered in evaluating an individual. The first axis contains the types of disorders usually handled by the mental health professions, while the second covers more enduring difficulties. The majority of the DSM is devoted to describing the categories on these two axes. The five axes used in the DSM are:

Axis I: Clinical Syndromes

Axis II: Developmental Disorders and Personality Disorders

Axis III: Physical Disorders and Conditions

Axis IV: Psychosocial and Environmental Problems

Axis V: Global Assessment of Functioning

A diagnosis should include a statement for each axis. It is possible for an individual to show behaviors that would be classified as two or more disorders on any one axis and, of course, as two or more disorders on different axes. Axis I is for the various mental disorders, and each diagnostic category is assigned a specific number. Axis II, for the developmental and personality disorders, also has a specific number for each category. Axis III requires a medical diagnosis. For Axis IV, there is a checklist of nine broad categories of psychosocial and environmental problems, such as problems with the primary support group, housing, occupation, or education. Axis V requires a global assessment of the individual's functioning. Here is an example diagnosis:

Axis I: Panic Disorder with Agoraphobia
Alcohol Dependence

Axis II: Dependent Personality Disorder (provisional, rule out Borderline Personality Disorder)

Axis III: Alcoholic cirrhosis of liver

Axis IV: Psychosocial problems: anticipated retirement and change in residence with loss of contact with friends

Axis V: (Current and past levels of functioning are reported in different ways)

Reaching this type of diagnosis is a logically complicated process. The DSM-IV includes decision trees to guide the process. Part of the decision tree for the differential diagnosis of anxiety disorders is presented here:

- Symptoms of irritation and excessive anxiety or worry, avoidance behavior, or increased arousal not attributed to a psychotic disorder? If yes, go to:
- Organic factor that initiated and maintained the disturbance has been established? If yes, go to organic decision tree. If no, go to:
- Recurrent panic attacks? If no, go to:
- Fear of being in certain places in case of an incapacitating or extremely embarrassing symptom? If yes, diagnosis is agoraphobia without panic disorder. If no, continue with tree.
- Back to recurrent panic attacks, if yes, go to:
- Fear of being in certain places in case of having a panic attack? If yes, diagnosis is panic disorder with agoraphobia. If no, diagnosis is panic disorder without agoraphobia.

Box 3.3 Example Political Controversies in Revising the DSM

The professional and political conflicts involved in developing a system of diagnosis of mental disorders became quite public during the 1987 revision of the DSM-III, known as the DSM-III-R, and continued through the next few years until the publication of the DSM-IV. *The Diagnostic and Statistical Manual of Mental Disorders* is published by the American Psychiatric Association, and critics charge that it is biased toward the therapeutic theories and professional needs of psychiatry. For decades, psychologists, social workers, and others have complained that they are not sufficiently consulted in the process of developing the diagnostic categories for the DSM.

At least three new categories proposed for the DSM-III-R and the DSM-IV aroused particularly strong opposition from psychologists, social workers, feminists, and others. These three were originally called masochistic personality disorder, premenstrual dysphoric disorder, and paraphilic rapism. Feminist critics called the original language for these categories "antifemale" and argued that they could easily be used to reinforce negative attitudes toward and discrimination against women.

Along with other groups, the APA Committee on Women (1985) charged that the psychoanalytic term *masochistic personality disorder* would be disproportionately applied to persons who engaged in apparently self-defeating behaviors and who stayed in situations that appeared to be harmful to them. For example, women whose husbands beat them would be considered to have a psychopathological condition, while the aggressive husbands would not. The Committee on Women stated,

> A large and well-developed body of research in the area of victimization would suggest that many of the criteria of this proposed diagnosis are, in fact, normative responses to the experience of having been victimized. . . . In a worst-case scenario, it is possible to imagine a battered woman with children who leaves her batterer and files for custody of the children, but loses it because she is diagnosed as having Masochistic Personality Disorder, while her batterer (for whom there exists no corollary diagnosis) appears more "normal" and functional. (pp. 1, 5)

In response to such criticisms, the name of this category was changed to "self-defeating personality disorder" in order to make it equally applicable to men. Many groups continued to oppose its inclusion, but it ended up being included.

The proposed category of premenstrual dysphoric disorder (PMDD) would obviously be applied only to women, and critics charged that it attempted to create a mental disorder for the known gynecological disorder of PMS, or premenstrual syndrome. The American Psychiatric Association Committee on Women, the Committee on Women of the American Psychological Association, the National Association of Social Workers, and others opposed this category. Defenders of the category argued that it would help women by legitimizing the monthly depression of those who have it and by allowing them to receive treatment for it. Critics continued to oppose the inclusion of this category because: it creates a gender-specific mental disorder, it reinforces stereotypical views of women as victims of "raging hormones," it can be used as a "scientific excuse" against women in the workplace, and there is insufficient evidence for it, among other objections. It was placed in the DSM-III-R appendix but was dropped in the DSM-IV. Instead, a depressive personality disorder was added.

The category of paraphilic rapism would appear likely to be used to diagnose mostly men, yet feminists objected strongly to it. In addition to citing research that did not support the creation of such a category, the APA Committee on Women (1985, p. 5) stated, "It appears to add little to the understanding of individuals who engage in sexual assault. Additionally, it would seem to provide an instant insanity plea for anyone charged with rape." At one point the name was changed to "paraphilic coercive disorder," but finally the category was dropped.

Some people argue that paraphilic rapism was dropped to placate feminist critics so that self-defeating personality disorder could be retained. Defenders of the DSM state that they create, change, keep, or eliminate various categories based on "scientific evidence," but critics still contend that "science" is being used to cover up a very political process. What do you think?

Criticisms of Diagnosis

Psychologists have been very critical of the use of the DSM in diagnosis. Surveys of psychologists show that the majority clearly disavow the DSM, saying they would prefer a new nosology based on better empirical research. Most psychologists believe that categories of behavior derived from good empirical evidence that is free of the medical model would lead to a more valid and reliable diagnostic system than the DSM.

Some people criticize the whole notion of diagnosis, regardless of the system, because diagnosing or classifying various disorders often leads to labeling. These critics argue that labeling people gives us a false sense of doing something helpful and useful, that labels always contain hidden value judgments, that labels are a way of controlling or devaluing others by objectifying them and making them "different," and that there is no mental "illness" or disorder to label anyway (Szasz, 1961).

Others believe that labels or diagnoses stigmatize a person, who may then be affected by a "self-fulfilling prophecy." Once people know that someone has been diagnosed as "schizophrenic" or "paranoid," they may act differently toward that person and induce the very behavior the label leads them to expect. Rosenhan's (1973) study of "sane" graduate students admitted to mental hospitals demonstrated how others then construed all their behavior as evidence of abnormality.

Furthermore, in the guise of being "objective," many DSM labels contain latent and not-so-latent value judgments. Many critics claim that the DSM is biased toward seeing all behavior as symptomatic of some disorder or other. Others (Kaplan, 1983) have argued that it is biased in a sexist direction in that certain male behavior is seen as normal or "human," while certain female behavior is viewed as deviant. There are diagnostic labels for primarily feminine behaviors, such as dependent personality disorder, without complementary diagnoses for masculine behaviors, such as an "independent personality disorder" (Caplan, 1987, 1991).

Diagnosis is also criticized as being a mechanism of social control. The medical model and its attendant system of diagnosis is perceived by some critics to be a way for society to allow mental health professionals to become the social control agents of various irritating deviant members of society. If an irritating deviant, such as a loud drunk, is labeled as having the "illness" of "alcohol dependence," then doctors and psychiatrists can legitimately control that behavior.

It can be argued that diagnosis is neither totally desirable nor totally undesirable. The question is, do the benefits of diagnosis outweigh the drawbacks? Some medical labels, such as sexually transmitted diseases and AIDS, carry a social stigma, but a correct diagnosis has important benefits, such as a cure. Much research demonstrates the social stigma attached to mental illness labels. Is there any evidence that diagnosis has positive consequences, such as determining the type of treatment required? In actual practice, individuals often receive the type of treatment that is available, regardless of diagnosis. An adequate cost–benefit analysis of diagnosis has yet to be done.

Despite the criticisms of diagnosis and the DSM, it seems likely that the recent trend to medicalize mental disorders ensures that psychologists will often be involved in assessment in order to help make diagnoses. Thorough knowledge of the diagnostic process, the latest DSM, and the scientific or political process by which it is developed is essential for professional psychologists. It is still possible that psychologists will organize themselves and their body of scientific knowledge to create an alternative to the DSM and, we trust, a superior system of classifying psychological disorders.

Program Evaluation and Accountability

Similar in a way to some research on psychotherapy, program evaluation or outcomes assessment attempts to determine whether an entire department, program, or agency is effectively doing its job. "Accountability" was a popular word in the 1980s, and it seems to be back in vogue at the beginning of the twenty-first century. Accountability means that a program is held to demonstrating its effectiveness in reaching its stated goals. If taxpayers or private charitable foundations fund a program to treat drug addicts, for example, they naturally want to know if their money is well spent. They may want to know if the program really does reduce drug use among the clients and by how much. If the program promised other benefits, such as an increase in gainful employment among the clients, it is accountable for demonstrating that it does that, too. Taxpayers, foundations, and insurance companies not only want effectiveness demonstrated, but they are also interested in cost-effectiveness. The program may be effective, but is it too expensive? Is there a cheaper but equally effective way to treat drug addicts?

At present in the United States, most programs that provide social services or treat psychological problems must engage in program evaluation and conduct outcomes assessments as a condition of funding. Demonstrating the effectiveness of programs runs into the same sorts of difficulties that research on the effectiveness of therapy does. How can effectiveness be defined and measured in a way that is acceptable to scientists, clients, taxpayers, and other interested parties?

Professional psychologists employed as program evaluators have developed a number of methods for assessing outcomes. Some assessments rely on easily obtained statistical information. For example, a child abuse treatment program may keep track of the number of client contact hours and the number of parents who are reported for child abuse during and after treatment. If more client contact hours coincide with fewer abuse reports, then the program's outcomes are good. Other outcomes assessments use a multitude of measures, from client self-ratings and psychological test scores to community focus groups. For example, a program to treat drug addicts may administer several psychological tests to clients when they first join the program and then again when they leave to see if treatment has produced positive changes on measures of depression, impulse control, and other variables.

Even when program evaluation is well designed from a scientific point of view, there may well still be problems. In the case of child abuse, is a reduction in incidents of abuse all we want to accomplish? Clearly it is a social good to reduce child abuse, but might we also want to increase the confidence and competence of the abused children? Might we want to make sure that they learn to trust others, control their anger, and refrain from abusing their own children when they grow up? What if it can be demonstrated that a program accomplishes all of these goals, but it costs a half a million dollars per child to do so?

Critics of program evaluation argue that it diverts resources better spent on programs and that it can make it appear that we are doing something about a problem when we really are not. The "No Child Left Behind" act is criticized for these reasons. Some groups of people believe that public education is not doing its job, that public schools are failing. No Child Left Behind was enacted to address this supposed crisis and improve public education by holding the schools accountable and measuring their outcomes. It is called No Child Left Behind because one of the goals is that all children will perform at grade level. Furthermore this act requires schools to test children's performance in certain subjects several times a year and show a certain amount of improvement in test scores. Schools that improve are rewarded with resources and those that do not improve sufficiently lose resources. The rationale for this act is that the federal government sets, assesses, and enforces standards, but leaves it to the states and schools to decide how best to achieve them.

One criticism of this act is that it is based on a faulty understanding of assessment. Test scores are defined by the norms of a representative sample. In any large representative sample, there will be large variation in the range of scores. In most tests of school achievement, grade level norms are set at the point where half the representative samples for each grade pass and half fail. Thus it is logically impossible for all children to perform at grade level. In addition, it is logically impossible for every school to show improvement as defined in the act. Since schools' test results are reported as percentiles, 10% of schools will always be in the bottom 10%. It is possible for a school to show improvement in test scores but still remain in the bottom 10% and therefore be considered a failing school.

Critics also charge that teaching and learning time is lost to test taking, that teachers "teach to the test" and neglect other areas and that the tests are not adequate measures of what schools are supposed to accomplish. Schools are not just for learning certain testable information but should also serve the community and produce good citizens and maybe some artists and musicians, too. Finally, critics argue that simply measuring something doesn't bring it about. (Weighing the pig doesn't make it get fat, as farmers say.) However, it is cheaper to institute a testing program than to make any number of changes that have been proven to improve schools, such as reducing class size, increasing teachers' salaries, or providing teachers with adequate resources. Whether you approve of it or not, No Child Left Behind is the largest federal experiment in outcomes assessment in U.S. history. While there are constant arguments about how best to hold programs accountable, it is clear that program evaluation and outcomes assessment will remain an important part of professional psychology.

In Conclusion

This chapter described the theory and general methods of psychological measurement and assessment in research, clinical work, and program evaluation. It also discussed the reliability and validity, cost-effectiveness, and social uses or misuses of psychological tests. Because clinical psychologists are trained to research, develop, administer, score, and interpret psychological tests, tests will remain an important part of professional psychology. Through constant research and the help of computers to analyze and integrate this research, psychological tests will continue to improve and find new applications. Because people have always wanted to be able to predict human behavior, psychological tests will continue to be used and possibly misused. Educating the public, as well as students of psychology, about the nature and meaning of psychological assessment may become an important ethical obligation of psychologists.

METHODS OF CLINICAL ASSESSMENT

LaTisha M., age 8, rarely attends school, where she is in the third grade, because of headaches and stomachaches. Although she did well in kindergarten, she began to have difficulty with learning to read in the first grade. When she was in second grade, LaTisha was pushed from some playground equipment and sustained a head injury, which went untreated. Now when she does attend school, she alternates between being withdrawn and disruptive. LaTisha's mother has six other children, and she rarely has time to pay attention to LaTisha except when she complains of illness. The school is beginning to demand that LaTisha's mother get some help for her, but the mother does not know where to begin.

What can be done to help this child? Before we can answer this question, we need to evaluate several aspects of her current functioning. Because her difficulties are related to school, it seems reasonable to assess her intellectual and cognitive abilities. Because of the headaches and the head injury, neuropsychological assessment would also be appropriate. Obviously, the stomachaches and headaches require a separate physical examination. Finally, because of the hints of emotional, behavioral, and family problems, personality and behavioral assessment should be included. It may also be necessary to request other information, such as school reports, and further evaluations, such as by a speech pathologist or educational psychologist. Obviously, interviews with the mother and the child before and after any assessment procedure are necessary.

The Interview

Despite all the technology and tests being developed, old-fashioned interviewing as a method of assessment remains popular. Interviews are useful when clients are first seen, in assessments, and in diagnosis. Their use in psychotherapy is well known.

A good psychological interview both obtains information and helps the client. Assessment interviews are goal oriented, and the interviewer bears the responsibility for guiding the interview so that all necessary information is obtained while at the same time rapport and good communication with the client are established. The interviewer should ask questions matter-of-factly with a nonjudgmental attitude and listen and observe carefully. Most interviews require privacy, generally in the confines of a quiet, professional office, but interviews outdoors and in other settings are possible. If a great deal of information is given, unobtrusive note taking may be necessary. Standardized protocols for conducting different types of interviews have been developed and published.

The Intake Interview

When a client first contacts a therapist, hospital, or agency for services, intake interviews are conducted to determine the nature of the individual's problems and to decide whether the psychologist or agency has the competence and facilities to help with such problems. These interviews usually take 45 to 90 minutes and can follow a structured, question-and-answer format or be relatively unstructured. The results of the interview may be utilized to make a diagnosis, prognosis, or treatment plan, so a sufficient amount of relevant information must be elicited to meet these purposes.

Besides identifying data such as name, age, address, family members, educational or occupational status, and the like, the information sought in an intake interview will focus on the presenting problem, that is, what brought the individual in for services. It will include the client's description of his or her problems and symptoms, when they began, what brought them on, and what the client has tried to do about them. Questions about the client's past psychological history, medical history, and personal history may also be asked. Any information from other sources, such as school reports or psychological tests, if available, may be collected. The goal is to obtain as much information as possible in order to determine the next step to be taken to help the client.

The Mental Status Exam

The ***mental status examination*** is the formal part of an interview that assesses the client's current mental functioning. It is often conducted when individuals are seen in an emergency room or admitted to a psychiatric ward. Usually fairly structured, this interview may include clinical tests such as asking the patient to repeat a series of digits backward, answer questions about current events, or subtract 7 from 100 serially. The typical mental status exam tries to cover the following areas:

1. General appearance and behavior. Is the person neat or disheveled, walking straight or not, alert or stuporous, avoiding eye contact, slow moving or agitated?
2. Speech and thought. Is the person's speech coherent, understandable, excessive, nonexistent? Is thinking logical, peculiar, confused, grandiose?

3. Consciousness. Is the person conscious, clear, confused?
4. Mood and affect. Is the person's prevailing mood sad, elated, irritable, appropriate, inappropriate?
5. Perception. Is the person hallucinating, and if so, when?
6. Obsessions and compulsions. Does the person engage in repetitive behavior or reveal intrusive thoughts? If so, are they seen as real or symptomatic?
7. Orientation. Does the person know what time, day, and year it is?
8. Memory. How are the person's long-term and short-term memories?
9. Attention and concentration. Is the person distracted, preoccupied, able to concentrate?
10. General information. Can the person name the president, six large states, the capitals of a few countries?
11. Intelligence. What level of education has the person attained? Are the questions in number 10 answered well?
12. Insight and judgment. Does the person seem to have insight into her current situation? (Judgment often seems to be assessed by whether persons agree that they are in need of treatment!)

The Case History Interview

Sometimes done during an intake interview, the case history interview attempts to elicit the client's personal and family history and social situation. The purpose is to provide a broad background and context for the individual's current difficulties and to identify strengths and resources as well as difficulties. Most adults provide their own social history, but in the case of children, people who are developmentally disabled, or people who are incompetent, parents, family members, or caretakers may provide the information. The typical case history interview will ask individuals or their caretakers about their present situation; their family history; their early development and birth; their past and current health; their education; their sexual development; and their marriages, divorces, and children, if any. The interview may ask the client to give a self-description, and, after the client does this, ask if the client has anything to add or ask.

Pretest and Posttest Interviews

If the above interviews indicate that psychological tests would be useful in assessing the client's problems, it is helpful to interview the person before and after the testing. A pretest interview helps establish the rapport and trust needed for the individual testing process. It should also explain the testing procedures to the client, including the kinds of tests to be administered, their purposes, and how the results will be used. Most people hold various preconceived notions about psychological tests, and care must be taken to elicit and correct any misperceptions, to answer clients' concerns, and to allay their fears.

After subjecting a person to several possibly disquieting psychological tests, it is ethical and humane to have a posttest interview in order to give the client feedback. It may be necessary to explain the tests again (most people are too anxious to listen well the first time), to go over the client's misperceptions and concerns again, and to address any new questions or fears the testing may have raised. Although there is professional disagreement about how much people should be told about their own test results, we believe that sensitive feedback coupled with a thorough explanation of the tests and their limits can be very therapeutic. We have also found it useful and helpful to ask clients to offer their own interpretations of what they think their test results mean.

Reliability and Validity of Interviews

The reliability of interviews will depend on how structured they are and how reliability is assessed. For example, observer reliability of diagnoses reached through the mental status exam is fairly good, but the observer reliability of diagnoses with less structured interviews is low. Because people change and because different interviewers will ask different questions, test-retest reliability of interviews can also be quite low. Having a clear goal in mind, establishing a precise definition of what is being assessed, developing specific interview questions to elicit the information sought, and providing appropriate training for interviewers all improve the reliability of interviews.

The validity of interviews is assessed in a variety of ways, depending on the purposes of the interview and the theoretical orientation of the evaluator. For example, one measure of predictive validity examines the correctness of the diagnosis reached through an interview and the success of the treatment plans the results indicate. Studies on the predictive validity of interviews (including job interviews) have not been positive, but in actual practice, numerous treatment decisions and diagnoses are made based on interviews alone.

Clinical Uses of Interviews

Clinical uses of interviews have been described above for each type of interview. Interviewing is inevitably part of all clinical assessments and interventions. Diagnoses and interventions should be based on several kinds of information and not on the basis of interviews alone, although that is often the case. Depending on the skill of the interviewer, interviews can provide valuable additional information when clinical assessments are conducted.

Intellectual and Cognitive Assessment

Although covering the years of controversy over the definition of intelligence is beyond the scope of this book, let us briefly outline some of the points of contention. Early researchers considered intelligence to be a general factor (*g*-factor) or characteristic that is manifested across a wide range of behaviors so that a person of high intelligence will be superior to others in many different ways. Later psychologists argued that intelligence is a collection of different kinds of abilities, all relatively independent of each other so that a person may be high in logical intelligence but low in artistic intelligence. The second controversial issue has to do with whether intelligence is inherited and relatively unchangeable or environmentally determined and open to improvement. In spite of the differing opinions about intelligence, psychologists have developed a number of tests designed to measure it. In response to the above issues, some have argued that a better term for intelligence tests is cognitive ability tests (CATS) and that they should simply be regarded as a systematic way to gather samples of school-related skills and behaviors in a structured setting.

The Stanford-Binet

The first so-called intelligence test was published in 1905 (Binet & Simon, 1905). At the turn of the twentieth century, the Paris school system had asked Alfred Binet and his colleagues to develop a test that would predict which children would do well in school and which children would not, so something could be done about the latter. Note the assumption that if children fail to benefit from schooling, it must be because of some (measurable) defect in the children, not because of any inadequacy in the educational system. Many critics think that the tests are still used to label and discriminate against children, rather than to change education or tailor it to individuals' needs.

Binet did as he was asked, and he did it brilliantly. He developed tests that directly sampled the skills needed in school, such as verbal comprehension, numerical skills, logical reasoning, visual discrimination, fine motor coordination, and the like. He developed standardized tests of these skills and administered them in standardized ways to many children. Because of this standardization, the performance of different children could be compared directly.

In addition, he developed the concept of age norms. He noted how many children of a particular age in a standardization group passed specific test items. Test items that half of 6-year-olds passed were called 6-year items. By this method, the scores of children could be directly compared across ages. A 9-year-old who passed the 6-year items and failed the 7-year items was considered to be the intellectual equal of an average 6-year-old.

Binet's test was modified in the United States by psychologists at Stanford University (Terman, 1916). Revisions of it are still in use today as the Stanford-Binet Intelligence Scale. The Stanford-Binet is administered individually by a trained psychologist. It can be used to test individuals from age 2 years to adult. The raw scores of the standardization groups are statistically transformed by a formula into IQ (intelligence quotient) scores, which are presented in tables in the test manual. A particular testee's raw scores are then compared to the tables to obtain an IQ. An IQ of 100 represents the average or mean score for an age group. The standard deviation is set at 16. If a particular individual achieves an IQ score of 116 on the Stanford-Binet, we know that she or he scored one standard deviation above the mean of the standardization group of the same age, or about 84% higher than most people of that age.

Up until the fourth (and current) edition of the Stanford-Binet, it produced only one overall IQ score, so it was difficult to assess an individual's strengths and weaknesses. Furthermore, the test items were different for each age. For example, a 3-year-old might be asked to identify body parts on a picture of a child, copy paper folded into a shape, match geometric designs, copy a circle, and determine whether two drawings match or not, while an 8-year-old might be asked to define words, compute math problems, and do analogies. Critics viewed this situation as unsound, because in fact different skills, perhaps even different types of intelligence, were tested at different ages.

The fourth edition contains major changes in the Stanford-Binet. There are now four general classes of tests, each with several kinds of subtests for ages 2 to adult. The four types of tests are verbal reasoning, quantitative reasoning, abstract/visual reasoning, and short-term memory. It is now possible to analyze a person's strengths and weaknesses, but because some of the subtests still differ for different ages, the Stanford-Binet is still criticized for evaluating intelligence differently at different ages. On the other hand, one of the strengths of the test is that it can be used with such a wide age range, and it is quite possible that there are developmental differences in the organization of cognitive skills and intelligence at different ages so that different types of tests would be required.

The Wechsler Tests

Beginning in the 1940s and making later revisions, David Wechsler and his colleagues have developed an intelligence test for children ages 5 to 16, the Wechsler Intelligence Scale for Children (WISC); one for adults, the Wechsler Adult Intelligence Scale (WAIS); and another for children ages 4 to 6, the Wechsler Preschool and Primary Scale of Intelligence (WPPSI). All have been revised, and the WISC is now in its fourth version, WISC-IV.

Like the Stanford-Binet, the Wechsler tests are based on the norms of large standardization groups for each age, and the raw scores are transformed through a statistical formula into IQ scores, which are summarized in tables. The early Wechsler tests differed from the Stanford-Binet in that they were divided into two parts: verbal subtests, which assess verbal skills such as vocabulary and comprehension, and performance subtests, which tap nonverbal skills such as matching symbols and copying designs. Three separate IQ scores were obtained with the Wechsler intelligence tests: verbal, performance, and full scale, unlike the single IQ of the old Stanford-Binet. Also unlike the Stanford-Binet, which contains different subtests for different ages, the Wechsler tests gave all individuals the same subtests, which contain items of increasing difficulty so that older or brighter people answer more items within each subtest. In fact, all current Wechsler tests consist of similar subtests. Box 4.1 describes some example subtests.

The 1991 WISC-III contained several important changes from the earlier versions. While the age-related norms were updated, the test items were also revised to make them more interesting to children; items that were unfair to certain cultural

Box 4.1 Some Example Subtests of the WISC-IV

Similarities: A series of pairs of words are presented orally and the subject explains how they are alike. This subtest is part of *verbal comprehension*.

Block Design: A set of two-dimensional geometric patterns must be copied as fast as possible using two-color cubes. This subtest is part of *perceptual reasoning*.

Digit Span: A series of orally presented number sequences must be repeated verbatim for Digits Forward and in reverse order for Digits Backwards. This subtest is part of *working memory*.

Coding: A series of simple shapes or numbers are each paired with a simple symbol. The subject draws the symbol in its corresponding shape or under its corresponding number, according to a key, as fast as possible. This subtest is part of *processing speed*.

groups were eliminated; and new subtests were added. Furthermore, the WISC-III was subjected to much research and factor analysis, and four factors, or clusters of scores, were found. In WISC-IV, these factors are called verbal comprehension, perceptual reasoning, working memory, and processing speed. It is now possible to obtain IQ scores on these four indexes, in addition to the full-scale IQ score. The WAIS-III and WPPSI-III also produce several types of IQ scores. For the Wechsler tests, the IQ mean is set at 100, and the standard deviation is set at 15. Furthermore, the raw scores of each subtest are transformed into standardized scaled scores with a mean of 10 and a standard deviation of 3. These subtest scaled scores can be profiled in order to compare relative strengths and weaknesses. In addition, the Wechsler group has developed the Wechsler Memory Scale (WMS) and the Wechsler Individual Achievement Test (WIAT), among others. These two tests can be used with the IQ tests to produce a very comprehensive picture of an individual's cognitive abilities and functioning. The Wechsler intelligence tests are now used more often than the Stanford-Binet.

Other Intellectual and Cognitive Tests

There are many other intelligence scales, some with special uses. For example, the Peabody Picture Vocabulary Test can be used to test children and adults who have a problem speaking English, perhaps because they are not native English speakers or because they have a speech disorder. Test takers are presented with four pictures and asked to point to the picture that represents a certain word. For example, children may be asked to point to a "car," while adults may be asked to point to "imbibe" or "bovine." The raw scores are converted to IQ scores, which compare fairly well to the IQs from other tests. This test is short and easy to administer, and it may provide a better estimate of a speech-disordered person's intellectual functioning than a Wechsler test.

An addition to the field of intellectual assessment of children is the Kaufman Assessment Battery for Children. It is suitable for children ages 2 to 12. This test has two unique features: It tries to assess the functions of the right and left hemispheres of the brain, and it tries to separate the measurement of skills or "intelligence" from that of fact-oriented or acquired knowledge. The separation of measurements is an attempt to answer the frequent criticism that intelligence tests really measure cultural and acquired knowledge and are therefore biased in favor of middle-class, white people.

There are even intellectual tests for babies. The Bayley Scales of Infant Development—Second Edition (BSID-II), for ages 1 to 42 months, consists of three parts, with scales designed to assess mental development, psychomotor development, and quality of behavior. Norms for this test are based on a sample of hundreds of young children, and a developmental age equivalent score can be determined for mental and psychomotor development. This test may be used to make an early identification of children with developmental delay so an early intervention can be made.

Achievement tests are frequently given with intelligence tests. It is often important to know how the level of global functioning measured by the intelligence tests compares to the level of academic achievement. Discrepancies, such as a child with a high IQ and low achievement, require explanation. There are many group and individual achievement tests, but the Wide Range Achievement Test (WRAT) is an example. It is short and straightforward in administration and scoring. It assesses three areas of achievement: reading, spelling, and arithmetic. An individual's scores in the three areas are both age normed and transformed into grade equivalents.

Reliability and Validity of Cognitive Ability Tests

It is generally agreed that properly administered intelligence tests are highly reliable, by both internal consistency and test-retest measures of reliability. For the Stanford-Binet, internal consistency correlations were reported to be in the .80s and low .90s range, and test-retest correlations for intervals of two to eight months were reported from the .70s to the low .90s. Reliabilities of the Wechsler tests may be even higher, with internal consistency for the WAIS-III ranging from .93 to .97 and test-retest reliabilities for short intervals ranging from the .70s to the high .90s (Sternberg, 2000). It should be pointed out that the intelligence tests were constructed so that they would be reliable. Careful standardization and using transformed scores contribute to these tests' reliability. However, an individual may show large changes in IQ scores over time if there are changes in any number of important variables, such as health, motivation, mood, type of education, or psychological disorder.

The validity of intelligence tests is much more debatable, as discussed in chapter 3. Recall that validity refers to the accuracy or appropriateness of the interpretation of the results of a test: Do IQ tests really measure intelligence, as they are often interpreted to do? Naturally, the answer to this question depends on the definition of intelligence. The theoretical argument over the nature of intelligence becomes important outside of academia when the lives of individuals are affected by decisions based on intelligence test scores.

Like many subsequent psychologists, Binet developed a pragmatic definition of intelligence—it was whatever the tests he was constructing measured. Spearman (1904) originated the theoretical definition of intelligence as a unitary factor, which became known as general intelligence or *g* factor. He considered intelligence to be an innate, global capacity that runs through and accounts for all the different skills and abilities a person may have. Other researchers have refuted the idea of intelligence as a unitary factor and have argued that there are types of intelligence that are not being measured by current intelligence tests. Gardner (1983) identified at least seven different kinds of intelligence: linguistic skills, logical and mathematical skills, visual and spatial conceptualization, musical skills, bodily kinesthetic skills, interpersonal skills, and intrapersonal knowledge. Each kind of intelligence functions semiautonomously and has its own form of memory, learning, and perception. Gardner argued that our culture values only the first two kinds of intelligence and they are what intelligence tests measure, not "true" intelligence.

One type of evidence used to assess the validity of intelligence tests is predictive validity. What do the tests predict? Career success? Happiness? Income potential? No, they predict school grades, because they sample school-related tasks and skills. And what do school grades predict? College grades. And college grades predict graduate school grades. Do these grades predict success or income? The evidence is mixed (Ceci & Williams, 1997).

Validity becomes a special concern when cognitive ability tests are applied outside their culture of origin. It can be argued that ability tests can be considered items of symbolic culture (Greenfield, 1997) that are constructed within racial, cultural, and socioeconomic contexts (Helms, 1997). In that case, the racial, cultural, and socioeconomic characteristics of the test maker, test giver, and test taker will influence test results and can undermine test validity. Given the increasing cultural diversity of the United States, this possibility becomes an important issue.

The controversial nature of the validity of intelligence tests for different ethnic groups came to public, as well as professional and academic, attention with the publication of a book called *The Bell Curve* (Herrnstein & Murray, 1994). One chapter of this book argued that racial differences in IQ are inherited, and this point sparked a great deal of public and scientific debate. Although not many addressed the point that there is little evidence for the existence of "races" in the first place, many have argued that there is little evidence for the book's thesis (Neisser et al., 1996) and that there are major errors in the book's statistical analyses (Fischer, Hout, Jankowski, Lucas, Swindler, & Voss, 1996).

The question of the validity of intelligence tests is important because of the social uses to which the tests are put. Although IQ tests are often used to help children receive the most appropriate and helpful educational experiences available to them, they are at times used to label certain people, to lay the blame for their failure in school on them rather than on the educational system, and to assign minority group children disproportionately to special education classes, as was discussed in the case of Larry P. in the last chapter. If these tests do not really measure intelligence, if there are indeed many types of intelligence that people could use if the culture valued them, then these uses of intelligence tests represent a social injustice. Test validity is more than a theoretical issue of interest to psychologists; it has real-life consequences for some people and for society.

Clinical Uses of Intelligence Tests

At present, in clinical practice, the Wechsler scales are used more frequently than the Stanford-Binet or any other intelligence test. Some tests may be infrequently used but valuable in certain circumstances, such as using the Peabody to assess people with language difficulties. The WPPSI may be used to test very young children when there is reason to suspect developmental delay and the parents are trying to obtain special services. The WAIS is often used to assess adults who have lost some degree of cognitive functioning because of illness or injury. The Kaufman is also used in neuropsychological assessment. In such cases, it is necessary to estimate the prior level of intelligence by knowing the person's education and occupational level and possibly by asking family members about the person. The comparison of present intellectual strengths and deficits to the estimated prior intellectual level can be useful diagnostically and in planning treatment or rehabilitation.

The WISC is useful in differential diagnosis and in identifying causes of difficulties in school. Take the case of LaTisha M., for example. The WISC may suggest evidence of neuropsychological disorder or a learning disability, and appropriate kinds of interventions could be planned. On the other hand, if in fact she performed well in all areas of the test, then the reasons for her school difficulties are not intellectual deficits, and other evaluations would be necessary. Achievement tests would be useful at this point. Whether her achievement scores were appropriate for her intellectual level or much lower than would be expected is important in explaining her school difficulties.

Many psychologists regard intelligence tests as methods for gathering behavioral observations in different structured settings. They observe how the child copes with the stress of the test, the kinds of verbal answers given, and the nonverbal behavior and physical coordination demonstrated during performance tests. A child who exhibits a great deal of motor activity throughout the WISC may be anxious or hyperactive. It is possible that LaTisha M. may exhibit anxiety by complaining, refusing to answer, or losing concentration during certain subtests. If she were to put block designs together in a rapid, systematic fashion, it would lead to different conclusions than if she did them slowly, in a haphazard, poorly planned, or uncoordinated manner.

The content in responses to certain questions can be analyzed in terms of what they imply about the child's worldview, social perceptions, attitudes, and the like. A rebellious middle school boy one of us tested revealed a surprisingly positive attitude toward the police in his reply to the test question asking why we have police. He said "They protect us" and that he wanted to be one when he grew up. A completely different social perception would be revealed if LaTisha M. were to answer the same question by saying that "We don't need them. They just hurt you." If a child is asked to explain such an answer, additional information about her reasoning and understanding of social relationships and implicit social rules can be obtained.

These few examples give an idea of how the intellectual tests are used in clinical practice. Assessment of children with learning disabilities almost always includes the WISC, and researchers are finding ways to analyze WISC and WAIS subtest scores for what they indicate about specific forms of neurological impairment (Sparrow & Davis, 2000), as discussed in the following section.

Neuropsychological Assessment

The field of neuropsychology studies the relation between brain and behavior, and neuropsychological assessment involves a set of procedures designed to detect the presence, extent, and type of organic brain damage or neurological impairment in individuals through evaluating the behavior that is related to brain functioning. As researchers learn more about the brain and its contribution to behavior, as well as behavior's effect on the brain, physiological and neurological factors must be taken into account in all forms of assessment, including personality assessment, and we can expect that neuropsychological assessment will become an increasingly important part of the occupation of psychologists.

Another and unfortunate reason for the growth in neuropsychological assessment is the increase in brain damage in our society in recent decades. Because of advances in medical technology, the lives of severely head-injured people, who would have died in the past, are being saved. The law requiring special seats and restraints for babies and small children has had some unintended consequences. It is true that car seats save lives, but they also produce specific types of brain damage in accidents. For example, in a head-on collision, the restraints stop the baby from going through the windshield, but they stop him very suddenly while his brain continues to travel forward and hit the front of the skull, thus creating frontal lobe damage.

Research on the brain has grown exponentially, especially in the 1980s and 1990s with the technological development of computerized ways of imaging and studying the brain. The idea that parts of the brain affect behavior differently is now well accepted. The earlier work on split brains, which demonstrated different skills in the right and left hemispheres of the brain, is well-known enough that people make remarks such as "That artist is so right brain." Of course, in real brains the hemispheres are connected and work together, so the concept of hemispheric dominance is somewhat misunderstood by the public.

A controversial issue throughout history has been whether functions are localized in certain parts of the brain or whether the brain is *equipotential* and any part can have any function. As usual, the final answer seems to be both. Although many functions are localized, the brain is highly plastic, with a great deal of individual variation, and it appears that if part of the brain is destroyed, other parts can take over its functions, at least in some cases. One of our graduate students suffered severe brain damage at birth so that only a thin outer layer of brain tissue remained intact, yet this student achieved well-deserved A grades.

Because some functions are localized to some degree in specific parts of the brain, the location of a brain injury will determine the nature of the resulting behavioral deficits, as shown in box 4.2. For example, the right and left hemispheres of the brain differ in that certain abilities related to sequential reasoning, vocabulary, and detail analysis appear to be preferentially handled in the left hemisphere of the brain in most individuals, while abilities related to holistic reasoning, spatial relations, and implied meanings appear to be handled by the right. Brain damage to the left hemisphere may harm speech. However, because the brain is plastic, injuries to certain parts of the brain do not necessarily predict the type of behavioral deficits that will result. Neuropsychological assessment is necessary in order to determine the exact nature of behavioral deficits in any kind of brain disorder so treatment can be planned.

The causes of brain damage are many. Accidents are a leading cause of brain trauma. Blockages of blood vessels in the brain, known as vascular accidents or

Box 4.2 Some Examples of Disorders of Learning, Memory, and Behavior Associated with Neurologic Injury

Temporal Lobe. Left temporal lobe damage is associated with impaired memory for verbal material, while damage to the right temporal lobe is linked to an inability to recall nonverbal material, such as faces or geometric drawings.

Frontal Lobe. Damage to the upper middle frontal lobe is associated with inhibition of information processing. Front lesions are linked to a disinhibition of stimulus-response reactions, characterized by impulsivity and hyperactivity.

Parietal Lobe. Parietal lobe damage has been associated with impaired performance of order memory tasks for auditory and visual information.

Cerebral Cortex. Injuries of the cerebral cortex have been associated with distractibility.

Cerebellum. In laboratory studies, damage of the cerebellum is associated with loss of previously learned conditioned responses in animals.

From: Lauerman, J. (1992, May/June). Neurologic impairment: Understanding the effects on learning. *Headlines*, pp. 12–15.

strokes, can cause certain parts of the brain to die, as can a cerebral hemorrhage, or rupturing of the blood vessels, and brain tumors. Degenerative diseases, such as Alzheimer's, are well-known causes of organic brain disorders. A variety of environmental toxins harm the brain, as in mercury and lead poisoning. Nutritional deficiencies also harm the brain, especially in children. Lack of oxygen during difficult births and toxins, diseases, and poor nutrition during pregnancy are important causes of damage to the developing nervous system and brain.

Symptoms of brain disorder also vary. Disturbances in perception, inability to smell, slurring of speech or inability to speak, a change in coordination, headaches, a sudden change in emotional reactivity, or a deterioration in intellectual functioning all may indicate the presence of neurological damage. These symptoms must be differentiated from similar ones seen in some psychoses or even malingering. Other types of brain impairment are subtle and may become evident only when complex tasks are encountered, as in learning to read. It is obviously important to understand the cause of such symptoms so appropriate treatment can be developed.

Neuropsychological assessment is likely to increase in importance in the psychological assessment field. There is increasing emphasis on biology and the brain in psychology. With the development of sophisticated brain imaging methods, research on brain and behavior interactions is growing. A person considering a career in neuropsychology or neuropsychological assessment will probably want training in the latest medical imaging technology in addition to the tests discussed below.

Single Neuropsychological Tests

Because of the complexity of the brain and of brain–behavior relations, neuropsychological assessment is also complex, generally requiring the use of several types of tests. However, in previous decades, single tests were developed to detect the general presence or absence of brain damage. The oldest neuropsychological test is the Bender-Motor-Gestalt test (Bender, 1938). Short and easy to administer, it involves copying geometric designs, a task commonly incorporated into psychoneurological test batteries. It consists of a series of nine geometric designs, each on a small card. The test taker is given a blank sheet of paper and a pencil and asked to copy the designs as they are presented one at a time. The test taker must be able to perceive the design and then draw it, hence a measure of visual–motor coordination. The copied designs are scored for their accuracy and their preservation of the *gestalt*, or overall form, of the designs. Designs that are poorly done considering the age of the child would suggest that there is impairment in the child's visual–motor coordination, which would be due to some organic brain dysfunction. Some examples of Bender designs are shown in box 4.3.

Another figure copying test, the Rey Complex Figure Test (Osterrieth, 1944), also called the Rey-Osterrieth Complex Figure, is in use with children and adults. The test consists of one very complicated geometric drawing. One way this test is administered is to have the individual copy the figure with different colored pencils so that her strategy for copying the design can be analyzed for specific types of neurological deficit. Another way includes having the person redraw the figure from memory after 30 minutes. Normative data from hundreds of children and adults have been collected for this test. The Rey and the Bender may be used as a screening for brain damage or as part of a test battery, but an adequate neuropsychological assessment cannot be based on a single test.

Box 4.3 Some Drawings from the Bender-Motor-Gestalt Test

The drawings below represent five of those included in the Bender-Motor-Gestalt Test. The drawings by the 10-year-old girl are not perfect, but they are accurate representations of the designs she was told to copy. The drawings by the 11-year-old boy show some errors commonly made by children with learning disabilities.

Drawn by a 10-year-old girl with no learning difficulties:

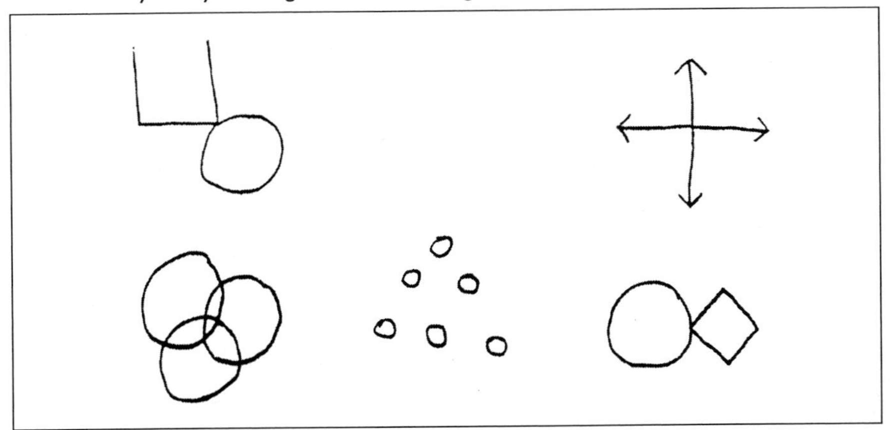

Drawn by an 11-year-old boy with learning difficulties:

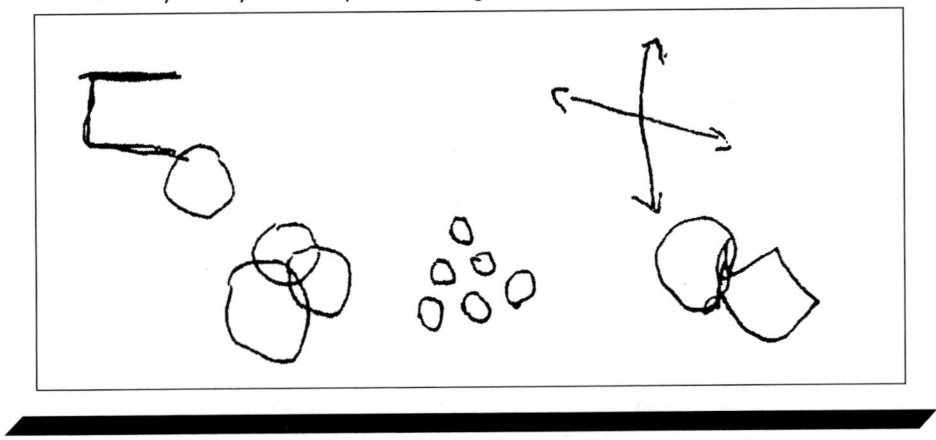

The Halstead-Reitan Neurological Test Battery

The Halstead-Reitan Neurological Test Battery is a complicated but comprehensive set of tests originally developed by Halstead and continually revised by Reitan and his colleagues (Reitan & Davison, 1974; Reitan & Wolfson, 2004). It is probably the most widely used test in neuropsychological assessment. To give you an idea of just how comprehensive it is, Reitan recommends allowing eight hours just to administer the test! Obviously, the testing should be broken up into two or more sessions.

Because of the long administration time, technicians sometimes administer all or parts of the test, leaving the intricacies of interpretation to the neuropsychologist.

The Halstead-Reitan includes several procedures: an intelligence test; aphasia tests; copying tasks; a memory test; tactile, visual, and auditory discrimination tests; speech, rhythm, and fine motor coordination tasks; form board problems; and more. New tests are occasionally added. Directions and research on the test are published in a variety of papers, and Reitan training workshops are offered to psychologists and physicians.

The Boston Process Approach

A group of neuropsychologists, physicians, and other professionals at Boston University School of Medicine have developed an approach to neuropsychological assessment of children with learning difficulties, known as the Boston process approach. They utilize a variety of well-known and new assessment techniques, but they interpret the results of these measures in terms of a theory that emphasizes the process by which the patient solves the problems presented by the tests. They emphasize that the meaning of test scores is context dependent, including the contexts of age, sex, socioeconomic class, developmental history, genetic background, handedness, developmental level, emotional style, and even the interactional style with the examiner. They consider behavior deficits to reflect the *intact* portion of the brain doing its best in the absence of the damaged portion of the brain, so that strengths, not just deficits, are examined.

Traditional neuropsychological tests and the WISC are analyzed in terms of this brain-world, context-dependent model. Among the many tests used in the Boston approach, children may be asked to perform difficult motor tasks, such as walking on the sides of the feet. How well children perform such tasks for their age and what sorts of behaviors are elicited by the stress of the tasks can provide trained observers with much information about the children's neurological functioning. Among the contextual variables taken into consideration in the process approach, the functioning of the examiner–child dyad is examined. For example, if the examiner feels his space is invaded by the child, then the child may have a social problem; if the examiner finds himself using very simple speech, then the child may have a language deficit; or if the examiner begins talking louder and louder, the child may have a hearing problem and need an audiologist.

Reliability and Validity of Neuropsychological Tests

There are special problems in determining the reliability of neuropsychological tests. Because they take so long to administer, a thorough evaluation may take several days, so internal consistency becomes essentially a measure of test-retest reliability. Patients with organic brain damage may be deteriorating or (preferably) improving, so that their performance will differ on subsequent tests. In spite of these problems, some studies indicate that reliability is adequate.

Validity of neuropsychological tests can be examined by several criteria. One measure of validity is the tests' ability to pinpoint the location of brain lesions, as determined by brain scans, the results of neurosurgery, or autopsy, as well as their ability to differentiate organicity from psychosis or other diagnoses. Predictive validity would include the effectiveness of interventions based on the test results. Studies (reviewed by Goldstein, 1997; Reitan & Davison, 1974; Ricker, 2004) indicate fairly good validity for the Reitan.

Clinical Uses of Neuropsychological Assessment

Typically, neuropsychological assessment is used with adults to assess stroke patients, head injury victims, or people with aphasia, amnesia, brain tumors, epilepsy, or senility, and with children to assess learning disabilities. In addition to use in medical research, neuropsychological tests are used for diagnosis, prognosis, differential diagnosis, and planning of patient care and rehabilitation. With children, they are used to evaluate the specific deficits involved in learning disabilities so that individually tailored educational intervention plans can be made.

As research advances and as knowledge of brain function improves, neuropsychology will continue to develop new tests and procedures to evaluate learning disabilities and other behavioral consequences of brain impairment (Allen, 2001). Appropriate interventions can be implemented only from a comprehensive picture of the nature of cognitive impairment. For example, it may be well-known that stroke patients have suffered specific kinds of brain damage, but neuropsychological assessment evaluates the precise consequences of this damage and the kinds of cognitive impairment, such as short-term memory loss or word retrieval difficulty, that are present so that appropriate interventions, such as memory retraining and speech therapy, can be designed. In the Boston model, behavior is assessed as a reflection of the intact brain coping with the damage, so that interventions are oriented to developing and training the intact part to compensate for the impairment.

Neuropsychological assessment is important in differential diagnosis. In elderly patients, for example, evidence of cognitive impairment may be erroneously interpreted as reflecting an organic disease when in reality cognitive abilities have been compromised by a psychiatric disorder such as depression. Costly and inappropriate treatments may be tried, and the failure to treat the depression may result in greater cognitive loss. With LaTisha M., it is important to know if her difficulties in school are due to psychosocial problems or to specific learning disabilities, because very different treatment recommendations would be made for each case. With brain-related interpretations of intelligence tests and other behavior, it may be that all cognitive assessment will be considered neuropsychological assessment.

Projective Personality Tests

Two major types of personality tests have been developed in the United States. The oldest type is the projective test. Test takers are given an ambiguous stimulus, such as a picture of a scene, an inkblot, or an unfinished sentence, and are asked to tell a story about the scene, say what the inkblot looks like, or finish the sentence. There are no objectively right or wrong answers to guide them. Clients must "project" their own thoughts, beliefs, and feelings onto the stimulus in order to make sense out of it. This is known as the projective hypothesis. The projective hypothesis also assumes that test takers will reveal their unconscious personality dynamics in their projected responses, because the ambiguity of the test and the test directions make it impossible to fake or to become guarded or defensive in their responses.

The other type of personality test is the objective or structured test. These tests usually require people to answer written questions with a pencil, hence their other name, pencil-and-paper tests. The answers required are usually short, such as true or false or agree or disagree, so that objective tests may take less time to administer and score than projective tests. Projective tests are somewhat like essay examinations, in which test takers must create their own answers from what they have in their minds, while objective tests are rather like multiple-choice examinations, in which test takers choose from among a limited number of given answers.

As you might guess from the projective hypothesis, projective tests grew out of the psychoanalytic tradition (see chapter 6) and were designed for the purpose of identifying the nature of psychological disturbance. Carl Jung first experimented with this idea at the turn of the twentieth century, when he developed a word association test to detect patients' unconscious conflicts and personality dynamics. The most famous projective test, the Rorschach inkblot test, was developed by Hermann Rorschach, a Swiss psychoanalyst, in the 1910s (Rorschach, 1921). The second most popular projective test, the Thematic Apperception Test (TAT), was created in the 1930s (Murray, 1938). The Draw-A-Person test (DAP) was developed in the 1940s (Machover, 1949); the House-Tree-Person test (HTP) was a later extension. Sentence completion tests were constructed in the 1940s and 1950s (Rohde, 1957; Rotter & Rafferty, 1950). It is apparent that the most frequently used projective tests are quite old.

Because they came from the psychoanalytic tradition, projective tests are based on certain theoretical assumptions. The people who developed the tests began with the assumption that what is bothering disturbed individuals is unconscious and must be discovered by indirect means. They also assumed that these unconscious difficulties centered on sex, aggression, early family relationships, and other specific issues. Thus, for the Rorschach, the inkblots chosen had portions that resembled sex organs, blood, and the like, while the TAT pictures portrayed conflicted relationships, childhood experiences, and the like. Projective tests were constructed from theory, not from empirical research.

The Rorschach

The Rorschach test consists of 10 inkblots printed on cards. Rorschach chose inkblots because they do not depict anything realistic and therefore would require persons trying to "see" something in them to project their own internal thoughts and feelings onto them. He made his inkblots just the way one usually makes inkblots—by dropping some ink in the middle of a piece of paper and folding it in half, thereby spreading the ink in a symmetrical pattern. However, Rorschach had specific theoretical reasons for choosing the shape, color, and order of presentation of his inkblots. For example, he started with an all-black, fairly easy inkblot, one that is often seen as a bat or a butterfly. His second card contained the addition of some red ink parts, which he supposed would throw test takers off guard and stimulate deep emotional responses. How they handled this stress and integrated the parts of the blot would indicate their coping abilities and degree of personality integration or disintegration.

The Rorschach is administered by psychologists to clients individually. The psychologist presents the 10 inkblot cards in the designated order one by one, and asks the client to tell what each might be. After the client responds to all 10 blots, the psychologist conducts the inquiry part of the test and asks the client to tell what aspect of each blot, such as its shape, color, or texture, made it look like that.

After the Rorschach is administered, it is scored and interpreted according to a complex system. There has been much controversy among competing systems as to the best way to score and interpret. In addition to Rorschach's original methods, Beck (1945), Klopfer (Klopfer & Kelley, 1942), Exner (1991, 2003), and others have developed scoring methods and interpretation rules, with Exner's system the most popular at present. Exner has spent years validating his system with extensive research, and he continues to modify and improve his system based on his empirical work. Even though the scoring and interpretation of the Rorschach is complex and beyond the scope of this book, you can easily imagine how a person whose response to the first card is "I see a raging dragon with his intestines hanging out" differs in important ways from someone whose response is "It looks like a butterfly."

The Thematic Apperception Test (TAT)

Perhaps because storytelling has been a human activity since ancient times, there are many projective tests based on storytelling. As already noted, the oldest and most frequently used storytelling test is the Thematic ***Apperception*** Test (emphasis added). There are special versions of the TAT for use with African Americans or Hispanic Americans. Other storytelling tests include the Children's Apperception Test (CAT); the Roberts Apperception Test for Children; the Blacky Pictures, which depict dogs; the Make A Picture Story (MAPS), which involves making up the picture as well as the story; and the Picture Projective Test (PPT), which uses photographs.

The TAT consists of 31 cards with drawings of people in various scenes. Because the TAT is supposed to be a projective test, the pictures are not drawn with photographic realism, but are in fact quite vague in many details to allow for individual projection. Certain pictures are supposed to elicit certain themes or issues that psychoanalysts assume to be important, such as authority, gender, and family relationships. In practice today a subset of 10 cards is generally given to individuals in a traditional order. Some psychologists develop preferences for certain cards over others, or they may vary the cards according to the nature of the test taker or the diagnostic question. For example, there is a card depicting a person alone at a window in a darkened room. This card is not often used, but psychologists may choose to use it if they are testing depressed and possibly suicidal individuals, for it tends to "pull" themes of loneliness, sadness, and sometimes suicide.

Like the Rorschach, the TAT is administered by psychologists to clients individually. The psychologist directs the client to make up a story about each picture: to tell how the story begins, what is going on in the picture, what the characters are thinking and feeling, and how the story ends. Differing systems for scoring and interpreting the stories have been developed for use in research or personality assessment. Interpretation depends on the psychologist's theoretical orientation. Those with a psychoanalytic orientation will analyze the stories for recurring themes of sex, aggression, and early family relationships. Others will examine the stories as to how the client handles issues such as nurturance or achievement, degree of social appropriateness or maturity exhibited in the stories, how well-organized and coherent the stories are, how reality based the stories are, and other variables.

Drawing Tests

The Draw-A-Person test is generally administered individually, but it may be given in groups. The administration of this test is simplicity itself. The psychologist gives clients a blank piece of paper and a pencil and asks them to draw a whole person. If clients express doubt, the psychologist may explain that this is not a test of artistic ability and any kind of whole person will do. They are then given another piece of paper and asked to draw a whole person of the opposite sex. Most people draw a person of their own gender first. Some psychologists ask their clients to describe the personalities of the persons they drew and to indicate their age, occupation, and other details. While the administration is simple, the interpretation of the DAP is complex and subject to controversy. For example, a large head is supposed to represent an emphasis on intellect, and sketchy lines on the head are supposed to represent anxiety about intellect. The validity of such interpretations is debatable.

The House-Tree-Person test is similar in many ways to the DAP. Clients are given a blank sheet of paper and a pencil and told to draw a picture with a house, a tree, and a person in it. The relations between the house, tree, and person are supposed to indicate how people view their world and themselves in it. Another version of this test has people draw the house, tree, and person on separate sheets of paper. Differing theoretical assumptions regarding what the house, tree, and person symbolize affect the interpretation of the test. For example, some psychologists believe the house symbolizes the mother and the tree the father, while others think the house reflects the nurturing side of the personality and the tree the achieving side.

The Kinetic Family Drawing test (KFD) involves having people draw a picture of everyone in their family doing something. The way the family members are depicted, their relative sizes, their facial expressions, and the relations between them may reveal how individuals see their families. For example, a child who draws her mother, father, and brothers all together in one room, with herself to the side, may feel left out or rejected by her family.

The Bender-Motor-Gestalt Test, described earlier, is sometimes interpreted to indicate characteristics of the personality. For example, someone who copies the designs quickly and confidently may differ from someone who copies them slowly and laboriously by counting the dots and curves in the lines. Some psychologists make symbolic interpretations as well, such as considering disconnected parts of designs as indicating distance in relationships or overlapping designs as indicating difficulty with boundaries. However, the validity of this use of the Bender has not been demonstrated.

Sentence Completion Tests

There are several sentence completion tests available, the Rotter Sentence Completion Test (Rotter & Rafferty, 1950) being perhaps the best known. Clients are asked to finish series of incomplete sentences, such as "Mothers are . . . ," "I hate . . . ," "I am very good at . . . ," "Girls are best because . . . ," or "Life can be very. . . ." The tests may be administered individually in oral form, with the psychologist reading the sentence beginning to the client, or they may be administered in written form, with the test takers writing down the completions. Again, there are several ways of scoring and interpreting these tests. You can easily imagine how a child who says "I am very good at nothing" differs in important ways from a child who says "I am very good at school and baseball."

Reliability and Validity of Projective Tests

It is difficult to measure the reliability and validity of projective tests, because the tests are scored, interpreted, and used in so many different ways, depending on the theoretical assumptions employed. Internal consistency may be considered irrelevant because it is assumed that different inkblots or different TAT pictures reflect different issues, and test-retest reliability may also be considered irrelevant because it is assumed that people change with time and in different situations. Most criticism is directed at observer reliability, because it appears from years of research that different psychologists analyzing the same set of Rorschachs or TATs may well produce widely divergent interpretations, even when using the same scoring system. Exner (1991, 2003) has tried to address this problem by making his scoring rules very precise and explicit and basing their interpretation on empirical research, and he reports reasonable levels of reliability with his methods. However, reviews of research have concluded that projective tests do not demonstrate adequate reliability (Lilienfeld, Wood, & Garb, 2000; Wierzbicki, 1993).

How to measure the validity of these tests is controversial because of differing theoretical assumptions. For example, it is assumed in the psychoanalytic tradition that people "identify" with the protagonists in their stories and thus reveal their own personalities in the behavior of the story hero. However, it is also possible that the hero represents cultural stereotypes, the star of a favorite TV show, what test takers think the test giver wants to hear, or even how test takers wish they were, but are not. Also controversial is whether projective tests have validity for cultures other than the Western tradition. On the one hand, projective tests, being vague stimuli, may elicit universal themes; storytelling exists in all cultures. On the other hand, it is unlikely that the meaning of stories or perceptions is universal across cultures.

Research on the validity of projective tests is mixed, but generally unsupportive (Lilienfeld, Wood, & Garb, 2000). The evidence for symbolic interpretations of the tests appears to be especially low. Interpretations of test behavior, such as drawing impulsively or telling incoherent stories, are closer to the data than symbolic interpretations and appear to have adequate validity in terms of predicting other, similar behavior. A literature review of studies on the TAT concluded that it does not exhibit adequate validity (Keiser & Prather, 1990). Studies by Exner and his colleagues (reviewed by Erdberg & Exner, 1984) have demonstrated the validity of specific sorts of Rorschach interpretations, such as quality of reality testing. Nevertheless, after reviewing the research on projective tests, Wierzbicki (1993) and Lilienfeld, Wood, and Garb (2000) concluded that projective tests are frequently used in ways that are invalid or not supported by research.

Clinical Uses of Projective Tests

Despite low demonstrated reliability and validity, projective tests continue to be used extensively in clinical practice for several reasons. First, there are the natural human tendencies to resist change and to attend to validating instances and not to disconfirming evidence. One of us tested a young man who had been diagnosed as schizophrenic, but there was evidence of brain damage on the Rorschach. As a result the admitting psychiatrist ordered a brain scan and found a previously unsuspected hematoma. The young man was saved from dangerous psychotropic medication and given proper blood thinning drugs. Another time, one of us tested a man who had been severely depressed, but requested discharge from the mental hospital. Despite appearing to be improved, he showed evidence on the Rorschach of continuing severe depression. The psychiatrist in charge of the case chose to ignore this evidence and released the man, who promptly bought a gun and shot himself to death the very next day. Such dramatic and fateful experiences may be more convincing of the usefulness of projective tests to practitioners than dozens of empirical studies, even though drawing conclusions based on a few personal experiences is not rational or scientific.

Second, professional psychologists use projective tests only in conjunction with other methods of assessment, as in a test battery. Projectives are interpreted tentatively and used as a source for hypotheses about a person, hypotheses that must be confirmed by other evidence. Often, in reporting the results of projectives, psychologists try to indicate the evidence for their inferences and interpretations.

There are at least four levels of inference used in making interpretations of projective tests. First, the level closest to the data of observable behavior is the task level. Some psychologists consider projective tests to be simply an opportunity to collect behavioral samples in a structured way. They will ask, how do individuals cope with and solve the problem presented by the test task? Do they work quickly or slowly, stick to the obvious or get creative, respond coherently or in a confused manner, include all the elements or leave some out? Second, the transactional aspects of the testing situation can be interpreted. How does the individual relate to the tester—with cooperation or resistance, with enthusiasm or anxiety, with overt or covert hostility? Third, the representational level of the test results, such as the types of things seen in the Rorschach or the content of TAT stories, can be analyzed. Are realistic or frightening things seen in the Rorschach? What is the nature of relationships as portrayed in TAT stories? Finally, interpretations at the symbolic level will depend on theoretical orientation, and this level requires the largest leaps in inference. Does a person's focus on black as a color on the Rorschach indicate depression? Does drawing a large head on the DAP indicate an emphasis on intellect? As noted above, the validity of projective tests is dubious, especially at the symbolic level of interpretation.

As implied by the example questions above, projective tests are often used to assess emotionally disturbed people in order to make a diagnosis or a differential diagnosis, to evaluate the nature and extent of the disturbance, or to make treatment plans. In the case of LaTisha M., such tests may help distinguish whether her difficulties are emotional or organic and reveal her perceptions of the problems in her family. As might be expected, the usefulness of these tests will depend on the clinical skill, as well as the theoretical orientation, of the psychologists using them.

Some psychologists make use of projective tests in therapy. Collecting TAT stories during a series of therapy interviews is a good way to get children to talk with the therapist and explore important issues indirectly and safely. The KFD also can be used in therapy with children as a way to talk about their family relationships. Some family therapists ask the entire family to draw one large KFD, and their drawing and how they go about making it can serve as topics for discussion.

Objective Personality Tests

There are many objective pencil-and-paper tests used in research and personality assessment. They are an economical use of the psychologist's time. Clients can answer the test questions by themselves, without any interaction with the psychologist after initial instructions are given, and answers can be written on machine-scorable answer sheets, which lend themselves to computer analysis. These tests can be administered, answered, and scored with a computer as well.

Burisch (1984) distinguished three major approaches to objective personality scale construction: empirical, inductive, and deductive. In the *empirical approach,* the test constructors know that people differ, but not how, so they determine the difference(s) empirically. They invent a lot of test items, give them to people who are known to differ in some way (say, anxious people and relaxed people), and then make their test up based on how the two groups differ in their answers. It doesn't matter what the test questions are about, because it has been empirically demonstrated that they differentiate anxious and relaxed people. In the *inductive approach,* the test constructors "discover" laws or personality structure by giving many people many test items and then subjecting their responses to mathematical analyses that determine which items go together. In the *deductive approach,* test constructors have a theory or definition of what they want to measure before they begin, and their theory or definition guides the choice of test items. They choose test items because they look like they fit, or they may ask the opinions of experts as to what items they should use. The differences in these three ways of constructing psychological tests will become clear as specific tests are discussed.

MMPI and MMPI-2: An Example of the Empirical Approach

The Minnesota Multiphasic Personality Inventory (MMPI), the personality test most frequently used by both professional and research psychologists, is an example of the empirical approach. The MMPI has a scale called Depression. People who were known to be depressed were compared to people who were not. Since it was not known how they were different, both groups answered hundreds of items, and the items that depressed people answered differently from nondepressed people were put in the Depression scale. There was no theoretical reason why depressed people should answer the items differently from the nondepressed—it was just an empirical observation that they did. Therefore, the items must measure something about depressed people, whatever it is, and they were put together in a Depression scale. Answers to these Depression items were then statistically transformed into scale scores with a mean of 50 and a standard deviation of 10. Several other scales were built this way.

The MMPI was developed by Hathaway and McKinley in the late 1930s and early 1940s (Hathaway & McKinley, 1943). It was originally developed to diagnose adult psychopathology in psychiatric and medical settings, but it is now used for many other purposes with individuals over 16 years old. (There is the MMPI-A for use with adolescents.) The MMPI consists of several hundred statements about life, opinions, likes and dislikes, family events, and similar things, about which people must make a forced choice between true or false, as the items apply to them. MMPI items range from statements such as "I like mechanics magazines" and "I am happy most of the time" to "I am worried about sex matters" and "At times I have a strong urge to do something harmful or shocking." Students (and psychologists, too) often have fun making up MMPI-like test items. See box 4.4 and try to make up a few yourself.

Despite its tremendous success, there were complaints about the MMPI. With 566 items, it was very long. Some of the items are seen as intrusive and possibly offensive. Since the MMPI scales were developed by comparing "abnormal" groups to "normal" Minnesotans from the 1930s, the norms for what is considered a "high" score appeared to be out of date. For example, a 1930s Minnesota farmer was not likely to have a high score on the Schizophrenia scale unless there was actually something seriously wrong with him. Today a high score for a college student who once experimented with drugs might not indicate any serious disorder. Another criticism was that the standardization group was composed of mostly rural white people, so that the norms did not apply to today's urban, multiethnic populations. Although the

Box 4.4 New, Improved MMPI Items

A favorite pastime of psychologists is developing new MMPI items. Over the years we have collected quite a few from various sources, including our students. The wording of these items is quite similar to many genuine MMPI items. Here are a few.

I like mechanics.

Cauliflower makes me sad.

I am not troubled by thoughts of housework.

I am sure most people would pick their noses if they thought they could get away with it.

I am excited by committee meetings.

As a child I was often an imaginary companion.

I feel like jumping off low places.

I think I would like the work of a chicken plucker.

I am bored by thoughts of death.

Sometimes I have difficulty remembering what I have done after hours of watching television.

I am not afraid to wash clothes.

My mother's third cousin was a good man.

I have used floor wax to excess.

Pedestrians are not to be trusted.

I cannot read or write.

Sometimes I find it hard to know what to say at an orgy.

Piercing screams make me nervous.

I am afraid of finding my self.

standardized norms were out of date and irrelevant to some groups, both "clinical lore" and computer programs had come through empirical research to take this kind of variation into account.

Nevertheless, the MMPI was revised in 1989 as the MMPI-2. Some offensive items were deleted, some items were updated, and norms based on new, multiethnic standardization groups were developed. Some new scales were added, including two posttraumatic stress disorder scales. The basic structure of the test remained the same.

As presently used, the MMPI and the MMPI-2 are divided into 10 empirically derived clinical scales:

1. Hypochondriasis (somatic problems and physical complaints)
2. Depression (sadness, hopelessness, depression)
3. Hysteria (using repression and denial as defenses)
4. Psychopathic Deviate (active family conflict, or possibly antisocial behavior, such as impulsivity, poor judgment, disregard for authority)
5. Masculine-Feminine (nontraditional sex role attitudes and behavior)
6. Paranoia (suspiciousness, hostility, and aloofness)
7. Psychasthenia (anxiety, phobias, obsessiveness)
8. Schizophrenia (being unconventional, withdrawn, confused, unusual in one's thinking)
9. Mania (impulsivity, optimism, high energy, impatience)
10. Social Introversion (nonsociability)

In addition to the 10 clinical scales, the test has four validity scales:

? (the number of omitted items)

L (a tendency to lie or present oneself in a favorable light)

F (an unusual items scale, suggesting a tendency to exaggerate difficulties)

K (defensiveness)

These four scales represent an attempt to build checks for validity into the assessment device itself. Obviously, if individuals fail to answer many items, it reduces the validity of their answers. The L scale is composed of socially desirable items that no one ever does, such as "I read all of the editorials in the newspaper every day." People who endorse many of these items are apparently trying to present themselves in a socially favorable way. This tendency to give socially desirable responses may reduce the validity of their answers. The F scale is composed of unusual items that are rarely marked by anyone. People who endorse many of these items may be "faking bad," confused, or unable to read. The K scale is supposed to measure the personality trait of defensiveness. It is added to the scores of some of the other scales as a corrective factor.

In recent years, many new scales have been constructed empirically from the original MMPI test, such as the Ego Strength and Anxiety scales. Because the MMPI was originally designed to detect psychopathology, the titles of the original 10 scales, as you can see, have negative connotations that are not appropriate for the many uses to which the MMPI is now put. Psychologists generally try to avoid the titles and refer to the scales by numbers.

In addition to the scores on individual scales, psychologists interpret the *profile* of the scores. The clients' scores on all the scales are drawn on a graph so that the peaks and valleys of the high and low scores can be seen, as in figure 4.1. This profile can then be interpreted according to clinical inferences or according to empirically derived rules. The MMPI was designed so that it could be interpreted with a "cookbook" of empirical rules, and several have been published. The individual's two or three highest scores are coded as a combination; the person in figure 4.1 represents a 4-2-6 combination. These combinations of scores can then be looked up in the "cookbook," which will summarize research on other individuals with that profile. Interpretation may consider several other aspects of the profile, including low scores. A high score on any one scale can be modified by high or low scores on other scales. For example, a high score on scale 4 suggests a tendency to be rebellious and to act out in socially unacceptable ways. However, a low score on scale 9 (energy) would attenuate this tendency, while a high score would increase it.

The Millon Tests: Another Example of the Empirical Approach

The Millon tests are later competitors of the MMPI. The Millon Clinical Multiaxial Inventory (MCMI) is similar to the MMPI in its construction and purpose. The MCMI is shorter, with about 175 items compared to over 500 for the MMPI-2. The scores and profiles on 20 scales are designed to give diagnoses that are similar to those

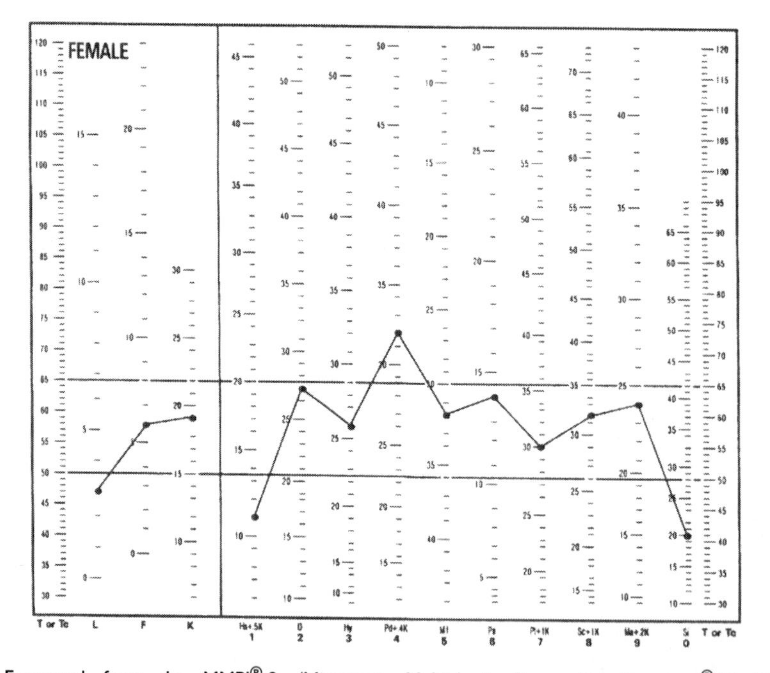

Source: Excerpted from the MMPI®-2 (Minnesota Multiphasic Personality Inventory®-2) Manual for Administration, Scoring, and Interpretation, Revised Edition. Copyright © 2001 by the Regents of the University of Minnesota. Used by permission of the University of Minnesota Press. All rights reserved. "MMPI" and "Minnesota Multiphasic Personality Inventory" are trademarks owned by the Regents of the University of Minnesota.

Figure 4.1 Example MMPI-2 Profile

in the DSM. While the 20 MCMI scales are empirically derived, as are the MMPI scales, the comparison group for each scale was not "normals," but the general psychiatric population. Thus, the MCMI is appropriate only for diagnosing psychopathology.

In addition to the MCMI, there are the Millon Adolescent Clinical Inventory and the Millon Behavioral Health Inventory. Each test is designed for use with specific patient populations in clinical settings, so the Millon tests may be more useful than the MMPI in certain cases. The Millon tests continue to be researched and revised by Millon and others (Millon, Davis, Millon, Escovar, & Meagher, 2000).

The Millon tests are best scored and interpreted by computer. The computer-generated report gives the clinician a list of possible diagnoses on Axes I and II of DSM, a personality description based on both Millon's personality theory and empirical factors, and recommendations for treatment and therapy. Some have accused Millon of making his tests scorable and interpretable only by his computers as a way to control the market for his tests and to increase his profits, but Millon argues that he controls his tests for ethical reasons and to ensure that the latest research is always used.

The NEO Personality Inventory—Revised (NEO-PI-R): An Example of the Inductive Approach

In the second type of personality scale construction, the inductive approach, a personality structure and its test items are "discovered" by giving large numbers of people large numbers of test items and subjecting the responses to a statistical procedure called factor analysis. Factor analysis reveals responses that consistently go together and therefore are assumed to measure some "real" aspect or dimension of personality. What that dimension is may be inferred by examining the content of the items that statistically go together.

The NEO Personality Inventory—Revised (Costa & McCrae, 1992) is designed to allow a comprehensive assessment of adult personality. A great deal of personality research agrees that five empirically derived factors (also called the Big Five) can account for most of the variance in personality tests—Neuroticism, Extraversion, Openness to Experience (the NEO part), Agreeableness, and Conscientiousness. Within each of the five factors or domains, there are six facets. For example, the facets of Extraversion are Warmth, Gregariousness, Assertiveness, Activity, Excitement-Seeking, and Positive Emotions. The makers and users of this test, which was originally developed as a measure of the "normal" personality, are researching clinical uses for it. For example, the utility of the NEO-PI-R in diagnosing personality disorders (Morey et al., 2002) and predicting responses to therapy (Ogrodniczuk, Piper, Joyce, McCallum, & Rosie, 2003) has been studied.

This paper-and-pencil test consists of 240 statements about the self to which the individual indicates strongly agree, agree, disagree, or strongly disagree. These responses are assigned points and summed for raw scores on the five factors and their facets. The raw scores are compared to norms and can be profiled and then interpreted, somewhat like the MMPI. The empirical basis of this test appears to be sound, although its clinical uses are in development.

The Beck Depression Inventory (BDI): An Example of the Deductive Approach

The deductive approach to personality scale construction assumes that a great deal is already known from theory and research about the personality characteristics to be measured. This knowledge governs the formulation of the test items. Test items may be invented by the test maker, or experts may judge which of a number of items best reflects what is known about the characteristic to be measured. With the BDI, much was already known about depressive symptoms, and items were created to assess them.

As the name implies, the Beck Depression Inventory was developed in the 1960s and 1970s by Dr. Aaron Beck, a cognitive behaviorist, to assess the presence and severity of depression in adults and adolescents (Beck, 1972). This test, revised in 1996 as the BDI-II to be more in line with DSM criteria for depression, consists of groups of four statements, each describing more severe versions of a depressive symptom. An example group of four statements follows:

0 I do not feel sad.

1 I feel sad.

2 I am sad all the time and I can't snap out of it.

3 I am so sad or unhappy that I can't stand it.

Other groups of statements deal with pessimism, past failure, agitation, worthlessness, loss of energy, concentration difficulty, loss of pleasure, guilt, crying, and other symptoms of depression. Test takers are given written instructions to circle the statement in each group that best describes how they have been feeling during the past two weeks. Points are assigned to each statement in a group, with 0 being the statement indicating no symptom and 3 being the most severe statement of the symptom. Points are summed, and although the test is not normed in the way the MMPI is, a specific cutoff score is considered to indicate severe depression. The BDI has been subject to extensive research, and it has found wide application in clinical practice. In addition, Beck has developed tests for anxiety, suicide ideation, obsessive-compulsive symptoms, and other scales.

Another inductive test, the Myers-Briggs (Myers, 1962, 1977) is based on Jung's theory of the basic dimensions of the personality. In his theory, and on the test, there are four theoretically independent dimensions of personality: Extraversion-Introversion, Sensing-Intuition, Thinking-Feeling, and Judging-Perceptive. Items for the test were developed because they appeared or were judged by experts to measure these theorized dimensions. An individual's responses are scored so as to result in a "profile" of the four dimensions. For example, a person with an ENFP profile would be high in Extraversion, Intuition, Feeling, and Perceptive. The manual lists all the possible profiles and describes this one as a person who prefers to be with others, looks for options rather than known facts, makes judgments according to personal values rather than logic, and prefers spontaneity over careful planning.

Reliability and Validity of Objective Tests

The internal consistency and reliability of objective personality tests range from low to moderately high, depending on the type of test. For example, the reliability of the computer-scored MMPI is respectably high. Internal consistency of the separate scales is in the .70s, and even test-retest reliabilities range from the .50s to the .90s. Other tests show lower levels of reliability.

Arguments over the validity of objective tests such as the MMPI, the Millon tests, and others would seem open to settlement by empirical studies. While it may remain forever debatable whether the MMPI is really measuring "hypochondriasis" or "psychasthenia" (whatever that is), there are literally thousands of studies demonstrating that the MMPI can adequately predict many things, such as whether someone will benefit from a certain kind of medical treatment. MMPI profiles can also predict which alcoholics will recover and which chronic pain sufferers will benefit from surgery, to give just a few examples. The MMPI is often used to make these kinds of predictions with a fair degree of success. Several hundred new studies on the MMPI are published every year, so it would appear to have acceptable validity, at least for a substantial number of researchers in the United States. Millon (Millon et al., 2000) also reports studies demonstrating the validity of his tests. As with projective tests, the use of objective tests in other cultures is questionable.

Clinical Uses of Objective Tests

Objective personality tests are used for a variety of purposes, besides the typical goal of diagnosis and differential diagnosis. New applications of the MMPI are being researched all the time. Many of them appear to be valuable and useful extensions of the test and psychological knowledge. For example, using the MMPI to predict which chronic pain sufferers would benefit from back surgery (Turner, Herron, & Weiner, 1986) would save medical expenses and unnecessary suffering from surgery that won't help. Predicting which form of psychological treatment will best help particular clients is a valuable use of objective tests.

In the case of LaTisha M., it is apparent that objective tests are not appropriate for assessing children. If she were a college student with similar problems, dropping grades and failing to attend classes, the MMPI could be used to see if she was experiencing depression, anxiety, or unusual thoughts that would explain her difficulties. If she reported depression, then the BDI could be used to assess its severity. If she were admitted to a hospital, the Millon could be used to reach a diagnosis. In all three cases, the test findings would suggest certain treatment directions.

As with the projective tests, objective tests are sometimes used in therapy. For example, some family therapists ask everyone in a family to take the Myers-Briggs. Each family member's profile is discussed and explained in a way that also educates the family about the nature of different communication styles. When misunderstandings arise, the therapist can point out that they are not anyone's "fault," but rather the result of differing communication styles. Families can learn to problem solve these differences, rather than becoming defensive and placing blame.

Behavioral Assessment

Although the techniques of behavioral assessment are quite old, its recognition as a separate type of assessment is more recent. No books on the subject were published before the mid-1970s, but now there are many. Two journals in the field, *Behavioral Assessment* and *Journal of Behavioral Assessment,* were founded in 1979. Since then, research and applications of behavioral assessment have proliferated, and the field continues to expand and change.

Behavioral assessment is derived from the empirical and theoretical foundations of behaviorism and behavior therapy (covered in chapter 10). Behaviorists do not accept the traditional concept of the personality, and radical behaviorists deny it exists. Behaviorists look at people in terms of their behaviors in specific situations. Rather than assessing underlying personality characteristics, they examine interactions between behaviors and situations. Rather than looking for "signs" of enduring personality characteristics, they examine "samples" of behavior and situations.

In ***functional analysis***, behaviorists analyze the stimuli that precede a behavior and the consequences that follow it. Behaviors are precipitated by certain stimuli or situations, and they are learned and maintained because of their consequences. Only by identifying the conditions that elicit a behavior and the consequences that maintain it can appropriate interventions to change that behavior be designed, all without making inferences about the "personality" of the behavior emitter.

Furthermore, behaviorists assume that behavior has multiple causes, that the environment and the person interact to cause behavior (reciprocal determinism), that individuals have behavioral skills as well as deficits, and that mediational variables such as social support systems, cognitive coping strategies, past experiences, and physiological responses or disorders are important in determining behavior. The functional analysis of behavior attempts to study all these factors, because the assessment of any one factor in isolation will result in an inadequate or incorrect conclusion. Because of its ties to academic behaviorism and its empirical hypothesis-testing paradigm, behavioral assessment values quantification of variables, objective observation, and assessment and intervention within controlled conditions. Therefore, behavioral assessors obtain information about the rate, duration, and intensity of target behaviors and the conditions under which they occur.

Most behaviorists would agree that methods of behavioral assessment include interviews, various kinds of observation, exposure-based methods, self-monitoring, psychophysiological measures, and behavioral questionnaires. Although more controversial, neuropsychological assessment, projective methods, intelligence tests, computer-assisted assessment, and other techniques may also be included in behavioral assessment. Because behavioral assessment is a rapidly growing and changing field, any list of its methods would soon be outdated, but we can describe some of the techniques most widely used today (Ramsay, Reynolds, & Kamphaus, 2002).

Behavioral Assessment Interviews

All behavioral interventions require some form of interview before they are attempted. The behavior therapist must first ask clients the nature of their problems and when and where they occur. Interviews are necessary to define the problem(s), target the behavior(s), and set therapy goals. Compared to nonbehavioral interviews, behavioral interviews tend to be more structured, more focused on overt behavior, more oriented to environmental causes of behavior, less interested in the past, and more quantitative.

Naturalistic Observation

In this method, two or more trained observers enter the client's natural environment (home, classroom, hospital ward) and systematically record the occurrence or nonoccurrence of predefined behaviors. Behaviors to be sampled in this way are carefully selected and defined prior to observation. They may be undesirable behaviors to be decreased, desirable behaviors to be increased, or behaviors with causal significance to be analyzed. For example, observers may go into the homes of obese individuals to observe their eating patterns or into bars to observe the drinking behavior of alcoholics.

Analogue Observation

Observations of behavior are made in a controlled environment that is different from but similar or analogous to the client's natural environment. Role-playing is a form of analogue observation often used to assess social skills. A shy client may role-play a scenario of being more assertive with the therapist role-playing the client's boss or date. The behavior avoidance test (BAT) is another type of analogue assessment. Clients are asked to approach a feared object, such as a snake or hypodermic needle, and their behavior is carefully observed and recorded.

Participant Observation

A family member or other involved person who is not professional is asked to monitor the target behavior. For example, parents may be asked to keep a record of all instances of tantrums thrown by their difficult child.

Self-Monitoring

Clients are asked to observe and record the occurrence or nonoccurrence of their own predefined behaviors. Smokers may be asked to record all cigarettes smoked, when, where, what they were doing as they smoked, how much they did or did not enjoy it, and what they were thinking about when they decided to smoke.

Psychophysiological Measures

Behaviorists have developed a number of measures that utilize an individual's physiology. Measures of brain waves, eye movements, skin temperature, pulse, muscle tension, respiration, penile erections, skin conductance, and blood pressure have been used in the behavioral assessment of headaches, phobias, high blood pressure, pain, anxiety, smoking, sexual dysfunctions, compulsions, and many other problems.

Behavioral Questionnaires and Checklists

Behavioral clinicians utilize a number of self-report techniques. Written questionnaires, symptom inventories, behavior checklists, and rating scales are often used in behavioral assessment. For example, a questionnaire could be used to collect information on what, when, where, how much, and how often someone eats. A fear survey may ask people to indicate the presence or intensity of the fear of different objects. Or a rating scale could ask clients to rate their levels of anxiety in different example situations. Compared to personality questionnaires, behavioral questionnaires tend to be shorter, more specific, and more focused on the occurrence and frequency of behaviors than on enduring traits.

One behavioral assessment method that is frequently used in both research and the clinical assessment of children is the Achenbach Child Behavior Checklist (CBCL), developed in the 1980s (Achenbach & Ruffle, 2000). Having both teacher report and parent report versions, the behavior checklist consists of over 100 normal and problematic behaviors with brief descriptions. The teacher or parent checks the behavior if it occurs and rates whether it occurs sometimes or often. The listed behaviors are clustered into meaningful scales for which extensive age-related norms have been developed. In the teacher's report version, there are six adaptive scales, such as Working Hard and Behaving Appropriately, and nine behavior problem scales, such as Anxious and Aggressive. The profile, or pattern of high and low scores on the various scales, can be analyzed for behavioral strengths and weaknesses in order to design and focus appropriate interventions. The CBCL is also useful for assessing improvement as a result of therapy.

Product-of-Behavior Measures

Product-of-behavior measures are records of data generated by the target behaviors themselves. For example, weight is often used as a product-of-behavior measure of eating behavior. Such assessments have the advantage of being objectively measurable and easily obtained as a by-product of the behaviors to be modified by the intervention procedures.

Radical Behavioral Assessment

The radical behaviorists, discussed in chapter 10, utilize all of the above behavioral assessment methods, but they emphasize the unique individual in her historical and environmental context. Thus, their relatively idiographic approach to behavioral assessment leads to the frequent use of self-monitoring or other methods that are designed for specific individuals and are not standardized. For example, an agoraphobic would be periodically asked to complete a standard one-mile walk with specific stopping points to rate anxiety. The radical behaviorists emphasize "clinically relevant behavior" and how it functions in its context. For example, there can be no universal definition of social skills in radical behaviorism. A behavior is socially skilled if it functions as a skill in a specific situation in relation to certain other people when performed by an individual with a specific learning history.

Reliability and Validity of Behavioral Assessment

Because of the strong empirical foundation of behaviorism, the reliability of behavioral assessment methods is relatively high. In general, the more structured and objective the assessment procedure, the higher its reliability will be. Thus, more structured interviews, such as those used in behavioral assessment, result in higher reliability than unstructured ones. In the case of observations, careful training of the observers is crucial for observer reliability.

As you might expect, the validity of the empirically derived behavioral assessment methods are mostly well researched. Furthermore, the results of such research lead to changes in the methods in order to improve validity. The ultimate test of the predictive validity of the behavioral assessment methods is, of course, whether they lead to effective behavioral interventions, and they often do.

Clinical Uses of Behavioral Assessment

Behavioral assessment is used most often in conjunction with behavior therapy. A general list of purposes, in addition to empirical research, would include identifying target behaviors to modify, identifying alternative (desirable) behaviors to replace or reduce undesirable ones, identifying causal variables so interventions can be made at that point, developing a functional analysis of the environmental and social situation in which the client is embedded, designing intervention strategies, and evaluating and modifying the intervention(s).

In the case of LaTisha M., the CBCL may be used to indicate behavioral strengths and weaknesses. In her case, it may be more useful for trained observers to go to her school to observe her behavior and its antecedents and consequences in that situation and to her home to observe the same. It is possible that certain frightening situations elicit illness behaviors that are rewarded with attention and sympathy from the teacher, the mother, or even siblings and friends. An intervention designed to reduce the attention she receives for illness behaviors and to increase the attention she receives for assertive and independent behaviors could be designed.

Vocational, Aptitude, and Interest Tests

Professional psychologists are involved in many other forms of assessment, from measuring physiological responses to assessing organizational dynamics and making employment decisions. We cannot cover them all in one chapter, but we will cover one final area. Assessment of vocational skills and potentials, aptitudes, and career and life interests is often done by counseling and educational psychologists.

Vocational, aptitude, and interest tests are used to help parents, schools, and individuals make educational and occupational decisions. They are supposed to measure people's talents, interests, and potentials, characteristics that should be related to what sorts of education and careers they would do well in. They are not intelligence tests, which supposedly measure a global ability to do well in school (some view this as "scholastic aptitude"). And they are not achievement tests, which are supposed to measure level of performance already achieved in various subjects. Rather, these tests attempt to identify specific talents or unknown potentials or patterns of interests to predict how individuals will "fit" in certain careers or educational programs.

These tests, especially aptitude tests, have been criticized for serving gatekeeper functions. The most common use of aptitude tests is in college admissions. Universities require minimum scores on the Scholastic Aptitude Test (SAT) of the College Entrance Examination Board for entrance, and the real-life consequences of this test are well-known. Television viewers watched Bart Simpson's aptitude test go to be scored at an institute very similar to the College Board, and the sign over the door said "Determining Your Destiny Since 1923."

Nevertheless, many individuals desire assistance in "discovering" their talents and making career decisions. There are many group and individual vocational and interest tests designed to help them do so. Among the best known—and the ones most often used by professional psychologists—are the Strong Interest Inventory and the Kuder Occupation Interest Survey.

Strong Interest Inventory

First developed in the 1920s, the Strong Interest Inventory was constructed using the empirical method of contrast groups, like the MMPI, and new norms were developed in the 1980s. It includes over 300 items, such as "Watching an open-heart operation," "Sports pages in the newspaper," and "Outspoken people with new ideas," for which test takers indicate their interest by marking "Like," "Indifferent," or "Dislike." These items were administered to national samples of hundreds of women and men in nearly 100 different occupations. The contrast sample consisted of several hundred women and men not identified by occupation. Their answers were compared to the answers of those in different occupational groups to identify those test items that statistically distinguished each occupational group from the general group. It is assumed that if an individual's answers on the Strong inventory match the interest patterns of certain occupational groups, then that person would be likely to find satisfaction in that vocation. There are also Basic Interest scales on the Strong, and these scales indicate low, moderate, and high interest in categories such as nature, science, art, religious activities, and sales.

Kuder Occupation Interest Survey

Begun in the 1930s and published in several different forms, the Kuder Occupation Interest Survey is composed of 100 triads of work-related activities, such as "Read lessons to a blind student," "Keep records of experimental results," and "Interview people in a survey of public opinion." For each triad of activities, the test taker indicates the most preferred and least preferred activity. This procedure results in a rank ordering of preference for the different kinds of activities, and the individual's pattern of ranked interests can be related to certain college majors and to occupational groups to indicate possible educational and career goals.

Other Tests of Talents

There are numerous other tests used in vocational and career counseling and assessment. There are other interests tests, such as the Career Assessment Inventory or the Career Occupational Preference System. There are tests of mechanical abilities, such as the Bennett Mechanical Comprehension Test; tests of spatial ability, such as the Minnesota Form Board; tests of artistic talents, social intelligence, managerial talent, and many others. A comprehensive career assessment will include interviews, interest tests, personality tests, possibly intelligence tests, and other tests the psychologist deems necessary for the particular individual. Counseling and thoroughly reviewing the results of the tests are part of the vocational assessment process.

Reliability and Validity of Vocational and Interest Tests

According to the research done for their manuals, the reliability of both the Strong and the Kuder tests is high—in fact, close to the reliability of intelligence tests. Because aptitude and interest tests are used to make long-term decisions about education and careers, it is important that their predictive validity be high. According to several studies, between one-half and three-fourths of subjects in studies on predictive validity choose college majors (Hansen & Swanson, 1983) or enter careers (Campbell, 1966; Campbell & Hansen, 1981; Spokane, 1979) that would be predicted by their scores on the Strong. The Kuder predicts careers accurately about half the time (Zytowski, 1976; Ihle-Helledy, Zytowski, & Fouada, 2004). While a 50% correct prediction rate may not sound high, it does, in fact, represent good predictive validity for a psychological test.

Clinical Uses of Vocational and Interest Tests

Vocational and aptitude tests are not designed for use with children, so we shall make LaTisha a college student again, this time with poor grades and anxiety attacks. Her difficulties may be due to a mismatch between her interests and aptitudes and her chosen college major. Her poor grades and anxieties may be due to trying to pursue a major or a career for which she is unsuited, perhaps because her parents expect her to or perhaps because she is unaware of her own preferences. Giving LaTisha vocational and interest tests would help her examine her aptitudes and abilities, her interests and preferences, and her educational and career options. While vocational and interest tests are often used alone when career choice is the issue, they are also used with other psychological tests to help discover explanations for difficulties.

Psychological Tests on the Internet

Along with the phenomenal growth of the World Wide Web has come a growth in the number of psychological tests available on the Internet. Tests have been put on the Internet for entertainment, for personal growth, as part of research, for teaching purposes, and for other assessment purposes. There are even Web sites that describe how to fake certain results on certain tests. These developments were never anticipated by those who created psychological tests or by those who use them professionally and ethically.

Psychological assessment focuses on the individual and the referral question and consists of interpreting and integrating information gathered from more than one psychological test and from more than one source. Professional psychologists know that a single test score in isolation is meaningless. The Internet cannot provide psychological assessment, only test scores. While a Web site may try to provide norms and interpretation, it is very possible that Internet test scores are inaccurate and not interpreted appropriately (Naglieri et al., 2004). Furthermore, there are many obsolete and poorly designed tests on the Web, and people are not trained to distinguish these from good tests. An incorrect or negative test score can have harmful effects on an individual, even if psychologists know the score is meaningless.

Additional concerns with Internet testing include confidentiality, test security, and test validity. People may be reluctant to take tests on the Internet for fear that their scores will become public, although there are technological ways of guarding confidentiality. Many psychological tests are copyrighted, but as the music industry learned, it is extremely difficult to maintain security over intellectual property on the Internet. Traditionally, psychologists have not allowed clients to take tests home, because it is believed doing this would allow more people to become familiar with the tests, thereby affecting their validity. Now anyone can access them any time. As people become familiar with psychological tests and practice taking them, test validity may decrease.

Despite these problems, Internet testing finds many uses. Many corporations have job seekers apply over the Internet and screen them by having them take some form of test. The possibility that an applicant will fake or get help with their responses can be dealt with by administering another test in a secure location after the initial Internet screening. People can gain useful information about themselves, as when they take a vocational test on the Web. Researchers can gather tremendous amounts of data by posting tests on the Internet. Tests can be easily updated on the Web. People with disabilities or those who live in rural areas with no psychological services have access to psychological tests on the Internet.

Professional psychologists are beginning to take advantage of Internet testing in their assessments. The possible clinical applications are many; for example, a client could self-monitor his levels of depression or anxiety by periodically taking a test on the Internet and the therapist could keep tabs on the client without having to see him. Since the Web and its problems are not going away, psychologists must make sure that people are educated about the limitations of Web testing, work to increase Internet test security and validity, and ensure that Internet tests are used appropriately and ethically.

In Conclusion

Intelligence tests remain psychology's big success. They are the most frequently used individual psychological test in clinical practice. They have been constructed such that they have the highest reliability of all psychological tests, although questions about their validity remain controversial. Neuropsychological assessment is poised to become psychology's next big success. Already extremely useful in diagnosing and designing interventions and rehabilitation for the increasing numbers of brain-injured people in our society, neuropsychological tests will improve in reliability, validity, and clinical utility as current research continues to help us understand brain structure and functioning and to pinpoint brain and behavior connections.

The fate of the projective tests seems more questionable. Projective tests produce a wealth of fascinating data, and they may lead to interesting interpretations and hypotheses, as demonstrated in the report on Jimmy S. in box 4.5. However, their validity and cost-effectiveness remain problematic. Because of their use in both research and professional practice and the constant development and revision of objective psychological tests, the enduring popularity of objective personality tests seems assured. A great deal of research demonstrates the utility of the MMPI for a multitude of purposes. Vocational and interest tests also remain vital in both research and clinical practice. The Internet poses a wealth of opportunity and problems for psychological test users and takers.

Cost effectiveness and ethical considerations remain important issues in psychological assessment. When developing or utilizing a psychological test, professional psychologists must ensure that it is reliable and valid and that the cost in time and money is worth it. Professional psychologists must also ensure that their tests are used appropriately and fairly. Tests should not be used alone to make decisions about people, but rather they should be considered as one piece of evidence in a context of other information.

Box 4.5 Example Evaluation Report

PSYCHOLOGICAL EVALUATION REPORT

Name: Jimmy S.

Address: 200 Main, Downtown, CA

Date of birth: November 2, 1988

Age: 17 years

Gender: Male

Grade level: 12

Dates of testing: 11/18/2005 and 12/7/2005

Tests administered:
Wechsler Adult Intelligence Scale
Turner School Achievement Test
Bender-Motor-Gestalt Test
Rotter Sentence Completion Test
MMPI-2
Self-Monitoring Behavioral Assessment
Strong Interest Inventory
Administered by: Lisa Dee, Ph.D.
Licensed Clinical Psychologist

Referral:
School recommended assessment for an explanation of Jimmy's recent withdrawn behavior and poor performance in school.

The privacy of this report is protected by law. This report may contain data or comments that should be interpreted by those trained in psychological assessment procedures to prevent misunderstandings about the findings or recommendations. Scores reported herein reflect functioning during this session and may or may not relate to later functioning.

Presenting Problem

Jimmy S. appears to be experiencing a severe case of "senioritis." His previously excellent grades have dropped upon starting his senior year in high school. He appears to have lost interest in school and after-school activities. His mother, who accompanied him on the first appointment, reported that he is listless and sleeping a great deal. Jimmy says he is "just tired."

continued

Behavioral Observations

Jimmy S., a good-looking 17-year-old Caucasian American boy of average size, arrived for the testing session somewhat disheveled, clad in torn jeans and a wrinkled T-shirt. Jimmy was polite and mostly cooperative. He alternated between paying attention and being inattentive, between being interested and uninterested in the tests.

Social History

An interview with Jimmy and his mother revealed a typical, middle-class upbringing. He was an only child, born to a college professor mother and lawyer father. His mother reported an easy birth and that all of his developmental milestones were normal. He always did well in school, and in fact, tested high enough in sixth grade to be recommended for gifted classes. Because he wanted to stay in classes with his friends, Jimmy chose not to go into the gifted classes. He was active in sports in middle school, but dropped them in favor of drama club in high school. He and his mother denied the possibility of any substance abuse.

Jimmy and his mother agreed that they had always gotten along well. They also agreed that Jimmy's father had a short temper and was often absent from the family. Although the deadline is fast approaching, Jimmy has not yet completed any college applications, is undecided about which university he would like to attend, and doesn't know what he wants to major in. He stated, "I don't think I really want to grow up."

Evaluation Results

Wechsler Adult Intelligence Scale. Although he is a bit too young for the WAIS, it was decided to use this test since he had scored so highly on an intelligence test in sixth grade. Jimmy seemed to enjoy the tests, and he worked on them in a careful manner. He scored one to one and a half standard deviations above average on all subtests. Clearly, the explanation for Jimmy's current difficulties in school does not lie in cognitive ability.

Turner School Achievement Test. Jimmy did not enjoy taking the achievement test and complained that there were too many tests like it at school. He went through it quickly and without the degree of care he had shown in the WAIS. His grade equivalent scores were at his actual grade level in all areas. These average scores are not in line with his above average cognitive abilities.

Bender-Motor-Gestalt Test. Jimmy's performance on the Bender-Gestalt was appropriate for his age. He copied all designs quickly but accurately. They were placed neatly on the page, almost as if he had taken it before. It is unlikely that Jimmy has any perceptual-motor difficulties.

Rotter Sentence Completion Test. The examiner read the sentence beginnings to Jimmy and asked that he complete each one orally. He seemed resistant to this test at times and fanciful at others. He said he couldn't think of endings to several sentences, and when encouraged to try, he seemed embarrassed by what he said. Most of his sentence completions were typical of adolescents, but he completed several sentences with words like "confused," "can't decide," and "unknown." For example, he completed LIFE IS "confusing" and MOTHERS ARE "I can't decide what they are." Other sentences were completed in quite a dramatic way. For example, he completed GIRLS ARE "mysterious creatures who plague us and please us and lead us astray" and I AM "so complicated that no one can figure me out, including me, and where I'm going to end up, nobody, and I mean nobody, can foretell." Jimmy seems to feel confused, indecisive, and unable to act.

House-Tree-Person Drawing Test. For the HTP, Jimmy drew from left to right a small tree with many detailed twisted branches, a large very detailed house with many windows with curtains and trim on the roof, and a tiny little boy, with blank eyes. The small boy may reflect low self-esteem or a low sense of entitlement. The blank eyes may suggest denial or avoidance. The twisted tree and detailed house may reflect Jimmy's dramatic interests.

If a psychodynamic inference is made with the assumption that the house represents the mother and the tree the father, then it may be that Jimmy feels overshadowed by his parents. He may see them as more successful than he is. In this context, the blank eyes may indicate that he cannot see his himself or possibly his future as clearly as theirs. Alternatively, his parents are seen as so successful (detailed, competent drawings of house and tree) that compared to them he is a nothing (blank eyes). Another hypothesis is the blank eyes express fear of leaving the shelter of his parents.

If we assume that the house represents affiliation motivation and the tree represents achievement motivation, then it may be that Jimmy's achievement motivation is not as high as other motives or needs. This interpretation is in line with his behavior when he did not take gifted classes so he could remain with his friends.

MMPI. Jimmy completed the MMPI at home. His profile indicated that his responses were valid and not defensive. Jimmy's highest score was on Scale 2, Depression, which was somewhat above average. His scores on all other scales were within the average range, except for two low scores, Scales 9 and 10. Clearly, Jimmy is depressed. The low score on Scale 9 reinforces the indication of depression. The low score on Scale 10 reflects Jimmy's sociability and social skills.

Self-Monitoring Behavioral Assessment. Between the two testing appointments, Jimmy was asked to keep a daily record of the times he slept and the times he engaged in physical activity. He readily agreed, and at the second testing session, he brought in a fairly detailed daily log. He had indeed been sleeping 12 to 16 hours per day. There was virtually no physical activity. Asked what he did when he was awake, he said he either attended school, watched TV, or played video games. Excessive sleeping is a symptom of depression.

Strong Interest Inventory. The results of the Strong suggested that Jimmy would do well in a career as an artist, a counselor, or a teacher, and not as a salesman, businessman, or lawyer. His interest was highest in art, nature, and people.

Summary

Jimmy exhibited several strengths in his psychological testing. He exhibited good social skills during the testing, and his interests as measured by the Strong inventory and Scale 10 on the MMPI tend towards people and social activities. He has above average cognitive ability in all areas tested by the WAIS. The fact that his current achievement scores are only at grade level suggests underachievement for some reason. The MMPI and the self-monitoring behavioral assessment strongly indicate depression. While depression may account for the poor grades and relatively low achievement scores, the reason for the depression is less clear. Medical causes should be ruled out by a physical examination, and the severity of the depression should be assessed by the Beck Depression Inventory.

Possible reasons for his depression are suggested by the results of the projective tests. He may feel overshadowed by his successful parents, that he cannot measure up to them, that there is no use trying. It is safer to remain confused, undecided, and avoidant. Since he is a senior in high school, the expectation is that he is about to leave home for college, and he may be afraid to leave the safety of his family. This fear may both confuse and shame him, leading to depression. He may be unable to handle the pressure of his parents' and society's expectations for him. After doing so well most of his life, he may be feeling helpless and incompetent in the face of his inability to handle this pressure. As he said, "I don't think I really want to grow up."

continued

Provisional Diagnosis

Axis I: Major Depression or Dysthymia
Diagnosis deferred, pending further assessment

Axis II: None

Axis III: Excessive sleeping and tiredness
Diagnosis deferred, pending medical examination

Axis IV: Psychosocial stressors: Parental and societal pressure to mature

Axis V: Serious impairment in school functioning

Recommendations

A physical examination is highly recommended in order to rule out a medical cause for Jimmy's excessive sleeping and listlessness. The Beck Depression Inventory is recommended to assess the severity of Jimmy's depression and to help determine if he is suffering a major depression or dysthymia. If his depression is severe and there is no medical explanation, an evaluation by a psychiatrist for antidepressant medication is recommended. If it is very severe, inpatient treatment may be considered. Individual counseling for Jimmy is highly recommended, as is behavior therapy. Behavior therapy should be designed to reduce his sleeping behavior and increase his activity level. Individual counseling should be designed to help Jimmy with the life decisions pressing on him, to increase his sense of self-efficacy, and to deal with his feelings about his parents. Seeing a college or vocational counselor would also help Jimmy decide on a college, major, or job. Immediate action as recommended is essential to get this intelligent, sociable young man back on track and to prevent the worsening of his depression and feelings of incompetence and helplessness.

THE USE OF STANDARDIZED ASSESSMENT MEASUREMENTS SHOULD NOT BE EMPLOYED AS THE SOLE CRITERIA IN DEVELOPING A TREATMENT PLAN OR IN THE PLACEMENT OF AN INDIVIDUAL.

5 Research in Psychotherapy

Psychotherapy has existed as a formal practice for a little over 100 years. For nearly 50 of those years it was not studied scientifically, until Carl Rogers began recording and studying therapy sessions in the 1940s. Even then, research on psychotherapy remained controversial for many years, so much so that we felt a need to justify the importance of researching psychotherapy in earlier editions of this book. At the present time psychotherapy research remains controversial—but for different reasons. Few any longer argue, as some psychoanalysts and gestalt therapists once did, that psychotherapy is a process that is not amenable to systematic research and that such research is not necessary. Now the argument is over how research should be conducted and then used to guide practice. We live in an era of "accountability," where in many different fields, such as in medicine and education, people who provide services are being asked to show that there is evidence justifying what they do. This demand for "evidence-based practice" in the field of psychotherapy can come from health care agencies and those who pay the bill for psychotherapy, from governmental agencies, or from professional interest groups. In this chapter, we first consider why it is important to systematically research psychotherapy. Then we consider some basic ways psychotherapy research is conducted. We next follow that with an overview of research findings, focusing primarily on outcome research—that is, research on whether psychotherapy helps or not. We also briefly consider some aspects of process research—research on what happens in psychotherapy. Finally we conclude with a discussion of the current controversies revolving around evidence-based practice, especially the particular form of it known as empirically supported treatments.

Why We Need to Study Psychotherapy Empirically

There was once a debate over the need for doing research on psychotherapy. Because of the difficulty of the task, many practitioners dismissed attempts to study the effectiveness of psychotherapy scientifically. Guntrip (1973) made one typical argument. He said that psychotherapy is so individualized that it is difficult, if not impossible, to study it using normal experimental methods. Similarly, Simkin and Yontef (1984) said, "Gestalt therapists are singularly unimpressed with . . . ***nomothetic research methodology***. No statistical approach can tell the individual patient or therapist what works for him" (p. 306; emphasis added). They went on to say that each gestalt session is an experiment, and so constant research is being done on each individual client. As we shall see, there are those who agree that normal experimental methods may not be the ideal empirical method for studying psychotherapy. But even if this were true, that does not mean research on it cannot be done. And, at the present time, mainstream opinion in psychology is that psychotherapy *can* be studied (and frequently is) using experimental methodologies.

Those who argue that psychotherapy is too difficult to study empirically typically say that empirical research is not needed because the truths of psychotherapy have been experienced by people over and over for themselves through the countless times people have been in psychotherapy. For instance, both psychoanalysts and gestalt therapists have sometimes argued that anyone who doubts the truth of their viewpoint will discover the truth if he undergoes analysis or gestalt therapy. The basis of this type of argument is that you can learn "truths" from direct experience that you cannot gain from books or empirical research. A related argument is there are plenty of case histories, written up by both therapists and clients, illustrating the effectiveness of psychotherapy. So what more do we need?

Anecdotal case histories (essentially self-reports of therapists and clients) can provide ideas about how therapy works. But such evidence by itself is too unreliable to serve as the basis for systematic conclusions. We shall try to illustrate this and why systematic research approaches are needed.

Is seeing believing? Can we just trust the testimonials of therapists and clients who say that they have observed that a given form of psychotherapy works? There are two issues involved. First, how do we decide if someone has improved or not? Second, even if we believe the person has improved, how do we know that the therapy contributed to this improvement? More specifically, how can we decide if it was the specific ingredients of the therapy that helped?

It is often on the basis of experiences in therapy that people become firm believers in a particular theoretical approach. Psychoanalysts become convinced that problems are based on repressed feelings from early childhood. Behaviorists become convinced that problems are a matter of conditioning. Humanists become convinced that problems stem from a lack of self-acceptance and the fragmentation of the person into intellectual and emotional sides. And cognitive-behaviorists become convinced that problems depend on what clients think to themselves. The experience of seeing an apparent cure may be so vivid that the therapist believes that what she has seen verifies the "truth" of her theory.

How valid and trustworthy is experience in therapy for supporting the truthfulness of particular theoretical beliefs? By itself, not very valid. Let's say that you are about to work with your first client. He enters your office, complaining of chronic and pervasive anxiety. You've decided from reading this book that a short-term psychoanalytic approach to therapy makes sense to you. You look for a recurring relationship theme related to events in his early childhood. You discover that he was criticized a lot as a child by his father. You see that he now chronically expects criticism. Underlying that is a lot of unconscious resentment and hostility. You help him become aware of this pattern. As you do this, he gets in touch with his anger and resentment toward his father. After several sessions, he reports that he feels better, and soon the anxiety seems to have diminished to a manageable level. You are amazed at the efficacy of your method; you stand a picture of Freud on your mantle, and put fresh flowers before it daily.

Or you prefer the behavioral approach. You help your client examine his life and find that he becomes anxious in situations in which he must assert himself, though he had not previously noted the connection. Since he is a traffic policeman, you realize that he is likely to feel anxious frequently. You create a series of hierarchies of situations in which he feels anxious. You teach him deep relaxation. You have him imagine these situations in a state of relaxation and you practice assertion skills with him. After 10 to 20 sessions the client happily reports that he rarely feels anxious. You are highly impressed with your behavioral approach and begin to carry a picture of Joseph Wolpe in your wallet.

Depending on your point of view and how you worked with the client, you might become convinced of either the "truths" of the psychoanalytic or the behavioral approach. Experience can be a powerful persuader. Yet, in reading the two examples above, you may already have seen the problem in claiming that "facts" about personality and psychotherapy can be learned from therapy sessions alone. If many of Freud's observations are "facts," why are they repeatedly confirmed in psychoanalytic sessions but not in behavioral sessions? If the behavioral view is correct, why is it not confirmed in psychoanalytic sessions? If we can discover "facts" through our direct experience in psychotherapy, then how come Carl Rogers, Joseph Wolpe, Albert Ellis, Aaron Beck, Carl Jung, Alfred Adler, and Fritz Perls all started out doing psychoanalytically oriented psychotherapy but later developed theories that have little in common with psychoanalysis, or with one another? It should be obvious that the kinds of experiences therapists and clients have in therapy, no matter how vivid and compelling, do not provide a reliable basis for knowledge. Seeing may be believing, but neither seeing nor believing is necessarily knowing.

Why are conclusions drawn from the therapy experience not reliable? One reason is that people tend to "see" what they expect to see. For instance, there are several of Freud's cases, which he presented as successes, where later reports by the clients themselves indicated they were not so successful. Freud "saw" success where perhaps there wasn't success. There is also reason to believe that Freud had already developed a belief in the sexual basis of neurosis before he began to "see" it in his clients. Freud developed the idea that problems are based on early childhood, and analyst after analyst carried that idea into therapy with them. Analysts encourage their clients to talk about early childhood and then, when change occurs, attribute the change to reviewing early childhood. Cognitive therapists have their clients talk about their dysfunctional cognitions and then attribute change to that. Client-centered therapists focus on clients' feelings, so assume it is something about that process that creates change.

Therapist preconceptions also probably shape the kind of material that the client brings out. It has been argued (Hobbs, 1968) that Freudian clients get Freudian insights, Jungian clients get Jungian insights, and so on. Over the course of many sessions, a good deal of material compatible with the therapist's point of view will be highlighted and discussed. It is not surprising that both the therapist and client become convinced that what they have discovered is the "truth."

But what about the client? Change experiences, when you gain an insight and suddenly feel transformed, are powerful, and experiences that include a lot of emotion are also compelling. If people experience a great deal of emotion, they may believe that somehow something important must be happening. Yet these experiences are not necessarily reliable as a source of knowledge about what is causing change. Let us take an example from psychoanalysis. Guntrip (1973, pp. 176–177) reports a case of a client who came to therapy for treatment of depression. In addition, he had a chronic sinus condition. Through the analysis process, he remembered that he had been left alone to nurse his dying mother, but the day of her death remained a total blank. One night, the forgotten memory of her death burst into his consciousness. He remembered that she had gone mad at the end and had died cursing him. This memory had been so horrible he had repressed it. When the memory was recovered, his sinuses opened, and the fluid poured out.

It is not implausible to suspect that something about this moment may have helped the man's sinuses to unblock. Such an experience is quite dramatic. Both therapist and client are likely to conclude that the repression of the memory "caused" the sinus condition and the recovery of the memory "cured" it. But there is no obvious connection between his blocked sinuses and his mother's madness. And even if there were (suppose she had yelled at him, "You're so stuffy!"), would that have proven that the repressed memory caused the sinus condition? Would the clearing up of the sinus condition after recovery of the memory prove that recovering the memory was the cure of the sinus condition? The answer to both questions is no.

Any highly emotional experience, in the proper context, might have a direct impact on the body. The specific content of the memory may have had nothing to do with the physical effect, except to make it seem more plausible. What may have been important was the emotional impact of recovering the memory. Intense emotional experiences are often associated with change, regardless of the belief system they are associated with. It is not implausible to imagine that this same man goes to a Christian evangelist, has a highly emotional conversion experience, is told by the preacher that his sinuses will open, and, lo and behold, they do. Or he goes to a primal therapist, "recovers" some primal pain from early childhood, and his sinuses open.

Still another possibility is the power of suggestion. The client recovers this emotionally charged memory and says to himself, "This must be it!" Unconsciously, he convinces himself that this was the cause, and the power of suggestion causes his sinuses to open.

We are not saying that these alternatives (and there are others) are the correct ones. We simply want you to see that you cannot conclude from one person's individual experience that it was specifically the recovery of the particular repressed memory that was therapeutic. (Again, we are using psychoanalysis to illustrate a point that applies to any of the therapy systems.) In addition, we do not even know for sure that it was the therapy that caused the memory to surface into consciousness. Perhaps some random event happened that day to bring the memory to consciousness. So we may not conclude that the therapy was responsible for the sinuses opening.

Further, you cannot conclude that the repressed memory caused the problem, either. Suppose there is an apparent connection between the memory and the clogged sinuses; the mother did say, "You're so stuffy!" There is certainly a similarity between this experience and the client's symptom of a stuffy nose. But because two things are similar does not mean that one caused the other. It is easy to find past experiences that "fit" current problems in retrospect. Probably all of us can find some experience in our childhood that is like some problem we are having now. But that does not mean that those experiences caused the present-day problems. It is tempting to conclude that I dislike myself now because my father was overly demanding, but there is no inevitable connection between the two. Many people who had an overdemanding father do not dislike themselves as adults.

The fact that it is easy to search one's past and find things that "explain" one's present was demonstrated in one research study (Ross, Lepper, Strack, & Steinmetz, 1977). Students were given the history of a person. Some were told that he went on to have a career as a politician, while others were told that he went on to commit suicide. Neither group had any difficulty in finding things in the history that "explained" the eventual outcome, though both groups were working with identical past histories for the person.

It is possible that what is therapeutic about an insight or explanation in therapy has nothing to do with the truthfulness of that insight or explanation. Jerome Frank (1974, 1982) suggests that therapy operates by combating demoralization. Insights and explanations help if they make the client's experience seem sensible. An insight or explanation need not be true if it gives a person some hope and if it suggests some things the person can do to manage her life. Suppose you "learn" in therapy that your low self-esteem was "caused" by your father's constant put-downs. It does not even matter if this is true. If you believe it is true, you may decide, "Well, I don't have to put myself down just because he did." Or, "That was his opinion, and he was pretty screwed up himself." In other words, the explanation may be therapeutic anyway. Donald Spence (1982), a psychoanalyst, argued that psychoanalytic interpretations are therapeutic because of their coherence-making qualities, not because of their truth. Kelly (1963) found that plausible-sounding interpretations, based on no theory, were often therapeutic. So, just because an interpretation is therapeutic does not mean it is true, and just because it isn't true does not mean it won't be therapeutic.

Finally, and perhaps most importantly, therapists and clients are both immersed in the process of therapy. Their memories of what happened will not necessarily be reliable. The therapist may write up a coherent, compelling case history, based on her memory and her notes, but both her memory and what she chose to write in her notes were the events that captured her attention. She did not systematically observe the process. Similarly, the client's memories will be biased. As an illustration of this, consider the fact that if you read some of Freud's earlier published versions of cases and compare them to later published versions, there are significant differences (presumably as Freud's understanding shifted). Single case histories based on either clients' or therapists' recollections can be a rich source of information, but additional study is needed using other methods before conclusions can be drawn. This is a general principle in science: that multiple methods of study are usually needed to truly understand a phenomenon (Rozin, 2001).

We hope by now you see that it is difficult to draw reliable conclusions from experience in therapy about whether therapy works, what in therapy works, or what the causes of psychological problems are. Therapy sessions are an important source of ideas and hypotheses, but by themselves they do not provide reliable evidence as to what works and why. What is needed is more systematic, observational processes, which is the essence of science. Next we consider some of the issues involved in obtaining more reliable evidence.

Methods in Psychotherapy Research

Ultimately, scientific research involves being able to establish the existence of relationships in the real world with a certain degree of reliability. One wants to be able to say that *x* is reliably associated with *y*, for example, "psychotherapy on average helps people feel better," and "insight in psychotherapy under the right conditions is useful." There are a number of different research strategies that have been used in psychotherapy research. Traditionally, psychotherapy research has been *quantitative*. The general approach in ***quantitative research*** is to devise some way to measure the variables that the researcher is interested in and then to relate them to one another, typically using statistical methods. There are many issues in quantitative research, including how best to measure the complex behavior and feelings of human beings, as discussed in chapter 3. When researching psychotherapy, the issue of how to define and measure the relevant variables, including how to decide which variables are indeed relevant, is especially difficult, as we shall see.

More recently, a second approach, called ***qualitative research***, has gained favor with some who believe that traditional quantitative designs are either inappropriate or incomplete for capturing the phenomena of psychotherapy. We will first discuss the use of quantitative research methods, and then briefly consider qualitative research.

Quantitative Research Methods

Quantitative research methods used in psychotherapy research can generally be broken down into experimental and nonexperimental methods. The dominant nonexperimental method is to measure some variable you are interested in and then to see how it correlates with some other variable. For instance, one might measure the level of empathy shown by the therapist and relate that to how much the client changes. When this is done (Bohart, Elliott, Greenberg, & Watson, 2002) the average correlation turns out to be about .32, indicating a moderately strong relationship.

A limitation of correlational research is that, by itself, it can tell us if two things vary together, but not if one causes the other. For instance, does the therapist's empathy cause clients to get better, or is it possible that the kinds of clients that get better in therapy are easier to relate to, thereby causing higher levels of empathy in the therapist? Correlational methods must be augmented by other methods if one wishes to infer a causal relationship. One such augmentation is the use of a statistical procedure called "structural equation modeling." We shall not describe this procedure here. We merely mention it to show that there are ways of inferring the likely existence of causal relationships from nonexperimental research.

The best way of estimating whether there is a causal relationship between two variables is the use of the experimental method. The experimental method relies on control and manipulation of the variables being studied. The use of the ***control group*** in psychotherapy research exemplifies this idea.

Suppose someone goes to therapy and gets better. In order to say that the therapy worked, a researcher would like to be able to say that it was the therapy that helped her get better. However, it is possible that something else going on in the client's life caused the change, not the therapy. A client may improve when she gets a job or when her husband recovers his love for her. Many of the changes in children are simply due to the maturation process. It is even possible that certain disorders have their own natural course, like a cold or the flu, and the client would eventually get better even without therapy. There is some evidence that this is true for many cases of depression.

The most common way of demonstrating that it is the form of therapy that is associated with the production of the change is to use a control group. One group of clients receives the therapy, and another group (the control) does not. A bare outline of the procedure is to have, for example, 40 depressed clients, with 20 assigned to the treatment group and 20 to the control group. The assignment is done randomly, so that the chances are pretty good that the two groups are approximately equal, that is, that one group does not differ in any systematic way from the other group. Change in the individuals in both groups is measured at the end of treatment. If the clients in the therapy group have changed more than those in the control group, it is concluded that something about the therapy caused the change.

The procedure is not as simple as the outline sounds. First, there are ethical problems in putting people in a control group because they are being denied treatment that they may need. Second, control groups often do not remain untreated. Individuals who are not receiving the therapy being researched may go to some other therapist or talk to a friend, doctor, or minister (some of whom have had counseling training).

One of the ways devised to handle some of these problems is the waiting list control group. Since there are waiting lists at many clinics anyway, there is nothing unethical about placing some clients in the waiting list control group. Clients are randomly assigned either to available therapists or to the waiting list control. After the research treatment period, people on the waiting list are given treatment. People on waiting lists may be less likely to seek treatment elsewhere, so the waiting list control group may remain somewhat more pure. One problem with the waiting list is that clients will not wait indefinitely. It is difficult to use, for instance, in studies of a two- or three-year psychoanalysis.

Even if it is found that the treatment group does improve more than the control group, can it be concluded that it was really the specific properties of the therapy itself that caused the improvement? No. It could simply be that the attention given the clients or the power of suggestion or their belief that they would get better was the agent of change. One way some psychologists have attempted to compensate for these possibilities is to try to use ***placebo*** control groups. The issue of placebos has received extensive attention in both medicine and psychotherapy. In medicine, placebos are regularly used in research. In testing a new drug, for example, some patients are given the drug and others are given an inactive sugar pill, but are told they are being given the drug. In many studies, placebos have been found to cause some improvement. Pill placebos have been used in some studies of psychotherapy, for instance, on depression (Elkin et al., 1989). In other studies, a placebo control group might be given a pseudo-treatment, a treatment that is really expected to do nothing, but is given as if it is a real treatment. However, a problem with placebo psychotherapy treatments is that they are difficult to design so that they possess all but the presumably "operative ingredients" that make the real therapy work (Mahrer, 2004). For instance, Mahrer has suggested using the following as "placebo therapists." Get actors and have them play the role of someone "who is fascinated with just everything about the patient, the patient's thoughts, hopes, worries, early childhood, hobbies, everything, . . . who [acts] wise, sage, knowledgeable, seasoned and experienced" (Mahrer, 2004, pp. 34–35). He concludes that the odds might be on the placebo therapists! Along these lines, Wampold (2001) has argued that most of the placebo treatments that have been used in psychotherapy research are inadequate.

Defining Change

Whether one is using experimental or nonexperimental methods, the quantitative researcher must find a way of measuring the variables he is interested in. Suppose you have an untreated control group or a placebo group being compared to a therapy treatment group. Now you have to decide how you are going to measure change. To do that, you have to decide what you mean by change. And this turns out to be perhaps even more complex than the issue of control groups.

What is change in therapy? How could you tell if your client had improved? Perhaps the most obvious answer is by noting an improvement in the client's presenting complaint. If a client came to therapy because he was drinking too much, change might be if he is no longer drinking, that is, if there is symptom removal. However, many therapists have more grandiose goals for their clients than the clients themselves have (Bergin & Lambert, 1978). They want to "reorganize the personality" or "get the client to trust his feelings, take responsibility," and "think rationally." Many therapists assume that symptoms are the result of a more pervasive, underlying disorder. Substance abuse may reflect difficulties with self-esteem or interpersonal relationships. Anxiety may reflect a distorted cognitive style or a denial of one's potential. Conversion disorders may represent attempts to manage fear. Most psychological disorders, such as schizophrenia, personality disorders, conversion disorder, substance abuse disorders, and so on, are generally thought to represent organized patterns of symptoms, not collections of isolated symptoms (only the behavioral view has systematically questioned this). If symptoms are believed to represent some underlying disorder, therapists will not be interested in symptom removal or improvement but in changes in personality traits, emotional experiencing, self-esteem, and cognition.

Another difficulty with looking at change in terms of symptom removal is that often there is no simple, clear symptom. There may be multiple symptoms, and therapy may help some, but not others. For instance, the borderline personality syndrome consists of several symptoms, including impulsiveness, difficulty being alone, boredom, identity problems, anger, and depression. Or the presenting complaint may not be a clear-cut symptom, such as "drinking" or "fear of going out of the house." For example, a client may complain of being depressed, feeling that life is meaningless, or of having difficulties in managing children, relating to a spouse, or relating to superiors at work.

Furthermore, what therapists see as change depends on their theoretical viewpoint (Mahrer, 2004). A behaviorist might focus on symptom removal and behavior change; a humanist on increased self-acceptance, responsibility taking, and emotional experiencing; a cognitive behaviorist on progress toward a flexible, differentiated cognitive system. In addition, what is considered a positive change varies. Generally, the therapist has a set of values about change derived from her theory of therapy. The client may have another. And relatives and friends of the client may have still another.

You, as a therapist, are not only interested in change per se, you are also interested in positive change. And what you define as positive change depends in part on your values. Therefore, it is possible that people with different values will see change differently. Your client, a depressed, middle-aged woman who has spent her adult life being a housewife and mother, starts therapy complaining of depression. Her children are now leaving home, and her life feels empty. Through therapy, she begins to feel that she has spent her life living for others and that she wants to do something in the way of a career herself. As she begins to make these realizations, her depression lifts. Both she and the therapist see these changes as positive, but will her traditional husband who believes that a woman's place is in the home? Or a 17-year-old boy is referred to therapy because his parents are worried that he does not show proper interest in girls. The therapist discovers that he is gay, and therapy consists of helping him accept this side of himself. This may or may not sit well with the parents if they hold traditional values.

It has generally been accepted that change in therapy is multidimensional (Strupp, Horowitz, & Lambert, 1997). Different therapies concentrate on different types of change in the personality or behavior, and change looks different from different vantage points in the person's life. In fact, Stiles, Shapiro, and Elliott (1986) have argued that psychological normality is heterogeneous, in contrast to physical health. Different therapies have differing definitions of psychological health, and they may all be right for different individuals.

At the same time, there is currently pressure to define change in terms of the alleviation of specific problems, particularly as defined in the Diagnostic and Statistical Manual (DSM). Agencies that fund psychotherapy research, perhaps responding to the demands of the marketplace and to those who pay for mental health care, are increasingly interested primarily in research studies that explore the effectiveness of therapies in alleviating DSM disorders (Goldfried & Wolfe, 1996).

Measuring Change

In the days when psychoanalysis ruled the roost in psychotherapy, change was usually defined in terms of change in personality structure. Thus, someone who wished to demonstrate that therapy worked would use various personality tests to measure change. Since client-centered therapy emphasizes self-acceptance, research on therapy conducted by client-centered therapists used measures of self-acceptance, such as self-esteem scales. With the ascendancy of the behavioral perspective in the 1960s, an increasing emphasis was placed on behavioral measures. It was argued that changes in personality structure and self-acceptance were meaningless unless they manifested themselves in observable behavior change, and so, behavioral measures were favored over personality measures.

Behavioral measures, self-acceptance measures, and personality tests are ways of measuring change. Another way to measure change is to use a client's self-report before and after therapy. The client may be asked to rate the degree to which he has improved on the target symptoms that brought him to therapy. Or he may rate his behavior in various areas, such as in functioning socially and at work. Or he may rate himself on self-acceptance or on various personality traits. There are simple personality inventories in which the client checks off adjectives that he believes describe him.

If the client provides one source of measurement of change, the professional psychologist provides another. In research studies, it is common to have the therapist rate the client's progress, often making the same kinds of ratings the client might be asked to make about himself. Or a professional psychologist assesses the client's personality from tests such as the MMPI, Rorschach, and TAT administered before and after therapy. The psychologist interprets results of the projective tests (for example, to see if ego strength has increased or tendencies toward denial and repression have declined) and look at changes in scores on objective test scales. For instance, Rogers, Gendlin, Kiesler, and Truax (1967) found that clients of therapists who were high in warmth, empathy, and genuineness showed reductions on the "schizophrenia" scale of the MMPI.

A professional psychologist or psychiatrist may be used as a neutral observer or rater. The client undergoes a structured interview with a neutral psychologist or psychiatrist who preferably does not know whether the client was in therapy or in a control group. This neutral observer rates the client on a number of scales, for instance, how much anxiety or depression the client is exhibiting.

Another source of measurement of change is an informant's report, that is, a rating of the client made by some person in the client's life. For example, a client's wife may be asked to rate his personality or behavior before and after therapy.

Still another measurement of change involves attempts to assess behavior change directly. These may include ratings of behavior by others and more "objective" measures of behavior. We have already discussed behavioral measures in chapters 3 and 4 but will briefly review their use in psychotherapy research. An early example of an objective measure of behavior change is one that has been used in research on fears of snakes (Lang, Lazovik, & Reynolds, 1965). Before treatment with systematic desensitization, clients with fears of snakes were asked to approach a cage with a snake in at as close as they could. Some were so afraid of snakes that they were not even able to enter the room in which the cage was placed. After treatment, the same procedure was used. Most clients were able to approach the cage and look at the snake, and some were even able to pick it up.

Most behavioral measures involve direct or indirect observation of behavior. A relative may keep track of the number of times the client loses her temper or drinks or engages in whatever target behavior is being modified. In hospitals, nurses and attendants usually do the observing. They keep track of the target behaviors on some kind of behavior rating form. An indirect way of observing behavior is to use tape recordings of family interaction patterns or to set up role-playing situations. These are less desirable than observing behavior in real life, but sometimes observing behavior in real life can be difficult. A role-playing situation may be set up, for instance, in which a client asks his boss for a raise. The effectiveness and appropriateness of his assertive behaviors can then be rated.

We have not previously mentioned the single subject research design used by behaviorists. This strategy avoids the necessity of having many subjects to serve as treatment and control groups. Behaviorists sometimes use an individual subject as her own control. Before therapy begins, the target behaviors are observed in the situations in which they occur and a baseline of the frequency is established. For instance, before treatment starts, it is observed that on the playground, a boy commits an average of four aggressive acts per 15-minute observation periods. Behavioral observations are made again after treatment is initiated. If it has worked, the rate will have changed; in this case, perhaps it drops to one incident every 15 minutes. The effect of the treatment can be further studied by withdrawing or reversing it. Suppose the treatment for the aggressive boy was reinforcing positive behavior and ignoring negative behavior. Suppose, also, that before treatment, it had been observed that the child was ignored when he acted positively and received a lot of attention (in the form of criticism and punishment) when he acted up. Upon the return to those responses to his behavior, the number of aggressive acts increases again to four incidents every 15 minutes. When the therapeutic strategy is resumed, once again the rate decreases to one incident every 15 minutes. This demonstrates that it is the therapeutic strategy that has caused the improvement, without the use of control groups. Unfortunately, such a design is most appropriate to behavioral treatments and is far less applicable to approaches such as psychoanalysis or gestalt (how would you reverse the treatment of "insight into the past"?).

Objective records can be used as a measurement of change in psychotherapy. Some studies use grade-point average in school, and several studies have found increases in the average as a result of therapy. Other objective indexes that have been used include hospitalization rates, incarceration rates, and number of clients receiving therapy who are unemployed versus unemployed control subjects.

A particularly important subgroup of objective indexes for some disorders are physiological measures, such as blood pressure, heart rate, galvanic skin response (which reflects anxiety), penile tumescence (when sexual dysfunction is the target symptom), and brain wave response. These measures are usually used when the disorder being treated involves stress or anxiety or when the treatment used includes relaxation, meditation, or biofeedback methods. Weight loss or weight gain are obvious biologically based measures when the problem being treated is either obesity or ***anorexia***.

Since each of the many ways to measure change has its limitations, it is usually recommended that multiple measures, utilizing different sources of information, be used (Strupp et al., 1997). These will often include various measures of changes in symptoms filled out by both therapist and client, and possibly an assessment done by an independent mental health professional.

Qualitative Research Methods

In recent years, qualitative research designs, already used in other research areas such as sociology and anthropology, have become more popular in psychology

(Camic, Rhodes, & Yardley, 2003). Some qualitative researchers have argued that experimental designs are inadequate to capture the complex interactive process that is psychotherapy. Psychotherapy is not like a medication that can be simply administered to a large group of subjects and its effects measured and compared to a placebo control group. Instead, psychotherapy is a give-and-take, back-and-forth process between therapist and client. The process that emerges is different for each therapist–client pair, and the solutions that emerge are often unique. Therefore, to compare a treatment group to a control group, as if a common "treatment" were being uniformly applied to all clients (as is the case with medication) simply is not an adequate way to learn about psychotherapy's effectiveness. Some qualitative researchers reject control group experimental designs entirely; others do not reject them, but believe they must be complemented by qualitative methods in order to achieve a full understanding of how psychotherapy works.

Qualitative research operates on a different set of assumptions than the control group design. Many qualitative researchers believe that the best way to achieve a scientific understanding of psychotherapy is through intense analysis of individual cases. A qualitative researcher might collect data on a sample of clients in psychotherapy by periodically interviewing them, by having them fill out questionnaires, and/or by taping the therapy sessions. Then, using various qualitative descriptive and interpretive methods, the researcher tries to understand the experience of the clients and its relationship to the processes that occurred in therapy. Procedures are used that serve to minimize biases in interpretation. What is achieved is an intense understanding of individual cases, from which generalizations can be drawn about psychotherapy experiences in a broader sense.

So far, qualitative research has been used more to study the processes occurring in psychotherapy than the question of psychotherapy's effectiveness. For instance, Rennie (2002) played tapes of therapy sessions back for both clients and therapists and asked them what they were thinking about at key moments during the process. Using qualitative methods to analyze clients' responses, Rennie demonstrated that clients are much more active during the therapy process than most models of psychotherapy hold. Clients do a lot of thinking to themselves, privately working on their problems as they talk to the therapist, but often they do not share these thought processes with the therapist. They use their own empathic understanding of the therapist to work with or around the therapist, depending on how understood they feel by the therapist. Watson and Rennie (1994) demonstrated how actively clients work to symbolize their experience and feelings and reflect on them to discover new meanings and make personal changes.

There is one innovative approach to using qualitative research to answer the question of whether psychotherapy is effective. This is Robert Elliott's (2001a) Hermeneutic Single-Case Efficacy Design (HSCED). This design actually relies on both qualitative and quantitative data. On the quantitative side, over the course of therapy clients fill out weekly measures of their problems and goals. On the qualitative side, clients are periodically interviewed during therapy, and after therapy. Data on significant events in their lives are also gathered. Ideally, individual therapy sessions are recorded, providing another source of both quantitative and qualitative data. Then a causal reasoning process is used to infer (a) whether the client has changed or not, and

(b) whether the change can be attributed to therapy. Principles are established for making these causal inferences. For instance, even if it is clear that the client has changed, in order to attribute the change to therapy there must be good reason to reject the possibility that some significant life event caused the change (for instance, a depressed person getting better because he got a job). One interesting insight that comes out of the more in-depth intensive analysis that an individual therapy case gets using the HSCED is how complicated the change process is. This is masked in typical quantitative research studies where change is assessed on a few measures.

Qualitative designs have become increasingly accepted in recent years, and there have been attempts to establish criteria for their reliability and validity (Stiles, 1993). Qualitative designs tend to be favored by researchers studying psychotherapies that rely on more open-ended, discovery-oriented, and relational methods, such as many psychodynamic, humanistic, feminist, and constructivist approaches. However, some traditional quantitative researchers remain uncomfortable with qualitative research. We would point out that one of the most influential scientific theories of all time, evolutionary theory, was based on qualitative data gathered by Charles Darwin. Qualitative research, like quantitative research, has its limitations. That is why ultimately we believe it is the use of multiple methods that holds the best chance of arriving at thorough understanding of the phenomena we are interested in.

Other Problems in Psychotherapy Research

In addition to some of the problems associated with doing research on psychotherapy mentioned above, we shall briefly discuss a few more. Follow-up is another problem: How long after therapy should clients be followed to see if change has been maintained? Following clients for any length of time is difficult; clients may move, die, or otherwise become unavailable.

Or suppose you want to compare psychoanalysis to behavior therapy. You should probably have several psychoanalysts and several behavioral therapists in your study. But do all psychoanalysts or behavioral therapists proceed identically? What if different kinds of persons become psychoanalysts and behavioral therapists? Suppose some personality characteristic differs between these kinds of persons and suppose that affects the outcome of therapy? One of the recent answers to this dilemma is to use ***treatment manuals*** to standardize the way therapy is delivered. We shall discuss treatment manuals and the controversy over them later in this chapter.

By now we hope you realize that it is complicated to provide an answer to the question: "Does the so-and-so approach to psychotherapy work?" For similar reasons, it is often quite difficult to know why a therapy works. Is it the personality of the therapist or the elements in the therapy that the particular theory claims are important? Is it factors that no one is aware of? We also hope that by now you see that believing you can tell how a therapy works by personal experience, either as therapist or client, is simplistic. Return to the examples at the start of the chapter and ask yourself: Would the client have changed without the therapy? Has the client changed? If change has occurred, is it because of insight, getting in touch with feelings, combating dysfunctional cognitions, or desensitization? Could it have been that any of those techniques would have worked because they all give the client a sense of hope? Could it have been that the therapist was a supportive, encouraging person? Are the therapist's perceptions of change accurate? How permanent and stable are the changes? What would you have to do to begin to answer these questions?

The Effectiveness of Psychotherapy

There are two general kinds of psychotherapy research: outcome research and process research. ***Outcome research*** deals with the effectiveness of psychotherapy. ***Process research*** deals with the processes that go on in therapy interactions. An example of process research is a study by Brunnink and Schroeder (1979), in which they compared the verbal behavior of psychoanalytic, gestalt, and behavior therapists. As expected, there were several differences. For instance, gestalt therapists were more active in providing direct guidance and used more self-disclosure than psychoanalysts.

Process and outcome research can be linked; a study can attempt to relate differences in therapy process to therapy effectiveness. For instance, researchers could see if the differences between gestalt and psychoanalytic therapists in verbal behavior relate to differences in effectiveness. Our review of psychotherapy research below will focus primarily on outcome research.

As previously noted, it has only been in the last 50 years that intensive efforts have been made to study the question of psychotherapy's effectiveness scientifically. Perhaps the event that triggered these efforts was a report by Hans Eysenck. Eysenck (1952) searched the literature for published reports of success rates for different psychotherapies and for different psychotherapy institutes. He collated these rates for neurotic patients and found a success rate of 44% for psychoanalysis and 64% for various other approaches. In order to know if these rates meant that therapy worked or not, Eysenck attempted to find a recovery rate for neurotic patients who did not receive psychotherapy. He discovered data on two such groups of patients and calculated that they had a ***spontaneous recovery rate*** of 72%. The apparent conclusion from Eysenck's data was that at best, there was no evidence that therapy worked, and at worst, the less therapy one had, the better!

However, Eysenck's report had many scientific problems (Bergin, 1971), and its conclusions could not be accepted. Its main function was to stimulate research on the question of psychotherapy's effectiveness. During the intervening years, a large number of research studies on the effectiveness of psychotherapy have been conducted, with a wide range of patients, over a wide range of types of problems, and across different kinds of therapies. Before we review current research conclusions regarding psychotherapy's effectiveness, we must briefly mention a method that has increasingly come to be used to estimate whether psychotherapy is effective or not, that of meta-analysis.

Meta-analysis is a statistical procedure that is applied to the results of all available studies on a certain topic. From the procedure, an effect size is calculated. An effect size is something like a standard deviation. It is a way of calculating how much the average effect due to a particular treatment is above the mean or average effect of those who are not given the treatment. The numbers given for effect sizes are not easily interpretable by themselves, but we can give you an approximate idea of what they mean. Smith, Glass, and Miller (1980), who introduced the use of meta-analysis to the study of psychotherapy, located 475 studies in which some kind of therapy was compared to some kind of control group. The overall effect size for psychotherapy was 0.85. This means that the average person who received therapy was better off than 80% of the persons who did not. For comparison's sake, the effect size for nine months of instruction in reading in elementary school in improving reading scores is 0.67 (Smith, Glass, & Miller, 1980, p. 88). The effect size for cigarette smoking increasing the probability of getting lung cancer is 0.60 (APA Commission on Psychotherapies, 1982, p. 137).

Is Psychotherapy Effective?

Lambert and Ogles (2004) have done an overall review of the research on psychotherapy. They reviewed a number of meta-analyses done since the Smith, Glass, and Miller (1980) one, and find that the effect sizes range from .47 to 1.05. Although there is some inconsistency in the results, the evidence is clear that psychotherapy is at least moderately effective. In fact, there is more research on the effectiveness of psychotherapy than on any medical treatment (Messer, 1994). Separate research studies have shown the effectiveness of various marital and family therapies (Sexton, Alexander, & Mease, 2004).

Is One Approach to Therapy Superior to Another?

In their meta-analysis, Smith et al. (1980) found that cognitive therapies, hypnotherapy, and systematic desensitization at first appeared to be the most effective. Psychodynamic, client-centered, gestalt, rational-emotive, transactional analysis, behavior modification, and various eclectic behavioral treatments were around the average in effectiveness. Despite the apparent superiority of some of the cognitive-behavioral therapies, Smith, Glass, and Miller concluded that on closer analysis, there was no evidence that cognitive and behavioral therapies in general were superior to verbal therapies. They reached this conclusion for a variety of reasons, including the fact that behavioral treatments used different kinds of measures of effectiveness than verbal therapies and in studies where the two were pitted against one another directly, there was no clear superiority.

This particular finding has been called the "dodo bird verdict," based on *Alice's Adventures in Wonderland* in which the dodo bird judges a race and proclaims that everyone has won and all must have prizes.

We will briefly review one classic research study that exemplifies the dodo bird verdict. The study by Sloane, Staples, Cristol, Yorkston, and Whipple (1975) compared psychoanalytically oriented psychotherapy to behavior therapy. A group of clients with diagnoses of either personality disorder or neurotic disorder were randomly assigned to psychoanalytically oriented treatment, behavioral treatment, or a waiting list control group. Three psychoanalytic therapists and three behavioral therapists, experienced, outstanding representatives of each approach (two of the three behavior therapists were Joseph Wolpe and Arnold Lazarus), conducted the therapies over a four-month period. The research group assessed the clients right after the end of treatment, and again a year after beginning treatment. Assessment of therapeutic outcome included several personality inventories; ratings by patients, therapists, and informants; assessment by an independent assessor; and analysis of target symptoms. On target symptoms, both therapy groups improved more than the control group. On assessments of more global improvement, the two therapies were again rated as generally equal, though there were some instances in which behavior therapy appeared to be superior. No specific client characteristics appeared to relate generally to therapeutic outcome, but there was some evidence that "acting-out" patients did better in behavior therapy.

The dodo bird verdict has been controversial ever since it was first articulated. The idea that all therapies work about the same has troubled people for several reasons. For one, it is troubling to those wedded to particular approaches and who believe in their superiority. Second, given the wide differences in how different therapies proceed, it is surprising that they could all be effective. Yet, although there are individual research studies where one approach outperforms another, many other studies continue to find no difference. Wampold et al.'s (1997) meta-analysis also found evidence supporting the dodo bird verdict. Lambert and Ogles (2004) found that overall, evidence continues to support the conclusion that differences in effectiveness between therapies on average are negligible.

Nevertheless, the issue is far from settled. Those who believe that specific treatments are needed for specific disorders point to studies where one kind of therapy works better for a specific disorder than does another therapy. For instance, several studies have found that behavioral exposure achieved superior results with agoraphobics (people with a fear of open places) compared to cognitive therapy (Emmelkamp, 2004). In reply, Wampold et al. (1997) point out that the existence of individual research studies where one therapy outperforms another therapy does not contradict the dodo bird verdict because, statistically, the number of such studies does not exceed what one would expect to find by chance: if you do enough research studies, by sheer chance some will find one approach to be superior to another. Additionally, findings where one therapy outperforms another are complicated by the "researcher allegiance effect": when one study finds a given approach to be superior to another, it is typically the approach that is the favorite of the researcher conducting the study. Luborsky et al., (1999) found a correlation of .85 between the allegiance of the researcher and outcome in the study. When researcher allegiance effects are controlled for statistically, differences between therapies tend to disappear.

This is not to say that there are not instances where it is likely that one form of therapy works better than another. Some have suggested that for the more severe disorders specific approaches may work better (Lambert & Bergin, 1994).

Why does the dodo bird verdict matter? If it is true that, for the most part, different therapies work about equally well for most disorders, this suggests that (a) the specific theories and techniques that different approaches prize so much may not be that important, (b) there may be common factors that operate across all therapies, and (c) the idea that specific treatments are needed for specific disorders, such as is true in medicine, may not be true. This latter factor poses a problem for psychotherapists in that most psychotherapy is now paid for by health insurance. Insurance companies tend to think along the lines of medicine. They expect that specific treatments will be needed for specific disorders. Indeed, they typically demand treatment plans based on the client's diagnosis. If it turns out that it doesn't really matter which approach to therapy is used for most problems, this implies that diagnosis is also not particularly useful. The upshot is that some psychologists are afraid that this will make psychotherapy look suspect in the eyes of the health care industry.

Yet, there are other findings that are compatible with the dodo bird verdict. For instance, there is evidence that the therapist providing the therapy may be more important than what therapy is being provided (Wampold, in press a). There is also evidence supporting the importance of the idea of common factors. Of particular importance is the therapeutic relationship. Evidence suggests that the relationship is at least as important, if not more important, than techniques. Lambert and Barley (2002) estimate that the relationship and other common factors account for about 30% of why therapy works, and techniques account for about 15%. In medicine it would be surprising to find that the relationship between physician and patient was twice as important as whatever specific treatment procedures the physician used. (The other two factors that contribute to success are the client and factors in the client's life—40%, and placebo effects—15%, according to Lambert & Barley).

A cautionary note here is that there are varying estimates of over 250 to 400 different therapy approaches in use today, and many of these approaches have not been researched. It is important to bear in mind that the conclusion that "all psychotherapies are equivalent" bears only on those therapies that have been researched.

Other Research Findings

Psychotherapy is not equally effective for all problems or for all clients. Generally, it has been shown to be effective for anxiety, depression, marital problems, and various types of specific behavioral problems. It has not been generally shown to be effective for schizophrenia (although it has been shown to be helpful with selected subsets of schizophrenics), and it has at best been only modestly successful, if at all, with various kinds of antisocial behavior.

In terms of the length of therapy, most researchers believe that the evidence has not supported the idea that long-term therapy is more effective than short-term therapy, as traditional psychoanalysts have held. Howard, Kopta, Krause, and Orlinsky (1986) conducted a meta-analysis of research on over 2,400 clients. Their analysis showed that approximately 50% of patients are measurably improved by the eighth session of therapy, and 75% are improved by the twenty-sixth session. This evidence supports the recent shift in the field toward brief psychotherapy. There is even evidence that a number of patients have benefited from a single session of therapy, leading to the development of single-session therapies (Rosenbaum, Hoyt, & Talmon, 1990). However, it must be noted that such relatively rapid improvements most likely take place in less disturbed patients with less serious problems (Lambert, Shapiro, & Bergin, 1986). Westen, Novotny, & Thompson-Brenner (2004) have found evidence that therapy often takes longer in real-life settings than it does in research studies.

Along these same lines, a *Consumer Reports* survey (Seligman, 1995) found that people who reported staying in therapy longer also reported receiving more benefit. In addition, Blatt and Ford (1994) have provided evidence that long-term, intensive, psychoanalytically oriented treatment can be effective, more so for clients who are concerned with issues of self-definition, self-worth, and self-control than for clients who are concerned with relationship issues. The *Consumer Reports* study has been criticized for its methodological limitations (Jacobson & Christensen, 1996), but these studies taken together suggest that the rush to briefer and briefer forms of psychotherapy may be a bit premature (Miller, 1996).

Making Sense of the Dodo Bird Verdict

As of the late 1980s, many psychotherapy researchers had generally accepted the conclusion that all of the major psychotherapies worked about equally well. The question then became why. Are there basic common factors in all the therapies that are responsible for their effectiveness? Or is it possible that different therapies and techniques work better for different psychological conditions, but when averaged together, they all looked about equally effective? Or, does focusing on specific processes in therapy lead to better understanding how change occurs? We review each of these three possibilities below.

The Therapeutic Alliance as a Common Factor

A large number of common factors in different therapies have been proposed (see chapter 14). However, few have been researched. The one for which there is the most support is the therapeutic relationship, or, as it is now called, the ***therapeutic alliance***. The therapeutic alliance appears to be the single most important curative factor in therapy, outweighing the importance of techniques or of differing approaches (Lambert & Barley, 2002). Some research (Horvath, 1995; Luborsky, McLellan, & Woody, 1985) found that measures of the alliance between therapist and client were the strongest predictors of whether the therapy would be successful. Other research has found that even in the case of prescription of antidepressant medication, the relationship between physician and client made a powerful difference in whether the medication was helpful (Krupnick et al., 1996).

It was Carl Rogers who originally proposed that the therapeutic relationship was a primary curative agent. As noted in chapter 8, his further claim that it is three general therapist qualities—warmth, empathy, and genuineness—which make the difference has only partially been supported by the data. They are important, but the evidence does not support the claim that they are necessary and sufficient. Modern conceptions of the therapeutic alliance focus on three aspects of the relationship—the bond, the goals of therapy, and the tasks of therapy. A good therapeutic alliance includes a strong bond between therapist and client (and this is where warmth, empathy, and genuineness play a role). In addition, it includes an agreement between therapist and client on the goals to be pursued in therapy and the procedures and tasks to be used to attain these goals.

The therapeutic alliance is not seen as something the therapist establishes alone but rather as a product of the collaboration between therapist and client. Thus, both client and therapist contribute. In this regard, Henry, Schacht, and Strupp (1986) found that greater therapist levels of "helping and protecting" and "affirming and understanding" were associated with positive therapeutic outcomes. However, they also found evidence that client behaviors contributed to how well a therapist was able to provide good therapeutic conditions. For instance, client behaviors of "disclosing and expressing" were related to the therapist's being more helping, affirming, and understanding, while client behaviors of "walling off and avoiding" were more associated with negative and hostile therapist behaviors. The most intriguing finding of this study was that the same therapist, using the same techniques, could come across with one client as "affirming and understanding" and with another as "blaming and belittling." This suggests that the presence of helpful behaviors in the therapist is partially dependent on the behavior of the client.

Differential Treatments for Different Problems

There is much current controversy surrounding the hypothesis that different therapies are needed for different conditions. Several reviewers of the research have concluded that on the whole, with a few exceptions, research findings have tended to contradict this idea (Bergin & Garfield, 1994; Wampold, 2001). For instance, a wide range of therapies seem to be of approximately equal effectiveness for the treatment of depression, including medication, cognitive therapy, and client-centered therapy. In a study by *Consumer Reports* magazine, data was collected from readers who had been in therapy. No differences were reported in effectiveness among differing approaches for any problems (Seligman, 1995). On the other hand, there are cases in which specific approaches seem to be differentially effective. One study by Stiles, Barkham, Shapiro, and Firth-Cozens (1992) found that clients' problems that are vaguely formulated or unfocused responded better to interventions of a psychodynamic or humanistic variety, while clients with well-formulated, specific, and focused problems responded better to more prescriptive (cognitive-behavioral) interventions. Using criteria for ***empirically supported treatments*** (ESTs), which were formerly known as empirically validated treatments (see below for a discussion of these criteria) there are some disorders for which only cognitive-behavioral treatments have been shown to be effective, such as panic disorder and borderline personality disorder. This is particularly true for some childhood disorders (Kazdin, 2004). However the problem in concluding that these are evidence for the idea that specific treatments are needed for specific problems is that other approaches have not been researched using the specific EST criteria for these disorders.

While it makes intuitive sense that there will be cases where specific treatments may be needed for specific disorders, it has been surprisingly hard to demonstrate that this is true in most cases. Overall, Seligman (2002) has concluded that, with a few exceptions, there is generally no evidence that specific treatments are needed for specific disorders. Yet we must point out that this conclusion remains controversial (Norcross, Beutler, & Levant, in press).

A different possibility is that different treatments may not typically be differentially effective for different *problems,* but different treatments may work better with different *types of individuals.* This is the strategy pursued by Larry Beutler and his colleagues (e.g., Beutler, Harwood, Alimohamed, & Malik, 2002). In a series of studies, Beutler and colleagues have shown that clients who are highly "reactant" (i.e., they are highly autonomous and become resistant if they feel others are trying to control them) do better with more nondirective treatments, while more dependent clients do better with more directive treatments.

As you will see below, the issue of whether different treatments are needed for different problems is far from settled. It is likely that both sides of the controversy are right: For many problems, it may not matter which approach to therapy is used, while for others, it may matter greatly.

Understanding the Process of Change

Believing that evidence shows that different theoretical approaches to psychotherapy all work about the same, some researchers decided that it would be profitable to turn their attention to a closer examination of what actually occurs in therapy. A number of researchers began to do intensive analyses of the process of psychotherapy. Two approaches to trying to understand the process of change are (a) Rice and Greenberg's (1984) task analysis, and (b) ***discovery-oriented research*** (Elliott, 1984; Mahrer, 2004). Both of these approaches attempt to identify important events in the psychotherapeutic process and then study what actually occurs in a therapy intervention.

Task Analysis

Task analysis starts by developing a model of the change process on a specific therapeutic "task" and then studying a number of actual "performances" to see how well they fit the model. The model is revised to fit with what has been learned from studying these actual performances. Then the model is once again compared to new examples to see how well it fits. Greenberg (1984) has used this approach to study the process of resolution in the gestalt "two-chair" procedure. The client "task," for instance, is to resolve a "split." A ***split*** is an experience in which the client feels at odds with herself; part of her may be wanting to leave her marriage, and the other part may be criticizing her for that. In the gestalt two-chair exercise, the client role-plays the conflict. In one chair, she acts out the role of the "internal critic," in this case, the side that is saying "you should stay in the marriage." Then she switches chairs and acts out the role of the "want" side, in this case, the side that wants to leave the marriage. She continues back and forth, switching sides, until some resolution is reached. Greenberg notes that several studies have found that this procedure is effective in helping the client with the "task" of resolving a conflict. By studying a number of actual "performances" of this task, Greenberg was able to develop a model of how the process goes when it results in successful resolution. Among other things, the process seems to work best when the "critic" side "softens" in its approach to the "want" side. Consistent with the point we made above, a perusal of Greenberg's work provides a good deal of concrete information that practicing clinical psychologists can actually incorporate into their practice.

One of the most important ideas to come out of Rice and Greenberg's (1984) work on task analysis is the idea of a "therapeutic marker." Their general strategy is to identify ***markers***, that is, behavioral signs exhibited by the client that suggest that the client needs to work on a certain therapeutic task. For instance, the marker for the use of the two-chair technique is that the client is expressing a split—"I feel like leaving my marriage, but then I feel like I'm a bad person for wanting that. I should stay in it." The presence of a marker can then be used to choose a particular therapeutic intervention that will be of assistance at that moment. In other words, identifying a therapeutic marker helps the therapist to make effective moment-by-moment decisions. Greenberg, Rice, and Elliott (1993a) have identified several other therapeutic markers that suggest the therapist use specific interventions at specific moments. A number of other researchers have identified other therapeutic markers relevant to their approaches (e.g., Safran & Segal, 1990).

Discovery-Oriented Research

A related development has been that of "discovery-oriented" research (Elliott, 1984; Mahrer, 2004). Mahrer has suggested that therapists try to identify what they believe are significant events in therapy sessions. They collect many instances of that kind of event, and then look for patterns. The researcher can then begin to identify the kinds of therapist operations and procedures that bring about this kind of event and look at the relationship of that event to the ultimate therapeutic outcome. Mahrer and Nadler (1986) have identified a list of what different therapists have considered to be ***good moments*** in therapy, that is, moments that are hypothesized to be important in creating therapeutic change. These can include the client exploring and expressing emotions, expressing insight or understanding, expressing feelings toward the therapist, or talking about personal, self-related material. Mahrer, White, Souliere, Macphee, and Boulet (1991) found that the therapist telling the client to describe, show, express, and "be" an emotion when the client was having difficulty accessing emotions helped facilitate a good moment of expressing emotion. Mahrer, Gagnon, Fairweather, and Cote (1992) identified criteria that denote whether a therapy session has been a "very good one" or not.

Elliott (1984) has suggested that an important process for learning about what actually happens in therapy is the use of "interpersonal process recall" (Kagan, 1984). Elliott identified moments in therapy when clients made "insight" statements, following therapist interpretations. These sessions were taped, and the client and the therapist later listened to the segment of therapy that included the insight statement and talked about what they were experiencing at the time. From this, Elliott was able to develop a model of an "insight event." An insight event appeared to run through four phases: the client begins to process the information offered by the therapist; the insight occurs; the client experiences a sense of newness, relief, accuracy, and helpfulness; and the insight leads to further exploration and new learning.

Research from studies such as these seemed to offer concrete, helpful information for practicing therapists. As of the late 1980s, it appeared that this would be the direction in which psychotherapy research would be heading: toward a more detailed, fine-grained, intensive understanding of how in-session processes facilitated change. However, under pressures described below, psychotherapy research made an abrupt about-face and returned to the study of whether specific treatments work for specific disorders.

Evidence-Based Practice

As the payment for health care is increasingly controlled by the government and by insurance corporations, there has been an increasing demand for health care service providers to demonstrate that the treatments they are providing work as they say they do. Along with this has come a call for the development of treatment guidelines in both medicine and mental health care. Treatment guidelines specify what treatments are to be used for particular disorders. An agency of the federal government, The Agency for Health Care Policy and Research, has been busy developing treatment guidelines for a wide range of medical and psychological disorders. In 1993, this agency published treatment guidelines for depression. Treatment guidelines, ideally, are based on the best empirical evidence available for treating a particular disorder. However, those who develop treatment guidelines always have their own point of view and interpret evidence in terms of that point of view. As a result, politics and science commingle in ways that lead to controversy in the health care arena.

Health care agencies and corporations have not been happy with the general statement that "all psychotherapies work about equally well." If they are to pay for psychotherapy for a particular disorder, they want to know *which* specific psychotherapy treatment has been shown through research to work for that disorder. Further, many clients themselves want to know if a particular treatment is going to help them with their particular problem. The result has been increased pressure on psychotherapists to demonstrate that particular psychotherapy treatments work for particular disorders. This has changed the face of psychotherapy research (Goldfried & Wolfe, 1996). Research has swung away from the study of psychotherapy processes back to a study of questions such as: "Does cognitive-behavior therapy work for eating disorders?" "Does client-centered therapy work for depression?" "Does brief psychodynamic therapy work for anxiety attacks?" Proponents of each of the major therapies are setting out to "empirically support" their approaches for the treatment of specific disorders in order that they not become obsolete, excluded from treatment guidelines and, therefore, from compensation by those who pay the bill for mental health treatment. In general, in both the United States and Europe, there have been movements afoot to develop guidelines for the practice of "evidence-based" psychotherapy, that is, using psychotherapy in ways that are supported by empirical research. Below we consider some of the developments with respect to this general trend.

What Is Evidence-Based Practice?

Generally, evidence-based practice of psychotherapy is based at least in part on empirical evidence. Defined this way it is hard to imagine anyone objecting. The problem is: What does it mean to base practice on empirical evidence? Does it mean that practice should be evidence-*driven,* based only on research utilizing strict experimental designs, as some advocates of the empirically supported treatments approach (see below) have held? This would mean that therapists would follow specific manuals for treating specific disorders and make no major decisions on their own (Lampropoulos, 2000).

Or, does evidence-based practice mean that practice should be evidence-*informed,* meaning that therapists use research knowledge but integrate it in with their own expert judgment of the individual case? Even then, what evidence should we use? The evidence of years of psychotherapy research that shows that all major bona fide therapies are approximately equally effective, no matter what the disorder being treated? The evidence that shows that the effectiveness of therapy may primarily be a matter of common factors, such as establishing a good relationship with the client, which cut across different approaches? Or evidence showing that therapists should use certain general change principles that cut across approaches? Or should it be the kind of evidence favored by the empirically supported treatments movement—evidence collected using carefully controlled experimental designs modeled after those used for drug research? And finally, what about the client? Doesn't the client have a say in what kind of therapy he receives and in what kinds of evidential bases matter most to him or her? These are issues currently being debated.

Treatment Guidelines and the APA Template

We previously mentioned the guidelines for the treatment of depression published by an agency of the federal government. These guidelines are a perfect illustration of how science has become completely mixed up with politics in the health care arena. This governmental agency, under the influence of medical thinking, concluded from its review of the research that the use of medication is the treatment of choice for severe depression and that depression is a "chronic illness." Many psychologists would not only contest the idea that depression is a chronic illness, but they also would hold that the available evidence indicates that psychotherapy alone is equally as effective as medication and that it is debatable whether combining it with medication is better than psychotherapy (or medication) alone. Further, psychotherapy has a lower relapse rate than medication. This suggests that making medication the treatment of choice for depression is not compatible with the research evidence and unduly favors medication over psychotherapy (see the results of a recent research study that found that cognitive therapy was as effective as drugs in treating severe depression; *Philadelphia Inquirer*, 2005).

In order to counter what psychologists saw as a biased reading of the evidence on the treatment of depression, the APA developed a template for evaluating and constructing treatment guidelines (Task Force on Psychological Intervention Guidelines, 1995). This template provides empirical criteria for deciding whether a given set of guidelines for therapeutic practice is justified by the data. The template's criteria include both efficacy and effectiveness of psychotherapy. *Efficacy* has to do with what we described earlier in the chapter: doing careful experiments using control groups. These studies must be done, in essence, by studying specific treatments for specific disorders. In addition, the template mandates that the *effectiveness* or *utility* of the psychotherapy must be studied, that is, the effectiveness of the therapy must be studied under real-life conditions.

The reason for the distinction between efficacy and effectiveness or utility is that many carefully controlled experimental studies of psychotherapy are done in ways that have little to do with the conditions under which psychotherapy is practiced in real life. For instance, in real life, if a client comes to a therapist complaining of feeling anxious all the time, the therapist works with the client regardless of whether the client perfectly meets the criteria for the diagnosis of generalized anxiety disorder and regardless of whether the client has other problems (e.g., depression, personality disorder). Yet in many of the carefully controlled research studies on therapy, clients are excluded from participating unless they meet strict criteria. Thus, in one study on a cognitive-behavioral treatment for generalized anxiety disorder, of the over 500 clients who were referred to the researchers for possible inclusion in the study, nearly 450 were rejected as not meeting the researchers' criteria (Borkovec & Costello, 1993). These researchers found that their cognitive-behavioral treatment was effective. However, one can ask how useful such information is to a practicing clinician, given that nearly 90% of the clients referred for the study (presumably because they were feeling anxious) were not included. That this is a genuine concern is illustrated by the findings of Weisz, Weiss, & Donenberg (1992) that psychotherapy with children practiced in the field was not as effective as psychotherapy practiced under carefully controlled research conditions.

The APA template thus encourages us to take a broader look at the scientific evaluation of psychotherapy, by looking at both questions of efficacy (can the psychotherapy be demonstrated to work under carefully controlled conditions?) and effectiveness (how well does it work under real-life conditions?). However, the template itself was criticized by proponents of psychotherapies whose methods and purposes do not easily fit into a model of psychotherapy as a specific "treatment for a disorder." There are still many therapists who believe that diagnosis and treatment of specific problems is not the proper goal of therapy. Instead, their goal is to promote deeper relational connections, self-awareness and insight, and deeper levels of a capacity to experience self and life. This includes many psychodynamic and humanistic therapists, feminist therapists, and constructivist therapists. Many of them believe that the template's criteria favor psychotherapies that can easily be evaluated using traditional experimental research methodologies, and they worry that the template might ultimately be turned against their preferred approaches. They lobbied to have nonexperimental and qualitative research methods, which fit their approaches better, included in the template's criteria, and this has come to pass in a 2002 revision (American Psychological Association, 2002)

Evidence-Based Practice and Empirically Supported Treatments

The issue of evidence-based practice in psychotherapy was crystallized by a task force of Division 12 of the APA (Task Force on Promotion and Dissemination of Psychological Procedures, Division of Clinical Psychology of the American Psychological Association, 1995), which published a set of guidelines for deciding which psychotherapy treatments had been empirically "validated" along with a list of treatments that had met their criteria. The criteria were similar to the criteria used in studies of drugs to show that a particular drug was effective. In order to be considered an empirically validated treatment, now called empirically supported treatment (see below), a particular psychotherapy had to be shown to be effective for the treatment of a particular disorder using what is called a *randomized controlled clinical trial design*. This is an experimental design in which the treatment had to be compared to a placebo control group or to another treatment of known effectiveness. The treatment had to be shown to be effective in two different studies. In addition, the treatment had to be *manualized.* Manualization means that the procedures to be used to treat a particular disorder are described in fairly intensive detail in a "treatment manual." A treatment manual is meant to insure that therapists in a research study all practice the therapy in the same way. Many psychotherapy studies in recent years have used treatment manuals. The task force held that manualization was good not only for research purposes but also for the training of therapists.

Second, the therapy study was essentially required to use a population of clients who all had the same disorder. This was in marked contrast to many earlier studies of psychotherapy in which the treated group of clients might have included a wide range of disorders. From the perspective of a health care agency, a study showing that cognitive therapy works on a group of clients with different diagnoses does not tell very much about how it works for any *specific* diagnosis. Therefore, the empirically validated treatments criteria included a requirement of demonstration of how a specific treatment worked for a specific problem or diagnosis. Thus the client population receiving treatment had to be carefully specified in terms of what kind of problem was being treated.

Using these criteria, the task force came up with a list of specific psychotherapies to treat specific disorders that met its research criteria. These were called "empirically validated treatments," and other approaches to therapy that did not meet the task force's criteria were labeled "experimental." Further, because many of the research studies on psychotherapy conducted in earlier years had not been manualized and had not been done on specific treatments for particular disorders, the task force concluded that these studies were null and void under the new criteria. They then stated that the old conclusion that all therapies were about equally effective could now be discounted. The task force went on to recommend that its empirically validated treatments be taught in graduate programs. Other writers who supported the idea of empirically validated treatments suggested that it was unethical not to use empirically validated treatments and that therapists who avoid using them should be subject to malpractice suits. It was often claimed that patients deserved empirically validated treatments.

Controversy over Empirically Supported Treatments

The term "empirically validated treatments" has gradually been replaced by the term "empirically supported treatments." This changed in common usage because the whole idea of ever "validating" a therapy has been criticized. It has been noted that at best, all one can ever do is gather data that empirically *support* the use of a given therapy, but there is always more that can be known about how a therapy works and who it works for. Thus, "validation" is an ideal never to be achieved. We shall use the term "empirically supported treatments" (ESTs) from here on.

The publication by the task force of Division 12 of the American Psychological Association of its list of ESTs was met with immediate controversy (e.g., Bohart, O'Hara, & Leitner, 1998; Garfield, 1996; Goldfried & Wolfe, 1996). Many criticisms were made, some of which we mention. First, the list of ESTs was almost exclusively cognitive-behavioral, with only a very few psychodynamic and humanistic treatments included. This is not surprising because of the task force's criteria: Cognitive-behavioral treatments are easily manualized and easily studied as treatments for specific disorders, while psychodynamic and humanistic therapies are typically more open-ended. They are not viewed as specific treatments for specific disorders, but rather as explorations in underlying personality, philosophical, and life-structure issues that lead to resolution of symptoms. Further, under the task force's criteria, many therapies, such as client-centered therapy, which had substantial empirical evidence to back up their effectiveness under the old research criteria, now found themselves banished to the group of "experimental" (i.e., empirically unsupported) therapies.

Second, many psychotherapy researchers objected to the specific research criteria that were chosen to identify ESTs. These criteria eliminated a large body of research that had suggested that many "bona fide" psychotherapies (Wampold, 1997), such as psychodynamic psychotherapy and client-centered therapy, had already been empirically supported using other accepted research criteria. If it is true that in general different psychotherapies are not needed for different, specific disorders, then stipulating that a therapy will only be considered empirically supported if it has been studied for a specific disorder is unduly restrictive and not in itself empirically justified.

Third, many clinicians worried that the list would supersede their use of their own clinical judgment as to what was best to use with their particular clients. They would be forced to apply an EST, for instance, to a particular client with panic disorder, when their own clinical judgment might suggest doing something else. They further worried that this document would give health care agencies ammunition in further being able to tell clinicians what to do with their clients.

Fourth, many argued that the task force's conclusions were not justified by the empirical evidence available. Many of the studies on the task force's list could be criticized as being irrelevant to how psychotherapy is practiced in the real world because they were done under carefully controlled research conditions (see the previous discussion of efficacy versus effectiveness). In fact, cognitive-behavior therapy for generalized anxiety disorder is on the task force's list, and we noted above how one of the studies supporting it excluded nearly 90% of the kinds of clients who might seek such a therapy in real life. In this regard, Goldfried and Wolfe (1996) reported a story of one psychotherapy researcher joking that the first law of psychotherapy research is not to use real clients. Westen et al. (2004) have noted that most of the research on ESTs is on a carefully controlled group of patients who have only one disorder, when in fact 50%–90% of the patients who seek out therapy in real life have multiple problems.

In addition, Westen and his colleagues have intensively studied the evidence on empirically supported treatments for a variety of disorders and have seriously questioned how empirically supported they actually are. For instance, the empirically supported treatments done under carefully controlled research conditions have tended to be rather time-limited in length. While at the end of the research study it appears that many clients have changed, follow-up evidence often suggests this is not the case. While many improve, most do not recover, and many seek further therapy within 18 months after the research study they were in. Furthermore, success rates are modest. Depending on how you define success, between 54%–63% of individuals with panic disorder benefit from the EST studied. With depression, results are even less impressive; anywhere from 78%–88% of those studied relapsed or sought further therapy.

Fifth, many have objected to the requirement of the manualization of therapy. It has been held that manualization of therapy makes therapy a "paint-by-numbers" process (Silverman, 1996), negating the necessary flexibility that the therapist must have to be effective. In real life, therapists do not follow manuals; they try one thing, and if it doesn't work, they try another (Seligman, 1995). Therapy is a complex, interactive process. Manualization, it is held by some, destroys therapist spontaneity and fails to capture the most important quality in therapy—that of the relationship. Duncan and Miller (in press) have reviewed the research on treatment manuals and have argued that the evidence does not support the idea that they make therapy more effective.

Sixth, even though the task force did not specifically require that research studies use DSM diagnoses, it did require that they "carefully specify" the types of clients being treated. By this they meant that the therapy had to be studied as a treatment for a particular kind of disorder or problem. This, too, does not fit with how therapists practice in real life. A client may come in with one problem, but during therapy, the problem may shift, and new goals may emerge. Or the therapy may work on multiple problems at the same time. Many therapies are not specifically focused on problem removal in any case.

Finally, as with the American Psychological Association template, it has been argued that the criteria for deciding that a therapy is empirically supported favor psychotherapies designed along the lines of the medical model, that is, as specific treatments for specific disorders, and discriminate against therapies not so conceived. Qualitative research methods and findings from qualitative studies, for instance, are not given much weight in the task force's criteria.

Defenders of the task force's work have argued in reply that studies are now being done that examine empirically supported treatments under more real-life conditions. So far, the evidence is promising (Ollendick & King, in press). Second, Ollendick and King (in press) argue that the evidence shows that ESTs work better than non-EST therapies (although Wampold, in press b contests this). Third, the guidelines were never meant to be used to dictate what clinicians did exclusively. Clinicians would always need to use their judgment as well. Further, defenders have argued that all therapies can be manualized and that treatment manuals are important to make sure that therapy is provided in a standardized and competent way. However, treatment manuals are never meant to be followed rigidly to the exclusion of what is happening with a particular client. Defenders have also suggested that those who complain that their favorite therapies are not on the list get busy doing the research to empirically support them. They argue that therapies will need to be empirically supported in the future to remain viable. Finally, they reiterate their argument that EST criteria provide the most stringent and clear-cut test of the effectiveness of a psychotherapy and patients deserve therapies that have been rigorously tested and shown to be effective.

Are There Multiple Ways to Be Evidence-Based?

In the United States, until recently the EST approach was the dominant way to think about evidence-based practice. However, this was not true in other countries. In England, for instance, evidence-based practice was more broadly conceived (Goss & Rose, 2002).

For the EST approach, the only way to practice in an evidence-based way meant to use a specific treatment for a specific disorder that had been manualized and empirically studied. This approach to evidence-based practice assumes that (a) specific treatments for specific disorders are needed, and (b) the operative ingredients in therapy are the treatments. However, we have already seen that the idea that specific treatments are needed is questionable in many cases. Wampold (in press b) has argued that there is no evidence that using ESTs improves practice. Wampold (in press a) argues that research shows that the therapist is much more important than the therapy being used. And, as we have previously pointed out, there is research suggesting that the therapeutic relationship is more important than specific treatments. So, are the EST criteria really justified? If you are an effective therapist and you use a therapy approach that has generally been supported by research, and you create good therapeutic relationships, are you not practicing in an evidence-based way regardless of what specific treatments you use for a given disorder? There are many who would say "yes."

In fact, one major alternative to the EST approach is the "empirically supported relationship" approach, created by a task force of a different division of the American Psychological Association, the Psychotherapy Division 29 (Norcross, 2002). This was created as a corrective to the overemphasis on treatments in the EST approach. Norcross and colleagues had a variety of experts review the research on the importance of various aspects of the therapeutic relationship and concluded that a number of aspects could be considered to be empirically supported in their contribution to therapeutic effectiveness.

Still another approach to evidence-based practice is to focus on empirically supported principles of practice (Beutler & Johannsen, in press; Bohart, 2005; Grawe, 1997). One empirically supported principle of practice, of course, is to establish a warm, empathic, and effective therapeutic relationship. Another one is to help the client have mastery experiences (Grawe, 1997). Another is to structure therapy around the client as active self-healer (Bohart, in press). The idea of empirically supported principles is that there are certain change principles, and some are specific to the treatment of certain disorders, but others are general to the practice of therapy. Westen et al. (2004) have made a similar suggestion, saying that instead of ESTs we have "empirically-informed" psychotherapy, where the therapist incorporates evidence on principles of change into practice. Practicing in this way, the therapist is practicing in an evidence-based way, but in a way that allows more flexibility than the EST approach.

Allowing for flexibility is important to many practitioners because prior research had shown that all "bona fide" therapies could be considered empirically supported (Wampold, 1997), but the EST group threw them out because they did not fit their particular criteria. That meant that many supporters of other approaches to therapy felt disenfranchised (Bohart et al., 1998) despite being empirically supported. The use of empirically supported principles of practice allows therapists to practice in evidence-based ways, but from a variety of perspectives, all of which in a general sense have been shown to be useful.

The field of psychotherapy in the United States now appears to be moving away from equating evidence-based practice with ESTs and towards broader and more flexible ways of construing evidence-based practice. A presidential task force of the American Psychological Association (Levant, 2005) has defined effective evidence-based practice as including three aspects: the best available empirical evidence, clinician expertise, and the client's personal values and cultural background. The best available empirical evidence can come from many different sources, including correlational studies and qualitative research. Thus "evidence" is defined more broadly than in the EST approach to evidence-based practice. In addition, the new APA criteria include clinician expertise, mandating that it is the clinician who must decide which evidence is relevant in a particular case. This then becomes more of an "evidence-informed" than "evidence-driven" approach to evidence-based practice. No matter how evidence-based practice is construed in the future, it is likely that there will be increasing pressure for therapists to show that what they do is "evidence-based."

Measuring Outcome in Clinical Practice

The trend toward demanding specific evidence on effectiveness is filtering down to the level of the individual practitioner. There are increasing demands that individual practitioners be able to document their effectiveness in working with different types of disorders. Some managed care companies already require therapists to periodically administer questionnaires to their clients to monitor therapy progress. Various proposals for how to do this have been given. Some have suggested using individualized scales with which clients rate their progress toward the goals that have been set at the start of therapy. Others have suggested using standardized tests. In either case, it is likely that at least in some contexts, practitioners will be required to measure how much each of their clients has improved, keep records, and be able to demonstrate their effectiveness in working with different types of problems.

One typical approach is to have clients fill out a short, well-validated symptom checklist at the end of each session. Based on a large accumulation of data, feedback can be given to the clinician as to whether this particular patient is improving at a rate comparable to other patients with similar problems. Such feedback has been found to significantly increase therapeutic effectiveness, even more so than using empirically supported treatments (Lambert & Hawkins, 2004). In Europe this is one of the favored methods of doing evidence-based practice, only it is often called "practice-based evidence" (Barkham & Mellor-Clark, 2000).

In Conclusion

The state of psychotherapy research is in great flux. There is increased pressure to do research demonstrating psychotherapy outcome—that is, that specific treatments work for specific disorders—at the same time as many believe that a more fruitful research avenue to follow would be to forget about studying different approaches to psychotherapy and instead study the specific change processes that occur. The promise of using psychotherapies that have been supported by empirical research is that consumers can be offered treatments that have shown some reliability in alleviating the problems that brought them to therapy. It seems important, as well as ethical, to study psychotherapy and to discover what is most helpful and efficient. Different research methods and criteria are favored by different researchers, but methods and criteria that may be optimal for some approaches to psychotherapy may not be optimal for others. We hope that three trends will develop. First, researchers will stay "methodologically open," allowing different therapies to be studied with methods appropriate to their structure and purposes. Second, any who hold that a particular approach to psychotherapy works will support, encourage, or conduct research on that approach. Third, all clinicians will use research to guide and inform their practice, but they will not use research to constrain and dictate what they do in working with their partner in the whole enterprise—the client.

PART III

Psychotherapeutic Approaches

Sigmund Freud and Psychoanalysis

I treated a young lady who suffered for six years from an intolerable and protracted nervous cough. . . . Every other remedy had long since shown itself powerless, and I, therefore, attempted to remove the symptom by psychic analysis. All that she could remember was that the nervous cough began at the age of fourteen while she boarded with her aunt. She remembered absolutely no psychic excitement during that time, *and did not believe there was a motive for her suffering* [italics added]. Under the pressure of my hand, she at first recalled a large dog. She then recognized the memory picture; it was her aunt's dog which was attached to her, and used to accompany her everywhere, and without any further aid it occurred to her that this dog died and that the children buried it solemnly; and on the return from this funeral her cough appeared. I asked her why she began to cough, and the following thought occurred to her: "Now I am all alone in this world; no one loves me here; this animal was my only friend, and now I have lost it. . . ." That was, therefore, the pathogenic idea: People do not love her, everybody else is preferred; she really does not deserve to be loved, etc.

—Sigmund Freud, "Psychotherapy of Hysteria"

. . . [O]ne analysand with marked obsessive-compulsive problems, based as is usually the case on an unconsciously maintained anal orientation to himself and his world, would at times grunt, groan, and writhe on the analytic couch in his efforts to force out some of his thoughts and feelings; finally he would appeal to the analyst explicitly for help in "getting it out." Upon analysis, this conduct proved to be a reenactment of his ambivalence during and after toilet training with respect to holding on to or letting go of his stools; it was also a reenactment of his conflictual retentive-expulsive actions in other areas of his life. In his childhood he often had ended up requiring help from his mother in completing his evacuations. It also

> emerged that he derived some secret masturbatory pleasure from the considerable and prolonged anal stimulation occasioned by his intermediate "paralysis."
>
> —Roy Schafer, *Language and Insight*

> The idea that a neurotic is suffering from a sort of ignorance, and that if one removes this ignorance by telling him facts (about the causal connection of his illness with his life, about his experiences in childhood, and so on) he must recover, is an idea that has long been superseded, and one derived from superficial appearances. . . . if knowledge about his unconscious were as important for the patient as the inexperienced in psychoanalysis imagine, it would be sufficient to cure him for him to go to lectures or read books. . . .
>
> —Sigmund Freud, "Observations on 'Wild' Psychoanalysis"

Psychoanalysis had been the most influential approach to psychotherapy. Originally developed by Sigmund Freud, psychoanalysis has provided many insights into both the process of psychotherapy and the nature of psychopathology. Many of Freud's insights have been incorporated into other approaches to psychotherapy that may diverge widely from psychoanalysis in other respects.

Psychoanalysis has spawned a host of creative offshoots. Taken all together, these are called the "psychodynamic" set of views. Psychodynamic views of the person hold that the personality is an organized system of forces and counterforces. Different dynamic theorists may disagree on what forces in the personality are important, but all usually include the need to protect against psychologically painful wishes, thoughts, feelings, or experiences as one of the major forces that drives the person. One of the major ways this is done is to deny painful aspects of the self or personality and keep them from awareness. Some of the theorists who have developed out of psychoanalysis are Jung, Adler, Rank, Reich, Sullivan, Horney, Fromm, Erickson, and Hartmann. More recent developments are object relations theory and Kohut's self psychology. In this chapter we will look at Freud's view of psychopathology and psychotherapy ("classical" psychoanalysis). In the next chapter we will consider the views of those who have followed Freud, examining in some detail modern relational approaches such as object relations theory and self psychology.

Theory of Personality

Hidden Meaning and the Concept of Repression

The core idea in Freudian psychoanalysis can be seen in the first two quotations at the start of the chapter. In both cases, the client's overt symptomatology (the cough in the first case and the difficulty in "getting it out" in the second) is actually not the problem. Rather, the symptoms are expressions of meanings hidden deep in the personality structure. The hidden meaning of the cough has to do with feelings of loss, of being alone, and of being unlovable. The second client's difficulty in getting his feelings and thoughts out is an expression of underlying conflicts over the act of defecation. The idea that overt behavior contains hidden meanings (Cameron & Rychlak, 1985) implies that there is a kind of "secret code" to overt behavior that must be deciphered if we are to help the client modify his actions. It is not sufficient to treat the symptoms themselves. Treating the overt behavior will be useless unless the hidden meanings are dealt with. In order to deal with them the client must become aware of them, and that is the ultimate goal of Freud's psychoanalysis. However, as the last quote at the start of the chapter indicates, intellectual knowledge about hidden meanings is not sufficient for therapeutic change to occur. Therapy must include reexperiencing the feelings and affects that accompany the hidden meanings. For instance, it would not be enough for the woman to know intellectually that conflicts about being lonely and being unlovable were underlying her cough. She would have to experience the feeling of being alone and unlovable for her awareness of these hidden meanings to be therapeutic. We will discuss why this is so later.

Most of Freud's original work was done with patients who used to be diagnosed as suffering from the neurotic disorder of conversion hysteria. Conversion hysteria is now called *conversion disorder.* Because for Freud (and, indeed, for many modern psychoanalysts) the concept of neurotic disorders was so important, we will briefly describe it. Basically neurotic disorders are disorders in which individuals have one or two symptoms that interfere with their functioning, but otherwise they are in touch with reality. This differs from psychosis, in which individuals are "out of touch" with reality, and personality disorders, in which individuals have pervasive characterological difficulties in the personality.

In ***conversion disorders***, clients suffer from one or more physical symptoms that mimic physical illnesses. For instance, a client may lose sight or hearing or speech, with no detectable physical cause for the loss. In fact, tests will often reveal that the client's eyes respond to light, ears to sound, and so on. Breuer and Freud (Freud, 1895/1937) originally treated conversion disorders with hypnosis. Under hypnosis the client was asked to recall when the particular symptom began. They found that the symptom was associated with an emotionally charged, forgotten memory. When this memory was recovered, the symptom would vanish. For instance, Anna O., Breuer's most famous client, developed the symptom of being unable to drink out of a glass and swallow water. The incident she had forgotten was one in which she had unexpectedly discovered her maid allowing a dog to drink out of a glass. Anna O. recalled feeling repulsed and disgusted. With the recovery of the memory, and her disgust, the symptom vanished, and she was able to drink easily from a glass.

It was such experiences with clients that led to Freud's view of psychopathology and then to his theory of personality. The client suffers from a symptom that disrupts the client's life. The symptom seems irrational and inexplicable; it does not appear to make sense. Furthermore, the client is unable to control the symptom consciously. However, there is a reason for the symptom at another, nonconscious level. Thus, the overt symptom is a disguised manifestation of a hidden meaning. In particular, the underlying meaning involves an emotional conflict of some sort. Though the emotional conflict is not in consciousness, it nevertheless manifests itself in overt behavior.

We may now ask why this memory is forgotten. Why was Anna O. unable to recall the dog's drinking out of the glass? Freud's answer was that such things are forgotten because they are painful and thus are blocked out of consciousness. Freud arrived at this conclusion by finding that some clients seemed to resist remembering the feelings that had been forgotten. From this, Freud ultimately developed the concept of ***repression***; that is, some emotionally conflictual material is excluded from consciousness because of its painful nature.

But why did the excluded material continue to influence behavior? Why was it not simply hidden and forgotten? Freud's answer was that it remains active because it is emotionally charged. It "clamors" for expression. Breuer and Freud used the term *strangulated affect* to capture this idea. The method of cure was to make these emotions available to consciousness, thereby allowing them expression and discharge. This idea is usually called *emotional catharsis.* Freud later abandoned the idea that catharsis is what makes therapy work, but he retained the idea that unconscious material remains active because it has a kind of "charge" (or "energy") attached to it.

It is important to distinguish the concept of repression from that of dissociation. With repression the mind deliberately (albeit unconsciously) pushes out of awareness painful material. It is as if this material is "buried" underneath consciousness. But the organized "self" of the person remains the same. Thus I may not want to know about impulses that are not congruent with my self-image, so I repress knowledge of them. With dissociation some kind of psychological trauma is so shocking that the mind is split and certain experiences get separated. One can still experience them consciously, but one has to enter into a dissociated state to do so. Individuals who have suffered serious trauma may enter dissociated states where memories or flashbacks of the trauma come back to them. The problem is that these memories are not integrated and can disrupt normal functioning. In extreme dissociative states the individual may have different, multiple personalities (Dissociative Identity Disorder in DSM). Freud emphasized repression, but modern trauma workers focus more on dissociation.

You now have the basics of Freud's view of psychopathology and personality. Certain conflictual material is excluded from consciousness because it is too painful. However, because it is emotionally charged, it remains active in the personality, resulting in overt behavioral symptoms. Full awareness (including allowing oneself to experience the emotions consciously) results in alleviation of the symptoms. These are Freud's theoretical hypotheses to explain the observations that recovery of forgotten, emotionally charged memories seemed to be related to the disappearance of hysterical symptoms. We mention this because other theorists have other ways of explaining these observations. With this in mind, we will now look at how Freud extended the above ideas to a whole theory of personality and psychopathology.

Metapsychology

We will be discussing Freud's metapsychology, which is what is most disputed by many modern psychoanalytic theorists and practitioners. The ***metapsychology*** consists of Freud's belief that the personality is fundamentally an energy system whose business is the regulation and discharge of both sexual and aggressive energy and his belief that the mind consists of three processes or structures: the id, the ego, and the superego.

As Freud extended his work, he began to find that the removal of symptoms in his hysterical clients did not effect a total cure. Other symptoms would pop up. This led Freud to believe that the ultimate causes of the person's problems lay deeply buried in the personality. In the second quote at the start of the chapter the man's problems in "getting it out" are not based on a single, emotionally charged memory, but on the repression of a whole set of experiences with toilet training when he was a child. As Freud continued to delve into the buried memories of his clients, he came to believe that psychological problems were not usually the result of a few highly charged emotional memories (traumatic memories), but rather the result of patterns of repression of meanings and associated experiences in early childhood.

In addition, Freud believed that many of the buried memories revolved around sexual themes. It is now unclear to what extent Freud actually found these themes in his clients' repressed memories and to what extent he went looking for them (see Masson, 1985). It is known that theorists both prior to and at the time of Freud (including Freud's friend Wilhelm Fleiss) were speculating that many psychological problems had their origins in sexual repression (Ellenberger, 1970). Freud was working during the Victorian era, a time of sexual repression, and it would not be surprising if sexual conflicts figured prominently among the emotional difficulties people had. Further, it was also about this time that Freud began his own self-analysis and began to uncover themes of repressed sexuality in himself. As a result, Freud began to believe that repressed sexuality lay at the core of psychopathological behavior. His clients' reports of early childhood sexual experiences with adults led to the formulation of his seduction theory. This theory held that it was the repression of actual traumatic memories of childhood molestations that caused neurotic behavior. However, Freud began to believe that many of these seductions had in fact not taken place. This led to the crucial idea that what had been repressed were frequently not memories of actual experiences, but memories of primitive sexual wishes and fantasies that were too painful for the individual to acknowledge consciously. Some scholars now believe that his original idea of repressed genuine sexual abuse was correct (Masson, 1985).

Freud later developed the idea of the regulation of aggressive energy in the form of what he called the death instinct. He developed this idea in part as a way to explain the carnage of World War I. He believed we each have competing "life" (or sexual) instincts and "death" instincts. The death instinct is supposedly an impulse to die or to return to inert matter. It is turned outward as aggression, as a defense to keep us from killing ourselves. Many analytic theorists do not accept the concept of the death instinct, though they may believe in an aggressive instinct. For our purposes, we will mainly talk about the development and regulation of sex and aggression, not the death instinct.

If, during development, various infantile sexual or aggressive wishes and fantasies are unacceptable to consciousness, they will be repressed (pushed out of consciousness). Repression leads to fixation, that is, if some wish is repressed, the developmental "stream" is arrested at that point. The infantile wish, with its accompanying energy, remains alive and active. The "trick" for the personality is to find an outlet for the repressed wish and simultaneously to keep it unconscious and hidden. The way to do this is to let the wish out in a disguised form. Much of personality—overt behaviors, values, beliefs, goals, job and mate choices, recreational choices—consists of disguised outlets for primitive, childhood repressed wishes and conflicts. It is not only people with psychological problems who have repressed wishes and fantasies, but all of us. For Freud, personality was the system of controls and restraints we develop in the first five or six years of life to regulate and channel our repressed primitive wishes, fantasies, and conflicts. Our early childhood experiences are the primary determinant of our current personality functioning. To quote a typical psychodynamic viewpoint (Adelson & Doehrman, 1980),

> [Psychoanalysis] holds that in truly important moments of one's life one is unwittingly held captive by the past. Whom we marry and how the marriage fares; the work we choose and how well we do it; whether we have children and when and how we raise them and feel about them; when we become ill and how we survive or fail to—all these and other vital events of the life course can be understood in depth only after we have a sufficient understanding of the personal past. (p. 100)

Defense Mechanisms

Although all of us have repressed wishes, most of us, while we may have our troubles, do not develop persistent neurotic symptoms. Nor do we become alcoholics or consistently act in impulsive or self-destructive ways. Whether or not we end up relatively "symptom free" depends on how our personalities regulate our repressed wishes and fantasies. For Freudians, that ultimately depends on the crucial, formative experiences with the family in early childhood.

Perhaps the most socially adaptive way of handling repressed wishes and conflicts is sublimation. In ***sublimation***, the repressed desire is channeled into some socially acceptable outlet. For instance, aggressive feelings may be channeled into being a highly competitive athlete. Sexual wishes associated with defecation and the anal stage of development (discussed below) may be channeled into creative activity, such as painting and sculpting. Or, early childhood wishes and conflicts may get channeled into founding the most influential of all theories of personality and psychopathology.

But sometimes we are unable to sublimate. Then we must rely on other ***defense mechanisms*** that distort reality to some slight degree. The concept of defense is a pervasive one in psychoanalytic theory. Psychoanalysis holds that the most fundamental factor in psychic development is avoidance of painful or threatening information. Repression is the fundamental way most of us have of avoiding painful information. In order to maintain repression, and to try to protect the ego from anxiety, we utilize defense mechanisms.

Denial is the simplest of these. ***Denial*** is the refusal to recognize the real nature of one's behavior. A person may act quite seductively, for instance, but deny there is any sexual intent to his behavior. Another person may exhibit symptoms of anger, such as a flushed face, angry expression, and angry tone of voice, yet deny that she is angry. Denial is the mechanism most commonly used by alcoholics. Long past the time when friends, neighbors, employers, and doctors have told an alcoholic that he has a drinking problem, the alcoholic will deny that he has a problem.

Rationalization is giving a plausible and acceptable reason for one's behavior and feelings in order to hide one's real motives. A rationalization we frequently heard in college was from male students who would claim that they bought *Playboy* magazine "for the articles" (but, of course, they never bought any other magazine with similar articles and stories). Alcoholics often combine rationalization with denial. For each lapse into excessive drinking, the alcoholic will have an excuse. It was because she was depressed or she had to join the office party and so on.

With ***projection***, the individual attributes to others the wishes, aims, and motives he cannot accept in himself. If a person has a lot of repressed hostility, he may see other people as dangerous and hostile. He may adopt a defensive, suspicious view of other people and be constantly on the lookout to protect himself from their malicious intentions and purposes. If a person has repressed his sexual impulses, he may angrily criticize what he sees as everyone else's preoccupation with sex. Projection allows some gratification of the repressed impulses by allowing them into consciousness but protects the individual by ascribing the impulses to other people.

Most of us are familiar with displacement. In ***displacement***, we deflect our feelings onto another less threatening target. Often we do this consciously. We get angry at our boss and come home and yell at our kids. With true displacement, however, this is done unconsciously. We actually believe we are angry at our kids and deny that our anger is toward our boss.

In ***reaction formation***, the individual acts in a way that is diametrically opposite to what he unconsciously wants. Thus, if a person has a good deal of unconscious hostility, she may act like an uncompromising pacifist on the surface or she may strongly condemn contact sports or violence on television. Conversely, a person with strong repressed dependency needs may intensely value toughness, physical violence, and contact sports. We should point out that neither being a lover of violent sports nor being a pacifist is necessarily a reaction formation against unconscious impulses. Perhaps a better index of reaction formation would be the rigidity with which beliefs are held, an unwillingness to tolerate or even consider different points of view. For psychoanalysis, rigidity of belief systems is usually a sign of defensiveness. A conflict area can often be identified by the degree of emotion invested in surface issues associated with it. The person cannot be flexible because she is protecting herself in that area. A fully functioning person is able to consider other points of view, even though he may come to identify strongly with one particular perspective.

With ***intellectualization***, the individual "understands" and acknowledges that she "must have" certain repressed impulses. Knowledge of the impulses, but not the impulses themselves, is thereby allowed into consciousness. For instance, a client may intellectually accept that she had incestuous feelings toward her father, while still repressing the actual feelings and impulses themselves.

With ***compensation***, the individual deals with frustration and inadequacy in one area by investing in another area. Thus, an individual who has underlying feelings of physical inadequacy as a male (he is not athletic or handsome) may compensate by becoming highly competent at intellectual pursuits. Conversely, an athlete who feels intellectually inferior may overinvest in his athletic skills.

According to psychoanalytic theory, defense mechanisms involve mild distortions of reality, but they are functional and necessary. In fact, all of us need to be able to regulate negative, conflictual feelings in order to function. Denial, for instance, may be important in certain professions, such as the military, where one must be able to "deny" one's fear in order to function. Intellectualization may help emergency room physicians deal with the very painful experiences they face. There are more or less mature defenses (Vaillant, 1995). More mature defenses help us control our conflictual fears and negative emotions but allow us to behave productively and effectively. For instance, Vaillant considers altruism to be a mature defense.

However, if defenses become too rigid or are overused, they may unduly constrict the individual's functioning. And what happens when an individual's defenses fail—

when they fail either to provide a sufficient outlet for unconscious impulses or to control the warded-off feelings, wishes, and impulses, and these threaten to break into consciousness? It is at this point that neurotic symptoms appear.

Psychopathology and Anxiety

For Freud, neurotic anxiety appears when one's defenses begin to break down. It is a signal that forbidden unconscious impulses are breaking into consciousness. Generalized anxiety disorder and panic disorder, in which free-floating anxiety is experienced, are examples. The person is overwhelmed by anxiety and cannot pin down any particular cause because the cause is unconscious: The anxiety is a signal of danger from within.

Other neurotic disorders also develop when unconscious impulses get intensified and threaten to break into consciousness. Symptoms develop that, like the defense mechanisms, allow some expression of the unconscious impulses but disguise their nature. Because more extreme measures are now needed, the symptoms that develop are likely to be socially dysfunctional. For example, in order to control unconscious conflicts over sexuality, an individual may develop a phobia about being outside in crowds (where he is afraid he might unconsciously "lose control"). If unconscious hostile and rebellious impulses are threatening to break through, a person might carry "rule following" to the extreme or develop elaborate obsessive-compulsive rituals to control the impulses. She may wash her hands 200 times a day in order to quell anxiety by washing away those "dirty," unconscious, hostile, rule-breaking impulses.

Why does this happen? Usually it happens because some event intensifies a person's unconscious conflicts. If a person has strong unconscious hostility, he may shy away from situations in which he might be tempted to lose control. He may avoid, as an example, being in situations where he has the power to take out his hostility on others. Being in such a situation may provide so much unconscious temptation that he needs to develop some neurotic symptomatology to keep his defenses in order. For instance, suppose this person is a lawyer who is made a judge with the power to impose sentences. The possibility that his unconscious hostility may now come out in harsh, punitive judgments may be so threatening that he develops a neurotic symptom such as compulsively keeping his workspace neat to the degree that he cannot pay attention to his cases.

What happens if neurotic symptoms don't work as defenses? What happens if even they fail in keeping unconscious material out of consciousness? The person may then experience a psychotic episode, which can essentially be seen as a disintegration of the ego (the ego is discussed in the next section). Unconscious material now floods into consciousness. While Freudian psychoanalysis attempts to help the average neurotic to gain insight into his defenses, with psychotics, the Freudian approach is the opposite. It tries to shore up defenses and restore the ego.

Developmental Stages and Id, Ego, and Superego

We have now seen how repression and other defense mechanisms function to keep material unconscious and how psychopathology develops when they do not work. Now we will look at personality development both in terms of Freud's concept of the mind and various stages of development.

Freud held that there are three "structures" or components to the mind: the id, the ego, and the superego. At birth, the person is all ***id***. The id is the biological storehouse of primitive impulses. It is all "want." Since it is pure desire, it has no concept of reality—others don't exist, reality doesn't exist, and time doesn't exist. At birth, the infant has no concept of itself as a separate human being, of others as human beings, of itself and the world as separate, of time, or of the difference between reality and fantasy.

The first stage of personality development, which lasts from birth to about one and a half or two years, is the oral stage. It is called oral because during this stage, the mouth is the primary erogenous zone, that is, sexual gratification is gained primarily through oral stimulation. This is why the infant not only nurses, but also is constantly putting things into its mouth.

The most crucial thing that happens at the oral stage is the beginning of the development of the ***ego***. The ego develops both as a result of biological maturation and as a result of interaction with environmental demands. At birth, the infant is all id, but soon learns that its needs will not automatically be met whenever it wants. As a result, the infant begins to develop a concept of reality. It must learn to develop a concept of itself as separate from the world. It must develop concepts of external "objects" that will help it gain gratification. Objects are any things that populate the external world. Among the objects that an infant must form concepts of to view reality accurately are chairs, tables, floors, cribs, bottles, spoons, and so on. Among the most important object concepts the child needs to form are concepts of other people. In forming concepts of objects and of the external world, the child needs to realize that fantasies and reality are separate. The ego can be thought of as the "executive" part of the personality. It is the part that learns to perceive reality accurately in order to help the id get its demands met as effectively as possible. If at this stage (through severe neglect, extreme overindulgence, inconsistent experience) a strong ego does not begin to develop, the person will be predisposed to having psychotic experiences under stress in later life. Other oral fixations (the stopping of the developmental process in the oral stage) may lead to dependency, alcoholism, overeating, or a constant need to be loved and "nourished" by others.

The ego continues to develop during the anal stage, which lasts from about age one and a half to three. In this stage of personality development, the anus becomes the primary erogenous zone, and the child gains sexual gratification through the act of defecation. Parents' attempts at toilet training will be interpreted as infringements on the child's freedom to indulge in instinctual gratification. Thus, the anal stage is when the issue of socialization becomes prominent. The developing ego must learn to control and regulate impulses. The child is confronted with the need to regulate its bodily activities in order to follow societal rules and will experience anger at the parents for imposing restrictions on gratification of its bodily pleasures.

If the anger is repressed, the child may become on the surface a rigid, orderly, rule-following person, concerned with cleanliness. Underneath is a great deal of "dirty" anger. This is the anal-retentive pattern. For the anal-retentive, rules and rituals become defense mechanisms for binding and controlling unconscious hostility. In addition, the individual may engage in undoing rituals to overcome unconscious guilt over the buried anger and rebellion. Undoing rituals are like atonements. Undoing can be used to overcome unconscious guilt over sexuality as well, as when individuals need to shower or wash their hands after making love. The ritualistic nature of defenses developed at this stage lay the basis for obsessive-compulsive neurosis, in which individuals may have to shower for hours a day or engage in other extreme undoing rituals.

If the anger is not repressed, the child may repetitively act out his anger, constantly trying to prove his independence. In effect he is "defecating all over everyone," and this is the anal-expulsive pattern.

The phallic stage is the most important one, according to Freud. It is the stage during which the third component of mental functioning—the superego—develops. It occurs between the ages of four and six. Though most of Freud's clients were women, the phallic stage is named after the male and is one example of why Freud has often been accused of being sexist. During the phallic stage, sexuality becomes localized in the genitals. Of particular importance during this stage is the Oedipus complex. The male child presumably begins to develop sexual feelings toward his mother and wants some kind of sexual contact with her. As a result of this, he views his father as a rival and may harbor primitive fantasies of wanting to murder his father and take his place. However, the male child becomes afraid that if the father finds out about these feelings and wishes, the father will castrate him. This castration anxiety leads the child to repress both his rivalrous feelings toward his father and his lustful feelings toward his mother.

The way the male child resolves the Oedipal crisis is to identify with his father (and be able to possess his mother vicariously as a result). This identification leads both to an adoption of the male sex role and to the development of the ***superego***. The superego is formed out of the internalized (or "introjected") values of the parent. It consists of both the parent's moral values (essentially the "conscience") and a perfectionistic standard of what a good person should be like (the "ego-ideal"). If the values of the superego are harsh or unrealistic, the individual will be constantly plagued with feelings of guilt and failure. The individual may have a need to punish himself and may set up situations where others are rejecting or punitive. The individual may unconsciously cause painful accidents to happen and, in the extreme, may have unconscious suicidal wishes that get expressed in self-destructive acts (for instance, through reckless driving).

The "female Oedipus complex" (sometimes called the Electra complex) is similar in its general outlines to that of the male. However, there are some important differences. According to Freud, little girls note that they are missing something that little boys have. This is called penis envy. The girl's desire for her father is not only sexual, but is based on the desire to obtain a penis as well. Because girls do not fear being castrated, there is less fear to lead to repression. As a result, girls develop less strong superegos than boys (Freud, 1925/1961). Girls resolve penis envy by identifying with the mother and accept the ability to have a baby as a substitute for a penis.

Between age six and adolescence is the latency stage, during which the child is busy regulating the repressed impulses from the Oedipal period. Psychoanalytically, this is why children at this age are often so fascinated with rules and the establishment of order in their lives. At adolescence, the genital stage, the upsurge of sexuality reawakens Oedipal conflicts. The adolescent's task is to not allow incestuous feelings to surface into consciousness. Rebelliousness against the parents and intense love affairs with peers are ways of distancing and redirecting the incestuous wishes so that they do not become conscious. If handled effectively, these desires will be tamed and sublimated, and the adult personality will be established.

With the phallic stage, the three major mental structures are all established. The mind can almost be thought of as a kind of stage with three actors on it. The three voices are in constant contention, and psychopathology can be seen as the conflict among them. The ego bears the brunt of coordinating the primitive wishes of the id, the limitations imposed by reality, and the moral restrictions of the superego. Repression complicates matters. Primitive wishes and impulses are repressed and kept out of conscious awareness, partly to satisfy the moral values of the superego. Repression weakens the ego's ability to deal realistically with the world. A particularly harsh superego may lead to extreme and debilitating repression. On the other hand, a particularly weak superego may lead to psychopathic behavior.

Not only are primitive wishes and fantasies repressed, but parts of the ego itself are unconscious. This is necessary for repression to occur. After all, repression is a kind of unconsciously "deliberate" avoidance of painful material. If this avoidance were conscious, it would not work, so the act of avoiding itself must be performed unconsciously. As one of our children said about something she was trying to forget, "I have to forget that I've forgotten, too. Otherwise I'll remember it." Therefore, repression means that forces unknown to the ego may be controlling behavior. As a result, the person will engage in behavior for reasons unknown to the conscious ego. Such behavior will be consciously experienced as "irrational" or "ego-alien." It is such an experience that often propels a person to seek therapy.

To sum up, the Freudian view of personality and psychopathology is that both ultimately rest on unconscious self-deception. Behavior is under the control of hidden meanings that are hidden because they are too painful to be consciously acknowledged and known. For Freud, these hidden meanings revolve around primitive sexual and aggressive impulses. As part of this self-deception, we must also, of necessity, distort external reality via defense mechanisms such as projection and displacement. Thus, most of us live in a world where objective reality is obscured by shadows from our past. These shadows also distort our perception of our own inner reality of feelings, thoughts, and motives. Each of us lives in a reality of our own construction, contrived to protect us from painful self-knowledge. Therefore, none of us lives fully in touch with external or internal reality. For most of us, the distortions are compatible enough with social reality that we are generally functional. For some of us, the distortions are discrepant enough, and the resulting behavior deviant enough, that our behavior is dysfunctional and in need of treatment.

Psychotherapy

The goal of classical Freudian psychoanalysis is to "lift repression" (Freud, 1937/1963). Freud said, "Where id was there shall ego be." However, it is rarely the case that all repression is lifted. Often, some repression is lifted and some is reworked so that it is not so incapacitating (Freud, 1937/1963). Following from this, the goal of psychoanalysis is to gain insight into and conscious awareness of the hidden meanings influencing behavior. This involves overcoming resistance, which is the main work of therapy.

How does awareness and the lifting of repression cure? Before therapy, the ego is not able to control behavior effectively because it is being guided by forces of which the ego is unaware. When the ego becomes aware of these forces, they can be controlled consciously and channeled into suitable outlets. It is important to note that insight does not eliminate the previously unconscious primitive impulses. A man's awareness that he has primitive wishes to kill his father and sleep with his mother does not relieve him of these impulses, but it does allow him to control them, rather than being controlled by them. Luborsky said that what changes in psychoanalysis is the function that controls and regulates a wish or need, but "the wish, need or intention . . . changes relatively little" (1984, p. 20). (In chapter 7 we will look at some recent psychoanalytic theorists' views of what happens when a person gains insight.)

While the impulses themselves may change relatively little, learning that these impulses are there helps people discriminate between reality and their primitive wishes, fantasies, and feelings. A person may come to therapy because he feels that people in authority are always putting him down. In therapy he may find that he is displacing onto authority figures unconscious perceptions of his father. He may discover that he could never face up to perceiving his father as critical because he would then have to face up to all the buried anger he has toward him. He can now separate what people in authority are really saying and thinking from what he is displacing onto them. Thus, an important consequence of lifting repression is the ability to see reality more clearly.

The ultimate goal of therapy for Freud is to facilitate the individual's ability to love and work (Ekstein, 1974). Freud did not believe that the goal of therapy is to make a person "happy." In fact, he saw therapy as "replacing neurotic misery with common unhappiness." One of the major achievements of therapy is an increase in the person's capacity to tolerate ambivalence and conflict or to live with "uneasiness" (Bettelheim, 1982). In relegating happiness to a secondary place among goals for healthy functioning, Freud's thought is compatible with many other theorists, including Rogers, Perls, and Beck.

Free Association

So how does classical psychoanalysis go about facilitating insight? Originally, Freud used hypnosis. However, he abandoned hypnosis early in his work. For a while he used a technique in which he placed his hand on the client's head to "suggest" that she remember (see the second quote at the start of the chapter). Eventually he abandoned this, too, in favor of the method of free association.

You might be thinking that hypnosis seems like the answer. Hypnotize patients, ask them to recover memories from early childhood, and therapy should be easy and quick. Why spend years in psychoanalysis? But Freud did not think this would work. The reason is that finding the buried memories is but a part of the therapeutic process. More important is going through the process of confronting yourself, learning how to dig into your past, and learning how to face up to your defenses. Using the easy magic of hypnosis to leapfrog defenses and resistances to get to "the truth" is bad therapy. You might be able to leapfrog these obstacles, but Freud wants you to clear the roads of them, so to speak. Thus, psychoanalysis needs to be a process done with relatively full awareness. After all, what you want is to be able to relate to yourself in a fully conscious way. You need to learn to do this by slowly and painstakingly confronting obstacles to full awareness as they arise. As you work through and discard or modify each obstacle or defense, you do indeed get closer to the buried childhood memories. But in addition, you have already become less defensive and more flexible and better able to tolerate painful self-knowledge.

Freud devised a technique to allow the person to stay conscious: *free association.* He believed that nothing psychological happens by chance. This is called ***psychic determinism***. Any thought that appears in consciousness is there for some reason. No matter how trivial or irrelevant, it is likely to be connected to some unconscious dynamic material. Normally, people control their stream of thoughts. For example, in conversations with others, we focus our thoughts and what we say on the conversation. We screen out, ignore, or do not give verbal expression to irrelevant thoughts and to thoughts that we judge to be socially inappropriate because they are hostile, sexual, or embarrassing. Freud wanted to relax the censoring activity that accompanies normal consciousness, so that deeper dynamic associations to surface thoughts could become conscious. So he instructed his patients to say whatever came to mind, regardless of how apparently irrelevant or inappropriate it was. In order to facilitate this, the client would lie on a couch, and Freud would sit behind him. This was presumed to reduce the demands of a normal social situation, where one converses face to face and does not let one's mind wander to whatever associated thoughts come up.

Suppose a client is discussing how loving his wife is and what an ungrateful wretch he is for not being more attentive to her. Suddenly he thinks of something that seems totally irrelevant—how much he hates spinach. It may turn out, through subsequent exploration, that it is no mere chance that this thought surfaced at that point. There may be an unconscious link between "spinach" and "wife." Perhaps the wife is so "loving" that he feels she treats him like a child. Since "being made to eat your spinach" is a fairly common image associated with being a child, the thought of spinach at that point makes sense. After this link is established, further exploration might uncover feelings of being smothered, and still further exploration, feelings of anger, and finally, feelings of being castrated. The unconscious is seen to follow a kind of emotional logic in how one thought flows into another. Topics are organized together based on their emotional associations, and it is this organization that the analyst hopes to tap into. But what does the analyst do while the client free associates?

Therapist Interventions

Psychoanalytic interventions are largely a matter of timing. Good analytic interventions first prepare a context for insight to develop and then facilitate the development of that insight. At first, the therapist will do relatively little other than listen. She may ask questions such as "What does spinach remind you of?" or "What else comes to mind?" Such questions will help the client explore his experience, and eventually, certain aspects of the client's experience will become more crystallized and focused.

When the context is sufficiently crystallized and developed, the analyst may broach an interpretation. An interpretation is a response designed to increase client insight. It attempts to bring into consciousness some thematic material that is unconscious. For the context to be sufficiently crystallized, the topic under discussion must have been explored enough for certain themes to be nearly apparent to consciousness. In addition, at the moment an interpretation is made, the context must be "affectively" alive, that is, the emotions associated with the underlying themes must be present or nearly present in consciousness. Put another way, a good interpretation works when it relates to something that is currently "on your mind," something you are currently "working on." Most of us have had the experience of being emotionally involved in talking about a problem (say, about our boss). At that moment, if a friend makes a response such as "He sounds like a real idiot" or "I bet you feel you can't show your real stuff around him," it will very likely feel relevant at that moment and help us crystallize our feelings about the boss. But if the same comments are made an hour later, when we are thinking about something completely unrelated, they will feel pallid, flat, and useless.

According to many psychoanalysts, interpretations are supposed to be short and couched in concrete, vivid, everyday language. Both of these requirements relate to the need for an interpretation to have a concrete emotional impact (we will discuss this later). In addition, interpretations are supposed to address material that is near the surface of consciousness. We have already mentioned that interpretations are made only when sufficient material has been examined by client and therapist so that the common underlying theme is apparent. After the client has related several instances of feeling disgruntled at his wife's taking care of him, the theme that he feels he is being treated like a child almost pops out, and it is at this point that interpreting this to the client will facilitate therapeutic insight.

Interpretations need to deal with material that is already nearly in consciousness so that therapy proceeds gradually. One cannot simply jump to a deep vertical interpretation, for instance, that the client is suffering from castration anxiety. There are three reasons for this. First, one goal of psychoanalysis is to gradually work through the blockades the person has constructed against awareness of the unconscious impulses. Deeper material is presumably more anxiety provoking and better defended. It is easier and less anxiety provoking to recognize that "I feel my wife treats me like a child" than it is to realize that "I felt overmothered and castrated as a child." As the client gradually confronts deeper and deeper material, the ability to tolerate the anxiety associated with deeply buried memories increases (this process is not unlike that of systematic desensitization, discussed in chapter 10).

The second reason insights must be acquired gradually is that insight is therapeutic only if it is affectively meaningful. (We will discuss this in the next section when we discuss the therapeutic conditions of change.)

What happens if interpretations are badly done? (We hope this section will discourage you from playing amateur psychoanalyst with yourself, friends, or relations.) We have said that the affective context for an interpretation must be carefully prepared. If the client, for instance, were to say to his wife, "Don't tell me to eat my spinach!" it would do no good for her to retort, "You are rebelling against me only because you didn't feel like a man when your mother told you what to do." Not only is the interpersonal atmosphere a very unsafe one for the client to consider the truth of such a remark, but the careful exploration needed to make such an interpretation therapeutically useful has not been done. Such an interpretation, even if true (and, of

Using interpretation with pets.

course, without the exploration, you don't know it's true—you're only guessing) will not be therapeutic. All the intervening resistances to insight have not been worked through, and the result of such an interpretation might be only to make the client more defensive.

Breaching defenses too quickly may make the client feel bad about himself. The client has presumably been overmothered as a child. This may make him unusually sensitive to criticism from mother figures. But, of course, all he knows is that he feels bad about himself when his wife criticizes him. His conscious context, then, is to take comments about himself as criticisms. So when a mother figure (his wife) tells him he was overmothered as a child, he will not take this as an insight-gaining, repression-lifting interpretation, but as a criticism. While this might be especially true if the interpretation is done by someone close to the person, the same thing can happen with inappropriately timed interpretations done by analysts. Thus, interpretations that go too deep too fast will not be therapeutic. They may actually be harmful, may lead to overwhelming anxiety, and could result in disintegration of the ego and increased psychopathology.

Therapeutic Conditions of Change

It is possible for people to have knowledge about themselves that is totally useless to them in terms of therapeutic change. Such knowledge, even if accurate, may actually shore up defenses, rather than lead to their disappearance. This happens if the knowledge is in the form of an intellectual insight. Freud found early (see the third quote at the beginning of this chapter) that the knowledge that transforms is knowledge that is emotionally meaningful. Put another way, insights that are acquired without an accompanying emotional experience will not be therapeutic. For instance, somewhere at the basis of your character, according to psychoanalytic theory, are Oedipal feelings. If you are a male, somewhere deep inside you is primitive lust toward your mother and hatred toward your father. If you are a female, you harbor hidden feelings of lust toward your father and hatred toward your mother. Yet we venture to guess that most of you have no awareness of such feelings. Presuming that analytic theory is true, such buried feelings play a role in whatever personal failings you may have. Now, we have just told you that those feelings are there in you. You have acquired (if you believe us) intellectual insight. Have you noticed any magical transformations in yourself? Have you suddenly found all your conflicts or self-doubts vanishing? Probably not.

The reason is that your knowledge is purely intellectual, abstract, and hypothetical. What you know is that you must have hated your father or mother. That is different from experientially knowing that you hated your father or mother. You have no direct awareness of such feelings, no direct personal memories of hating your father or mother (or lusting after one or the other). To acquire therapeutic insight is to relive the emotion of hating. To remember your personal experience of the feelings will be to reexperience them in the therapeutic context. Thus, you must recover the deepest and most personal part of your memories—your feelings—in order for insight to be therapeutic.

Even after a person achieves early childhood insights that are accompanied by emotional reexperiencing, there is no magical change. But how can this be so, since we said that the goal of psychoanalysis is to lift repression? We have already partially answered this in our discussion of why Freud abandoned hypnosis. Basically, feelings and behavior must be worked through. The working-through phase of therapy is the longest. Clients must learn how derivatives of early childhood feelings have been woven into the fabric of their whole lives. They need to examine specific events to find where the unconscious feelings are coloring and distorting their perceptions of situations and relationships. For example, you might examine an instance of anger at your boss to see if unconscious hatred of a parent is coloring your reactions. Insight does not magically lead to change. It is rather a precondition to change, because change actually occurs during the working through process.

Television and movie portrayals of instantaneous and magical therapeutic change are seriously distorted. A client has a hysterical symptom, such as blindness. The doctor discovers the reason—the client saw his wife in the arms of another and became hysterically blind to deny what he saw. The doctor confronts the client with the truth. The client resists: "No! No!" The doctor repeats the truth, more loudly. Finally the patient faces up to it: "You're right! . . . I can see!" Most therapists agree that change is slow and gradual. In a small survey of over 30 therapists of all persuasions done by one of us, only one therapist reported a case in which change was sudden and instantaneous as a result of an insight (Bohart, 1979).

Dreams and Resistance

We have now seen that the major therapeutic tool of psychoanalysis is interpretation. We have also seen that insight must be accompanied by emotional reliving and working through in order to be therapeutic. Now we will discuss two sources of data that the analyst uses in facilitating therapeutic change. For Freud, dreams were the "royal road to the unconscious." Freud believed that dreams express unconscious wishes and conflicts in symbolic form. Therefore, they can be used to acquire insight. The client is asked to free associate to the dream symbols in order to discover their unconscious meaning.

Resistance provides another general source of data about repression. The basic phenomenon is that no matter how much people may consciously wish to change (especially if their symptoms are painful), unconsciously, they do not wish to change. To change is to undo the repression that protects them from painful unconscious memories, and therefore, they will unconsciously resist treatment.

Resistance manifests itself in many ways in therapy. It may show up in difficulties in free association ("I can't think of anything at all to say"), in missing or being late for appointments, or in wasting most of the appointment talking about trivia. A client may try to seduce the therapist, literally or figuratively, to keep the therapist from forcing confrontation with the unconscious. Aside from literal sexual seduction, a person may try flattering the therapist, buying her gifts, or wanting to be "friends" outside of therapy. The client may resist by belittling or berating the therapist or by deciding therapy is a waste of time or through a temporary "flight into health," insisting that problems are solved after a few sessions.

The phenomenon of resistance to change is noted by therapists of most persuasions. However, there are different ways of interpreting the cause of resistance, as you shall see later on in this book. The psychoanalytic interpretation of resistance is that it occurs because the client is getting close to unconsciously avoided and painful memories.

The analyst may confront resistance. Confrontation is essentially a kind of interpretation in which the therapist attempts to make the client aware of what the client is really doing and the consequences of the behavior. For example, the therapist may present the possibility that there is some underlying motive to the client's repeated missed appointments. Good confrontation, as with good interpretation in general, does not force insight. The client may be confronted with the idea that something underlies the missed appointments, but then the client and therapist will explore to find out what it is.

Confrontation is a response that is especially susceptible to misuse. It is too easy for the therapist to use confrontations as punishments or manipulations. For instance, a client may really feel therapy is not working. For the therapist to say, "You only feel that because unconsciously you don't want to get well" could be a dangerous response. It may manipulate the client into staying in therapy when indeed it isn't working. It would be more appropriate in such a situation for the therapist to be more open-minded and help the client explore the possibility that resistance underlies the desire to terminate, rather than to assume that is the reason.

The Therapeutic Alliance and Transference

As mentioned previously, the therapeutic alliance refers to the working relationship between therapist and client. The analyst must be able to establish a good working relationship with the healthy part of the client's ego. This involves the therapist's demonstrating some degree of caring and understanding towards the client. However, for Freud the potential healing aspects of a caring, empathic relationship were of secondary importance. The primary healing element was the achievement of insight. Over the years the relationship between the therapist and the client has become more central as a healing element (see chapter 7).

However, Freud discovered early on that the client's unconscious issues interfered with the working relationship. This led to the development of the concept of transference. As you'll recall, overt relationships to people and to the world are derivatives of unconscious conflicts. In particular, the way adults perceive and relate to significant others is almost invariably tinged by unconscious feelings and wishes they had toward the significant others in their early childhood. Thus, people transfer onto others feelings and reactions they had toward their parents. This is done not only to use other people as outlets for disguised wishes, feelings, and fantasies, but also as a defense against recognition of these wishes and fantasies. A man may sublimate his lustful feelings toward his mother by transferring them onto other women in his adult life. And by having an outlet for these feelings, he is able to maintain the repression so that he never has to face up to their true nature. This partly explains why people may get involved in the same kind of destructive relationship time and again. For instance, the client who was overmothered may continually seek out women who dominate him and with whom he can feel simultaneously protected and rebellious.

The therapist, as part of a significant relationship, becomes a target for transference of significant emotional themes from childhood. The client, for instance, may see any friendly, helpful gestures by the analyst as signs that the analyst will "mother" and protect him. Certainly he will wish for the analyst to mother and protect him. To the extent that he initially sees the analyst as fulfilling these infantile wishes, he will see the analyst as wonderful and therapy as wonderful. This is positive transference. However, as soon as the analyst does not act in accord with his unconscious wishes and fantasies, he may begin to feel lost, frightened, and even angry. If the client begins to feel angry toward the analyst, this is negative transference. Even if he unconsciously sees the analyst as the good, all-protective mother, he may exhibit negative transference toward the analyst. After all, unconsciously, he both likes the safety of being overmothered and resents feeling emasculated. So he may begin to see the analyst as trying to belittle him.

In order to use the transference therapeutically, the analyst attempts to remain relatively anonymous and neutral in demeanor. It is often said that the analyst attempts to act like a "blank screen" onto which the client can transfer images of childhood relationships. This does not mean that the analyst acts like a personality-less robot. It simply means that she does not share her personal reactions to things. She may nevertheless convey warmth and empathy to the client and not be phony or assume a false facade. By remaining relatively neutral in expressing opinions and judgments, the analyst allows the transference to become clear. If the client accuses the analyst of being critical of him, this must be a transference since the analyst has not expressed judgments.

Therapist neutrality is also designed to frustrate the client's unconscious desires for the therapist to provide gratification for the client's unconscious wishes. This also fosters transference.

The transference relationship is so important therapeutically because the client acts out the core of his neurotic problems right in therapy. Insight into the unconscious dynamics of these problems can be acquired as the problems are lived out and experienced directly. We have already seen that interpretations are most effective if timed to coincide with affectively alive context, and the transference relationship is certainly that. The client feels treated like a child by experiencing the analyst as treating him like a child, and in this affective context, he may gain insight into how he constructs reality.

In order to handle the transference relationship well, the analyst must be careful not to let her personal reactions intrude. However, in order to do this, the therapist must be aware of her own countertransference. Remember that all people have unconscious memories that color their current experiences. If therapists are to react clearly and objectively to their clients, they must be aware of what kind of unconscious transference relationships they are projecting onto their clients. If the therapist has an unconscious need for approval, for instance, she may be devastated by a client's negative transference and may react in a way that has no therapeutic benefit or even impedes the process. In order to be aware of countertransference, the psychoanalyst must undergo a training analysis herself.

Recently, a shift in psychoanalytic thinking has occurred in that analysts now believe that countertransferential reactions are therapeutically useful. The analyst must still be able to separate her own personal reactions from more "objective" perceptions of the client, but personal reactions can often provide important clues to what clients are thinking and feeling and to what may be going on with them at an unconscious level. Thus, analysts now try to understand their countertransferential reactions and use them to develop hypotheses about the client.

Mechanics of Psychoanalysis

Classical Freudian psychoanalysis is a lengthy affair. Freud himself often saw clients six days a week and complained that the one-day break would set the analysis back. Modern analysts usually see clients three to five times a week. A full-fledged analysis usually lasts several years. Furthermore, since analysis is never complete, clients often return periodically (Malcolm, 1981).

Because it is believed that making too many concessions to the client, such as allowing sessions to run long or going for walks, may increase resistance, the client is seen in a fairly rigid format. He is usually billed for missed appointments, rarely allowed more than the traditional "50-minute hour," and rarely seen in settings other than the therapist's office.

As a procedure that involves meeting several times a week over a period of years, classical psychoanalysis is obviously expensive. Its high cost is part of the reason for the development of modern shortened versions. We will discuss these short-term approaches to psychoanalytic therapy in chapter 7.

Recent Issues in Psychoanalysis

Historical Truth versus Narrative Truth

Freud likened his therapy to archeology. The therapist is like the archeologist who searches for ancient relics of lost civilizations, digging down through layer upon layer of ancient civilizations until he reaches the bottom. The therapist engages in a kind of psychic excavation of the personality, seeking buried "truths" from the deepest layer of early childhood.

Based on this archeological model, analysts have believed that the memories clients ultimately uncover (often after years of analysis) represent historical truth, that is, they are actual memories of what really happened to the client or what the client really fantasized about as a child. Donald Spence (1982), himself a psychoanalyst, challenged this view. We cannot reproduce all of Spence's argument here, but basically it is that psychoanalysis cannot be said to be uncovering historical truth. Rather, it has to do with replacing old, dysfunctional stories about one's past, with new, more functional stories. This view is not only advocated by Spence, but by many other modern analysts, including Schafer (1992).

Many of these authors draw on psychological research that has demonstrated that memory is reconstructive. What is remembered in the present is influenced at least as much by our present state of mind as it is by what happened in the past. Therefore, our memories of childhood are always interpretations of what our childhood was like rather than the literal, "historical" truth.

Most of us are aware by now that what we see in any particular scene is partially determined by how we are looking at it. Different observers can see the same scene quite differently and give differing accounts of it. In psychoanalysis, a crucial change is the acquisition of a different interpretive scheme. Most of us do not have a view of the world that includes constructs such as "Children sexually lust after their parents." We learn in psychoanalysis to see the world through such an interpretive framework, and that interpretive framework is then brought to bear on our own memories. Do we actually "recover" memories of having lusted after our parents? Or, do we learn to see our behavior and interpret our feelings as meaning that we lusted after our parents? Spence points out that this is simply undecidable. There is no way to verify empirically the "truth" or "falsity" of these memories. Indeed, in some sense, the question of truthfulness is meaningless. What is meaningful is the fact that the interpretive scheme we learn in psychoanalysis creates more of a sense of order in our experience.

Narrative truth has to do with how well an explanation makes an individual's "life story" a sensible coherent whole. But what purpose does this kind of "truth" serve? Fingarette (1963) suggests that the development of a coherent explanation for symptoms reduces anxiety. A coherent explanation helps "make sense" of behavior. By itself the consequent reduction in anxiety helps the individual to manage behavior better. Having a sensible explanation for a symptom robs it of its "power," so to speak. The person is not so frightened or mystified by it and is therefore more confident that she can control it without letting it disrupt her life. In addition, a good explanation will suggest ways of coping. In some sense, whether or not your overreaction to criticism is actually due to how your father treated you is beside the point, but having that explanation helps you cope. You might be able to say to yourself, "Oh, there I go again. Now remember. Part of this is my father, so let me just stop a minute and sort out what is real here."

The obvious problem with Spence's view is that it makes people wonder if just any old explanatory system can work. In work with some rural clients who were not psychologically sophisticated, George Kelly (see chapter 11) made up interpretations, based on no particular theory, and found that they could be therapeutic. We do not believe, however, that any old explanation will do. The explanation has to be "plausible," and we take this to mean that it must "fit the facts." As long as an interpretation is plausible and fits a client's memories of experience, that may be all that is needed for therapy to occur.

Narrative views of psychoanalysis are controversial (Eagle, 1984; Westen, 1998). However, they are controversial primarily if taken to an extreme: that there is no historical truth in a person's reconstruction of his childhood. A reconstruction of childhood is a current perspective, interpretation, and "story" about one's past, and it most likely must contain elements of historical truth in order to be therapeutically effective.

Child Abuse and the Seduction Theory

Early in Freud's work, he believed that his patients were suffering from repressed memories of actual traumatic events of having been sexually abused, or "seduced," as children. He later came to believe that most of his clients had not actually been abused, but that what had been repressed were infantile wishes and desires.

Masson (1984), as well as others such as Miller (Greif, 1992), have argued that the seduction theory was correct and that Freud's clients probably had been molested as children. Summit (1987) has argued that some of Freud's early work was a masterful description of the relationship of child abuse to psychopathology. However, Freud changed his mind. Summit says that during Freud's time, it was taken as ridiculous on the face of it that adults did such things to children. Thus, when Freud came out with his seduction theory, he was heavily criticized. Sometime thereafter Freud revised his theory so that instead of presenting a radical view of adults as sexual molesters, he presented a radical view of children as having sexual lusts and fantasies. Freud then saw his patients not as suffering from real abuse but from their own infantile wishes.

Masson (1984) goes on to accuse Freud of having modified his point of view in order to make his views acceptable to his medical colleagues. The implication is that Freud "sold out" on the truth in order to buy acceptance. Many others, such as Summit, have pointed out that at the time in Victorian Vienna, people simply were unaware of the extent of child abuse. Freud's rejection of the child abuse theory, therefore, would not represent intellectual dishonesty so much as ignorance about the extent of child abuse. Furthermore, Freud never denied that in some cases actual abuse had occurred.

The importance of the controversy lies in how we view clients' problems. Are they a response to real traumatic events, or are they simply a result of fantasies? Briere (1989) mentions that there are cases of abused women going to therapists who tell them that their abuse memories are "really" fantasies of what they unconsciously wanted! In light of recent information about the prevalence of childhood sexual abuse, it does not seem improbable that many "Oedipal fantasies" were indeed memories based on actual childhood experiences. Some researchers now believe that childhood abuse is at the heart of a variety of disorders, including some anxiety disorders, some depressions, borderline personality, and multiple personality (e.g. Briere, 1989).

Of course, it is not an either/or issue. The key event in psychopathology from a Freudian standpoint is that in using mechanisms such as repression, individuals cut off from conscious experience aspects of themselves. In some sense, it may not matter whether these cutoff elements are fantasies or memories of actual events.

Research Evaluation of Psychoanalytic Theory and Therapy

Once upon a time, one of the most telling criticisms that could be launched against psychoanalysis was the lack of research done to investigate its premises. However, in recent years, this situation has changed (Westen, 1998). Especially with regard to the study of psychotherapy, vigorous research projects on various aspects of psychoanalytic theory and psychotherapy have been conducted in both the United States and Europe. In the next section, we will review research findings relevant to several psychoanalytic premises, from both psychoanalytic and nonpsychoanalytic investigators.

Effectiveness of Psychoanalysis

How effective is long-term, intensive psychoanalysis? At one point in history advocates argued that because psychoanalysis was the lengthiest and most intensive of all approaches to psychotherapy, it had to be the best. Although research has not supported that claim, in recent years evidence has it to be effective. For instance, studies by Sandell et al. (2000) have found that psychoanalysis resulted in greater symptom reduction than comparison short-term treatments. Blatt and Ford (1994) have found some evidence that long-term, intensive psychoanalysis of the object relations variety (see chapter 7) can be effective. On the other hand, a study of psychoanalysis at the Menninger Clinic (Kernberg et al., 1972) involved 42 clients over a 20-year period. Some were seen in regular analysis (an average of 835 hours), others in a shorter version of psychoanalytic therapy (an average 289 hours). For the most part, there was no evidence that clients who had regular analysis improved more than clients who had the short-term analysis, though there were some clients for whom regular analysis did work better. Of course by today's standards, when psychotherapy is typically 50 sessions or less, both of these treatments can be considered "long term."

There is also evidence that psychoanalytically oriented psychotherapy, which is a shorter form of psychotherapy that utilizes psychoanalytic principles, is effective. From the results of their meta-analysis of many studies of psychotherapy, Smith, Glass, and Miller (1980) calculate an average "effect size" of 0.69 for psychoanalytic approaches. They also find an effect size of 0.89 for dynamic-eclectic therapies, which are therapies based on dynamic principles but are more eclectic in techniques than psychoanalysis. Basically, the larger the effect size, the more substantial the amount of change. The highest effect sizes calculated have been around 1.0 for some of the behavior and cognitive therapeutic techniques. (See chapter 5 for an explanation of effect size.) To date, no therapy has demonstrated an effect size sufficiently higher than the others to conclude that one is superior. The effect sizes mentioned for psychoanalytic approaches are in the average range, meaning these approaches are indeed effective and about as effective as other approaches. Several other studies have suggested that short-term psychoanalytically oriented therapy is effective (Luborsky, Singer, & Luborsky, 1975; Sandell et al., 2000).

Some psychoanalytic proponents claim that their therapy is superior, because it cures the underlying disorder while other approaches are superficial. This argument rests on the assumption that psychological problems are grounded in deep early childhood experiences that must be worked through in order for change to occur. However, evidence suggests that many so-called superficial treatments are quite effective and that their positive benefits persist long after therapy has been terminated (Nicholson & Berman, 1983). Long-term, in-depth therapy may have other positive benefits in addition to symptom removal, but therapy can remove symptoms without deep exploration.

Aside from the question of psychoanalytic therapy's overall effectiveness, is there any evidence demonstrating the effectiveness of its key components? Orlinsky, Grawe, and Parks (1994) summarize a number of studies showing that interpretation is usually, but not always, positively associated with therapeutic outcome. Henry, Strupp, Schacht, and Gaston (1994) summarize a series of studies on interpretations of the client's transferential reactions to the therapist. The researchers conclude that transference interpretations can be damaging if there are too many of them and are more likely to elicit client defensiveness, but they can be effective if they are accurate, delivered with low frequency, and given to relatively high-functioning clients. Fitting in with this, the suitability of an interpretation to the client's problem appears to be important to the effectiveness of an interpretation (Messer & Warren, 1990).

With regard to transference, Luborsky, Crits-Christoph, and Mellon (1986) have also studied transference reactions in therapy and found evidence to support several of Freud's formulations. For instance, a client's core relationship problems were found to manifest themselves in a variety of relationships in the client's life and in relationship to the therapist. There was also evidence that this relationship theme could be found in the client's memories of early childhood. Other evidence from Luborsky and his colleagues indicates that therapy alters the transference relationship, though it does not entirely eliminate it (Luborsky, Crits-Christoph, & Barger, 1991).

Psychoanalytic Personality Theory

We now turn to a brief evaluation of psychoanalytic hypotheses on personality and psychopathology. Westen (1998) identifies five basic propositions of psychoanalytic thought. We shall consider three here. The first is that much of mental life is unconscious. The second is that unconscious conflicts can influence behavior. The third is that early childhood plays an important role in shaping personality. A corollary of this is that personality is relatively stable from childhood on. Westen reviews relevant evidence and concludes that each proposition has some empirical support.

The Unconscious

With regard to the first two propositions having to do with unconscious mental processes and conflicts, Westen (1998) notes that there is evidence for the existence of unconscious thought, emotion, motivation, and defensive processes. Measures of what are called implicit attitudes have shown that people can consciously espouse nonprejudicial attitudes while holding unconscious prejudiced attitudes (Banaji & Hardin, 1996). In a series of studies, Silverman presented sentences to subjects at a speed so rapid that perception was subliminal (not producing a sensation that is consciously perceived) (Silverman & Weinberger, 1985). In one study subjects unconsciously saw the sentence "beating dad is okay," which is presumed to relate to an unconscious childhood wish to better one's father. Subjects who saw this sentence did better at playing darts than subjects who saw the sentence "beating dad is wrong."

There is also evidence for defensive processes. Morokoff (1985) had female subjects view an erotic videotape. They were asked to report how arousing they found the tape. A physiological measure of vaginal activity was also taken. It was found that women who had high levels of guilt over sex reported that they did not find the videotapes arousing, even though the vaginal measure showed that they had found it even more arousing than had women who were low in feelings of guilt over sex. In other studies in which words were presented to subjects at a very rapid exposure speed and the subjects were asked to report what they saw, subjects did not recognize certain emotionally charged words as rapidly as neutral words, even though the words could be shown to have been perceived unconsciously (Kostandov & Arzumanov, 1977; Shevrin, 1973).

There has been a great deal of controversy over the concept of repression with respect to the recovery of memories of childhood sexual abuse. Many believe that childhood sexual abuse experiences are so traumatic that people repress them, either partially or entirely. These memories sometimes surface in psychotherapy, especially if the therapist has encouraged the client to search for them. The problem is that the recovery of memories in therapy cannot be taken as reliable evidence for the existence of repression because some have argued that therapists are capable of suggesting or implanting such memories. However, there is evidence to suggest the possibility that memories of childhood sexual abuse can be lost or forgotten. Williams (1992) studied 100 women who, as children, had been sexually abused. Their abuse had been carefully documented at the time because they had been taken to hospital emergency rooms for treatment and for collection of evidence. The women were located and interviewed 17 years later, and it was found that 38% of them did not remember the abuse. On the other hand, there is also evidence to suggest that memories can be implanted in therapy. Loftus (1993) found that it was possible to successfully implant a false memory in a 14-year-old boy of having been lost in a shopping mall as a little child, although some have argued that a memory of being lost is different than a memory of abuse.

Although there is evidence for the existence of unconscious processes, it is not clear that Freud's view of the unconscious is the correct one (Wilson, 2002). For one thing, Freud's unconscious is a repository of primitive impulses. Yet some research suggests that unconscious information processing can be more creative and sophisticated than that (Wilson, 2002). Furthermore, although there is evidence for a disconnect between what is known consciously (for instance, between consciously reporting that an erotic videotape was not erotic while unconsciously responding), there still is no conclusive evidence that it is repression that causes the disconnect. Further, the hypothesis that the repression of early childhood experiences is a significant factor in causing psychological disorders remains to be confirmed.

Personality Development

One of the cornerstones of psychoanalytic theory is the idea that children around the age of five or six experience the Oedipal conflict of sexually desiring their parent of the opposite sex, while viewing the parent of the same sex as a rival. To date there is no empirical evidence supporting the idea of an Oedipus complex in children, and many experts on child development reject the idea (e.g., Brophy, 1977). They argue that to the extent that a child does experience Oedipal feelings, it is a response to a real situation being set up by dysfunctional parenting, rather than something all children undergo.

We have seen that many psychoanalytic thinkers consider childhood events to be the primary determinant of the most important aspects of adult functioning. In this chapter, we consider the question of whether adult personality is indeed formed in early childhood. At the end of chapter 7, we will consider the further questions of whether problems in early childhood are the causes of adult psychological problems, and whether the "foundational" view of personality is valid.

Basically, evidence does not support the hypothesis that personality is largely finished or formed in early childhood. Chess and Thomas (1984), for instance, studied a sample of children from infancy into adulthood. In another study, Chess (1979) concluded,

> We now have to give up the illusion that once we know the young child's psychological history, subsequent personality and functioning are *ipso facto* predictable. On the other hand, we now have a much more optimistic vision of human development. The emotionally traumatized child is not doomed, the parents' early mistakes are not irrevocable. (1979, p. 112)

Livson and Peskin, based on their developmental studies, concluded "neither past nor present, neither childhood nor adolescence, nor any era of adulthood is fixed in its effects or of higher priority in its contribution" (1980, p. 84). These research studies suggest that while early childhood is one important time of life, it is not necessarily more important than any other. They also suggest that early effects on personality can be modified and even undone by later events.

Vaillant (1995) studied a sample of males from late adolescence into mid-adulthood, and found evidence for significant changes in personality as people mature past their adolescence. McCrae and Costa (1990) concluded from their research, as well as their review of other research, that personality continues to develop into early adulthood and only finally becomes "fixed" around age 30.

The fact that personality in general continues to grow and change into early adulthood, however, does not mean there is no stability from early childhood into adulthood. Block and Block (1980) found evidence of stability in what they call "ego control" and "ego resiliency," that is, the degree to which the individual can control and regulate impulses and feelings and the degree to which the individual exhibits flexibility in coping. A complicating factor for Freudian theory, however, is that it is now known that genetics contributes to personality. It is possible that what stability does exist from early childhood into adulthood in personality development is genetically based.

Is Character Structure as Fixed as Freudian Theory Presumes?

There is another implication that emerges from the view of personality as something that is primarily fixed. Classical Freudian psychoanalytic theory holds a largely intrapsychic view of behavior. That is, a person's present behavior problems (as well as other, more normal aspects of that person's personality) derive primarily from internal factors such as character traits that have been developed and fixed in early childhood. Such a view minimizes the impact of current situations on a person's behavior, implying that behavior largely reflects a person's internal personality dynamics. Thus, if someone seems obsessed with detail at work, Freudian theory assumes that this reflects an underlying character trait of orderliness, which developed during the anal stage of development. It would be expected that this person would appear to be orderly in a wide variety of other situations in his or her life: at home, while making travel arrangements, on vacations, perhaps even during sex.

This view is to be contrasted to other views we consider in this book that ascribe progressively more importance to the here-and-now situation in creating psychopathology. In the next chapter, you shall see that for one modern variant of psychoanalysis, self psychology, the here-and-now interpersonal situation plays an important role in determining a person's behavior. For self psychology, a person's transferential reactions to the therapist during therapy are not simply a manifestation of that person's unconscious personality dynamics but instead are a complex interpersonal event, coshaped by the person of the therapist and the dynamics of the client. Similarly, Paul Wachtel's integrative psychodynamic perspective (to be covered in chapter 14) ascribes significant importance to the here-and-now situation as well as to intrapsychic factors from childhood.

To what degree does the pervasiveness in behavior implied by classical psychoanalytic theory exist? Do people exhibit the degree of orderliness in widely differing situations in their lives that this view implies? Do individuals diagnosed as having a borderline personality disorder, for instance, characteristically act borderline, in situation after situation, relatively independent of what is going on? Kroll (1988) noted that borderline behaviors wax and wane. People labeled borderline may act borderline in some situations and not others. They may act borderline at some times and not others. Further, individuals diagnosed as having a borderline personality disorder at one point may, even within a few years, be diagnosed as having some other kind of personality disorder. The point is that the borderline's behavior does not exhibit the degree of stability that a traditional view of personality structure might imply. In general, there has been a great deal of controversy over the years concerning the degree to which behavior primarily reflects a person's character versus the degree to which it primarily is a result of the situations people are in. The current consensus is that people are probably more changeable than a traditional view of character structure implies but that there is some consistency in personality. At the same time, behavior is also significantly influenced by the situation (Feshbach, Weiner, & Bohart, 1996).

The same applies to psychological problems. While some problems may primarily owe their existence to early childhood factors, others appear to be heavily influenced by a person's current situation, with early childhood factors playing only a secondary role, or no role at all. Many would argue that present events, such as stress, play a major role in creating adult psychopathology (Bloom, 1984). Many cases of depression appear to reflect here-and-now factors more so than childhood factors. Brown and Harris (1978) attributed 80% to 90% of the causes of depression in women to "provoking agents," such as loss, poor housing, and family alcoholism. Also, vulnerability to depression is greatly enhanced by the lack of a good social support network. This is not to say that childhood events are of no importance. Brown, Harris, and Bifulco (1986) found that the death of a parent enhanced vulnerability to depression in these women. Nevertheless, the stresses in adulthood appear to play a significant role, although a vulnerability may be created by a childhood event. As another example, Hobfall (1989) argued that women who stay in abusive relationships are not doing so primarily because of individual personality factors (though low self-esteem can play a role), but because of problems in current resources. Many women stay in abusive relationships because they do not have the here-and-now resources to leave.

In sum, research suggests that personality in general is not fixed in early childhood as Freud assumed and that many behavior and psychological problems are more influenced by current situations than classical Freudian theory has assumed. At the same time this does not rule out the importance of early childhood in the creation of certain aspects of psychological disorder. We shall consider this issue more fully in the next chapter.

In Conclusion

Freud has had such an enormous impact on our Western intellectual tradition in general (including the fields of psychology, philosophy, literature, and history) that it would be impossible to discuss all facets of his influence here. Among his many contributions are a major theory of personality, and a whole set of ideas about how to help people change. It would be inaccurate to say that Freud "created" psychotherapy, because many of the ideas and processes had been around before he was. However, Freud can be said to be the foremost figure in having formalized all these diverse ideas and processes into the discipline of psychotherapy. In a generic form, many of Freud's insights about the nature of the change process have held up, although Freud's interpretations of these insights have been challenged. Many of the "common factors" among the differing approaches to psychotherapy (see chapter 14) were first given prominence by Freud. For instance, Freud noted that sheer intellectual knowledge was not sufficient to produce personal change, that the affective, feeling side of the personality was important, that nonconscious processes and lack of personal awareness played a significant role in behavior, that what happened in the therapeutic relationship was an important part of the change process, and that helping people to "free their minds" from rigid constrictions imposed by learned ways of thinking and perceiving was central to change. In addition, Freud called attention to the importance of self-deception and the avoidance of painful feelings, wishes, and thoughts in personal functioning. He also alerted us to how childhood experiences can have significant impact on adult behavior. Even as relational views of psychoanalysis (see chapter 7), existential-humanistic views (see chapters 8 and 9), cognitive views (see chapter 11), and strategic views (see chapter 13) put their own spin on many of these insights, they are following the path first started on by Freud.

In particular, we believe therapists will continue to utilize some of the insights of Freud, including the following: (a) Childhood experiences play a role in some (though perhaps not all) psychological problems. Therapists will use this insight to understand how a person's early experiences may have led him or her to make personal developmental compromises and to adopt coping strategies that made sense when the person was a child, but that now get in the person's way. They will use this understanding to identify important life themes in the individual's life, themes that indicate the nature of the person's enduring struggles. (b) At least some psychological problems have unconscious components that the person does not have access to or understand. Such components may not be involved in every problem, but knowing that such unconscious components can exist will help therapists with cases in which they do play a major role. (c) Clients often bring their problems into the therapy situation (transference) and problems can therefore be worked with in an *in vivo* sense. This insight converges with the emphasis on the relationship in existential-humanistic and some cognitive and behavioral approaches. (d) Therapists' own personal reactions (countertransference) can be used therapeutically. Once again, this insight already forms a component of some existential-humanistic and cognitive-behavioral approaches. (e) One of the major blocks to therapeutic progress is the client's defensive need to protect him- or herself in the therapy session. Helping clients find ways of reducing their need for self-protection so that they can "come out" and engage their energies in the pursuit of change will continue to be one of the major tasks of therapists. (f) The development of self-awareness is one of the major components involved in personal change and that awareness must not be just intellectual awareness but experiential awareness as well.

Relational Approaches to Psychoanalysis

In recent decades, a revolution has taken place within psychoanalysis. This revolution has consisted of the increasing influence of object relations theory, attachment theory, and self psychology. The shift to these perspectives within the psychoanalytic camp is important because these perspectives overlap with other important perspectives on psychotherapy. Object relations theory and attachment theory, with their emphasis on internal representations of the self and of others, share commonalities with cognitive theory. Self psychology, with its emphasis on empathy and the interpersonal nature of the person, shares commonalities with both humanistic and systems theories.

These perspectives continue developments that began almost as soon as Freud first articulated his views in the early 1900s. It did not take long for dissenters to appear within the ranks of Freud's own inner circle. First Alfred Adler and then Carl Jung broke with Freud's emphasis on the human being as primarily a creature driven by sexual and aggressive impulses. Later, many other theorists, such as the neo-Freudians Eric Fromm, Erik Erickson, and Karen Horney, also dissented, placing greater emphasis on the importance of the ego and on social relationships. We shall briefly review the contributions of some of these early dissenters. Then we shall consider object relations theory, attachment theory, and self psychology in some detail. Finally, we shall consider a related development: that of brief forms of psychoanalytic psychotherapy.

The Neo-Freudians

There have been so many creative offshoots from traditional Freudian psychoanalysis that we cannot consider them all here. In this chapter, we will briefly review the contributions of Jung and Adler, perhaps the two most famous theorists to develop out of psychoanalysis.

Adler

Alfred Adler (1929, 1964) was Freud's contemporary and a respected psychiatrist in his own right when he studied with Freud. He subsequently rejected many of Freud's ideas. Like many others, Adler rejected Freud's emphasis on sexuality and the unconscious as crucial forces in personality development. He called the system he developed "individual psychology."

Adler emphasized the unique individuality of each personality. In contrast to Freud, who viewed the personality as fundamentally split into conflicting components, Adler saw the personality as unified. Adler also focused on the conscious side of the personality. Like later ego analysts, Adler believed that the strivings of a rather rational, organized self accounted for much behavior. He emphasized people's thoughts and beliefs and how they affected behavior. He felt that the relationship of this self to other people ("social interest") and the striving of this self toward future goals ("fictional finalism") were also important. Adler stressed the ongoing social environment as a cause of behavior more than Freud did. For this reason, some view Adler as one of the forerunners of the community psychology movement (see chapter 15).

Adler is perhaps best known for his concepts of the inferiority complex and striving for superiority. He began with the idea of "organ inferiority." He argued that people born with certain physical defects (such as deafness, poor vision, lameness) would organize their personalities around compensating for the feelings of inferiority engendered by the defect. Later he came to believe that feelings of inferiority as a result of being a small, weak child are universal. Some individuals would successfully compensate for their feelings of inferiority and achieve a great deal, while others would fail to do so and would develop feelings of insecurity or grandiosity or other symptoms. The negative personality characteristics surrounding the attempt to deal with these feelings were called an ***inferiority complex***.

For Adler, the basic dynamic motivating force within the personality is striving for superiority. This basic force is normal and inborn and continues throughout life. All people strive for self-esteem, perfection, and completion in all their behaviors. This dynamic force results in achievement and fulfillment in most individuals, although each expresses these strivings in different ways. Some strive for superiority by being successful in their occupations, others by being loving or creative. Disturbed individuals may express their strivings for superiority in less desirable ways, such as becoming tyrannical at home or being viciously competitive. Unlike Freud, Adler was an optimist, and he believed that the normal, inborn motivation for humans is a prosocial striving for accomplishment and achievement.

Adler's approach to therapy was active, kindly, and "commonsensical." He appealed to his patients' rationality and supported their general strivings and goals. He often worked with children, and he would invite family members, teachers, and other involved adults to attend therapy sessions. He would support the child and explain the child's view to the surrounding adults, somewhat like family therapists do today. He also tried to make the child's and the family's goals explicit, so they could all agree to work together.

This brief summary cannot do justice to Adler's theory, which also included a personality typology and extensive discussion of people's styles of life. Style of life referred to the person's individuality, ways of handling problems, methods of compensation for feelings of inferiority, and specific goals and ways of achieving them. Like Freud, Adler believed the style of life was set in early childhood and continued in the same direction throughout adulthood. Adler began the notion that people's earliest memory indicates the basic direction of their life. (The earliest memory of one of us is taking a nap!)

Although Adler still has followers with their own journal, *The American Journal of Individual Psychology*, his system never became as famous and popular as Freud's. However, his ideas were important precursors of many currently popular ideas—an emphasis on the social nature of the person, an emphasis on how people construe their personal realities, and an emphasis on an individual's personal vision of her future and her goals.

Jung

Carl Jung (1933, 1956) studied under Freud when he was just beginning his psychiatric practice. Like Adler, he disagreed with Freud's emphasis on sexuality. His extensive theory of personality, called analytical psychology, was considerably more mystical and philosophical than Freud's. However, his therapeutic practices were generally similar to Freud's. Jung emphasized dreams even more than Freud. The kinds of interpretations he made also focused on symbolic and archetypal meanings underlying behavior, in addition to meanings from early childhood.

Like Freud, Jung believed that psychic energy coursing through personality structures causes behavior. However, while this energy derives from biological processes, it is not particularly sexual. This energy motivates behavior whose goal is the actualization and fulfillment of the self, an idea similar to Adler's striving for superiority. In this respect, Jung's theory presaged both recent developments in psychoanalysis and humanistic approaches.

Like Freud and unlike Adler, Jung emphasized unconscious determinants of behavior. He divided the unconscious into two parts—the personal unconscious and the collective unconscious. The personal unconscious contains repressed and forgotten memories from infancy and childhood. It is unique to the individual, depending on the types of childhood experiences the individual had.

The collective unconscious is transpersonal and shared by all human beings. It is the foundation of the entire personality structure and contains inherited memory traces embedded in the brain. These include memories from humankind's ancestral past and prehuman nature. For example, humans are predisposed to know God, since the memory traces of countless preceding generations' experiences of God are in the collective unconscious. Jung wrote that the collective unconscious contains centuries of wisdom and experience.

Archetypes are the "primordial images" or "universal thought forms" found in the collective unconscious. After centuries of experiencing similar issues, the human brain evolves archetypes to deal with each issue. Like all evolutionary structures, archetypes help us survive. Some archetypes are so important to our evolutionary survival that they have formed important subsystems within the personality structure. Jung wrote especially about the persona, shadow, anima-animus, and self archetypes. To simplify greatly, the persona is the socially conventional mask we all wear; the shadow is the darker, animal side of human nature; anima represents the feminine in men and animus represents the masculine in women; and the self is our striving for unity and wholeness. Jung wrote extensively about the self and its strivings for actualization.

Jung developed a complex personality typology of eight major types based on two major life orientations—extraversion and introversion—coupled with four psychological functions—thinking, feeling, sensing, and intuiting. Extraversion is an outer-directed orientation to life; introversion is inner directed. A person could be a thinking introvert, who spends all her time alone reading philosophical works; a feeling extravert, who constantly creates emotional scenes with other people; a feeling introvert; and so on.

Jung's impact has perhaps been greater in fields other than psychology. His contributions to philosophy, art, literature, metaphysics, and history are acknowledged by many. His ideas are complex, unsystematic, and subjective. An idea such as the collective unconscious is untestable and in its pure form is not accepted as a scientific hypothesis today. However, many cognitive psychologists do believe there may be inborn ways of organizing information, somewhat like archetypes.

Other Neo-Freudians

Many highly creative therapists and theorists have arisen from the psychoanalytic perspective. These include Karen Horney (1945), Harry Stack Sullivan (Mullahy, 1952), and Erik Erikson (1968). What is common to these theorists is a greater emphasis on the importance of relationships to others in determining personality and psychopathology than is found in classical Freudian theory. Horney's three orientations to life—moving toward people, moving away from people, and moving against people—stress relationships. Erikson saw development in interpersonal terms. For instance, the key development at Freud's oral period is for Erikson the development of "basic trust." Furthermore, Erikson saw development as continuing throughout the life span, instead of being largely completed by age five. His approach has become increasingly influential in the field of developmental psychology. Harry Stack Sullivan believed that we develop a concept of the "good me" based on what is acceptable to our parents. Those aspects of ourselves that we consider to be the "bad me" are split off from consciousness. With his emphasis on the "good me" and the "bad me" and their development as a result of relationships to others, Sullivan was a precursor of object relations theory.

Along with a greater emphasis on the importance of interpersonal relations in the development of personality, these and other theorists also generally placed greater emphasis on the ego than did Freud. For Freud, the ego developed out of the id, and its main function was to mediate between the id and reality. ***Ego psychology*** (for instance, Hartman, 1964) saw the ego as having greater autonomy. Humans consisted of more than the management of sexual and aggressive instincts. Rational thought, creativity, and so on, all had their own independent existence. In this respect, these theorists were also precursors of the developments to be considered next.

Contemporary Perspectives

Modern relational psychodynamic theory emphasizes the primacy of relationships in human development (Mitchell, 1988). Three approaches have particularly contributed to this: Object relations theory (Cashdan, 1988; Hamilton, 1988), attachment theory (Bowlby, 1988), and self psychology (Kohut, 1984; Stolorow, Brandchaft, & Atwood, 1987). Each views the development of a cohesive, functional self or identity as fundamental. Each focuses on the importance of interpersonal patterns in understanding an individual's psychological problems. These approaches now constitute the predominant influences on the current psychoanalytic scene. Further, their influence is seen in other approaches to psychotherapy, such as cognitive therapy, and in fields as diverse as social psychology and developmental psychology.

These developments continue trends noted in the previous section. For Freud, psychological development was primarily a matter of mastering and regulating sexuality and aggression. Relationships with "objects" in the environment, including other people, ultimately only occurred because at some unconscious level they served the purpose of discharging sexual or aggressive drives. Love of another person, for instance, could be for the purposes of gaining unconscious gratification of sexual drive, even if that gratification were obtained only in highly disguised forms. Or, it could be a defense against unconscious aggressive wishes. In addition, all forms of "higher" human activity, such as learning, studying, writing novels, composing music, or exploring science, are also unconscious, displaced forms of dealing with sex and aggression. Thus the "higher" in human behavior is really an expression of the "lower"—more basic biological impulses—as is the need for relatedness to others. Psychotherapy becomes the process of helping people become aware of the roots of their problems in early childhood sexual and aggressive wishes and fantasies.

We have already noted how various theorists who followed Freud discounted Freud's emphasis on sex and aggressive wishes and impulses in various ways. Most gave greater importance to ego functioning than Freud did and saw the "higher" activities of the human, such as art, philosophy, or science, as arising from an "autonomous ego," rather than as being derivatives of sexual and aggressive wishes. In a similar manner, many emphasized the importance of interpersonal relationships in human life for their own sake, over and above sexual and aggressive aspects. Sullivan, for instance, believed that it was the interpersonal context that was most important to people's development, and Adler believed that concern for others was crucial to full human development.

Object Relations Theory

According to Harry Guntrip (1973), important precursors of object relations theory were the ideas of Melanie Klein (1932/1975) and Harry Stack Sullivan. Other important figures (see St. Clair, 1986) associated with this approach are D. W. Winnicot, W. R. D. Fairbairn, Otto Kernberg, Margaret Mahler, and James Masterson (Masterson, 1981, 1985). Object relations theorists generally reject part or all of Freud's metapsychology, that is, his concept of id, ego, and superego and the idea that the personality is an energy-regulating device. Some substitute a rather complex metapsychology of their own, which we will only briefly touch on later.

Self-Structure and Integration of Aims

> A person is a whole self and so unique that it is impossible to find, among all the millions of human beings that have existed and do exist, any two who are exactly alike. When a baby is born, he contains a core of uniqueness that has never existed before. The parents' responsibility is not to mold, shape, pattern, or condition him, but to support him in such a way that his precious hidden uniqueness shall be able to emerge and guide his whole development. (Guntrip, 1973, p. 181)

It is apparent from this quote that we have come a long way from Freud. Whereas Freud saw development in terms of regulating and expressing sexuality (and later, aggression), ***object relations theory*** focuses on the development of a separate, differentiated, integrated, cohesive self. Certainly the regulation of sexuality and aggression is an important issue for the development of a differentiated, cohesive self, but so are hunger and needs for closeness, attention, competence, mastery, and others.

Object relations theory is thus more comprehensive than Freud's psychoanalysis. Sex and aggression are important, but they are only a part of the whole story. A fully developed self is unique. It is also creative, flexible, and self-regulating. It is true to itself, and behavior flows from its own plans and schemes, rather than from some externalized image of how it should be (a "false self"). The most crucial factor in the development of a true self is relationships to other people, particularly the mother. As we said in the previous chapter, relationships with other people are seen by psychoanalysts as a subcategory of relationships with objects in general. Hence, even though the object relations theorists are most interested in relationships with people, they call them "object relations." Now read the following quote with the understanding that the word people can be substituted for object and see what it means to you. "The entire process of growth, disturbance, and restoration of wholeness as an ego or personal self depends upon the ego's relations with objects, primarily in infancy, and thereafter in the unconscious . . . interacting with object-relations in real life" (Guntrip, 1973, p. 95).

Along with the emphasis on the development of the self in the context of relationships to other people comes a deemphasis of Freud's view of the mind as composed of id, ego, and superego. For Freud, the id was a biological repository of primitive sexual and aggressive energies. But if sex and aggression are energies that build up and clamor for discharge, people have a need to act aggressively or sexually regardless of what is going on in their lives. For Freud, relationships with other people are based on their being sources of need gratification. It is important for an individual to be liked or loved by other people, because people are vehicles of sexual gratification. All motives, such as the need to achieve, to have power over others, to have positive self-esteem, to be loved, are all ultimately secondary to the basic needs of discharging and regulating sexuality and aggression.

Many object relations theorists reject the view that sexuality and aggression are instinctual energies that build up and clamor for discharge (Eagle, 1984; Guntrip, 1973). They believe that both sex and aggression have a biological component, but neither are instincts in the generally accepted meaning of the word; that is, they are not energies that build up and need to be discharged or reduced. In rejecting an energy model of motivation, object relations theory is in accord with most modern views of needs and motivations (Weiner, 1980). According to Guntrip, sex is better thought of as a biologically based appetite. An appetite may increase in intensity if a person is not able to engage in the desired activity, but there is no energy that builds up if the person does not engage in it. For example, if one has an interest or "appetite" for going to classical music concerts, one's desire to go may increase if one has not been for a while, but there is no buildup of "classical music energy." Freud's energy idea implies that people need to discharge the energy in order for pleasure to occur. Such a view makes orgasm the ultimate goal of sexual activity and makes any sexual activity without orgasm appear to be ultimately incomplete. This is quite out of keeping with modern views of sexuality. In fact, this view is now seen as one of the causes of sexual problems. Sexual activity and becoming aroused may be experienced as pleasurable whether or not they lead to orgasm. If sex is an energy that needs to be discharged and dissipated, then this does not make sense. If sex is an appetite, then it does make sense.

Similarly, if aggression is an instinctual energy, then we as species would periodically have to act aggressively in order to dissipate this energy. But while most modern theorists believe there is a biological basis to aggression, they hold that it is a response to threat rather than instinctual energy. We may learn to enjoy aggression for its own sake, but that is because aggression, like sex, can come to serve other needs in the personality. There is no aggressive energy that needs to be discharged.

If the self is the focus of development, and not sex and aggression, then what is the self? Morris Eagle (1984) defined the self

> as a biologically evolved adaptive hierarchical structure coordinating a wide range of subordinate functions. In as complex a system as a person, one would expect the evolution of a superordinate structure whose main functions would include the coordination and fulfillment of a wide range of the person's interests and needs. (p. 207)

Thus, the self is an organization that attempts to coordinate a host of goals, desires, aims, and values. For instance, at any given moment you may have a host of conflicting aims and goals. You may feel hungry, tired, and bored with your studies. Yet you may have the goal of passing the test tomorrow, which may relate to other goals of becoming a psychologist, pleasing your parents, maintaining your self-esteem. You may also have a desire to please your spouse, who wants to go out, or to pay attention to your children. The individual needs an organizational structure that can prioritize competing aims, desires, and feelings and bring some coherence to how the individual goes about meeting them. That is what the self is and what it does.

Eagle goes on to suggest that some of our aims are infantile and some are not available to conscious awareness, having been split off and disavowed, usually in early childhood. He sees persons as

> attempting to carry out a variety of aims—some in conflict with each other and others harmoniously, some infantile and others more mature, and all with varying degrees of conscious awareness and of acknowledgment as one's own aims, ranging from full conscious awareness and acknowledgment to total lack of awareness and disavowal. (p. 123)

Disowned or disavowed aims imperil adequate functioning of the self.

> A superordinate structure or self-organization which excludes and dissociates a wide range of strivings and aims does not adequately reflect one's welfare and is therefore carrying out its adaptive functions poorly. (p. 207)

Thus, if persons have disavowed certain primitive wishes in early childhood, their self-organization cannot function adequately. These wishes still influence their behavior, but cannot be integrated and coordinated with other aspects of their personality because they are not available to awareness.

This way of looking at the self provides a better explanation of what happens in therapy than classical analytic theory. Classical analytic therapy makes repressed impulses conscious, but then what? You can't go have sex with your mother or father. All you can do is make sure these impulses don't distort your view of the world. But what do you do with them? In object relations theory, aims are influenced by their place in the whole self-structure and take on different meanings depending on how they are integrated into the personality. The problem with repression is that certain primitive childhood aims are split off from the self-structure and therefore are not given a chance to be integrated effectively. Conscious awareness in therapy allows these aims to be integrated in the adult self and therefore modified.

Consider a client who gets in touch with infantile rage toward his father, who often slighted him. In classical analytic therapy, what does a person now do with this rage? We have had clients get in touch with such rage, only to feel worse, saying, "Now what do I do?" Our answer was that the rage needs to be worked through until the client can "let go" of it. This may involve forgiving the father, which itself involves relinquishing demands that the father (or all people, including oneself) be perfect. It also involves recognizing the father's humanness. Finally, it involves the realization that the client is now an adult and no longer needs to feel so threatened by such slights. These learnings fundamentally alter the rage so that it either goes away or becomes considerably less intense.

We will now look at one of the most commonly accepted object relations views of the development of the self.

Mahler and Separation-Individuation

Margaret Mahler (Mahler, 1968, 1971; Mahler, Pine, & Bergman, 1975) conducted observational studies of mothers and children to arrive at her model of development. For her, development is primarily a matter of separation and ***individuation***; that is, the child must separate herself from other objects and the external world and develop a sense of her own uniqueness as an individual. According to Mahler, the child in the first month of life is in the stage of *normal autism.* In this stage, the infant is largely unresponsive to external reality, being more preoccupied with internal stimuli. The infant could be described at this stage as *narcissistic.* She has no interest in the external world; in fact, she does not even have a concept of the external world. External objects, such as the mother, are not seen as external objects, and their presence may only be dimly sensed as an accompaniment of need gratification. The infant may believe that her desires are all that is needed to make the mother magically appear to satisfy them.

From the second or third month, the child begins to attend to the world. At this stage, known as *normal symbiosis,* the child cannot distinguish between his own efforts to get his needs met and the mother's responses to his needs. The child may now be aware of external stimuli, particularly of those associated with the mother, but the child does not perceive the mother as an external object (a separate person). In effect, the child experiences himself as fused with the mother, as sharing a common boundary with the mother. When the mother feeds the child, for instance, the child perceives the mother's arm and the bottle as part of his own body feeding himself. Thus, when the mother does not immediately gratify the infant's hunger, the child perceives his own self as inflicting pain and frustration.

At about four months of age, the separation-individuation process begins. The first phase of the process, from about four months to 10 months, involves the infant's development of a sense of *bodily separation* from the mother. At this stage, the child begins to realize that he and the mother are physically separate. This realization, however, is anxiety provoking, and the child will periodically "check back" with the mother in order to reassure himself of her presence. The next phase, from about 10 to 14 months, is that of *practicing.* Early practicing involves gradual acquisition of motor skills that allow further separation from the mother. Practicing begins when the infant begins to walk. This is the peak period of the child's omnipotence. The child acts as if he is on top of the world, and can master anything, as a whole new world is opened up to him by his ability to move around. However, this sense of omnipotence is still linked to the psychological presence of the mother as the child's "security blanket."

Before we discuss the next phase, we should discuss the mother's activity during the whole maturation process. For development to be successful, the child must experience "good enough mothering" (Winnicot, 1965). A good enough mother is not a perfect mother who meets all of the child's needs, but rather a mother who is "good enough" to positively encourage and support the development process in the child. A good mother enjoys her child and is comfortable holding him. Mahler believes that how and when a mother holds her child conveys to the child a whole host of attitudes. As the child begins to separate and individuate, the mother is neither too distant nor too close. An overprotective, smothering mother holds a child when she needs comforting rather than when the child needs comforting. This behavior may stifle the child's initiative and moves toward autonomy. It inhibits the child's ability to develop a sense of herself as separate from the mother and to develop her capacity for independent judgment. A distant, rejecting mother may also be harmful because she does not provide a safe place of support to which the child can return after venturing out into the world. The child needs both a sense of support from the mother as she challenges the world and some freedom to explore. A distant, rejecting mother may allow freedom, but provide no support. Her child will never successfully separate and individuate because she will forever long for union with the mother. She will fantasize union with the mother because that is the only way she can control her own anxiety in response to her mother's abandonment or neglect.

One other factor of good enough mothering is that the mother be able to act as a "holding environment" (Winnicot, 1965) or a "container" for overwhelming emotions the infant might feel. When the infant is experiencing anger or pain or fear the mother can "hold," soothe, and contain these feelings so that the infant feels safe and is not overwhelmed by them. This allows the infant to learn how to master these strong emotions herself.

It is particularly important that the mother effectively balance support and freedom in the next phase of separation-individuation, that of *rapprochement*, which occurs from about 14 to 24 months. Some object relations theorists hypothesize that many different kinds of psychopathology, including borderline personality disorder and eating disorders such as bulimia, have their roots in this developmental phase. During rapprochement, the child becomes more aware of her separateness from the mother. Her joyous sense of omnipotence vanishes as she begins to recognize her separateness. She begins to feel small, deflated, weak, and helpless. This is the beginning of the rapprochement crisis. The child must master the fact of her separateness from the mother. In addition, it is during this time that the child becomes aware of gender differences, and thus, analytic theorists see it as the beginning of a person's identity as a male or female.

During rapprochement, splitting is used as a defense mechanism. All object relations theorists discuss splitting. However, some assume that it begins to happen earlier in development than Mahler, according to whom it primarily occurs during rapprochement. For these other theorists, such as Cashdan (1988), ***splitting*** is the first and most primary way we evaluate and judge the world, separating things into "good" and "bad" based on our affective responses to them—that is, how much they please or displease us. Thus, the roots of splitting may develop earlier than the rapprochement period.

For Mahler, as the child begins to form a representation (or image) of the mother as a separate person, the child is confronted with some painfully contradictory information. Mother is good, a rewarding source of pleasure and support, but she is also bad, a frustrating source of criticism, punishment, and saying no. It is too painful for the child to perceive the "good" mother as having bad qualities, so the image of mother is split in two. When mommy is being nice, the child's image is of the "good mother"; when she is being critical, the image is of the "bad mother." In other words, the mother is perceived as all good or all bad, depending on how she is acting, and the two images are not integrated. Similarly, the child splits her own self-image into the "good me" and the "bad me." When the child is being praised by the mother, she feels good and sees herself as all good. When she is being criticized, she feels bad and sees herself as all bad, rotten through and through.

The point here is that the child's self-image is unfinished. First, the child judges herself completely in terms of how the mother is responding to her: She is bad if the mother is critical of her. Second, the child engages in global, either-or thinking: I cannot be both good and bad at the same time; I am either all bad or all good. Thus, the child does not have an integrated image of a whole self, consisting of good and bad aspects. Similarly, the child does not have an integrated image of the mother or, by extension, of people in general.

A concrete example of splitting is when the baby feels weak and helpless and reaches out to the mother. Suppose the mother is unable to respond to these needs appropriately. The baby is helpless and cannot afford to get angry at the mother. So the baby "splits off" her helpless, needy baby side. She must also split off her anger toward the mother because it is too threatening to be angry at the mother. It is better to feel "bad" than to feel weak and needy and angry at the mother. In later life, this person will have difficulty in interpersonal relationships, immediately feeling "bad" about herself whenever someone else doesn't meet her needs, or even contradicts or disagrees with her.

All children use splitting as a defense mechanism at a certain point in development, but it is crucial that the child develop whole object representations and emotional object constancy. With good enough mothering, the child eventually overcomes her defensive need to separate good and bad images of the mother. She will be able to unify them into an image of a whole person. She will also be able to develop whole object representation of her self-image. Then, when her mother is critical of her, she will not see the mother as all bad, nor will she see herself as all bad. By extension, as an adult, she will not completely devalue people just because they do something that displeases her, nor will she idealize them, just because she feels attracted to them, and expect them to be perfect in her terms and to meet all her needs. Because she is able to see people as having both good and bad qualities, she will develop emotional object constancy; that is, she will be able to maintain a constant emotional reaction toward someone. Being able to separate a person's actions from the person, she will be able to continue to love the person, even if the person engages in some behavior that displeases her.

In addition to being able to maintain positive feelings toward a person, it is sometimes necessary to be able to maintain negative feelings toward someone. For instance, women who are battered by their husbands are often unable to maintain negative feelings toward their husbands. As soon as the husband apologizes and acts repentant, the wife "forgets" her negative reaction to him.

The achievement of emotional object constancy and whole object representations happens during the final phase of the separation-individuation process. This phase of *consolidation of individuality* occurs at 24 to 36 months. The person who achieves these goals can maintain self-esteem even in the face of failing at something, can continue to like and prize others even if they do not live up to expectations, and can maintain a "good self" image without needing to please others continually. The person will be able to continue to develop his true self, that is, to separate his own intentions, perceptions, and goals from others.

Psychopathology

We have already mentioned some of the things that can go wrong during the sequence of separation-individuation. In general, object relations theorists hold that early problems in relationship to the mother or primary caretaker create structural weaknesses in the self that predispose the individual to various forms of psychopathology. They particularly believe that early disturbances are important in the formation of serious and difficult to treat problems such as eating disorders and personality disorders. An example is someone who exhibits symptoms of borderline personality disorder. The assumption is that a person with this diagnosis has failed to establish whole object representations and emotional object constancy. As a result, the individual may be unable to form stable, enduring relationships, constantly fluctuating from intense love and involvement to intense disappointment. He may be unable to establish a stable, cohesive identity in terms of an integrated set of goals, values, and self-perceptions. This may lead to unstable vocational pursuits—frequent job changes and inability to settle on and pursue some career. The individual may exhibit a pattern of impulsiveness as the result of these instabilities. Because the individual has not developed a stable inner self, he may need constant emotional stimulation from outside to feel alive and involved. Thus, he may invest himself in casual or promiscuous sex, use of drugs, and gambling.

Because he has not learned emotional object constancy, his emotional responses may be intense but momentary. He may be afflicted with intense feelings of hostility that come and go. If he does not completely establish a sense of self as a separate object—if he feels fused with the mother—he will continually search for the "ecstasy" of the fusion experience. He may seek intense, immediate personal encounters (such as promiscuous or casual sex) in which he can temporarily experience that sense of fusion, but then when he is alone, he will feel depressed, empty, and abandoned.

Bowlby and Attachment Theory

John Bowlby's (1988) ***attachment theory*** integrates psychoanalytic ideas with evolutionary theory. Bowlby assumes that infants are biologically predisposed to form attachments with adult caretakers. This is because infants could not survive very long on their own, so it has been evolutionarily advantageous that they form bonds with adult caretakers. Similarly, adults are biologically predisposed to form bonds with their children. The attachment bond between infant and mother is a joint product of both of them. That is, mothers may find some infants more "cute and cuddly" than others, and bond more easily with them. On the other hand, no matter how cute and cuddly an infant is, some mothers may be inept at forming good, secure attachment bonds.

A good attachment bond with the mother provides a "secure base" from which the growing infant can gradually move out to explore the world. It also provides a context in which the infant develops an internalized "working model" of relationships with people. ***Working models*** consist of: (a) an image of the self, (b) an image of others, and (c) an image of how relationships with others work. It is important to note their interpersonal nature: they are not of self alone, but of self-relating-to-other. In other words, we first develop an image of self as part of relationships. If early childhood relationships with the mother (and later with the father) are dysfunctional, then the child develops flawed models of both the self and of relationships.

These models persist and influence later development. For instance, if the mother does not provide a secure base, the child may be afraid to explore relationships with others when she goes to school. This may negatively impact her relationships both with her peers and with her teachers. This may in turn negatively impact her ability to learn, both in terms of her schoolwork and in terms of how to relate to people. In addition, working models usually persist into adulthood, affecting both love and work relationships.

Another important consequence of secure attachments is that the child develops the ability to effectively reflect on herself and her behavior and to empathize with other minds. Early childhood abuse particularly interferes with these developments, contributing to the development of personality disorders, such as antisocial, borderline, and narcissistic disorders (Fonagy, et al., 1996).

Bowlby's theory has had considerable influence in many areas of psychology beyond clinical psychology. It is now one of the major theories of childhood development. It has also been extensively researched. We shall consider this research in a later section.

Kohut and Self Psychology

A third major new approach to psychoanalysis is that of self psychology. Self psychology is sufficiently revolutionary compared to other analytic theories, and some writers treat it as a unique perspective in its own right, rather than as a form of psychoanalysis (Messer & Warren, 1990). Self psychology is also much closer to the humanistic theories of client-centered therapy (see chapter 8) and existentialism (see chapter 9) than other psychoanalytic approaches (Kahn, 1985; Tobin, 1990).

For Heinz Kohut (1971, 1977), the growth of a stable, cohesive, unique self is the basic issue in personality development. Other issues, such as how the parents handle toilet training during the anal stage or how they react to the child during the phallic stage, make sense only if we see them in terms of the process of self-development, and psychopathology is seen as a result of thwarting this process.

Self-objects are crucial in the person's development of a cohesive self. A self-object can be thought of as a person who supplies an important set of functions for the developing self, though some writers have stressed that it is more appropriate to talk about self-object functions than about self-objects, since the crucial things are really the functions themselves.

Consider a small infant within the first year of life. At that point, according to Kohut, he has no "self" (though he does have the innate potential to develop a self). At that point in development, his sense of self is fragmented and incoherent. It is through the responses of important caretakers that he begins to develop an organized core "nuclear" sense of self, along about the second year of life. The caretaker engenders this development by providing certain functions that the infant is unable to provide for himself. The most basic mode of such support is through empathy. The mother, through her empathic responses to the infant, conveys to him that he is a self: unique, distinctive, and worthy of being understood and responded to.

The mother also supports the child's developing self by helping the child with tension regulation, that is, by providing for the child's basic needs. More importantly, the mother provides psychological support. In order to develop a cohesive self, the child must develop mature ambitions, ideals, and positive self-esteem. He must develop the ability to support himself in the face of frustration and to nurture and empathize with himself. If the mother is unable to respond when the infant is experiencing some troubling emotion such as anger or anxiety, those troubling emotions will not be integrated into the developing self-structure and will trouble the individual the rest of his life, threatening psychological disorganization when they are reawakened (Stolorow, 1992).

Initially, these self-supportive functions are provided by the mother, if the child is lucky enough to have good mothering. Early in childhood, the child will have grandiose and exhibitionistic needs for attention and admiration. In order for the child to develop a sense of her own self-worth, the mother must engage at this stage in empathic ***mirroring***—that is, the mother must be able to experience and respond to the child's "look at me" behavior with appreciation and joyfulness. If the child rarely or never gets empathic mirroring, then she never has the kind of appreciative support she needs to grow. Anyone who has been around small children will have experienced their "look at me" behavior. One must be "properly appreciative" in order for the children to develop a sense of their own self-worth.

At the same time, mothers (and other self-objects, such as fathers) are not always available to provide empathic mirroring. Mother may be busy, or Father may be tired. There will be inevitable failures in empathic mirroring. However, if a self-object always provided empathic mirroring, the child would never learn to take over this function herself. In optimal development, the periodic failures of empathic mirroring allow the child to learn to provide her own self-support. At times when the mother is unavailable, the child can model the mother's empathic response and "talk" internally to herself as the mother would. Put in Kohut's terms, a "transmuting internalization" occurs, in which the function of self-support provided by the mother gets internalized and built into the individual's own self-structure. Optimal empathic mirroring from the mother leads to a modulating and softening of the grandiose and exhibitionistic tendencies of the child and to the development of healthy, mature self-esteem, ambitions, and assertiveness.

The very young child also has a need to idealize his caretakers. As adults, we can still have this need. When we are learning in a new area, for instance clinical psychology, we may have a tendency to idealize and then pattern ourselves after certain figures, say, Freud, Rogers, or Kohut. These figures embody our ideals, and it is through them that we develop our own ideals. As adults, of course, we are not directly soothed by these figures, but the presence of someone whom we can idealize is emotionally soothing.

For a child, it is reinforcing to the self-image and self-esteem to be soothed and nurtured by someone who is idealized. Thus, idealizing the mother helps the child feel good about himself. If the mother is empathic, the child will eventually develop the ability to soothe himself. He will also internalize the ideals of the parents. Further, he will grow out of the need to idealize the mother and, by extension, other individuals as well. As the child develops the ability to soothe himself, he no longer needs to see the person who soothes him as perfect.

Another need that the young child has is to feel a similarity to other people and a feeling of belonging ("twinship"). As adults, for instance, we experience this twinship need when we are pleased to meet someone whom we feel is a great deal like ourselves. The child's ability to develop this aspect of herself has to do with her ability to establish sociable relationships with others.

The development of these three "poles" of the self—the grandiose, exhibitionistic pole; the idealizing pole; and the twinship pole—leads to the achievement of a cohesive nuclear self by sometime in the third year of life if all goes well. This cohesive self includes the functions of both healthy self-assertiveness and an internalized image of parental goals and ideals. This process of "self- structuralization" leads to a child who will ultimately be able to regulate her own emotions, be assertive, take responsibility for herself, pursue and develop her own ambitions and goals, form healthy relationships with others, empathically minister to her own self when distressed, and empathically relate to others.

Once we have achieved a healthy nuclear self, do we no longer need other people? No, according to Kohut. Self psychology is not a theory of separation-individuation as is object relations theory, where the healthy outcome is a separate, autonomous self (Tobin, 1990). To the contrary, the healthy self exists in an *intersubjective field* (Stolorow, 1992); that is, the healthy self always exists in relation to others. There is no such thing as a self completely separate from other people. Thus, all of us will continue to need support from others throughout our lives. We will continue to need empathy, connectedness in the form of twinship relationships, people to idealize, and so on. These functions mature with age; that is, they take more mature forms, but they don't disappear. Thus, developing a "nuclear self" is not quite the same as becoming separated and individuated as in object relations theory. A cohesive, functional, nuclear self is really a structured set of interactive functions: the ability to make decisions, to choose ideals and goals, and so on.

Self psychology thus postulates a radically different view of the human being in contrast to Freud's view, to object relations theory, and to most traditional Western theories of the self. Its view is compatible with modern feminist interpretations of the self, recent developments in the view of the self in client-centered therapy (see chapter 8), the "field" view of the self postulated by Gestalt theory (see chapter 9), and systems views of the self (see chapter 13).

Kohut's (1984) version of the Oedipus complex is different from Freud's. Kohut assumes children enter the Oedipal stage joyfully if they have had a healthy environment until then. For Kohut, the primary issues of the Oedipal stage are not sex and aggression, but affection and assertiveness. The young male child begins to explore his affectional capacity in relation to his mother and his assertive capacity in relation to his father. The converse happens for the female child.

At this age, assertion and aggression are often not sufficiently differentiated for the child, and neither are sex and affection. As a result, if the parents handle the situation badly, assertion degenerates into aggression and affection degenerates into sexual wishes. Thus, according to Kohut, the Oedipus complex as Freud portrayed it is actually not universal, but a product of poor parental management. If the mother has conflicts over sexuality herself, she may be put off or threatened by her child's affectional moves. Her sense of threat may inadvertently sexualize these affectional moves for the child. Similarly, if the father is threatened by the child's assertion, then the situation may become a competitive, rivalrous one, leading to feelings of hostility toward the father.

For Kohut, castration anxiety is actually a metaphor for disintegration anxiety. Anxiety is fear of the self's disintegration or a sense of the self as disintegrating, in contrast to Freud's view of anxiety as a signal that the repressed is about to break through into consciousness. Kohut's view of penis envy should also be mentioned. For Kohut, penis envy in the girl is a result of failure on the part of parents and culture to prize the uniqueness and individuality of the female. It is a metaphor for the girl's diminished sense of self due to her parents' and society's masculine bias.

Even if as children people receive adequate empathic responding from their parents, they continue to need self-objects throughout their lives. One of Kohut's interesting ideas is that anyone who supports a person's self-development can function as a self-object. For instance, you may find one theorist in this book with whom you really resonate. That theorist will be a self-object for you. As you read about that theorist and find your developing ideas mirrored and supported in the theorist's work, that mirroring and support will further the development of your own ideas. Rock stars are often self-objects for teenagers, and for young adults a self-object is often a respected teacher or supervisor. Of course, we all want self-objects in our romantic relationships—someone who "prizes" us and likes us for who we are.

Psychopathology

Psychological problems occur when parents or other caretakers do not provide the supportive, empathic context for the development of a coherent nuclear self. The self remains fragmented, and the child never develops certain of these important self-functions, such as the ability to set goals or soothe the self. As an adult, these disturbed self-functions will manifest themselves in disturbed relationships, both with others and with one's work.

For instance, the child who does not receive healthy empathic mirroring at an early age may develop a narcissistic personality disorder. This disorder is characterized by an incessant need to be the center of attention and to be loved and admired. The person also has fantasies of unlimited success. Some narcissistic people, who have not successfully internalized an idealized image of their parents, may continually search to merge with people whom they can idealize. The self-esteem of narcissistic individuals depends on the availability of people who can admire them or of people they can identify with and idealize. When they do not have these things, or when they engage in behaviors that are less than admirable, they respond with shame and rage rather than with the more mature emotion of guilt.

It is important to realize that the adult is not simply "acting like an infant" whose development has been arrested at a very early age. The adult's narcissistic behavior is an attempt at the present time to get the kind of emotional support he needs in order to resume growing. In other words, dysfunctional adult behavior is not merely a repetition of childhood behavior; it is an active attempt to cope, to get what is needed to grow, in the present. In fact, contrary to object relations theory, where psychopathological behavior is primarily a manifestation of an immature ego, for self psychology, psychopathology is a manifestation of the particular interpersonal relationship the person is in.

Relational Concepts

Later relational theorists, such as Stephen Mitchell (1988), building on ideas such as those of self psychology, have argued that "the basic unit of study is not the individual as a separate entity . . . but an interactional field within which the individual arises and struggles to make contact and to articulate himself. . . . Mind is composed of relational configurations" (pp. 3–4). That is, your experience of self in any given moment is always a product of your history plus whom you are with at the moment. Even if you are alone, your mind is basically relational, which means that emotionally you are never really alone, because everything you are doing is always relational, at least mentally. The meanings that you apply to what you are doing are always grounded in your past and present relationships with others, even if they are not present. You may be at home painting a picture, but even that is an intersubjective experience in that you are always implicitly planning to show it to others, seeing it through the eyes of others (as well as through the eyes of yourself), and so on. There simply is no such thing as a separate, developed, autonomous "self" from which your behavior flows, independent of the context of others.

This has been called a two-person psychology in contrast to a traditional one-person psychology. In a one-person psychology whatever the client does in therapy is presumed to come out of the client's internal psychological processes, with the therapist staying in a neutral observer role. In contrast, in a two-person psychology it is assumed that the dynamics between therapist and client account in part for the client's behavior. Therapists are not neutral objects unaffected by the client, but instead inevitably react to clients as persons. Mitchell (1997) has argued that because therapists and clients are caught in a two-person system, therapists get dragged into the repetitive ways clients create problems in their worlds. One way to change this is to find new and better ways of being with the client and try to interest the client in doing the same.

Approaches to Psychotherapy

Both self psychology and object relations theory have led to specific ideas about psychotherapeutic practice. In contrast, attachment theory has been primarily a theory of personality development. It has not specifically led to a particular form of psychotherapy. In fact, attachment ideas have influenced a wide range of therapists of different orientations, from psychodynamic to experiential (chapter 9), to cognitive (chapter 11). We shall focus on self psychology and object relations theory in this section.

In addition to these approaches to therapy, we shall consider a related development in psychoanalysis, that of relatively brief forms of psychotherapy. Among the problems associated with classical psychoanalytic therapy are its lengthiness and its expense. This is also true to some extent of object relational treatment of borderline personality and of Kohut's treatment of narcissistic personality.

Self Psychology and Object Relations Theory

There are several similarities between self psychology and object relations approaches to therapy. First, both approaches stress the importance of therapist empathy. Empathy is used in classical psychoanalysis, but its primary use is to help the analyst gain insight into the client. In contrast, both object relations and self psychological approaches assume that empathic failures in childhood have contributed to the adult client's problems. Therefore, it is important that the therapist provide empathy as a way of helping the client "contain" strong unruly emotions and affects and integrate them into the personality. For these approaches, empathy itself is a major vehicle of therapeutic change. This is particularly true in self psychology (Rowe & Mac Isaac, 1991), where the provision of empathy by the therapist actively institutes a condition for maturation and growth of the self.

Second, most therapists in both approaches value insight into childhood roots of adult problems, but to a lesser degree than in classical psychoanalytic therapy. It is helpful to learn how one's adult problems are based on parenting failures in childhood. However, the corrective experience of the here-and-now therapy relationship itself is also valued. Masterson (1981), an object relations therapist, calls therapy an "experiment in individuation." Change occurs through the experiential reliving of early childhood conflicts in therapy, and through that reliving, the maturational process is freed for the individual to develop a more differentiated and cohesive self. For some object relations therapists, such as Cashdan (1988), insight into the past plays a very little role, and therapy is primarily concerned with helping clients gain insight into how they are unconsciously structuring present relationships.

According to Kohut, when pathological early childhood experiences are revived and reworked in therapy, the therapist can provide the empathic conditions missing in childhood (including the occasional failures of empathy necessary for transmuting internalizations to occur). In these circumstances, "the accretion of psychological structure that optimally should have occurred during normal development is now belatedly occurring in the therapeutic milieu" (Kahn, 1985, p. 900).

Guntrip (1973) has perhaps most forcefully expressed the idea that through the experiential quality of the therapy relationship, growth can be achieved.

> I cannot think of psychotherapy as a technique but only as the provision of the possibility of a genuine, reliable, understanding, and respecting, caring personal relationship in which a human being whose true self has been crushed by the manipulative techniques of those who only wanted to make him "not a nuisance" to them, can begin at last to feel his own true feelings, and think his own spontaneous thoughts, and find himself to be real. (p. 182)

Third, these therapeutic approaches advocate the selective use of therapist self-disclosure. For instance, the therapist may reveal her feelings of ignorance or clumsiness in attempting to understand the client. Or the analyst may reveal her own occasional needs to use the client as a self-object (Wolf, 1983). For Kohut, a parent may have been unable to provide empathy because his or her own self-development was incomplete. As a result, the parent may have been more interested in gaining emotional support from the child, rather than in giving it to the child. Self-disclosure by the therapist may help the client realize that the therapist is not there to use the client for her own needs. This may help the client to overcome feelings of resistance and defensiveness and, therefore, to grow (Wolf, 1989):

> Since in essence, resistance is nothing but fear of being traumatically injured again, the decisive event of its analysis is the moment when the analysand has gained courage from these self-revelations of the analyst to know that the analyst does not need to feed on the patient to achieve cohesion and harmony. (pp. 500–501)

Guntrip also believes that the therapist should be a real person in therapy, at least more so than in traditional analytic therapy. In a somewhat related fashion, Masterson (1981) will abandon therapeutic neutrality to confront clients with the destructiveness of some of their behavior.

Fourth, both approach the transference relationship differently than classical psychoanalysis. For Freud, transference relationships were ultimately patterns of resistance. For self psychologists, they may involve resistance, but they are also expressions of the self's needs from early childhood. Needs for mirroring and for idealizing will be expressed in therapy. In the mirroring transference, the infantile, grandiose self demands continual empathic approval and attention from the therapist. In the idealizing transference, the client wishes for the therapist to be the all-powerful person who can fix all the client's problems. While it is acceptable for the analyst to provide some mirroring, it is often through failures in empathy that these two transferences get resolved. Through failures in empathy, the client is reminded of the unempathic parent. These experiences are then relived, but because they are relived in the context of an overall empathic relationship, growth of the self occurs.

For object relations therapists, a major key is to work with the *projective identifications* of the client. Projective identification is a defense mechanism in which the client projects unwanted aspects of the self onto another person and then attempts to control

Projective identification from pets.

those unwanted aspects via interactions with that other person. Suppose you are unconsciously uncomfortable with your sexual desires. You may project them onto another person, and then see that person as being sexual and seductive toward you. Now you are able to feel sexual, because the other person is acting sexually toward you. With projective identification, the individual may unconsciously manipulate the other person into actually acting out the unconscious projection. Thus, the individual may act unconsciously sexual in order to manipulate the other person into being sexual toward him. Another example of projective identification is that of a prison inmate who, at Christmas, felt lonely, and so he called his wife to "cheer her up" (Robert Rosenbaum, personal communication, June 1993). In other words, he projected his loneliness onto his wife and then tried to control those feelings by taking action toward her.

Thus, projective identification creates a specific kind of transferential relationship in which the client unconsciously tries to manipulate the therapist into feeling and acting in a way that the client unconsciously needs. An important part of object relations therapy is to make the client aware of how she is unconsciously "setting up" certain kinds of interpersonal patterns (Cashdan, 1988).

Finally, object relations therapy and Kohut's therapy have similar goals: the development of the self. For object relations theory, this includes separation of the self from the mother and forming differentiated and integrated representations of both the self and others. According to Masterson, this manifests itself in increased client autonomy and the ability of the client to take responsibility for himself and manage his life in a constructive manner. In addition, it should lead to a capacity for creativity, intimacy, and flexibility. For Kohut, the goal of therapy is the development of a cohesive self that has realistic ambitions and goals, is able to be creative, intimate, and flexible, and is able to make its own judgments and maintain its own self-esteem.

Brief Forms of Psychoanalytic Psychotherapy

Lester Luborsky (1984) has outlined his supportive-expressive approach to psychoanalytic psychotherapy. This relatively brief form of psychotherapy can be practiced on an open-ended basis or on a time-limited basis, in which case it usually lasts less than 25 sessions. Strupp and Binder (1984) have developed a time-limited dynamic therapy that lasts 25 to 30 sessions. We will also consider interpersonal psychotherapy (Gottlib & Schraedley, 2000). There are other approaches to brief psychoanalytic psychotherapy (reviewed in Strupp and Binder), but we will focus on these three. In general, these brief forms of psychoanalytic psychotherapy are utilized with relatively "more healthy" clients, that is, clients who may have some significant symptom, but whose functioning in general is relatively adequate. Other brief psychodynamic approaches include those of Davanloo, Mann, and Malan (reviewed in Strupp & Binder, 1984). Among the virtues of these approaches is that all have been presented as psychotherapy treatment manuals. This relatively recent innovation in writing about psychotherapy developed because of the need to standardize treatment for purposes of doing research on psychotherapy. The treatment manuals are more concrete and specific in describing treatment than many other writings on psychoanalysis.

Supportive-Expressive Therapy

Luborsky's supportive-expressive psychoanalytically oriented therapy is based on the assumption that a core conflictual relationship theme (CCRT) is at the center of a person's problems. This relationship theme developed from early childhood experiences, but the client is unaware of it and its relation to childhood experiences. Therapy is oriented toward increasing the client's awareness of the theme. It is assumed that the client will have better control over behavior if she knows more about what she is doing at the unconscious level. This knowledge is acquired through reliving childhood experiences. Interpretations must be done only with strands of the CCRT that are close to awareness and not heavily defended against in the therapeutic moment. As we have said, knowledge alone does not change previously unconscious wishes and needs. However, it does lead to an increased ability to master and control them consciously. Luborsky says that the change "may be considered to have enabled the person to function at a higher level of organization" (1984, p. 21). The transference relationship is important in that the CCRT will probably be lived out and enacted in relationship to the therapist. A supportive, empathic relationship is considered crucial, and Luborsky speculates that compared to the acquisition of insight, the relationship may be the more potent therapeutic factor.

Luborsky's supportive-expressive psychotherapy begins with a "socialization interview" in which the client is told how psychotherapy proceeds, what is expected of the client, and what the therapist will do. In the initial, supportive phase of therapy, the therapist attempts to listen nonjudgmentally, demonstrate acceptance and understanding, support defenses and activities that bolster positive functioning, and encourage a "we" feeling. In the expressive phase, the therapist is more active: listening, responding, and listening further.

Time-Limited Dynamic Therapy

What is common to Strupp and Binder's time-limited dynamic therapy approach and to most brief forms of psychodynamic therapy is that it focuses on dysfunctional interpersonal relationship patterns, as opposed to early childhood sexual and aggressive wishes. Time-limited dynamic therapy is based on the assumption that earlier difficulties with significant others have given rise to patterns of interpersonal relatedness that originally served a self-protective function but are now anachronistic, self-defeating, and maladaptive. Central to these problems are deficiencies in self-esteem, the inability to form satisfying interpersonal relationships that gratify the person's needs for closeness, and interferences with autonomous adult functioning (Strupp & Binder, 1984, pp. xiii–xiv).

In childhood, the person experiences a disturbed pattern of interpersonal relationships, from which he develops organizing themes that form a rigid, habitual way of construing and acting in current relationships. These patterns are hidden from the self because of "the ubiquitous human tendency to hide from oneself painful experiences and their aftermath" (Strupp & Binder, 1984, p. 32). The client unconsciously believes these patterns will bring him security and nurturance in current relationships. Relationships are defensively distorted in order to protect the self as the person strives to achieve these primitive, unconscious forms of intimacy. Time-limited dynamic therapy attempts to identify and concentrate on these "focal issues."

Strupp and Binder believe that these central relationship issues will manifest themselves in the therapeutic relationship and that reexperiencing them in the transference relationship will be therapeutic. The therapist attempts to help the client become aware of the symbolic meanings of his behavior, but this needs to be done when "an appropriate affective context exists" (1984, p. 136). At the same time, intellectual reconstruction of the past is deemphasized. In fact, Strupp and Binder assume that it is impossible to really recover the past. The most important quality of a therapeutic relationship is that it is a human one. Learning occurs not through acquisition of abstract knowledge, but "rather it is the result of a human experience in which he or she feels understood and in which this understanding is given new meanings" (1984, p. 45). While it is true that transference involves bringing past relationships into the current, therapeutic relationship, Strupp and Binder assume that the client's feelings toward the therapist also include some real aspects of the here-and-now relationship. The therapist is to use her own feelings as signals of how the client is attempting to structure their relationship. Empathic listening is important, and the therapist is encouraged to engage in honest self-disclosure if necessary and appropriate.

Interpersonal Psychotherapy

Interpersonal psychotherapy had its roots in the interpersonal psychodynamic theory of Harry Stack Sullivan. It was first developed for work with depression, and emphasizes the importance of disturbed interpersonal relationships in the genesis of depression. There is some research to support this supposition, such as evidence that shows the relationship of depression to marital problems and as the genesis of psychological disorder. What is different about this approach from other psychodynamic approaches is that it emphasizes current difficulties as well as childhood difficulties in interpersonal relationships as the cause of depression. There are four major types of interpersonal problems: grief over some kind of loss, role disputes (such as between husband and wife), role transitions (such as getting married, having a child, retiring), and interpersonal deficits (lack of social skills).

Interpersonal psychotherapy is short term (12–16 sessions) and specifically addresses one or two of the four types of interpersonal problems. If the problem is grief, the therapist facilitates healthy mourning. If the problem is role disputes, the emphasis is on adaptive communication. If the problem is a role transition, again the focus is on mourning if loss is involved and on acquiring new skills for the new role. Finally, interpersonal deficits are addressed by helping individuals develop better communication skills. In essence, the interpersonal psychotherapy approach stresses the development of acceptance (for instance, through mourning loss), and the development of more adaptive communication and other skills. Thus, even though the approach has psychodynamic roots, the actual practice is an integrative form of psychodynamic talk therapy and cognitive-behavioral skills training. Interpersonal psychotherapy has empirical support for the treatment of depression (Gottlib & Schraedley, 2000).

Summing Up Recent Approaches

As we have pointed out, object relations therapy, self psychology, and the brief therapies have some common themes. First, they place greater emphasis on the curative power of the therapeutic relationship itself than does classical psychoanalysis. Second, they place less emphasis on change through insight and reconstruction of the past and more emphasis on change through reliving significant early childhood relationship issues in the context of therapy. Third, they allow the therapist to be more flexible than in classical analysis and encourage the therapist to provide empathy as a vehicle of therapeutic change and to use self-disclosure, when therapeutically appropriate, to help overcome resistance. Finally, all emphasize the importance of ruptures in interpersonal relationships as being the cause of psychological problems and the repairing of interpersonal relationship patterns as being the cure.

Evaluation of Relational Psychoanalytic Approaches

After a brief mention of psychotherapy research, our evaluation below primarily focuses on object relations theory and its hypotheses about early childhood and about self-representations in psychopathology. We particularly focus on the issue of the extent to which early childhood is foundational in influencing later development.

Research on Psychotherapy

A study we reviewed in the last chapter on intensive long-term psychoanalytic psychotherapy is specifically a study of object relations therapy. This study found evidence for its effectiveness for clients with personality disorders (Blatt & Ford, 1994). A combined interpersonal psychodynamic/humanistic approach has been shown to be effective with depression (Shapiro, 1995). In one study, brief psychodynamic therapy was shown to be effective with problems such as anxiety, depression, and interpersonal problems (Piper, Joyce, McCallum, & Azrin, 1998). A meta-analysis of research on brief psychodynamic psychotherapy approaches has shown them to be as effective as nonpsychodynamic approaches (Crits-Christoph, 1992) for a variety of problems. This latter is a particularly important finding in an era of brief therapy and managed care.

Research on Child Development

Both Freud's classical version of psychoanalysis and the modern relational approaches place a heavy emphasis on the impact of early childhood on the development of personality and psychopathology. Both adopt a "foundational view," that is, that early experiences form a strong or weak foundation for later development. In the previous chapter, we reviewed research findings suggesting that, in general, personality is not fixed in early childhood, and that many forms of psychopathology are influenced in important ways by here-and-now situational factors. In this section, we will take a closer look at development in the first few years of life. We first evaluate several aspects of Margaret Mahler's view of development. In so doing, we shall consider the work of Daniel Stern (1985). We then take a broader look at the impact of the first few years of life on later development, and in so doing, consider attachment theory.

Views on Mahler's Separation-Individuation Model of Development

Mahler held that during the first month of life the infant was in the stage of normal autism and lived in an "autistic shell," unresponsive to the outer world. We now know from a great deal of infant research that this is not true. Infants are highly responsive to the external world from birth on, and that capacity grows rapidly within the first few months of life.

More importantly, the idea that infants do not have a separate sense of self but instead experience themselves as fused with their mothers also does not appear to be true. To quote Ulric Neisser (1988), a cognitive scientist

> Certainly by 3 months of age (and probably from birth), the infant perceives much the same sort of world that we do: a world of distinct, solid, and permanent objects of which she herself (or he himself) is one. . . . The old hypothesis that a young infant cannot tell the difference between itself and the environment, or between itself and its mother can be decisively rejected. (p. 7)

Stern (1985), in an influential psychoanalytic view of child development, also has argued that evidence does not support the idea that infants ever confuse themselves with their mothers. Stern believes that everything we know about infants supports the idea that infants have a sense of self as a separate entity from near birth onward.

Stern argues that there are several different senses of self, and that they develop at different times. The most basic sense of self, that of the self as a physically distinct entity, which is the source of its own actions and experiences, develops very early, within the first few months. Later, around 18 months of age, the young child begins to develop the ability to think about herself in the form of concepts, and begins to develop a concept of self. Stern argues that it is at this level of the self that the things object relations theorists talk about might happen. That is, as the child begins to develop concepts about her own traits and characteristics, her own values and beliefs, the child might confuse her view of herself with her mother's views of her.

Stern further argues that the process of separation-individuation is not something that begins and ends in the first three years of life, but is something that people continue to work on and struggle with throughout their lives. Stern's work has also demonstrated how early childhood influences might persist into adulthood. Stern gives several examples of children's interactions with mothers who are acting dysfunctionally, and how these interactions might create enduring patterns. For instance, one mother persistently forced her child to look at her and engage in play when the child clearly was feeling overstimulated and was trying to avoid her. The result was a child who (a) hadn't learned how to terminate interactions that were stressful and overwhelming, and therefore (b) might enter interpersonal situations with an avoidant, defensive stance. In another case, the only way a young child could get his depressed mother to interact with him was by very actively pursuing and initiating contact. A few years later, this child was already a "social clown," trying to be the life of the party in social interactions.

In sum, Mahler's description of the developmental sequence of the child appears to have some flaws in it. Children do not appear to confuse themselves with their mothers at a basic level. Further, they are highly responsive to environmental stimulation even at birth. On the other hand, Daniel Stern's work provides models of how very early interactions with adult caretakers might establish long-standing dysfunctional relationship patterns.

Are Early Experiences Foundational in Creating Psychopathology?

There is a pervasive view in our culture, influenced by psychoanalytic views, that very early childhood (around the first two years of life) is of crucial importance in terms of later development. Presumably, early "damage" during this period can irrevocably harm the person (unless the person goes into therapy), creating serious personality problems in later life. Many object relations theorists, for instance, argue that borderline personality disorder results from damage occurring within the first two years of life, particularly at the rapprochement stage. To what degree is it true that very early experiences are generally foundational in this sense?

With respect to borderline personality disorder, Mahler (1971) herself concluded that parental conflict during the rapprochement period was not the primary cause of borderline personality disorder. She noted in the sample of subjects she had followed into adulthood someone who had become borderline even though the rapprochement period had been nonconflictual, and others who did not become borderline, despite having had highly conflictual rapprochement periods. In general, researchers now reject the idea that borderline personality disorder is a product of a specific developmental failure at a specific time of life in a specific process, such as separation-individuation (Marziali, 1992). The development of borderline personality disorder is a complex process involving constitutional, biological, and many environmental factors (Marziali, 1992).

Other research suggests that what happens during the first two years of life is not as inevitably foundational as object relations theorists suppose (Kagan, 1996). As we noted in chapter 6, researchers on child development now believe that no one developmental period is any more primary, foundational, or crucial in development than any other one. Kagan (1984) cites several studies that show that neglect within the first two years of life need not leave permanent damage if children later receive good supportive home environments. Gaensbauer and Harmon (1982) found that abused infants who were separated from their parents and placed with nurturing foster mothers were able to respond with considerable adaptability and resilience.

Werner and Smith (1982) followed a large sample of children from infancy into adulthood. They concluded, "As we watched these children grow from babyhood to adulthood, we could not help but respect the self-righting tendencies within them that produced normal development under all but the most persistently adverse circumstances" (p. 159, as quoted in Kagan, 1996).

What this means is that the idea that early events create a kind of damage to internal psychological structures that then persists relatively unchanged unless modified by intensive psychotherapy is not necessarily true. Other evidence shows that problems in childhood do not necessarily continue into adulthood. Several researchers have looked at the issue of whether pathology in childhood portends pathology in adulthood. Their conclusion is that neurotic and adjustment disorders do not portend psychological difficulty in adulthood, whether or not the child has had therapy (Cass & Thomas, 1979; Dohrenwend, Dohrenwend, Gould, Link, Neugebauer, & Wunsch-Hitzig, 1980; Eme, 1979). For instance, Dohrenwend and his colleagues conclude that "most neurotic children become normal adults" (p. 23).

On the other hand, while negative early experiences may not inevitably doom a child to later problems, there is considerable research suggesting that it can increase the probability. Some research (Garmazy, 1986; Weintraub, Winters, & Neale, 1986) has also found that depression in the parent affects the development of the child. Block, Block, and Keyes (1988) found that low ego control at ages three to four predicted marijuana use at age 14. Abuse experiences have particularly been associated with the development of at least some borderline personality disorders (Briere, 1989; Links, 1992; Marziali, 1992), as well as with the development of a variety of other problems (Briere, 1989). Briere has argued that the symptoms of borderline personality disorder, such as impulsiveness; inability to form stable, lasting relationships; lack of a stable, organized identity; and so on, are natural consequences of living through the terrifying experience of having been sexually abused.

Similarly, in one study of girls raised in institutions, Rutter (1986, p. 8) found that "adverse experiences in childhood were associated with substantially worse psychosocial outcomes in early adult life." However, Rutter also found that "marriage to . . . a well-functioning man who provided a supportive relationship was associated with a marked improvement in functioning. Good experiences in adult life can lead to important psychosocial gains." The loss of a parent can predispose a child to depression in adulthood. However, Rutter suggests that the long-term effects of a death on a child

> probably stem as much from factors consequent upon the death as from the death itself. These other factors include such hazards as the break-up of the home, frequent changes of caretaker, changes in family roles, financial and material disadvantage, the effects of bereavement on the surviving parent, and the arrival of a stepparent.

Thus, the loss may affect development because it creates a continuous envelope of adverse experiences, such as family and financial instability.

Research on attachment theory (which is extensive—a search for articles in journals of the American Psychological Association alone turned up over 100 for just the years 2000–2005) shows a relationship between early experience and later development. There are ways of measuring whether the mother has formed a secure or insecure attachment bond with the infant (Main, 1996). There are also ways of measuring how adults form attachment bonds (Main, 1996). Overall, studies have shown correlations between being insecurely attached to the mother in infancy and later problems in social relationships as well as in academic performance in elementary school. For instance, Moss and St.-Laurent (2001) found that children who were securely attached to their mothers at age six had higher scores on communication, cognitive engagement, and mastery motivation at age eight than insecurely attached children. Schneider, Atkinson, and Tardif (2001) reviewed 63 studies and concluded that securely attached children had better peer relationships. Crowell, Treboux, and Waters (2002) measured the attachment style of adults before they entered into marriage. Seventy-eight percent later showed that attachment style in their marriages. Other research has shown that the attachment style of parents, measured before they have children, predicts the kind of attachments parents form with their children (Steele, Steele, & Fonagy, 1996).

Of particular interest is the *disorganized* attachment style exhibited by some children (Main, 1996). These children exhibit disorganized and confused behavior when attempts are made to assess their attachment to their mother. This style is associated with parental abuse. These children are at the highest risk for psychological problems (Main, 1996). Not only are these children affected psychologically, their physiology shows signs of having been negatively impacted. They are also at a higher risk for dissociation (Liotti, 2004).

Thus, there is evidence that insecure attachments in infancy may be associated with later problems. However, we once again caution that early childhood experiences do not doom children to later problems. For instance, although Schneider et al. (2001) found that insecure attachments to the mother were associated with later problems relating to peers, the relationship was only small to moderate; that is, many children who have such insecure attachments do not turn out to have later problems relating to peers.

In sum, negative childhood experiences are implicated in the genesis of psychopathology. However, negative early experiences do not necessarily leave indelible marks that are not erasable without intensive therapy. To the contrary, there is evidence that children are resilient and that as long as they get good support and parenting somewhere along the line, early damage can often be repaired. Overall, the genesis of both personality and most forms of psychopathology is probably a complex process that involves many experiences over time and does not generally appear to be the product of specific events or interactions at specific times.

Object Relations Theory, Self-Representations, and Psychopathology

Object relations theory holds that psychopathology is a result of disturbed representations of self in relation to others, and that this results from negative childhood experiences. There is some evidence supporting the object relational idea that individuals diagnosed as having a borderline personality disorder do have less complex and less developed internal representations of people than do "normal" individuals (Westen, Lohr, Silk, Gold, & Kerber, 1990) and that having less complex and less developed internal representations of people is associated with pathogenic developmental experiences such as neglect and abuse (Westen, Ludolph, Block, Wixom, & Wiss, 1990).

Similarly, Blatt and Wild (1976) reviewed studies suggesting that individuals with less well-developed boundary concepts exhibit more psychopathology. Boundary concepts have to do with the ability to tell where one object begins and another leaves off (e.g., be able to tell where the self begins and the other person leaves off). For instance, Blatt and Ritzler (1974) measured boundary disturbances with the Rorschach inkblot test. They found that schizophrenics with more severe disturbances exhibited greater difficulties in reality testing.

Silverman and Weinberger (1985) report on research in which the sentence "Mommy and I are one" was presented to subjects at a speed so rapid that it was subliminal (not producing a sensation that is consciously perceived). In a series of studies this subliminal perception was found to reduce psychopathological symptoms and to improve performance on mathematics tests. In one study (Palmatier & Bornstein, 1980), smokers receiving behavior therapy were broken into two groups. One group received several subliminal exposures to the "Mommy and I are one" message in addition to the behavior therapy. This group had a much higher rate of maintaining abstinence from smoking than the group that did not receive this message. Similar results have been found with treatment of a variety of other disorders (see Silverman & Weinberger, 1985, pp. 1, 301).

In sum, there is evidence supporting the object relational hypothesis of disturbed representations of self in relation to others in individuals with psychological problems.

In Conclusion

Relational approaches to psychoanalysis have revolutionized psychoanalytic theory and have had significant influence on nonpsychoanalytic theory. The idea that psychological problems occur at least in part because of disturbed interpersonal relationships is widely accepted. Interpersonal approaches provide models of relationships and self-development in childhood that help clinicians develop detailed descriptions of adult pathology. Many therapists in practice find that such conceptualizations help them, particularly with difficult, "personality-disordered" clients (Tobin, 1990). Underlying these formulations are attempts to outline the emotional conflicts and tempests involved in primary relationships with the self and others, and interpersonal psychoanalytic accounts vividly capture these conflicts and tempests. Attachment theory in particular has become and will continue to be an important theory in the study of child development, and ongoing research on that theory holds promise of helping us to understand just how early relationships may affect adult psychopathology.

Relational approaches have facilitated the development of brief forms of psychodynamic therapy. These forms rely on identifying problematic interpersonal themes in an individual's life. The presence of these themes can also be looked for in the transference relationship with the therapist. Identification of such a "core conflictual relationship theme" (Luborsky, 1984) helps focus the therapist's efforts. Research currently supports the effectiveness of brief forms of psychodynamic therapy.

The focus on interpersonal relationships has also led to the development of other new, psychodynamic theories, which we did not have space to review in this chapter. These include approaches such as the work of the Mount Zion group (Weiss, Sampson, & The Mount Zion Psychotherapy Research Group, 1986) who hold that clients in therapy engage in unconscious "testing" to try to undo dysfunctional beliefs learned in early childhood, and Horowitz's (1987) "states of mind" model, which holds that at any given moment, our behavior is guided by the state of mind we are in, and that state of mind is made up of internal models of ourselves in relationships. Wachtel's (1997) integrative cyclical psychodynamic theory (reviewed in chapter 14) also fits into this group.

Relational models have also brought psychodynamic thinking closer to other approaches. Their emphasis on the development of internal models of the self and of relationships brings them close to cognitive theories. Their focus on the here-and-now relationship in therapy brings them close to humanistic theories. And self psychology's focus on the mutual relationship between therapist and client brings that theory closer to systems theories (chapter 13) and feminist theories (chapter 15). As such, relational psychodynamic theories are having an impact on nonpsychoanalytic approaches and appear to be the wave of the future in psychodynamic theorizing.

CLIENT- AND PERSON-CENTERED THERAPIES

I had been working with a highly intelligent mother whose boy was something of a hellion. The problem was clearly her early rejection of the boy, but over many interviews I could not help her to this insight. I drew her out, I gently pulled together the evidence she had given, trying to help her see the pattern. But we got nowhere. Finally, I gave up. I told her that it seemed we had both tried, but we had failed, and that we might as well give up our contacts. She agreed. So we concluded the interview, shook hands, and she walked to the door of the office. Then she turned and asked, "Do you ever take adults for counseling here?" When I replied in the affirmative, she said, "Well then, I would like some help." She came to the chair she had left, and began to pour out her despair about her marriage, her troubled relationship with her husband, her sense of failure and confusion, all very different from the sterile "case history" she had given before. Real therapy began then, and ultimately it was very successful.

This incident was one of a number which helped me to experience the fact . . . that it is the client who knows what hurts, what directions to go, what problems are crucial, what experiences have been deeply buried. It began to occur to me that unless I had a need to demonstrate my own cleverness and learning, I would do better to rely upon the client for the direction of movement in the process.

—C. R. Rogers, *On Becoming a Person*

Rogers's method brought it home that the decisions a person must make are inherently that person's own. No book knowledge enables another person to decide for anyone. That goes for life decisions and life-style as well as, moment by moment, what to talk about, feel into, struggle with. Another person might make a guess, but ultimately personal growth is from the inside outward. A process of change begins and moves in ways even the person's own mind cannot direct, let alone another person's mind.

—E. T. Gendlin, "The Politics of Giving Therapy Away"

The insights and conclusions above capture the "prime directive" of the client-centered approach to psychotherapy, an approach that falls under the broader category of the existential-humanistic approach. The existential-humanistic perspective places the most emphasis on the person as the author of his own life. The client-centered approach originated with Carl Rogers with the publication of his book, *Counseling and Psychotherapy*, in 1942. In later years, Rogers and his colleagues began to broaden the application of client-centered principles from psychotherapy to areas such as education, medicine, and organizational psychology. In the last few years of his life, Rogers devoted his efforts to the promotion of world peace by facilitating group encounters between warring factions in different countries, such as between Blacks and Whites in South Africa, and Protestants and Catholics in Northern Ireland. With the expansion of client-centered ideas to areas other than psychotherapy, Rogers renamed his approach ***person-centered***. The person-centered philosophy has since spawned several new approaches to psychotherapy.

In this chapter, we shall consider client-centered theory and the practice of client-centered therapy. In the next chapter we will consider two of the offshoots of client-centered therapy and the person-centered approach: those of Eugene Gendlin's (1996) "focusing-oriented psychotherapy" and the emotion-focused psychotherapy of Leslie Greenberg, Robert Elliott, and their colleagues (Greenberg, Rice, & Elliott, 1993; Elliott, Watson, Goldman, & Greenberg, 2004).

Client-Centered Therapy: Model of the Person

The fundamental concept of client-centered therapy is to respect and facilitate the self-propelled and self-generated growth process in the individual. Perhaps it is easier to explain this by describing what a traditional client-centered therapist does not do. First, the therapist does not give specific advice about solving problems ("Why don't you try being honest with her?"). Second, the therapist does not give general advice on strategies for living ("You should live in the here and now"). Third, the therapist does not judge or condemn ("It is all right to get angry with your mother"; "You are a bad person for having gotten drunk"). Fourth, the therapist does not label ("You are a psychotic"). Fifth, the therapist does not develop a treatment plan for the client ("First we will work on your lack of assertiveness, then on your anxiety"). Sixth, the therapist does not interpret the meaning of the client's experience ("You are not really angry at me; you are really angry at your father").

The fundamental concept, that the therapist is to respect and facilitate the self-propelled growth process in the individual, is based on two premises. The first premise is that there are many possible personal realities. No one is in a position to judge someone else's reality as being less correct, more distorted, or less adequate than someone else's reality (Rogers, 1980). The second premise is that if the personal reality of an individual is respected by others and a basic trust is demonstrated toward that person, then a self-propelled growth process will move in a positive, life-affirming direction.

Multiple Realities

Most people believe that somewhere "out there" is "a" reality, and ultimately there is one correct way of viewing it. For instance, most of us would agree with the Freudian view that people misperceive and distort reality from time to time. Certainly we would think that a person who thought that people on television talk shows were secretly talking about him or who saw things no one else did was distorting reality.

At the same time, most people are aware that there are different ways of experiencing reality. Is there, for instance, a "correct" way of experiencing anchovy pizza? We are personally convinced that those who like anchovy pizza are distorting reality, but they would probably say the same about us. It is clear that people accept differences in tastes in music, clothing, and food and in preferences for hobbies, choice of careers, and so on.

Furthermore, different cultures have different ideas about how people should live. Although they may accept differences within limits, they do have ideas about what is appropriate, or correct, in different settings. For instance, there are very few settings in our culture in which it is correct, or even acceptable, to be nude. The list of "correct" and "incorrect" ways to live is quite extensive and includes both moral and legal rules. Thus, people recognize that there are variations in how individuals experience certain aspects of reality, but they believe that everyone should experience some aspects the same way, the "correct" way. If someone does not perceive or experience one of these aspects in that way, the person is said to be "distorting" reality or "out of touch" with reality. Many of Freud's notions are based on this idea. For instance, the concept of transference assumes that patients distort their perceptions of the psychoanalyst by transferring onto the analyst feelings they had toward their parents. The defense mechanisms are also Freudian concepts that include the idea of distortion or misperception of reality. Cognitive therapy (see chapter 11) also includes the idea that client problems are based on distortion of reality. A person's depression may be a result of overfocusing on the negative, for instance.

Rogers argued that there are ***multiple realities.*** To believe that someone is out of touch with reality or is distorting it is to believe that there is a correct way of viewing reality. Rogers believed that reality is relative to each person's point of view, and therefore there is no possible way for any human to determine which is the "correct" view, if indeed there is a correct view. Rogers was a "constructivist" (we discuss constructivism in more detail in chapter 15).

This premise sounds simple, but it can lead to disturbing questions. Must we respect the reality of a Hitler? What about a woman who believed her child was possessed by the devil and threw her out of a tenth-story window? To deal with this issue, we will turn to Rogers's second premise.

The Meaning of Acceptance

What about respecting the reality of a Hitler or the woman who killed her child? If we trust the experience of all clients, could the therapist not end up supporting and facilitating murder, child abuse, rape, robbery, or other acts most of us see as negative? Rogers's (1967) answer to this is that the self-actualization or growth process is positive. "I find it significant that when individuals are prized as persons, the values they select do not run the full gamut of possibilities. I do not find, in such a climate of freedom, that a person comes to value fraud and murder and thievery" (p. 26). Rogers asserted that individuals who are prized and trusted will naturally choose "prosocial" values. He believed that there was an internal process, called the actualization process, which would unfold in positive, prosocial directions *if* given the proper interpersonal conditions.

Rogers believed that accepting and trusting others leads to their showing concern and care for other people as well as their own self-actualization. What does it mean to prize, trust, or accept another's experience? Does this mean the therapist should agree with the way clients view the world, or support and positively reinforce any behavior? What if the therapist disagrees with a client's views and sees his behavior as destructive?

For Rogers, to accept or trust another's reality does not mean to agree with it or approve of it. It means to acknowledge nonjudgmentally that it is what the other actually perceives. Put another way, an accepting attitude means listening nonjudgmentally. A client who has been labeled paranoid schizophrenic by a hospital medical staff may say that the police are always following him around in helicopters and that he is planning to retaliate by blowing up the police station. Does acceptance mean saying "I agree with you. Go to it"? No. It means acknowledging that the client really does experience the police as out to get him. Wanting to blow up the police station is a logical (but not reasonable!) outcome of the way the client is experiencing the world. Either agreeing with the client or telling him that he is wrong or crazy would be making a judgment. But as the therapist does not agree that the police are out to get the client and certainly does not want him to blow up the police station, what does she do? Rogers distinguished between accepting another's way of experiencing the world and accepting his behavior. A parent can accept and understand a child's desire to stick her finger in a flame (it is bright, it is pretty, the child is curious), while certainly not allowing the child to go through with the act. Thus, one can respect and accept another's experience of the world while not supporting or encouraging certain behaviors that might flow from it. An example of a lack of acceptance would be a parent who not only stops a child from putting her finger in the flame but also tells the child she is wrong or bad for even wanting to do this.

A therapist might want to go further than restraining destructive behavior and express disagreement with the client's experiencing. How is this done? Eugene Gendlin (1967) suggests that therapists can express a viewpoint if they offer it as their own. They would not say, "You are wrong" or "You are crazy for seeing the police as dangerous," but they might say, "I don't agree with you. I don't see the police as out to get you." The latter way of expressing a viewpoint implies a respect for and acknowledgment of the client's perspective that the former does not.

In sum, the prime directive of client-centered therapy is to accept and respect the experience of the client. This means acknowledging that there are multiple ways of viewing reality. Acceptance requires neither approval of the client's perspective or actions nor agreement with them.

Because of his emphasis on respecting the worldview of each individual client, Rogers was against labels. He preferred that the therapist relate to the client as another person rather than as a "schizophrenic" or an "obsessive-compulsive." Psychiatric labels carry the implication that there is something "wrong" with the person (e.g., a "borderline personality disorder"). In addition to being judgmental, labels tend to pigeonhole and categorize. Therefore, they may blind the therapist to the uniqueness of the individual.

Personal Constructs and Values

Personal constructs is a term borrowed from George Kelly (1955). Kelly's idea was that people organize their lives in terms of their constructs, or concepts, about people, events, and even physical reality. Values can be considered a subset of constructs that have a positive or negative component. People have private values—about what constitutes attractive physical appearance and how important physical appearance is; moral values—about killing, telling the truth, and stealing; and conventional values—about being a good member of society, driving on the right side of the road, wearing clothes in public. Examples of personal constructs and values are: (a) I tend to be a hardworking person (a construct about the self); (b) I believe Carl Rogers's ideas about human nature are wrong; (c) That person is a rat! (d) People who don't look at you while they are talking are trying to hide something; (e) It is wrong to feel angry toward one's parents.

Congruent with his belief in multiple realities, Rogers believed it is important that people hold their personal constructs and values tentatively. He said that in the early stages of therapy "personal constructs are rigid, and unrecognized as being constructs, but are thought of as facts" (1961, p. 134), but later, "the ways in which experience is construed are much loosened" (1961, p. 141). Finally, in the highest stage of development, "personal constructs are tentatively reformulated, to be validated against further experience, but even then, to be held loosely" (1961, p. 153).

To put it another way, Rogers seemed to be advocating that people act like good scientists in regard to their personal beliefs and treat personal constructs as hypotheses, rather than as fixed, objective facts. Values and beliefs about themselves and others are all to be treated as imperfect formulations about reality. As with scientific theories, they may be mistaken, and people must be open to challenging even their most deeply held values if they run into experiences that call them into question. This does not mean one cannot be committed to a set of values or personal constructs, just as scientists may be committed to a point of view but still hold open the possibility that future experience may prove them wrong.

To hold personal constructs tentatively means to move away from rigid, absolute "shoulds" (Rogers, 1961, p. 168). If individuals see their values as fixed, unchanging facts, then they must follow them. They have no choice. Rogers wanted people to choose their values on the basis of what makes sense to them, not to adopt values because some authority said that is how one should be. He wanted individuals to challenge and test their values to see if they make sense. Chosen values lose their "should-like" quality; they become something the person wants to do because they make sense to the person. Rogers believed values are meaningful only if so chosen.

Process Orientation

Rogers saw fully functioning individuals as being ***process oriented:*** they see life as a process of becoming and they focus on doing. People are creatures whose nature is characterized by change, which means that the fully functioning person is continually open to the reevaluation of values, goals, and attitudes about life. In this regard, the individual does not even have a fixed "self." As the individual grows and changes, more complex, differentiated, and organized forms of self-organization evolve. In some important sense, you are not the same person you were when you were 14 years old, and your attitudes, values, and self-concept have undergone some alteration to reflect this change. Of course, there are probably also many continuities. For instance, perhaps you valued achievement at age 14 and still do. But your view of what achievement is has probably altered (perhaps from being a rock star or a famous athlete to getting a good job as a psychologist). Further, you have probably been learning to coordinate your striving for achievement with other aims and goals (such as maintaining a relationship, or pursuing a personally meaningful avocation such as music or drama). Therefore, while you are still "the same" in many ways, you are also different.

A process orientation also involves focusing attention on the doing of things rather than on their outcomes (Rogers, 1961, p. 171). Being overly focused on the outcome of actions can lead to excessive preoccupation with self-evaluation. People are inclined to evaluate themselves in terms of success or failure: "I am a good person" if I succeed; "I am a bad person" if I fail. This excessive preoccupation with evaluation draws attention away from the process of doing and prevents people from investing all their energies in the doing of the activity. Paradoxically, by focusing on how well they are succeeding, they may increase their odds of failure. This does not mean they do not have to try to do things well. For instance, to play a guitar, you have to finger the right chords. But if you are worried about the final outcome, that is, whether you will be judged a success or a failure, you are actually drawing attention away from the doing (from the moment-to-moment business of fingering the right chords), and as a result, you may do poorly. From Rogers's perspective, people should focus on what they did "wrong" not to evaluate (I was bad) but instead to learn how to improve.

People who are overly concerned about the outcomes of their actions are probably concerned with whether they are good or bad people. To ask whether "I am good or bad" or whether "I have good traits or bad traits" is to treat yourself as if you have a fixed self. From a Rogerian perspective, it is no better to have a fixed positive self-concept than to have a fixed negative self-concept. Fully functioning individuals have no fixed beliefs about themselves at all and in this sense may not even think about their "self" at all. In other words, if you never worry about whether your successes or failures mean you are good or bad and if you focus on how you are doing this task at this moment, then you are concerned with learning from your success or failure, not with whether you are good or bad.

Internality, Authority, and Individualism

Rogers's emphasis on individual views of reality led him to reject authority. No one possesses the correct answers as to how others should live their lives. This includes parents, the school system, society at large, and religion. Does this mean people should not ever listen to authority? No. But they should not accept what authorities say simply because they are the authorities. People must always take responsibility for listening to and evaluating any idea, no matter what its source, to see if it makes sense to them. Adopting an idea only because a teacher, parent, religious leader, or therapist says it is so may lead to conflict between the adopted value and what a person feels. Fully functioning individuals are autonomous, self-directed, and congruent; that is, their behavior arises from a chosen set of values that are in accord with their perceptions and experience.

Some client-centered therapists have argued that Rogers's emphasis on individualism and autonomy is a reflection of Western, masculine values and is not in keeping with the values of many other cultures in the world, or with the values and experience of females in Western culture (Holdstock, 1990; O'Hara, 1992). These writers are part of a trend that argues that Western psychology's emphasis on the importance of individualism, autonomy, self-direction, having firm self-boundaries, directing oneself from within, and being separate reflects certain cultural values rather than reflecting truth about the nature of human beings. They point out that in many other cultures, the boundary of the self is fluid, is not fixed where the individual's body ends, and often extends to include one's family and even one's social group. In many cultures "I" am my family or my group. Behavior is a product of a field of forces, of which the individual is a part, rather than emerging primarily from processes within the individual. These authors would argue that being influenced by others is a natural part of being human. One's sense of self is intimately linked to one's relationships, and the idea of a separate, autonomous self may be a myth. For them, freedom to be oneself would mean finding oneself within the matrix of one's relationships with others, rather than by separating oneself from such a matrix.

This view paradoxically fits with other aspects of Rogers's views while contradicting his emphasis on individuality and autonomy. Rogers held a "field" view of human functioning, and Rogers himself certainly believed that optimal functioning included care and respect for the uniqueness and empowerment of all people. That is, he believed that people's behavior arose from a field of forces (see the related views of Gestalt therapy in chapter 9, and systems theory in chapter 13), of which factors inside the person are only a part. Yet, in his desire to support and respect the uniqueness of individuals, he sometimes wrote as if we could completely separate ourselves from the influence of others.

To put these ideas together, some modern person-centered theorists would hold that becoming oneself only has meaning when it happens in the context of continuous dialogue, with interaction with, and concern and respect for others. The trick is to "be oneself" and be interrelated with others, to be both "I" and "We" at the same time.

Experiencing

As noted above, the fully functioning person holds constructs tentatively, does not adopt them just because they are offered by an authority, and continually evaluates them against his or her own experience to see if they make sense. But what is this "experience" against which values and constructs are checked?

You may have heard that it is good to "get in touch with feelings." Often, client-centered therapy is seen as emphasizing this process, and one of the techniques of client-centered therapy is called ***reflection of feelings,*** in which the therapist mirrors back to the client the therapist's understanding of the client's subjective experience. Yet actually, it is more accurate to say that client-centered therapists want us to "listen to our experience."

Freud was the first to point out that an affective component seems to be necessary for psychotherapy to work. This is not surprising, since problems are frequently based on the fact that bodily or emotive responses are incongruent with intellectual beliefs. You may feel like eating, though intellectually you decide you should lose weight. Or you might intellectually decide it would be good for you to study, but you find yourself wanting to watch TV. Since the bodily or affective level seems to be so integrally involved in personal problems, it is not surprising that psychotherapy must involve it in some way. Clearly, if we were able to decide intellectually what was good for us and always and easily put it into operation, few therapists would be needed (see chapter 14). But exactly how the emotive or bodily component plays a role in psychotherapy and mental health is open to debate. For Freud, it was a matter of "getting in touch with" primitive childhood fantasies that carry an emotional charge. In other therapies, such as primal therapy (Janov, 1970), it is a matter of getting in touch with a buried reservoir of pain and then expressing and discharging it. In many existential or humanistic approaches, it is a matter of "getting in touch with feelings," which means being willing to acknowledge and label one's anger, sadness, or fear.

Client-centered therapy, based primarily on Gendlin's theory of ***experiencing*** (Gendlin, 1969), has a somewhat different view of the role of the affective component. Experiencing is a broader construct than "emotion." People are said to experience feelings. The goal of client-centered therapy is to help clients become able to experience feelings and to listen to their experience. In the process of experiencing a feeling, it is more important to listen to the experience of the feeling than to the feeling itself.

Experiential Knowing

What is experience? That's a difficult question, and perhaps we can begin to answer it by appealing to your "experience." Let us break down "knowing," or acquiring knowledge, into two components. The first is intellectual and verbal. This is the kind of knowing you are engaged in right now. You are reading words and thinking about what they mean. The second kind of knowing is experiential. This is knowing that seems more visceral, gut level, sensory, and nonverbal. The difference is not hard to illustrate. Reading a description of being kissed romantically is not the same as experiencing being kissed romantically. There is a kind of "knowing" about being kissed romantically that is beyond what can be conveyed in words. In fact, if one were to try to describe what it feels like to be kissed romantically, the words would come from the experience. They are attempts to verbally encode the experience and, as such, they can never do more than convey part of it. What one knows about being kissed romantically at an experiential level will always be more than one can put into words.

The nonverbal, bodily way of knowing includes the processing of sensory and muscular information. Emotions are bodily events and may be particularly important guides to bodily ways of knowing. However, we know more things in an experiential or bodily way than emotions. We can know how we feel, but we also know how things taste, how some things feel when we touch them, and how it feels to know how to play a musical instruments.

If you were asked to describe what it feels like to be kissed romantically, you would probably try to describe the bodily sensations that are associated with the experience. You might use metaphors and analogies: "It feels like you are melting for a moment," "It feels like two parts being joined together," "There is a sense of quickening, or excitement, a sense of letting go." Similarly, in describing being rejected, you might say, "It feels like I was kicked in the gut" or "It feels like I was thrown out the door." Again, you are using metaphorical language to try to "capture" that set of bodily sensations that were your experience of being rejected.

"Getting in touch with feelings" for a client-centered therapist, then, means listening to and trying to capture the felt meanings of experience. It does not mean identifying emotions, though that may be a useful route into experiential knowing. More important is the nonverbal sense of what objects and events are felt as meaning. If you feel loved, that probably includes a whole set of experiences you have shared with the person who you feel loves you. If you feel anger, that is because you are experiencing the interaction with another person as anger provoking. Thus, paying attention to feelings is important because they are an indication of how you are experiencing a particular situation or relationship.

What is true for each individual is what that individual knows experientially. This does not mean it is objectively true or experientially true for other people. For instance, you may know that you experience eating anchovy pizza as unpleasant, even if it is judged good by others. Since there is little societal pressure to like anchovy pizza, you are allowed to "follow your own feelings" in the matter. But what happens when an individual's experiential sense disagrees with something society holds to be objectively true and seems to care about? For instance, what if your experiential sense is that you care little about financial success, but society says you should care about it and evaluates you on the basis of it? Rogers seemed to believe that people will be affected more by their experiential sense than by their intellectual beliefs. If they do not actually "follow" their experiential sense, they will still be influenced by it in experiencing conflict between it and what they think they "should" do.

Did Rogers believe that people should always follow their experiential sense? Remember, this is different from emotions. For instance, if I am feeling anger, does that mean I should express or act out my anger? No. To experience anger means to experience a situation as anger provoking. If I experience the situation as anger provoking, does that mean it is anger provoking? Again, the answer is no. That is certainly how I am construing the situation at an experiential level, but that does not necessarily mean my construction of the situation is objectively true. Yet, at the same time, I have little control over my experiencing the situation that way. The crucial thing is to listen to it. While it may be inaccurate in an objective sense, it is nevertheless how I am experiencing the situation at a gut level. Furthermore, it may be correct, because I may have picked up cues from the situation at a gut level of which I was not consciously aware.

Listening means trying to capture the meaning of experience. For instance, you might say, "I feel you dislike me." There are some psychologists who would say that such a statement is inaccurate. Rather, you should say, "I think you dislike me." However, to say "I feel you dislike me" is to say that your experience around this person is like your experience around people who have later proven to dislike you. And you may experience this even though intellectually you have no evidence that this person dislikes you. You could express this as "I think you like me, but I feel as if you don't."

It is against this experiential sense of things that the individual's personal constructs are to be checked to see if they "make sense." While Rogers did not claim that a person's experiential sense is always correct, he did believe that dialogue between the conceptual and experiential levels was necessary. These two levels are different, equally valuable "voices" or perspectives, and both need to be listened to and integrated to make the best possible decisions for the self. A person may be able to resolve incongruence by listening to the experiential level to try to grasp the meanings implicit in it. Gendlin suggests that such a process leads ultimately to an integration of the intellectual and experiential in regard to whatever issue is at hand.

Psychopathology

From the client-centered perspective, psychopathology occurs when individuals do not hold constructs tentatively, do not listen to experience, and, as a result, are not able to creatively grow and change. When individuals are functioning optimally and encounter a problem, failure, or a personal setback, they are able to listen to their experience, search for what is new or different in this situation compared to their old constructs, and use that information to creatively learn and evolve. In other words, they are able to function more intelligently, and both Zimring (1990) and Van Balen (1990) have argued that client-centered therapy works by helping individuals function more intelligently.

When people proceed dysfunctionally, they are unable to listen to their experience, and so cannot discern what is new and different in this situation, and therefore cannot learn and form creative new ways of dealing with life's problems. This happens because such people experience incongruence between what they think ought to be and what they experience. Ultimately, all forms of psychopathology—anxiety, depression, alcoholism, rigid behavior, psychotic episodes—result from such incongruence.

Thus, psychopathology results from not accepting or listening to that important source of information about how one finds oneself in the world—one's experience. The case of Janet is an example. Janet appeared to be distant, unemotional, and unfriendly. She was planning to be a doctor. Then, one day she was very different. She was friendly and warm. She said that she had finally admitted to herself that she did not want to be a doctor and had changed her major to art. From a Rogerian perspective, Janet had adopted the ideal that she should be a doctor. In order to pursue this goal, she had consistently denied her own feelings and her own experiential sense of what she enjoyed, what felt meaningful to her. It affected her whole personality.

The above should not be construed to mean that you should never take a class that you find boring. Even though a class may be boring, it might be experientially meaningful to take it anyway, because you know at a feeling level that the class fits your goals. Rather, you should pay attention to the experience of a class as boring to see what it means. Does it mean that this class is boring, or is it that you are feeling bored with the whole field? If it is the latter, you may wish to reevaluate your career goals.

Why do people not listen to their experience? Rogers said that this occurs because in childhood, people are taught that their acceptance or worth as individuals is dependent on their meeting someone else's standards. Children are born with a primitive and undifferentiated ***organismic valuing process*** through which they directly experience what is meaningful or life-enhancing for them. The valuing process will grow and differentiate if children are allowed to stay in touch with it. However, parents and schools teach rules as to what children should be and think, and the question of whether those rules make sense to the children is never raised. In fact, if children protest that the rules do not make sense, they may well be punished.

For Rogers, emotional disturbance is caused by child-rearing practices that do not convey positive regard for the child. By putting ***conditions of worth*** on the child, the parent forces the child to ignore its organismic valuing and thereby creates incongruence. It is this incongruence that causes trouble in development. Incongruence occurs when the child does not trust or listen to her own internal capabilities for experiencing and making judgments about what are the best and most effective things to do and ways to be. A condition of worth is basically a message conveyed to the child that "you as a whole person only have worth when you conform to my ideas of what you should be."

Rogers thought that the organismic valuing process is the innate way that humans have to learn positive or prosocial behavior and that it can become a reliable, valid, and important source of information and guide to action. Humans find it innately rewarding or reinforcing to be kind to each other, to relate to each other, to be affectionate and helpful, and so forth. It is only when the child learns to ignore organismic valuing that behavior goes awry.

Rogers did not advocate letting children follow only those rules or perceptions that make sense to them. For instance, Rogers was not saying that the child has the right to stick her finger in a flame because the rule against doing it doesn't make sense to her. However, insisting that the child follow the rule should be done without telling her that she is bad or wrong or stupid for wanting to stick her hand in the flame. Even if there are occasions when children have to conform to a rule that does not make sense to them, at the very least, the parent tries to convey positive regard and not to invalidate the child's experience.

If children are told that their experiential sense is bad or wrong often enough, they will begin to distrust it, perhaps even to deny it. They will become "other-directed" and depend on authorities to tell them what is correct. They will adopt rules and perspectives in a rigid, either/or manner and lose the ability to be spontaneous or creative and to effectively self-regulate and evolve. Then, when life poses challenges to them, they are unable to rely on their own internal resources for self-change and growth, and may experience various forms of psychological breakdown instead.

Psychotherapy

Therapeutic Process

The process of psychotherapy for Rogers is the restoration of the individual's ability to use all of himself to creatively and intelligently cope with life's challenges. This occurs primarily through the process of self-acceptance. If clients can adopt a nonjudgmental, self-accepting attitude toward themselves, then they can learn to tune into their experiential sense of things. As this occurs, they hold constructs more tentatively and become more flexible, less structure-bound, and more autonomous.

This view of therapy does not mean that clients will automatically or magically find answers to all their questions. For Rogers, life is a continual growth process in which people are periodically challenged to develop and expand their skills in living. "Self-actualized" people are not perfect, are not always happy, are not even always congruent with themselves. Rather, they are people who accept the fact that they will be periodically challenged and at those times are willing to reevaluate their personal constructs. They are willing to face the anxiety and disorganization attendant on the struggle to solve a new life problem and move ahead. Rather than "self-actualized," it would be more accurate to call them "self-actualizing." Rogers said, "I believe they would consider themselves insulted if they were described as 'adjusted,' and they would regard it as false if they were described as 'happy' or 'contented,' or even 'actualized'" (1961, p. 186). They know they will not do everything perfectly and that there will be times of unhappiness. But because they view life as a process rather than expecting it to be some fixed state of bliss, they try to learn from their mistakes and to live with the unhappy times in order to move forward.

The ability to trust all of their inner, life feelings as well as thoughts, does not mean that they magically find the right answer to life dilemmas. Rogers said, "[One's] organism would not by any means be infallible. It would always give the best possible answer for the available data, but sometimes data would be missing . . ." (1961, p. 191). A person may feel confusion because a major life decision, such as getting divorced, must include many pros and cons. If the individual can experience the pros and cons (I enjoy being around her, but I enjoy not having to answer to someone), then he can have a direct experiential sense of the whole conflict. But that experiential sense will not be one clear feeling, such as "leave" or "stay." Rather, it will include the whole experience of the situation and how one experiences one's goals. Gendlin says the person experiences the problem as a kind of "all that."

Tuning into one's whole inner experience of the problem, then, means focusing one's attention on all the "inner voices" that constitute the different sides of the problem and listening empathically to all of them. As a person does this, different meanings separate out, and the person begins to get in touch with how he experientially weighs components of the dilemma (My enjoyment of her feels more important than my desire for freedom). In addition, as the person attends to how each component of the dilemma feels, a kind of constructive process takes place. According to Gendlin, as the person attempts to capture experiential meanings in words or images, there is a kind of momentary experiential resolution of some aspect of the problem and a "felt give" or sense of relief. Ultimate problem resolution is made up of many such momentary bits of integration, building on one another.

Thus, for Gendlin and Rogers, one important aspect of therapy could be said to be a creative process of synthesizing new, more complex, and more integrated ways of perceiving and experiencing the self and the world. Resolution of particular problems flows from this, often by finding creative ways of synthesizing what appear to be "either/or" aspects of experience into "and's." For instance, a client may feel "either I stay single in order to have as sexually free a life as I want and lose the positive aspects of being married, or I get married and have those positive aspects, and lose the freedom to have multiple sexual relationships." This may seem like an irresolvable conflict between two mutually contradictory choices. However, as the client listens to his experience, he may find an "and" between the two apparently conflicting poles. He may discover that there are ways to incorporate a feeling of diversity within his marriage in such a way that his needs for the adventure of playing around are satisfied.

The creative aspect of client-centered therapy needs to be emphasized. The goal of the process really is to liberate and facilitate the client's creativity. Clients find creative new solutions to their life dilemmas that neither therapist nor client could have predicted in advance. Following the work of the Nobel prize-winning chemist Ilya Prigogine (Prigogine & Stengers, 1984) who found that systems threatened with disorganization can often spontaneously leap to a higher level of organization, client-centered therapists believe that individuals who are struggling with problems in their lives can, under the proper therapeutic conditions, evolve new, more integrated, creative syntheses that help them find new ways of handling problems.

Client-centered therapists therefore do not presume to know what the proper solutions are for their clients. Rather, they believe in providing optimal conditions under which the clients' own creative capacities for self-regulation and self-evolution can operate. For instance, sexual abuse is seen as one important cause of some adult psychological problems, such as borderline personality disorder (Briere, 1989). There are many therapists who, if they believe that their client has been sexually abused, believe that therapy must focus on the abuse as the major issue. Thus, the therapist makes the decision for the client as to what needs to be worked on in order for the client to improve. In contrast, a client-centered therapist seeing an abuse victim would work with whatever problem the client wanted to work on, in the belief that as the client's own self-creating and self-restoring capacities get mobilized, the client will spontaneously begin to deal with the abuse herself when it is necessary for her to face it in order to creatively move forward.

To sum up, the process of psychotherapy includes two elements. First, clients learn to listen to and accept their experience. As they do this, they become more flexible and more self-directed and begin to hold constructs tentatively. Second, the acceptance of all inner experience mobilizes the client's own creative, self-evolutionary, self-restorative capacities, allowing the client to forge creative new solutions to her life problems and to develop new, more integrative and organized ways of dealing with life.

Role of the Therapist

There has been an evolution in the role of the client-centered therapist (Hart, 1970). In the 1940s, the therapist was to remain relatively anonymous and create a warm, accepting climate in which the client would feel free to engage in self-exploration. In the 1950s, therapist empathy was stressed. The therapist was not only to convey warmth, but also to make an active effort to understand the client's subjective experience through the reflection of feelings technique developed at this time. The stereotypical picture of the client-centered therapist is based on this period.

In the late 1950s and early 1960s, there was a further evolution. Rogers (1957) published a paper suggesting that it is the therapeutic relationship itself that is therapeutic. More important than the therapist's professional training, theoretical point of view, or techniques are certain personal qualities. Therapists who have these qualities will be effective; those who do not have them will not be. This bold and far-reaching statement implied that a person could be a psychiatrist, a psychologist, or a barber and be an effective therapist if the person had certain crucial personal qualities. It also implied that the crucial qualities were independent of whether the person was a Freudian, Rogerian, Jungian, or behaviorist.

What are these personal qualities? Rogers listed several in 1957, but they have generally been reduced to three major groups: nonpossessive warmth, empathic understanding, and genuineness (we use the names given them by Truax and Carkhuff, 1967). We will discuss each quality in turn and try to identify its therapeutic value.

Nonpossessive Warmth

Nonpossessive warmth is a general name for a quality or set of qualities called, variously, unconditional positive regard, prizing, acceptance, respect, caring, or even nonpossessive love (Rogers, 1965). These all refer to the following: First, the therapist must positively prize or care for the client. Second, this caring must be nonpossessive, a quality related to the idea of acceptance. Third, the therapist must not only care for the client in a nonpossessive way but must also treat him with respect as an autonomous individual, equal in value to the therapist. Caring is probably therapeutic because it builds trust and is a motivator. Clients are more likely to reveal themselves to, take chances with, and try hard for someone they feel cares about them.

Nonpossessiveness is related to acceptance. Possessive caring is caring with an attempt to control the other. Being nonpossessive in therapy means acknowledging clients' autonomy, accepting their choices, and not imposing one's will on them. As we have stated before, acceptance does not mean approval. It means responding to others nonevaluatively, acknowledging and listening to them nonjudgmentally. Possessive parents or lovers are always either approving or disapproving of the behavior of the child or of the romantic partner. Nonpossessiveness contributes to therapeutic effectiveness because most people are averse to feeling controlled or judged by another. Feeling controlled or judged may motivate clients to rebel or make them feel unsafe.

Respect for clients' individuality and autonomy goes hand in hand with nonpossessive acceptance. The therapist's attitude of respect reinforces clients' belief in themselves as capable of making decisions for themselves. Some parents seem to care for their children in a way that does not include respect. For example, by being overprotective, they convey the message that the children are incompetent to take care of themselves. Respect also implies trust in the client. An attitude of trust should increase clients' trust in themselves and in the therapist, with a resultant lowering of defenses. As respect and trust increase, so will clients' openness to communications from the therapist.

Empathic Understanding

The term "empathy" has many different meanings in the psychological literature (Bohart & Greenberg, 1997). For some it refers to an emotional sharing between two people. Others believe themselves to be empathic if they are warm, concerned, and showing that they care. However, for client-centered therapy, empathy is primarily a matter of *understanding* the other person's point of view. Empathic understanding involves the ability to enter clients' worlds and to see things from their frame of reference. This is more difficult than it may seem. To be accurately empathic, one must be able to *decenter*, a concept borrowed from the work of Piaget (Cowan, 1978). ***Decentering*** is the ability to step outside of one's own perspective and, through imagination, guess at how things would look and feel from someone else's perspective. For adults, it is relatively easy to imagine how someone else is seeing the physical world. For instance, it is not hard for students to imagine what the classroom looks like physically to the professor as he or she lectures, even though the students are not at the podium. It is quite another thing for students to imagine how a teacher is experiencing the lecture material and the classroom situation. The experiencing of any given situation is based on how the person is construing that situation, which is based on that person's prior experiences. Since everyone's experiences are different to some extent, it may be difficult for one person to guess how another is construing a situation. It may be relatively easier if the two people are similar in many ways (Henschel & Bohart, 1984). The greater the difference in prior experience, the greater the difficulty in achieving empathy. Yet true empathic ability is probably demonstrated more in situations when a person is trying to grasp the experience of someone quite different (Henschel & Bohart, 1984), perhaps even somebody he does not like, approve of, or agree with. This also means that therapists must be careful not to mistake recalling their own experiences for having an empathic response. True empathy is not how you would feel if you were in the client's shoes, but an attempt to guess at how she feels, that is, how you would feel if you were she, in her shoes.

How does a therapist "be" empathic? We have described empathy as an ability, but it is not something that one simply "has." Rather, empathy is an active process, a skill that must be practiced. Rarely will a person have a magical flash of insight in which the person just "knows" how another is experiencing the world. Usually, a person can achieve that knowledge only through a laborious process of listening, adjusting guesses, and listening some more. Here is how it goes: The client has said that he has been dumped by his girlfriend. You make a guess at what he is experiencing, based on your own experience in such situations and your general knowledge of the experience of others in such situations. You state your guess, and then you listen to see if you have guessed right. You will know from the client's response. This response will be given in words and body language. If the client says, "Yes, that's it!" then you probably hit it. If the client hesitates and says, "Yes, that must be it," then you know you didn't. If your guess is accurate, the client will know right away. It will "feel right" to him. If the client has to hesitate, then at an experiential level, what you said did not feel right, even though at an intellectual level the client decides it "must be right." So you listen, and based on what cues the client gives back to you, you make another guess, and then you listen further.

Achieving empathic understanding can take time because it requires clarifying communication between the therapist and the client. Empathy involves learning the client's private language. For example, when the client says "My girlfriend dumped me," you may take that to mean "I feel rejected," but perhaps the meaning the client attaches to that statement and wants to convey to you is "People always mistreat me." Therefore, empathy is normally achieved over a period of time in therapy. Empathy will develop more quickly if therapists are willing to suspend judgment and their own private way of interpreting words and behaviors.

Reflection of feeling is a technique that was developed in the 1950s as a means for the therapist to convey empathic understanding of the client back to the client. A reflection may start out "It sounds like you feel . . ." or "You're saying that . . ." but it may also simply be an empathic restatement of what the therapist thinks the client is experiencing. Reflection of feeling is actually a misnomer. Several studies have shown that Carl Rogers only referred to feelings about 25% of the time in his reflections, and even then his purpose was to check his understanding of the client's experience, not to empathize at a feeling level. Most often, his reflections focused on meaning. A far more accurate name for the technique would be "reflection of the meaning in subjective experience." To give an example:

CLIENT: I failed the test! Boy, does that screw things up! I'm behind on my other classes, but now I'm going to have to devote extra time to this one.

REFLECTION (OF FEELING): Oh no! It feels so threatening to have failed that test. And now to have to study extra, that's so frustrating and overwhelming!

REFLECTION (OF MEANING): Failing the test means you're going to have to change your plans, and devote more time than you would have to that class, and you're behind already.

REFLECTION (OF FEELING AND MEANING): It almost sounds like you're feeling a little desperate. How can you get caught up on your other classes, and devote extra time to this one?

Notice that the reflections do more than repeat what the client just said. Often, people think of reflecting as nothing but parroting, as in the following parody:

CLIENT: I'm feeling depressed today.

COUNSELOR: You're feeling depressed today.

CLIENT: I think I'll kill myself.

COUNSELOR: You think you'll kill yourself.

CLIENT: I'm going to jump out the window.

COUNSELOR: You're going to jump out the window.

CLIENT: I'm jumping out the window.

COUNSELOR: You're jumping out the window.

SOUND FROM BELOW: Plop!

COUNSELOR: Plop!

Good reflections do not simply repeat back to the client what the client has already said. At the very minimum, they paraphrase. For instance, a simple paraphrasing of the client's statement about being depressed might be, "You're feeling down today." Most reflections, however, go beyond what the client actually said to try to capture more of the flavor of the client's experience than the client put into words. The presumption is that the client's words summarize or convey a fraction of the client's total experience in the moment. Good reflections guess at what some related aspects of that experience might be. In the examples of reflections, each one goes beyond the client statement to make a guess at what the client is experiencing at the moment but did not say. For instance, the first reflection presents a guess that the client is feeling frustrated and overwhelmed, although this was not stated by the client. The reflection is a step in the constructive activity of empathic understanding. If the client responds to the reflection with "Boy! That's for sure!" the therapist guessed correctly and may have moved closer to the therapeutic goal of being able to guess what it feels like to be that client. If the client says, "No, it's more like I'm feeling picked on by life. I'm being treated unfairly," then the therapist has also moved forward in gaining an understanding of the client's subjective world.

Using reflection with pets.

Reflection differs from interpretation (see chapter 6) in that while both guess at the meanings that underlie the client's statement, reflection tries to stay with meanings that are within the client's current awareness. Interpretation attempts to uncover hidden meanings of which the client is unaware. For instance, an interpretation of the client's statement about failing the test might be, "Is it possible that your failing the test means that you don't really like that class?"

Empathy and reflection are presumed to be therapeutic for the following reasons: First, empathy, along with warmth, creates a sense of trust. Second, feeling understood is often by itself therapeutic. Simply knowing that someone else can understand what she feels may make a person feel less alone and more "normal." Third, empathy and reflection focus the client's attention on her inner experience. In effect, they train the client to listen to and to try to capture the meanings in her own experience. Thus empathy is directly teaching the skill Rogers believed is so important in living.

Genuineness

The third important quality for therapists to possess is genuineness. Other words associated with this quality include congruence, honesty, authenticity, openness, and self-disclosure. Genuine people show congruence. This means that their outer actions align with some facet of their inner thoughts and feelings. Put another way, what they say and what they do are accurate reflections of some aspect of what they are currently thinking and feeling. In this sense, they can also be called honest and authentic. However, genuineness must be distinguished from the terms openness and self-disclosure, although they are related. Self-disclosure and openness are more like things people do. They disclose their problems to another; they are open about private thoughts and feelings with one another. However, people can be genuine, yet not be open or not self-disclosing. And people can self-disclose and be incongruent or phony. Suppose we asked you to tell us about your sexual fantasies. You might feel that it is none of our business. You might act congruently with that feeling and choose not to tell us. In that case, you are being genuine, but you are not being open and self-disclosing about your sexual fantasies. Conversely, you might feel it is none of our business, but because some psychologist told you that the healthy person is open and self-disclosing, you go against your feelings and tell us. In this case you are being open, but you are being incongruent and you are not being genuine or congruent.

People never express or act on everything they are thinking and feeling. They always select. While a professor lectures to a class, she may be simultaneously experiencing (a) a desire to communicate ideas on the class topic, (b) a concern that the students understand what is being said, (c) hunger, (d) anger at her landlord, and (e) dislike of the awful shirt the man in the first row is wearing. If the professor were to try to express or act on all these things, her behavior would be confused and confusing. Instead, she selects those parts of her experience relevant to the situation to express in behavior. It is relevant to act on a desire to communicate and on a concern for the students. It is irrelevant to interject "I'm hungry" or "That darn landlord!" or "That's an awful shirt!" Is the professor being phony because she does not say these things? No. She is being congruent, because what she does say and do is an accurate reflection of the part of her experience that is relevant to the situation. As we said before, people always select. We never act on or verbalize everything we're thinking and feeling. If we did, we would engage in unending monologues and no one else would get a word in edgewise.

While therapists should always be genuine, they should only selectively and judiciously self-disclose. Generally, they should self-disclose only when it is relevant to the therapeutic interaction. Then they need to self-disclose in ways that facilitate the therapeutic process. Gendlin (1968) states that when the therapist does self-disclose, it must be done in a way that is more growth producing than if it were done by "the person on the street." Many people in everyday life are "honest" in insensitive, critical, and disparaging ways. In therapy, the therapist must give feedback in a way that promotes growth. This includes making "I" statements instead of "you" statements ("I am uncomfortable with the way you are treating your child" versus "You are a terrible parent"), giving specific information in a nonblaming way, and often noting the positive as well as the negative.

Genuineness is therapeutic in combination with warmth and empathy because it promotes a genuinely positive, growth-oriented relationship in which clients can learn to trust and listen to themselves. In addition, self-disclosure appears to be therapeutic for several reasons. First, there is a modeling effect. If the therapist wishes the client to open up, then some gesture of opening up on the therapist's part might provide a model. The therapist is also modeling the idea that one doesn't have to be perfect. Second, by being genuine and by selectively self-disclosing, the therapist is demonstrating trust in the client ("Gee, the therapist trusts me enough to share some private things with me"). Third, self-disclosure can give immediate feedback to the client on the impact of his behavior. Fourth, self-disclosure can create a sense of empathy. Judiciously timed, selective self-disclosure about the therapist's own experiences can demonstrate empathy and understanding of the client's feelings. Fifth, if the therapist's self-disclosures are offered tentatively, this gives therapist and client the opportunity to explore together what is going on in the relationship and to clarify each other's perceptions.

From Client-Centered to Person-Centered

Rogers's statement that therapy is a function of the quality of the relationship, the emphasis on the qualities of warmth, empathy, and genuineness, and Gendlin's theory of experiencing changed the client-centered approach for many of its followers from a specific set of therapeutic techniques to a philosophy of therapy (Lietaer, 1990). Prior to this change, many therapists believed that they could use any technique—behavioral, gestalt, analytic—as long as they maintained the qualities of a good therapeutic relationship and as long as the technique was used only when it was experientially meaningful for the client. Then, with this change, the client-centered approach became a model for the eclectic practice of therapy for many therapists. Hart (1970) discusses an informal study in which tapes of various client-centered therapists were identified by expert listeners as representing a range of other therapies, such as Adlerian or rational-emotive.

This shift from a specific way of practicing therapy to a general philosophy of the person, along with the application of Rogers's ideas to education, medicine, childrearing, and international relations, eventually resulted in Rogers's changing the name of his approach to "the person-centered approach." Person-centered theory holds to the following general hypotheses: First, there is a belief in the intrinsic potential of each person to creatively grow in life-enhancing directions. Each person is ultimately the expert on his or her own process of development, and the person-centered theorist has trust in each person's capacity for self-development, self-righting, and self-creation. Second, there is a belief that the provision of the three therapeutic conditions of warmth, empathy, and genuineness is most fundamental in providing the conditions under which this client capacity for self-growth can function. Within this general framework, a number of different approaches to psychotherapy have evolved, and we shall now discuss the evolution of different ways to practice client-centered therapy itself.

Traditional client-centered therapy is a nondirective process in which the therapist empathically listens to the client as she explores her experiences. The therapist may also self-disclose, but the major activity of the therapist is to empathically listen to and reflect the client's communications. The therapist is a companion on the client's journey, and it is believed that by being a good companion, the therapist helps the client alter that journey in more growthful directions. The therapist is nondirective in two important ways. First, the therapist does not direct the client to focus on specific content or kinds of issues. That is, the therapist does not direct the client to explore childhood, childhood abuse, family relationships, or the client's dysfunctional conditions. Second, the therapist does not generally provide directions for how the client is to explore. That is, the therapist does not try to direct the process of therapy, either. The client chooses what to talk about, how to talk about it, when to shift to something else, when to focus on feelings, when to talk about thoughts, when to talk about the past, and so on. Ultimate faith is placed in the client's ability to feel her way into the right directions for creative growth and to explore in the manner that best suits her.

Rogers's emphasis on the therapeutic conditions of warmth, empathy, and genuineness as necessary and sufficient for therapy to take place led many client-centered therapists to expand how they practiced. This was especially true because of the increased emphasis on therapist genuineness. If you as the therapist are listening to your client discuss his problems with assertion, and the thought crosses your mind that there is a method—assertion training—that might be of assistance to your client, and you keep that thought to yourself because you are trying to be "nondirective," then you might be acting ingenuinely. Thus, in the name of genuineness, therapists began to share some of their own thoughts on clients' issues when they were sensitively relevant to what the client was dealing with. This meant that the therapist might mention the possibility of assertion training to the client, for instance. Many client-centered therapists began to incorporate techniques and ideas from other approaches into their practice, although the stance of the therapist was not one of the expert "fixing" the client, but rather one of a "companion sharing with" the client.

With this shift, the old stereotype of all client-centered therapists as simply reflecting client feelings no longer held. Despite the shift toward a more active therapist role, client-centered therapists still held to the belief that it was ultimately the client who would choose what was good for him. The therapist was more like a "consultant" who offered empathy, genuineness, and warmth, as well as ideas, feedback, and suggestions.

More active, directive approaches to psychotherapy, based in person-centered theory, developed. These "experiential" approaches are considered in the next chapter. Currently there is some controversy in the field of client-centered therapy between those who advocate more of a "pure traditional" approach to client-centered therapy and those who are willing to use techniques such as experiential and process-experiential therapies. Traditional client-centered therapists believe that these approaches are no longer truly nondirective, and in that sense no longer truly client-centered, which is why some (Brodley, 1988b) have argued that there is a family of person-centered therapies, of which pure client-centered therapy is one member, and process-experiential and experiential therapies are other members.

Evaluation of Client- and Person-Centered Therapies

Research

Carl Rogers has often been seen as the "father of psychotherapy research," and client-centered therapy is the most well researched of the experiential-humanistic approaches. Meta-analyses have confirmed its effectiveness (Elliott, 2002; Elliott, Greenberg, & Lietaer, 2004). Some research studies have compared various versions of client-centered therapy to behavioral approaches (Grawe, Caspar, & Ambuhl, 1990) and psychodynamic approaches and have found client-centered therapy to be equivalent in effectiveness to these other approaches. For instance, Eckert and Biermann-

Ratjen (1990) compared client-centered with psychodynamic group therapy in the treatment of personality-disordered clients and found equivalence in effectiveness. In another study, client-centered therapy for depression led to changes equivalent to those brought about by cognitive therapy (Greenberg & Watson, 1998). Ends and Page (1957) found that a client-centered group therapy approach as an adjunct to inpatient hospital treatment for alcoholism led to higher rates of abstinence at an 18-month follow-up than either a psychodynamic group therapy approach or a learning-based approach. Overall, studies have found client-centered therapy to be effective with a wide range of disorders, including anxiety disorders, personality disorders, and even with some schizophrenics (Bohart, 2003).

Rogers and Sanford (1985) summarized research done in foreign countries on psychotherapy, the teacher–student relationship, and the use of encounter groups. These studies are reported as demonstrating the effectiveness of the person-centered approach. Specifically, teachers high in the facilitative (therapeutic) qualities were found to be more effective. The encounter groups were utilized with a variety of populations, from neurotic students to businesspersons to cancer patients. Generally, these participants gained positive benefits from their encounter experiences.

In sum, a substantial body of evidence demonstrates the effectiveness of the person-centered therapies for a wide range of disorders.

Therapeutic Conditions

The hypothesis that high therapeutic conditions of warmth, empathy, and genuineness are both necessary and sufficient for therapy has been extensively explored. Research summaries have supported the effectiveness of these conditions. Bohart, Elliott, Greenberg, and Watson (2002) conducted a meta-analysis of 47 studies on empathy and found that it bore a moderate relationship to positive therapeutic outcome. Farber and Lane (2002) reviewed the evidence on the relationship of positive regard (warmth) to therapeutic outcome and also found evidence of a moderately positive relationship. Along these same lines, Miller (2000) concluded from his survey of the research, particularly on the treatment of addictions, that love or caring might be the primary healing element in therapy. The evidence on congruence or genuineness has been more mixed, but is still on the positive side (Klein, Kolden, Michels, & Chisholm-Stockard, 2002).

However, the relationship of the therapeutic conditions to outcome is not strong enough to state that it is either *necessary* or *sufficient* for change to occur. Nevertheless, Rogers appears to have been correct in believing that these qualities play an important role in facilitating change. Overall, Rogers's hypothesis that the relationship is the most important curative factor in therapy has consistently received support. Evidence shows that the therapeutic alliance is more important than techniques across therapies as diverse as cognitive, psychodynamic, and humanistic (Lambert, 1992).

Experiencing

Gendlin's hypothesis that clients who are working with their inner experiencing in a productive way in therapy will be more likely to benefit from therapy has been extensively researched. Several studies on client-centered therapy found that clients who were high in this ability appeared to benefit more from therapy (Gendlin, Beebe, Cassens, Klein, & Oberlander, 1968). Other studies on other kinds of therapy have produced mixed results, though on balance, higher levels of client experiencing have been associated with therapeutic change (Klein, Mathieu-Coughlan, & Kiesler, 1986).

Gendlin and his colleagues (Gendlin et al., 1968) suggested that their analysis of the data on client-centered therapy found that the ability to relate to one's experience did not increase to any great extent over the course of therapy. Instead, it appeared that people high in this ability had entered therapy with high levels. Therapy then helped them to utilize this ability to change, but it did not teach the ability. It was because of these results that Gendlin developed his "focusing" procedure (see chapter 9) as a way of facilitating the experiencing process in those who were not good at it when they entered therapy. However, this particular finding—that clients who do well in therapy enter it with higher levels of experiencing—has been disputed (Brodley, 1988a).

Other research on the ability to relate to oneself experientially (or to focus) has found that it relates to creativity (Gendlin, 1969) and even to longevity in elderly people (Gendlin, 1981).

The Self-Healing Client

Rogers believed that psychotherapy was primarily a process of the therapist supporting the client's capacities for self-healing and self-righting. Bohart and Tallman (1999) and Duncan and Miller (2000) have concluded that evidence supports this view. For instance, one explanation for why all therapies seem to work about equally well is that it is the client who takes what any given therapy offers and makes it work. Other research shows that humans are more resilient than once thought and that many clients are able to self-right using self-help procedures. Still other research (Rennie, 2002) has shown how clients are highly active in how they pursue their goals in therapy.

Theory

Client-centered theory is primarily a theory of personality *process* rather than of personality *structure*. That is, it is a theory of the person as an active, organizing process moving toward the future. It focuses on how people, when they are functioning most effectively, are continually and actively using their own experience to revise their personal constructs, to change, and to create better ways of dealing with life. However, in this focus, client-centered theorists have provided few ideas of how individuals remain the same. We have seen in the evaluation of psychodynamic theories that people probably change more than these theories assume. However, it is also the case that they remain the same in various ways, and client-centered theory has not developed models of what is enduring in personality, as have psychodynamic theories.

Another problem with client-centered theory is that the client-centered therapist's intense focus on the individual tends to result in a view that all psychopathology arises from the client's inability to trust himself. First, such a view ignores biological factors. Second, it ignores the possibility that social, ecological, and systems factors may create psychopathology, even in people who are congruent. As an example, Haney, Banks, and Zimbardo (1973) found that some students who were otherwise free of any apparent signs of psychopathology became brutal or experienced psychological breakdowns when put in the roles of guard or prisoner in a mock prison setup. Finally, Watzlawick (1978), a family systems theorist (see chapter 13), has argued that often, pathological behavior arises from being congruent. He suggests that pathological behavior is behavior that has worked in the past, but is dysfunctional in the current situation, although the person does not recognize this. When things continue to go wrong, the person tries harder to make things go right by increasing the behaviors that worked in the past. Increasing the now dysfunctional behaviors simply makes matters worse. Yet the person is behaving in what appears to him to be a congruent manner; he's doing what he believes.

Still another problem has been an intense individualistic orientation in client-centered therapy. Rogers (1977) believed that social changes do not result from attempts to change society at a collective level but from creating personal change within individuals. Yet the individual and society are two parts of a balanced system. In order to create self-actualizing people, it would seem that we must change society, not just try to foster actualization in individuals. But to change society, we must understand all political, cultural, and social forces that are involved. Rogers tended to ignore or distrust this level of analysis.

There are other problems with the Rogerian focus on the self. These problems are shared with other theories such as object relations theory, gestalt, and existentialism. All of these theories in one form or another see the fundamental event in the development of mental health as the development of an integrated, autonomous, separate, actualized self. It is assumed that only an autonomous, actualized self can maturely relate to others. Therefore, for all these theories, good relationships to other people follow self-actualization. However, it has been argued that the emphasis on individuation and development of selfhood is culture-specific and may reflect the high value Western cultures place on individualism. In contrast, Asian personality theories (Pedersen, 1983), for example, stress the development of the person through relationships. What Asian theories see as healthy, Western theories tend to see as unhealthy: an "other" orientation, the positive value of dependency, and so on. And the reverse is true; for some Asian theories, "self" doesn't really even exist, and an emphasis on self-actualization is contrary to optimal development. Similarly, many modern feminist theorists (e.g., Jordan, Kaplan, Miller, Stiver, & Surrey, 1991) have argued that the emphasis many theories place on development of separateness and autonomy over interdependence and connectedness to others reflects a masculine cultural bias. Whether there is a correct theory, we do not know. The important thing is to realize that emphasis on self-actualization and autonomy may reflect "actualization" of cultural values as much as it reflects "fundamental truth" about personality development.

In terms of psychotherapy, client-centered therapy is the purest of the "discovery-oriented" approaches. Discovery-oriented approaches to therapy begin with the idea that change ultimately occurs through clients making their own individual discoveries of their own individual "truths." Psychoanalytic therapy is primarily a discovery-oriented approach, but psychoanalytic therapists have some specific ideas about what clients need to discover in order to change, and so have some directive elements to them. Some client-centered therapists adopt a radical nondirective stance, believing that if the therapist directs the client in any way, he gets in the way of the client's own self-directed growth process. It is because of this that the therapist wishes to encounter the client free of preconceptions in order to relate to the unique person that the client is. Because of this, most client-centered therapists do not want to diagnose. Nor do they wish to make treatment plans for the client. Many client-centered therapists do not even like Gendlin's focusing approach or the process-experiential approach because they are *structured* discovery-oriented approaches. That is, while the ultimate goal is still for the client to discover her own truth and solution, process-experiential therapists and those who follow Gendlin's approach believe the therapist can facilitate discovery by structuring therapy with the use of certain techniques.

This radical nondirective stance makes it philosophically difficult for some client-centered therapists to use techniques and procedures when they might be helpful. For instance, with a client with a sexual difficulty, there are techniques that can be useful. Yet Rogers himself, with his increased emphasis on the therapist's genuineness later on in his life, was acceptant of client-centered therapists who believed that they could suggest and utilize techniques without imposing on the self-directed growth process of the client. It does not appear that there is anything inherently contradictory about a therapist suggesting a technique, if she does it in a way that truly respects the client's right to (a) say no if it does not fit, and (b) learn from it in his own way. Similarly, there is nothing inherently contradictory about labeling and diagnosing, and treating clients as unique individuals. The issue depends on how therapists use their constructs. To use client-centered theory itself, it depends on whether therapists hold their constructs tentatively. It is unfortunately true that diagnosis has been used to label and pigeonhole clients by therapists who fail to recognize them as individual, unique persons. If the therapist holds her constructs tentatively, using them as tools to "get to know" the client, rather than as fixed truths about the client, then constructs about the client should not obscure the client's uniqueness.

A further, practical problem with the radical nondirective stance is that it does not fit well with the current managed care environment (see chapter 16), where therapists are expected to diagnose their clients and to develop treatment plans for them. Therapists who truly want to practice in a traditional client-centered way may have to practice outside of the health care establishment.

In Conclusion

While only a minority of therapists currently identify themselves as client-centered in a pure sense, Carl Rogers has been rated as the most influential of all psychotherapists, including Freud (Smith, 1982). This is because his ideas have influenced many therapists who are eclectic or of other theoretical orientations. Rogers's emphasis on the importance of the therapeutic relationship has been almost universally adopted. Many believe that the relationship is the primary curative factor, even if they are not client-centered in orientation

We believe that the emphasis on the relationship was one of Rogers's two major insights and that this insight will continue to play an important role in how therapy is conducted. In particular, Rogers's emphasis on empathy has spread from a focus on its importance in the therapeutic relationship to an increasing interest in its growth-producing potential in parenting relationships (Feshbach, 1997) and in society at large (Goleman, 1996).

The second major insight concerns the client's own self-healing potential, or what Rogers called "self-actualization." While most therapists do not use the term self-actualization, it seems clear that clients have an enormous capacity for self-healing and self-righting (Bohart & Tallman, 1999). To quote Bergin and Garfield (1994), based on the most comprehensive review of psychotherapy research to date:

> Another important observation regarding the client variable is that it is the client more than the therapist who implements the change process. . . . Rather than argue over whether or not "therapy works," we could address ourselves to the question of whether or not "the client works!" . . . As therapists have depended more upon the client's resources, more change seems to occur. (p. 826)

Orlinsky, Grawe, and Parks (1994, p. 278), based on their comprehensive research review, say, "We view psychotherapy as 'the activation through the process of interpersonal communication of a powerful endogenous therapeutic system [in the client] that is part of the psychophysiology of all individuals and the sociophysiology of relationships." Therapists of many persuasions are increasingly coming to trust, rely on, and utilize their clients' own creativity and self-healing capacities (Bohart & Tallman, 1999; Gold, 1994), and this is particularly true of therapists who follow brief, "solution-focused" approaches (Duncan, Hubble, & Miller, 1997). For instance, Duncan et al. (1997) have shown in a study of "impossible cases"—clients who have repeatedly failed to have been helped by prior therapy—that the therapist's reliance on the client's frame of reference and own creativity led to the occurrence of change. Thus, as therapists learn to utilize clients' own self-healing potentials more, we believe they will become more effective (Bohart & Tallman, 1999).

Experiential and Existential Psychotherapies

> I do my thing, and you do your thing
> I am not in this world to live up to your expectations
> And you are not in this world to live up to mine.
> You are you, and I am I.
> And if by chance we find each other, it's beautiful.
> If not, it can't be helped.
>
> —Fritz Perls, quoted in *Fritz*

In the previous chapter we considered one of the most important existential-humanistic approaches in the work of Carl Rogers. In this chapter, we will look at the other major approaches in this perspective: experiential psychotherapies, including gestalt therapy and existential therapy.

The Concept of the River

Of all the major approaches, the existential-humanistic approach places the most emphasis on individuals creating and directing their own lives. For this approach, the very essence of the person is the freedom to shape and reshape her own life and identity. The personality is viewed as a continual process of growth and change. The individual never possesses a fixed self, or character structure, or identity. People are "open systems," continually interacting with the environment, taking in information, and growing and changing as they creatively deal with a continual influx of information. The most appropriate metaphor for the personality in the humanistic approaches is "the river." Although the river can be said to have an identity, it is never the same from one moment to the next or one place to the next. Its nature at any given moment is influenced by where it has been, where it is going, where it is now, and what happens to it at any time in the past or present.

Humanists believe that if early childhood events are still influencing a person it is because the person, as the author of his own fate, is still allowing (often unconsciously) them to do so. Personality is not so much something that is built up inside from experiences as it is something that the person actively maintains through choices. The radical emphasis on growth, change, and choice means the humanistic approaches place a heavy emphasis on creativity and the individual's reaching his full potential.

Humanistic approaches also generally see the human being holistically. No part of the human is disowned or seen as somehow "lower" or "less human" than other parts. Humanists generally reject Freud's view of the person as split into relatively "higher" (ego) functions and relatively "lower" or more primitive (id) functions. Sex and aggression are not seen as primitive, selfish impulses in and of themselves. They are primitive and selfish only if the person chooses to express them that way. If owned and acknowledged, these parts can play creative, life-actualizing roles in personality development. By the same token, the emotional and intuitive functions are not seen as things to be controlled. Subjectivity, fantasy, and intuition are all regarded as sources of growth and creativity.

As part of the river metaphor, humanistic approaches see life as an ongoing process of *meaning making*. This means that we are continually forging and reforging the meaning in our lives. The things that are meaningful to us as adolescents shift and fade as we get older, get jobs, and raise families. New things become meaningful. This process continues until the end of our lives. A key part of effective coping, and indeed a key part of psychotherapy, is to create new meaning in the face of personal disorganization, loss, or tragedy. Some research (Tedeschi, Park, & Calhoun, 1998) has found that those who are able find meaning in traumatic experiences are among those who are more likely to grow from trauma rather than be devastated by it.

Experiential Psychotherapy

If you continue on in the field of clinical psychology, you may increasingly encounter the term ***experiential psychotherapy***. There is a tendency now to refer to all the existential-humanistic approaches, including client-centered therapy, existential therapy, and gestalt therapy, as forms of "experiential" psychotherapy. This is confusing because there are also a number of specific approaches to psychotherapy that have been named "experiential." Mahrer (1993) has noted that there are more than 20 different therapies that include the word "experiential" as part of their name.

Therefore, it is important to keep in mind that when you read about "experiential psychotherapy," the term could be referring to virtually any existential-humanistic approach, or any of the 20 or more different approaches that specifically call themselves experiential. What the experiential approaches have in common, in contrast to cognitive-behavioral and psychodynamic approaches, is a relatively stronger emphasis on direct experience in therapy as a key part of the change process. It is only a relative difference, because all therapies are experiential to some degree (see chapter 14). However, experiential therapies are more likely to (a) stress the activation and experience of emotion; (b) focus on how people are experiencing their lives, more so than on how they are thinking about their lives; (c) activate the imaginative, experiential side of the personality; (d) use experiential activities and exercises, such as gestalt role-play exercises; and (e) focus on immediate sharing of experience, in one form or the other, between therapist and client.

In this section we shall consider four different experiential approaches: Gestalt psychotherapy, Gendlin's focusing-oriented approach, Greenberg and colleagues' emotion-focused psychotherapy, and Mahrer's experiential psychotherapy. The approaches of Gendlin and Greenberg and colleagues grew out of client-centered therapy. Gestalt psychotherapy and Mahrer's experiential psychotherapy have independent roots.

Gestalt Therapy

> In 1970 a terminally ill Fritz Perls was in bed in a hospital in Chicago. At about nine o'clock that evening he kind of half got up with all this paraphernalia attached. The nurse said, "Dr. Perls. You'll have to lie down." He sort of went back down and then almost sat up and swung his legs out a bit. Again she said, "You must lie down." He looked her right in the eye and he said, "Don't tell me what to do," fell back, and died. (Robert Shapiro, as quoted in Shepard, 1975, p. 192)

If there was ever an apostle of "doing your own thing" among the major theorists of psychotherapy, it was Fritz Perls. For Perls, the emphasis on individual self-determination and responsibility was central (as is reflected in the epigraph at the beginning of this chapter). Perls has been virtually synonymous with gestalt therapy and is considered by many to be its founder (or "finder," as Perls said).

Actually, gestalt was cofounded by Perls, his wife, Laura Perls, and a philosopher, Paul Goodman. Perls became the most visible figure and achieved almost guru status on the West Coast in the late 1960s. For many years, people thought of gestalt therapy in terms of Fritz Perls. Yet there is a good deal of diversity among therapists who identify with the gestalt approach, and many do not share Perls's emphasis on "rugged individualism." In fact, Perls's individualistic emphasis actually contradicts other aspects of gestalt theory, as we shall explain. While Perls was preaching rugged individualism on the West Coast, other gestalt therapists, especially those in the eastern United States, were developing a form of gestalt that emphasized interaction and "contact" over "doing your own thing."

Theory of Personality and Psychopathology

Gestalt therapy is a field theory (Kaplan & Kaplan, 1985) in that it holds that one must look at the total configuration of interrelationships in a person's life to understand his behavior. This configuration includes the person's past experiences, beliefs and values, expectations, current momentary desires and needs, current structure of life, including where he lives, his relationships and work, and finally, the immediate situation he is in at the moment. The word ***gestalt*** (German for "shape" or "form") refers to this configuration of integrated parts. In the academic gestalt theory of perception, it is assumed that humans have an innate tendency to form "good" gestalts in a field and an innate ability to detect the "figure," or most important part of a perception, from the "ground," or surrounding elements. The analogy in gestalt therapy, as discussed later, is that healthy people naturally function in complex fields by forming experiential gestalts to guide action.

The state of every element in a field is determined in part by its interaction with every other element in the field. A simple analogy would be a stew. Carrots in a stew made with lamb will taste different from carrots in a stew made with beef. Beef in a stew made with carrots will taste a little different from beef in a stew without carrots, and so on. Thus, the nature of each element in the stew is partly determined by the whole configuration of the stew, and the whole configuration is determined by the interaction of the elements.

This is also true of people, according to gestalt. Psychologically, a person exists at each moment in a field consisting of past experiences, self-image, beliefs, values, attitudes, hopes and fears for the future, significant relationships, career, neighborhood, material possessions, and culture. The field also includes the person's current biological state, momentary needs and desires, and immediate situation (the physical environment, the people present, what is going on). Behavior and experience will be determined at any given moment by the interaction of all these elements. Because there is always some change in some element of this field, the individual is never exactly the same person as she was at any time before. Every day you sit down to breakfast something will be different, if only that you have another day's experience to throw into the "stew." But in addition, the people around you will have changed, and there may be some changes, however small, at work also.

Such a view is a nonlinear perspective on the causes of behavior, experience, and identity. It is the entire configuration that determines behavior, experience, and identity; they cannot be attributed to any one element in the configuration. A linear view traces behavior directly to one or several elements. Suppose a woman is acting rebellious at work. Classical psychoanalysis might hold that her rebellion is caused by the childhood trauma of having an overcontrolling and domineering father. A cognitive view might hold that her rebellion is caused by her dysfunctional belief that she must have her own way. A behavioral view might hold that it is caused by the situational factor of having coworkers who reinforce acting rebellious around the boss. According to gestalt theory, these three factors, plus others, are all part of what is leading to the behavior.

Let us look at another set of examples of how the person experiences the current situation in terms of all the other elements in the field. If you are hungry, you will be acutely aware of the presence or absence of food in the situation; if you are in class, your hunger may change your experience of the situation, so that the psychology professor's highly interesting lecture may seem boring and trivial. Or, if you believe psychology is irrelevant to your future plans, you may experience the lecture as boring and trivial. Or, if your past experience has included a large number of academic failures, you may believe that whether or not you listen in class is irrelevant to how well you will do on the test, and you may find it difficult to experience the lecture as involving. Conversely, your hunger, which you experienced as pressing in the classroom situation, may fade completely into the background if the terribly attractive person you have had a secret crush on for weeks suddenly comes over and asks for your help with today's lecture notes.

The past will take on different roles in a person's current behavior depending on the other elements present. There is no simple linear relationship between the past and the present. The same past experience may play a destructive, disintegrative role in one "stew" and a constructive, integrative role in another. Your past failure experiences in class may interact destructively with usual classroom situations. They may contribute to a configuration that leads you to behave self-destructively by not paying attention and by believing that you will probably fail anyway. But the same set of experiences may interact in a quite different manner with a different classroom situation. Suppose as part of the psychology class, you are assigned to spend 10 hours at a child care center. While there, you notice a child who seems to be having trouble with the class material and who seems to have a negative self-image as a result. Your own experience leads you to establish an immediate empathy with the child. Through your support and empathy, the child begins to change for the better, both in terms of his self-image and in terms of his performance. This, in turn, increases your own feelings of competence. You return to class with a more positive self-image, a greater sense of motivation, and perhaps now begin to do better yourself. The role played by the past, as with any other element in the stew of your current experience, changes as a function of all other elements present and how those elements blend together.

All the elements we have been discussing form a dynamic whole with each here-and-now situation. The situations individuals live in from moment to moment are, in some sense, part of them. Who they are at any given moment is partially determined by the situation. The "self," from this point of view, is not an internal structure existing somewhere within the person. Rather, it is an ever-shifting, ever-changing part of the ongoing organizational field of experience. The self is really a concept that is part of the stew. It is a concept that helps people to organize the field of their experience in an adaptive way. As with any other concept, its meaning will shift and change in response to other elements present.

Contact

The self, therefore, exists at the contact boundary between the person and the current situation. The process of healthy functioning rests on maintaining healthy, full, and open contact with one's experiential field. That means staying in contact with what is present in the moment in oneself, and staying in contact with what is present in the moment in the situation. When a person is able to stay in full contact with self and situation, she is naturally able to fully and creatively utilize all aspects of herself to make the best choices possible for herself at that time, given her needs, her values, her goals, and the natural constraints and limits present in the self and the situation.

Full contact can best be thought of in terms of a fluid flow of information. That is, the person's attention is not fixated on one part of her experience to the exclusion of other parts. Rather, attention is free to scan the whole field of experience. Early experiments with animals found that very hungry animals were so overfocused on food that they were unable to "creatively" find ways around barriers to get to that food. Instead they would simply try to break through the barrier over and over (Bruner, 1986).

In a like manner, one of us had a client who had been an executive in a big corporation but had been laid off when the corporation went bankrupt. He was so overfocused on the idea of finding exactly the same kind of job that he began to lapse into despair when his efforts of several months to find such a job led nowhere. He said he felt he had come to a dead end in a road. There was a big wall and no way to get over it. The therapist attempted to "free up" his attention by asking him to imagine that he was facing a big wall at the end of a road. What does one do? After a few moments, he thought: "Well, one can back up and find a way around that wall." The therapist and the client worked with confronting dead ends metaphorically with this analogy for the rest of the session. Soon after this session, the executive announced that he had found an ad in the newspaper for a job doing something different than he had been doing, and at a lower salary, but he decided to apply for it. He did apply for and get that job, and the happy ending of this story is that he was ultimately able to get back into a position comparable to the one he originally held.

Overfocused attention that limits full contact can be caused by many factors: rigidly held values and goals, overly intellectual attempts at problem solving, unacknowledged needs and emotions, and the use of various defense mechanisms. These should be thought of as ways of trying to make or maintain contact with self and world, albeit in dysfunctional ways. For instance, unacknowledged needs and emotions may be a way of trying to maintain contact with people you care about, who you are afraid will reject you if you do acknowledge such needs and emotions.

There is an obvious similarity here between the ideas of gestalt and the ideas of psychoanalysis. That is, disowning or not acknowledging certain parts of oneself, or using defense mechanisms, interferes with effective functioning. The difference is that gestalt emphasizes that these are things the person is actively doing in the moment to try to keep his life organized and flowing along, albeit in dysfunctional ways.

Organismic Self-Regulation

Gestalt therapists believe that if the individual is able to maintain full, open contact with self and situation in each moment, he will be able to make effective choices. They have held that there is a natural organismic self-regulating process by which the whole person can integrate all the available internal and external information into a functional gestalt so as to "know" or "sense" what is an optimal direction to go in at any given moment. Within the field of a person's experience, whatever is the most important direction for the client to go in will become "figural," that is, will stand out against the "ground" of the rest of his experience. If this "figure" does not lead to action, it becomes ***unfinished business***. For instance, hunger can be an incomplete or unfinished part of the field of experience, and it will have a tendency to become figural. However, it will become figural only if it is the most pressing incomplete experience present. In our earlier example, hunger became figural during a lecture, but if an attractive classmate asks for help with lecture notes, hunger may temporarily recede into the background as the less pressing experience in your current field.

Some ***incomplete gestalts*** come from the past. If a woman has a good deal of unresolved anger toward her father, this may "lurk" in the background until the proper situation brings it forth. Then, as she is dealing with a boss who reminds her of her father, that unfinished business may become figural, influencing her reactions to her boss.

According to Simkin and Yontef (1984, p. 18), the "field will form itself into the best gestalt that global conditions will allow." If free attention is available, the person's subjective experience will fluidly shift and flow to best integrate what is happening in each new situation with the person's short-term and long-term goals and needs. Psychological problems are due to interferences with this natural tendency. In other terms, pathology is an interference with the person's creative problem-solving capacity.

Open contact allows the individual's full organismic capacity to "know" how to operate. That is, functional knowing is a whole-body affair, not just a matter of intellectual, cognitive analysis. We not only know with our thoughts, but with our intuition and "guts" as well, and intuitive, gut-level knowing is often wiser than intellectual knowing.

We have seen that gestalt values full, present-centered awareness, but living in the here and now does not mean pretending that the past did not exist or that the future will not occur. It simply means being fully present in one's awareness of both outer and inner experience, which allows people to bring all of their resources to bear on coping with the flow of their lives as they are being lived in the present moment. It means to live in the moment, but not for the moment. People's experience will include relevant aspects of their past, as well as relevant aspects of their future goals. If people are fully present, these will all be organismically integrated into their current field of experience.

Psychopathology

What gets in the way of being able to be fully functioning in this manner? People are born with the ability to organismically self-regulate, but they lose it if they lose contact or if they learn to split experience up and to categorize rigidly. Categorizing our experience can be helpful as long as we recognize that categories are conceptual tools that help us cope with life and not rigid, absolute fixed realities. It is useful to categorize our experience into "inner" ("inside me") and "outer" ("outside" in the environment). It is useful to categorize part of our experience as "thinking" and part as "feeling." However, the problem is that people are taught to think of these categories as real. In other words, they learn to apply their category systems rigidly and do not even recognize that they are category systems. Therefore, they believe that self and environment are literally and rigidly separate, that feeling and thinking are separate and different, and so on. To make matters worse, they are also taught to categorize some of their experience as "bad" or "sinful."

People are also taught to regulate behavior by external rules and to distrust their feeling and intuition. As a result, they come to believe that the only "good" way to function is to be intellectual, objective, and rational. Both because of the "shoulds" they learn and the labeling of some experience as "bad," they may completely disown some of their experience. For instance, we may completely disown our angry feelings, because it is "bad" to feel anger and we "should" always be kind.

Responsibility

The splitting of experience interferes with the person's spontaneous ability to regulate himself. The person must instead rely on external guidelines rather than on his own ability to organismically self-regulate. Thus, he is not "response-able." By being "response-able," gestalt theory means taking responsibility for oneself and being present-centered. To be fully aware of one's inner and outer situation is to be able to make optimum choices for oneself at any given moment.

Responsibility defined this way means that I am responsible for my choices. It does not mean that I am not responsible to others, although it has sometimes been

Using gestalt with pets.

interpreted that way, including by Perls himself. Perls seemed to be preoccupied with maintaining his independence from others, as the story about his death and his gestalt prayer illustrate. The gestalt prayer presents a noninvolved image of interpersonal relationships. The "I do my thing . . . you do your thing" idea is an image of ships passing in the night, which, if they just happen to be sailing along on the same course, sail along together for a while. But that is not an image of involvement. The prayer implies, "I don't want your wishes, demands or desires to infringe on me in any way. I want to be free to do my own thing, with no responsibility to you."

Therapeutic Approach

The gestalt goal is not to help the client resolve the particular problem that she brings to therapy. The gestalt belief is that the presenting complaint is merely a symptom of a style of living that is the true problem. The focus of gestalt therapy is to increase the individual's ability to maintain full contact and awareness with the current situation and, through that, to reclaim her power to make effective choices through organismic self-regulation. Remember that what gestalt means by an "increase in awareness" is not the acquisition of insight. The goal is to increase the client's ability to stay present-centered and be aware in the moment.

As a result, gestalt is a highly experiential therapy. Gestalt does not proceed like verbal therapies, where the therapist and client sit around and talk about the client and his problems. In fact, some gestalt therapists see "talking about" problems as an avoidance of here-and-now experiencing, and they will not allow it to take place. Instead of having clients talk about problems, the gestalt therapist will interact in ways designed to facilitate full, immediate contact in the here and now. This may include focusing on the here-and-now relationship between the therapist and client. It also can include the use of various exercises that have been developed by gestalt therapists in order to do this.

Since the main goal of gestalt therapy is to increase contact in the moment, one of the most basic techniques is to have the client simply report what he or she is now aware of in order to train present-centered attention. The client will be asked to begin every sentence with "Now I am aware of." This will often demonstrate how difficult it is to stay present-centered, as the client will usually stray off into rumination or self-analysis.

Similar to the "now I am aware of" exercise is the "stay with" exercise. The client is instructed to stay with a thought or feeling. Remaining attentive to a feeling may lead to the emergence of some incomplete gestalt or issue the client needs to deal with. Both the "now I am aware of" and the "stay with" exercises can be seen as directly training present-centered attention.

Other techniques enhance the client's experiential focus. Gestalt is a holistic approach, and it is believed that often nonverbal expression conveys what a client is experiencing more accurately than her words. The client may be asked to exaggerate a gesture or tone of voice to enhance the actual experience of what she is saying. For instance, if the client says in a meek tone of voice, "I feel angry," she may be asked to say it louder. If a client is fooling with her wedding ring as she talks about her depressed feelings, the gestalt therapist may have her exaggerate the gesture and talk from her experience of the gesture: "Now I am slipping my wedding ring on and off my finger. I have a lot of ambivalence about my marriage." If the client is blinking a lot, the therapist may ask her to role-play her eyes: "I am my eyes. I am blinking as fast as I can to hold the tears in."

Another technique is to have a client substitute the phrase "I won't" for "I can't." Often, clients will say, "I can't confront my boss" or "I can't control my sexual feelings." This is a signal that the person is splitting off certain aspects of experience and not being response-able. By saying "I won't confront my boss" or "I won't control my sexual feelings," the individual focuses his attention back to his organismic experiencing. He may decide that he does not want to control his sexual feelings or confront his boss, because that is "organismically wise" for him. However, at least now he is able to be response-able.

Perhaps the most well-known experiential exercise used by gestalt therapists is role playing. For instance, to work with a dream, a client will act out parts of the dream. Perls's view was that the parts of a dream, including nonhuman objects such as chairs, cars, or houses, represent different aspects of the self and feelings. One client dreamed of an old road that had fallen out of use when a new superhighway was built nearby. When asked to role-play this road he said, "I'm an old, neglected road. For years I was the center of attention, but even then people used me. They used me and broke me down and then they abandoned me. No one cares about me. I'm just falling apart."

One role-playing exercise is called the "empty-chair" or "two-chair" technique. It is used to help clients resolve internal conflicts and their feeling about conflicts with others. The client sits facing an empty chair. If the problem is an internal conflict between different aspects of the self, the client is asked to pretend that one side of the conflict is sitting in the opposite chair. The client role-plays one side. Then the client switches chairs and role-plays the opposite side. If, for instance, you were having a conflict over studying one Sunday afternoon because you wanted to watch TV, you would be asked to place the side that watches TV in the empty chair and to role-play the side that wants you to study. Then you would change chairs and role-play the side that wants to watch TV. It might go as follows:

> ***Side A:*** You should study. You'll never graduate and get a good job if you don't. You're bad for wanting to watch TV. You just want to do nothing but lie around.
>
> ***Side B:*** But I only wanted to watch the football game. I need time to relax. I can study later. You demand too much.

The chair switching continues until some integration between the two sides is achieved.

> ***Side A:*** It's just that I feel so incompetent. I study and study but don't feel I'm getting it. Then I get desperate. I'm feeling really vulnerable and scared about my future.
>
> ***Side B:*** But then I feel like escaping when you feel like that. I don't like feeling incompetent. It's easier to watch TV.

Through the dialogue, the feelings of vulnerability that are the heart of the conflict emerge. Once you can "own" your feelings, you can deal with them, ultimately freeing you to choose or not to choose to study on any given Sunday afternoon.

The conflict over studying is an example of what Perls called the "top dog–underdog" conflict. The "top dog" is the "should" side, or the "internal critic" side, which is always judging and criticizing the self. The "underdog" is the "want" or "don't want" side. Greenberg (1984) has researched the process of resolution using the two-chair technique. He has found that the critic side starts out expressing itself in terms of shoulds and demands on the other want or don't want side, which Greenberg terms the experiencing side. Eventually, through the role-playing exercise, the critic side begins to soften, and moves away from being a harsh critic. As this happens, the experiencing side moves away from being defensive. The critic side begins to express the feelings of vulnerability that underlie the shoulds and the demands. As that happens, both sides begin to find that they are on the same "side," and some integration is reached.

The same role-playing technique can be used to help a person resolve "unfinished business" with interpersonal conflicts. If, for instance, you are still struggling with feelings that you were neglected and unloved by your father, you would pretend that your father is sitting in the empty chair opposite you. You would role-play your side of the conflict, switch chairs, and role-play your father's side. Again, you would continue the dialogue until some integration occurs. But what is achieved by this role playing? After all, no matter how successfully you use the technique in your therapy sessions, your real father might still act as unloving as ever. When you role-play your father in the empty-chair technique, you may begin to realize that just because he rejects you, you don't have to reject you. You begin to separate out his view of you from your view of you. You begin to take back the power to be in charge of your own life. You may be able to say: "I love you and want you to understand. But if you do not, that is you. I will still love you, but I will not feel bad about myself. I will still feel congruent and whole within myself. I would like your approval, but I do not need it."

There are other gestalt techniques and exercises that we will not present here. The important point is that for many gestalt therapists, techniques are secondary to maintaining full, present-centered contact with the client. While Perls tended to remain distant and uninvolved, many current gestalt therapists respond openly and interactively to their clients. Furthermore, they may integrate ideas from other approaches into their practice.

Gendlin's Focusing-Oriented Psychotherapy

According to Eugene Gendlin (1996), therapy is effective when it impacts in a directly experiential manner. Gendlin (1967) and his colleagues studied the therapy process by rating samples of successful and unsuccessful therapy. They concluded that when therapy worked, the client was, on the average, engaging in an experiencing process, and when therapy did not work, the client was not.

For Gendlin and his colleagues, engaging in an experiencing process is the activity of focusing inwardly on felt experience, listening empathically to it, and letting words and concepts come from that experience. In other words, it is the process of listening to and articulating one's inner, felt meanings. Clients may explore their problems in intellectual, abstract ways that will have no concrete, felt, therapeutic effect. Or, they may explore by constantly referencing their own inner experiential reactions. This is when therapy happens.

The focusing-oriented psychotherapist, according to Gendlin, tries to guide the client to focus on her inner experiencing in a therapeutically productive way. What is talked about is not important. Rather, how the client is exploring is what is crucial. Does the client "feel" what she is talking about, and is the client able to refer inwardly to that "feel" and talk from that "feel"? Gendlin called the ability to do this "focusing" ability. He went on to develop a specific technique called ***focusing*** (Gendlin, 1996) to facilitate it. Focusing is a structured procedure in which clients silently refer inwardly, try to suspend intellectual analysis, and then quietly listen in order to sense or feel what their experience is saying to them. When words come from their experience, rather than being applied to their experience by intellectual thought from above, a felt shift in experienced organization occurs. Clients experience a sense of something coming more clearly into focus that they can feel is right for them. The focusing process is one of repeated steps. Clients may not get "the answer" to their problems all at once. However, over time, focusing leads to greater clarity about what is bothering them, with the development of a more subtle and differentiated way of responding to the problem.

Gendlin and his colleagues suggested that all therapists are being helpful when they facilitate such an experiencing process, be they psychoanalytic, cognitive, or behavioral. Therapists can use many different techniques to facilitate this experiencing process. They can respond empathically; they can self-disclose; they can use ideas and concepts from other theories, such as object relations theory or psychoanalysis; or they can use techniques from other approaches, such as gestalt and behavioral techniques. The only criterion is that the idea or technique not be imposed on the client, but only used if it is experientially meaningful for the client.

Gendlin's focusing-oriented therapy arose from client-centered therapy. Gendlin believes that the therapist's warm, empathic, and genuine "being with" the client is fundamental. Gendlin trusts the client's own inner process to develop wise solutions. However, Gendlin is more directive than a traditional client-centered therapist in that he specifically responds in a manner designed to more efficiently facilitate the experiencing process.

Emotion-Focused Psychotherapy

An important theoretical development in person-centered theory was the work of David Wexler and others (Wexler & Rice, 1974) to apply an information-processing interpretation to client-centered therapy. Despite Rogers's emphasis on feelings, his theorizing has always had a cognitive, information-processing flavor. For instance, getting in touch with feelings is seen informationally:

> Often I sense that the client is trying to listen to himself, is trying to hear the *messages and meanings* which are being communicated by his own physiological reactions. . . . He comes to realize that his own inner reactions and experiences, the *messages* of his sense and viscera, are friendly. He comes to want to be close to his *inner sources of information*. (Rogers, 1961, p. 174, italics ours)

> This leads to the client's having access to all of the available data in the situation. . . . He could permit his total organism, his consciousness participating, to consider each stimulus, need, and demand, its relative intensity and importance, and out of this complex weighting and balancing, discover that course of action which would come closest to satisfying all his needs in the situation. (Rogers, 1961, p. 190)

Thus, the work of Wexler and his colleagues is an extension of an idea already implicit in Rogers's own work.

Wexler (1974) suggests that the therapist is a "surrogate information processor." What therapists do is direct clients' attention to ignored or neglected aspects of information (that is, feelings and experience), help clients sort out and differentiate relevant from irrelevant aspects of this and other information, and then help clients integrate the information into new and more effective cognitive structures for interacting with reality. Empathic responses are seen as active shapers and facilitators of information processing. They draw out the implications in what clients say, focus attention on selected aspects of client communication, and model and suggest ways of integrating or synthesizing differing themes in what clients say.

Following up on this work, Greenberg, Rice, and Elliott (1993b) developed a comprehensive integrative approach to psychotherapy originally called ***process-experiential psychotherapy,*** and more recently called ***emotion-focused psychotherapy*** (Elliott, Watson, Goldman, & Greenberg, 2004). Their approach is a unique integration of the more systematic therapy formats of cognitive and behavioral approaches with the client-centered belief in a self-propelled growth process. It also integrates ideas from both gestalt therapy and Gendlin's focusing-oriented approach. As a specific, brief, structured experiential-humanistic approach, emotion-focused therapy is more compatible with the current managed care climate than is "pure," open-ended client-centered therapy, and is currently being empirically supported by research.

The basic theory is that psychological problems occur because clients are unable to pay attention to the information available in their own emotional reactions. If clients are able to access emotions and emotional meanings, they will be able to reorganize the cognitive belief structures and the emotional patterns that have been guiding their dysfunctional reactions.

Emotion-focused psychotherapists are systematic in how they intervene to help clients grow and change. They look for *therapeutic markers* to help them decide exactly how to intervene at a particular moment. Recall from chapter 5 that a therapeutic marker is some kind of behavior exhibited by the client that signals or marks that the client is struggling with a particular kind of emotional problem or "task." The therapist then picks an intervention that will best help the client explore and resolve that particular emotional processing task.

One kind of marker is called a ***problematic reaction point.*** Clients who exhibit this marker talk about some kind of incident in which they have said or done something about which they feel self-critical. This marker leads to the use of the intervention called ***evocative unfolding.*** The therapist guides clients to explore the incident in vivid detail, using empathic reflections that are designed to be highly evocative of the experience of the scene itself. As clients are able to vividly reenter the scene, they discover the way they are viewing the situation that triggered their reaction. This helps clients resolve the problematic feelings. In addition, clients are able to reevaluate that way of construing things and change it if necessary. We consider this process in more detail under the heading of "task analysis" later in this chapter.

A second kind of marker is the *split.* Here clients exhibit a split between a "want" and a "should" as in our example where one part says "you should be studying" and the other part says "I don't want to study." The emotion-focused therapist uses the gestalt two-chair technique to help clients resolve the split. A third marker is *unfinished business.* As mentioned previously, the client is asked to make up a dialogue, this time between herself and the person she has had problematic experiences, "unfinished business," with. This usually helps clients come to terms with the problems generated in their relationship with the other person. For instance, a client who has been sexually abused by her father may feel damaged and unable to get the sense of betrayal she feels towards her father out of her mind. Through the role-playing procedure she may come to realize that she is a whole person no matter what her father did and be able to let go of her feelings of being damaged. Along with this she may change her relationship with her father. She may forgive him, or decide that he does not merit forgiveness. In either case she moves beyond what he did to feeling stronger in herself and focusing her attention on making her own life better.

A fourth marker is ***meaning protest*** (Clarke, 1996). The client describes a life event that violates some important cherished belief. The client also exhibits emotional protest; that is, he shows that he is upset over this violation. The client also expresses confusion or a lack of understanding about the experience. An example of such an event may be any unexpected trauma, such as one that violates a belief in the predictability or fairness of life. The goal of the therapist is to help the client "create meaning" from the event. The process includes helping the client identify and specify the cherished belief that has been violated and using empathic reflections and questions to help him reflect on the role and place of the cherished belief in his life. This process leads to revision of the cherished belief in a more adaptive direction.

As with Gendlin's focusing-oriented psychotherapy, emotion-focused therapists believe that the therapist must be warm, empathic, and genuine. Further, they also believe that it is the clients who actually find the resolutions to their problems. Emotion-focused therapists believe, however, that the systematic use of interventions at specific marker points help clients in the exploratory process.

Mahrer's Experiential Psychotherapy

Alvin Mahrer's (1989) experiential psychotherapy is based on the idea that the goal is to activate a person's deep inner experiencing potential. Basically, Mahrer assumes that through their upbringing, people develop an operating personality on the "surface." That is the relatively programmed side of the person, through which the person operates on a day-do-day basis. However, this "operating" side of the person often blocks the creative potential for a deeper inner experiencing. Mahrer's goal in therapy is to get people in touch with this deeper inner experiencing.

Mahrer's approach is unusual. He has both client and therapist recline in large easy chairs. Both therapist and client keep their eyes closed throughout the session. Sessions last as long as they have to; that is, there is no fixed time limit, though most sessions usually conclude in about one and a half to two hours. The client talks about anything she wants. The therapist uses four basic steps to help the client access her inner experiences.

The first step is to facilitate the client's being in a moment of very strong experiencing of emotion. This could be anger, sadness, happiness, love, or fear. The most important thing is that strong emotion is accessed. The therapist does this by putting himself in the client's shoes and verbalize the kinds of feelings and emotions he thinks the client is experiencing. The therapist is very dramatic, using loud vocal tone and vivid phrases and images to heighten the client's emotion. For instance, with a woman client who came in complaining of neck pains, Mahrer and the client accessed the client's "devilish" side. That brought laughter as the client imagined using her neck pains to get out of going to work (Mahrer, 1989). During the second step, the therapist facilitates appreciation of the inner experiencing that has been accessed. For example, the laughter accessed in step one was associated with the client's "devilish" feelings. This inner experiencing was allowed to be, and the client was allowed to "indulge" in it. In step three, the goal is to help the client disengage from her normal operating personality and be able to more fully accept and "be" this inner experiencing. In order to do this, the therapist asks the client to recover memories from childhood where this inner experiencing had been activated. For instance, this client remembered incidents when she had been devilish as a child. Finally, in step four, the therapist gives the client a chance to use her imagination and explore what life might be like if she could more fully be this inner experiencing. For instance, this client imagined being "devilish" in her life, quitting her job, and going on a vacation with her husband.

Mahrer's approach to therapy is not explicitly problem oriented. At no time in this therapy session with this client were techniques designed to make the neck pains go away explicitly used, nor was any attempt made to understand the unconscious meaning or the genesis of the neck pains. Yet, after this and several other sessions,

Mahrer reports, the pains disappeared. Mahrer's belief is that the goal of his therapy is to access the client's potential for new experiencing, and nothing more. How this becomes concretely instantiated in changing the client's actual life is up to the client. For this reason, Mahrer believes that each of his therapy sessions is a complete "therapy" in itself. There is no continuity from one session to another unless the client brings up the same issue. What is talked about at the next session may be completely unrelated to what was talked about in previous sessions.

Existential Therapy

Philosophical Background

Existential psychotherapy is based in a philosophical approach called phenomenology, developed by Edmund Husserl (1964). Husserl's goal was to suspend acceptance of all concepts about reality in order to get to things that could not be doubted about reality: pure phenomena. Imagine looking at all things that come into your consciousness as though they were images on a movie screen. Imagine examining them while suspending all judgment about what they are, what they mean, or what they consist of. To the extent that you can do this, you approximate what Husserl was striving for. For example, you see someone acting "crazy." Can you suspend your judgment that he is acting "crazy"? Can you suspend your tendency to characterize his behavior at all? It is impossible to suspend all preconceptions, but the phenomenologists tried to approach this ideal. Their cry was "To the things themselves!"

One example of the ***phenomenological method*** in psychology is the work of R. D. Laing (1967). Laing wished to study schizophrenia without any preconceptions. So he suspended the idea that the schizophrenic is mentally ill, crazy, or incomprehensible. In trying to look at the schizophrenic without preconceptions, Laing concluded that the typical Western view of schizophrenia was based on the worldview and preconceptions of those judging the schizophrenic as ill or disordered. Laing proceeded to arrive at a very different view. Basically, he argued that schizophrenia can be a growth experience wherein the schizophrenic, by shedding a false, socially imposed identity and descending into madness, is able to reclaim his own true inner potential. If this process is respected and supported rather than judged and interfered with (for instance, with the administration of drugs), the schizophrenic can come back to reality as a more whole person than before. Laing's views have not generally found favor among Western psychiatric professionals. However, there is some evidence that for some schizophrenics, treating them as being on a growth experience can be beneficial (Mosher, 2001). Mosher and his colleagues created a place in the San Francisco Bay area in California called Soteria House. There, schizophrenics were not subjected to typical psychiatric treatment. They were not given drugs, unless over time it became clear that the milieu of Soteria House was not helpful to them. Instead they were offered caring, supportive, empathic relationships. Outcomes were better than outcomes of schizophrenics in more typical treatment programs.

Another important philosopher who influenced the existential approach was Martin Heidegger. Heidegger's philosophy was based on Husserl's phenomenological approach, but went in a different direction (Frings, 1968; Schmitt, 1969). He held that humans, in contrast to objects, exist as interactive entities with reality. People are activities rather than fixed objects, in constant dialogue with their surroundings. At any given moment, the individual is a creative construction of both past history and current situation. As a result, the individual is never the same from moment to moment. Heidegger would have considered the belief in a fixed personality structure, including the various labels, such as borderline, passive, or narcissistic personality, to be an inauthentic way of relating to ourselves and others. People do not "have" personalities; they constantly create and re-create their personalities through their choices and actions.

Inauthenticity is an attempt to deny the existence of choice. Jean-Paul Sartre (1956) suggested that people become anxious when they face the fact that they are responsible for themselves and their choices. The concept of a fixed identity reduces anxiety. Thinking of myself as a "good" person becomes a substitute for examining my behavior and making choices on the basis of rightness or goodness. If I define myself as a borderline personality, then I no longer have to consider myself responsible for my impulsive acts. In order to avoid the anxiety of choice, we all seek fixed identities, such as "being a doctor" or "being an honorable man." Yet what really counts is not who we are, but what we do, that is, how we choose to behave.

Every time people make choices they open up new possibilities both in themselves and in the world. For example, if I act cruelly toward someone, I "bring out" the negative in myself and, perhaps, reciprocally in that person. If I act caringly, I may allow potential positive aspects to come forth.

Humans are thus the creatures through which reality "knows" itself. An individual's actions allow what has previously been only potential, or "hidden," in reality to be articulated. The most important kind of knowing is knowing how. Knowing how is the kind of knowing involved in doing. For instance, learning how to play the guitar brings forth potential in the player and musical potential in an object. Intellectual knowing about facts is less useful. Therapy should involve learning how to be human, rather than learning about oneself, that is, about one's past. People need to learn how to listen to themselves, how to be in tune with their nature as creatures in transition.

With this brief summary of its philosophical basis, we will now look at existential psychotherapy. We will not concentrate on different existential theorists by name, but we will list here some of the important names: Ludwig Binswanger (1963), Medard Boss (1963), J. F. T. Bugental (1976), Salvador Maddi (Kobasa & Maddi, 1983), Rollo May (Schneider & May, 1995), and Irving Yalom (1981). A closely related approach is Victor Frankl's (1963) logotherapy. An important recent existentialist is Kirk Schneider (Schneider & May, 1995).

Theory of Personality and Psychopathology

For the existential approach, the primary fact of human existence is that people are free to create their own meaning and identity in life. But can anyone be anything he or she wants? The answer is obviously no. There are limits. People must accept finiteness as a fundamental fact of existence. Humans are finite in two senses: (1) reality imposes limits, and (2) everyone ultimately dies. Reality places limits on people in several ways. We are limited by our biology and by the time and place into which we are born. Being born with a handicap, into a starving Ethiopian family, or as a black slave in 1800 would all impose certain limitations.

But there are two ways of thinking about limits: to see them as restricting freedom or to see them as making the experience of freedom of choice meaningful. Limits and freedom are two sides of the same coin. There could be no freedom without limits. If you could choose to be anything you wanted at any time, then both freedom and choice would lose all meaning. If you could have anything you wanted at any given moment, then you would never really have to choose.

Thus, freedom and choice are mutually interdependent. The individual is free within the limitations imposed by the facts of his existence to create life in any way he can. The individual is free to choose how he will deal with limits. He can view them as immutable barriers and give up, or he can accept them as challenges. If you lose the use of your legs in an automobile accident, you can withdraw from activities or you can learn to maneuver in a wheelchair and continue with your life. Some limitations cannot be transcended. If you are in prison, sentenced to be executed, you may be unable to escape or get the sentence changed. However, you can still choose how you spend your last days and how you approach death. The challenge is to do as much as possible with what one has. Each individual can be creative and forge something meaningful out of whatever life has given him. Existentialists call the courage to face up to adverse circumstances in life the "courage to be" (Tillich, 1952).

The individual's choices not only create the meaning of her life and being, but they also influence the meaning of events surrounding her. The existential view can properly be considered a "field" or "systems" view of behavior. As the meaning of a word is determined by the rest of the sentence it is embedded in and the meaning of a sentence may change if one word is changed, the meaning of any event in an individual's life is determined by the whole web of meanings she has attributed to herself and the world. How the individual sees herself and the world may change if the meaning of some important event in her life changes.

Therefore, people create the structure of their own lives, and each choice moves them along their life paths. But at any moment they can choose to alter the path. Right now your choice to continue reading this chapter is in some sense "creating" who you are. In reading this chapter, you are acting on your perception of your interests and values at this moment. Perhaps you are a student planning a career in psychology, but perhaps you are not a good student. Perhaps you feel awkward around others and have low self-esteem. If, as you read, you grow more and more bored, you might toss the book away and go change your major the next day. Perhaps you change to dentistry. Pursuing dentistry, you associate with different people and take different courses. Now you may find new aspects of yourself opening up. Your values may change and your self-image may improve. You discover that you are so interested in dentistry that you do well academically. Instead of feeling stupid, you now see yourself as motivated and capable. Before, you may have seen yourself as awkward, dull, and romantically undesirable. Now you find yourself talking with enthusiasm to another person who is interested in dentistry, and romantic sparks begin to fly. Your self-image in that area begins to change also.

If people create their life structure and identity through their choices, why does anyone choose a miserable or self-defeating existence? One answer to this is that they are often unaware that they are choosing. They may not have had any experiences that allow them to realize that they have a choice in how they move through life. A woman who grows up in a family and community where the message is that a woman's place is in the home may accept that message as objectively true. She will not see the possibility of any choice over her role as a woman.

Many existential theorists also stress the denial of the possibility of choice. According to May and Yalom (1984), people deny choice because of anxiety. They point out that existentialism is a "depth psychology," similar to psychoanalysis, but existentialists believe that what is hidden is the possibility of choice, not sexual and aggressive impulses. To avoid anxiety, people avoid their own potential. Often, they try to actualize an image of what society says they ought to be. They ought to be businesspeople rather than artists, married rather than single, heterosexual rather than homosexual, religious rather than nonreligious, or whatever. They deny the possibility of choosing to be anything other than what society says they should be, and they become anxious if they sense that they may not fit these images. They deny themselves knowledge of their true wants and goals in order to try to fit these images.

But these attempts to avoid anxiety do not always work, and anxiety may be a signal that an individual is living an inauthentic existence. Two cases illustrate this point. A man was going for his doctorate because his parents strongly wanted a Ph.D. in the family. About three years into his graduate program, just about the time he had to pass three comprehensive exams to advance to his dissertation, he became anxious and depressed. The interesting thing was that he became anxious and depressed after passing the first two exams with outstanding performances. He found he could not even study for the third. An existential view would be that as the man approached completion of his degree, the lack of fit between that goal and his own feelings grew more pronounced. After a stormy period of depression, anxiety, and several suicide attempts, he finally took an "existential leap" and dropped out of school. He got a job as a social worker helping underprivileged families, and his depression and anxiety vanished; when last heard of, he was living a normal life. In this case, anxiety and depression were signals of inauthencity, rather than repressed instincts (psychoanalysis), dysfunctional cognitions (cognitive approaches), or conditioning (behavioral approaches).

Another case was a woman in an unfulfilling marriage. She was distant, cold, and reserved, seemed vaguely "out of touch" all the time, and was usually somewhat negative and depressed. Some friends described her as a basically negative person who liked to see the worst in the world. Finally, on facing up to the lack of fit between herself and her marriage, she left it. By taking this "existential leap," she was able to move out of living an inauthentic existence, and this freed up other aspects of her personality. She became more warm, open, and vital.

For existentialists, anxiety results from denial of one's authenticity and potential. But we said earlier that it was to avoid anxiety that people deny their ability to choose in the first place. According to existentialists, people deny their ability to choose to avoid the basic anxiety associated with human finiteness. For existentialists, anxiety is unavoidable. To live is to have to choose. But to have to choose is to face up to the basic uncertainty of life. Whenever we make a choice, we are literally betting our lives. By choosing to read this book and to pursue your college career, you are betting that a college degree will be good for you in some way. The problem is that you may bet on a career only to find there are no jobs available in your field when you graduate. Or there may be jobs, but you discover that you want to change fields or that you aren't as talented in your field as you would have liked. To live authentically is to face up to the fact that there are no "safe" choices in life. And, eventually you will die. If you happen to have made "wrong" choices, time may run out before you can rectify things. Thus, death is the ultimate source of anxiety, and the ability to face up to one's own death is a precondition to authentic living. Terror management theory, a recent approach based on existential ideas, holds that self-esteem is in part a defense against death anxiety. Some research supports this view (Pyszczynski, Greenberg, Solomon, Arndt, & Schimel, 2004). For instance, in one study, individuals rated their self-esteem higher when reminded of their mortality by being near a cemetery.

Existentialists do not hold that one choice is necessarily superior to another. Any choice involves risk. The woman mentioned above was taking a risk by leaving a marriage (she might be unhappier outside it; she might have been able to work things out), and she was taking a risk by staying in it (she might miss a happier existence; she might not be able to work things out). Telling yourself "I must get a Ph.D.," or "I must stay married," or "I must remain a full-time housewife" reduces anxiety. Then you do not have to make a choice either way. But even though you do not know it, you are making a choice—you are choosing not to face up to the reality of your situation. Other ways you might deny the reality of choice is by drinking too much or taking drugs. You might become dependent, hoping others will make choices for you. You can pretend the future doesn't exist and become an impulsive creature of the moment, thereby denying that choice has some future impact. From an existential perspective, all psychopathology results from an attempt to deny choice.

The inauthentic person does not integrate the past, present, and future in his choices. He may avoid choice by thinking in terms of the future: "I'll be myself as soon as I've gotten a good job" or "a good relationship." He may idealize others, thus denying the basic imperfection and uncertainty of life. Or, he may pursue happiness. Victor Frankl (as quoted in May & Yalom, 1984) said that happiness is something that cannot be pursued, it is something that can only ensue. In other words, happiness is a by-product of creative involvement in the world. The "more we deliberately search for self-satisfaction the more it eludes us, whereas the more we fulfill some self-transcendent meaning happiness will ensue" (May & Yalom, 1984, p. 380). Finally, the person living an inauthentic life will often have stereotyped and undifferentiated values, probably swallowed whole from others rather than authentically chosen. As a result, inauthentic patterns of living often consist of attempts to force oneself and the world into rigid, preconceived patterns. Often, the values are treated as objectively real, and the person does not even realize they are chosen.

Psychotherapy

The existential approach is really more of a point of view on psychotherapy than a specific psychotherapeutic approach. The existentially oriented therapist can use any technique or approach, as long as it is used in a way compatible with existential ideas. Some of the earlier existentialists, like Ludwig Binswanger, were psychoanalytic in many respects. Some modern existential therapists practice more like gestalt therapists, others more like client-centered therapists. Nevertheless, there are some general ideas and principles of existential therapy.

The ultimate goal of existential therapy is to get the client to become aware of her own goals in life and to make authentic choices. Put another way, the goal is to set people free (May, 1981). Therapy can be seen in all cases as helping clients "de-restrict" themselves, as helping people to grow. In order to do this, clients must confront themselves and what they have been avoiding. This means confronting their own anxiety and, ultimately, their own finiteness. Often, it is the deepest potentialities that are denied in order to control anxiety. To choose potential is to take a risk, but there will be no richness in life, no joy, unless people confront the possibility of loss, tragedy, and ultimately, death.

One of the first things a client needs to do is to expand awareness. That means to become aware of the potential he is denying, the means he is using to maintain the denial, the reality that he can choose, and the anxiety associated with choice. In order to help him do this, the therapist uses the two basic tools of empathy and authenticity. Empathy is used as a form of the phenomenological method. The therapist attempts to respond to the client without preconceptions. An empathic and nonjudgmental attitude may allow the client's inner world to surface.

The other important tool is the therapist's authenticity. To be authentic, the client has to learn that he does not have to play roles, that he does not have to be perfect or what he is "supposed" to be, that he does not have to deny aspects of his own experience, and that he can take risks. Therefore, the therapist must model these qualities and try to be a "real" person in therapy. But what does it mean for the therapist to be "real" in therapy? We considered this question in our discussion of genuineness in chapter 8. It is important because we are aware of a number of instances in which, in our opinion, the concept of "realness" in therapy has been abused by individuals labeling themselves "existential therapists."

In existential therapy, being real or authentic means that the therapist is present—fully "there" in the moment, with total attention on what is happening in the therapy room. She is tuned in to the client, tuned in to herself, and tuned in to what is going on between them. She is not half there while the other half is immersed in theoretical thoughts about the client. Being fully present also means that the therapist is in the relationship as a real person, allowing herself to be affected by the client, and using how she is affected to respond therapeutically in an immediate way to the client. If the goal of therapy is for the client to be authentic, then it is important that the therapist model authenticity by sharing her immediate impressions and reactions to the client with the client. In essence, it is a matter of giving the client immediate personal feedback. However, it is important to give that feedback in a useful, respectful way.

Effective and helpful feedback is first "owned" by the therapist, that is, presented as her personal reaction and not as the objective truth about the client. Second the therapist acknowledges that it is *her* perception; that is, it could be unique and idiosyncratic to the therapist. Third, it is given in the form of an "I" statement, which is framed in a way to give specific helpful feedback rather than in a blaming or criticizing way (e.g., "I get bored when you focus on describing what your wife is doing wrong rather than giving me your personal feelings and reactions" versus "You're talking nothing but dry, intellectualized drivel"). Fourth, effective confrontations and shared personal reactions are most helpful when they address clients' strengths—that is, rather than merely telling clients what they are doing wrong, the therapist gives them a sense of what she thinks they are capable of doing right.

Beyond empathy and authenticity there are few techniques that are specifically existential. However, Frankl's logotherapy, which is generally considered a form of existential therapy, has contributed two: paradoxical intention and de-reflection (Frankl, 1963). Paradoxical intention is similar to paradoxical intervention, used by family therapists (see chapter 13). The client is urged to wish for the very thing she fears or to engage in the behavior she fears. Thus, a person with a fear of germs would be instructed to deliberately get herself dirty. De-reflection, used in cognitive-behavioral approaches, is based on the premise that focusing too much on problems exacerbates them (as an example, think of the last time you tried to get a melody out of your head). The therapist tries to shift the client's attention. This is not to teach the client to deny or repress. Rather, if the client's attention can be directed to positive aspects of his life, the negative will not loom so large and may fade away. The best cure for shyness, for instance, is to get so involved in a social situation that you "forget" to worry about how you are being seen by others.

Evaluation of Experiential and Existential Approaches

Effectiveness of Therapy

Focusing-oriented psychotherapy has not been studied extensively in an empirical way. However, there is evidence that it can be effective for coping with cancer, dealing with weight problems, and working with public speaking anxiety (Greenberg, Elliott, & Lietaer, 1994). Elliott, Greenberg, and Lietaer (2004) reviewed 10 studies on Gestalt therapy for a variety of psychological problems. They found that the average client in Gestalt therapy improved significantly. Three studies compared Gestalt therapy to a control group. The average effect size was .64, suggesting moderate effectiveness. Emotion-focused therapy has been found to be equivalent in effectiveness to cognitive therapy (the current "treatment of choice") for the treatment of depression (Greenberg & Watson, 1998). Other research has shown that it is useful for helping people who were sexually abused as children to resolve feelings of unfinished business (Paivio & Greenberg, 1995).

There is little controlled research on either existential psychotherapy or Mahrer's experiential psychotherapy. However, we have previously mentioned the positive results of the work of Mosher (2001) and colleagues using an existentially based growth-oriented model to facilitate recovery from schizophrenia. Schneider (2003) argues that there is evidence for many of the postulates of existential psychotherapy, including its emphasis on the importance of the authentic relationship, the use of experiential techniques, and emphasis on the client as the ultimate self-change agent (see chapter 8). Mahrer (1996) has extensively researched his approach to therapy by carefully examining tapes of therapy sessions. He has found evidence to support the importance of emotional activation. He has also found evidence of clients making changes such as ridding themselves of the bad feeling that they brought into therapy.

In some cases there is evidence of clients making significant personality changes as shown in the therapy tapes.

In a recent review of research on experiential approaches to psychotherapy in general (including client-centered therapy, gestalt therapy, process-experiential therapy, and related approaches), Elliott et al. (2004) found that the evidence for the effectiveness of experiential therapies is equivalent to the evidence for the effectiveness of cognitive and other psychotherapies.

There is evidence supporting the effectiveness of some of the specific tasks used in emotion-focused psychotherapy, such as using evocative unfolding at problematic reaction points (Rice & Saperia, 1984), and using Clarke's "creation of meaning" task to help clients overcome traumatic experiences (Clarke, 1996). The gestalt role-playing techniques have also received empirical support. For instance, studies by Greenberg and colleagues (Greenberg, 1984) demonstrated the efficacy of the empty-chair technique in helping a person resolve conflictual feelings. The technique was also found to get the client experientially involved in the therapy process more quickly and immediately than the Rogerian technique of reflection of feelings.

Theoretical Evaluation

The group of experiential and existential perspectives can be generally criticized in several ways. First, some psychologists find experiential and existential terminology vague. Terms such as "living in the here and now," "taking responsibility for oneself," "authenticity," and "staying with one's feelings" are open to a wide range of interpretations. Such vagueness not only can lead to widely differing applications of the terms (with some resulting abuses), it also can make it difficult to study experiential and existential approaches empirically. Further, it is confusing to the beginning therapist. What is "living in the here and now"? How do you know if you are being "authentic"?

In the past, this vagueness sometimes led to abuses. These are not as common now, but there were cases where, in the name of "holding people responsible," clients were blamed for their problems. Additionally, while effective authenticity can be therapeutically helpful, there were also abuses of authenticity in the past. Fritz Perls, for example, was reputed to maintain that he was not responsible for what happened to a client in therapy because clients are responsible for themselves. Sometimes, in the name of authenticity, therapists were "honest" in confrontive and unfeeling ways that were harmful to vulnerable clients.

A second criticism has to do with the discovery-oriented nature of existential and experiential approaches to psychotherapy. By "discovery-oriented" we mean that the goal of the therapy is to help clients discover their own solutions to their problems. At a deeper level, the goal is to help clients live a more authentic and meaningful existence. However these are not necessarily the goals of many clients. They want to get over their drinking problem, or lose weight, or rid themselves of anxiety or depression. They are after quick and efficient targeted ways to achieve these ends. They may prefer approaches (such as cognitive-behavioral) that have methods specifically designed to alleviate the problem they have come to therapy to resolve. On the other hand, some existentialists (e.g., Schneider & May, 1995) would reply that their approach to therapy offers the possibility of a deeper, more meaningful engagement in life. Not all clients may want this, but after symptom removal, some do.

The traditional approaches to experiential and existential practice, gestalt therapy and existential therapy, are relatively unstructured. Therapists learn a set of principles. Then their training primarily consists of their own experiences in therapy workshops. The goal of these approaches is spontaneity and the capacity to improvise in the moment. After all, the goal of therapy is to "set the client free" to be more spontaneous, so therapists need to model this themselves. However some therapists (and some clients) want a clearer agenda and a clearer direction for how therapy is to proceed. Mahrer's experiential psychotherapy and emotion-focused therapy provide more specific structure for practice than do the older humanistic and existential approaches, while preserving the discovery-oriented essence. Schneider's (Schneider & May, 1995) work on existential therapy also moves in that direction.

Another criticism that can be levied against these approaches is that there is little evidence for their theories of what causes psychological problems. Is an anxiety disorder, for instance, primarily a problem of a crisis in personal meaning—not being able to make an authentic choice about one's life path? There is little evidence for such a view. There is also little evidence for the gestalt view that it is an inability to maintain full contact in the moment, which in essence causes all psychological problems. And conceptually, if it is a lack of maintaining full contact that causes *all* problems, why does it show up in so many different forms (e.g., anxiety disorders, depression, eating disorders, substance abuse, and so on)?

A final criticism of these approaches is not really a criticism so much as an observation. In the current mental health climate, when insurance companies pay for psychotherapy, it is going to be difficult for therapists whose focus is to help clients discover new meaning in their lives and to live more authentically to receive payment for their services. It may well be that they may have to practice outside of the typical health care system.

In Conclusion

Experiential and existential approaches are discovery oriented in their therapy focus. That means that their goal is to provide a context within which clients have the opportunity to consider important personal issues about how they are living life, to discover new possibilities for themselves, and to create and develop new personal pathways. As such, they are not specifically symptom-focused. Existential-humanistic therapists generally do not look with favor on DSM diagnoses and prefer to work in an open-ended exploratory fashion, rather than to decide on a specific treatment plan in advance, targeted to removal of client symptoms. As such they do not fit well into the current managed care climate. Yet many clients appear to prefer such approaches and even pay out of pocket for them rather than see a brief, symptom-focused therapist through their health care plan. Thus, it is likely that existential-humanistic approaches will flourish outside of the health care system as an alternative therapy for those who want more than symptom removal.

In this regard, existential-humanistic approaches are unique in that they emphasize the whole human being, in the terms that people use to describe and experience their own lives—as creatures who make plans and have goals, wishes and needs, thoughts and experiences, relationships, and a future. In contrast, psychodynamic approaches emphasize unconscious forces and their impact on conscious experience, and cognitive approaches focus on whether the person's thoughts are logical and scientific. Behaviorism sees the person as a collection of responses, and systems theory sees the person as a "cog" in a system. None of these focuses on the experience of the whole person as an organized, planning entity. It is likely that this aspect of existential-humanistic thought will continue to be of importance.

Existential-humanistic principles have already been incorporated into other approaches, and in that sense will continue to exert influence. First, existential-humanistic approaches take growth and change seriously. As such, they give central attention to the creativity of the person. Second, existential-humanists were among the first to take the idea seriously that the person is to some degree the constructor of his or her world. Following from this is an emphasis on choice and individual responsibility. These emphases can now be found in recent psychoanalytic thinking and in cognitive views. Third, existential-humanists were among the first to emphasize the role of meaning, its creation and modification, as a central part of psychotherapy. This also is now a part of most other approaches. Fourth, existential-humanistic thinking was among the first to adopt a "systems" view of personality, emphasizing the interpersonal, interactive nature of the human being. Fifth, approaches such as gestalt have contributed useful techniques to the therapist's "kit." Sixth, the development of Gendlin's focusing-oriented psychotherapy, emotion-focused therapy, and Mahrer's experiential psychotherapy contribute systematic, structured existential-humanistic approaches. Emotion-focused therapy in particular has considerable research support.

Finally, ***positive psychology*** (Snyder & Lopez, (2002) is a broad-based recent movement that incorporates many of the topics first studied by experiential, existential, and client-centered theorists (chapter 8). Positive psychology emphasizes the positive in human beings: their strengths, courage, compassion, wisdom, the search for meaningfulness, empathy, love, forgiveness, acceptance, authenticity, creativity, resilience, and positive motivation. Carl Rogers (chapter 8) was one of the first to study the person's capacity for growth in the face of adversity (resilience). Existentialists also have emphasized humans' capacity to "bounce back" and to create meaning in the face of adversity. Carl Rogers has been given credit for making empathy popular in the United States. Experiential therapists such as Leslie Greenberg and Alvin Mahrer were among the first to emphasize the adaptive potential of emotions. Compatible with existential, client-centered, and experiential approaches, positive psychologists have questioned the negative focus on pathology in DSM and have argued for the need for a diagnostic system that focuses on human strengths and virtues.

BEHAVIORAL APPROACHES TO THERAPY

A 34-year-old man had a severe fear of being in an automobile. This had started four years previously when his car had been struck from behind while he was waiting for a red light to change. He had been thrust forward so that his head, striking the windshield, had sustained a small laceration. He had not lost consciousness, but a surge of panic had swept over him, brought on by the thought "I am about to die." The fear became connected to the car's interior and spread to all car interiors. During these four years he had been unable to enter a car without great anxiety. Driving was out of the question. That fear was entirely due to classical autonomic conditioning.

—J. Wolpe, *The Practice of Behavior Therapy*

Much confusion about the etiology of neurotic fear emanates from the assumption that it is quite different from that of normal fear. . . . There is in fact no basic difference. Just as some normal (i.e., appropriate) fears develop on the basis of classical conditioning and some on the basis of information (cognitive learning), the same is true of neurotic fears. What differentiates normal and neurotic fears is the character of the stimulus situation to which the conditioning has occurred. If that stimulus situation is objectively either a source of danger or a sign of danger, the fear is appropriate or "adaptive"; if it is neither, the fear is neurotic.

—J. Wolpe, *The Practice of Behavior Therapy*

One day you are walking down the hall in the psychology building on campus when a research assistant beckons to you from a laboratory door. "Want to see something weird?" "Okay," you say, following the assistant into the lab. "See anything unusual about this rat?" she says, reaching into a cage and grabbing a fat, glossy, white rat by the scruff of the neck.

"No, it looks like a normal rat," you conclude after a careful examination of 1.5 seconds.

"Well, watch this." She carries the rat over to a large box with lights and wires attached to it. There is no top on the box and it is divided into two compartments with an opening between them. One compartment is painted all white and the other dark brown. "What will happen if I put the rat in there?"

"Well," you consider, trying to remember what you know about rats, "the rat will probably explore the compartments, and it will probably stay mostly in the dark compartment." (You suddenly remembered that rats prefer darkness to light.)

She lowers the rat into the dark side of the box, and almost before its paws can hit the floor, it shoots through the doorway into the white compartment, and there it stays, sniffing around.

"How peculiar," you say, because you are absolutely certain that you recall Professor Lecturn telling the class that rats prefer dark areas. "Maybe it just doesn't know any better," you suggest. "Let's see that again."

Obligingly, the assistant places the rat in the dark compartment again. Again, it rushes to the white side and stays there. She repeats this activity several times, and the rat always runs to the white side without the slightest hesitation. She even inserts a door into the opening between the compartments, which can be opened by a lever in the dark compartment. When she then puts the rat in, it rushes to the lever, pushes it, and scurries through the open door into the white side. Since you (and Professor Lecturn) could not possibly be wrong about normal rat behavior, there must be something wrong with this particular rat. "Wow," you say, "what an abnormal rat!"

"You think so?" the assistant asks. "What if I told you that there used to be an electric grid on the floor of the dark compartment? This rat received a huge electric shock in there."

"I see," you nod knowingly. "But there's no electric grid in there now, so it's impossible for the rat to get shocked again."

"That's the neurotic paradox. The learned behavior remains even though the conditions for the original learning no longer hold."

"Why doesn't the rat eventually learn that no shock is coming?"

"It would under certain circumstances," she admits, "but there are several theories about why it doesn't under these conditions. One possibility is that when the rat runs into the white side, its fear is reduced, which is highly rewarding, so the behavior of running to the white side is constantly being reinforced by fear reduction."

You nod as if you understand and remark, "So this is a perfectly normal rat after all."

"Yes, when you know its learning history."

Foundations of Behavior Therapy

The set of therapeutic interventions known collectively as behavior therapy resulted from the application of scientific behavioral theory and methods to the treatment of psychopathology. The foundations of behavior therapy lie in learning theory, and the theoretical assumptions behind behavior therapy techniques begin, like learning theory, with the philosophical belief that methods for dealing with human behavior problems should be based on the scientific method. Another fundamental assumption is that all behavior is determined and that the variables determining it can be discovered and changed.

Behaviorists differed most drastically from previous theorists of psychotherapy in their insistence that abnormal behavior is not fundamentally different from normal behavior and that the abnormal "symptom" *is* the disorder and not a symbol of unconscious conflict. The same laws of learning apply to all behavior, both "normal" and "abnormal." Abnormal behavior is simply the normal, lawful response to abnormal learning conditions. Abnormal behavior can be changed by changing these learning conditions. In essence, behavior therapy is very optimistic.

Early behaviorism also differed from traditional psychotherapy in its opposition to mentalistic notions of the mind and its emphasis on objectively observable behaviors and situations. Strict behaviorists, such as B. F. Skinner (1938, 1971), believe that behavior can be explained by the principles of learning and conditioning, without using what goes on in the person's head as an explanation. It is not that behaviorists deny the existence or importance of thoughts and feelings (or genetic predispositions), but rather they think that these internal behaviors should be subject to the same scientific investigation as behavioral factors. Until they are, such factors have no explanatory value, and scientific rigor requires an emphasis on observable behavior.

Box 10.1 One Flew Over . . .

Many years ago, a psychologist sat quietly in a staff meeting while two psychoanalytically oriented psychiatrists argued for an hour about the patient they had all seen recently in intake. The patient was an attractive 17-year-old woman who was suffering from anxiety and a severe phobia of birds, which kept her from being able to go out to school or work. One analyst argued strongly that the fear of birds symbolized her fear of heterosexual encounters, since the birds unconsciously represented penises or "cocks." The other analyst argued, equally vociferously, that the fear of birds represented her fear of her latent homosexuality, since at that time and place "bird" was slang for young woman or "chick."

During intake, the psychologist had asked the patient why she thought she was so afraid of birds. The patient immediately described an incident when she was four years old and visiting her aunt's farm. As punishment for some naughty act, the aunt locked her in the henhouse for a few minutes. In her attempts to escape from the henhouse, the crying child probably frightened the chickens. She vividly recalled the hens squawking and flying about, hitting her with their wings and scratching her face and arms. She remembered feeling terrified, and she avoided birds ever after.

When the analysts finished arguing, the psychologist ventured to report the client's history. The analysts paused for only a moment before uniting against the psychologist and asserting that the henhouse incident was merely a "screen memory" invented to rationalize the phobia. Nevertheless, the psychiatrists agreed to allow the psychologist and her young colleague to try out a new approach to treatment based on the assumption that the fear was a conditioned response and that unconscious conflicts need not be dealt with.

The treatment (described in box 10.2) was successful in that the patient's fear was reduced and she was able to leave her house and obtain a job. It is not known if the young woman developed substitute symptoms for the phobia as would be predicted by psychoanalysis, but she did not come back to the agency in the four years the psychologist worked there.

Most of the basic assumptions in the behavioral view can be seen in the story of the "abnormal" rat at the beginning of the chapter. Mowrer and his associates did a series of experiments similar to the one described in the rat story during the 1940s and 1950s (Mowrer, 1947; Mowrer & Lamoreaux, 1946; Mowrer & Solomon, 1954). Even earlier, in 1920, John B. Watson (Watson & Rayner, 1920) is supposed to have attempted the first demonstration that "abnormal" behavior is learned in humans as well as rats, and in 1924, Mary Cover Jones demonstrated how such "abnormal" behavior could be unlearned.

A Brief History of Behavior Therapy

Watson reported that in an experiment, he classically conditioned a fear of white rats in 11-month-old Albert (Watson & Rayner, 1920), although some scholars question the veracity of the tale of Little Albert (Harris, 1979). Prior to Watson's intervention, Little Albert had enjoyed playing with a white rat. Watson paired a loud, frightening noise with handing Little Albert the rat, and he did this a few times. Soon Little Albert cried at the sight of a rat and tried to crawl away, and he showed the same fear reaction to any white, furry object. Watson had demonstrated that an abnormal behavior such as a phobia could be learned. He even wrote, "It is probable that many of the phobias in psychopathology are true conditioned emotional reactions" (Watson & Rayner, 1920, p. 14).

In the case of Little Peter, Mary Cover Jones (1924) demonstrated that phobias could be unlearned. She taught a three-year-old boy with a fear of rabbits to like them. By bringing a caged rabbit closer and closer while Little Peter was eating, his fear was gradually eliminated, supposedly because the feared object became associated with the pleasure of eating.

Despite these early studies, it was to be several decades before behavior therapy was established as an identifiable school of therapy. In the 1950s Joseph Wolpe, a psychiatrist from South Africa trained in psychoanalysis, became interested in Pavlov's research and theories. As you know, Pavlov conditioned dogs to salivate at the sound of a bell. Wolpe saw that phobias could be explained as conditioned fear responses. He believed they could be treated by conditioning a new response to the fear stimulus, a response that would interfere with or inhibit the fear response, that is, a response that would be incompatible with the fear response, something that could not be done or felt at the same time as fear. Jones had chosen eating as a response incompatible with fear. Wolpe chose deep muscle relaxation, also known as progressive muscle relaxation (Jacobson, 1938). Wolpe taught his patients to induce deep muscle relaxation in themselves, and then he gradually introduced verbal descriptions of the phobic object, with the aim of replacing the conditioned fear response with the conditioned relaxation response to the feared stimulus. He called this method ***systematic desensitization*** or reciprocal inhibition (Wolpe, 1958).

This method was an immediate hit among U.S. clinical psychologists, who then turned to their own rich background of behaviorism with new appreciation. Pragmatic American psychologists realized that at last, here was a theory and technology that could challenge psychoanalysis in explanatory and treatment power. This realization coincided with the post-World War II increase in demand for psychological services for people with a wide variety of problems and economic resources. Behavior therapies promised to be a quick, relatively inexpensive, and highly effective way of meeting this increased demand.

Before going further into the types of behavior therapy, we should first review some of the basic principles of behaviorism.

Principles of Learning

In traditional learning theory, there are two basic types of conditioning, or learning. The first, ***classical conditioning,*** has also been called ***respondent conditioning*** and Pavlovian conditioning. The abnormal rat at the beginning of the chapter was classically conditioned to fear the dark box. Modern learning theory has changed, and behaviorists now argue that what the animal is learning in classical conditioning is not a conditioned response, but rather *associations* between stimuli. The animal learns which cues predict certain events, and there is evidence that only stimuli that are useful in prediction can be conditioned. However, since this is not a book on learning theory, we will not cover every aspect of learning, but trust that the following review is sufficient to help you make sense of the rest of the chapter. The second basic type of learning, ***instrumental conditioning,*** has also been called ***operant conditioning*** and Skinnerian conditioning.

Classical/Respondent Conditioning

Classical conditioning was first demonstrated by the Russian biologist I. Pavlov in his famous experiments with dogs. Pavlov was actually trying to study digestion when he discovered classical conditioning and then turned to a whole new career in neuropsychology. Each dog was hooked up to a device so that its saliva drained out of a fistula into a beaker to be measured. Pavlov introduced measured amounts of food into a dog's mouth and measured the salivation response. Soon he noticed that the dogs began to salivate when they saw him approaching with the food, and they even began to salivate at the sight of the experimental harness. While this ruined his digestion research, he became intrigued and began to study this process systematically. He rang a bell immediately before introducing the food into the dog's mouth, and he paired the bell and food several times. Soon the dogs salivated to the sound of the bell, even if no food followed.

In Pavlov's experiment, salivation is the ***unconditioned response*** to the ***unconditioned stimulus*** of food. Salivation is the natural or automatic response to food. The bell, rung just before food was given, is the ***conditioned stimulus,*** and salivating to it, instead of to food, is the ***conditioned response.*** In other words, salivating to a bell is not a natural, automatic response, but is a conditioned, or learned, one. It has been thought that any stimulus that occurs around an unconditioned stimulus can become associated with it, as the sight of Pavlov and their experimental harness became associated with food for Pavlov's dogs.

Classical conditioning occurs only with behaviors that are automatic, perhaps even unconscious responses to things—for example, reflexes such as salivation and emotions such as fear. The rat described at the beginning of this chapter was classically conditioned to fear the dark compartment. The automatic or unconditioned response to the unconditioned stimulus of electric shock is fear. The cue of the dark compartment was close in time and place to the rat's perception of the shock, so the dark compartment became the conditioned stimulus to the conditioned response of fear.

Instrumental/Operant Conditioning

The most famous example of instrumental or operant conditioning is B. F. Skinner's bar-pressing rat. In Skinner's experiments, rats learned to press a bar, which released a pellet of rat chow into a food cup. It is called instrumental because the conditioned or learned response of bar pressing is instrumental in obtaining the reward of food. It is called operant because the behavior being conditioned or learned is voluntarily put forth by the organism, rather than being an automatic response to a stimulus as in classical conditioning. The conditioned response of bar pressing precedes the rewarding stimulus of food. Recall that in classical conditioning, it is the opposite: The conditioned stimulus precedes the conditioned response.

Extinction

Another type of learning is called extinction. ***Extinction*** occurs when the association between stimulus and response no longer holds, as when rewards are no longer delivered after the operant response, and the organism learns to stop making the conditioned response. A rat presses its bar and no food falls into the food cup; the rat is said to be *on extinction.* It may give the bar a few more quick presses—still no food. Gradually, it gives up pressing the bar altogether. Bar pressing has been *extinguished.* Classically conditioned responses can also be extinguished. If Pavlov rang the bell many times without delivering food, the dogs would gradually stop salivating to the bell. Notice that extinction is an active learning process, not simply forgetting or fading. The rat *learns* that bar pressing does not result in food, and the dog *learns* that the bell is not associated with food. A behavior is said to be strongly conditioned, or *resistant to extinction,* if it takes a long time, or many trials of doing the behavior for no reward, to extinguish.

Generalization and Discrimination

Generalization occurs when a response learned under one set of conditions is made in other situations. A child who whines for snacks before dinner and gets rewarded for it may generalize this learning to whining for snacks before lunch, whining for toys as well as snacks, or whining for things at school as well as at home. ***Discrimination*** is the opposite. A rat may learn that bar pressing leads to food only when a green light shines in its cage and not at any other time. A child may learn that whining leads to rewards at home, but not at school.

Social Learning

Social learning theorists such as Bandura (1977) have argued that another type of learning, imitation or ***observational learning,*** is important in humans. Humans and other primates are great copiers of others, and it may be that most human learning is a result of imitation. All that is necessary for this type of learning to occur is for the person to observe someone else engaging in the behavior. In many experiments, Bandura (1969) and his colleagues demonstrated that humans will imitate almost anyone, including film and cartoon characters, but they are more likely to imitate models who are warm and nurturant and who have high status and power than to imitate mean, low-status models. They are also more likely to imitate models who are rewarded for their behavior than models who are punished for their behavior.

Reward and Punishment

The reinforcement in operant conditioning has been defined several ways. One seemingly circular definition is that reinforcement is anything that strengthens the behavior that precedes it. "Strengthening," to behaviorists, seems to mean increasing the likelihood of performing a behavior. Any consequence contingent on a behavior that increases the likelihood of that behavior is said to reinforce the behavior.

Currently, a reward is defined as either the delivery of a positive stimulus, such as food, or the removal of a negative stimulus, such as turning off a loud noise. Delivering a positive stimulus is also called ***positive reinforcement;*** removing a negative stimulus, as in stopping a loud unpleasant noise, is called ***negative reinforcement.*** A punishment can also be positive or negative: either the delivery of a negative stimulus, such as an electric shock (and called, just to make things difficult, positive punishment), or the removal of a positive stimulus, such as interrupting beautiful music or docking someone's allowance (called negative punishment).

What constitutes a reward for most people? Food is obviously a reward to a hungry rat. But rewards are rarely that obvious in human learning, and much of our behavior does not seem to be followed by any obvious reward. In humans, an important reward seems to be the attention of other human beings. We are a social species. We work with people, we talk to them, we go out to lunch, we play cards, we goof off and hang out together. What is the reward? Just the pleasure of interacting with others seems to be enough.

There is evidence that the reward of human attention has drive properties—we need it and are motivated to try to obtain it. In an early experiment (Gewirtz & Baer, 1958), children who had been deprived of human attention for 20 minutes worked longer and harder at a subsequent boring marble-dropping task for the simple reward of an adult's saying "Mm-hmm" and "Fine" than children who got lots of attention before the task. This is similar to a food-deprived rat's working longer and harder at bar pressing for food than a well-fed rat. We say the rat is hungry—it has a drive or need for food. People may have a similar need for attention.

Furthermore, if people are deprived of attention, they may resort to unpleasant or "abnormal" behavior to get it. Even if the form of attention they receive for abnormal behavior is disapproval or punishment, it appears that they prefer this to being ignored. Most of you can probably remember a really obnoxious kid in your elementary school who made the other children laugh or bothered them and was repeatedly scolded or threatened by the teacher. When that kid did work quietly, probably everyone ignored him. A child who does not seem able to get enough attention by prosocial methods may resort to disturbing or disturbed behavior in order to get it. Such behavior is called *negative attention seeking,* because both the behavior to get attention and the attention it gets are negative.

Postmodern, radical behaviorists (discussed below) argue that it is futile to try to define what is rewarding for everyone. Food and attention appear to be universal rewards, but they are not. For example, anorexics find food aversive, and very shy people may find attention, even warm praise, to be punishing. Radical behaviorists go back to the earlier definition of reinforcement as any consequence that strengthens a behavior. As such, reinforcement will be different for each individual, depending on that person's learning history and the situational context. In the therapy situation, therapists must pay attention to client behavior in order to determine what reinforces a particular behavior in a specific individual.

Many experiments have studied how the timing of rewards affects the speed and strength of conditioning. Rewards can be given after every instance of an operant response, for a 100% reinforcement schedule, or after every few operant responses, for a partial reinforcement schedule. In real life, it is unlikely that rewards ever arrive on a 100% reinforcement schedule. In general, 100% reinforcement results in faster conditioning than partial reinforcement, but partial reinforcement results in stronger conditioning. The more unpredictable the partial reinforcement schedule, the more resistant the behavior is to extinction. Place a rat who has received food variably for every tenth to twentieth bar press on extinction, and it will take that rat a long time to learn that no food is coming for any bar press.

Human behavior is most often rewarded on some type of variable partial reinforcement schedule, which is probably why it is so difficult to break some bad habits. An hour before dinner, children start whining for snacks. Their parents tell them no, because dinner is almost ready. On the tenth whine, exasperated parents cave in and give the children snacks. Then they wonder why the next night the children start in whining for snacks before dinner. On a schedule of partial reward, whining has been inadvertently and unfortunately strongly conditioned and made resistant to extinction.

The Development of Abnormal or Unwanted Behavior

Behaviorists believe that just the basic principles of learning—classical conditioning, operant conditioning, extinction, imitation, generalization—can account for behavior, both normal and abnormal. Abnormal behavior, bad habits, and other unwanted behaviors are learned in the same way as normal or desired behaviors. Because a behavior that seems odd or abnormal was acquired by the basic learning principles, it will make sense when its learning history is known. And it should be possible to change it by applying those same learning principles.

It is easy to see that phobias might result from experiences like the electric shocking of the rat in the dark compartment. A ***phobia*** is a strong fear of something that does not elicit fear in most people. Since most rats prefer dark places, we could say that, compared to other rats, the behavior of the rat that always ran away from the dark looked abnormal. When it is known that the rat had been shocked in the dark compartment, its behavior makes sense. A fear-evoking event may classically condition a phobia in humans as well.

Let us turn to the example of the young woman, described in box 10.1, who was severely afraid of birds. As a child, she was locked in a henhouse and "attacked" by the frightened chickens. She was classically conditioned to fear chickens, harmless stupid birds that do not ordinarily elicit fear in the human heart. In her case, the sight of chickens was paired with the experience of being locked in a small enclosure with scratching, squawking, pecking creatures, an experience that would naturally be frightening to a small child, if not to all of us. The sight of chickens, which was paired with the unconditioned stimuli of attacking chickens, became the conditioned stimulus for the conditioned fear response. Furthermore, this response generalized, so that the sight of other birds also frightened the girl. She had developed a bird phobia.

Why didn't this fear extinguish with time, as the girl grew up? This phenomenon is the so-called ***neurotic paradox.*** The conditioned fear remains, even though the original conditions for learning it are no longer present or relevant. The rat's fear of the dark compartment remains even though the electric grid floor has been removed and the rat is no longer shocked when it is placed in the compartment. In the case of the bird-phobic woman, the fear of birds remained even though the fearful event was long in the past and in everyday life, birds don't attack or injure people.

There are several explanations for the neurotic paradox. One possibility is that the amount of time it takes to run away from or avoid the feared stimulus is shorter than the amount of time it takes for real fear to build up and be extinguished. The rat runs away from the dark compartment before it has a chance to learn that it won't be shocked. If the rat were to be locked in the dark compartment, its fear would build up, no shock would follow, its fear would decrease, and the classically conditioned fear of the dark compartment would eventually be extinguished.

Another explanation for the persistence of the phobia is that the operant behavior of running away or avoiding the feared stimulus is repeatedly rewarded with anxiety reduction. When the rat is put in the dark compartment, it starts to feel fear and quickly runs into the white compartment, where it immediately feels better because its fear is reduced. This reward is a so-called negative reinforcement, in that the reduction of the unpleasant fear is rewarding. Thus, the avoidant or phobic behavior is repeatedly rewarded through the reduction of fear, and it will therefore persist. For years, every time the young woman saw a bird, she would feel afraid, walk away from it, and immediately feel better, so that the avoidance of birds was a highly rewarded and well-learned behavior. To summarize, then: A phobia is the result of operantly conditioned avoidance behavior that is rewarded by the reduction of classically conditioned fear.

Behaviorists believe that complex neuroses and other abnormal behaviors, not only phobias, are also learned. "Symptoms" are operant behaviors rewarded by the reduction of classically conditioned fears. Let's look at one more example of how abnormal or unwanted behavior is learned—temper tantrums. Most small children throw one or two temper tantrums at some time or other. This behavior is not abnormal, although it is definitely unwanted. However, some parents inadvertently train their children to throw tantrums excessively, and then it becomes abnormal. Such parents tend to fail to reward desired behavior and to pay attention only to undesired behavior. We have seen that most humans find receiving the attention of other humans highly rewarding. Children will do a lot of things to get their parents' attention: "Look at me! Watch this! See the doggy, Mommy!" A stressed parent may ignore these normal and fairly pleasant attempts to get attention. She may also be so relieved when the child plays quietly by himself that she goes off to rest and so fails to reward this type of "good" behavior with any attention. (It could be said that desired behavior is on extinction.) In stressed families, the level of reward is often low for all behavior. The child may then throw a tantrum, a behavior that is difficult to ignore, especially if it is done in the middle of the supermarket. The parent is forced to pay attention, even if that attention is scolding or punishing, and the child has learned a guaranteed way to get the parent's attention. The parent has rewarded the child for throwing the tantrum by paying attention. In a low-reward family, a child may throw more and more tantrums to get attention until it is a well-learned behavior. The parent has not planned to train the child to throw tantrums, but failing to reward desired behavior and paying attention to undesired behavior has had that result.

By now you have probably thought of some examples of abnormal behaviors that learning theory cannot explain. Not all children in low-reward families learn to throw temper tantrums. It is possible that not all children locked in a henhouse would develop a bird phobia. Not all phobias are associated with an identifiable childhood trauma. Some adults can reason themselves out of early learned fears. Not all survivors of car crashes develop a fear of driving, but some do. How can learning theory account for such individual differences? How can a behaviorist explain such apparently complicated disorders as schizophrenia, which includes hallucinations and bizarre thinking? How could someone learn such a thing as an anxiety neurosis, when the aversive feeling of anxiety is experienced almost all the time?

Behaviorists have developed a number of theoretical and empirical arguments to counter such criticisms. For example, H. J. Eysenck (1967) reported evidence that there are genetic differences in conditionability, which would account for the fact that some people become phobic after car accidents and some do not. In general, behaviorists counter criticisms of their theory by arguing that if we could obtain a sufficiently accurate learning history for each individual, we would find appropriate explanations for her or his behavior. However, a detailed discussion of all the criticisms and defenses of the behavioristic view is beyond the scope of this book. Behaviorists' final argument is that even if we are not certain precisely how all abnormal behavior is learned, we can nevertheless change it by applying learning principles. Abnormal behavior can be unlearned and new behavior can be learned.

Behavior Therapy

There are behavioral treatment methods based on all the learning principles previously discussed. In addition to Wolpe's method of classically conditioning new responses to feared stimuli, there are behavior therapies based on extinction, classical conditioning of aversive responses, operant conditioning with rewards, imitation, and combinations of these methods. Different forms of behavior therapy have been developed to treat every type of psychological disorder, as well as to modify bad habits, to eliminate unwanted behaviors, and to teach new skills. Behavior therapies have been developed to treat disorders from depression and obsessive-compulsive neurosis to borderline personality disorder, as well as phobias. We shall cover only a representative sample of the many behavior therapies currently available.

For a definition of behavior therapy, let us turn to the Association for the Advancement of Behavior Therapy:

> Behavior therapy is a particular kind of therapy that involves the application of findings from behavioral science research to help individuals change in ways they would like to change. There is an emphasis in behavior therapy on checking up on how effective the therapy is by monitoring and evaluating the individual's progress. Most behaviorally oriented therapists believe that the current environment is most important in affecting the person's present behavior. Early life experiences, long-time internal psychological or emotional conflicts, or the individual's personality structure are considered to be less important than what is happening in the person's life at the present time. The procedures used in behavior therapy are generally

intended to improve the individual's self-control by expanding the person's skills, abilities, and independence. (AABT, 2001)

Most behavior therapies share certain assumptions. All behavior is learned by the same principles. Behavior can be unlearned and changed. Therapy methods are tied to experimentally verified principles of behavior. Research and assessment are integral parts of behavior therapy. Therapy techniques are specified and defined clearly and concretely, so they are testable. The outcome of therapy is evaluated empirically with measurable behavior changes.

Behavior therapies also emphasize the importance of the relationship between the therapist and client. Therapy must begin with an interview between therapist and client, in which the nature of the client's problem and its appropriateness for behavioral treatment is assessed. The initial interview may include some of the behavioral assessment techniques described in chapter 4, such as questionnaires or observations. Trust and understanding between therapist and client are assumed to be essential for the success of treatment. If the therapist is to reward behavior changes, then the therapeutic relationship must have rewarding qualities. Behavior therapists recognize the role of therapist warmth and empathy to enhance that relationship.

Initially, a detailed history of the client's problems is taken, including when and how the problems began, their frequency (or baseline), what the environmental stimulus of the problems is, and what solutions the client has tried so far. The therapist tries to clarify with the client precisely what the client hopes to accomplish in therapy. The therapist will also try to cast these goals in behavioral terms: What type of behavioral changes will the client and therapist have to see in order to know that therapy has been successful and the goals have been reached?

Behavior therapy may involve using more than one method for more than one client problem. In a way, all behavior therapists are eclectic. Despite this variety, most behavior therapies include at least these five steps in their procedures:

1. Assess and evaluate the client's problem.
2. Choose the best therapeutic method for addressing the problem.
3. Educate the client about the method, including exactly what will be done and the likelihood of success.
4. Apply the therapeutic method.
5. Evaluate the success of treatment.

Exposure-Based Treatments (Classical Conditioning Methods)

The assumption behind behavior therapies based on classical conditioning is that abnormal behavior is due to inappropriate, classically conditioned emotions, especially fear and anxiety. These emotions then motivate avoidance and other behaviors that are rewarded by anxiety reduction. Since the Pavlovian methods share the feature of exposing the client in various ways to the feared object, these methods are now called exposure-based treatments. It is also argued that these methods do not work because of classical conditioning, but rather, they work because they increase the individual's sense of coping and mastery. Again, because this is not a book on learning theory, we will leave this issue and move on to a description of the treatments.

Desensitization

Originally called ***reciprocal inhibition,*** systematic desensitization has already been described as a treatment for phobias, fears, and anxiety, based on classically conditioning a new response that is incompatible with fear and anxiety. The basic idea is that a person cannot be relaxed and afraid at the same time. The client is trained in deep muscle relaxation, a response that is incompatible with fear. In addition, the therapist and client create an anxiety hierarchy. This hierarchy lists aspects of the fear- or anxiety-producing objects, events, or situations from least frightening to most frightening. For example, an anxiety hierarchy for a snake phobia might be a snake in the next county, a snake in the next room, a snake in the same room in an escape-proof cage, a snake on the floor, a snake touching the client. Then the hierarchy and the relaxation are put together to create systematic desensitization. The client is desensitized, that is, made less sensitive, to what he previously found frightening. See box 10.2 for details.

In vivo (Latin, "in life") ***desensitization,*** also called graduated exposure, is a logical extension of systematic desensitization, and it is often used to assess the success of

Box 10.2 And One Flew Under . . .

In the systematic desensitization of a phobia, the therapist and client first develop a hierarchical list of phobic situations. Together they work up a list progressing from the least to the most anxiety-provoking situation. There must be enough items on the list so that there are only small increases in anxiety associated with each step. The bird-phobic woman in box 10.1 and her therapist developed the following anxiety hierarchy:

Looking out of the window at the street
Looking out of the window and seeing one bird in a tree
Looking out of the window and seeing many birds
Walking outside with no birds in sight
Walking outside with one bird down the street
Walking outside with several birds in view
A bird flying near to her
A bird hopping toward her
An injured bird at her feet
Picking up the injured bird
Touching a healthy small bird
Touching a large bird

The next step in systematic desensitization is to train the client in deep muscle relaxation. There are several methods of teaching muscle relaxation, including hypnosis and tape-recorded suggestions. The therapist may train relaxation by directing the reclining client to tense and relax the various muscles of her body, noting the different sensations until she can easily relax all the muscles deeply. The physiological response of muscle relaxation is incompatible with the physiological response of anxiety. Therefore, when the items on the anxiety hierarchy are introduced, the relaxation response should prevent the anxiety response. Additionally, a new response, relaxation, is being conditioned to the anxiety-provoking stimuli.

Once the client has mastered relaxation, the therapist begins to describe items on the anxiety hierarchy, starting with the first item. The therapist invites the client to imagine all that procedure. Systematic desensitization relies on imagining the phobic element, and behaviorists have often criticized it as being too cognitive. Furthermore, it is possible that clients could remain relaxed with the image of the phobic element, but become frightened in its actual presence. In vivo procedures gradually place the phobic person in contact with the actual feared object or situation.

The possibilities for exposure treatments in the hands of creative therapists are endless. For example, fear of flying is treated by asking the client to engage in behaviors that gradually approach getting on an airplane, such as phoning for a flight reservation, then driving to the airport. The client may be required to sit in an airplane on the ground and then finally to take a short flight. As another example, a technique called cue controlled/active relaxation involves clients learning to *attend* to their feelings of anxiety as a cue to begin their relaxation exercises while they go about their daily lives.

Eye Movement Desensitization and Reprocessing (EMDR)

EMDR therapy, developed by Francine Shapiro (1995) is another exposure technique. EMDR is a desensitization procedure, but instead of relaxation, therapist-led

---

the details of an item on the list. The therapist describes sensory details to help make the image vivid and stresses the client's positive feelings. For example, for the item "Walking outside with several birds in view," the therapist may say: "You are walking outside on a beautiful fall day. The sun is shining, you are walking comfortably, and you feel confident and strong. You can hear a breeze rustling the trees, and you can hear the leaves crunch under your feet as you walk. The air smells fresh. You can hear the cheerful chirping of some small birds in the trees. You keep walking, enjoying their songs. You can see some birds in nearby yards. They are hopping around looking for things to eat. They are very pretty with the sun shining on their feathers. You continue walking past the birds, who do not appear to notice you. You are enjoying your walk in the fresh air, the sunshine, the chirping birds, the beautiful day."

The therapist proceeds to cover each item on the anxiety hierarchy, describing the situation in detail, as long as the client remains relaxed. If the client begins to tense her muscles or states that she is experiencing anxious feelings, the therapist may reinstitute muscle relaxation procedures or go back to a less anxiety-provoking item on the hierarchy. It may take several sessions for the client to imagine every item on the anxiety hierarchy while remaining completely relaxed.

The bird-phobic woman was able to complete her anxiety hierarchy in two sessions. Graduated exposure was then used. A bunch of feathers was tied to a clothesline pulley so that she could recline and relax and still pull the feathers closer to her at a speed that was comfortable for her. The therapist helped her remain relaxed by giving relaxation suggestions while she pulled the feathers closer. The therapist also described the feathers vividly as they came closer. When the client felt she could, she touched the feathers, then held them, then brushed them over her arms and face, while the therapist continued to give relaxation suggestions and to describe the feather sensations. Then a caged, tame parakeet was connected to the pulley, and a similar procedure was carried out.

Finally, when the client tolerated the close presence of the caged bird well, the therapist put her hand in the cage and petted the parakeet to model touching a bird. The client was encouraged to do the same, and she was able to do so. This part of the treatment took three sessions and the client was successfully desensitized to a phobic object.

---

eye movements performed by the client are paired with images of what frightens or disturbs the client. Clinical evidence suggests that EMDR is a quick, effective treatment for posttraumatic stress disorder, although research studies do not always support this conclusion (Shapiro, 2002a). Shapiro proposes that EMDR actually changes the way the brain processes the traumatic experience and memories of it, so her theory fits in with recent thinking on brain–behavior connections, but it may work like other exposure methods (or vice-versa). As an interesting aside, Wolpe strongly supported EMDR (Shapiro, 2002b).

Extinction

Implosive therapy or flooding is both an extension of the desensitization work and a direct application of academic research on extinction (Stampfl & Levis, 1973). Rather than conditioning a new response, why not just massively extinguish the fear all in one go? Like the rat kept in the dark compartment, people forced to remain in a frightening situation will have to stop feeling afraid after a while. It is physiologically impossible to remain strongly afraid for more than 20 or 30 minutes. So if a person could be induced to stay in the frightening situation, rather than immediately running away and feeling better, then the fear should extinguish, according to learning research. Implosion involves making the client vividly imagine all aspects of whatever is frightening until she becomes relaxed. An in vivo version keeps the client in the actual frightening situation until the fear is extinguished and relaxation replaces it. In both cases, the constant presence of a supportive, trusted therapist is crucial. A technique known as *response prevention* is also considered an extinction procedure. Used to treat obsessive-compulsive disorder and bulimia, the procedure involves exposing the client to the stimuli that elicit the compulsive behavior and then preventing the client from engaging in the response. Because extinction methods require a great deal of control over the client and because they often elicit anxiety, they are used only in certain cases.

Punishment

Aversion therapy involves the use of an unconditioned aversive stimulus to classically condition fear or aversion to a previously attractive stimulus in order to create an avoidance response or to suppress undesirable or unwanted operant behavior. For example, one of us helped in a research project years ago in which an electric shock was paired with an alcoholic drink in order to reduce drinking. Through classical conditioning, the previously attractive stimulus of the drink should become aversive, so that the person will avoid the drink or suppress the operant behavior of drinking.

Obviously, there are ethical problems with punishing people. In the experiment on drinking just described, the shock level, which was set by the participants themselves, had to be set so high to have any effect that it left holes in the arms of the alcoholics. Aversion therapy is not often used, but it has been used in the treatment of bad habits such as smoking, overeating, or nail biting. Except in the treatment of bad habits, aversion therapy alone has not been demonstrated to be an effective treatment. It appears that the aversion gradually wears off or extinguishes and must be periodically reconditioned.

Covert sensitization is the use of an imagined punishment in place of an actual aversive stimulus to create new learning. Almost the opposite of desensitization, covert sensitization may be used to create classically conditioned anxiety to teach an avoidance response. For example, a dieter may be asked to vividly imagine a favorite food with worms all over it (an aversive stimulus), so that disgust or fear will be conditioned to the food and the person will avoid it in the future. This procedure is similar to the use of aversion, but avoids some of the ethical problems associated with the use of punishment.

Skills Training (Operant Conditioning Methods)

Behavior therapists who use operant conditioning methods assume that many types of abnormal behavior, such as shyness or even schizophrenic symptoms, are due to a lack of skills or to a poor environment or both. Shy individuals lack the social skills to understand and make contact with other people. It follows that the needed skills can be taught. Abnormal behavior may result from an environment that inadvertently rewards that behavior and fails to reward desirable behavior. Again, such an environment can be changed, mostly by developing the skills of those who deal with the "abnormal" behavior, such as the parent. With operant methods, the collaborative role of the therapist is emphasized. The therapist acts as an instructor or consultant to guide the client or parent in choosing and making changes.

Social Skills Training

Social skills training, formerly called assertion therapy, was originally designed to help shy, retiring people become better able to deal with other people. It includes a variety of training techniques for several social skills and is used with diverse types of clients individually and in groups. It is based on operant conditioning in that the operant behaviors of social skills, such as conversation, asking for dates, and dealing with bosses, are rewarded by praise from the therapist or by the success of the behaviors themselves.

Social skills training is widely used to treat shyness. In addition, it has proven useful in teaching developmentally disabled adults how to be more effective in a confusing world and how to protect themselves from possible exploitation. It is also used in conjunction with other forms of therapy to train new responses to substitute for abnormal behaviors that are being eliminated.

The social skills taught vary according to what the clients believe they need. Some shy clients wish to learn to make conversation in many social situations. Some clients are not shy but want to learn to deal more effectively with specific individuals, such as bosses, or in specific situations, such as negotiating a raise at work. Among the skills and situations covered in such training are asking for dates, turning down dates, making requests or successfully giving orders to others, refusing requests or orders, starting conversations, making social conversation, negotiation, asking for a raise, dealing with aggressive or difficult coworkers or customers, dealing with sexual harassment, and asserting independence from guilt-inducing parents. For such social skills to be effective, clients must also learn to understand other people's feelings, to be nonjudgmental and uncritical of others, to curb their anger or aversive behavior, and to increase their awareness of the effect of their behavior on others. They must learn to pay attention to the nonverbal behavior of others and to alter their own nonverbal behavior so that it has the effect they intend. Social skills are complex, and they must be broken down into specific parts so they can be taught.

The techniques most frequently used to teach these complex social skills are lecture, modeling, and role playing. Therapists describe social skills to their clients, explain how they work, and advise clients what to try. They demonstrate social skills by acting them out in front of the client, saying what they want the client to say, pointing out their own nonverbal behavior. They then ask clients to role-play. The client may role-play the target person, such as a boss or parent, while the therapist plays the client and demonstrates what the client should do. Then the client role-plays his own role while the therapist role-plays the target person, so that the client has a chance to rehearse the demonstrated social skills. In groups, clients role-play individuals and social situations for each other. For example, the entire group may pretend to be at a cocktail party, and they practice initiating and carrying on social conversations.

Shaping and covert practice are also sometimes used by therapists to teach social skills. ***Shaping,*** also called successive approximation, involves the client making closer and closer approximations to the desired response. Each step closer to the desired behavior is rewarded with praise from the therapist or group. A shy person cannot be expected to go to a party and start several lively conversations right away. The first step may be simply to go to a party. The next step may be saying "Hello" to just one person, then speaking to two people, and so on. In ***covert practice***, the person imagines performing the social skills competently. The shy person is asked to imagine carrying on lively conversations.

An important element of social skills training is feedback. As clients rehearse and role-play, the therapist and group members give feedback on the effectiveness of the rehearsed social skills. They point out which aspects of the performance need to be improved and which were done well. The more specific the feedback, the more useful it is. Videotaping the role play is an effective way to give accurate feedback.

The rewarding behaviors of the therapist are an important part of social skills training. Warm praise for successful social skills performance reinforces the behavior. The status, power, warmth, trustworthiness, attractiveness, and other personal attributes of the therapist affect how rewarding the praise will be. The importance of the therapist–client relationship in the effectiveness of behavior therapy is clear.

Most social skills therapy includes practicing the skills in the real world. Specific homework assignments are often given. A shy man may be required to ask a specified woman for a date before the next therapy meeting. A woman may be assigned to say no to at least one request at work by the following week. Such assignments are clear and precise as to what the client is expected to do, and the behavior is practiced beforehand. Usually, the therapist thinks the client has a reasonably good chance at success, but the emphasis is on performing the social skill in the real world, rather than on whether it succeeds or fails. Since the behavior is being done at the direction of the therapist, the therapist will take the blame for failure but praise the client for success.

Contingency Management

A set of behavioral management techniques known as ***contingency management,*** also called behavior modification or applied behavior analysis, utilizes operant conditioning principles. These behavior-changing methods involve the planned use of rewards to increase wanted behavior and extinction to decrease unwanted behavior. The environment is fixed. Rewards are made contingent on desirable behavior and are not given for undesirable behavior. These methods are used in many different settings, including businesses, schools, institutions for the developmentally disabled, and prisons. We will describe operant methods used in parent training or child behavior modification, the token economy in mental hospitals, and contingency contracting.

Parent Training. Modifying the problem behaviors of children is often accomplished by training the parents to use operant techniques. Therapists teach the parents these techniques in group classes, to couples, or individually with such methods as role playing and videotaping. Basically, parents are taught to reward behavior they want in their children and to remove the rewards for behaviors they don't want. In addition, parents must learn how to communicate clearly to the children what they want done, to be consistent in delivering behavioral consequences, to reduce their own aversive and ineffective parenting behaviors, and to give appropriate rewards. Once again, a seemingly simple operant procedure turns out on examination to require complex behavior changes. Even something as seemingly natural and simple as rewarding a child for being "good" is extremely difficult for some parents to learn. Some parents are opposed to the use of rewards on principle, because they see it as "bribing" the child, who should "want" to be good for goodness' sake. Others have difficulties being warm or affectionate, perhaps because of their own deprivation. These kinds of problems must be addressed before operant techniques can be used effectively.

There are many programs to train parents to modify their children's behavior. Gerald Patterson's program at Oregon Research Institute (Patterson & Chamberlain, 1994; Reid, Patterson & Snyder, 2002) is well documented, researched, and evaluated, and it is fairly representative of others. Patterson argues that behavioral disorders in children are a result of parents' reliance on what he calls aversive control, that is, reliance on scolding, punishment, screaming, nagging, and the like to try to control their children. The relatively powerless children engage in disruptive, defiant, or destructive behaviors in an attempt to control their parents, because they learn aversive control from their parents through imitation. These parents also tend to use few rewards, either because they don't know how or they don't feel like being rewarding because of stress or anger. Because of the low level of rewards, the children may engage in aversive behavior just to get their parents' attention. A vicious cycle is set up in which the parents try to control the children with punishment, which makes the children hurt and angry and more likely to be unpleasant, which makes the parents use more punishment, and so on.

Among some cultural groups and socioeconomic classes, physical punishment in the form of spanking and hitting is a common and socially acceptable form of child discipline. People from such groups disbelieve or are offended by the insistence of middle-class, white therapists that such punishment should not be used. However, there are sound empirical reasons why physical punishment should be avoided. First, the principle of classical conditioning indicates that because the parent is paired with pain, the child will come to fear the parent and the parent will lose the ability to be rewarding. Second, the principle of imitation indicates that what children learn when punished is to hit people smaller than themselves. Third, any use of punishment as a method of control always leads to the need for a constant policing function, because children soon learn to discriminate that they should refrain from the undesired behavior only when the parent is around. Finally, parental reliance on punishment leads to the vicious cycle of aversive control described above.

Patterson tries to break this cycle by teaching the parents to increase their use of rewards and to stop all use of punishments and threats. Instead of punishment, extinction in the form of a procedure called time-out, described below, is used. There are several steps in Patterson's program.

The child and the family must be assessed so that an appropriate behavioral program can be designed. Patterson has worked mostly with school-age children with behavior problems of aggressiveness and noncompliance. Similar behavior modification methods have been used to treat temper tantrums, excessive sibling fighting, hyperactivity, disruptive school behavior, stealing and lying, and any sort of frequent unpleasant behavior used as negative attention seeking.

Once the problem has been defined and assessed, Patterson involves both parents and target child in deciding on the behavior modification program. What the child must do is discussed, specified clearly, and agreed on. For example, it might be specified that the child must obey parental requests to do household chores by the second time he is asked. The consequences of behavior are discussed. For example, if the child obeys the first parental request, he will receive a certain reward; if he obeys the second, he will receive a certain other reward; and if he does not comply, he will be placed in five minutes of time-out. All of the specified behaviors and consequences may be written down in a behavioral contract, which parents and child sign as an indication of their understanding of the treatment program and their agreement to try it.

The nature of the rewards is open to negotiation. Different children find different things rewarding. Some children prefer monetary rewards, some prefer objects such as toys or bicycles, and others prefer time spent with a parent in an activity of their choice. Parents and children agree on a formula for the distribution of rewards that takes into account the number of behaviors being modified and the frequency with which they occur. For example, each act of compliance with a parental request may be worth 10 cents, or the child must comply with parental requests 90% of the time for six weeks in order to get a bicycle. Charts with points or check marks are used to keep track of performance and rewards. The charts are kept in an accessible place, such as on the refrigerator door, and each and every rewarded behavior is noted carefully. Patterson also tries to teach parents to give social rewards such as attention and praise when the points or money or other concrete rewards are given, so that concrete rewards can eventually be eliminated.

Time-out is used to eliminate unwanted behavior or as a consequence for not performing wanted behavior. Unwanted behavior and noncompliance are assumed to be reinforced and maintained by the attention they gain. Even if that attention consists of punishment, it seems that some children prefer it to being ignored. So the solution to such problem behavior is to remove the reward in order to extinguish it.

Time-out involves removing children from the rewarding situation to a place where there are no social rewards, and so it can be viewed as an extinction procedure. (It can also be seen as a negative punishment in that it is the removal of something positive.) A bathroom, a porch, even the child's own room or a corner of the living room can be used for time-out. It should be some relatively uninteresting but safe place where children will not be getting attention. In practice, the punishment aspects of time-out are avoided, because the parents are already too reliant on aversive control. Rather, they are taught to be matter of fact and nonthreatening when using time-out.

Time-out should not be frightening, so children should not be locked up and small children should be able to see their parents. Time-out needs to be only a short time, such as five minutes. For very young children two minutes of time-out is a long time. Children have a different sense of time from adults, and five minutes without human attention can seem very long to them. Some therapists suggest giving children a clock or a timer so they can see how long time-out will take.

Some parents express surprise or even outrage that time-out is so short and seems to be such a mild consequence. After all, they have been grounding their children for weeks at a time, although without much success. They need to be convinced that time-out is not a punishment and that five minutes of the removal of social rewards is sufficient. Even children may say, "Oh, time-out! Big deal! What's five minutes?" The first time children must go into time-out, they may well act nonchalant. However, that first time-out is often more difficult than children or parents anticipate. Parents are instructed that they are to add five additional minutes for every instance of unacceptable behavior during time-out. If the child swears, yells, kicks the door, breaks things, leaves the time-out area, or even calls the parent, then five more minutes must be added. That first time-out may well end up being more than 40 minutes long. However, the second time-out is likely to be 20 minutes and subsequent ones only five.

It is essential that parents use time-out consistently for every behavior they agreed it was to be used for. It is also important that it not be viewed as a punishment, used as a threat, or randomly invoked without prior agreement. Parents are encouraged to apply time-out in a matter-of-fact manner, without criticism or yelling. Most parents who apply time-out correctly and consistently find that it does not have to be used often after the first few times. They also find it far more effective than the nagging and yelling and punishments they had tried before. However, because it is difficult to administer time-out properly, especially the first few times, people should not even begin a program utilizing time-out unless they are deeply committed to using it properly and consistently. If time-out is used inconsistently, the child's unwanted behavior ends up receiving partial reinforcement, which only strengthens it.

Evaluation research studies of behavior modification programs such as Patterson's find that it is an effective treatment for child behavior disorders. In addition, parents tend to feel happier and more competent after treatment, as do the children. Parents report that they are able to generalize the principles they learn in treatment to other aspects of child raising and family life. Other behaviors of the child often improve, as well as the treated behaviors. Another frequently reported result is that the behavior of siblings of the treated children also improves (Reid, Patterson, & Snyder, 2002).

Parent training can be combined with attempts to modify children's school behaviors. Teachers may agree to keep behavior charts at school, which can be sent home for the parents to reward. For example, for every half hour that children sit and work quietly, the parents can give praise and points toward an agreed-on reward.

Behavior modification principles are sometimes used (and sometimes misused) in classrooms for all the children. Teachers attempt to reward desired child behaviors with praise, gold stars, tickets, and prizes. Teachers also try to implement time-out for disruptive negative attention seeking. Placing the child in time-out outside the classroom can be an effective technique for eliminating such behavior. Using time-out to shame or punish children, making it too long, or keeping children in the classroom during time-out so that they still receive peer attention are common misuses of time-out. However, research indicates that well-conducted behavior management programs in schools are effective in reducing classroom disruptions and increasing the academic progress of all the students (Jackson & Panyan, 2002; Kiraly & McKinnon, 1984; Zirpoli & Melloy, 2001).

Token Economy. Token economies are behavior modification programs that were developed for use in psychiatric wards in hospitals, classrooms, and institutions for the developmentally disabled. Token economies are based on operant procedures, and rewards are given for desired behavior and not for undesired behavior. Since it is difficult to give actual rewards for each desired behavior, tokens are commonly given to patients instead, hence the name of the programs. When sufficient numbers of tokens are collected, patients can exchange them for designated rewards, such as 10 tokens for a pack of cigarettes or five for an extra dessert. Undesirable behavior, such as psychotic talk or failure to show up for therapy appointments, may either be ignored or have a consequence such as being docked tokens.

One of the pioneers of token economies, Ted Ayllon, originally used food as a reward in an experimental behavior modification program on a locked ward of very disturbed schizophrenics (Ayllon & Azrin, 1968). Ayllon thought that it was possible that the schizophrenics were rewarded for their withdrawn behavior by concerned nurses coming to spoon-feed them in bed. Ayllon altered the conditions on the ward so that only patients who showed up at the dining room by a certain time were allowed to eat. Despite staff concerns that the very disturbed patients would starve to death, all patients were eating in the dining room within four days. Then Ayllon changed the conditions so that patients needed tokens to get in the dining room, and various positive behaviors, such as dressing themselves or talking to others, were rewarded with tokens.

Everyone would agree that food can be a powerful reward. However, patients' rights advocates have argued that people in mental hospitals have basic rights to care, protection, and treatment, and these rights certainly include the right to eat. Buying privileges or special items with their tokens has replaced food as a reward.

Critics have charged that token economies are manipulative methods of social control, used against helpless mental patients. Defenders argue that token economies mimic the real world, in which people have to work for the reward of money. The "real world" argument seems to be substantiated by the fact that in many token economies, there is a flourishing black market in tokens. Patients make counterfeit tokens, play poker with them, steal them, trade them with each other for things, and hoard them, just like people do with ordinary money.

In general, evaluation research on token economies suggests that they are effective in making psychiatric wards fairly pleasant and cooperative places (Ayllon & Azrin, 1968) and that patients on token economies are less likely to return to the hospital than patients on regular wards (Glynn, 1990). However, token economies are not often used on psychiatric wards today. It may be that the development of effective antipsychotic and antidepressive medications have made them unnecessary.

Contingency Contracting. In contingency contracting, also called individual behavior contracting, the therapist and client make a formal agreement or contract about certain consequences of certain acts by the client. If the client performs a difficult assignment, such as losing a certain number of pounds or practicing a certain social skill in public, the therapist will give an appropriate reward. For example, a therapist and client may contract that the therapist's fee will be reduced 10% when the client loses five pounds, or they may contract that the client will be free to buy a new outfit after a specific weight loss. Some behavior therapists request that clients deposit a sum of money at the beginning of a behavior modification program. The reward may then be to return part of the fee.

The contract may specify punishment-like consequences for certain client behaviors, too. With ***response cost,*** positive reinforcers are withdrawn to suppress an unwanted behavior. Tokens, points, or privileges may be withdrawn. Or the failure to perform the contracted behavior may result in a "fine." Donation of the sum deposited at the beginning of treatment to a cause the client dislikes may be used as a consequence for failure to comply with the treatment program. For example, a liberal client gives a deposit of $100 prior to treatment, and if he fails to comply with the agreed-on treatment, his money will be given to the Republicans. The potential for creative uses of contingency contracting seems great.

Self-Management

As implied in the name self-management, behaviorists can teach individuals to use operant and contingency management techniques to modify their own behaviors, as shown in box 10.3. Such behavior modification treatments use self-monitoring, self-reward, and techniques of problem solving and coping as well as contingency contracting. Clients set a goal to modify certain behaviors, keep a chart of the frequency and context of the behaviors, and apply appropriate rewards for achieving the goals. It is surprising, but true, that simply recording the frequency of unwanted behaviors often results in their reduction. Perhaps increased awareness of behavior makes it easier to change.

Self-monitoring involves keeping track of the targeted behavior, including when and in what context it occurs. Self-reward allows clients to give themselves a chosen reward. Self-reward follows Grandma's Rule: "First you work, then you play." For example, in smoking-reduction programs, clients keep count of the number of cigarettes smoked and the situations when smoking occurs. If the number of cigarettes falls below a certain number in a day, clients reward themselves with a dinner out, a movie, or whatever. Clients are also trained to reward themselves with self-approval for meeting behavioral goals. People who are trying to modify a bad habit are frequently critical of themselves, and they need to learn to attend to and reward their positive behavior.

There are special techniques used in self-management. With ***problem-solving training,*** clients are taught first to define and assess the problem; second, to recognize their reaction to it, such as anger, which might be part of the problem; third, to generate several alternative solutions or responses to the problem; fourth, to evaluate the solutions and decide to act on one; and, fifth, to assess the effect of the attempted solution. Coping and coping imagery exercises may be part of problem solving. The therapist and client review possible ***coping strategies*** for the client's problem, and the client imagines using them in various situations. In reviewing coping strategies, the therapist may teach coping skills that the client lacks or has not thought of before.

Box 10.3 Self-Management of Study Habits

Susan F. transferred in her junior year from a community college to a state university and found her grades there dropping. She became anxious, and she could not seem to find the time to study regularly. After reading about self-management in a psychology class, she decided to try to modify her study habits. She defined her problem as an inability to study for longer than about half an hour and a lack of a regular study time. She decided to assess her current study behaviors before attempting to change them.

For one week she kept a chart of her behavior after her classes were done for the day. She made entries every hour, described what she was doing and where, how she felt, and what she was thinking. For example, for Tuesday she had written

4:00 Sitting in living room staring at philosophy book. Feeling lonely, worried. Thinking I'll never get this stuff.

5:00 In the middle of baking chocolate cake in kitchen. Feeling hungry, but happy at prospect of cake. Thinking I should be studying, what's the matter with me?

6:00 After I called Maria, she came over for dinner and cake. Feeling happy, having fun, not lonely. Thinking I better study later or else.

At the end of the week, Susan examined this chart. She noticed a pattern that when she sat down to study, she would begin to feel anxious and lonely and to think that she was stupid. Often she would then find something else to do, especially baking or visiting friends. Later in the day she would be too tired to study, and she would berate herself for her stupidity.

Susan considered several possible solutions to her problem and decided to implement this plan. After classes, she would come home, have a healthy snack such as a banana or apple, rest for 15 minutes, and then study for one hour, a goal that she thought she could accomplish easily. If she began to feel anxious, she would tell herself, "I can easily study for one hour, and studying will improve my grades. I have gotten good grades before, and I can do it again. It's only one hour." If she began to think self-critical thoughts, she would tell herself, "I am an intelligent person, and when I finish studying, I will feel good about myself." When she completed an hour of studying, then and only then would she reward herself with a visit to a friend or a piece of cake after dinner. After five weekdays of keeping this schedule, she planned to reward herself with a nice dinner out with a friend. She continued to keep the behavioral chart in order to keep track of her success with maintaining an hour a day of studying and to make herself substitute calming thoughts when she felt anxious and praising thoughts when she felt self-critical.

At the end of the week, Susan evaluated her success. She was able to keep to her plan. She was tempted to berate herself for studying "only" one hour per weekday, but she decided that she should be proud for accomplishing so much so quickly. She had read that it was important to set achievable goals and to reward oneself for success. The second week, she increased her study time to two hours per weekday, and rewarded herself with two dinners out with friends. The third week, she increased her study time to three hours per weekday, and rewarded herself with a new shirt. By that time, she had had two examinations and the best reward of all, higher grades. Her anxiety had abated, she felt less lonely since her rewards involved visiting friends, and she felt more in control of her life.

In addition to its use in individual therapy, self-management is now often used in business and education. Employees and students are taught self-management techniques in order to improve company functioning and student learning. Furthermore, a structured, modularized teaching program designed to give medicated schizophrenics the information and skills needed to self-manage their illness has been developed by the Veterans Administration (Eckman, Wirshing, Marder, & Liberman, 1992).

Punishment

Delivering punishment for operant behavior is rarely used because of ethical concerns. However, punishment has been used to quickly suppress severely psychotic behavior such as self-injury in retarded or autistic children (Lovaas & Simmons, 1969). Defenders of the practice of shocking autistic children for biting or hitting themselves argue that it is preferable to the amount of injury the child would receive if extinction were used. They agree that punishment should be used only when other methods fail. They also point out that eliminating the psychotic behavior allows the child to make use of other forms of psychotherapy.

Rather than the therapist delivering an actual punishment, the client may be asked to imagine negative consequences (a punishment) to unwanted operant behavior. This technique is similar to the covert sensitization described under aversion techniques. For example, a kleptomaniac may be asked to imagine what would happen if he shoplifted. The therapist may guide his imagery so that he imagines going home with the stolen object, waiting anxiously in his apartment wondering if he will be caught, having the police arrive at his door and arrest him in front of all the neighbors, going to jail, and so on. Another alternative to punishment is response cost, described earlier.

Self-administered punishment is sometimes used to modify bad habits. For example, a cigarette smoker or nail biter may put a rubber band around her wrist and use it to give herself a painful snap every time she reaches for a cigarette or bites her nails. Such a technique may be part of a larger self-management program. A 12-year-old girl we know invented a self-management technique that utilized response cost. To make herself complete reading assignments quickly, she would check the required book out of the library and refuse to return it before she had finished reading it. The threat (and sometimes the payment) of mounting overdue fines motivated her to finish reading the book.

Social Learning Methods

Like many behavior therapists, those who use social learning methods assume that it is not necessarily important to know the cause of abnormal behavior. They assume that normal behavior can be learned in its place, whatever its causes, through the normal social learning process of imitation or modeling. Rather than desensitizing or extinguishing fearful feelings, social learning theorists argue that nonphobic behavior can be learned by watching others. Through demonstration and ***role playing,*** the therapist models appropriate social behavior. According to ***social learning theory,*** the client learns social skills by observing and imitating the therapist. For example, a snake phobia is treated by having the client observe the therapist handling a snake. Then the client is encouraged to copy the behavior. ***Modeling*** is probably an important component of social skills training and other forms of therapy. Even in a talking psychotherapy such as psychoanalysis or client-centered therapy, the client may be learning important relationship skills by observing and imitating the therapist.

Covert modeling, similar to covert practice, is imagining another person engaging in the desired behavior. A therapist may tell a child a story about another child who successfully stops fighting with his siblings and learns other ways to get attention. It is assumed that imagining a successful model facilitates learning new behavior that is similar to the model's.

Broad Spectrum Behavior Therapy

So many new methods of behavior therapy have been developed that the field has become diverse and eclectic. Behavior therapists tend to be pragmatic and ingenious in trying new methods, and they select and combine techniques to fit individual clients. Multimodal behavior therapy, now called broad-spectrum therapy, represents a systematic eclecticism. It is an assessment and therapy framework that encompasses elements of all the above behavioral methods as well as cognitive-behavioral therapy and rational-emotive therapy. It is associated with the work of Lazarus (1981). Psychological disorders are viewed in terms of seven modalities—behavior, affect, sensation, imagery, cognition, interpersonal relationships, and drug/biological aspect—which result in the clever acronym BASIC ID. Clients are assessed as to their functioning in each of the modalities, and a specific treatment plan is made for each of the seven. For example, a shy client may show passivity and compliance in behavior, for which assertion training is prescribed; anxiety and fear in affect, for which desensitization is prescribed; images of helplessness and ridicule in imagery, for which coping imagery exercises are taught; perfectionism in cognition, for which cognitive disputation (described in chapter 11) is done; avoidance and withdrawal in interpersonal relations, for which risk-taking assignments are given; and excessive eating and coffee drinking in the drugs/biology aspect, for which diet and exercise are prescribed.

Postmodern Behavior Therapy

As behaviorist Neil Miller did over half a century ago (Dollard & Miller, 1950), postmodern behavior therapists have recast the usual sorts of therapeutic interventions into behavioral terms. A group known as radical behaviorists (Hayes, Follette, & Follette, 1995; Hayes, Strosahl, & Wilson, 1999; Hayes, Follette, & Linehan, 2004; Jacobson, 1994; Kohlenberg & Tsai, 1991, 1994, 2000; Linehan, 1993; Linehan, Armstrong, Suarez, Allmon, and Heard, 1991; Linehan, Cochran, & Kehrer, 2001; Rizvi & Linehan, 2001) has called for behavior therapy to return to B. F. Skinner's experimental analysis of behavior. Not only do they criticize behavior therapy as just a collection of techniques that no longer have much to do with behaviorism, they also argue that Skinner has been misrepresented and misunderstood by behavior therapists in the past. Contrary to common beliefs about Skinnerian behaviorism, radical behaviorists place importance on understanding, thinking, and feeling (called private behaviors) not just on "observable" (public) behavior, seriously consider genetic determinants of behavior, and are interested in early childhood determinants of behavior.

In the radical behaviorists' view, behavior therapy can never be a method that is applied to everyone, but rather, it must be idiographic. Each behavior therapy intervention must be designed for a specific individual, because behavior is a function of learning history, genetics, and the situational context, all of which will vary greatly among different people. Even when two people appear to be in the same environment to an outside observer, they are actually in different environments because they have different learning histories and so experience the context differently. A therapeutic intervention can be designed only by a functional analysis of all of these variables as they affect a specific person.

A *functional analysis* examines the function of a behavior in its particular context, rather than examining the behavior itself. For example, a radical behaviorist would not focus on the avoidance behavior in phobias but would analyze the function of a specific individual's avoidant behavior in its situational and historical contexts. As another example, there can be no universal definition of social skills in radical behaviorism. A behavior is socially skilled if it *functions* as a skill in a specific situation in relation to certain others when performed by an individual with a specific learning history.

In traditional behavior therapies, therapists use similar rewards such as money or praise for everyone. By doing so, they are using reinforcement that is chosen by the therapist and may be experienced as arbitrary by any one individual. Radical behaviorists argue that reinforcers will vary from person to person, and they emphasize natural reinforcement and the contingencies that occur in "the real world." They observe which therapist behaviors and which situational factors reinforce the desired behaviors of a specific individual in therapy and then use those as reinforcers. By consciously using their own genuine behavior that they have observed during therapy as strengthening desired client behaviors, radical behavior therapists claim to be using "natural," rather than "arbitrary" reinforcement.

Although our review of radical behaviorism necessarily simplifies a complex theory and cannot cover it all, we will look at one other concept. Skinner originally made the distinction between direct contingency control versus rule-governed behavior. Traditional behavior therapies emphasize the first one: public "observable" behavior that is rewarded or punished by an external stimulus, such as temper tantrums being rewarded by parental attention. Radical behaviorists have reemphasized the importance of the second distinction. Also called indirect contingency or verbal control (Hayes et al., 1995), rule-governed behavior refers to behavior that is guided by verbalized thoughts or feelings. Recall that radical behaviorists consider thoughts and feelings to be behavior like any other, only private, and therefore governed by the same principles as all behavior. Thus, thoughts and feelings are learned, and they can be verbalized to one's self (i.e., kept private) or to another person (i.e., made public). Depending on the situational and historical context, these verbalizations can become rules that influence observable behavior. For example, a woman may have learned "Girls are afraid of snakes" and be likely to develop a snake phobia, while another woman may have learned "Snakes make fun pets" and be likely to handle snakes. The behavior of avoiding or handling snakes is said to be rule governed. On the other hand, the snake-avoiding behavior of people who live in a jungle infested with poisonous snakes is said to be under direct contingency control (i.e., controlled by external reinforcers). The concept of rule-governed behavior allows radical behaviorists to account for individual differences, for the effects of cognitions and emotions on behavior, and for the effectiveness of verbal therapy.

After this brief review of radical behaviorism, let us now turn to some of the treatments developed by radical behavior therapists. Each has its own name, leading to an "alphabet soup" of acronyms. Functional Analytic Therapy (FAP) emphasizes an intense, emotional relationship between client and therapist that functions both to elicit and to reinforce relevant client behaviors. Acceptance and Commitment Therapy (ACT) encourages client acceptance of difficult or disturbing feelings and thoughts, not by altering these private behaviors, but by placing them in a new context. Dialectical Behavior Therapy (DBT) is designed to treat borderline personality disorder by behaviorally teaching clients to modulate their extreme reactions. As discussed in chapter 13, Integrative Behavioral Couple Therapy (IBCT) teaches couples to accept each other, rather than engaging in self-defeating behaviors such as trying to change the partner. As you will see, and as radical behaviorists ironically note, their therapeutic interventions appear to be more similar to psychodynamic, client-centered, existentialist, and other interpersonal therapies than to traditional behavior therapies.

Functional Analytic Psychotherapy (FAP)

Because Kohlenberg and Tsai's (1991, 1994, 2000) Functional Analytic Psychotherapy (FAP) emphasizes an intense, emotional relationship between therapist and client as the vehicle for behavioral change, it is best suited for people with difficulties in close relationships or other interpersonal problems. The context of therapy is designed to elicit the client's problematic behaviors, and these behaviors are changed by the natural reinforcers of the therapist's reactions in the therapy session. (The client inevitably shapes the therapist's behavior, too.) FAP opposes the use of arbitrary reinforcers chosen by the therapist; rather, genuine reactions of the therapist are used to reinforce improvements in client behavior as they occur. For example, FAP would not address shyness by teaching assertive behavior and rewarding it with therapist praise. Rather, in the context of therapy that fosters closeness and trust, a FAP therapist's behavior would naturally evoke shy behavior, which in FAP would be called socially avoidant behavior and would be dealt with as discussed below, and any assertive behavior that occurred would be shaped and reinforced by the therapist's genuine reaction, such as "I feel close to you when you tell me what you really want." If this response led to client behavior change, then the therapist would be reinforced.

FAP requires the therapist to pay attention to clinically relevant behaviors (CRBs) as they occur in the therapy session. There are three types of CRB. The first are behaviors related to the client's presenting problem; for example, a person who complains of social anxiety avoids eye contact during the session. The second type of CRB is improvements in client behaviors that occur in the session; for example, this socially avoidant client asks for an extra session. The third type of CRB refers to clients' talking about their own behavior and what seems to cause it, as when they make interpretations on their own; for example, this same client may say, "I freeze up when other people look me in the eye and I think they are going to judge me."

FAP recommends five "rules" for therapist behavior to help develop the therapist's own rule-governed behavior. The first one, to watch for CRBs, is the core of FAP. In therapy, the main consequence of client behavior is the therapist's reaction.

By attending to CRBs, the therapist can react naturally to them and thus promote the necessary genuine, intense, emotional relationship between client and therapist.

The second rule is to evoke CRBs. Depending on the client's presenting problem, the therapist can do a variety of things to elicit the clinically relevant problematic behavior during therapy. When that behavior occurs in session, the therapist can then react according to the fifth rule, described below, to help the client deal with it then and there. The therapist should also provide for the development of improved clinically relevant behavior. Any technique from free association to homework assignments that provides the opportunity for the client to try out an improved behavior is acceptable in FAP.

The third rule is to reinforce improvements in CRB as they occur in session. The therapist must be alert to the significance of even small behavior changes as potential improvements for specific clients. For example, an extra session requested by a socially anxious client may be inconvenient for the therapist, but a FAP therapist would recognize the significance of this particular client making a direct request as an improvement in CRB and so would reward the assertive behavior by readily agreeing to an extra session. On the other hand, the same request by a client whose problems include demanding, overly dependent behavior would not be reinforced.

The fourth rule is to observe the potentially reinforcing effects of therapist behavior in relation to client CRBs. Following this rule involves the therapist making a functional analysis along the lines of observing which of her own behaviors strengthen which client behaviors and which have the opposite effect. For example, a therapist may observe that when she responds warmly and enthusiastically to her socially anxious client's self-disclosing statements, the client changes the subject. With this particular client at this time in therapy, warmth is not reinforcing the improved clinically relevant behavior of talking about feelings. The therapist may find that listening neutrally leads to more self-disclosing statements by this client.

The fifth rule is to give interpretations of variables that affect client behavior. Statements of functional relationships between the client's behavior and other variables help clients become aware of problematic clinically relevant behavior and what brings it about. In addition, giving such interpretations models the third type of CRB, those that involve making observational statements of one's own behavior, for the client. For example, a therapist may interpret, "When I make a positive remark about you, you look away and change the subject." This interpretation points out the first type of CRB and models the third type of CRB. It will also lead to an intense interpersonal discussion that may evoke the second type of CRB, improved behaviors.

If followed, the rules of FAP lead to the intense relationship required for developing and reinforcing therapeutic change. This therapy then looks more like interpersonally based psychodynamic therapy or client-centered therapy than like traditional behavior therapy. It has been integrated with cognitive therapy (see chapter 11), resulting in FECT: FAP-Enhanced Cognitive Therapy (Hayes et al., 1999).

Acceptance and Commitment Therapy (ACT)

As with other radical behavior therapy, the Acceptance and Commitment Therapy (ACT) of Hayes and his colleagues (Hayes et al., 1995, 1999, 2004) requires a strong therapeutic relationship between therapist and client. Within this context, the goal of ACT is to support the client's acceptance of unacceptable or disturbing thoughts and feelings without needing to avoid, escape from, or control them. Recall that thoughts and feelings are (private) behaviors like observable (public) behaviors. Trying to avoid certain thoughts and feelings may lead to self-defeating behavior in specific individuals in certain contexts. While most adult psychotherapies deal with clients' thoughts and feelings, ACT does not try to alter these private behaviors but rather to place them in a different context. There are five phases in this treatment.

The first phase of ACT involves "creative hopelessness." The therapist confronts clients with the hopelessness and futility of their past attempts to avoid or change their unacceptable or disturbing thoughts and feelings. In the second phase, clients are encouraged to examine their own experiences to identify how self-defeating it is to try to control their thoughts and feelings. This part of ACT is similar to strategic therapy's observation that the solution is the problem (see chapter 13 for details of strategic therapy); that is, the client's "solution" to unacceptable feelings, trying to avoid experiencing them, actually becomes the problematic avoidance behaviors.

In the third phase of ACT, the goal is to help people distinguish between themselves and their behavioral reactions. To the extent that people can separate the "I" from what "I do, think, and feel," the more they can allow themselves to experience unacceptable feelings without feeling threatened. For example, clients are encouraged to say "I am having the thought that I am stupid and cannot give my oral report," rather than "I am stupid and can't give my oral report."

In the fourth phase of ACT, "letting go of the struggle," clients are encouraged to experience rather than avoid negative thoughts and feelings. Interventions that look like the reflections of client-centered therapy or the paradoxes of strategic therapy are used to achieve this goal. In the fifth phase, the emphasis on committing to and implementing changes most closely resembles traditional behavior therapy. In all phases, the therapist flexibly makes use of exercises, homework, metaphor, and various verbal interventions, including reflection.

Dialectical Behavior Therapy (DBT)

Marsha Linehan (1987, 1993; Linehan et al., 1991, 2001; Marra, 2005) has developed a program of behavior therapy originally designed for people with borderline personality disorder. Called Dialectical Behavior Therapy (DBT), it is grounded in the assumption that social interactions and personal growth are a result of a dialectical process, which involves an action leading to a reaction resulting in a synthesis. However, it is assumed that borderlines are stuck in going back and forth between extremes of emotion and behavior without ever learning a new synthesis, or middle ground. They are highly emotionally aroused and sensitive to threat all the time, so the focus of therapy becomes self-management of affect rather than behavior or cognitions as in traditional behavior or cognitive-behavioral therapy.

Linehan contracts with borderlines to attend her program for a year and then the contract is renegotiated, but generally, therapy with borderlines is very long-term, because they need a great deal of help. She tries to establish a collaborative, consultative relationship with the client, emphasizing problem solving so that the client's needs are met and the therapist's needs (for client improvement) are also met. It is essential that there is a positive relationship between therapist and client so that therapist responses are sufficiently reinforcing to effect client change. Creating this positive relationship may involve warmth, attentiveness, availability, genuineness, and reciprocal self-disclosure.

There are three components to DBT for borderline personality disorder. Clients attend a weekly psychoeducational group, which teaches behavioral skills, assertion, affect regulation, cognitive restructuring, problem solving, and coping, typical behavioral techniques we have described earlier. In addition, acceptance and mindfulness (paying attention to and experiencing emotion) are special skills taught in DBT. The second component of the treatment program is telephone contact, and clients phone the therapist when they need help with applying the skills learned in group to the real world. On the telephone, the therapist focuses the client, who, like most borderlines, is in a state of perpetual crisis, on how to solve the current problem by asking the client to define the problem, describe what led up to it, review the skills that can be applied to the situation, and then decide what to do about it.

The third component is weekly individual therapy. Here, the relationship with the therapist is used as a reward in shaping improved behaviors, as is done in Functional Analytic Psychotherapy. Borderline clients first agree on certain behavioral goals, and they are allowed to continue therapy only if they maintain the agreement to work on those goals. The therapist must ensure that competent and improving behaviors are rewarded with the therapist's time and attention, because it is easy to inadvertently reward incompetent or even suicidal behavior by attending to it more than to competent behavior.

In individual therapy, agreed-on target behaviors are organized hierarchically, and in each session the therapist and client first address behaviors that have occurred in the highest target area before discussing other issues. The first therapeutic target behavior involves the elimination of suicidal and self-destructive behavior. The second is the reduction of therapy-threatening behavior, such as not attending therapy, not talking about important issues, and the like. The third target behavior on the list involves work and living skills necessary to maintain an adequate life. Fourth, core skills for emotional control are addressed. Finally, if there are no issues left in any of the previous areas, the specific goals of the individual client are discussed.

While many of the behavioral methods used in DBT are similar to those used in other behavior therapies, Linehan has developed some new techniques for use with borderline clients. One of these is ***validation.*** According to Linehan, borderlines have been raised in families that invalidate their experience so that genuine emotion becomes highly threatening. The therapist validates the client by listening carefully to the client's experience; by reflecting accurately to the client the therapist's observation of the client's thoughts, emotions, and behaviors; and by finding the "nugget of truth" in the client's present situation that would naturally make the client feel and behave that way. For example, if a client feels that the therapist doesn't like her, rather than invalidating her experience by denying any dislike, the therapist addresses what the client thinks she is doing that is unlikable. The focus then becomes teaching client how to elicit the behaviors, such as liking her, that she wants in other people.

Others (Rizvi & Linehan, 2001; Marra, 2005) have extended DBT to treat additional disorders and have conceptualized dialectic conflicts typical of each. DBT is suitable for disorders consisting of high emotionality or arousal, including anxiety and depression. Because of their strong, unpleasant emotions, disturbed people engage in avoidance and escape strategies that prevent them from going through the dialectical process and learning to deal with their emotions. Furthermore, the escape and avoidance behaviors are often self-destructive, such as engaging in risky sexual behavior or heavy drinking. Clients are taught psychosocial coping skills to replace their escape and avoidance behaviors. Emotion regulation, distress tolerance, and other strategic behavior skills are also taught. In addition, clients are taught acceptance and mindfulness, so they can experience their negative emotions and complete the dialectic. Mindfulness, nonjudgmentally paying attention to emotional states as they occur, can thus be seen as an exposure or desensitization method.

Evaluation of Behavior Therapy

Behavior therapy is unique in its emphasis on research, assessment, and empirical verification of efficacy. Because of this emphasis, a large body of knowledge has developed to help in the evaluation of behavior therapy. The field has matured sufficiently to recognize its weaknesses as well as its strengths.

The research on behavior therapy, including theory and practice, is so extensive that it would be impossible to do justice to it in this chapter. Many experimental studies and many meta-analytic studies attest to the effectiveness of most behavior therapies to improve human functioning in many ways. Recall from our chapter on research in psychotherapy, it is difficult to define improvement to everyone's satisfaction. Behavior therapy is highly successful in reducing symptoms, although the definition of symptom and whether symptom removal is the only goal of therapy remain controversial. Behavior therapy leads to other improvements that some people value. For example, with Patterson's behavioral treatment of acting-out boys, it was found that there was improvement in the behavior of siblings as well as the client (Reid, Patterson, & Snyder, 2002). In another example, behavioral marital therapy for alcoholics and their spouses not only led to reduced drinking but also to happier marriages, as long as relapse prevention was included (O'Farrell et al., 1996).

Meta-analytic studies have found higher than average effect sizes for most behavior therapies (see Emmelkamp [2004] for a review of this research). Since higher effect sizes indicate higher therapy effectiveness, it is safe to conclude that behavior therapy is effective according to research.

Criticisms of Behavior Therapy

Many past criticisms of behavior therapy centered on theoretical disagreements between different schools of thought. Critics claimed that because their theory was the correct one, behavior therapy was wrong, not "deep enough," or just missed the point. For example, psychoanalysts criticized behavior therapy for not treating the underlying unconscious conflict, just the superficial symptoms.

Behavior therapy is criticized as not being behavioral at all. Systematic desensitization is criticized as relying on cognitions and "imagining" the phobic stimulus. Radical behaviorists argue that what is called behavior therapy is merely a collection of behavioral techniques that have very little relationship to genuine behaviorism.

Behavioral technology is applied too quickly, too enthusiastically, and with too many modifications, so that it frequently loses its ties to empirically verified behavioral principles. Precisely how is a technique, such as playing the role of asking for a date, based on behavioral principles? Pairing all the stimuli surrounding lighting up a cigarette with electric shock seems a clear case of classical conditioning and the use of punishment. However, what kind of behavioral technique is making the client chain smoke many cigarettes fast until he is exhausted and nauseous? Does giving it the name "massed practice" make it a behavioral method? Can it be considered a technique of aversion therapy? Or is it an example of reverse psychology? It may be that practitioners generalize or modify behavioral techniques without considering their theoretical or empirical rationale, until some methods do not appear to be related to the known principles of learning.

Behavior therapy is criticized for being open to incorrect applications and deliberate misuse. The principles of behavior therapy seem clear and easy to understand, but inexperienced individuals unfamiliar with the empirical foundation of behaviorism may try to apply the principles in inappropriate ways or to inappropriate problems. Attempting to extinguish depression by ignoring talk of sadness or suicide would be an obvious example of misapplication, and we mentioned earlier how time-out is sometimes used incorrectly in schools.

Since behavior modification involves the deliberate manipulation of reward contingencies so that desirable behavior is increased and undesirable behavior is decreased, critics contend that it is or can be misused to serve merely a social control function, or to manipulate or even oppress people. Behavior therapy is accused of being coercive and manipulative, promoting social conformity, and limiting freedom of choice. Critics are concerned with who decides what is desirable behavior to be rewarded and what is undesirable behavior, since value judgments are inherent in such decisions. They also point out that behavior modification methods are often used with relatively powerless groups, such as developmentally disabled children or mental hospital patients.

Defenders of behavior modification point out that any procedure can be misused and that care must be taken to serve the best interests of the clients. Furthermore, they say, rewards are being given out in all social situations, and children and mental patients are being managed and manipulated all the time anyway. With behavior modification, the value judgments as to which behaviors to reward and which not to reward are made explicit and therefore open to criticism and change. In other words, defenders argue, behavior modification is just ordinary social behavior made conscious and deliberate and out in the open. Finally, they conclude, proper contingency management techniques are highly effective for helping individuals change in directions they themselves wish to go.

Aversion therapy and the use of punishment have been especially criticized, for ethical reasons. Interestingly enough, B. F. Skinner himself argued against the use of aversives in many of his writings, for in addition to punishment being morally questionable, he thought it did not work very well.

Radical behavior therapy may be open to the criticism that it merely gives new labels to what is usually done in interpersonal talking therapies. Unlike traditional behavior therapies that remain very different from other forms of psychotherapy, radical behavior therapies creatively utilize techniques borrowed from therapies from psychoanalysis to cognitive-behaviorism, and they lend themselves to the possibility of theoretical integration with other therapies.

New applications and new forms of behavior therapy are being developed every day. Some critics believe that behavior therapies are developed and implemented without adequate research. Behaviorists' pride in their emphasis on empiricism may clash with pragmatic desires for quick, inexpensive psychological treatments.

Strengths of Behavior Therapy

A large body of research demonstrates that behavior therapy is at least as effective as other forms of therapy. (Much of this research is covered in this chapter and in chapters 5 and 11.) There is extensive empirical support for radical behavior therapy (Hayes, Follette, & Linehan, 2004). Behavior therapy is a cost-effective form of treatment, an aspect that becomes increasingly valued in our society. Even though behaviorists do not meet the ideal of empirically evaluating every treatment before it is implemented, behavior therapists subject their methods to empirical research far more frequently than any other group, except client-centered therapists. And this research tends to support the effectiveness of behavior therapy.

As brain–behavior connections are increasingly researched, biological evidence of behavior therapy's effectiveness may appear. A landmark study conducted at the UCLA Neuropsychiatric Institute examined the brain functioning of people with obsessive-compulsive disorder before and after treatment with medication or behavior therapy. They found that *both* successful drug therapy *and* behavior therapy led to similar identifiable changes in the brains of the participants (Baxter et al., 1992). Thus, there is evidence that effective changes in behavior can actually cause changes in the brain.

From a values orientation, a strength of behavior therapy may be that it is essentially egalitarian. Although criticized as potential social control agents, behavior therapists see themselves as "giving away" their knowledge to clients. They fully explain their procedures and their theoretical and empirical rationales. They describe the empirically verified effectiveness of their methods. They do not "interpret" their clients' questions about their methods as "resistance," but respect their clients' right to know by answering their questions fully. Once clients have their therapists' knowledge, they can use it to achieve any goal they desire.

In Conclusion

Behavior therapy at its best is essentially a cooperative enterprise between therapist and client. The client may define the treatment goals, and the therapist may describe and explain the methods to reach them. They can mutually agree on a clear plan of action and then work together to implement the treatment plan. This egalitarian approach undoubtedly contributes to a good relationship between therapist and client. A good therapist–client relationship is certainly central in radical behavior therapy, and it may be the essential ingredient for behavior therapy's effectiveness.

Cognitive and Cognitive-Behavioral Approaches to Psychotherapy

> We take the stand that there are always some alternative constructions available to choose among in dealing with the world. No one needs to paint himself into a corner; no one needs to be completely hemmed in by circumstances; no one needs to be the victim of his biography.
>
> —G. Kelly, *The Psychology of Personal Constructs*

> Change is mediated through cognitive processes, but the cognitive events are induced and altered most readily by experiences of mastery arising from successful performance.
>
> —A. Bandura, *Social Learning Theory*

Suppose a parent tells his young child that he is not allowed to draw on the walls of his room with his crayons. Later, the parent discovers the child drawing on the living room walls. The parent becomes angry and spanks the child. Asked why he became angry, the parent says, "He knew better. He was drawing on the walls because he was deliberately being naughty." Asked why he chose spanking as a method of discipline, he replies, "I spanked him because if you spare the rod, you spoil the child. It'll probably whip some sense into him."

How would a cognitive psychologist explain this anger at the child and the choice of spanking as a method of discipline? First, the cognitive psychologist would assume that the anger is based on the parent's perception and interpretation of the situation. From a cognitive perspective, anger is a response to the perception that the other person could have controlled his actions (Weiner, 1982). Thus, the feeling of anger is based on the interpretation that the child was "deliberately being naughty" and that he "knew better."

But perhaps he didn't. Little children often are quite literal, and they do not necessarily interpret things as we do. The child may not have known that he was doing anything wrong, believing that he had been told only not to draw on his own walls. If the parent had interpreted the situation this way, he probably would not have felt quite as angry.

The action of spanking was also based on the father's interpretation of the situation. Believing the child's actions were deliberately naughty, he concluded that severe measures were called for. He may have said to himself: "He must not be allowed to act defiantly that way. That is an awful way to act." His choice of spanking came out of his beliefs about appropriate methods of discipline, and these beliefs were probably based on his own experience as a child. The choice may also have been influenced by his perceptions of self-efficacy, that is, his self-perception of his ableness or competence to handle the situation effectively. He may have perceived himself as unable to influence the child's behavior in other ways, for instance, through dialogue. In sum, a person's actions in a situation are determined by his perceptions of the situation, his ideas about the best way to handle the situation, and his perceptions about his own skills and competencies in the situation. In addition, interpretations and cognitions influence how a person feels about the situation.

Generalizing this to abnormal behavior, the cognitive perspective sees cognition as mediating or causing both psychopathological feeling states and behavior. Psychotherapy becomes, directly or indirectly, the attempt to modify these cognitions. Cognition includes our perceptions and interpretations of situations, our behavior schemes for handling situations, our values and beliefs, and our perceptions of ourselves and of our own competencies. As you shall see, cognitions do not necessarily have to be conscious, and some perspectives give cognition a place of more central importance than others. For instance, social learning theory does not see the direct modification of cognition through verbal communication as a particularly effective therapeutic strategy. In contrast, both Aaron Beck's (1986, 1987, 1990) cognitive therapy and Albert Ellis's (1973; 1979a, b, c, d; 1984) rational-emotive therapy rely extensively on verbal communication as a therapeutic approach.

Cognitive and cognitive-behavioral therapies are rapidly becoming the most influential set of approaches at the present time. They have somewhat different lineages. Cognitive therapy developed on its own. George Kelly was the first important cognitive therapist. Two other major cognitive therapists who shaped this approach are Albert Ellis and Aaron Beck.

Cognitive-behavior therapy developed out of behavior therapy. The difference between cognitive and cognitive-behavioral therapies is a matter of emphasis. Cognitive therapies utilize behavioral techniques, but emphasize cognitive ones. Cognitive-behavioral therapies utilize cognitive techniques, but emphasize behavioral ones. Goldfried (1997) has illustrated the difference by comparing the work of Donald Meichenbaum (a cognitive-behaviorist) with the work of Aaron Beck (a cognitive therapist), both working with the same client, Richard, in a set of famous films (Beck, 1986; Meichenbaum, 1986). Richard is a divorced, suicidal man who has interpersonal problems including anger management. Meichenbaum, the cognitive-behaviorist, helps Richard find more adaptive ways of expressing his anger (a behavioral strategy). Beck, the cognitive therapist, helps Richard cope with his suicidal feelings by learning how to challenge his dysfunctional beliefs (a cognitive strategy).

To make matters confusing, both cognitive and cognitive-behavioral therapies are currently often referred to as *cognitive-behavioral* therapies. Thus, when you hear about cognitive-behavior therapy, you often will not know if it refers to those therapies that represent the cognitive therapy stream or those that represent the cognitive-behavior therapy stream. In either case, cognitive-behavior therapies have become influential because (a) they are brief and efficient; (b) they are highly structured and systematic; (c) cognitive-behavior therapists spend a considerable amount of effort researching their approaches and demonstrating empirically that they work; and (d) they are typically developed as highly structured, specific treatments for specific disorders. Thus, they fit well with the current health care climate.

In this chapter we shall first consider the transition from behavior therapy to cognitive-behavior therapy by taking a look at an important theoretical development that helped lead behavior therapy to adopt cognition—that of Bandura's social learning/social cognitive theory. Next, we shall briefly consider the work of one of the pioneers of cognitive-behavior therapy—Donald Meichenbaum—and afterwards describe some modern examples, such as Borkovec's treatment for generalized anxiety disorder and Barlow's work on panic disorder.

We shall then consider the "cognitive stream" of development—the work of George Kelly and the work of perhaps the two most influential cognitive therapists, Aaron Beck and Albert Ellis.

Transition from Behavior Therapy to Cognitive-Behavioral Therapy

Traditional behaviorism had little use for cognition. Because cognition was not directly observable, the belief was that it was not scientific to talk about it. To the very last, B. F. Skinner (1987) refused to see any value in cognitive psychology, blaming it (along with humanistic psychology) for supposedly interfering with the development of psychology as a science of behavior. Of course nowadays scientists have developed sophisticated ways to study cognition, and a cognitive revolution has transformed psychology. Virtually every subarea of psychology, from experimental psychology to developmental psychology, to personality and social psychology, place the study of cognitive processes at center stage.

Albert Bandura

The shift from behaviorism to cognitive-behaviorism in the realm of psychotherapy began in the 1970s. One of the major contributors to this shift was the work of Albert Bandura. Bandura was a codeveloper of social learning theory (also considered in chapter 10). Bandura has since redubbed his approach "social-cognitive theory" (Bandura, 1986).

Perhaps the best way to introduce social learning theory is to compare it to behaviorism. Traditional behaviorism assumed that learning was the automatic association of a stimulus with a response. Such an automatic association was "strengthened" by reinforcement, and behavior was a function of the consequences. In order for learning to occur, a behavior had to be performed and reinforced. Learning was essentially a trial-and-error process, in which an organism emitted a variety of behaviors until one was reinforced.

Bandura (1986) took this view to task. He asserted that all learning is cognitively mediated. A stimulus comes to be associated with a response because it comes to have predictive value. If a shock is repeatedly paired with a light, a person avoids the light, not because the light itself has become aversive, but because it has become predictive of shock and pain. Thus, what people learn are ***expectancies.*** They do not develop conditioned responses to stimuli unless they are aware of the relationship between the stimulus and response, that is, unless they are aware that the stimulus predicts the onset of reinforcement or punishment.

Furthermore, Bandura argued that the idea that reinforcement "strengthens" associations between stimulus and response is a metaphor and not literally true. He suggested that reinforcement leads to learning because reinforcers are information givers and incentives. For instance, many social reinforcers, such as good grades on tests or teachers' approval, are reinforcing in part because they give the information that the student is on the right track. If a person is told that shock is a signal for a correct response, shock will function as a positive reinforcer (see, for instance, Dulany, 1968). In general, Bandura said that behavior is more a function of its anticipated consequences than of its immediate, real consequences.

Bandura went on to point out that most important human learning is ***vicarious learning.*** People do not learn most of the important skills in life by performing trial-and-error responses until one is reinforced. They would not be likely to survive long if that was the way they learned. It would be a highly inefficient way to train surgeons or automobile builders, for instance, if they had to do things by trial and error until they finally got them right. Instead, most important learning takes place through observation and instruction. People learn through watching others' behavior, reading books or gathering information from other media, and receiving instructions.

People learn both how to interpret situations and what to do in a given situation. Bandura was one of the first investigators to note the relationship between being abused as a child and becoming a child abuser as an adult (Bandura & Walters, 1959). An abused child might learn that when a person with more power gets angry at a transgression by a person with less power, the person with more power has the right and obligation to use the infliction of physical pain as a punishment. No one explicitly verbalizes this as a rule, but it is modeled by the parent's actions. When the abused child becomes an adult, she may enact this same pattern of behavior. If she becomes a leader of a country, she may use it as a principle of national policy.

Situational Specificity of Behavior

A key concept for many social learning theorists is that of the situational specificity of behavior. Traditional views of the person, such as those within psychoanalysis, believe that each individual has an enduring personality structure made up of an organized pattern of character traits. A person might be described, for instance, as having the traits of cleanliness, friendliness, conscientiousness, optimism, extraversion, and assertiveness. Such a view assumes that this person's behavior is primarily determined by her character traits; that is, she is generally expected to be friendly, assertive, extraverted, and clean.

However, Bandura, as well as social learning theorists, believes that behavior is situation-specific. Behavior is guided by the expectancies in a specific situation. If a person acts assertively in some situation, it is not because she has an internal trait of assertiveness, but because she has learned to expect that assertiveness is effective in that situation. Because her behavior is guided by what she has learned to expect in different situations, she might act quite differently in a different situation. If she had learned to expect that quiet deference is the most effective behavior in a different situation, she would probably act deferentially.

Therefore, many social learning theorists do not believe that people will necessarily exhibit consistency of behavior in different situations. Bandura describes an autistic child who was calm, well behaved, considerate, and cooperative when the child's father was home, but at other times she was destructive and undisciplined (Moser, 1965, as reported in Bandura, 1977a, p. 86). Now, which is the "real" child? According to social learning theory, both are, because the child's behavior is different in different situations.

The idea of situational specificity can explain why psychologists, psychiatrists, and other mental health professionals have difficulty predicting violent behavior. Often, they are asked to predict if an individual in a prison or mental hospital is likely to be violent if released. Typically, such predictions are based on the idea of personality character structure: Does this individual still exhibit character traits of a violent nature or not? Examples of violent crime committed within days of release by someone who was judged nonviolent by professionals support the idea that the situational specificity of behavior is often more important than the individual's personality structure in predicting what he or she will do. Bandura (1986) has argued that those we label as "aggressive" or "violent" do not act aggressively or violently most of the time. It is more useful to find out *when and where* they act aggressively or violently in terms of efforts to modify their behavior.

Self-Efficacy

Perhaps Bandura's most enduring contribution is the concept of ***self-efficacy*** (Bandura, 1996). Self-efficacy is a person's self-perception of competence to enact a behavior or to handle a given type of situation. For example, some of you may have a sense of self-efficacy as an auto mechanic and others may not. In our example of the parent who spanked his son for writing on the walls, we suggested that he may have chosen spanking because he felt he could not influence his son through dialogue. If this were because he perceived himself as not good at verbal persuasion, then we would say he had a perception of low self-efficacy as a communicator.

Bandura has argued that an increase in self-efficacy is the common underlying dimension of effectiveness of psychotherapy. A perception of low self-efficacy has a number of negative consequences. It leads to avoidance. People are likely to avoid situations in which they feel incompetent. Thus, if you believe that if you go outdoors, you will be overwhelmed by a panic attack that you cannot manage, you will stay indoors. Defensive behavior, then, is a response to perceived low efficacy. People act defensively when they believe they cannot handle something. In essence, then, defensiveness is the converse of a feeling of mastery.

Along with avoidance, low self-efficacy leads to a tendency to give up too soon. As a result, a person does not persist long enough to find out if she can master a situation. In addition, low self-efficacy leads to a tendency to self-monitor in a self-destructive manner. The person observes her own efforts to cope with a situation and engages in negative self-evaluation. Such self-conscious rumination has a tendency to further disrupt behavior. A person who is absorbed in thoughts of how badly she is performing is no longer focusing on the situation and therefore cannot respond to it adequately. For example, if you feel sexually inadequate, you may focus on how well you are doing, not on your partner or the stimuli that make sex pleasurable. As a result, you may do things mechanically, and you are not likely to respond adequately to your own or your partner's sensations and reactions. Low self-efficacy can be seen to relate to a variety of disorders including phobias, substance abuse, depression, and anxiety disorders. We further consider the impact of ***negative self-monitoring*** next.

If a person feels incompetent in a particular situation, he may begin to observe himself critically, looking for signs of dysfunction, and because he is no longer focused on the situation, he acts less competently. When you are doing something, it is disruptive to continually focus your attention on yourself rather than on the task and on your behavior. Such self-consciousness can also intensify negative mood states (Buss, 1980).

Bandura (1986) suggested that there are ways to use self-monitoring effectively. Effective self-monitoring does not focus on what momentary success or failure means in terms of personality, self, or future. Rather it focuses on the situation and task: "What does this situation demand?" "What did I just do? Did it work? If not, why not?" "What resources do I need for my next task?" As you shall see, Meichenbaum's cognitive-behavioral therapy is an attempt to replace disruptive self-monitoring processes with more effective ones. Sex therapy also does this by trying to deflect the client's attention from self-evaluation to enjoyment of the activity. Attempts to modify dysfunctional, self-focused attention are also parts of Ellis's and Beck's cognitive approaches.

Following on Bandura's ideas, Goldfried (1995) has argued that many of the changes in behavior therapy are primarily changes in self-efficacy. For instance, a person who is afraid of some situation may be repeatedly exposed to that situation until he overcomes the fear. Goldfried argues that what is being learned is a sense that "I can" handle the feared situation. Similarly, the learning of skills (see chapter 10) increases one's sense of self-efficacy.

In fact, Bandura has argued that raising the level of perception of self-efficacy is the most potent therapeutic change event and that verbal persuasion is probably the least effective way to do this. He states quite forcefully that "performance-based" therapeutic interventions are more effective than verbal ones. While verbal persuasion can be useful in modifying fears that have not been reinforced by direct experience and that are primarily a matter of misinformation, it is relatively ineffective in modifying fears that have been learned through direct experience or that have been heavily reinforced. Basically, Bandura argues that direct experience is a much more potent teacher than words delivered in a therapeutic setting. For this reason, he believes therapy must include situations in which individuals actually engage in successful mastery experiences, and the therapist must arrange therapeutic tasks so that mastery experiences occur.

Bandura states that a potent way of learning, in addition to direct experience, is observation. Both direct performance and observation are considerably more experiential than verbal persuasion. Most of us can sense the difference between being told "Snakes aren't dangerous" and seeing someone like us learn to overcome his or her fear of snakes. Bandura has demonstrated that observing someone else overcoming fears helps the client overcome his or her own fears.

Donald Meichenbaum

Donald Meichenbaum (1977) was one of the pioneers of the development of cognitive-behavior modification. Showing his behavioral roots, he initially did not talk about "thinking" but rather about "self speech." He focused on how we talk to ourselves. According to Meichenbaum how we talk to ourselves is crucial in determining how we behave and feel. Meichenbaum pointed out that children talk to themselves all the time as they play and practice new skills. It is through such self-guiding speech that people learn to direct and control much of their behavior. For example, when you first learned how to drive, you most likely guided your first attempts with self-speech. Talking to yourself is actually quite adaptive, if you say the right things. And that is the crux of Meichenbaum's cognitive-behavioral therapeutic approach.

Maladaptive self-speech can contribute to psychological problems. Someone who says things to herself that are disruptive and distressing, such as "I can never do anything right. What's the use?" may give up on tasks or engage in dysfunctional behavior, such as drinking, to avoid the tasks. The absence of adaptive self-speech makes dysfunctional behavior more likely. Furthermore, if a person does not have effective self-guiding strategies for handling a situation, then she is likely to employ ineffective, maladaptive coping methods.

One of Meichenbaum's general therapeutic strategies was to retrain how clients talked to themselves. The retraining attempted to eliminate dysfunctional self-speech and to increase adaptive self-speech. In some of Meichenbaum's original work, this was done quite systematically. First, the therapist modeled the kind of self-speech the client was to learn to use. This, as with each of the succeeding steps, might be done several times. The client then practiced the self-speech aloud, then whispering, and finally silently. The practice was repeated until the desired type of self-speech became habitual. An extensive body of research by Meichenbaum and others (reviewed in Meichenbaum, 1977) supported the efficacy of this strategy for a variety of disorders.

Recent Cognitive-Behavioral Approaches

Currently there are so many cognitive-behavioral approaches that it would be impossible to synopsize them in one chapter. There are cognitive-behavioral approaches to modify panic attacks, generalized anxiety disorder, posttraumatic stress disorder, obsessive-compulsive disorder, depression, and eating disorders, among other things. Cognitive-behavioral approaches have also been developed to help children. One example of this is for children with anxiety problems, such as fear of going to school (Silverman & Treffers, 2001).

Specific Cognitive-Behavioral Treatments for Specific Disorders

One of the advantages of cognitive-behavioral therapies is that they can be specifically designed for specific disorders. Thus, if a therapist is seeing a client with a particular type of problem, there may be a particular cognitive-behavioral treatment designed specifically for that disorder. Further, because cognitive-behavioral treatments consist of specific combinations of cognitive and behavioral strategies, it is possible to write treatment manuals that outline the specific treatment for a particular disorder. So far, cognitive-behavioral treatments have been developed for depression, generalized anxiety disorder, panic disorder, social phobia, irritable bowel syndrome, bulimia, chronic pain, chemical dependency, suicide, marital problems, obsessive-compulsive disorder, schizophrenic hallucinations and delusions, and personality disorders (Beck, 1995; Chambless et al., 1998). We shall consider two examples.

Borkovec and his colleagues have developed a cognitive-behavioral treatment for generalized anxiety disorder. Generalized anxiety disorder is characterized by pervasive anxiety not specifically tied to environmental events or cues. In one research study (Borkovec & Costello, 1993), in the behavioral part of the treatment, clients learned to monitor their reactions and to disrupt anxiety with the use of a variety of relaxation responses and by learning to focus attention on present experience. In the cognitive part of the treatment, clients first practiced imagining themselves using their anxiety-reducing relaxation skills to control their anxious feelings in various situations. In addition, they learned various skills of cognitive restructuring, such as how to identify and combat dysfunctional, anxiety-arousing cognitions. The research study found that the cognitive-behavioral treatment was superior to a "nondirective" approach patterned after early client-centered therapy in helping reduce symptoms of generalized anxiety disorder.

Panic attacks are full-blown, intense anxiety attacks that include bodily symptoms such as a racing heart, dizziness, sweating, and so forth. In Barlow's (1988) cognitive-behavioral treatment for panic disorder, clients engage in activities that induce panic-like symptoms in the therapy session. These include engaging in exercises to stimulate the experience of cardiovascular symptoms, and hyperventilation to stimulate some of the respiratory symptoms. Engaging in such exercises, clients expose themselves to the panic symptoms, and the behavioral part of the treatment is that exposure itself can help clients get over anxiety symptoms. Then, in addition, cognitive procedures are used in which clients learn to identify the catastrophic thoughts that occur when they have these bodily symptoms. They learn to reinterpret these experiences as normal bodily processes. They also learn to challenge other, more basic cognitive errors. Research has shown this procedure to be successful in eliminating or reducing panic attacks in most clients.

Cognitive Psychotherapy

As we noted at the start of the chapter, there have been two streams leading to the development of what is now called by the umbrella term "cognitive-behavior therapy." We have considered the first stream: that leading from behavior therapy to cognitive-behavior therapy. The second stream has to do with the development of cognitive therapy. We will first look at the work of George Kelly (1955). Kelly was a pioneer in applying cognitive ideas to understanding personality and to psychotherapy. Because he died before the "cognitive revolution" took place, his work is less influential than it deserves to be. We will then consider social learning theory, attribution theory, Aaron Beck's cognitive therapy for depression and personality disorders and Albert Ellis's rational-emotive therapy. We will also review examples of some of the specific cognitive-behavioral treatments developed for specific disorders, such as Borkovec's approach for generalized anxiety disorder and Barlow's approach for panic disorder.

Kelly's Construct Theory

George Kelly was a clinical psychologist and college professor. He also coached the college drama club. As a clinician interested in behavior change, Kelly noticed that some drama students permanently changed their behaviors as a result of playing certain roles in plays. Kelly decided to apply role playing as a therapeutic method with students who sought counseling. To account for the changes he observed using this method, Kelly developed the first comprehensive cognitive theory of personality and therapy. He also developed an assessment device, called the repertory grid, to detect individuals' cognitive structures. Kelly published his ideas in 1955, then died a few years later. His work did not become well known in the United States. However, his theory has become popular in Britain, where Bannister, Fransella, and others continue to use some of his ideas.

Cognitive Constructs

Kelly's theory of personality begins with his fundamental postulate: A person's processes are psychologically "channelized" by the ways in which he or she anticipates events. The construction corollary is that a person anticipates events by construing their replications. What these statements mean is that individuals make sense of the world by developing cognitive categories that they can then use to try to predict, that is, anticipate, events. Furthermore, these cognitive constructions of the world determine behavior, or, in Kelly's words, "psychologically channelize" people's "processes." For example, the young child is confronted with complexity and chaos when she first notices the world around her. However, certain events repeat themselves; there are regularities even in the complexity of reality. Children may notice that there are big people and little people. Big people smile, say goo-goo, and give food and help; little people play, yell, hit, or grab things. It becomes useful for survival and comfort to notice this difference between big people and little people. Children develop a cognitive category of adult versus peer. They can then use this category to anticipate help from adults and no help from peers. They will then behave in help-seeking ways toward adults and not toward peers. Their behavior is "channelized" or determined by the way they construe events.

Kelly elaborated an entire personality theory about these ***cognitive constructs.*** There are individual differences. People will construe the same events differently, and they will develop different numbers and types of cognitive constructs, which can be organized in different ways. A person's construct system is organized with some all-embracing categories such as "good" versus "bad" and some subordinate categories such as "morally good," "esthetically good," "sensately good," and so on. While the cognitive construct system is always organized, it may be well organized or poorly organized (or fragmented), with some constructs incompatible with others. It may also be permeable (open to change) or impermeable (rigid). People are motivated to extend and define their cognitive systems. They are motivated to elaborate the system they use to make sense out of the world in order to be better able to predict and control what happens to them.

As implied above, some cognitive construct systems are better than others at helping people cope with reality. Several characteristics of cognitive constructs lead to behavior problems or mental disturbance. A simplistic system, with few cognitive constructs, will lead to trouble, because the person will constantly be confronted with new data that cannot be understood or anticipated with the system. For example, a person who sees the world in simplistic black-and-white or good-versus-evil terms will have difficulty dealing with the multitude of grays in life. There are just too many events that are not clearly good or evil. Similarly, a cognitive system that is too rigid will cause difficulties when it cannot account for everything. A paranoid person who rigidly sees everyone as untrustworthy will not be able to determine who to relate to or who can be trusted. On the other hand, a system that is too permeable will not help the person make sense out of the world at all. Psychosis, with its intruding and confusing thoughts and its lack of contact with reality, is an example of too permeable a cognitive system of constructs.

Kelly developed the repertory grid to assess what an individual's cognitive constructs are and how they are organized. The repertory grid consists of the names of people important to the individual with spaces for descriptions of these people. The examiner asks the client to describe these people and then to compare pairs of them, asking how they are alike and how they are not alike. The examiner gradually elicits the cognitive constructs the client uses to make sense out of the behavior of the people around him. By analyzing these responses, the examiner can determine what in the client's construct system is causing problems. For instance, a young man having difficulty relating to women may discover that his construct system divides people into kind and unkind, and trustworthy and untrustworthy, with females always seen as unkind and untrustworthy. To relate to women, this young man will have to change his construct system so that the male–female dimension is independent of his other categories.

Therapeutic Methods

Kelly prescribed a form of behavior therapy in order to change such troublesome cognitive construct systems. He believed that the individual develops a particular construct system because his particular life experiences make these constructs useful. In the case of the young man, perhaps his mother and other important female figures were unkind, withholding, and unreliable. However, now his cognitive constructs get him into trouble. If he anticipates that women are going to be unkind to him, he will behave toward them as he would toward any unkind, untrustworthy people—defensively and perhaps with hostility. This behavior may then induce women (who may or may not be kind, but who won't understand his hostility) to be unkind and hostile in return. Then his cognitive constructs will be validated, and he will continue to avoid or be hostile to women. Kelly would try to get this young man to behave in such a way that his old cognitive constructs will be invalidated by new data; new experiences will force him to develop new cognitions.

Kelly's technique was to write out a role for a client to play in his everyday life for a couple of weeks. He emphasized that it was "just role playing," just an experiment, so the client wouldn't become anxious over performing correctly or failing. He made the role just slightly different from the way the client usually acted. The role could not be so different that the client wouldn't be able to do it or to make sense out of the new data it generated. However, it had to be different enough so that others would perceive the client's behavior as different and behave differently toward him than they had in the past. This would provide invalidating experiences for the old construct system and force the development of new constructs. The client was supposed to play the role with everyone for a couple of weeks. Specific behaviors in specific situations might also be assigned as homework from time to time. The client then discussed the resulting experiences with Kelly, who helped the client integrate the new data and the old cognitions.

Let us use the young man as an example. Kelly might have written a role such as this for him: "You are a strong, self-confident, but gentle man, especially protective of and kind to women. You help women in conversations by asking them questions about their interests, listening carefully to their answers, and showing concern for their difficulties. You also like to have fun, and can occasionally tell a joke." If this young man even partially succeeds with this approach to women, he will elicit warm and kind behavior from them, rather than the hostile and defensive behavior he provoked before. These new experiences provide new data that do not fit his old constructs of women being unkind and untrustworthy, leading him to construe women differently, which will change his behavior toward them.

Kelly's approach was novel for its time and anticipated many of the recent developments in cognitive therapy and such behavioral techniques as assertion training. He reported great success with it among his young, changeable college student population. Research in England suggests that the repertory grid is a useful assessment procedure in clinical and research settings and that variations of Kelly's therapy are suitable for many types of problems. In recent years, there has been a resurgence of interest in Kelly's approach. This has been because personal construct theory intersects with the idea of constructivism (Feixas, 1990; see chapters 13 and 15) and can provide a basis for psychotherapy integration (Neimeyer, 1988). That is, it can be argued that we experience the world through our constructs, and that different approaches to therapy work primarily by changing our construct systems.

Beck's Cognitive Therapy

The single most influential cognitive approach is that of the psychiatrist Aaron Beck. Beck's work was originally on depression (Beck, Rush, Shaw, & Emery, 1979), and it has been expanded for use with a wide range of psychological problems including anxiety disorders (Beck, Emery, & Greenberg, 1985) and personality disorders (Beck, Freeman, & Associates, 1990). We shall review Beck's approach to depression in some detail and then briefly consider the cognitive approach to personality disorders.

Cognitive Therapy for Depression

Some people, we say, look at the world through rose-colored glasses. Beck's cognitive view of depression assumes that the depressive's glasses are of a somewhat more dusky hue. Beck holds that the symptoms of both depression and anxiety are a result of the client's cognitions about the world. In particular, a ***cognitive triad*** characterizes the depressive's thinking: a negative view of herself (low self-esteem), a negative view of her personal future, and a negative view of her current experiences. For instance, one of us had a young woman client who was convinced that things would "never get any better" for her. That was because she was "all screwed up as a person." If she were asked how her week was she would say, "Terrible."

Depressives also exhibit basic errors in information processing that contribute to their negative perceptions. They tend to magnify negative things and minimize positive things. For instance, every week the client (mentioned above) would begin her session by reporting that her week had been "terrible"; she would then be asked to review her week day by day. It was invariably discovered that she had had both negative and positive experiences that week. When she said her week had been "terrible," what she had done was magnify the negative and minimize the positive. One week the big "negative" was that her mother had insulted her, while the positive experience, which had not even been mentioned at first, was that she had been promoted in her job.

Depressives also overgeneralize. For example, if your relationship breaks up, you may conclude (if you are good at depressive thinking), "No one will ever love me." Still another depressive error is selective abstraction, in which a detail is taken out of context and then overgeneralized. Thus, in a whole conversation with someone there is perhaps one moment when things don't go well. A depressive will focus on that moment, take it out of the context of the rest of the conversation, and conclude that she made a fool out of herself and that the conversation went badly.

Another form of dysfunctional thinking is the making of dysfunctional attributions. ***Attribution theory*** is a social-psychological approach that has been adopted by clinical psychologists. Attribution theory holds that people try to explain the causes of their behavior by attributing the cause either to something in themselves or in the world. Weiner (1982) has shown how the kinds of attributions we make influence how we feel. Martin Seligman's ***learned helplessness*** theory (Abramson, Seligman, & Teasdale, 1978) is based on how we attribute the causes of our successes and failures. In particular, depressed people tend to attribute the causes of their failures to things about themselves that are global ("my whole self") and fixed and unchangeable. In other words, the depressive sees herself as being at fault for her difficulties and, in addition, believes that she is at fault because of some fundamental flaw in her character. Therefore, she not only sees herself as being at fault for her difficulties, but she also feels helpless to do anything to change or to control negative events.

More recently, Seligman (1990) has argued that adopting an optimistic explanatory style is more functional than adopting a pessimistic one. Optimists tend to take credit for their successes and do not blame themselves for their failures. When something goes wrong, they do not generalize from that to assume that things will never go right. Seligman cites a number of research studies suggesting that optimistic baseball teams do better than pessimistic ones, presidential candidates who espouse optimistic philosophies tend to win, and optimism can enhance immune system functioning.

A predisposition toward depressive thinking is learned in early childhood. Beck assumes that children think in global, absolute, either/or ways and that in depressives, these primitive ways of thinking are carried forward into adulthood. In particular, they are maintained in the form of primitive, simplistic schemas learned in early childhood, such as "In order to be happy, I have to be successful in whatever I undertake"; "To be happy, I must be accepted by all people at all times"; "If I make a mistake, it means that I am inept"; and "I can't live without you" (Beck et al., 1979, p. 246).

In particular cognitive therapists (e.g., Beck, 1987) hold that there are two general kinds of schemas that predispose people to depression. Some individuals have schemas that emphasize their dependency on others ("To be happy, I must be accepted by all people at all times"), while others have schemas that emphasize achievement-related concerns ("I must do everything perfectly"). Those with dependent predisposing schemas will be vulnerable to becoming depressed if they suffer a significant interpersonal setback, such as the loss of a relationship. Those with achievement-related predisposing schemas will be vulnerable if they suffer a significant setback in the achievement-related realm, such as the loss of a job.

Therapeutic Goals

Cognitive therapy is a systematic, structured, problem-solving approach. It is generally time-limited and rarely exceeds 30 sessions. Each therapy session has an agenda, in contrast to the free format of psychoanalysis or client-centered therapy. Beck believes the therapist should be warm, empathic, and genuine, as does Carl Rogers (see chapter 8). However, in contrast to Rogers, he does not see these conditions as sufficient for therapy to take place. Rather, the therapeutic relationship is important because it is the source of learning. Among other things, the therapist is a model of what he is trying to teach. If the therapist is judgmental or moralizing, that will merely reinforce the primitive, judgmental thoughts of the client.

The ultimate goal of cognitive therapy is to identify dysfunctional cognitions, including dysfunctional attributions, see how they trigger and generate depressive feelings and behavior, and learn to modify them. It is important to note that Beck is not as interested in what the client thinks as in how she thinks. Beck even admits that on occasion, a depressive cognition may be accurate (for instance, somebody may ignore you because he really doesn't like you). Beck is not interested in teaching "positive thinking." He sees positive thinking as potentially as destructive as negative thinking. The issue is not whether the client likes or dislikes herself. The issue is whether she thinks in a mode of either "I am good" or "I am bad" depending on what happens. If she is stuck in this mode of thinking, she will say, "I am good" when things go right. But of course, that just sets her up for "I am bad" when she makes a mistake or things go wrong. It's better for her not to think in terms of "I am good" or "I am bad," depending on what happens, but rather to focus on what she does: "Did I do this well or not?"

Similarly, life, for Beck, is not the pursuit of happiness. Happiness is a by-product of activity. Though Beck has been accused of being a "positive thinker" (Hazleton, 1984), you can see that this is inaccurate. Beck does not think it is better to see a glass as "half full" than as "half empty." Instead, it is better to see it as containing four ounces of water (Beck et al., 1979).

Beck wants his clients to learn to test hypotheses. Even though occasional depressive cognitions may be accurate, depressives generate their depression through their dysfunctional errors in information processing and the cognitive triad. Beck attempts to teach clients to treat these ideas as hypotheses rather than as facts and then to test them against the evidence. The development of this hypothesis-testing attitude will lead to a much more flexible, nonjudgmental cognitive system that can handle an occasional negative cognition that is supported by the evidence. In initial sessions, Beck explores the client's difficulties and formulates a plan of action. The link between thoughts and feelings is demonstrated to the client, with examples. Then, two general lines of attack are used to combat dysfunctional cognitions. They are behavioral techniques and cognitive techniques.

Behavioral Techniques

Behavioral techniques are used first with more severely depressed clients. Severely depressed clients may have difficulty processing ideas and information. Therefore, cognitive interventions are often ineffective with them. For example, one client one of us worked with could barely say more than "This is stupid. I've got to get over this and get back to work." Trying to get her to explore her feelings and thoughts was unsuccessful. She would elaborate slightly, but then lapse back into "This is stupid. I've got to get over this and get back to work."

For such clients, behavioral interventions are used to help lift the depression. Getting the client to act counters cognitions such as "I can't do anything" or "I'm a vegetable." In addition, the therapist can get the client to begin to test his dysfunctional cognitions while engaging in the behavioral activities. As these interventions gradually help lift the depression, the client becomes open to cognitive interventions.

Beck does not believe that behavioral interventions can cure depression by themselves. The underlying negative cognitions that generated the depression need to be attacked as well, or the depression will return. Nevertheless, doing something is a good "cure" to lift the depression temporarily.

Beck utilizes several behavioral interventions. The *daily activity schedule* is an hourly record kept by the client of all his activities, no matter how trivial. It helps counter the dysfunctional cognition that "I never do anything." In addition, the client is often asked to rate each activity for the amount of pleasure and the amount of "mastery" it gives him. The amount of mastery is the sense of accomplishment one gets from doing something. This also often gives the therapist insight into the client's dysfunctional cognitions. For instance, one client's daily activity record (Beck et al., p. 130) rated wallpapering the kitchen as 0 for mastery and pleasure and rated getting up, getting dressed, and eating as 1. How could wallpapering provide even less of a sense of mastery than getting up? The answer lies in this depressed client's distorted, perfectionist perceptions of his achievement (see box 11.1), which the therapist was able to explore with the help of the mastery-pleasure ratings.

Another behavioral intervention Beck uses with depressed clients is a series of *graduated task assignments.* A client for whom getting out of bed is an accomplishment may be assigned the task of brushing his teeth and shaving. After he has mastered that, he may be assigned the task of fixing himself breakfast and going for a walk. The next week, the assignment may include reading the paper and looking at the want ads. The strategy is to pick activities that slowly and gradually return the depressed client to full functioning. However, it is important to pick tasks that are within the client's grasp. To say to a seriously depressed client who can barely get out of bed, "You'll feel better if you go look for a job," will probably contribute to his depression rather than help it. It is too big a leap to go from getting out of bed to looking for a job. In addition, Beck stresses that the goal of the activity is the doing of it, rather than the accomplishing of it. The client is told that no one accomplishes everything he or she sets out to do and that the important thing is to treat the activity as a learning experience.

Another behavioral technique is ***cognitive rehearsal.*** Severely depressed clients often cannot handle a complex task assignment, because they have difficulty in concentrating and thinking. As a result, they will "self-destruct." They will forget directions or they will fail to anticipate crucial prerequisites to getting the task accomplished. For instance, a client whose task assignment is to go look for a job may forget to get clothes washed the day before, or may forget to arrange for transportation. These things may dawn on the client only at the moment when the client is preparing to leave. Without clothes or transportation the client cannot carry out the task assignment and the experience becomes another failure, confirming the client's self-perception of incompetence. To counter this, the therapist has the client rehearse the task, that is, go through the task step by step to discover what she will need to do to accomplish it. Such pitfalls are then discovered in advance, and the client can take steps to overcome them. In addition, the therapist can give the client suggestions as to how to handle unexpected pitfalls.

Box 11.1 Cognitions Involved in Mastery and Pleasure Ratings

Below is a sample of a dialogue between a depressed man who had rated his achievement in wallpapering a kitchen as providing no sense of mastery or pleasure. Note Beck's questioning technique to first uncover and then attack the dysfunctional cognitions involved.

THERAPIST: Why didn't you rate wallpapering the kitchen as a mastery experience?
PATIENT: Because the flowers didn't line up.
T: Your kitchen?
P: No. I helped a neighbor do his kitchen.
T: Did he do most of the work?
P: No. I really did almost all of it. He hadn't wallpapered before.
T: Did anything else go wrong? Did you spill the paste all over? Ruin a lot of wallpaper? Leave a big mess?
P: No, no, the only problem was that the flowers did not line up.
T: So, since it was not perfect, you get no credit at all.
P: Well . . . yes.
T: Just how far off was the alignment of the flowers?
P: (Holds out fingers about an eighth of an inch apart) About that much.
T: On each strip of paper?
P: No . . . on two or three pieces.
T: Out of how many?
P: About 20 to 25.
T: Did anyone else notice it?
P: No. In fact, my neighbor thought it was great.
T: Did your wife see it?
P: Yeah, she admired the job.
T: Could you see the defect when you stood back and looked at the whole wall?
P: Well . . . not really.
T: So you've selectively attended to a real but very small flaw in your effort to wallpaper. Is it logical that such a small defect should entirely cancel the credit you deserve?
P: Well, it wasn't as good as it should have been.
T: If your neighbor had done the same quality job in your kitchen, what would you say?
P: . . . Pretty good job!

Source: Beck et al., 1979, pp. 130–131.

Another technique used by cognitive therapists is *role playing.* Beck has found that depressed clients are often more critical of themselves than of others in the same situation (Beck et al., 1979). He has clients role-play what they would say to someone else who had their problem. In the example in box 11.1, Beck does this when he asks the client how he would feel about his wallpapering job if someone else had done it for him. One of us used this technique with a religious young man who felt guilty about masturbating. He had given it up and had been absolved by the elders of his church, who told him that the important thing was not to dwell on his past transgressions but to try to do better in the future. Yet he still felt guilty and anxious. In therapy, he was asked to pretend to counsel another young man with the same problem. He was much more forgiving toward this imaginary man than he was toward himself. When he realized this, his guilt and anxiety subsided

Cognitive Techniques

Once the depression has lifted sufficiently, the therapist can begin to concentrate on cognitive techniques. The first thing necessary is to make the client aware of the connection between his thoughts and his feelings. In order to do this, the client is given the assignment of keeping a *daily record of automatic thoughts.* Every time the client notices himself feeling depressed, he is to attempt to recover the thoughts that immediately preceded the onset of the depressed feelings. He is to record the objective situation, the thoughts he had, and the feelings they led to. For example, you are sitting in class and you suddenly begin to feel depressed. You realize that you had just noticed the attractive person near you who acts as if you don't exist. You record the situation: sitting in class, noticing the attractive person. You also record your thoughts: That person acts as if I don't exist. I'll never get a date. And you record your mood.

Initially, people often report that the depressed mood came on them without any thoughts. Beck believes that in these cases, there were thoughts present, but they occurred so quickly that the client was unaware of them. These are called ***automatic thoughts***, and they are the cognitive therapist's equivalent of the unconscious (Meichenbaum & Gilmore, 1984). Automatic thoughts are thoughts that have become so habitual that when they are triggered by some situation, they flit through the client's mind too rapidly for him to notice. Yet they stimulate depressive feelings. The daily record helps clients become aware of the automatic thoughts that precede their depressive feelings and can be used by the therapist to help clients modify their dysfunctional thinking pattern.

An additional assignment, besides the daily record of dysfunctional thoughts, is often made. Along with recording the situation, thoughts, and feelings, the client is asked to write down alternative, less dysfunctional ways of perceiving the situation. This has the effect of helping the client realize that she has been locked into one way of seeing the situation and that there are other ways. Generating alternative views of the situation encourages the hypothesis-testing attitude that Beck is trying to teach.

The main cognitive technique used by the therapist is *questioning.* Questions are designed to help the client explore and test dysfunctional cognitions. Note in the dialogue about wallpapering in box 11.1 that the therapist explores the possibility that the client's perception of failure as a wallpaperer might have a real basis—he made a mess, wasted wallpaper, and so on. It is clear in this example that the client's perception of failure is based instead on his perfectionist attitude. The therapist helps the client realize this through questioning. However, even if the client had made a mess, the cognitive therapist could then have explored the dysfunctional cognitions based on that situation, such as "I never do anything right," "I'm inept," and so on. Cognitive therapists use three general kinds of questions (Beck et al., 1985): "What's the evidence?" "What's another way of looking at the situation?" and "So what if it happens?"

It is important to point out that Beck uses questions rather than attempting to argue the client out of dysfunctional cognitions. Why doesn't he try to logically persuade the client that his beliefs are incorrect? People often react to depressives in everyday life by saying, "You did fine! I'm sure your neighbor didn't care about the misaligned flowers. Don't be so hard on yourself. Everyone likes you. You have to have more confidence in yourself!"

The depressive might respond with a short-lived good feeling or argue back, "But you don't really know me. Maybe the misaligned flowers aren't so bad in themselves, but they're just a symptom of the generally sloppy, careless way I live my life. Besides, you're just trying to cheer me up." After a few rounds of this the friend will go away feeling angry and frustrated. The friend may say to another friend, "Oh, he just likes to be depressed. He wants everyone to feel sorry for him." Anyone who has argued with a depressive has probably come away with such feelings. The perception that the depressive likes being depressed then becomes a further problem for the depressive, who begins to be rejected by the people around him, who no longer want to listen to him complain or to attempt to lift his depression. In yet another way, depression becomes a vicious cycle.

Trying to argue someone out of a deeply entrenched point of view is usually quite fruitless. Some research (Nisbett & Ross, 1980) has shown that people with deeply committed beliefs simply explain away or assimilate information contradictory to their belief system and paradoxically end up believing in it more than ever. Even if depression is based on a dysfunctional belief system, presenting contradictory evidence will have little effect. This is true for all of us whenever we have a deeply committed belief, be it religious, political, or psychological. Imagine trying to use logical argument and evidence to convince a committed Republican to be a Democrat or vice versa! Because it is difficult to argue a person committed to a belief system out of it, it is inaccurate to accuse depressives of "wanting to be depressed" when arguments fail. Beck holds that depressives would love to get out of the binds they're in if they could. They do not counter arguments because they want to stay depressed; they counter them because they are locked into a depressive belief system that they would be only too happy to escape from if they saw a way.

Beck uses a questioning technique to get the depressed person to challenge her own depressive cognitions. In Plato's *Dialogues*, Plato's philosophy is articulated through the main character of Socrates. Socrates does not expound or argue. What Socrates does is ask skillful questions to make the person he is talking to think it out until he arrives at Socrates's perspective. Arguing leads to defensiveness. People will often hang on to a point of view in an argument just to justify themselves and defend their own autonomy. The therapist who argues with a depressive may put her in the position of having to defend and justify her negative perspective. This can be circumvented by using the Socratic method—by asking questions to get the client to think it out so that she arrives at a less depressive view. In addition, it mobilizes the client's cognitive resources and trains her in a method that she can use at other times.

Beck's questioning technique, then, mobilizes depressives to challenge their own cognitions. Even so, the challenges must be repeated over a period of time before they sink in. One disconfirmation of a dysfunctional belief is rarely enough to change it. The insight must be acquired over and over again before the belief system will finally change.

In addition, Beck gives *homework assignments* so that dysfunctional cognitions can be tested against direct experience. A client may be instructed to test out the belief "My boss will never give me a raise" by asking for a raise. (If the boss does not give the client a raise, the dysfunctional cognitions generated by the client from that will be dealt with, and so the experience will be a productive learning one either way.)

Role of Emotion in Cognitive Therapy

Cognitive therapy has never ignored emotion, contrary to what some have believed. Cognitive therapists do respond empathically to client emotion. However, in recent years, emotion has become more emphasized as an important component of cognitive therapy. It has come to be believed that cognitions that are activated in the context of emotion are more easily changed than cognitions that are not so activated. That is, a person's negative cognitions about himself will be more readily challenged and changed when they are dealt with in the presence of the actual negative emotions generated by such cognitions. This has led to the idea of ***hot cognition***, that is, cognitions that are associated with emotions (Safran & Greenberg, 1982). In regard to this, cognitive therapists will now more actively work to elicit emotions in the belief that the activation of emotions makes the accompanying cognitions more available for challenge and reprocessing. With anxiety, for instance, the therapist may encourage the client to hyperventilate in order to recreate some of the anxious experience. At that moment, dysfunctional cognitions such as "Oh God! I'm having a heart attack," or "I'm having a panic attack and I'll totally self-destruct" can be challenged.

Cognitive Therapy for Personality Disorders

An extension of cognitive theory has been to the treatment of personality disorders (Beck et al., 1990). Beck and his colleagues believe that personality disorders, such as dependent personality disorder or paranoid personality disorder, are learned dysfunctional interpersonal strategies or schemas. These interpersonal strategies or schemas get triggered in various situations. As an example, whenever a problematic situation arises the dysfunctional schema or interpersonal strategy "I need help" gets triggered in dependent personality disorders (Beck et al., 1990, p. 32).

These dysfunctional schemas have been learned in childhood and chronically influence a person's behavior. For instance, the paranoid personality disorder is one in which the individual typically views other people with suspicion and often tends to react in a negative and aggressive way to others. This disorder is based on schemas in which such individuals portray themselves as righteous and mistreated by others, and their schematic views of others see others as basically mistrustful. This leads such individuals to be continually on the alert for signs of mistreatment and slights from others.

The goal of the cognitive therapist treating personality disorders is to change these dysfunctional schemas. Many of the same techniques used in cognitive therapy of depression and anxiety are utilized with personality disorders. However, to totally change such schemas is very time-consuming, and often a therapeutic strategy is not to totally eliminate them but to alter them so that they are less rigidly dysfunctional. With a paranoid personality disorder, the therapist might encourage the client to learn to trust some people in some situations or to test her dysfunctional beliefs more, so that she is not rigidly ruled by them.

In working with personality disorders, Beck and colleagues (1990) point out that sometimes long-standing dysfunctional interpersonal patterns cannot be modified without working with childhood experience. Childhood experiences are not worked with as extensively as in psychoanalysis. However, the cognitive therapist may have the client role-play an encounter with his mother or father, if that parent seems to be a major source of the learning of the dysfunctional schemas. In cognitive therapy, the client does not merely relive early childhood traumatic experiences, but during role play practices more functional, adult ways of responding to the person in question. In essence, this allows the client to reevaluate the childhood experience from an adult perspective and to relinquish old, dysfunctional attitudes that had developed from it. Once again, this can be seen as an extension of the idea of "hot cognition" mentioned previously: dysfunctional beliefs are best modified when their relevant affective, experiential aspects have been activated and are "alive."

Ellis's Rational Emotive Behavior Therapy

We have noted that one depression-causing cognition begins "I'll never. . . ." So when your third or fourth relationship doesn't work out, you say, "I'll never have a good relationship." You might even go further and say, "I'll never have a good relationship because I'm unlovable." We have shown how Beck would treat this. He would get the client to evaluate the evidence for these propositions and encourage the client to see that even a series of failures does not prove that his relationships will never work out. It is also obvious that it would be difficult to find evidence proving that he is unlovable. But there is another way to proceed. For Albert Ellis, founder of rational-emotive behavior therapy (called for many years "rational-emotive therapy"), the important question is "So what if you never did have a good relationship?" (Beck stresses this question in therapy for anxiety.) For Ellis, a client's answer to the question can be something depressing to him only if he makes it mean something depressing. For example, most people answer the question "What if I never have a good relationship?" by insisting "I must have a good relationship in order to be happy." In other words, if people didn't set such an absolute philosophical condition on their lives, the thought that they might never have a good relationship would not be threatening or depressing.

Causes of Psychopathology

Ellis claims that this kind of ***musturbatory thinking***, that is, this setting of an absolute standard for behavior and life is at the basis of most personal difficulty. Ellis (1979b) lists three groups of such ideas that "virtually all humans hold to some degree but that disturbed individuals hold more intensely, extensively, and rigidly."

> I must be competent, adequate, and achieving, and I must win the approval of virtually all the significant people in my life. It is awful when I don't. I can't stand failing in these all-important respects. I am a rotten person when I don't do what I must do to act competently and to win others' approval.

> Others must treat me kindly, fairly, and properly when I want them to do so. It is terrible when they don't. I can't bear their acting obnoxiously toward me. They are damnable, worthless people when they don't do what they must do to treat me satisfactorily.
>
> I need and must have the things I really want. The conditions under which I live and the world around me must be well ordered, positive, certain—just the way I want them to be. I must gratify my desires easily and immediately, without having to deal with too many difficulties or hassles. It is horrible when conditions are not this way. I can't tolerate their being uncomfortable, frustrating, or merely not ideal. The world is a rotten place and life is hardly worth living when things are not as they should be in this respect. (pp. 3–4)

These ideas are what Ellis calls irrational beliefs. They are absolute, rigid, intolerant, and demanding. But they are beliefs. Ellis is fond of quoting Shakespeare's Hamlet: "There's nothing either good or bad, but thinking makes it so." Ellis is especially interested in what people think they must have in order to be happy, how they must act in order to be a good person, what the world should be like, and how others ought to be. When Ellis holds that beliefs are irrational, he means that they cannot be empirically or scientifically verified. He says, "They can all be easily exposed and demolished by any scientist worth his salt; and the rational-emotive therapist is exactly that: an exposing and nonsense-annihilating scientist" (Ellis, 1973, p. 173).

Where do irrational cognitions come from? Ellis believes that all people are born with tendencies toward rational and irrational thinking as well as self-actualization. We all have them, even educated academics and intellectuals. People are born with a tendency to learn self-defeating behavior more easily than life-enhancing behavior, to remain attached to beliefs that do not work in various ways, to need to prove themselves superior to others, to demand rather than to want, to be overcautious, to be lazy, to be undisciplined, to have low frustration tolerance, to prefer the easiest way out of situations, and to be shortsighted. Though general tendencies to think irrationally may be inborn, specific irrational thoughts are learned from the person's culture. Even if they are learned in early childhood, however, they are kept alive because people continually reindoctrinate themselves.

According to Ellis, it is a person's cognitions about events that determine behavior, not the events themselves. The effect of cognition on behavior is represented by Ellis's famous A-B-C model. A is the objective event, B is the person's interpretation of the event, and C is the person's emotional or behavioral reaction. Most people tend to think that A causes C, but Ellis believes that while A contributes to C, B is the most important determinant of reactions. For instance, clients with borderline personality disorder feel they "cannot stand" being alone. But is it really true that they can't stand being alone? Or is that merely a self-perception on their part? Their perception is that A ("I am alone") leads to C (feelings of depression or panic). Ellis would suggest that this happens only because of intervening cognitions: "I do not like being alone," "I must not be alone," "I can't stand being alone." It is this set of intervening cognitions that causes the borderline's reactions of depression or panic, not being alone itself. Ellis suggests that the borderline person has made a non sequitur. He has followed a rational (sane) sentence, "I do not like being alone," with an irrational (insane) inference, "I must not be alone," leading to the perception "I cannot stand being alone" and feelings of depression.

Ellis also says people create problems by turning preferences into needs. There is a difference between the rational desire—I prefer to have a good income; it would be nice to have a good relationship; I prefer to be attractive and well liked, and the irrational need—I must have a good income; I can't stand to be without a loving fulfilling relationship; I must be attractive; and I deserve to be well liked. Ellis generally does not believe that "shoulds" and "musts" exist in nature and that people would behave much more sanely and rationally if they stayed at the level of their wants and preferences. Sounding very existential, he holds that the world just "is" and that people would be better off to accept that, rather than to make demands that the world be fair or just according to their perceptions. This is also true of the self. Ellis has argued that self-evaluation is probably the major cause of personal distress, along with musturbatory thinking. Positive self-esteem is just as bad as negative self-esteem. It is better not to judge or evaluate the self at all. In this, he agrees with Beck that it is rational to evaluate actions, but not the self.

Ellis illustrates the destructive consequences of self-evaluation, rather than behavioral evaluation, in the case of Myra, a woman who came to therapy feeling inadequate because she was unable to have an orgasm. He asks Myra to recount what she is thinking as she tries to achieve orgasm. It turns out that not only is she trying to have an orgasm, but she is also thinking that if she doesn't have an orgasm "wouldn't that be terrible, what a lousy sex partner I'd be . . . all that effort for nothing . . . how awful . . . how unfair . . . while so many other women have one so easily, with no effort at all!" (Ellis, 1979a, p. 71). A person dwelling on such thoughts cannot possibly be focusing on the pleasurable aspects of sex. Thus, the self-evaluation becomes a self-fulfilling prophecy. Ellis also talks about "disturbance about disturbance" (1979d, p. 48), which is thinking less of oneself for having problems. In addition to Myra's contributing to her own lack of orgasmic responsiveness, she also criticized herself and felt guilty for not being able to have an orgasm: "I must get orgasms like other women do, and I don't get them; that's awful! I can't stand it! I must be something of a turd for being so inferior to most other women!" (1979a, p. 69).

Therapeutic Methods

In terms of therapeutic practice, rational-emotive therapy is relatively short-term (usually not over 50 sessions) and utilizes techniques from a wide range of approaches. Rational-emotive therapists will use operant conditioning techniques, desensitization, assertion training, role playing, interpersonal skills training, modeling, imagery, shame-attacking exercises (see below), and bibliotherapy (the use of reading material).

However, its central technique is ***disputing***. As the name implies, disputing is the logical challenging of irrational beliefs. Ellis believes that he can identify and begin attacking a client's irrational cognitions within the first few minutes of the first session. An example of his technique is given in box 11.2. Ellis (1973) describes this method thus:

> The rational-emotive practitioner mainly employs a fairly rapid-fire active-directive-persuasive-philosophic methodology. In most instances, he quickly pins the client down to a few basic irrational ideas which motivate much of his disturbed behavior; he challenges the client to validate these ideas; he shows them that they are extralogical premises which cannot be validated; he logically analyzes these ideas and makes mincemeat of them; he vigorously and vehemently shows why

> they can't work and will almost inevitably lead to renewed disturbed symptomatology; he reduces these ideas to absurdity, sometimes in a highly humorous manner; he explains how they can be replaced with more rational, empirically based theses; he teaches the client how to think scientifically. (p. 185)

Ellis has noted, however, that disputing alone is frequently insufficient for psychotherapeutic change to occur. Most clients also require active, experiential exercises in order to test out their irrational cognitions. Because of the biological tendency to think irrationally it is difficult to correct irrational habits. One "insight" into irrationality will not suffice to change such an ingrained pattern of thinking.

It is important to note that Ellis's therapy involves an attitude of unconditional acceptance toward the client. The therapist does not judge the client as a person, even though he may vigorously attack some of the client's behavior and ideas. Ellis (1979a) points out that his client, Myra, occasionally irritated him:

> Not that I wasn't tempted, on several occasions, to really tell her off. But, with the use of RET (rational-emotive therapy), I kept reminding myself that she was not a louse even though her behavior was quite lousy. And I actually got myself to believe this and to convey my belief to her! (p. 83).

Furthermore, Ellis (1979c) states that the rational-emotive therapist respects the client's value system and does not impose his value system on the client. It is not the values themselves that are attacked, but rather their absolute, musturbatory quality.

Box 11.2 Ellis Disputes

This is the first part of an initial interview with a 25-year-old female client complaining of guilt, unworthiness, depression, and insecurity, among other things.

T: All right, what would you want to start on first?

C: I don't know. I'm petrified at the moment!

T: You're petrified—of what?

C: Of you!

T: Because of what I am going to do to you?

C: Right! You are threatening me, I guess.

T: But how? What am I doing? Obviously, I'm not going to take a knife and stab you. Now, in what way am I threatening you?

C: I guess I'm afraid, perhaps, of what I'm going to find out—about me.

T: Well, so let's suppose you find out something dreadful about you—that you're thinking foolishly or something. Now why would that be awful?

C: Because I . . . I guess I'm the most important thing to me at the moment.

T: No, I don't think that's the answer. It's, I believe, the opposite! You're really the least important thing to you. You are prepared to beat yourself over the head if I tell you that you're acting foolishly. If you were not a self-blamer, then you wouldn't care what I said. It would be important to you—but you'd just go around correcting it. But if I tell you something really negative about you, you're going to beat yourself mercilessly. Aren't you?

Source: Ellis, 1984, pp. 215–216.

Using rational-emotive therapy with pets.

For instance, if a client does something contrary to his own values, he will feel depressed, anxious, or guilty only if he believes that he is "an awful person" because of what he did. A more rational way of responding would be "I would prefer not to act that way. I'll try to do better next time." The rational-emotive therapist would not attack the person's values, but his rigid way of using his values.

In addition to disputing in therapy sessions, the therapist often gives the client the homework assignment of disputing her own beliefs. For instance, Myra worked at disputing the beliefs that she must have sex enjoyment easily and quickly and that she should have orgasms as other women do. She realized that although it would be highly desirable if she could, there was no evidence that she should, and that she was not a bad person because she was the way she was.

Many of the techniques that rational-emotive therapists use, such as the behavioral techniques, are discussed elsewhere in this book. We will briefly mention two others here. The first is ***shame-attacking exercises***. Because Ellis believes that shame is the essence of many disorders, he has clients attack this feeling. In these exercises, the clients deliberately make fools of themselves. Myra, for instance, was given the assignment of walking a banana down the street on a leash. Despite feeling foolish at first, she soon realized that nothing bad happened to her, and she actually began to enjoy the experience.

The use of imagery is another technique. It is based on the work of Maultsby (1975). Myra, for instance, was to imagine a scene of sexual failure. She was to imagine trying hard to have an orgasm, failing, and her husband's being critical of her. As she imagined these things, she experienced shame and depression. Her assignment was to imagine these scenes repeatedly, but to practice experiencing the more rational feelings of sadness and disappointment. Gradually, she learned that she could experience these feelings instead.

Comparison of Ellis and Beck

You may have noticed that the approaches of Beck and Ellis are similar. Although Ellis considers his therapeutic approach to be scientific, we believe that Beck places more emphasis on a scientific attitude than Ellis, and Ellis places greater emphasis on philosophical analysis. Both believe that clients make logical errors that lead to dysfunctional conclusions. However, Beck emphasizes testing hypotheses. Are the client's ideas true or false? Are they overgeneralizations? Can they be backed up by evidence? If the client says, "I will never have a relationship," the main thrust of Beck's approach is to demonstrate that this conclusion does not have any evidence to back it up. Ellis may do this also, but his main emphasis is on what the client believes to be the consequences of the statement, whether it is verifiable or not: "Even if it were true, does that mean you cannot enjoy life?"

As therapists, their methods differ also. Beck is certainly active in asking questions, structuring the therapy hour, and suggesting assignments and techniques, but he is relatively nondirective in his approach to the client's cognitions and beliefs. Beck never tells the client his beliefs are irrational or which beliefs to modify. Rather, he ultimately lets the client draw his own conclusions. Ellis is much more directive. He tells the client which beliefs are irrational and need modification. The technique of disputing by its very name implies this more confrontational approach.

Theoretical Advances

Cognitive approaches are becoming theoretically more integrative. Beck's cognitive therapy integrates and overlaps with ideas from a variety of approaches (Alford & Norcross, 1991). Meichenbaum (1995) considers the modification of meaning as the most important therapeutic event, and sees the therapist as a "co-constructivist" who not only helps clients combat dysfunctional cognitions and improve problem-solving skills, but also helps them develop new narrative theories of their problems (see chapter 15) and new ways to view themselves and the world.

A particular development in cognitive therapy is Safran and Segal's (1990) interpersonal approach. These authors state that most dysfunctional beliefs are inherently interpersonal, having been learned in interpersonal contexts and having interpersonal consequences, as George Kelly said years earlier. Their approach to cognitive therapy particularly emphasizes the interpersonal interaction between the therapist and the client. They assume that the client's dysfunctional beliefs about interpersonal interactions can hook the therapist into dysfunctional interpersonal interaction patterns. A dependent personality, for instance, may be able to hook the therapist into a cycle of taking care of the client. Or it may hook the therapist into feeling alienated by the client's dependency, which may exacerbate the client's tendencies to cling and try to establish dependency.

Safran and Segal place greater emphasis on the use of therapist empathy than is typical in cognitive therapy. They believe that empathy not only establishes a relationship, but also helps in accessing client's dysfunctional interpersonal beliefs. In addition to typical cognitive techniques, an important therapeutic goal is for the therapist to "unhook" from the client's dysfunctional interaction cycle. The therapist must consciously refrain from engaging in the dysfunctional behaviors that are being elicited by the client's dysfunctional belief system. The therapist may then give the client feedback on the behaviors that are contributing to the therapist's reactions. For these therapists, therapy is a kind of "learning laboratory" in which dysfunctional cognitions will actually be activated and challenged in the "live" context of the therapeutic relationship. In this respect, Safran and Segal's approach is an integrative cognitive therapy, including aspects of both client-centered and other humanistic approaches, as well as psychodynamic concepts.

Evaluation of Cognitive Approaches

Effectiveness of Psychotherapy

In general, the evidence for the effectiveness of cognitive approaches to therapy is quite positive. Cognitive-behaviorists are committed to researching their approaches and there is a large research literature on them (Emmelkamp, 2004; Hollon & Beck, 2004). With regard to Ellis's rational-emotive-behavior therapy, Smith, Glass, and Miller (1980) found an effect size of 0.68, which places it with psychodynamic, gestalt, and client-centered approaches in terms of effectiveness. A more recent meta-analysis of 70 studies also provides support for rational-emotive therapy (Lyons & Woods, 1991).

There is also good evidence for the effectiveness of Beck's cognitive therapy. Hollon and Beck (2004) review the research on cognitive therapy for depression and conclude that the evidence shows it is generally effective for reducing acute distress. The evidence on whether cognitive therapy outperforms medication is equivocal, but cognitive therapy generally does at least as well as medication. Other evidence shows that cognitive therapy can be effective for panic attacks and generalized anxiety disorder (Hollon & Beck, 2004).

There is also evidence supporting Barlow's cognitive-behavioral treatment for panic disorder (Hollon & Beck, 1994) and Borkovec's (Borkovec & Costello, 1993) cognitive-behavioral treatment for generalized anxiety disorder. For instance, Barlow's treatment for panic disorder has been shown to lead to superior results compared to no-treatment control groups, with over 85% panic free at the end of therapy (Klosko, Barlow, Tassinari, & Cerny, 1990; Barlow, Craske, Cerny, & Klosko, 1989). With regard to cognitive-behavioral approaches in general, the report on "empirically supported treatments" put out by a task force of the Clinical Psychology Division of the American Psychological Association listed over 19 cognitive-behavioral treatments as having received sufficient empirical support to be considered as "efficacious" or "probably efficacious" (Chambless et al., 1998). In sum, cognitive-behavioral treatments appear to be efficacious for a wide range of disorders.

Theoretical Evaluation

To what extent is it true that cognitions cause psychopathology, as Beck, Ellis, Seligman, Meichenbaum, and others suppose? This is a complicated issue and we cannot fully evaluate it here. However, research has shown that the relation between cognition and psychopathology is more complex than cognitive theories originally held them to be. There is evidence that depressed individuals do indeed exhibit negative beliefs about themselves, their futures, and the world. There is also evidence that they may make negative attributions to themselves (Solomon & Haaga, 2003). On the other hand, the evidence is mixed as to whether depressive thoughts play a causal role in depression. It is possible, for instance, that they develop as part of being depressed. Hammen (1985) concluded that the evidence supported this view. However, some recent evidence (Solomon & Haaga, 2003) suggests that those who are depressed have a predisposition to depression in the form of latent depressogenic beliefs that are then activated by stressful stimuli to precipitate a depressive episode. The good news is that cognitive therapy alleviates the depression. The bad news is that it does not appear to alter this underlying vulnerability to depression.

In particular cognitive therapists now hold that there are two general kinds of self-schemas that predispose people to depression, depending on the triggering event. Hammen (1985) mentions some evidence suggesting that people with dependent self-schemas (those who define themselves in terms of their dependency on others) are likely to become depressed when they suffer a negative interpersonal event, but not when they suffer a negative achievement event. Individuals with self-critical self-schemas (those who define themselves in terms of how successful they are) are likely to become depressed when they suffer a negative experience related to achievement. Beck's (1987) work takes such differences into account.

Further, cognitive theories have tended to suppose that depressives distort reality in a negative direction. Several studies have found that depressives do indeed focus on the negative more so than do nondepressives. However, research has shown that it is nondepressed "normals" who often distort reality (Taylor & Brown, 1988). Normals tend to believe they have more control over their fates than they really do, while depressives are more realistic in their assessments. Normals also see themselves more positively than others see them, while depressives are once again more realistic in their assessments. In other words, while depressives may be more negative, they may also be more realistic! In general, it appears that the perceptions of all individuals, not just depressives, is biased by their schemas (Dykman & Abramson, 1990).

Another difficulty is that the hypothesis that cognitions cause emotions may not be entirely true. While cognitions can cause emotions, there is some evidence that emotions can cause cognitions (Bower, 1981). Some findings suggest that depressive mood, for instance, can reduce the number of positive memories that an individual can recover. Overall, it is now believed that cognition and emotion reciprocally influence one another (Brewin, 1988).

One of the most important criticisms of cognitive approaches has been made by Sampson (1981). Basically, Sampson argues that cognitive approaches try to adjust the individual to fit in with social reality. The cognitive approach assumes that a client's problems are, so to speak, all in his head. If an individual is depressed, it is because he is distorting or engaging in musturbatory thinking. The possibility that his situation is objectively depressing is not taken seriously. Thus, cognitive therapists have little to say about unjust or oppressive social conditions that may cause abnormal behavior. The client needs to adjust his cognitions, and then everything will be fine.

The dangers in this seem obvious. If all of people's problems lie in how they conceive of events, then all that is necessary is for them to think differently about things. Should people change their cognitions in such a way that they will be happy? Yet perhaps depression, for instance, is a legitimate reaction to certain situations. Neither Beck nor Ellis appears to grant this as a possibility. A lower-class African American woman with few job skills, trying to support a family by herself, has reason to become depressed. The belief that she might never get out from under racism and poverty may not be distorted. The belief that she needs more money, not just that she would prefer to have more money, is not a distortion, either. The point is that cognitive approaches, in assuming that everything is in how people construct reality, appear to leave no basis for making judgments. If "there is nothing either good or bad, but thinking makes it so," why shouldn't we only think what will make us happy? How can we decide?

To be fair, however, both Beck and Ellis deal with this in their own ways. Neither Beck nor Ellis denies that sometimes things are objectively bad. What they really try to do is to help people deal productively with whatever is going on in their lives. Even if things are objectively bad, it does not help to catastrophize, to see oneself as fundamentally flawed and incapable of change, or to focus on how life "should" be if it were fair. What does help is to keep one's attention focused on what one can do (see discussions of the idea of a task-focus in Bohart & Tallman, 1999; Tallman, 1996). And this is precisely what cognitive therapy helps clients do.

Many criticisms of cognitive therapy can be subsumed under a general philosophical critique of the idea that one can say whether or not certain ideas are "true" or "false," rational or irrational, as if there were simple, objective ways of deciding such things. Kruglanski & Jaffe (1988), for instance, have pointed out that a person's beliefs are ultimately incapable of being proved true or false. Mahoney (1991) and constructivists (see chapter 15) have held that it is not so much whether a belief is true or false but whether it is viable and useful or not. Some people seem to be able to use self-criticism, even if exaggerated, productively (Norem, 2002). Kruglanski and Jaffe (1988) also point out that many of the things Beck considers "cognitive errors" cannot truly be considered errors. For instance, they note that whenever we form any abstraction, we are being "selective." Therefore, selective abstraction is not necessarily a cognitive error when we consider it among all of the other, but presumably less erroneous, forms of abstraction.

In sum, there are some difficulties with cognitive theory in its belief that certain kinds of beliefs can be said to be either rational or irrational. Perhaps, as several psychologists have pointed out, more important is the rigidity with which the belief is held, its unattainability, and how it is used by the person. As an example of this, Norem (2002) has found that ***defensive pessimism*** can be functional for college students. Defensive pessimists are those who catastrophize as they prepare to study for an exam, presuming that they are going to fail, and so on. Yet they use this catastrophizing to motivate themselves to study, and generally do quite well. This is different than the kind of pessimistic thinking that leads to feelings of hopelessness and paralyzes effort. In sum, even pessimism is not inherently dysfunctional.

A final criticism of cognitive therapies is that they treat psychological problems like "noise in the system" to be eliminated. A person's dysfunctional thinking is merely dysfunctional thinking to be corrected and "cognitively restructured." A person holding a very strong "should" is simply thinking irrationally and must learn not to think in terms of shoulds. A person experiencing panic or generalized anxiety is merely overattending to and misinterpreting bodily cues. What these accounts leave out is the possible functional significance of dysfunctional cognitions, shoulds, and misinterpretations. For instance, a person experiencing generalized anxiety may be overattending to bodily cues because she is feeling very vulnerable as she struggles with a difficult life choice concerning her career (chapter 9) or because she has had a childhood that makes her feel highly vulnerable about herself (chapter 7). A person may be thinking dysfunctionally because he is trying to be honest with himself and make himself face up to what may be the bleak reality of life (e.g., "I'll never have a good relationship"). A person may have difficulty letting go of a should because it represents a deeply held personal value for her. In our experience, there are clients who do not want to simply get over their worry by learning to relax in the presence of bodily cues. Rather, they prefer to explore what the anxiety means to them. Such a concept is only beginning to be taken into account in cognitive theories.

In Conclusion

Cognitive therapies and theories are currently the dominant approaches to psychotherapy in many professional circles, such as in clinical psychology programs in universities (although the most popular approach among practicing psychotherapists still is eclecticism—using ideas from a variety of approaches). Cognitive and cognitive-behavioral therapies have provided therapists with powerful, effective, and fast-acting methodologies. Their constructs are much more easily understood by people without professional training than the rather esoteric concepts of psychoanalysis and humanistic approaches. This means that the therapist is able to explain the therapeutic approach and goals to the client more thoroughly and quickly. Cognitive therapies, like the behavioral approaches, have the virtue of being systematic, planned, and structured, but they are more flexible than the behavioral approaches. In this respect, they may provide one of the most fruitful grounds for future integration of all therapies. Both Beck and Ellis are eclectic in their use of techniques in therapy. In addition, theorists such as Meichenbaum are providing theoretical models that may help integrate the contributions of many approaches.

In sum, cognitive therapies will continue to be "major players" on the psychotherapy stage for years to come. Further, cognitive ideas, such as that of the "schema," are now used by therapists of many persuasions, including psychodynamic and humanistic. It is possible that a cognitive "language" for talking about therapy will become the dominant theoretical language for the field.

Behavior and Biology

Sandy S., a 43-year-old married man with two teenage children, suffers from irritable bowel syndrome. With only a 10th-grade education, he has worked for many years without any possibility of advancement as a machinist in a large business. His wife also works, and since he shares some of the housework and tries to spend time with his kids, Sandy feels he never has time for his hobby, fishing. Sandy has gone to many doctors about his "stomach problems" to little avail. Sandy does not report feeling depressed, but he is "upset" over his physical problems and the inability of anyone to cure him.

In the worry and strain of modern life, arterial degeneration is not only very common but develops often at an early age. For this, I believe that the high pressure at which men live and the habit of working the machine to its maximum capacity are responsible rather than excesses in eating and drinking.

—W. Osler, *Lectures on Angina Pectoris and Allied States*

Relatively recent research on behavior and the brain has led to a paradigm of the unity of all aspects of a living organism, from its behavior and body to its environmental context. This view addresses the age-old question of the relationship between the mind and the body. As stated in the quote by Osler above, people have believed for a long time that psychological variables such as worry affect the body. Now the thinking is that the mind–body split is, in fact, artificial, that mind and body are a unity, each inevitably affecting the other. Some call this view the biopsychosocial model (Smith, Kendall, & Keefe, 2002). Health psychology and behavioral medicine have been in the vanguard of research on how behavioral changes can lead to changes in disease processes affecting the body and vice-versa. In addition, health psychologists have been leaders in developing applications of behavioral interventions in biological processes. Virtually all of the behavior therapies described in the last chapter and many of those described in the next have been applied to the treatment of a wide variety of medical disorders.

Since Roman times, some physicians have speculated that the mind affects the course of an illness, even whether an individual becomes ill. By the mid-twentieth century, it was generally accepted that at least in the case of the so-called *psychosomatic illnesses,* such as ulcers and hypertension, the individual's psychological state was an important determinant of the disease. Parallel to the development of clinical psychology, the first psychological interpretations of psychosomatic illness were psychoanalytic. It was thought, for example, that unmet, unconscious oral and dependency needs led to ulcers (Alexander, 1950). The growth of behavior therapy in the 1950s and 1960s led psychologists working in medical fields to turn from psychoanalytic to behavioral views of illness. The usefulness of the behavioral view was promoted in the late 1960s, when it was discovered that biofeedback (discussed later) could be used to help treat some medical disorders. Once biofeedback legitimized psychology's entrance into the medical field, many other behavioral techniques were applied to a variety of medical problems.

The holistic view of mind–body unity has interesting implications for psychotherapy in general. The thinking about older behavioral techniques such as desensitization and more recent ones such as role playing may be recast in terms of the biological consequences of changed behavior. For example, the behavior of enacting a new social skill during a role play may lead to biologically-based changes in perception and brain organization. Hypnosis, used in both health psychology and traditional psychotherapies, may or may not be a special biological or psychological state that creates positive changes in mind and body. The current emphasis on biology in medicine and science coupled with the biopsychosocial view means that the relation between behavior and biology will be of increasing interest to psychological researchers and practitioners.

Health Psychology

At present, in the United States and other developed nations, the major killer of humans is not disease caused by viruses and other pathogens, but rather harm to the body caused by individual behavior. At the turn of the 20th century, infectious diseases were the leading cause of death, but by mid-century the leading cause of death became chronic disease. Leading causes of death, illness, and injury include incorrect eating habits (too much food, too much fat, too much salt), drug and alcohol abuse, lack of exercise, vehicular accidents, and cigarette smoking. It is estimated that one fifth of U.S. deaths are related to smoking alone and that one third to one half are due to consequences of behavior (Barlow, 2004; Stefanek, Hess, & Nelson, 2005; U.S. Surgeon General, 1979). In terms of improving public health in the United States, the focus has shifted from controlling external factors such as germs and poor sanitation to changing individuals' behaviors, such as their eating habits or reactions to stress. It is only logical that psychology should be in the forefront in the treatment of these problems.

When it first became a recognized specialty in professional psychology, health psychology went by several names, such as behavioral medicine, clinical health psychology, medical psychology, and behavioral health, and the terms are still sometimes used interchangeably. It can be said that health psychology is the application of behavioral principles and methods to problems and disorders that have been traditionally labeled medical. Some scholars distinguish between health psychology, as the application of behavioral principles to prevent disease and promote health, and behavioral medicine, as the application of behavioral principles to the diagnosis, treatment, and rehabilitation of disease. However, we will use health psychology as the general name for this field and go along with APA Division 38 that health psychology deals with "the integration of biomedical information about health and illness with current psychological knowledge" (American Psychological Association, 2005).

Psychological involvement in health care grew into a definably separate field by 1978, when the APA established a new Division of Health Psychology (38) and the *Journal of Behavioral Medicine* began publication. Health psychology has continued to grow tremendously since then (Smith et al., 2002), and there are now several journals, such as *Health Psychology, Neuropsychology, Rehabilitation Psychology, Prevention and Treatment*, and others.

The rapid growth of health psychology has been attributed to several factors. First, there was the "discovery" of the behavioral components of disease in the last century. Second, there is the growing emphasis on "self-care." Once people are ill, the reality is that their health care is mostly self-care, and psychologists can help them take better care of themselves. The third trend pushing health psychology is the high cost of traditional health care, since behavioral prevention and treatment are usually more cost-effective than traditional care. In addition, health care is sometimes scarce, with rural people and poor people having less access to care, and health psychologists can make care available to these groups.

Theoretical Basis for Health Psychology

As a result of research and clinical experience, the philosophical underpinnings of both behavioral and biological medicine have evolved to an integrative, holistic view. Disease is seen as multifaceted and multidetermined. Not only do the behavior, conditions, and emotions of the individual interact with and influence the physiological, neurological, and immunological systems of the body, but the sick individual also interacts with and is affected by interpersonal, social, and environmental contexts. This view, known as ***reciprocal determinism***, implies that intervention at any of these levels affects all the others, because they function in an ongoing process of mutual interaction and influence. If mind and body are one, then interventions aimed at either are equally effective in producing positive change. In chapter 10, we have already mentioned the study done at UCLA that demonstrated that changing obsessive-compulsive behaviors led to observable changes in brain functioning (Baxter et al., 1992), results that support this point.

The old mind–body dualism allowed for psychology as a discipline to apply the scientific method to the study of the mind, but it also limited psychology to the "mental" realm and impeded the development of a holistic view of human functioning. Although the philosophy of biomedicine and all science has become more holistic, health care practice and policies are still dominated by mind–body dualism. Hospitals and health agencies are divided into departments of psychology, departments of internal medicine, departments of surgery, and so forth. Almost all health insurance policies divide coverage between mental health and medical-surgical health benefits, generally with lower coverage for the former than for the latter, although national legislation to require equal coverage of mental and physical disorders was introduced in 1996 and 1997. These divisions make it difficult to determine who is responsible for biofeedback treatment of surgically induced incontinence, for example. These "real world" divisions run counter to the increasing tendency of science to integrate and synthesize knowledge.

Interestingly, science is beginning to pinpoint the exact nature of the link between the mind and the body (and it is *not* the pineal gland, as Descartes thought!). The emerging field of psychoneuroimmunology studies the relationship between the immune system and psychosocial stressors, which appear to directly affect the functioning of the hormonal, autonomic, and immune systems of the body. Research with animals has demonstrated that stress can affect the immune system so that it cannot effectively fight microorganisms, toxins, or even tumors. Furthermore, it has been demonstrated experimentally that the immune system itself is open to suppression or enhancement through classical conditioning, so that modifiable learning may be of importance to immunocompetence (Ader & Cohen, 1985). If so, psychology has more than emotional support and coping skills to contribute to the treatment of allergies, AIDS, and other immune system disorders.

Interventions in Health Psychology

Distinctions are made between the *disease,* as what is objectively wrong with the person; *illness,* as the person's subjective experience of the objective disease; and *illness behavior.* Illness behavior includes adopting the role that people expect an ill person to play, such as defining and evaluating symptoms, seeking help, altering life routines, and the like. The psychological components of illness behavior are obvious, and it is easy to see that psychology could be important in illness, too. Evidence has accumulated that behavior affects disease as well.

Psychologists have a large body of proven skills for changing behaviors, including all of the principles of learning and techniques of behavior change described in the last chapter and the next. The same emphasis on the scientific method, objective assessment and empirical verification of efficacy, and the assumption that all behaviors are lawful responses to identifiable and changeable learning conditions comprise the foundations of health psychology. Just as behavior therapy has become eclectic and diverse, health psychology utilizes behavior change methods from other schools of thought, as well as learning theory.

Health psychology encompasses intervention in a wide variety of disorders with a wide variety of behavioral methods. The following list gives an idea of the range of activities of psychologists in behavioral medicine: assessment of candidates for back surgery or penile prosthesis surgery; desensitization of fears of medical and dental treatments; teaching skills to cope with pain; interventions to control vomiting associated with pregnancy and chemotherapy; cardiac rehabilitation; memory retraining for cognitive impairments due to strokes; consultation to improve health and safety at the work site; psychosocial services for oncology patients; psychoeducational self-management programs for asthma; coping strategies for rheumatoid arthritis; hypnosis for irritable bowel syndrome; prevention programs for addictions; assessment of neurological disorders; and many more. Health psychologists conduct research in these areas and others as well. They especially research the effectiveness of their methods, and the empirical support for the effectiveness of health psychology interventions is good (Taub, 2004).

The various behavior therapy methods that may be considered part of behavioral medicine can be grouped according to three major purposes. First, behavioral techniques are used to change physiological responses or learned symptoms that constitute or contribute to threats to health. Second, health psychology contributes to the improvement of health care delivery. Third, health psychology addresses known risk factors, that is, behavior that is known to increase risks to health, in order to prevent disease and illness.

Interventions in Disease-Related Behavior

One purpose of health psychology is to intervene in the disease process itself, through assessment, diagnosis, treatment, and rehabilitation. Some medical disorders are a result of some sort of physiological response. Tensing the muscles of the head and neck may cause headaches, producing too much stomach acid helps create ulcers, breathing incorrectly intensifies some forms of asthma. The research on biofeedback suggests that people can, to a degree, control such physiological responses when they become aware of them, and so it is possible they may be able to alleviate the resulting disorder. Other interventions can alter the course of disease. For example, cancer patients often develop food aversions to anything they eat before their nausea-inducing treatments. If, as a result, they eat less or restrict their diet, their ability to fight the disease is impaired. Deconditioning their food aversions and teaching coping skills will directly affect the course of their illness.

Rehabilitation is an important part of health psychology. It may not alter the disorder, but it helps people change their behavior so they can deal with the disorder. For example, behavioral therapists work with patients who have brain injuries as a result of accident or stroke. They retrain the patients' memories and teach them cognitive coping strategies. They may use biofeedback of muscle tension to retrain control over muscles paralyzed by a brain injury. Since the brain is relatively plastic, neurorehabilitation methods are being developed to use behavioral techniques to change the brain in a positive direction. For example, stroke-induced loss of control of the left arm can be treated by restraining the right arm, forcing use of the left arm and leading to reorganization of the undamaged part of the brain to control the left arm (Taub, 2004).

As another part of health psychology, psychologists intervene in "illness behavior" or "sick role behavior." It is possible that some people are rewarded with attention and sympathy for being in pain or for being sick. Called secondary gain, the attention and sympathy people receive for their symptoms may serve as a powerful reward for those symptoms. In that sense, symptoms are learned. Furthermore, patients may become socialized or trained by the medical bureaucracy to fall into sick roles that may become chronic. In such cases, behavior therapy techniques may help improve the medical problem.

Biofeedback, systematic desensitization, classical conditioning, operant conditioning, hypnosis, contingency management, and other methods have been used alone and in combination to successfully treat migraines, headaches, back pain, other chronic and acute pain, cancer, alcoholism, drug abuse, hypertension, asthma, insomnia, arthritis, gastrointestinal disorders, incontinence, enuresis, encopresis, anorexia, bulimia, irritable bowel syndrome, seizures, ulcers, vomiting, nausea, bruxism, head injuries, scoliosis, hives, attention deficit disorder, seizures, insomnia, and other disorders (Cohen, 2004; Prochaska, 2004; Schneiderman, 2004; Smith et al., 2002; Taub, 2004). In addition, stress, sleep, exercise, and diet are clinically modifiable behaviors of importance to immunocompetence. As already mentioned, it has been demonstrated experimentally that the immune system itself may be open to suppression or enhancement through classical conditioning, so that the behavioral treatment of allergies and other immune system disorders, including AIDS, is a possibility worthy of future research.

Interventions in Health Care Delivery

Behaviorists can assist in the improvement of health care delivery and collaborate with and assist physicians in a number of ways. Psychologists are involved with increasing patient compliance with medical regimens. Patient compliance is an interesting problem for medicine. All the diagnostic tests and medical advances in the world will not help if patients do not follow doctors' orders. Some surveys suggest that over half of patients do not take prescribed medicines correctly—they take them too much, not enough, or not at all. Patients often fail to keep follow-up appointments. Certain disorders involve difficult regimens to follow. The best example is diabetes, which may require a special diet and a strict regimen of medications for the patient's entire life. Teenagers are especially resistant to the treatment necessary for diabetes. Education, group therapy, contingency management, and other techniques are used to increase patient compliance.

Health psychologists can help patients cope with medical procedures, some of which are frightening, painful, or nauseating. Education, modeling, and role playing can prepare patients for procedures. Simply knowing exactly what is going to happen to them can reduce patients' anxiety. Explanations, discussions, slide shows, and demonstrations help adults. Some therapists use special dolls and puppets to demonstrate surgical and treatment procedures for children. The children's fears and questions can be addressed through playing out a doctor–patient scene. Some therapists use modeling through films that show children undergoing the same medical procedure as the patient.

Behavioral techniques can help patients control their pain when they must have painful diagnostic tests or treatments. Dental treatments, spinal taps, angiograms, and the like are often painful. Systematic desensitization, relaxation, guided imagery, hypnosis, and other techniques can help patients reduce or at least control their response to the pain. The same techniques can help patients reduce or control the nausea and vomiting that are the side effect of some chemotherapy for cancer.

Health psychologists often become involved in public policy related to health care. Conducting research on the many causes of illness, educating the public regarding these causes, and working in medical settings lead to the observation that, at times, the health care system itself gets in the way of effective treatment. Behavioral psycholo-

Using systemic desensitization to treat medical noncompliance in pets.

gists gain evidence and ideas for how to improve the entire health care delivery system and, consequently, the health of individuals. Psychologists thus become involved with public policy and political activities, in court cases, in legislation regarding health insurance companies, in training and licensing requirements, and other issues. For example, if psychotherapy is proven to be cost-effective for treating somatizing patients, individuals with diabetes and asthma, and patients recovering from surgery and heart attacks, then changes are required in the way we regulate hospital admitting authority, prescription privileges, health insurance reimbursement, and other health care delivery issues (discussed in chapter 16). It is also possible that if it seems evident that the way our society is organized creates health-endangering stress for some groups, psychologists must become involved in social action to change society.

Disease Prevention and Health Promotion

Some health psychologists emphasize preventing disease and promoting wellness. If research reveals that certain behaviors increase the probability of developing certain diseases, then it is clearly cost-effective and good public policy to reduce those behaviors and prevent the development of illness in the first place. If certain changes in behavior can be made and maintained, the amount of human suffering can be greatly reduced.

Health psychologists intervene in known risk factors. Certain behaviors, such as smoking and overeating, have been demonstrated by research to increase the risk of painful, disabling, and fatal diseases such as lung cancer, emphysema, and cardiovascular disorders. It follows that modification of these behaviors would decrease the health risks. A quick glance at the titles of articles in recent clinical psychology journals will show that obesity is the behavioral disorder most frequently mentioned, with smoking a close second. The treatment of these two risk factors is an important field.

Smoking and overeating are extremely difficult habits to modify. In the past, failure and relapse rates have been unacceptably high. Health psychology has entered the fray. A combination of behavioral techniques, including aversion therapy, relaxation, identification of signaling stimuli, negative practice, imagery, self-reward, contingency management, group therapy, exercise, hypnosis, and whatever else creative therapists think of, seems to be equally or somewhat more effective in modifying smoking and eating behavior than traditional methods of stopping these behaviors.

Stress inoculation methods and stress management programs continue to grow in popularity. It is assumed that if people can learn to control their reactions to stress, they will reduce the likelihood of developing stress-related diseases, such as hypertension, ulcers, headaches, and heart disease. Behavioral techniques are used to teach individuals to recognize the signs of stress, learn to relax, alter their priorities, and organize their time better. Relaxation training, hypnosis, guided imagery, desensitization, exercise, group therapy, assertion training, role playing, biofeedback, and meditation are often used to teach people how to relax their muscles, lower their blood pressure, lower their heart rate, or induce certain kinds of relaxing brain waves. Some health psychologists also consider changing the nature of our competitive work culture as a way of preventing the diseases that result from chronic stress.

Behaviorists are involved in educating the public regarding the prevention of health problems in the first place. The 1979 U.S. Surgeon General's report indicated that as much as half the mortality in the United States may be due to unhealthy behavior. It also stated that of the 10 leading causes of death, at least seven of them could be substantially reduced if people altered just six habits: poor diet, smoking, lack of exercise, alcohol abuse, maladaptive responses to stress, and failure to use appropriate antihypertensive medications (U.S. Surgeon General, 1979). Widespread changes in these six behaviors would substantially reduce morbidity and mortality due to heart disease, stroke, arteriosclerosis, emphysema, diabetes, cirrhosis of the liver, and psychological disabilities. Furthermore, even bacterial or viral diseases such as AIDS and SARS are spread and controlled primarily by the behavior of individuals.

Part of prevention is the early detection of disease. Psychologists teach the importance of self-examinations of the breasts and testicles in order to detect cancer in its earliest, most curable stages. The importance of proper diet, exercise, and rest in preventing disease is taught, along with specific techniques to increase the likelihood that individuals will begin and continue to engage in exercise or good diets. Teaching people to announce their plans to exercise or diet publicly, to enlist the support of friends, to reward themselves for meeting their goals, and to structure their environment to support their goals are some of the ways that behaviorists can educate people about disease prevention.

Health psychologists are sometimes involved in "wellness," the promotion of optimal health. The promotion of wellness behavior in entire populations of people would contribute to the reduction of addictions, for example (Prochaska, 2004). In addition to preventing disease, the active promotion of excellent health and general well-being is considered a social good. Maintaining low weight and eating a moderately low-fat, low-salt, low-sugar diet are important in wellness, but the greater emphasis is generally on exercise. Research suggests that regular aerobic exercise has numerous benefits, from reducing weight, improving cardiovascular functioning, and increasing physical strength, to reducing depression, improving mood, raising self-esteem, and increasing energy levels, as well as lowering the risks of certain diseases, such as heart disease, diabetes, osteoporosis, and chronic pain (Dubbert, 1992). With so many things in its favor, it is perhaps surprising that exercising regularly is so difficult for so many Americans. Education, group support, and contingency management techniques are used to teach and maintain regular exercise programs.

Some psychologists argue that we should be pursuing psychological wellness in addition to physical wellness. Psychological wellness is promoted through competence, resilience, social system modification, and empowerment. These concepts again suggest that psychologists become involved in public policy and social action in order to modify the social system and empower people for the sake of health and wellness.

Biofeedback

The use of biofeedback is now recognized as a separate, specialized *skill*, and professional psychologists, as well as physicians, physical therapists, and others can seek certification in its use from the Biofeedback Certification Institute of America.

Biofeedback is a treatment technique in which people are trained to improve their physical and psychological health by using signals from their own bodies. Here is the definition from the Association for Applied Psychophysiology and Biofeedback:

> Biofeedback is providing real time information from psychophysiological recordings about the levels at which physiological systems are functioning. Biofeedback does not need to involve the use of computers, electronic devices, etc. For example, a mirror is a perfectly good biofeedback device for many aspects of gait retraining. Electronic biofeedback devices are designed to record physiological functions non-invasively. Most record from the surface of the skin. The information recorded by surface sensors is frequently sent to a computer for processing and then displayed on the monitor and/or through speakers. The person being recorded and any therapist or coach who may be present can attend to the display of information and incorporate it into whatever process they are attempting to perform. The device does not send anything directly back into the person being recorded. The loop is completed only when the person being recorded attends to and uses the displayed information. (Applied Psychophysiology & Biofeedback, 2005)

While it can be used with any behavior, biofeedback is often used to make ordinarily nonconscious, nonvoluntary, automatic bodily responses evident by the electronic display of information taken from mechanical or electrical sensors. For example, ordinarily, your heart beats at a certain rate or changes its rate automatically without your awareness. When you are hooked up to an EKG machine, your heart rate becomes available to your conscious awareness. You can watch the monitor line and listen to the bleeps that represent your heartbeats. You are given immediate, ongoing visual and auditory feedback about the biological activity, hence the name biofeedback.

Theoretical and Empirical Basis of Biofeedback

Biofeedback was first developed by academic psychologists researching certain controversial questions about the nature of learning in the 1970s. Research psychologists were astonished to find that people could apparently learn to raise or lower their heart rate when they got biofeedback about the rate. They also found that many other nonconscious, automatic physiological responses, such as blood pressure, muscle tension, and brain waves, which had been thought to be nonvoluntary, appeared to be modifiable by learning. The early research suggested that biofeedback resulted in true learning curves and the acquisition of a new response. Subsequent research has suggested that this is incorrect and that biofeedback enhances a person's ability to make relatively small voluntary changes in physiological responses through increased awareness alone.

The interesting question remains, how does biofeedback work? As mentioned, it was originally thought that biofeedback led to the learning of new physiological responses or response patterns. However, some scholars believe that the positive effects of biofeedback are mediated through a generalized relaxation effect and through cognitive factors. Biofeedback may simply enhance people's ability to relax, and relaxation itself improves their health and well-being. Several cognitive processes are hypothesized to be an important part of biofeedback. It may increase individuals' sense of self-efficacy, that is, they become more confident that they can have an effect on their disorder, and so they do. Once people believe they have control over their problems, they feel less anxious and stressed. Although biofeedback has been thoroughly studied empirically, the reasons why it works are still open to question, as is the case with hypnosis, discussed below.

Interventions Utilizing Biofeedback

Rather than wait several decades as they did with other academic behavioral discoveries, clinical psychologists immediately saw that if such physiological responses could be modified, then perhaps patients could learn to control health-threatening physiological responses. Biofeedback technology has been used to treat several types of medical disorders. Biofeedback of blood pressure has been used to treat hypertension and migraine headaches; biofeedback of muscle tension has been used to treat headaches, backache, and stress; biofeedback of brain waves has been used to treat stress and teach relaxation; and biofeedback of heart rate has been used to treat anxiety and cardiac rate disorders, to give just a few examples.

The use of biofeedback in treating disorders has been extremely controversial in the past and still is somewhat controversial. For example, Roberts (1985) concluded that the research does not justify the use of biofeedback alone in therapy: it must be accompanied by other techniques. More recently, the Association for Applied Psychophysiology and Biofeedback has reviewed a great deal of research and concluded that the effectiveness of biofeedback has been adequately demonstrated for over 30 disorders, from attention deficit disorder to irritable bowel syndrome. The Applied Psychophysiology & Biofeedback (2005) Web site provides a complete list of medical and mental disorders for which there is evidence that biofeedback is efficacious.

Box 12.1 Behavioral Treatment of Headache

To demonstrate the specifics of treatment in behavioral medicine, we will discuss the headaches of Jan N. as an example. Jan is a 39-year-old Caucasian American, the single mother of very active, 7-year-old twin boys. She also works 50 hours per week as a stockbroker in a high-pressure investment firm. Jan has suffered from debilitating headaches all of her life, but since the birth of her sons, they have increased in intensity and frequency so that she cannot function at least one day per week. Over the years, she has sought medical help to no avail. The last physician she consulted recommended that she see a psychologist, Dr. Diane R. Although skeptical, Jan is desperate and makes an appointment.

There are certain basic steps in any behavioral treatment program, beginning with assessment and diagnosis. Diane and Jan will proceed through these typical steps. Note the similarity of these steps to problem-solving training and behavior therapy.

Step 1: Define the Problem

Generally, as part of one or two initial interviews, the therapist will ask the client to define the problem. The information collected will include current symptoms, precipitating events, pain history, assessment of physiological functioning (often from physicians' reports), assessment of psychological functioning, and thoughts and beliefs about headache.

There are two main types of headaches for which behavioral treatment is sought. Migraine, or vascular, headaches are attributed to a two-step process of a prolonged constriction of arteries in the head, followed by a rebound dilation of the arteries associated with the onset of pain. Muscle-contraction, or tension, headaches are attributed to excessive, sustained contraction of the back, shoulder, and neck muscles. Some believe this distinction is questionable and argue that all headaches involve excessive muscle contraction, with migraines simply being more severe.

As Jan describes her headaches, they do not appear to be migraines, and in fact, previous physicians have ruled out that diagnosis. She reports a life full of stress and that her headaches generally occur at the end of the week. She believes they are due to the pressure at work, but she also believes that she is being punished for success at work, that once the pain begins she is doomed, that she can never be a good mother to her sons because of her pain, and other anxiety-provoking beliefs. Diane observes that Jan does not sit in a relaxed manner, but rather exhibits hunched shoulders and a wrinkled forehead. She begins the process of educating Jan about the nature of tension headaches and how they can be modified.

Step 2: Generate Alternatives

The next step in behavioral treatment is for the therapist and client to work together to generate alternative conceptualizations of the problem and alternative ways of intervening. The therapist generally elicits information about strategies the client has used before and how effective they were. The therapist gives information about alternatives, explaining the rationale, research on effectiveness, and appropriateness of each for the client's particular problem. Clients are encouraged to employ existing skills, develop untapped resources, and learn new methods of coping.

In exploring alternatives with Jan, Diane discovers and points out to Jan that several things she tried in the past did in fact work. When she used to take a break to meditate in the afternoon, her headaches were less frequent. Diane suggests that the relaxation involved in meditation reduced Jan's muscle tension and that since Jan has skills in that direction, relaxation training might be appropriate.

continued

Besides relaxation training, other interventions have been found to be effective with headache, and Diane discusses them all with Jan. Hypnosis is useful for suggesting pain control and pain reduction and for teaching relaxation. Biofeedback is often used with headache. It might educate Jan about the level of muscle tension in her neck and shoulders and teach her how to reduce it. It may also facilitate "physiological insight" so she learns there is a connection between psychological and physiological processes.

Stimulus-control modification may help Jan identify and avoid the exact situations that bring on her headaches. If they cannot be avoided, then cognitive-behavior therapy may help her modify her anxiety-provoking and tension-raising thoughts about those situations. A thought-stopping technique may help her stop the vicious cycle of feeling a bit of head pain and thinking she is doomed and a terrible mother, thoughts that increase her muscle tension, which leads to more pain and more thoughts and so on.

Diane also suggests stress-coping group training, in which Jan would attend a small, educational, weekly group in order to learn coping strategies for stressful situations at work. The group would cover techniques for identifying cues that trigger tension, evaluating thoughts and responses to the cues, and correcting, modifying, and stopping thoughts that increase pain and instituting thoughts that are incompatible with further stress and tension.

Step 3: Evaluate Alternatives

The therapist alerts the client to typical advantages and disadvantages of each intervention strategy. Treatment recommendations will reflect the state of knowledge at that point. The client will be encouraged to anticipate the consequences of change.

Among all the alternatives, Diane points out to Jan that because of her experience with meditation, she may be able to use hypnosis and biofeedback effectively. Diane cites a study that found that both hypnosis and biofeedback were more effective in the treatment of headache of individuals high in hypnotizability. Diane also describes a study on stress-coping group treatment that showed significant improvement in headaches. Diane is trying both to describe the empirical efficacy of the alternative treatments and to instill hope and trust in Jan.

Step 4: Choose Alternatives and Implement

The client's level of commitment and the support available in the client's environment must be evaluated at this point. Several factors will determine the choice of treatment.

Because biofeedback and hypnosis do not seem to Jan to demand as much time and energy as the other alternatives discussed, and because she hopes for a quick solution, she prefers them to the others.

Diane begins with a series of biofeedback sessions, hooking Jan up to a special EMG machine that through painless electrodes attached to the skin detects muscle contraction and turns it into a high-pitched sound. This procedure helps Jan become aware of the level of muscle tension in her head, neck, and shoulders. By relaxing her muscles, she is able to lower the pitch of the machine's sound. After three sessions of biofeedback, Diane adds hypnosis to the sessions. These sessions include suggestions that Jan will be successful in lowering the tone in biofeedback, that she will be able to detect the cues that bring on headaches before they begin, that she will be able to relax her muscles and prevent the headaches, and that she will substitute a relaxing scene of a flower-filled meadow for her usual anxiety-provoking thoughts.

Step 5: Monitor Progress and Reevaluate

The therapist and client may need to evaluate the choice of treatment strategies based on the client's new experiential knowledge. Changes in treatment strategy may be necessary. Long-term follow-up contact may be necessary to refresh client skills.

After a few weeks of treatment, Jan reports some welcome relief from her headaches. However, she has a very bad one again and returns for treatment. Diane incorporates relapse prevention into the program, and tells Jan that occasional headaches do not mean the program is failing. She tells Jan of another study that demonstrated the usefulness of booster treatments for long-term maintenance of improvement.

Jan thinks she might like the stress-coping group after all. She also reports an unanticipated consequence of fewer headaches: she has to spend more time with her sons. She feels overwhelmed and inadequate with their activity and demands. Diane begins again with Step 1, now working on a definition of the problem as one of difficulty coping with the stress of parenting. She goes through the steps to recommend parent training and other alternatives. She and Jan will continue the process as long as it leads to effective interventions and worthwhile changes for Jan.

Hypnosis

Hypnosis is a remarkable phenomenon. Two people in a special relationship, one the hypnotizer and the other the hypnotized individual, engage in a conversation in which the hypnotizer tells the other to concentrate, close eyes, relax, and the like, and then gives suggestions for a variety of changes, including physiological responses, and they happen. While engaged in the activity labeled hypnosis, individuals can undergo physically painful experiences without reacting, alter other physiological responses such as blushing, "cure" palsied movements, and make seemingly difficult behavioral changes.

Like biofeedback, hypnosis is now a recognized *skill*, and psychologists, physicians, and others may gain training and certification in it. It has its own Division in the APA, 30, the Society of Psychological Hypnosis; its own professional organizations, the American Society of Clinical Hypnosis (www.asch.net), American Board of Professional Hypnosis, and the Society for Clinical and Experimental Hypnosis (www.sceh.us); and its own journals, such as the *American Journal of Clinical Hypnosis* and *Contemporary Hypnosis*.

Hypnosis has been used for centuries by everyone from shamans and entertainers to physicians and midwives, and it has wavered in and out of respectability over the years. The formal use of hypnosis in medical treatments began early in the nineteenth century, in Europe, when it was popularized by Mesmer. Then known as mesmerism, hypnosis was used in obstetrics as early as 1831 (Chertok, 1981) and in surgery even earlier (Spanos & Chaves, 1989). Freud originally used hypnosis in psychoanalysis but dropped it in favor of his own technique of free association. Mesmer eventually fell into disrepute, and his methods were ignored by the medical community for many decades. In recent decades, hypnosis was reintroduced as a behavior modification method in health psychology, where it was used with success, and as a result, it is now used in dentistry, medicine, and psychotherapy as well.

Hypnosis is extremely difficult to define, measure, and investigate. After many years of research and controversy, there is still little agreement as to what hypnosis is. Whether it is an altered state of consciousness, a trance, or simply deep relaxation is not known for certain. Most writers in the field of hypnosis settle for defining it simply as a heightened state of suggestibility. However, here is the definition from APA Division 30, the Society of Psychological Hypnosis:

> Hypnosis is a set of techniques designed to enhance concentration, minimize one's usual distractions, and heighten responsiveness to suggestions to alter one's thoughts, feelings, behavior, or physiological state. (Society of Psychological Hypnosis, 2005)

How is that state of heightened "responsiveness to suggestions" achieved? The techniques for inducing hypnosis and those used once the client is hypnotized vary tremendously, and creative therapists invent new ones every day. Hypnotic inductions may be direct or indirect, administered by a therapist or self-administered by the client. They may take a few moments or a half an hour. Induction may involve a quiet room, sitting comfortably, the hypnotist's soothing voice, and suggestions to relax and concentrate. For example, the hypnotist tells the client to stare at a certain point up on a wall and then says, "Your eyes are getting tired." Well, of course they would! However, it is believed that the client experiences the hypnotist's words as making an accurate prediction or as making a suggestion that must be obeyed, thus increasing the client's suggestible state. After several such inevitable suggestions, the client soon enters a state that both the hypnotist and the client consider to be hypnosis. It is believed that when clients successfully follow a series of suggestions to close their eyes, breathe deeply, and concentrate on certain stimuli, they are then more open to following other therapeutic suggestions.

There are a number of misconceptions about hypnosis, for example, that people can be made to do things against their will. One of the reasons for its questionable reputation may be that hypnosis is used for entertainment, such as in nightclub acts, when people do absurd things seemingly without awareness or will. It is debatable whether volunteers for such acts are "really" hypnotized. Rather, it appears that entertainers are experienced at selecting cooperative volunteers and persuading them to go along with the act. Hypnosis has also been negatively portrayed in horror films, making it appear that people can be made to murder or commit other terrible acts against their will. Research, of course, indicates that this portrayal is entirely unrealistic.

Hypnosis, despite its presentation in entertainment and films, is no more dangerous than other forms of behavior modification. A hypnotist cannot force people to do things, for hypnosis is basically a cooperative enterprise. Hypnosis cannot induce amnesia either, unless the person wants to forget. A layperson often views hypnosis as coercive, with the powerful or mysterious hypnotist forcing the hypnotized person to do things against his will. Even scientists fall into this sort of bias when they label people with high ability in being hypnotized with pejorative terms that imply passivity or "weakness," such as "suggestible" or "susceptible" to hypnosis. In fact, it is possible to view the ability to become hypnotized as a skill, with some individuals more able than others to enter into the hypnosis process.

Like biofeedback, hypnosis has been used in health psychology to treat a wide variety of disorders with various degrees of success (Flammer & Bongartz, 2003). Hypnosis has been used to treat asthma, posttraumatic stress disorder, gastrointestinal disorders, arthritis and other types of pain, skin conditions, nausea due to cancer treatments, dental distress, enuresis, irritable bowel syndrome, obesity, and many of the disorders treated with biofeedback. It is also used as a technique in behavior therapy, psychoanalysis, and other therapies.

Theoretical Explanations of Hypnosis

There seems to be sufficient evidence from well-controlled studies to conclude that, at least for people who are responsive to hypnosis, it is very effective in treating a variety of problems and disorders. There is much more controversy over why it works. There are many different theoretical explanations for hypnosis, but they can be grouped into two predominant views. One is that hypnosis constitutes a special state different from ordinary consciousness. In this view, hypnosis is an altered state of consciousness or trance brought about by the hypnotic induction procedures. It is argued that a trance can be observed in physiological changes such as flaccid facial muscles, pallor, and altered breathing. The special state view of hypnosis fits in with the holistic view that physiology and psychology are a unity.

The second major view of hypnosis is that it is not a special state, but simply a subset of everyday social and cognitive behaviors. Holders of this view argue that the empirical evidence indicates that hypnosis can be accounted for with the same concepts that are used to study behavior in other social situations (Kirsch & Lynn, 1995). For example, it is hypothesized that the "demand characteristics" of the hypnosis situation require a person to cooperate with the hypnotic suggestions, because everyone "knows" that that is how a hypnotized person is "supposed" to act (Orne, 1962). It is also possible that some people feel less threatened by and therefore less resistant to therapeutic suggestions when they cognitively attribute their obedience to the hypnosis and not to simply obeying someone else's advice. In the hypnosis situation, people may shift their perspective from an objective, possibly rigid position to an uncritical, accepting, possibly flexible perspective. The point is that their behavior can be explained with the same psychological principles that explain all social behavior.

It seems that professional psychologists more frequently hold the view that hypnosis is a special state requiring a special theoretical rationale and that academic psychologists more frequently believe that hypnosis can be explained with the usual principles of social, behavioral, and cognitive psychology. We will focus on one well-known contemporary example of each view. The theory of Milton Erickson will represent the special state view (Erickson & Rossi, 1979; Rossi, 1980), and the work of Nicholas Spanos and his colleagues will demonstrate the cognitive-behavioral perspective (Spanos & Chaves, 1989; Spanos, 1991).

Milton Erickson's Theory of Hypnosis

Probably the most famous hypnotist in the world, Milton Erickson died in 1980 without leaving a comprehensive written summary of his theories and methods, although he wrote numerous scientific articles. He was a very charismatic and effective hypnotist and therapist, and he greatly influenced many of today's prominent therapists. Although Erickson's work was not widely accepted when he was alive because hypnosis was not regarded as "scientific" then, his complex ideas are popular today.

Erickson believed that all forms of psychotherapy are based on suggestion and hypnosis. Hypnosis is related in Erickson's framework to the therapeutic paradox, as discussed in chapter 13. The paradox inherent in all psychotherapies is as follows. The implicit message is that the therapist will help the client change (after all the therapist is taking the client's money for that purpose!). However, most therapists explicitly state that the client is ultimately responsible for change and the client can change only if she wants to. So clients cannot disobey the therapist—if they change, they are obeying the therapist's implicit message (to change), and if they don't, they are obeying the explicit message (not to change unless they want to). Once clients obey the therapist at all, and under the therapeutic paradox they cannot help but obey one message or the other, then they are hypnotized in the sense that their suggestibility has increased and they are more willing to follow other helpful suggestions.

Despite professing a pragmatic, atheoretical stance, Erickson developed a complex theoretical rationale as to why hypnosis and indirect suggestions work. Based on his detailed and extensive observations of people's behavior, he believed that normal humans are composed of at least two "minds" or systems of knowing and experiencing the world. He called these the "conscious" and the "unconscious" (or "subconscious") minds, although he meant something quite different from Freud's use of these words. The "conscious" mind is composed of those thoughts, emotions, perceptions, and memories in awareness. It has its own needs and goals and ways of knowing and communicating. It is logical, slow to react, and thinks in a linear cause-and-effect fashion. The "unconscious" mind consists of an entirely different set of thoughts, emotions, perceptions, and memories, with its own needs and goals, which are not immediately available to conscious awareness. It is holistic, intuitive, quick to react, and, according to Erickson, wiser and more objective (although more literal and simplistic) than the conscious mind.

To Erickson, the "conscious" is the source of resistance and difficulties in life, while the "unconscious" contains valuable learnings and objective, experiential knowledge. For example, the unconscious knows how to walk—you walk every day without awareness. As long as walking remains outside of awareness, it is done perfectly well. When you become aware of how you walk, as when you become self-conscious about how you look to others, you start to have trouble doing it. As Erickson noted, his ideas about the conscious and unconscious minds are similar to present ideas about right- and left-brain functioning. The logical, linear-reasoning left hemisphere of the brain is similar to Erickson's conscious mind, and the holistic, intuitive, reactive, right hemisphere is similar to his unconscious mind. In fact, hypnosis may be seen conceptually as a way to confuse the logical left hemisphere so the therapist can directly access the right hemisphere, thus solving the therapeutic problem of access to the part of the personality that is organized to accept change, as discussed in chapter 14.

Erickson defined hypnosis descriptively "as an artificially enhanced state of suggestibility resembling sleep wherein there appears to be a normal, time-limited and stimulus-limited dissociation of the 'conscious' from the 'subconscious' elements of the psyche" (quoted in Havens, 1985, p. 249). This definition implies all the points of Erickson's theory of hypnosis. Like other definitions of hypnosis, Erickson's includes a state of increased suggestibility, which is different from other such states in that it is artificially enhanced, through hypnotic inductions. Note also that it allows the "unconscious" (or "subconscious"—he called it both) mind to separate from the "conscious." In everyday functioning, the conscious mind dominates the way people experience and function, and it cannot solve difficulties such as anxieties and symptoms. Hypnosis is time limited and stimulus limited; that is, it occurs only for a certain period of time and under certain circumstances. Furthermore, Erickson considered hypnosis to be a "normal" state, and in fact, he said that some of our best behavior (such as safe freeway driving) is done while we are hypnotized.

Thus, Erickson believed that hypnosis and suggestion "worked" in therapy because they circumvented the troublesome "conscious" and spoke directly to the wiser "unconscious." Hypnotic inductions confuse the logical "conscious," sort of putting it out of commission, allowing the "unconscious" to respond. By being illogical, vivid, and literal, hypnotic techniques allow the therapist to deal with the unconscious mind directly. Since Erickson considered the unconscious to be healthier and more sensible than the conscious, hypnosis enlists the patient's better self in the change process. The unconscious is able to solve problems that the conscious cannot, and it wants to change in positive directions, so it will follow therapeutic suggestions that the conscious mind may resist.

The Cognitive-Behavioral View of Nicholas Spanos

The belief that hypnosis is not a special state is almost as old as hypnosis. Unusual events appear to happen with hypnosis, and most people assume that unusual events require special explanations. Early in the nineteenth century, Mesmer claimed that his procedures worked because of changes in "animal magnetism" and the like. The nineteenth-century physicians who tried to discredit him (and succeeded) argued that there was no such thing as "animal magnetism" and that mesmerism could be explained as merely the effect of suggestion and expectancy.

By mid-twentieth century, psychologists began subjecting hypnosis to empirical investigation, and a great deal of scientific research has failed to demonstrate that hypnosis is a special state. Two major types of studies have been done. First, there are many studies in which the behavior of people subjected to a hypnosis procedure is compared to that of people not hypnotized. The vast majority of such studies find little difference in the behavior of the two groups. For example, people who are told while hypnotized that they can bear a painful procedure and people who are simply told they can bear it report similarly reduced levels of pain. Second, there are many studies in which hypnotized people make certain claims, but indirect measures suggest these claims are not accurate. For example, individuals hypnotized to forget certain words claim they cannot remember them, but they show changes in their galvanic skin response when presented with them. From such research it seems that the most parsimonious explanation of hypnosis is not that it is an altered state of consciousness, but rather, that it is continuous with other types of complex social behavior.

T. R. Sarbin (1950) was the first modern theorist to explicitly reject the idea that hypnosis is a special state. Using a theatrical metaphor, he viewed hypnosis as role enactment. In the minidrama of the hypnosis situation, the hypnotist and client act out their roles based on their perceptions, attitudes, and expectations about what is supposed to occur in hypnosis. Another researcher, M. T. Orne (1962) argued that the "demand characteristics" of the hypnosis situation explained why a person would comply with the suggestions of the hypnotist.

Nicholas Spanos and his colleagues (Spanos & Chaves, 1989; Spanos, 1991) have researched the cognitive-behavioral view of hypnosis. Spanos believes that hypnosis is not an altered state of consciousness requiring any special explanation. Rather, hypnosis is historically rooted, context-generated, goal-directed, motivated, interpersonal behavior. Hypnosis behavior is a strategic response to the odd hypnotic situation and does not reflect dissociation. Individuals respond to hypnosis according to their attitudes, expectations, and interpretations of the ambiguous hypnotic situation. Susceptibility to hypnosis is not a trait, but a skill that can be enhanced with training. Basically, according to Spanos, there is no evidence that a hypnotic trance exists at all apart from the meaning it has acquired in our culture.

All of the supposedly unusual aspects of hypnosis can be explained with cognitive-behavioral principles. In our culture, most people expect to feel passive and to do things involuntarily in situations that are labeled hypnosis. They also hold situational representations or schemas about what is supposed to happen in hypnosis, such as involuntarily closing their eyes and the like. They have self-schemas, too, and some individuals, who are "susceptible" to hypnosis, may value cooperation or "letting go."

As another example, let us look at the effect of hypnotic suggestion on reducing pain. In the cognitive-behavioral view, the individual is seen as an active agent who can engage in various types of cognitive activities in order to reduce or minimize the effects of noxious stimuli. Many studies demonstrate that nonhypnotized people can make use of such coping strategies as self-distraction, positive imagery, or positive self-statements to significantly increase their pain tolerance. Hypnosis merely encourages individuals to make use of these ordinary coping strategies.

Spanos and his colleagues also emphasize the social psychological principles of role enactment, self-presentation, and impression management. All people enact roles, such as student or spouse; all people actively present themselves in the best light; and all try to manage the impressions they make on others to affect the course of interpersonal interactions. Individuals seeking hypnotic treatment are motivated to enact the role of a hypnotic subject; they try to present themselves as good, hypnotizable clients; and throughout the hypnosis situation, they try to manage the impression they are creating as someone "under hypnosis." As a result, given our cultural expectations that people "under hypnosis" behave involuntarily and can be made to do unusual things such as bear pain or hold their arms very stiff, they may well comply with helpful suggestions for changes in their cognitions and behaviors.

Hypnosis Interventions

Today, hypnosis is used for many therapeutic purposes, from its many uses in health psychology, described earlier, to uncovering painful memories and reducing symptoms in other forms of psychotherapy. As with other behavioral methods, the first step in any treatment involving hypnosis is assessment. Assessment as to the suitability of hypnosis for the individual and his problem may involve an interview or a more comprehensive evaluation. Like other therapists, hypnotherapists must establish rapport with the client, explain the rationale for hypnosis, describe and discuss the intervention alternatives, and with the client, decide on a treatment plan and how to evaluate it. These steps should create a positive attitude toward hypnosis, relieve anxiety, foster a client's sense of control over the process, and engender hope and an expectation of change.

Hypnotic techniques can vary according to how direct or indirect they are. Indirect hypnotic inductions include techniques that increase the client's suggestibility without explicitly labeling them hypnosis. This form of induction may be successful with very resistant clients, those who insist they can never be hypnotized. For example, as the master of indirect suggestion, Milton Erickson would breathe with the same rhythm as a client until they were breathing in synchrony; then he would gradually change his breathing rhythm until the client was following his lead; and then he would make his therapeutic suggestions. Indirect inductions may also be given in the way the therapist uses language, for language has the interesting quality of containing both explicit messages (what is said) and implicit messages (what is not said but is logically implied). For instance, a therapist may ask a client when he would prefer to give up his symptom, on Wednesday or Thursday. While discussing the explicit message about which day, the client must accept the implicit message that the symptom is under his control and it is possible to give it up. It is very difficult for clients to resist these unspoken suggestions, and their indirectness may increase the client's willingness to follow them. More direct inductions include the more well-known orders to stare at a certain point, to close the eyes, to concentrate on certain situations, and so on.

Hypnosis has many uses in behavioral medicine, many already mentioned. Hypnosis has been demonstrated to be effective in treating both chronic and acute pain (Patterson, 2004). For example, it has been used to treat the symptom of chronic pain when other forms of medical treatment do not help. The relaxation may help control the pain, and new reactions to pain are suggested. If the pain cannot be removed, it can sometimes be moved to a less debilitating spot or reduced. Under hypnosis, the client is taught to experience chronic back pain, for example, as a pink spot that can be moved to the head or to the lower arm, where it does not hurt as much.

As a behavioral technique, hypnosis has helped remove a variety of symptoms, including phobias, tics, anxiety, chronic pain, enuresis, and bruxism. Similar to systematic desensitization, the hypnosis treatment for phobias, for example, includes suggesting that the client will not feel fear when near the feared object or situation and suggesting an alternative feeling, as described in box 12.2.

Besides symptom removal, hypnosis helps change or control problem behaviors such as smoking, overeating, drug abuse, or gambling. Interventions may include direct commands to stop the offending behavior, the use of guided imagery for increasing desired behavior, and suggestions that the client will not feel like doing the offending behavior anymore, that he will be able to control himself easily by doing specific suggested behaviors or thoughts, that he will do some alternative behavior. As an example, the treatment of overeating may involve a direct command to not feel hungry, the suggestion that the sight of food will lessen the urge to eat or make the client feel like doing something else such as drinking water, or guided imagery to change the client's image of herself as a pig to one of herself as a greyhound as a metaphor for the goal of therapy. The same techniques can be used to change bad habits such as procrastination or nail biting. This approach is similar to cognitive-behavior therapy (discussed in chapter 11).

Hypnosis appears to be useful in teaching relaxation and stress management. Hypnotic induction itself relaxes the client, and once the client learns how to use hypnotic techniques to relax, she can use them whenever needed. Besides directly teaching relaxation, hypnosis helps clients manage stress by suggesting alternative behaviors, thoughts, or emotions to experience when under stress. Rather than feeling rage in a traffic jam on the freeway or during a confrontation at work, the client may be taught to retrieve the image of a peaceful place, such as a beach or meadow, at stressful times and to substitute the peaceful feeling the scene induces for the anger or anxiety being felt. Reducing stress this way has numerous health benefits.

Hypnosis is also used in conjunction with other types of psychotherapy, and part or even all of the therapy can be conducted with the client under hypnosis in order to enhance the effectiveness of the therapy. Hypnosis has been used as an additional

Box 12.2 Hypnotic Treatment of a Bird Phobia

In the hypnotic treatment of a bird phobia (see chapter 10), the therapist will first explain the procedure, establish rapport, obtain informed consent, and then perhaps begin treatment with an induction such as the following:

> I'd like you to find a comfortable position in your chair, one in which you won't feel physically restricted in any way. Get comfortable, and you will probably want to close your eyes. And simply breathe, deeply, at your own rhythm, and as you do, as you inhale, imagine that you are drawing all the tensions in your body into your lungs, and then as you exhale, you expel all those tensions out of your body. Keep breathing, keep expelling tension, until you feel deeply, completely relaxed. Simply breathe, and listen to my voice, and no extraneous sounds will bother you. You'll begin to feel very relaxed and heavy, as though you were sinking down into a warm, safe place, deeper, and more completely relaxed. And as you find your breathing slowing, you'll also discover that you enjoy being in this place somewhere between sleep and consciousness, and you can let go, really let go, and slowly relax, even more with every breath. When you feel comfortable and fully ready, I'd like you to focus on a point on your right knee. Good. Now I'd like you to focus completely on a point on your right hand. When you've done that I'd like you to focus on a point in the middle of your forehead, and imagine that your entire being is focused and relaxed. You feel comfortable in your body in every way, you simply exist, deeply relaxed, unburdened, and totally free. You are very deeply, deeply relaxed and comfortable.

After the bird-phobic client is sufficiently relaxed and suggestible, the therapist may say:

> You are sitting in the peaceful meadow we talked about before. You see a bird, a beautiful red bird, singing sweetly in the sunshine, and you look at it calmly, you feel happy listening to its song, you enjoy watching its beauty. When you leave my office, you will see many birds, and they will remind you of the beautiful red bird, and you will feel glad to see them, glad that there are singing birds in the world.

More suggestions may be given, and at the end of the session the therapist may say:

> Now, as soon as you are ready, you will stop thinking about this good feeling, and bring your attention back to the present. You will feel rested, refreshed, and energetic. You will be able to remember all of this session that you wish to. When you are ready, open your eyes.

The similarity of this approach to systematic desensitization as described in box 10.2 is evident.

technique in almost all types of therapy, from psychoanalysis to the family systems approach. However, the success of treatment is not attributed to the hypnosis, but rather to the theoretical principles of whatever type of therapy is being done. For example, psychodynamic therapists sometimes make use of hypnosis in their psychotherapy. Simply put, the goal of psychodynamic therapy is the reconstruction of the personality, and this goal is achieved by working through unconscious conflicts, fears, and memories in order to achieve insight. Hypnosis can facilitate these processes. If an analytic client has difficulty retrieving early memories or resists important issues, hypnosis may be used to enhance memory, unblock resistance, or elicit unconscious material. Client improvement then is attributed to the psychoanalytic interpretation of this material and not to hypnosis. Sometimes, memories of early traumatic events can be discovered by regressing the client to younger ages. Hypnosis can be used to uncover ordinary memories, too, as when it is used to help eyewitnesses recall details of crimes. This brief description only hints at the complexity and creativity of therapists of all schools using hypnosis.

With self-hypnosis individuals learn to self-induce hypnosis. The therapist may also teach the client a specific cue under hypnosis, such as suggesting that the client will be able to enter into a deep, relaxing trance by concentrating on a point on the forehead or by saying certain words to himself, and the client can then use the cue for self-hypnosis any time he wishes. The uses of self-hypnosis are similar to those of ordinary hypnosis, but responsibility for trance induction and awakening is transferred to the client.

Finally, hypnosis may be used for personal growth. Hypnosis is useful for many types of self-exploration, from regression to retrieve early experiences to imagining conversations with important others. Some people believe hypnosis can enhance artistic expression, allowing an individual's full creativity to emerge. Some people believe hypnosis can help with spiritual growth by, for example, accessing the "cosmic unconscious," although personally, we have always tried to access the "comic unconscious." In short, hypnosis is used for many different purposes.

Psychopharmacology

The final area where biology and behavior meet that we shall consider is psychopharmacology and the use of psychotropic drugs that affect the brain in order to alter behavior and psychological disorders. The development of these drugs began in the mid-twentieth century, and since the 1980s, the precision and effectiveness of these drugs has greatly improved. When psychotropic drugs were first developed, psychologists often worked with prescribing psychiatrists to manage clients' medications. In 1967 the APA officially stated that psychopharmacology research and practice were a domain of psychology. By the 1980s the APA was discussing and studying the possibility of prescription privileges for psychologists, that is, the legal right of appropriately trained psychologists to prescribe medication for the treatment of psychological and behavioral disorders. (It should be noted that some psychologists in the military and certain other federal programs have had prescription privileges for decades [Clay, 2004].) The APA formally approved prescription privileges for appropriately trained psychologists and began advocating for them in 1995. They also developed training curricula and model legislation. By the turn of the twenty-first century, legislation to give prescription privileges to psychologists had been introduced in 10 states. New Mexico became the first state to enact such a law in 2002. This important change in the role of psychologists has been and will be resisted, and psychiatrists in New Mexico have reportedly spent $100,000 on lobbying to stop this legislation or repeal it (Practice Directorate Staff, 2005).

There is no reason to believe that psychologists cannot be trained to prescribe psychotropic drugs, just as general practitioners do. And there are several reasons to support prescription privileges for psychologists, especially health psychologists. Consider that the federal government, encouraged by the pharmaceutical industry and organized medicine, has been advocating that medication be the primary treatment for mental and emotional disorders, so psychologists need to be able to prescribe medication in order to keep practicing. It is estimated that depression accounts for up to half of the effects of disease and more than half of visits to physicians, yet most depressed people do not get proper treatment. If psychologists could prescribe medication, then more people could get proper treatment, and expensive physician time could be spent on something else. Certain groups, such as people living in rural communities, have little access to psychiatric care; psychologists could serve these groups. Many other nonphysicians have prescription privileges, including dentists, nurse practitioners, and physician assistants. It is clearly not necessary to attend medical school in order to prescribe appropriate medication. Psychologists, with far more training than primary care physicians have in biopsychosocial assessment and treatment of emotional and behavior disorders, deserve prescription privileges. Since many are working as health psychologists in medical settings, prescription privileges would enhance their effectiveness and range of treatment options.

Even within the field of psychology, there are those who disagree with the above arguments. Obviously, organized medicine and psychiatry are opposed, just as they were opposed to prescription privileges for dentists, nurse practitioners, and others, and just as they were opposed to the right of clinical psychologists to do psychotherapy in the first place. Some fear that psychologists will become "pill-pushers" like some doctors. Given their training and demonstrated expertise in behavioral and psychological treatments, it seems unlikely that many psychologists would become pill-pushers. Others fear increases in liability insurance premiums or that sufficient training will be expensive or unavailable. Finally, some are concerned that psychology will lose its distinct identity and that the status of non-prescribing psychologists will suffer. The field of psychology has undergone incredible change in the past and survived and flourished, so it is likely that it will do the same with prescription privileges. (See www.apa.org/apags/profdev/prespriv.html for an extensive discussion of this issue.)

Thousands of psychologists work in medical schools and settings already, and they often informally prescribe and monitor psychotropic medication. There is some evidence that with their behavioral training health psychologists help clients function with fewer medications and lower doses of medication. Health psychology is an expanding field, and prescription privileges will allow health psychologists to offer clients another option (Barlow, 2004).

Now that it is a well-accepted fact that certain behaviors can lead to disease and death and that disease can lead to behavioral and psychological problems such as depression, psychology has been recognized as a health care profession. The APA has pushed for this recognition and for psychology to be included in any of the constantly proposed changes to the health care system. With appropriate training, it should be possible for health psychologists to be primary care providers, both in private practice and medical settings (Feldman & Christensen, 2003; James & Folen, 2005). Just as primary care physicians must be alert to patients' behavior and social situation and deal with them somehow, psychologists with expertise in behavior and social situations can be trained to be alert for physical problems. Some people may prefer a health psychologist as their primary care provider, as for example those who participate in a large, confusing health maintenance organization. The convincing evidence for the biopsychosocial model may lead to many changes in the health care system.

Evaluation of Biopsychosocial Interventions

Not everyone is enthusiastic about the possibilities for using behavioral methods to treat medical disorders and psychologists' potential movement into primary health care. While many physicians welcome psychology's contributions to medical care, many oppose the entrance of psychologists into the field on the grounds that they are "practicing medicine without a license." Obviously, concerns over professional territory prompt this charge, as well as a desire to protect the public from inappropriate interventions. As the line between the mental and physical aspects of medical problems continues to blur, we can expect that psychologists will continue to develop effective behavioral techniques for helping sick people and that this controversy will also continue.

Some critics charge that the effectiveness of behavioral methods in this context is not proven and that insufficiently researched techniques are rushed into application. Applying unproven techniques to medical problems is often considered especially risky and ethically questionable, although we fail to see why it should be worse than applying unproven techniques to psychological problems. Fortunately, the behavioral tradition in psychology emphasizes a process of research and verification of efficacy.

Biofeedback and hypnosis have been criticized for a number of reasons, including their use in cases when they haven't been proven effective. Some critics are concerned that how they work is not really understood. Of interest to many people is the issue of the "truth" of what goes on under hypnosis, especially when hypnotically enhanced memories are used in court cases. Are memories recalled under hypnosis any more or less accurate than ordinary memories? Do people manufacture memories to please the hypnotist? Many therapists argue that the accuracy of recalled information is irrelevant, because even if invented, the memories experienced under hypnosis are psychologically important to the individuals who create them and can be used to benefit clients in therapy.

In addition, hypnosis is criticized for being manipulative in its direct attempts to control the client's maladaptive behavior, but the obvious reply is that all therapies try to change the client and hypnosis only does so explicitly. Control sometimes becomes an issue between the client and therapist during treatment, especially with resistant clients, and the use of indirect techniques in these cases to circumvent resistance is criticized as controlling and manipulative.

Despite years of research, hypnosis remains a fascinating theoretical enigma. Substantial evidence of its effectiveness tempts many therapists and clients to try hypnosis, but hypnosis is not for everyone. Not all clients are sufficiently cooperative or able to enter hypnosis, and hypnosis is clearly not appropriate for some clients, such as psychotics. Not all therapists are equally comfortable or competent with hypnotic techniques. However, it appears that hypnosis, like biofeedback, has achieved sufficient clinical success, especially in health psychology, that it is once again a respected therapeutic technique

Other criticisms of health psychology involve philosophical and ethical disagreements with certain interventions. For example, some people argue that "fat is a feminist issue." It is true both that one of the most frequently researched and treated behavioral medical problems is obesity and that far more women than men seek treatment for obesity. It is argued that both of these facts reflect our culture's unrealistic overemphasis on women being thin in order to be considered attractive and socially acceptable. Critics argue that psychologists should not be involved in "treating" the moderately overweight as if they were very overweight, but rather should direct their efforts toward increasing the acceptance of somewhat higher than average weight in the women seeking treatment themselves and in society at large.

Some critics believe that the increasing emphasis on psychological causes of illness leads to a tendency to "blame the victim." If it is believed that certain behaviors cause certain illnesses and if society begins to emphasize personal responsibility for illness, then it is a short leap to blaming people for failing to take the steps necessary to change their behaviors and thereby failing to prevent their illnesses. It is even possible that fiscal conservatives and health care corporations could use the belief in personal responsibility for health as a reason to cut funding for behavior-related illnesses. Health psychologists must educate the public regarding the distinction between encouraging personal responsibility for behaviors that are modifiable and not blaming people for being unable to change some behaviors or for becoming sick in spite of good health practices. After all, altering health risk behaviors changes only the *risk* or likelihood of illness—it does not guarantee health.

A great deal of research has been done on the effectiveness of behavioral interventions in health, and it generally supports the effectiveness of health psychology interventions (Smith, Kendall, & Keefe, 2002). It is impossible to summarize this large body of research here, but interested students could consult the Web pages cited elsewhere in this chapter for the latest findings.

Strengths of health psychology include its interdisciplinary orientation, its incorporation of the new scientific holistic view, and its emphasis on scientific empiricism. Although these factors are philosophically valuable, it is probably health psychology's cost-effectiveness that will ensure its place in American health care. The United States' annual per capita spending on health care is the highest in the world, yet our mortality rates and other measures of health are far from first in comparison to other developed countries. Physicians complain of being overburdened, and patients complain of lack of attention. Psychologists can address these problems by developing more effective and less costly health treatments, by preventing disease in the first place and saving those costs, and by doing some of the important educational and emotionally supportive interventions that physicians don't have the time or ability to do. All that remains is for health psychology to gather and present the evidence of its cost-effectiveness to the public and the funders of health care so that they will support its inclusion in the changing U.S. health care system.

In Conclusion

The growing scientific and public awareness of the interconnectedness of the psychological and physical aspects of human beings ensures the future growth of health psychology and biology-based interventions in psychotherapy. Therapeutic techniques such as hypnosis and biofeedback demonstrate the mind–body connection vividly. Research that demonstrates the effectiveness of behavioral interventions, including research suggesting that changes in behavior bring about observable changes in the brain and its functioning, indicate that psychology has many contributions to make to the field of medicine and public health. The roles of health psychologists are already many and will in future extend into primary care and prescribing medication. Health psychology's contributions may also include social action to change the causes of disease, as part of psychology's involvement in prevention.

Marriage, Family, and Child Therapy

Marsha and George have been married for seven years. They have two children: Jane is five and the second, Mark, is three. Marsha and George have felt that they have been growing apart in recent years. They do not spend as much time together. In addition, Mark, who is in preschool, has been acting somewhat shy and withdrawn.

How should these problems be treated? Where should a therapist start? In general, the problems of this family fall under the purview of the specialty called marriage and family therapy, a profession now licensed by a number of states. In addition, there are many other mental health professionals, such as psychiatrists, psychologists, or clinical social workers, who also practice in the general area of marriage and family therapy.

Marsha and George have problems that could be treated by any one of the three approaches we consider in this chapter. If they decided to focus on the problems of their three-year-old, they might take him to a therapist who specializes in working with children. If they decided to focus on their couple issues, they might seek out marital therapy. If it was decided that their problems involved the whole family in some way or other, they might receive family therapy.

These three specialties are considered together in this chapter because they are often interrelated, and practitioners who specialize in one often specialize in the others. Sometimes problems with children are a result of family or couple problems. Perhaps problems between George and Marsha have affected the family, resulting in Mark's acting shy and withdrawn at preschool. Other times, children's problems are entities in their own right. Perhaps Mark is a genetically shy child who needs special attention in order to thrive.

We shall consider each of these three approaches in turn. Before we start, we should note that the principles we allude to in doing couples therapy can be used (with appropriate modifications) with any couple. That is, we focus on the "normative" American couple: heterosexual and married. However, couples therapy can be used with unmarried couples and with gay and lesbian couples. Similarly, when we discuss "families" we use the "normative" model of a family: a father, mother, and children (and possibly a dog). However, this normative family is becoming increasingly nonnormative in the United States. Once again, the general principles of family therapy, with appropriate modifications, can be applied to the many other forms that families take in our current culture besides the traditional one.

Psychological Interventions with Children

Almost every school of therapy has a version for use with children. While the theories may be seen as equally applicable to children and adults, the methods of intervention must be altered for children. Children differ from adult clients in two ways. First of all, children almost never voluntarily request psychotherapy, and so children participate in therapy under at least some degree of duress. More importantly, children differ profoundly in their cognitions, perceptions, and emotions at different developmental stages, and they lack the maturity and cognitive development to benefit from interventions that rely on verbalization and self-examination. Most forms of therapy with children have substituted play for the largely verbal activities required of adults in therapy.

Psychological interventions for children have been developed to treat a wide variety of problems in a wide variety of settings. A distinction may be made between clinical child psychology, which deals with disorders, and pediatric psychology, which deals with child rearing and educational issues, but as with many specialties, there is a great deal of overlap in the types of problems addressed. Children may be treated for such disorders as phobias, anorexia and bulimia, childhood schizophrenia, autism, depression, mental retardation, asthma, headaches, or the aftereffects of child abuse or other trauma. Psychologists may also be consulted for such childhood issues as toileting, sibling rivalry, lack of friends, nightmares, and tantrums.

Psychoanalytically Oriented Therapy

It is probably not surprising that the historical development of child therapy began with psychoanalysis, during the 1920s in the United States. While Sigmund Freud treated a child called Little Hans by advising his father, it was left to two female analysts to develop methods for use specifically with children. Anna Freud (1928, 1946) and Melanie Klein (1955) are credited with establishing a theory and methodology of psychoanalysis to use with children. While both allowed play to substitute for free association, Klein emphasized the symbolic meaning of play and Freud focused on its ability to enhance the relationship with the therapist. Another early analyst, Levy (1939), used play to re-create and work through specific traumatic situations experienced by the child. About the same time, Alfred Adler (1930), an ex-follower of Sigmund Freud, developed his Individual Psychology for use with children and their families. His treatment emphasized allying with the child, teaching the child to compensate for deficiencies in the self and the family, and educating the family in better parenting methods. Many educators and child therapists continue to use Adlerian concepts today.

As with analysts who work with adults, those who work with children will interpret the meaning of dreams, daydreams, fantasies, and play activities, in terms of both transference issues and symbolic meanings about early or traumatic experiences and the child's family. The goal is to help the child negotiate the developmental stage according to the psychoanalytic theory of development and to increase the child's self-understanding and conscious control of behavior. Except for specialized private practice, psychoanalytic treatment of children is not common today in the United States, although psychodynamic concepts are used by many types of therapists.

Client-Centered Therapy

As with adult therapy, the next historical development in child therapy involved the Rogerian school. During the 1940s and 1950s, nondirective techniques were used with children, most often as a part of play therapy, discussed below. Virginia Axline (1947a, b) attempted to apply client-centered therapy to the treatment of children with reading and other problems. Agreeing with Carl Rogers that human beings are born with the capacity for prosocial behavior and self-realization, client-centered child therapists provide unconditional positive regard for their clients in an attempt to undo the damage caused by the parents' conditions of worth on the child's natural good qualities, and they reflect feelings in order to help the child connect with those tendencies. The emphasis is on the accepting, trustworthy relationship between the therapist and child, rather than on any specific techniques or theorized causes for problems in child development.

Play Therapy

Although Axline began in the client-centered school, play therapy soon became recognized as a special form of child therapy in itself. There are now many types of play therapy, including one based on Jungian theory, which utilizes special fantasy play figures in sand trays. Play therapy is sometimes criticized as a vague collection of assorted techniques, without a systematic guiding theory, but there are at least two major types of play therapy at present.

Classical Play Therapy

In classical play therapy, conducted in a moderate-sized playroom with a variety of toys and play and art materials, the therapist focuses on developing a warm, caring relationship with the child. The therapist accepts the child as she is, allows the child to take the lead in the sessions, and does not try to change the child or intervene in or direct the child's play in any way. The therapist creates a safe and permissive atmosphere so that the child feels free to express herself. The therapist attends to, accepts, and reflects the child's feelings in a manner that helps the child develop self-understanding. The therapist does not otherwise "help" the child, but rather, allows her to solve problems in her own way. The therapist sets limits only when required for safety and to help the child accept appropriate responsibility. In classical play therapy, it is believed that if the therapist consistently behaves in these ways, a therapeutic process will be generated in which the child's natural tendency toward growth will be enhanced. The emphasis is on the relationship and generating this process, rather than on specific therapeutic objectives or outcome goals. The general goals of classical play therapy are to help the child develop self-esteem, responsibility, and self-acceptance, to experience a sense of control, and to become more self-directed, as well as more socially appropriate.

Structured Play Therapy

Many modern child therapists believe that classical play therapy takes too long, is inefficient and vague, and most importantly, may collude with the child in avoiding facing difficult issues. Earlier beliefs that children should never be pressured to express certain feelings or discuss certain topics and that they will express feelings spontaneously if they are in an atmosphere of trust and safety are now considered likely to be seen by the young child as permission or even encouragement not to talk about certain issues, especially socially taboo topics such as child sexual abuse.

Structured play therapy, while acknowledging the importance of establishing an accepting, safe relationship between therapist and child, emphasizes specific therapeutic objectives. The therapist is active in directing and structuring the child's play, often arranging a specific activity for each session in order to accomplish specific goals within a certain time range. The therapist utilizes planned stories, metaphor, drawing activities, dolls, and puppet play to raise and explore specific issues with the child. Once the issue has been raised for discussion, the therapist may direct the child's exploration of feelings about the issue, explain that other people feel the same way, teach specific problem-solving or coping behaviors, or make other active interventions.

The traumatic experiences of a sexually abused child, for example, may never come up in classical play therapy, yet the abuse is the major reason for the child's disturbed behavior. Sexually abused children are motivated to keep their problem secret for several reasons, including the molester's threats about what will happen if they tell, a fear of disrupting the family, shame, and society's denial of the problem. In structured play therapy with a sexually abused child, the therapist may tell a story about an abused child or animal and ask the child what the person or creature in the story may feel or should do. The therapist may ask the child to draw a picture of a scared person and then ask a series of questions about the drawing, such as "What could be scaring this person?" Puppets can be used to talk about abuse indirectly, or dolls can be used to demonstrate what happened to the child. Abused children often find it possible to talk about the abuse as if it has happened to someone else—a doll, or a puppet—when they tend to deny and retract if asked about abuse directly. Once the abuse can be discussed, then the therapist will direct an exploration of the child's feelings of helplessness, shame, fear, and rage and help the child understand, accept, and redirect these feelings. Specific coping behaviors are also taught. Although this description of structured play therapy with sexually abused children is necessarily superficial, it is easy to see how different it is from classical play therapy.

Behavior Therapy

Behavior therapy is often used with children, generally in special classrooms or in family therapy, as described in chapter 10. Almost all special education classes and treatment facilities for disturbed children utilize behavioral methods to a greater or lesser extent. Rewards, points, or tokens are given for desired behaviors, such as sitting still, paying attention during a short lesson, or completing work, and time-out is commonly used for undesired behaviors. Critics argue that time-out is widely misunderstood and misapplied, with children spending long periods of time in unhelpful isolation. If so, it is possible that educators need improved training in behavioral principles. Teachers may also use behavior therapy with certain individuals in a regular classroom, especially if the child is involved in behavior therapy with the family.

Although children can be taught to self-monitor and change their own behaviors, more frequently parents are taught to use behavioral methods with their children instead of the ineffective or aversive methods they have been using. Parent Management Training (PMT) (Patterson, 1982) is a particularly effective form of this training. Often parents with problem children have gotten into dysfunctional interaction patterns where they try to modify their children's behavior with coercion, only to be met with oppositional, coercive behavior from the children. The primary goal of PMT is to modify interactions between parents and children that are characterized by coercion and replace them by interactions that reinforce prosocial behavior. Parents learn how to establish clear rules, provide positive reinforcement for appropriate behavior, deliver mild punishment, and negotiate compromises. Parents can be taught to specify clearly the behaviors they desire, to reward those behaviors appropriately, to ignore mild misbehavior, and to set appropriate limits for specific problem behaviors. Limit setting may include the use of time-out. Although designed to address specific behaviors, behavior therapy with children also enhances their feelings of self-esteem and competence. Similar changes are often observed in the parents.

Cognitive-Behavioral Therapy

Cognitive-behavioral therapy is beginning to be used with children to treat such problems as impulsivity, hyperactivity, conduct disorder, and even reading disability. In the latter, the aim is to stop the child's self-defeating self-speech and automatic thoughts and to replace them with coping thoughts. Typically, these children say to themselves things such as, "This is too hard. I'll never get it. See, I made a mistake. It's ruined. I may as well give up." The therapist may model a writing assignment by saying out loud, "Let's see, copying these words is difficult, but I can manage it. I'll start with the first letter. It's an A. I begin here and make this line go like this. Oh, I made a mistake, but it's good enough. I'll keep going. Now I need to make a line like this." By acknowledging the difficulty but reassuring the self that it can be done, by breaking the task down into its component parts, and by accepting mistakes, the therapist teaches reading-disabled children to modify their self-defeating thoughts and behaviors.

Health Psychology

A variety of behavioral and child therapy methods have been found to be beneficial in children's medical treatment. Children can be taught to use imagery or self-hypnosis in order to cope with painful medical procedures. Puppet or doll play to explain surgical procedures is useful in reducing children's fears and enhancing the outcome of surgery. Classical play therapy may help hospitalized children express themselves and retain a positive outlook through the stress of a debilitating illness.

Behavior therapy can increase compliance with difficult diets or other medical regimens. Just as behavioral medicine with adults is a growing field, new methods of intervening in the medical treatment of children are being developed every day.

Hypnosis is also used with children. For example, hypnosis has occasionally been used to help anxious and hyperactive children calm down and learn to calm themselves. Now available for children are audiotapes that contain a soothing hypnotic induction, which children can use to help themselves go to sleep or deal with other problems. The use of self-hypnosis in helping children cope with painful medical procedures has already been mentioned.

Although children are sometimes medicated for anxiety and depression, most frequently, children are given drugs for attention-deficit/hyperactivity disorder. The use of these drugs remains controversial. Drugs such as Ritalin may have negative side effects such as inhibiting growth, although research is resulting in improved drugs. Critics argue that children are drugged for the convenience of teachers and parents and that treated children misattribute their improvement to the drug and not to themselves. Defenders argue that these children suffer from a biologically based brain disorder and that it is unethical to deny them a needed biological intervention. Because drugs appear to be effective and quicker and cheaper than psychological interventions in the treatment of attention-deficit/hyperactivity disorder, their use is likely to continue and to grow.

Family Therapy

In some child guidance clinics in recent years, the family is required to participate as part of therapy for the child. Many therapists reject the notion that a child can have a problem or be treated for it in isolation from the familial context of that problem. A child is frequently the ***identified patient*** when a family becomes dysfunctional. In such cases, family therapy, as described later in the chapter, would be the treatment of choice.

Parents may be involved in therapy with children in other ways. For example, in behavior therapy, they may be taught to apply behavioral methods to modify undesired behaviors in their children. Even in classical play therapy, the parents (usually the mother) meet occasionally with either the child's or another therapist to discuss the child's behavior and to enhance the parents' support of the child's changes.

Group Therapy

As with adult therapy, children may be treated in groups of three to eight under the different models of therapy. For example, in psychoanalytic groups for children, interpretations of parental transference to the therapists or sibling issues between the children may be made. In behavior therapy, small groups of anxious, socially inhibited children may be taught assertive, sociable behavior. Play therapy is often quite effective in groups. In structured play therapy for sexually abused children, for example, two or three therapists with four to six children may meet for planned, guided play exercises directed to the issues of such abused children. The advantages of group therapy in such cases include modeling revealing the secret, the ending of the "pluralistic ignorance" of each child thinking that abuse has happened only to her or him, a reduction of shame and guilt, and the ability to practice problem solving and coping behavior with both peers and adults.

Marital and Couples Therapy

A marital or couples therapist's initial assumption is that problems of the individuals in the couple are caused by the malfunctioning of the couple as a unit, rather than solely by emotions or personality structures within either or both individuals. A couples therapist makes a point of defining clients' difficulties as a couple dysfunction, even if the couple enters therapy because of the disorder of one partner. In other words, most couples therapists assume that psychological problems lie between individuals, rather than solely within one partner or the other, though the couple's problems may manifest in the individual symptoms of one of the partners. Many theorists therefore view marital therapy as a subset of family therapy, and many of the ideas discussed in this section are similar to those of the family therapists discussed later.

When couples come into therapy with a problem, each partner is usually feeling threatened and is on the defensive. They may cope with this by blaming each other, by mutually withdrawing, or by blaming themselves. The result of this is the couple is usually focusing on *each other* as the problem, instead of seeing the problem as *their* mutual problem to solve. We believe that all couples therapists of different orientations strive to do three things. The first is to reduce threat, blame, and defensiveness. The second is to facilitate effective communication that helps the couple work together on their mutual problems. The third is to facilitate actual problem solving.

Here is a typical example. The wife wants the husband to take out the trash. In her childhood family, the man took out the trash, and it was a part of how he showed he cared for his wife. When her husband fails to take out the trash, she feels hurt and rejected. Perhaps she is unaware of these feelings, or perhaps she is afraid or ashamed to reveal them, but she does get hurt and then angry when he does not take out the trash.

In the husband's childhood family, perhaps the woman took out the trash, or perhaps there was a constant battle over the trash and the loser had to take it out. When his wife asks him to take it out, he feels pressured and threatened, and he experiences the request as an unreasonable demand, demeaning of his role in the family. However, he is also unaware or afraid or ashamed of these feelings, and he just feels angry.

How does this situation affect their communication? She, feeling hurt and let down, says, "Why didn't you take out the trash?" He, feeling nagged by this unanswerable question, says, "I didn't see it." She, feeling frustrated and further enraged at this evasion of her real message, shouts, "Are you blind? It's right by the back door where you left it all week!" He, feeling attacked, screams, "Are you crippled? Take it out yourself!" It goes on. She yells, "You never help, you worthless bum," and he returns, "Shut up, you bitch," or worse, "There's no need to get so irrational." You can see they won't be able to resolve the conflict this way.

Couples therapy involves techniques to promote effective communication to replace the blaming and shouting that characterize this couple. Couples therapists may focus on the precise nature of the problem and its accompanying experience. In therapy, the wife may cry, "He never contributes. He never helps." The therapist tries to narrow this blanket condemnation down to a specific example of nonhelping. Perhaps the wife remembers that he didn't take out the trash the night before. The therapist tries to elicit her version of what happened and how she experienced it: What was she thinking and feeling at each point? Her underlying feelings of hurt and rejection may be brought out. The therapist elicits the husband's version and his experience, with his underlying feelings of hurt and criticism. The spouses are usually surprised to learn what the other one really thought and was trying, however indirectly, to say. They may be surprised to discover that each one feels hurt and misunderstood. The therapist's next task may be to teach or elicit alternative ways of communicating about this issue so that productive problem solving can take place.

Much of couples therapy involves teaching the couple social skills. The therapist tries to model clear, direct, nonjudgmental, effective communication when talking to the couple and may also employ specific techniques to teach communication skills. One such technique is sometimes called mirroring. The husband is asked to tell his version of a conflict, and the wife is directed to listen carefully. She is then asked to say as precisely as possible what she heard her spouse say. He is asked if she got what he was trying to say and, if not, to say it again. It is surprising how frequently spouses cannot do this task. Even when they are given the specific assignment of listening carefully so they can repeat the message, they get caught up in thinking of a defense to what the spouse is saying or hear an attack when none is intended or simply are unable to hear anything other than their own projections or expectations. In other cases, the communicating spouses do not say clearly what they want to say. If they can be made aware of the misunderstanding, they may be able to restate or explain what they want and gradually learn to communicate more directly and clearly.

When a couple's communication skills are improved by these methods, they are able to solve their problems on their own with their new ways of communicating. Sometimes the therapist must continue to help the couple. Even with clear and honest communication, some conflicts are difficult to resolve. There may be profound differences in sexual desire or values about religion or child rearing. Compromises can be negotiated or tolerance for each other's differences can be taught.

Finally, some couples decide to divorce when the nature of their conflict is clarified. Whether marital therapists should always work to save a marriage or accept divorce as a reasonable solution is a controversy we will not address here. Also, it should be unnecessary to note that the principles of marital therapy apply to all intimate couples, married or not, heterosexual or not.

Psychodynamic Couples Therapies

Although most couples therapists work to improve communication and reduce blame and coercion (Greenberg & Johnson, 1988), they approach this in different ways. Therapists influenced by psychoanalytic theory try to help couples clarify the projections and expectations each partner is placing on the other, which have been carried forward from early childhood experiences. It is believed that individuals often choose as partners people who unconsciously fit into their dynamics from childhood: they tend to recapitulate their childhoods in one way or the other. Psychoanalytic therapists believe that these projections must be explored and clarified in order to facilitate positive, proactive communication.

A variant of psychodynamic theory—collaborative couples therapy (Wile, 2002)—takes a different tack. Wile believes that individuals act dysfunctionally with their spouses because they do not feel entitled to their feelings. Although this may have originated in childhood, it is very much a here-and-now experience. For instance, a husband may not feel entitled to feeling angry about his wife being so busy at work that she does not spend as much time with him as she used to. Not feeling entitled to the anger, the feelings may either leak out in hidden, passive ways, or come out in rigid, defensive explosions. Even individuals who, on the surface, are apparently acting as if they feel entitled to their feelings, by constantly expressing anger in a "definite" tone of voice at high volume, are likely experiencing self-disapproval at some level, which is why their expressions of anger seem rigid and exaggerated. Wile's goal is to help each partner reduce self-criticism and come to accept his or her own and each others' feelings. When this occurs, couples are able to "have" their feelings in more functional ways and communicate more effectively. Basically, Wile tries to get each partner to be on the other partner's side, and when this happens, there is no need to "negotiate" compromises, because compromises will often spontaneously occur. Wile's primary therapeutic tool is to model and coach effective communication so that each partner can "find his or her voice" in a way that reaches out to rather than turns off the partner.

Behavioral and Cognitive Therapies for Couples

Behavioral and cognitive methods have been adapted for use with couples, resulting in a number of different approaches.

Behavioral Couples Counseling

Behavioral couples counseling (Jacobson & Margolin, 1979) has two aims: to reduce or eliminate problem behaviors and to increase positive and effective behaviors. Usually, the goal of increasing positive behaviors is considered first. Partners are asked to list all the positive behaviors they would like the other person to perform. Then the partners work on increasing the frequency of these behaviors. For instance, they may have ***caring days:*** one spouse tries to maximize the positive experience of the other, and spouses are encouraged to surprise one another with positive experiences.

A key part of this is training and encouraging partners to show their appreciation for the positive behaviors of the other. In addition, the partners monitor the rates of pleasing events and keep records of daily levels of satisfaction.

The second part of counseling is aimed at reducing problems. This is attacked by teaching the partners effective problem solving. Problem solving breaks down into two phases: problem definition and problem resolution. To define their problems, clients are taught to state their complaints in brief, specific, nonblaming ways. They are also taught to state their feelings, to admit their own role in the problem, and to paraphrase the other person's viewpoint, even if it is not consistent with their own. An example of an effective problem definition, which includes a statement of feelings, is "When you let a week go by without initiating sex, I feel rejected" (Jacobson & Margolin, 1979, p. 230).

To resolve problems, clients are encouraged first to brainstorm, to come up with as many possible solutions as they can. They are to suspend judgment of the various options until as many have been generated as possible. Then they consider and evaluate each option. Finally, they are taught to negotiate and compromise until a solution is arrived at. This solution is recorded in writing.

Sometimes a contract is included. A contract may be set up with specific reinforcers or consequences associated with the performance or nonperformance of the behaviors involved. Thus, if one partner wants more sex and the other wants more affection, the provision of these may be made contingent on the performance of other behaviors that each desires in the other person, such as taking out the trash or not nagging so much. However, there is some controversy over the use of contracts and reward contingencies with couples problems (Christensen, 1983), and they are not used in all cases.

A general goal of the behavioral approach is to teach these problem-solving skills so that the couple can use them on their own. Couples are encouraged to set aside certain specified times to engage in problem solving and to refrain from attempting problem solving when they are in the midst of an emotional conflict.

Integrative Behavioral Couple Therapy (IBCT)

Christensen, Jacobson, and Babcock (1995) describe an integrative approach to behavioral couples therapy in which the idea of acceptance, typically found in humanistic and psychodynamic approaches, is incorporated along with behavioral techniques. Integrative Behavioral Couple Therapy (IBCT) is one of the radical behavior therapies, discussed in chapter 10. Like those therapies, it emphasizes acceptance. It is trying to change unacceptable feelings and thoughts that leads to problematic behavior in individuals, and trying to change one's partner is seen as the source of a couple's difficulties. Acceptance involves "letting go of the struggle" to change one's partner. Acceptance also encourages couples to use their problems as opportunities for developing a closer relationship, rather than to try to "solve" or avoid the problems.

IBCT develops individualized strategies for each couple based on a functional analysis (see chapter 10) of their attempts to communicate and attain intimacy within the therapy session, rather than assuming, as does traditional couples therapy, that there are universal criteria for good and bad communication in marriage. IBCT attempts to promote improved behaviors by creating intimacy-enhancing experiences in the therapy sessions and by ensuring that natural rather than arbitrary reinforcers follow when these behaviors occur.

There are four categories of acceptance-focused interventions in IBCT. In "empathic joining around the problem," methods to promote compassion and empathy toward the partner's formerly unacceptable behavior are used. In interventions that "turn the problem into an 'it'," couples are encouraged to join together against the problem and to view it as something outside of themselves about which to commiserate. Third, tolerance-building techniques are designed to prepare couples for the inevitable conflicts in their relationship and to desensitize them to conflict. Finally, self-care techniques teach people how to take better care of themselves so they are less dependent on their partners for giving them what they want.

For example, a couple battling over whose fault it is that they "never talk anymore" might be treated in the following way. Instead of arguing about whether the husband withdraws or the wife nags (a typical pattern addressed in traditional marital therapies), IBCT would encourage acceptance and focus on examples of intimate communication in the session. The couple might be encouraged to empathize with each other about how sad they are and how they miss their old conversations. "Not talking" is seen as something that has happened to them, not as something one person does or does not do to the other. The therapist may use the tolerance-building technique of pointing out the positive aspects of not talking. Of course, all the while, the couple actually *are* talking in the therapy session, and the therapist ensures that the natural reinforcer of feeling closer will increase the likelihood of their engaging in more talk outside the session.

Cognitive Approaches

Many behavioral approaches have increasingly incorporated cognitive techniques. Cognitive-behavioral couples therapy might include many of the previously mentioned exercises but will also help members of the couple identify and challenge dysfunctional cognitions and expectations. Cognitive approaches to couples therapy (e.g., Dattilio & Padesky, 1990) utilize many of the same cognitive challenging techniques discussed in chapter 11. There are three basic aspects to cognitive therapy with couples. First, the cognitive therapist tries to modify unrealistic expectations in the relationship. Second, the cognitive therapist tries to modify the making of faulty attributions to one another (e.g., "you don't *really* care for me"). Third, partners are taught procedures, such as the behavioral ones we have previously discussed, to avoid destructive interactions.

Experiential-Humanistic Approaches

The experiential-humanistic approach of Greenberg and Johnson (1988) focuses on the elicitation and expression of clients' subjective experience, particularly what they call "primary emotions." They believe that members of couples act defensively toward one another because they don't feel safe. The emotions they do feel and express are secondary emotional reactions, that is, defensive emotional reactions. For instance, a partner who frequently gets angry because he feels his spouse is not paying enough attention to him is using anger as a kind of defensive reaction to try to protect himself. Underneath the anger is a more primary emotion, such as fear or vulnerability. The goal of emotionally focused therapy is to help each member of the couple access these more primary emotions. Accessing primary emotion changes the nature of the couple's interaction. When the husband is able to express vulnerability and acknowledge how much he wants and needs his partner in a nondemanding, nondefensive way, the partner finds it easier to open up and share her primary emotions. Eventually, better collaborative communication is facilitated.

Another experiential-humanistic approach is that of Relationship Enhancement (Guerney, 1984). It is derived from client-centered therapy and is not only a form of therapy but is also a form of training that can be used to prevent problems in the first place. It can be used for a variety of relationships, such as for parents and children or for groups of individuals, and is not limited to couples. Some of the goals of Relationship Enhancement are: to help individuals understand their emotions, wishes, goals, and conflicts better; to help them learn how to better understand others; and to help them learn how to understand and resolve problems between themselves and others better. Relationship Enhancement is essentially a skills training approach and is therefore an integration of client-centered and behavioral ideas. Couples are taught the skills of effective expression, such as learning to show understanding for the other before immediately firing off a response. They are also taught the skill of being empathic, which includes learning how to listen intently, sense and "absorb" the other's mood, concentrate on the other's internal world, put oneself in the other's place, and then express one's tentative understanding in a functional manner. Along with these and other skills, couples are also taught problem-solving skills, in a manner similar to behavioral couples counseling.

Family Therapy

Most forms of family therapy view the family as a system. A ***system*** is a pattern of interrelationships among elements, such that each element of the system both determines and is determined by the other elements in the system. The behavior of any part of a system reflects the overall organization of the system and feeds back into the system itself. Furthermore, systems have often been thought to evolve toward a state of equilibrium, or "homeostatic balance." However, with respect to family systems, many theorists now question this notion. They question it because healthy families are not static. Although they maintain some sense of coherence, healthy families continue to evolve as they are confronted with each new developmental challenge: forming a marital unit, having one or more children, nurturing the children through the various stages of child development, the children growing up and leaving home, and finally the couple growing old together. In fact, it is precisely the capacity of a family to grow and change that could be considered the mark of a healthy family.

From a systems view, problems of individuals are seen, in part at least, as reflecting some kind of malfunction in the whole system. If a system is threatened, it may become closed and try to maintain a static sense of equilibrium. Thus, if a problem between husband and wife threatens to destroy a whole family system, a child may develop either a psychological or physical problem as a way of restoring balance. This is not consciously done by the child but rather is a response to the pressures and strains in the family system itself. The child's developing a problem may deflect the couple's attention from their problems and thereby serve to restabilize the system, at least to some degree.

Some family systems theorists believe that some families "need" their problems. If a therapist works only with the individual with the problem, say, the child who is acting dysfunctionally at school, this may not help. In fact, as the child gets better, someone else in the family may begin to develop a problem. One of our colleagues worked for some time with a family in which the members "rotated" problems. The father would periodically drink heavily, the daughter would periodically become rebellious and do things such as ditch school, and the mother would periodically become depressed. When the father was drinking heavily, the mother and the daughter would be problem-free. If, through therapy, the father began to reduce his drinking, either the mother or the daughter would begin to have a problem. When that problem abated, another member of the family would develop a problem. This went on for quite a while until the family system itself finally changed. The goal of family therapy, therefore, ultimately becomes that of reorganizing the family system so that it does not "need" a problem.

Returning to our example at the start of this chapter, it is possible that any one (or all) of the problems in this family represent a systems problem in the whole family.

The couple problem may be some subtle reflection of stresses and strains in the whole family system itself. The 3-year-old child's problems may similarly reflect a subtle dynamic in the family system itself. Family therapists would want to work with the whole family in this case to help fix things. Many family therapists believe that to work only with the individuals involved (say, the child) is useless, or worse than useless. They argue that the person who comes to therapy (again, perhaps the child) is merely the identified patient when the real patient is the entire family.

There are many different approaches to family therapy. Many of them correspond to each of the major schools of therapy we have covered previously in this text. Because they are largely extensions of the ideas and principles used in individual contexts, we will not cover these approaches, but instead focus on approaches that have made further contributions to the understanding and treatment of behavioral difficulties.

Approaches to family therapy vary along a dimension from those that, while systems-oriented, also focus on individual dynamics and processes to those that are more purely systemic. We shall first consider Murray Bowen's approach, which is systemic but also includes many psychodynamic ideas. Next we shall consider the views of Virginia Satir, which similarly are systemic but include many ideas from experiential-humanistic theory. Then we shall consider approaches that are more purely systemic: Minuchin's Structural approach and the strategic and solution-focused approaches of Milton Erickson, Jay Haley and Cloe Madanes, Paul Watzlawick, and Steven de Shazer.

Murray Bowen and Personal Differentiation

For Murray Bowen (1978), who was one of the first to designate his approach a family systems approach, the key issue in psychopathology is the degree of personal differentiation of each person from his or her ***family of origin***, that is, the family within which he or she was raised. Therefore, even though Bowen is a systems theorist, his approach has also been heavily influenced by psychoanalysis. For Bowen, ***differentiation*** consists of the ability to remain emotionally controlled while in the context of one's family and the ability to have a clear sense of one's own values, beliefs, and reactions separate from others. A truly differentiated person is able to think objectively about a situation and not be overwhelmed by emotion and to assert and own his values and beliefs without attacking or dismissing the values and beliefs of others.

For most people, there are areas in their relationships to their families where they remain undifferentiated. People remain ***fused*** or emotionally entangled with their families in various ways. The degree of lack of differentiation is an index of the individual's emotional disturbance. Bowen believes in a ***multigenerational transmission process*** for lack of differentiation. Lack of differentiation in the parents is transmitted to the children. An anxious mother who is not sufficiently differentiated herself, for instance, will project her anxiety onto a child. Bowen argues that this process may lead to progressively lower levels of differentiation generation by generation, ultimately resulting in the production of a psychotic child.

Lack of differentiation leads either to an inability to keep oneself separate from another or to a pathological, defensive separateness. Unresolved attachments to parents may be "resolved" by cutting off emotions. Thus, someone may yearn for emotional closeness, but defend against it. Either an inability to maintain separateness or a defensive separateness will lead to an unstable situation with a spouse. You will either be demanding things you feel you are not getting from your spouse or you will feel demands from your spouse.

In order to deal with the tension and instability, couples usually form a triangle with a third person. This means that a third person is drawn into the emotional system in order to provide a kind of stability. For instance, a wife who cannot feel close to her husband may devote herself to her child and distance herself from her husband. In states of relative calm, most triangles include two members who are relatively close to one another and one member who is an outsider, as in our example of the wife and child. ***Triangulation*** can occur because of an intergenerational instability. For instance, a son who has been overly close to his mother may marry in order to create some distance between himself and her. In states of high tension, more and more people may be included in triangles. Other siblings, relatives, and even neighbors may be included. Thus, a husband and wife who have been unable to deal with their tension by including one child may include more children. There may be a husband-wife-son triangle and a husband-wife-daughter triangle and perhaps even a wife-daughter-son triangle. One example of including members outside the family in a triangle is the extramarital affair.

Even though Bowen believes that fusion and lack of differentiation are passed down through generations and that ultimately an individual's problems have to do with lack of differentiation from the family of origin, Bowen does not necessarily work with the whole family. He believes the therapist can work with individual members of the family, but he prefers to work with the marital subsystem. One technique Bowen uses is constructing a ***genogram*** of the family. This is a diagram that shows the relationships of the husband and wife to their families of origin. Relationships are diagrammed in terms of fusion and emotional cutoff. Bowen may show the genogram to the family as a way of helping them gain insight into their difficulties.

The primary goal of Bowen's family therapy is to develop the autonomy of each family member. Part of this process is helping the spouses to become aware of how their relationships to their families of origin affect their relationships to each other and to their children. Thus, Bowen, values insight as a growth-producing mechanism. Bowen attempts to provide an atmosphere in which such learning can occur, modeling differentiation himself. For instance, husband and wife will attempt to triangle Bowen into their problems by trying to get him to take sides in an argument. Bowen attempts to avoid this by making sure that any statements he makes are identified as his own and by not being judgmental.

Bowen also tries to model and teach observation of the family system. In other words, he attempts to model separating objective observation of what is going on from overly subjective emotional reactions. His belief is that emotional reactions of anger, blame, sadness, anxiety, and so forth result from lack of differentiation. Therefore, by keeping the emotional climate of therapy toned down and by encouraging observation, he is facilitating differentiation. This approach differs from Satir's emphasis on feelings.

Bowen provides an atmosphere that facilitates differentiation also by having each spouse talk to him rather than to each other. For example, as the husband talks to Bowen, the wife listens. Afterward, Bowen may ask the wife for her reactions to what she heard. Bowen might then ask the husband for his reactions. This mechanism facilitates differentiation because it keeps the spouses from falling into old, undifferentiated patterns of argument, blame, criticism, and so forth, in which emotions run high.

It puts one spouse in the role of observer as the other talks. Again, Bowen differs from Satir, who encourages spouses to talk to each other.

Finally, Bowenian therapists encourage husband and wife to go back to their families of origin and confront them. They help coach the husband and wife so that they can interact with their families in different, more productive ways than before. This allows the husband and wife to engage in experiential learning in order to develop greater differentiation.

Virginia Satir and Dysfunctional Communication

Satir (1967) assumed that dysfunctional communication is a large part of families' problems. Dysfunctional communication results from the way the marital partners were raised as children and from their unrealistic, unspoken expectations of what the spouse will do for them.

Satir believed that every individual grows up with unspoken assumptions and rules learned from parents about the way families should work and how family life should run. In disturbed families, the spouses grew up with low self-esteem and chose their marital partners in the hope that the partner would supply the esteem they lack. Of course, a partner cannot do that, so these insecure people are doomed to disappointment. Furthermore, they tend to view differences with a partner as threats, as evidence that the other does not love them. However, differences are inevitable, because they come from different families with different unspoken rules. Since the rules are unspoken, disagreements about them are difficult to resolve. All of this leads to severely disturbed communication and disturbed family functioning.

Let us look at a typical case. The wife comes from a large family in which the men waited on the women. Since it was a large family, one had to be assertive and expressive to gain attention. The husband is an only child from a family in which the women waited on the men, and the men were quiet and unexpressive. When the couple first met, they were immediately attracted to one another. He, being quiet and unassertive, saw her as a fascinating, lively, mysterious creature who would love him and take care of him. She saw him as a strong, stable person who would love her and take care of her (wait on her). As the inevitable disappointment sets in, she comes to see him as a boring stick-in-the-mud, and he comes to see her as irrational, bossy, and overemotional. (It is not uncommon that the quality in a spouse that most aggravates a partner is the very quality that first attracted the partner.)

In addition to the disappointment of unrealistic expectations, this couple's low self-esteem makes them perceive differences between them as threatening to their relationship. When the husband does not talk to her or wait on her, the wife takes it as evidence that he does not love her. When she talks all the time and fails to wait on him, the husband concludes the same thing. Both their lack of confidence and the fact that they may not even be aware of their unspoken rules about family life prohibit them from discussing these rules. They are in pain, but they cannot talk about that, either. Their younger child develops symptoms: poor grades and noncompliance. The child's problems keep the family from falling apart and give the parents an issue they can agree to focus on. It is the child's symptoms that bring the family into therapy.

In weekly family therapy sessions, Satir tried to make the couple aware of all these processes. She took a family history from each spouse and pointed out how differently they were raised. She tried to elicit their unspoken assumptions and their feelings about behavior that differs from these assumptions. She helped them communicate more clearly and directly by reflecting their feelings and raising their intended meanings. She might have asked the clients to mirror one another's statements. Satir also interpreted the family's behavior as it occurred in front of her. Frequently, when the parents start to talk about a meaningful issue, the child with problems engages in distracting or symptomatic behavior. She may break things, start talking loudly about something else, twitch and squirm hyperactively, or throw a temper tantrum. Satir interpreted this behavior as the child's attempt to protect the parents from having to deal with the pain of their low self-esteem and their marital disappointments. The role of the child's symptoms in the family can thus be made clear to all.

Satir described five roles or basic modes of communication in families: placating, blaming, super reasonable, irrelevant, and congruent. In this disturbed family, the father is always super reasonable, never showing his true feelings; the mother placates him all the time, never showing her true feelings; the older child blames everything on everyone else; and the symptomatic child responds with irrelevant annoying habits and silly talk. Only congruent communication—messages that reflect a person's genuine feelings and intentions—can help solve family conflict. Satir tries to model and teach congruent communication.

Once the family has gained insight into the role the child's symptomatic behavior is playing in the family, the behavior is useless to protect the parents or to maintain family homeostasis, and it will be given up. In this respect, Satir is one family therapist who values the acquisition of insight. In addition, as the parents learn to communicate more effectively, their sense of competence and feelings of esteem improve. They are better able to tolerate each other's differences and to explore the meaning of those differences. The child learns a new role in the family, and they all learn communications and problem-solving skills. The entire family system functions better.

One significant difference between Satir's approach and other family approaches that emphasize communication is that Satir places a greater emphasis on feelings. Communication is not merely the communication of ideas and perspectives, but of feelings. Therefore, in addition to gaining access to unspoken family rules and assumptions, her approach focuses on becoming more aware of feelings, which are the intended meanings of most messages.

Minuchin and the Structural Approach

Salvador Minuchin's (1974) therapy, called ***structural family therapy***, is based on a view of the family as a hierarchically organized system. That means that the system has various levels and subsystems. For instance, there is the spousal subsystem (husband and wife relating to one another), the parental subsystem (husband and wife relating to one another in terms of the children and relating to the children), and a sibling subsystem. There may be other subsystems, such as ones that include grandparents or in-laws or subsystems organized by gender (female and male subsystems). These subsystems overlap, interact, and separate as the family goes about its daily functioning.

What goes wrong in disturbed families has to do with the characteristics of the subsystems. Difficulties can develop around boundary problems. In a well-organized family, there are clear, but not rigid, boundaries between various subsystems. For instance, there is a clear distinction between the parental and the child subsystems. In a disturbed family, that distinction may be blurred, as in a family in which there is an alliance of a mother and child against a father, or in totally child-focused families, in which the spouses have no relationship, or in immature families, in which no one takes the role of parents or where children have too much authority. In a well-organized family, the sibling subsystem is organized in a hierarchical manner appropriate to age, that is, children are given responsibilities and privileges commensurate with age. In a poorly organized family, older children may be treated like younger children, or younger children may be given responsibilities and privileges more appropriate to older children. In families with parental substance abuse, the children may be "parentified" and take on responsible roles beyond their capacity. In the well-organized system, distinctions are not too rigidly drawn. For instance, the parental subsystem is not so rigid that parents always act like parents and always put themselves in the role of authority.

There are two major types of dysfunctional family systems. In the ***disengaged family***, the subsystem boundaries are excessively rigid, and family members are disconnected from one another. This type of family is conducive to the development of antisocial personality in children. In the ***enmeshed family***, the boundaries are weak or unstable, and individuality is difficult to maintain. A disorder typical of this type of family is anorexia, which Minuchin sees as an attempt to assert autonomy and gain control over the self.

Minuchin's goal is to help families restructure their subsystems and to establish appropriate boundaries. He uses a variety of methods and takes an active and directive part in the therapeutic process. Some compare him to a freedom fighter trying to liberate the family from its destructive rules and roles. He learns the family's language and rules and joins the family system for a while. Once the therapist joins the family, it is a different system already. Minuchin may take sides in family arguments if he perceives that a family member has no appropriate allies. Sometimes he speaks for family members, putting their unspoken thoughts into words. He tries to provoke weak couples into strengthening their spousal subsystem. He may define a child as inappropriately parental and, by doing so, challenge the parents to ally with each other and to exert their authority. Minuchin directs family members to behave certain ways in homework assignments. He might put a weak father in charge of a symptomatic son for a week and tell the overcontrolling mother not to interfere. He sometimes exaggerates family patterns, for instance, by yelling in a family that yells too much.

One interesting aspect of Minuchin's method is his use of the family's seating arrangement in therapy sessions. He arranges the room so that family members have a choice of where to sit as they enter the room for the first session. How they sit is often a gauge of how the family interacts. Minuchin will actively rearrange seating to change the interaction. For instance, if overprotective mother and dysfunctional son sit together and father sits off to the side, son and father may be made to sit next to one another.

Strategic and Solution-Focused Approaches

In the early 1960s, the Mental Research Institute in Palo Alto, California, was a hotbed of innovation. Some of the biggest names in family therapy were there, including Virginia Satir, Don Jackson (whom we do not discuss here), Jay Haley, and Paul Watzlawick (two of the foremost strategic therapists). Collectively, their approach was known as the "communications" approach. From that base, Satir went off to develop her own communication approach, and Haley and Watzlawick went off to develop their "strategic" approaches. From them, as well as from others, developed the more recent "solution-focused" approaches, such as that of Steven de Shazer, which has much in common with strategic approaches.

Another influential form of strategic therapy was developed in Milan, Italy (Selvini Palazzoli, Cecchin, Prata, & Boscola, 1978). What is common to all of these approaches is the goal to design a strategy to change the problem behavior in either a family or an individual client. The goal of therapy is to remedy the problem behavior, not to gain insight, get in touch with feelings, assume responsibility, or challenge dysfunctional cognitions. Watzlawick (1978) argues that cognitive insight is not only therapeutically useless, but may be counterproductive. Thus, each intervention is individually tailored to a particular client's or family's problem. Strategic and solution-focused therapists are content to remove the problem behavior or symptom, without worrying about the dynamics supposedly underlying them. In this regard, these approaches are similar to behavior therapy.

Another important commonality is that the approaches all derive much of their therapeutic strategy from the work of Milton Erickson. Although some therapists think that Erickson's influence equals Freud's (Dowd & Milne, 1986), he is not well known among nonprofessionals. We will consider the work of three "teams" of modern strategic and solution-focused therapists: Jay Haley and his colleague Cloe Madanes (Haley, 1976; Madanes, 1984), Paul Watzlawick and his colleagues (Watzlawick, Weakland, & Fisch, 1974), and Steven de Shazer (1985). All are similar (though not identical) in their therapeutic strategies, but they differ most in their theories of psychopathology and personality and all draw on Erickson's work. Therefore, before we discuss strategic approaches, we will introduce Erickson's work.

Milton Erickson

We shall use a story to introduce Milton Erickson's work (Feldman, 1985; see also our discussion of him in chapter 12). A woman spent some time studying with him and then returned to her home city. She subsequently wrote Erickson complaining about her lack of results in trying to work the way he did. In the same letter, she incidentally asked for a recipe for cinnamon pie, which she had had at his home. In his reply Erickson did not address her concerns about her work. Instead, he merely gave her the recipe for cinnamon pie, with the comment, "Of course, every good cook must adjust the seasoning to suit their own particular taste" (Dammann, 1980, p. 200).

This story illustrates the indirect way Erickson communicated his messages. The woman was not directly told, "You need to adapt what you learned from me to your personal style," but the message was implied. Erickson was one of the most colorful therapists. The things he did were often startling, uncommon, and delightful. Perhaps what is most impressive about his work is that he was a pioneer. Now, years after his death (in 1980), he has become a highly influential figure. Yet, while he was alive, he worked in relative obscurity, engaging in a kind of therapy that fit no models popular at the time, for it was not Freudian, client-centered, or behavioral.

Erickson did not believe in the importance of insight or awareness for inducing personality change. Instead, he believed that the unconscious was a source of wisdom, and his therapy was designed to draw on that. In addition, Erickson believed that major change could be induced by first inducing smaller changes. Like a snowball rolling downhill, a small change could change the overall system of the personality or the family for the better.

Erickson is primarily known as a hypnotist, and that was one of his major tools. He believed that all therapy worked by suggestion. However, he devised many techniques to utilize the power of suggestion without the use of hypnosis. ***Paradoxical interventions*** are one example. Paradoxical interventions include ***reframing*** (or, "positive connotation") and *prescribing the symptom.*

Reframing is reinterpreting a behavior that a client sees as pathological in a positive way. For instance, de Shazer (1985) relates the case of a young woman whose problem was that she was unable to speak up around her fiancé. Instead of treating this as a problem, the therapist congratulated her on having learned the most important lesson in communication—how to listen. Her perception of her silence as pathological was reframed as something positive. In addition, she was told that she now had to learn another skill. She had to pay attention to her fiancé and try to detect when he was ready to listen.

With prescribing the symptom, the therapist instructs the client to perform the very symptomatic behavior the client is trying to eliminate, although not necessarily exactly as it occurs spontaneously. In one of Erickson's most well-known cases, a husband and wife who both wet the bed were instructed to deliberately wet the bed each night before they went to bed. The bedwetting soon stopped. Watzlawick (1985) relates the case of a man who was constantly arguing with his wife. He was instructed to go out on the weekend and pick arguments with others. After trying to follow this instruction, he stopped arguing with his wife.

While reframing and symptom prescription are perhaps the best known Ericksonian interventions, there are others, such as to give the client an apparent choice, but actually, the message left no choice. In addition, the message carried an indirect suggestion that the client would stop exhibiting the symptom. For instance, Erickson might say, "When are you going to stop the arguing—on Wednesday or on Thursday?" Such a message apparently presents the client with a choice, but takes for granted that the client will stop exhibiting the symptom.

Another Ericksonian technique was the use of ***teaching stories***, stories that convey a message metaphorically. Cameron-Bandler (1978) used this to treat a young man for premature ejaculation. First, the man was told that nothing could be done about his problem. Later, he was placed in a hypnotic trance and told a story. The essence of the story was that one could go on a "vacation" in one of two ways: one could either rush to the destination or take the slow route, enjoying the sights along the way. The message implied should be clear, and this teaching story appeared to cure the young man's difficulties.

An example of Erickson's belief that a small change could lead to much larger changes is given in Feldman (1985). The client was a depressed, angry woman who complained of hating Phoenix but was reluctant to go on a vacation. While she was in a hypnotic trance, Erickson suggested to her that while on vacation, she would be curious about seeing an unexpected "flash of color." This mobilized her to look for the unexpected, and of course, she did eventually see an unexpected flash of color in the form of a redheaded woodpecker flying past a tree. After seeing this, she continued to search for "color" in her life, and she eventually became someone who enjoyed traveling and was not depressed.

Erickson believed that one could use a client's symptom as part of the solution to his problem. In other words, instead of working against the client's symptom, he worked with it and turned it to the client's favor. Actually, this is the strategy that underlies his other techniques, such as reframing and paradoxical intervention. However, we will give an example in which the technique is used directly. A hospitalized patient believed himself to be Jesus. Many therapists would presume the belief is a defense and try to remove it by helping the client acquire insight into its defensive nature. These therapists would be working against the symptom. Erickson's approach was to mobilize the symptom positively. He said to the man, "I understand that you have experience as a carpenter." Thus, part of the symptom of believing himself to be Jesus was used therapeutically. Erickson was able to get the client involved in doing productive work, thereby lessening the need for the symptom in the first place.

Jay Haley and Cloe Madanes

For Jay Haley, all behavior is communication. Humans cannot not communicate. Even remaining silent conveys a message: "I don't want to talk." Communication occurs on more than one level at once. For instance, if you ask someone for advice, she may answer by saying "You should do so and so." What she suggests you do is the content of the communication. However, she has also agreed with your definition of the relationship as one in which you are helpless and she acts as the wise helper. For Haley, in addition to conveying content, communication serves to define a relationship in terms of who has power. He sees power, "who's in charge," as a basic issue in all human relationships.

Haley analyzes interpersonal relationships in terms of power arrangements and sees psychological symptoms as metaphorical communications through which the power relationships in a family system are expressed. For instance, a wife who wishes her husband to stay home with her may develop anxiety attacks. She is not consciously in control of the anxiety attacks, but at the same time, her husband must stay home in case she has one. Therefore, the message "Stay home with me" is conveyed metaphorically in the symptom of the attacks, and the symptom also serves the purpose of exerting power over the husband.

In a family system, a pathological behavior is some metaphorical communication about the family. For Haley, as well as for Watzlawick, the question of why pathological behavior occurs is not as productive as the question of what purpose it serves. Haley and many other theorists adopt a "functionalist" view, that is, they believe that pathological behaviors serve functions in the family (Bogdan, 1986). The functions are unconsciously generated; families are largely unaware of how the symptoms function in the family.

While Haley sees the process of symptom formation as largely unconscious, he does not believe that insight and awareness are important therapeutic goals. Instead, he advocates direct manipulation of behavior as it functions within the family system. The therapist must take charge and intervene in the family in such a way as to change the dysfunctional family system. Haley, Madanes, and others have developed a large set of techniques to apply to individual cases.

Before we describe the strategies, we wish to mention how such strategies are arrived at. First, these therapists often work with a one-way mirror. One therapist sees the family, while a group of other therapists observe through a one-way mirror. The intervention strategy used is devised by the whole team. In designing a strategy, Haley (1985) points out that great care must be taken to design a strategy that the clients will comply with. Therefore, as with many of the other therapeutic interventions described in this book, it takes a great deal of skill to successfully design a strategic intervention that both will be followed by the clients and will be effective. So, if you're having problems with your husband or wife, or children, or parents, it would be better for you to try something besides paradoxical interventions or other strategies discussed here.

One set of strategies used by these therapists involves restructuring the family. In one form of restructuring, other members of the family are asked to share the symptom. For example, one family came to therapy because the middle daughter was exhibiting problem behavior. Her siblings were "model" children. The family was told that it was unfair that the middle daughter carry the burden of being the troublemaker for the whole family. The family appeared to need a troublemaker, but the burden should be shared. Each of the other children was given the assignment of being the troublemaker for a period of time. This eliminated the middle daughter's problem behavior (Madanes, 1985).

In another type of restructuring, the normal power structure in the family is reversed. If a parent is acting irresponsibly, a child may be put in charge of that parent or of that parent's happiness. In one case, a mother was accused of physically abusing her children, who were generally unruly and uncooperative. One of the most uncooperative children (who, among other things, set fires) was put in charge of making his mother's life easier. This appeared to bring out the love and caring the child felt for the mother, and her abuse of the children stopped, as did the son's disruptive behavior (Madanes, 1984).

These therapists also use reframing and paradoxical interventions. For example, a young adult male was gambling so much he was seriously in debt and was draining the family funds (Madanes, 1987). His gambling was being supported by his mother and aunt, who would give him money to help get him out of debt. The therapist, rather than telling him to stop gambling, instructed him to gamble. However, the structure under which he gambled was altered. His mother and aunt had to go with him to the racetrack, tell him which horses to bet on, and then stand in line with him while he placed his bets, warding off any friends or acquaintances that might approach. In addition, the family was to hold nightly poker games in which the mother and aunt were to coach the young man on how to play. Though the mother and aunt did not know anything about gambling, they enthusiastically agreed to learn so they could play their parts. After rehearsing these procedures in therapy sessions, the young man disgustedly told the therapist that she did not know anything about gambling, but that it did not matter, because he was going to give up gambling, get a job, and pay his debts anyway. This is what he proceeded to do.

In the paradoxical intervention in the gambler's case, the behavior prescribed differed quite a bit from the spontaneous symptom. In some cases, the change is more subtle. For instance, if a husband and wife tend to argue in one room in their home, they will be instructed to argue deliberately, but in a different room. Or the timing of the arguments might be changed. The husband and wife might be instructed to set aside 20 minutes each day to argue.

Related to the use of paradox is an intervention in which the therapist talks about all the possible negative things that might occur if the problem is solved. The therapist implies that the family could not tolerate the elimination of the problem or even that it would be disastrous for the family to eliminate the problem and that they are at the best level of adjustment they can hope for. This intervention is thought to work by mobilizing the family's resistance. In order to prove the therapist wrong, they must change for the better (see box 13.1).

Paul Watzlawick and Constructivism

Paul Watzlawick is one of the foremost spokespersons for the viewpoint of ***constructivism*** (Watzlawick, 1984; see also chapters 11 and 15). Briefly put, constructivism holds that there is no "one true objective reality"; rather, each individual constructs his own reality and there are, therefore, multiple possible constructions of reality. Individuals' concepts of reality are like maps. Maps are representations of reality, but no map reproduces reality. Furthermore, different maps of the same territory can be drawn, and each may be useful in its own way. A geological map of an area will not look identical to a road map.

Does this mean that any construction of reality is equally acceptable? No. While we might not be able to say that any one view is the true one, we can say that some constructions work better than others. Watzlawick (1984) gives the example of a boat captain navigating a channel at night. There may be multiple "correct" routes that will get him through the channel. However, there are also clearly wrong routes that will lead to shipwreck. Watzlawick argues that the same is true of people's views of their world. For Watzlawick, therefore, we can never talk about the validity of an idea about reality, we can only talk about its viability, that is, is the idea helpful and useful?

Constructivism is a very popular notion in the area of family therapy at the present time. In general, constructivism leads to the idea that how we use language shapes and defines our realities. Therefore, if we can shift how we talk and think about our realities, those realities will shift. Constructivists believe that one of the goals of therapy is to change how we "language" our experience. Constructivists play with words and use paradoxes and the like to help shift the personal constructions through which individuals experience their world.

Paul Watzlawick's work is a prime example. For Watzlawick, psychological problems are actually attempts at solutions to life problems. Psychological problems occur when people attempt to solve new life problems with a solution that worked in the past or for old problems, but that does not work now. Often, when the old solution strategy does not work, people try "upping the dosage." Finally, they may even break down. Solutions themselves are based on how the individual is defining or "constructing" the problem. That is, a solution is based on an implicit premise about what the reality is and what the problem is.

Watzlawick (1985) gives the example of army ants, who have evolved a pattern of marching in a column. This strategy allows the colony of ants much greater flexibility in adaptation and survival than any one ant would have on its own. Yet, this life-enhancing strategy can become their downfall. If, by some accident of terrain, the lead

Box 13.1 The Function of Disruption

The therapist ushered the family into the therapy room, where an angry mother and her two oldest teenage daughters immediately sat together on a sofa and the youngest, the identified patient, sat in the chair farthest away. The mother reported that Wendy was being truant from junior high, failing several classes, lying, and stealing. As a single mother who worked full time and went to college at night, she just "couldn't take" any more disruption from her always difficult child.

Most of the therapy hour was spent eliciting each person's version of the family's difficulties, with the therapist empathizing with each individual's feelings and perceptions. The mother and two oldest daughters insisted that everything would be just fine if it weren't for Wendy. Her truancy was the final straw because the mother had to miss work to go to Wendy's school for a parent conference. Since Wendy sat far away, huddled sullenly in her chair, refusing to speak or look at anyone, the therapist empathized with how difficult it must be for her to talk with everyone against her and how distressed, embarrassed, hurt, and angry she must feel. Having made contact with each family member by validating her viewpoint, the therapist made her paradoxical intervention.

The therapist delivered this speech slowly and seriously:

> As you know, I believe the reason one member of a family shows problem behavior is because the entire family is in pain. And this family certainly is in pain. Everyone is busy, stretched to the limit, and stressed out. Mrs. G works, goes to college, raises a family alone. Each daughter goes to school, helps run the household, does chores and homework, tries to have a social life. It's just too much. But only Wendy acts out the family pain by doing bad things. She saves the rest of you from having to look at the kind of stress and pain you live under by being the bad one. In fact, she is sacrificing herself to save you, her loved ones, from having to experience your own pain. And she is sacrificing herself, because after all, she's the one who will have to pay. She must really love all of you a lot.
>
> But I don't want you to change too fast. If Wendy suddenly started being good, you'd all have to face your own pain, and you might not like that. So Wendy, during the next week, I want you to be truant as much as possible and continue lying. In fact, tell at least three really good lies. I want you to continue to sacrifice yourself and protect the rest of your family. Okay, I'll see you all next week at this time.

The effect of this intervention on the family was electric. They all immediately sat straight and listened carefully. Wendy sat up, leaned forward, and looked at the therapist as if she were crazy. The others looked between Wendy and the therapist in confusion. The mother started to protest that she didn't want Wendy to sacrifice herself in that way, but the therapist ushered them out of the room with promises to see them next week.

The next week, quite a different family entered the therapy room. Three cheerful daughters sat comfortably on the sofa together, and a beaming mother sat in a chair beside them. They reported that they couldn't understand it, but they'd had a great week together. For some reason Wendy went to school and did not lie or steal. They all got along well together and even had some fun together. No one could explain it. The therapist said that she was glad to see the family handling their issues so well and that they could call her in the future if they needed to. The family did not request another appointment for over a year.

ant starts to march in a circle and catches up to the last ant in the column, the ants will continue to march in a circle until they die. The strategy that evolved because of its survival value becomes a problem under the wrong conditions. The ants are "stuck."

For Watzlawick, therefore, the problem is that the individual, couple, or family is stuck in a construction of reality that is blocking them from finding creative, new solutions. It is as if they are looking at the world through blue-colored glasses, and therefore do not notice other colors that might help them resolve their problem. They are stuck, trying to do the best they can, rather than, as some other perspectives hold, unconsciously trying to maintain their symptoms because their symptoms are unconsciously gratifying.

How does Watzlawick propose to get a client unstuck? How would you help the ants? Would you put the lead ant on a couch and help it gain insight into its past? Would you have it focus on its feelings or felt meanings? Would you wonder what dysfunctional cognitions the ant has? Or would you simply place a stick strategically so that the circular pattern is broken up, allowing the ants to march forward once again?

For Watzlawick, therapy is a matter of using some intervention to break up the circle in which the client is stuck. He (1987) argues that insight is irrelevant to change and that change occurs all the time in everyday life without insight. If the old system is broken up, new, forward-moving behavior will take its place, and engaging in a new behavior can change a whole personal system for construing reality. This is a crucial point because Watzlawick believes that a simple change can result in a major, pervasive, personal change. In contrast, psychoanalysis, for instance, believes that changing one's personal construct system takes years of reviewing its roots in early childhood.

One of Watzlawick's key ideas is the distinction between ***first order change*** and ***second order change.*** People get stuck because they operate out of unquestioned assumptions about the nature of reality and, in particular, about the nature of the problem situation they are dealing with. For some "traditional" husbands, it is practically "bred in the bone" that the husband is supposed to be dominant; the wife is supposed to stay at home and not work. All people have unquestioned assumptions. They form part of their first order reality. When individuals attempt to solve problems, they operate out of those assumptions, without realizing they are assumptions. Then, when things go wrong, they do not question the assumptions underlying their actions, goals, and perceptions, but simply try to refine their strategies or actions in accord with those same old assumptions. For instance, someone sinking in quicksand may not question his assumption that some kind of vigorous action is needed to get out. So even when thrashing about does not help, he shifts to another kind of vigorous action (perhaps trying to swim and kick with his feet), rather than questioning his assumption that vigorous activity is an appropriate solution.

Watzlawick argues that what is needed is not a first order change, in which one simply tries new ways to solve the problem from the same old assumptions. What is needed is a second order change, in which the assumptions themselves are overthrown. The person has to be able to step outside of the old frame he puts on situations, to see them in a new way. A simple illustration of this is given in figure 13.1 and figure 13.2 (on page 354).

The therapist's task, then, is to induce second order change. This will get the system "unstuck" and moving again. Let us consider an example of someone who attempts to solve a problem by instituting first order changes. One of us knows of a family in which the wife, because of her own traumatic family background, is overprotective toward her teenage daughter. Because the woman was somewhat wild as a child, she is concerned about her daughter's becoming wild. So she is highly restrictive concerning her daughter's curfew time and her daughter's friends. If you think in terms of a system, you can imagine what might happen next. Such overprotectiveness generates rebellion in the daughter. She begins to exhibit some of the very behaviors the mother has been so worried about: cutting school, hanging around with people the mother dislikes, and acting rebellious at home. This convinces the mother that she was on the right track all along—the daughter is in danger of going down the wrong path. The mother therefore redoubles her efforts to control the daughter and becomes even more restrictive. Thus, her solution is to do "more of the same." This is the first order change she attempts. The basic premise underlying all her attempts to control her daughter is never questioned. A second order change in this mother's case might be to facilitate a shift in perspective so that she "sees" that focusing on the positive with her daughter, and building a positive relationship with her, in addition to or instead of trying to control her, might lead to better outcomes. Thus she might be told, "It is important that you persist in your efforts to monitor your daughter. However, in order for you to know her better so that you can do this more effectively, we believe you need to spend more time carefully listening to her. So we suggest the following. . . ."

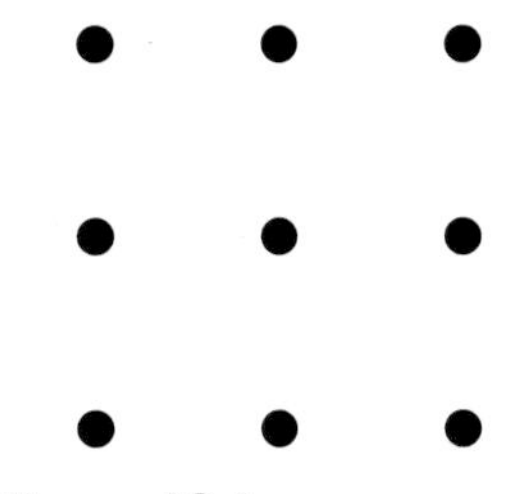

Figure 13.1
The problem is to connect all nine dots by drawing four lines without lifting the pencil from the page. See figure 13.2 for the solution.

How does Watzlawick propose to initiate second order change? Watzlawick argues that there are two languages: the verbal, logical, analytic language of the left brain and the language of image, metaphor, synthesis, and totality of the right brain. According to Watzlawick, "This language of the right brain does not explain; it creates, it evokes" (1978, p. 58), and it is in this language that therapists must speak. This is the language of strategic interventions, the language of concrete imagery, indirect suggestion, metaphorical communication, paradox, and jokes. It is this language that can create second order change.

Watzlawick's approach to therapy is quite brief, with the average being about six sessions per client (Watzlawick, 1985). The Watzlawick group uses many of the techniques we have already encountered (Watzlawick, Weakland, & Fisch, 1974). Among others mentioned by Watzlawick (1985) is the therapeutic double bind. The client is given an instruction that puts her in a paradoxical position. A woman client who said she "couldn't say no" was instructed to go around to each person in the room and say no to them. She said, "No! I can't do that!" Of course, by saying no to the intervention, she was saying no.

Watzlawick phrases his communications in such a way as to make "every success theirs" and "every failure ours." After a successful change the client might be told, "Amazing! You must have done something different. What did you do to make it a success?"

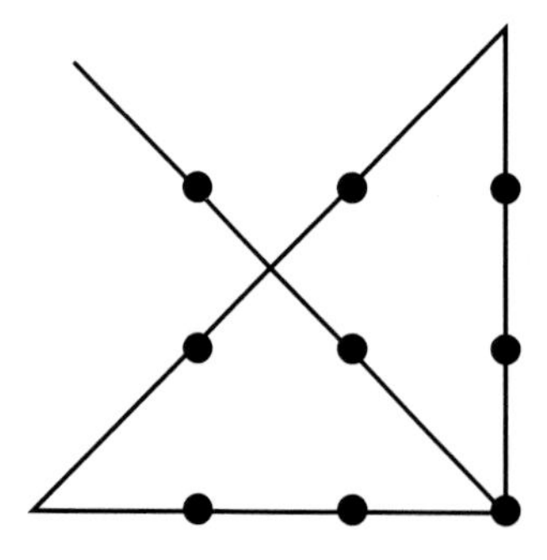

Figure 13.2
People have trouble with this problem because they see the nine dots as a square. They have to change that assumption and see the dots in a different way to solve the problem.

Steven de Shazer

De Shazer's approach is one of those called "solution-focused." The emphasis in solution-focused therapies is on the future: finding ways of helping people get where they want to go. Correspondingly, there is little or no emphasis on the past in terms of what "caused" the problem. In order to create solutions, solution-focused therapists rely on client strength and creativity, and in this regard, they share Carl Rogers's faith in the self-healing capabilities of people (Miller, Duncan, & Hubble, 1996). One of their most basic strategies is to help clients notice what they are doing right, or to remember when things were going the way they wanted them to go. In essence, solution-focused therapists believe that clients often already know how to solve their problems; they are just not paying attention to the ways to make things go better that they already know how to do, or were doing at one time.

De Shazer (1985) shares the idea that problems are most often the outcomes of attempts at solution, and he would agree with Watzlawick (1987) that pathology is a system that has run out of ways of dealing with a problem. On the development of the causes of the problem, the de Shazer position is compatible with other theoretical perspectives covered in this book. For instance, it could be that a problem has complex roots in the past. However, de Shazer believes that just because a problem is complex does not mean that it demands a complex solution. One could think of the story of Alexander the Great and the Gordian Knot, which no one could untie. Alexander's solution was to take his sword and cut it apart. There may well be solutions to problems that are quite simple, though the problem itself is quite complex.

De Shazer does not believe that the solution must exactly match the problem. As a skeleton key can be used to unlock a variety of locks, therapeutic solutions can unlock a variety of problems or complaints. In this respect, therapeutic solutions work by "unsticking" the client. They break up the old system, and de Shazer believes, as does Milton Erickson, that the clients actually then resolve the problem with new, creative solutions the therapist could never have anticipated or planned.

A key theoretical point of de Shazer's is a rejection of the traditional concept of clients' unconscious resistance to change. He says:

> I became more and more convinced that clients really do want to change. Certainly some of them found that the ideas about how to change did not fit very well. However, I found it difficult to label this as "resistance" when it seemed to be a message the clients were sending in an effort to help the therapist help them. . . . Over and over I found people sent to me by other therapists . . . to be both desperate for change and highly cooperative. (1985, p. 15)

The implication is that resistance may be as much a function of the therapist's interventions as it is a function of the client. Perhaps clients resist intervention techniques that do not fit them well. The de Shazer group works to minimize resistance and elicit clients' cooperation by complimenting clients on what they are already doing to try to solve their problem.

Many of the interventions used by the de Shazer group are based on the work of Milton Erickson and are shared by other strategic and solution-focused therapists. We will mention some we have not previously covered. De Shazer respects the reality of each client. If two clients give differing views of the problem, the therapist stays neutral and does not take sides. Rather, the therapist may mirror the conflict. However, it may be done in such a way as to put the couple in a "positive double bind," as Watzlawick does. In one example, a husband and wife were treated for cocaine abuse. They also were concerned about problems in the marriage. One partner believed the real problem was not the drug abuse, but their fights and arguments. The other thought it was the drugs that were causing the marital problems. The intervention given by the de Shazer group to the couple is described below. We will not reproduce the rather complex theoretical logic for this intervention here, but it is based on the fact that each member of the couple was seeing the problem in either/or terms.

> You've got a problem. It seems to us, Ralph, that your marital problems are being exacerbated by the drugs, or fogged over by the drugs, or perhaps even created by the drugs. Perhaps you need to, stop the drugs, just to see what is going on. But, on the other hand, we agree with you, Jane, that if you two were to stop the drugs, then there might be nothing there. And, you might not have time to create anything before the marriage broke up. In short, we don't know what the . . . you are going to do.
>
> I suggest you think about what I just said, and decide what actions you are going to take . . . first. (de Shazer, 1985, p. 52)

The interesting thing is that this intervention resulted in a two-thirds reduction of drug use by the next session and complete elimination of drug use by two weeks later, along with the development of new, positive marital activities. Follow-ups at six months and one year indicated no further drug use and infrequent arguments. In other words, a substance abuse problem and a marital problem appeared to be "cured" in two sessions!

Another intervention, similar to one used by the Watzlawick group, is to have the clients concretely and specifically define what they would like changed. Most clients come in and say things such as "We want our marriage improved" or "I want to get over being depressed" or "I want to stop being anxious so much." These are global, vague goals. Clients are asked to try to imagine concrete behavioral differences that could be used as an index of change for the better. For instance, for people who want their marriage "improved" it might be "spending one night together sharing a pleasant activity without fighting." For the depressive it might be "feeling calm and content while sitting at home on a Saturday night watching TV." For the anxious person it might be "stepping outside the door and feeling calm." The interesting thing is that the simple act of developing and defining such concrete goals is therapeutic. Clients find ways of bringing them about that are unique, creative, and not predictable by the therapist.

De Shazer, following Erickson, believes that change is not only possible, it is "inevitable," and this attitude is conveyed to the client. For example, the client may be asked, "What will you do when you have changed?" or "When do you think you will be over this problem—by next week or the week after?" A specific intervention is to tell a client to "pay attention to what you do when you overcome the urge . . ." (1985, p. 132). This may be used, for instance, with overeating. The client is told to pay attention to what he does when he overcomes the urge to eat. There are two parts to this intervention. First, it implies that the client can change, that is, he can overcome the urge to eat. Second, it focuses the client's attention on the positive moments when he succeeds and counteracts either/or thinking. De Shazer points out that things in life are rarely "always" or "never" and that always/never thinking is an example of the either/or thinking that is often involved in dysfunctional behavior. Overeaters often say, "I always overeat" or "I never can control my appetite," yet this is rarely true. Most dieters do overcome their urges to eat, frequently. They may fail at other times, but they do not always fail.

Summary of Strategic and Solution-Focused Approaches

The strategic therapists, discussed above, suggest ways of doing therapy that represent fundamental "paradigm shifts" from most of the more traditional ways of approaching psychological problems. Despite their differing theoretical orientations, these therapists all share a belief that the therapist's task is to intervene in such a way that the old, dysfunctional system is disrupted, freeing the system to develop and move forward in positive ways. They all believe that small, seemingly irrelevant changes can have a ripple effect, resulting in major and lasting changes within the individual client or the family system. They believe that instead of pitting themselves against the client's or family's problems, which could mobilize resistance, they should work with the symptoms in some way. Therefore, interventions frequently do not proscribe the symptom but rather place it in a different context. They also agree that insight into the causes of the symptoms is not necessary or important for change.

Finally, there is a fundamental orientation among many of the strategic and solution-focused approaches toward strengthening and enhancing positive functioning rather than trying to "fix" negative functioning. Because they believe that negative functioning is simply a result of a system getting stuck on a negative track, they believe that one can get the system back on a positive track by enhancing positive behavior. Essentially they believe that clients get stuck in a negative vicious cycle. Negative vicious cycles get created by clients' dwelling on the negative and by using the same old solutions that have not worked previously. Therapy can create a positive "vicious cycle." One way to break out of this is to have clients concretely imagine and remember how they have done things successfully in the past. O'Hanlon and Weiner-Davis (1989), for example, continually emphasize asking clients to focus on what they were doing when things were going well.

These approaches also emphasize the future more so than the past. "The future is more important than the past in determining present behavior," (Shlien, 1988), to quote a phrase that strategic therapists would agree with. They try to get clients to imagine positive outcomes because anticipating positive outcomes feeds back to influences present behavior to move in that direction. If one imagines negative outcomes, the feedback system will operate to have the negative image feed back and increase the probability of negative behavior.

More-Recent Approaches to Family Therapy

We will briefly consider three more-recent developments. The first, narrative therapy, is not specifically a family approach, although many of the contributors to its development came out of the family therapy tradition; it can be used in individual and couples therapy as well. The other two approaches are *multisystemic therapies* and may represent an important part of the future of family therapy.

Narrative Therapy

Narrative psychotherapies are one set of *postmodern* approaches. Postmodernism asserts that one fixed reality to which we all respond does not exist. To the contrary, the realities we live in are constituted by our cultures, our languages, and our individual life experiences. What we see as problems and how we see them as problems are constituted by our cultural experiences, our personal backgrounds, and are particular places in the world at any given time. There is no timeless "truth" about social reality. Accordingly, postmodernists have serious reservations about DSM, which treats psychological disorders as if they were objective facts.

Narrative therapy (Angus & McLeod, 2004) holds that our problems are embedded in how we tell the stories of our lives. Therapy becomes the "restorying" of one's life so that new possibilities are opened up. Michael White (2004), one of the most well known narrative therapists, gets the client to view the problem as an "it" so that the person can gain some distance from it and realize that "I am not my problem." This alone is therapeutic and helps counter paralyzing self-criticism. The therapist may also, through skillful questioning, get clients to reconstrue problems in a more constructive direction. For instance, in one case White worked with a family who had come because their daughter, Jill, had killed herself. The family didn't understand why this had happened, were consumed with sadness, and were wondering what they had done to contribute to the problem. As a result they were unable to make their peace with her death. Through skillful questioning, White was able to lead the family to remember the positives about Jill, and to get in touch with her strong will. Additionally they were able to get in touch with the reasons she did what she did. The suicide now seems sensible in terms of what they knew about their daughter, and they are now able to move on to honoring her life.

Narrative therapists, as with other postmodern therapists, do not portray themselves as the experts on their clients' problems. In fact, they adopt a stance of "not knowing" in therapy. From that stance they are able to ask questions in a curious and open way, which helps the clients make the discoveries that help them resolve their problems.

Multisystemic Approaches

Multisystemic approaches intervene not only at the family level but at the level of the family in its relationship to larger systems, such as an adolescent's peer network and relationships with schools. We shall consider two here: Multisystemic Therapy (MST) (Henggeler, Pickrel, & Brondino, 1999) and Functional Family Therapy (FFT) (Sexton & Alexander, 1999). MST is an approach designed for youth and families dealing with substance abuse problems and conduct disorders. MST pays more attention to extra-family systems than does traditional family therapy. It also pays more attention to individual developmental issues. The approach is present-focused and relies on a wide range of interventions from a variety of approaches that have been empirically shown to be helpful. Particularly important are behavioral interventions; the therapist may work with the individual client (usually an adolescent), with the parents, with the family, or with the siblings, whatever appears to be the best strategy for a given family and a given problem. The therapist may also work at the school or community level to modify systems that may have not been reinforcing adaptive behavior. For instance, teachers may be coached on how to best reinforce the child for effective behavior, and part of the treatment plan may include having teachers give regular reports to parents.

FFT is a behaviorally based approach that works on the family relational system. As with MST, FFT has been utilized primarily with families experiencing adolescent behavior problems. The basic premise is that the adolescent's problem serves some legitimate relational purpose in the family. There are three basic purposes it could serve: creating contact and closeness, creating distance and independence, or creating a vacillation between these two. The goal of the therapist is to assess the interpersonal functions of the behavior of each family member and then to assess how they interrelate. Therapy includes an educational component in which family members can learn specific skills, such as communication skills and problem resolution skills. Techniques used include a range of behavioral techniques such as modeling and systematic desensitization (see chapter 10). The therapist also tries to get family members to question their interpretations of what is going on so that they can reinterpret or relabel family interactions in less blaming ways.

FFT is multisystemic in that it assumes that larger systems such as those of the school and community impact on the family and filter through to affect the adolescent's behavior. However in contrast to MST, the focus of intervention is primarily on the family itself.

Multisystemic work is increasingly becoming popular in agencies that deal with problem children and adolescents. It makes sense that family therapists not only intervene at the level of the family but also deal with larger systemic variables that impact on the family. Research on MST and FFT has been quite supportive of their effectiveness (Sexton, Alexander, & Mease, 2004).

Evaluation of Marriage, Family, and Child Therapy

Effectiveness of Marriage and Family Therapy

Gurman (2003) and Gurman & Fraenkel (2002) have found, after reviews of the research, that the average effect size for couples therapy is 0.80 or greater, which means that any given couple is better off at the end of therapy than about 70% of couples who do not receive therapy.

The two approaches that have the most research support are Behavioral Marital Therapy and Emotion-Focused Therapy. There is also some evidence supporting the effectiveness of therapies with a structural or strategic emphasis. Also, couples therapy can play a remedial or preventative role as part of treatment of anxiety, depression, and alcohol abuse. Relationship Enhancement couple and family therapy also has an empirical base (Accordino & Guerney, 2002). On the other hand, in many cases the effects of couples therapy, although positive, are relatively modest (Sexton et al., 2004), and there is relatively little evidence on how long term the effects are.

With regard to family therapy, Shadish, Ragsdale, Glaser, and Montgomery (1995) found significant positive effects for behavioral, systemic, psychodynamic, and eclectic approaches. All appeared to be about equally effective. However, when specific disorders are considered, some approaches appear to be more effective than others (Sexton et al., 2004). For instance, for problems such as conduct disorder and substance abuse, FFT (Alexander, Robbins, & Sexton, 2001) and MST (Henggeler et al., 1999) have been shown to be effective.

In particular, several reports support the effectiveness of Minuchin's structural approach. Rosman, Minuchin, Liebman, and Baker (1978, as reported in Prochaska, 1984) report results on the treatment of 53 anorexics; they found that 86% achieved normal eating patterns. These writers also report successful outcomes for 17 chronic asthmatics and for the reduction of stress effects on children with diabetes. As with the research noted previously, there were no control groups, however. Informal evaluations of the effectiveness of strategic therapies have been carried out by those who practice it. Weakland et al. (1974) reported complete relief or significant improvement in 72% of their cases using the Watzlawick brief therapy approach. A follow-up on many of these, as well as other cases, found similar results (62% improvement), indicating that the changes wrought by this approach persist for some time after treatment. There was some evidence that there were positive changes in areas other than the specific presenting problems. However, their data do not meet stringent research standards. Success rates are largely based on clients' subjective reports, and no control groups were used. The de Shazer group tends to follow up their clients for six months to a year, and they report a similar figure of 72%. However, their results are subject to the same criticisms.

There have been a number of studies on the effectiveness of paradoxical interventions in particular. A tabulation by Orlinsky, Grawe, and Parks (1994) of 13 studies on paradoxical intervention found that all 13 showed positive results. This is better than the results for any other technique from any other therapy. Hill (1987) has done a meta-analysis of earlier research on paradoxical interventions. On the average, clients who received paradoxical interventions were better off than 84% of clients in untreated control groups, and better off than 72% of clients who received placebo treatments (see chapter 5). There was also tentative support for paradoxical interventions being more effective than nonparadoxical interventions. Hill holds that the evidence is particularly strong for the effectiveness of positive reframing, and somewhat less so for symptom prescription. Positive reframing is more helpful with depression, and many therapists believe that symptom prescription should not be used with depression. Hill's conclusions are based on a small number of studies (15) on a limited number of disorders (insomnia, depression, agoraphobia, procrastination, and stress). Therefore, it is not clear for what populations paradoxical interventions are appropriate, but the evidence is strong that they can be useful.

Effectiveness of Child and Adolescent Therapy

Reviews of research have indicated that psychological interventions with children are effective (Casey & Berman, 1985; Kazdin, 1994; Vernberg, Routh, & Koocher,

1992; Weisz, Weiss, Alicke, & Klotz, 1987). Research on humanistic play therapy has also shown it to be effective (Bratton & Ray, 2002). Similar to the findings with adults, children who undergo psychotherapy show improvement on a number of outcome measures significantly more frequently than comparison groups of untreated children. A more recent review (Kazdin, 2004) identifies a number of psychological treatments that have specifically been identified as evidence-based for the treatment of specific disorders, including anxiety, fear, phobias, depression, and oppositional and conduct disorder. Most of these treatments are cognitive-behavioral or behavioral in nature. Research now focuses on the question of what subgroups of children or adolescents will be helped by what methods and on the role of parents and environmental factors that may moderate the effectiveness of therapy.

Given the apparent increase in child abuse and child sexual abuse in the United States in the past decades, psychological services for children are much needed. In fact, economic factors are both increasing the incidence of these problems and causing cuts in the services needed to treat them, so that in most of the country, child service agencies are overwhelmed. Prevention would appear to be most cost-effective means of dealing with abuse, and many programs for the prevention of child abuse have been developed and demonstrated to be effective. Furthermore, the increasing number of children born to drug-abusing mothers and to mothers with AIDS means there will be an even greater demand for psychological services for children in the future. Again, an emphasis on prevention seems both humane and cost-effective, but the young casualties of our social problems still deserve help and effective treatment.

Modern child therapies are briefer, more directive and structured, and more goal-oriented than earlier ones. Almost all require the participation of the parents as part of the treatment. The necessity of combining knowledge of the child's developmental changes in cognition, emotion, and perception with the utilization of therapeutic interventions means that therapy must change as knowledge of child development improves. Future research must address the issue of how interventions made at one age are construed by the child at a later age and how early interventions can be made to "last" through the developmental changes of the growing child. Vernberg, Routh, and Koocher (1992) propose the concepts of "developmental psychotherapy" and "healthy versus deviant pathways" to deal with this issue. The focus in their model is on the therapist intervening to help a child regain his footing on a developmental pathway more likely to lead to adequate adaptation in later stages of life.

Theoretical Evaluation

Because the marital, family, and child approaches constitute a diverse collection, we will not evaluate them as a whole. However, there are criticisms that have been leveled specifically at strategic approaches that need to be considered. Many systems theorists believe that an individual client's symptom serves some functional significance in the family. In other words, the symptom is an unconscious strategy for dealing with some family issue. However, criticisms of such a view can be made (e.g., Bogdan, 1986). First, it is no more than an assumption or an indirect inference that the presenting complaints of the identified patient are meeting some family need. This is not directly observable.

Second, there are certain inconsistencies in the idea. For example, an adolescent's school problems might be assumed to serve to bring father and mother, who have intimacy problems, closer together. But if we assume that all family problems are an attempt to resolve some family imbalance, then what imbalance is the parents' intimacy problems attempting to resolve? This leads to an infinite regress.

Third, this viewpoint can be questioned from an "ecological" view of systems. In an ecological system, a balance among all forces present will evolve. For instance, in an area in which rabbits eat grass and coyotes eat rabbits, a balance evolves in which the number of rabbits is controlled by the amount of grass available and by the number of coyotes around. The number of coyotes is controlled by the number of rabbits available, and indirectly by the amount of grass available, and so on. It is true that changes in one part of the system lead to adjustments in other parts (e.g., a drought affecting the amount of grass will affect both rabbits and coyotes). But to argue that one element of the system changes in order to keep the system in balance would be like arguing that coyotes eat rabbits in order to keep the ecological system in balance. But that is not why coyotes eat rabbits. They eat rabbits because they are hungry, and their eating rabbits keeps the system in balance because the whole system interactively evolved that way. Bogdan (1986) prefers an ecological metaphor and argues that problems often evolve in family systems accidentally. Arguing from the work of Watzlawick and his colleagues, Bogdan suggests that problems evolve because "ordinary life difficulties are mishandled. And they persist because no one realizes that it is the mishandling that perpetuates the problem" (p. 35).

In a similar manner, the functionalist perspective can be criticized for minimizing the role of individual psychological variables. The assumption is that pathological behavior is always the result of the family system and not the result of any individual process. This perspective was originally developed in family theories of schizophrenia, in which it was argued that schizophrenics were actually the identified patients in pathological families. Case histories were given suggesting that families of schizophrenics were more disturbed in many ways than normal families. However, the functionalist perspective overlooks an alternative possibility. It is possible that having a disturbed family member, such as a schizophrenic, disturbs the family. Patterns of disturbance similar to those found in families of schizophrenics have also been found in families of children with other serious illnesses, such as leukemia. Having a sick child may affect the way the whole family functions. It would be most peculiar to argue that a child developed leukemia in order to bring his mother and father closer together. An ecological system point of view could handle the fact that an individual member of the system could be disturbed, and that disturbance could then disturb the rest of the system. This could then become an accidental dysfunctional feedback loop.

Furthermore, the systems theory depends on the idea that each element of the system has some identity of its own, independent (at least partially) of its place in the system. A system with coyotes and rabbits will be different from a system with sheep and raccoons. Some systems theorists seem to discount the idea that each individual in the family system has his or her own personality, which plays its role in the overall family system. To really understand a family system, one has to take into account the individual characteristics of the members of that system, just as one must know that an ecological system has rabbits and coyotes in it instead of sheep and raccoons. There is nothing fundamentally incompatible between the ideas that family members have their individual personalities (and problems) and that they are part of an interactive system.

Another major criticism of strategic approaches has to do with their manipulativeness. Strategic therapists do not value insight. They do not believe that change occurs by making clients aware of their own problems so that clients can consciously initiate and control their own changes. Instead, it could be said that the therapists institute change by playing tricks on clients.

The therapists might reply that all therapy interventions are manipulations, so why not do them consciously and deliberately? This is an argument that behaviorists used to make in response to criticisms that they were manipulative. Haley (1985), who has been openly assertive about the therapist's using manipulation to help the client, has made fun of the idea that if a therapist does something without deliberately trying to manipulate and it works, that is somehow all right, while if the same thing is consciously done as a manipulation, it is not. Furthermore, it could be argued that these manipulations work. People are better off afterward and with a lot less investment of time and trouble than with so-called insight therapies.

An argument against manipulative intervention is that it does not empower people. One of the important current movements in psychology is the idea of "giving psychology away" (Larson, 1984). The idea is to develop techniques that people can use to manage their own lives. Strategic therapy may eliminate symptoms, but it does not empower individuals to change their lives on their own if further problems arise. It seems to imply that people must be "operated on" when they are stuck, rather than unstick themselves. Psychoanalytic and humanistic approaches do not merely wish to get the client unstuck, to get rid of symptoms, but to develop the client's own self-management skills. Perhaps that is why they take longer.

While all strategic and solution-focused therapists plan their interventions and use paradoxical techniques, not all of them accept the manipulative model of theorists such as Jay Haley. They use the techniques not to manipulate the client into some specific outcome, but to free the client to solve the problem creatively. De Shazer points out that the actual solutions clients come up with to their problems are unique, developed by the clients themselves, and not predictable by the therapist.

Another criticism is leveled at the range and permanence of strategic approaches. Advocates of other approaches sometimes question whether changes brought about in such a brief time, using such noninsight methods, can have any enduring quality. They argue that in such a short time, these approaches cannot cause change that persists and that they will not work with enduring characterological problems, such as addictions and personality disorders. Certainly, cures of substance abuse that appear to take place in two sessions, as with the case of de Shazer we reviewed earlier, will be greeted with skepticism by those who believe that psychological problems represent ingrained behavior patterns.

In response, Watzlawick (1985) has pointed out that even if it were true that a client might eventually have to return to treatment with a new problem or a recurrence of the old, that does not invalidate the treatment's success. He notes that no one expects medical doctors to effect cures of infections so that the patient will never get another infection. Furthermore, there is no evidence that the changes wrought by analytic or humanistic approaches are any more permanent. In fact, not only does analysis take years, but people frequently return to it with recurrent or new problems.

Finally, strategic therapists point to cases of supposedly chronic characterological problems that they have helped, such as bulimia, substance abuse, and antisocial behavior in adolescents. However, individual case histories do not prove that the strategic approach is generally effective with such problems, and strategic therapists do not present any systematic evidence showing that it is. Though it may be true that they have helped individual cases of substance abuse, personality disorders, or other problems that are typically seen as longstanding and difficult to treat, further research will have to demonstrate that these approaches can be generally effective with such problems.

Finally, bear in mind that published successes achieved by these approaches have usually taken place under unusual circumstances. They have occurred at institutes, such as Watzlawick's brief therapy institute in Palo Alto, California, or de Shazer's institute in Milwaukee. In these institutes, families or couples are typically seen by one therapist, while a team of other therapists watch through a one-way mirror. The intervention given to the family or couple has been designed by the whole team. We know of colleagues who trained in the strategic or solution-focused approach, but they have found it more difficult to put into operation in private practice where one does not have a team of colleagues watching through a one-way mirror. Under these circumstances, these colleagues have reported that it becomes more difficult to use such interventions with the degree of success reported by these institutes, and these colleagues report having to resort to other approaches in addition to strategic ones.

In Conclusion

Aside from the contributions of specific procedures and approaches for working with families, couples, and children, the two major contributions of family and couples perspectives that will continue to be influential have to do with viewpoints. The first is the recognition that people exist in and are influenced by larger relational units (e.g., the system idea). Systems ideas offer an important corrective to the highly individualistic biases of most traditional psychological theories. The idea that, at least in part, "you are who you are with" implies a major shift in how we are to view human beings. Family systems theorists were the first to advocate this idea. Now they are being joined by multicultural, feminist, psychodynamic, and humanistic theorists who are arguing that interpersonal relationships, and, at a larger level, cultural relationships play an important role in defining who individuals are and in influencing how they function. It is as yet unclear how this is going to play out in practice, but it would seem likely that new models will evolve that take both individual and systemic factors into account.

The second major viewpoint comes from strategic and solution-focused therapies. These therapies have given us a totally new view on how to provide treatment. First, they hold that to focus on finding the causes of a person's problems is simply irrelevant. Instead, we should be focused on finding solutions. Second, in order to do this, we should not be focusing on pathology, but rather on strength. We should focus on the positive about people, and locate and enhance their strengths. Focusing on strengths often leads to individuals finding solutions to their problems much more quickly than they would if the focus were on pathology. Along with this, strategic and solution-focused therapists have provided a whole armamentarium of procedures that seem in many cases to facilitate change quickly. In this sense, strategic and solution-focused therapists have been a major force in the development of brief psychotherapy. Especially because of its fit with the modern health care climate, which requires brief psychotherapy, it seems likely that strategic and solution-focused viewpoints and methods will continue to exert an influence.

The third viewpoint contributed by family systems theorists is that of constructivism, which, while not totally a creation of family systems theorists, has been given major impetus by them. We discuss constructivism further in chapter 15.

PART IV

CONTEMPORARY ISSUES

Psychotherapy Integration

Convergence in Psychotherapy

Surveys have found that the majority of practicing clinical psychologists perceive themselves as eclectic (Norcross, 2005); that is, they use techniques and concepts from a variety of theoretical sources. One of the reasons for this may be research findings that suggest that each of the major approaches to psychotherapy is approximately equivalent in effectiveness to the others (see chapter 5). Knowing that differing approaches can all be effective, practitioners have been more likely to borrow what is useful from each one.

Along with the tendency toward eclecticism in practice, there has been a growing interest in finding commonalities among differing approaches and ways of integrating them. Prior to the 1970s, there had been sporadic efforts in this direction. Dollard and Miller (1950) attempted to translate Freudian concepts into behavioral terminology. Gendlin (1996) proposed that all therapies worked by influencing the client's experiencing process. Frank (1961) was among the first to propose that there were nonspecific factors common to the effectiveness of the various approaches.

The movement toward integrating approaches to psychotherapy has been mushrooming in recent years. There is now an international society for the study of psychotherapy integration: the Society for the Exploration of Psychotherapy Integration. There is also a professional journal devoted to the topic. The Society for the Exploration of Psychotherapy Integration currently has over 800 members and holds conventions each year. Between 1980 and 1995, more than 50 books were published presenting various integrative and eclectic views of psychotherapy.

Types of Psychotherapy Integration

Recent interest in integrating approaches has taken several directions. There are generally considered to be three different orientations toward psychotherapy integration: technical eclecticism, common factors, and theoretical integration (Norcross, 2005; Stricker & Gold, 2003). However, another approach, assimilative integration (Messer & Warren, 1990), has also been identified. We shall briefly review each of these major approaches to psychotherapy integration and then consider our view of some of the convergences in the field of psychotherapy.

Technical Eclecticism

The term *technical eclecticism* refers to the idea that the therapist will be eclectic, that is, she will borrow or use techniques and procedures from different approaches. Technically, eclectic therapists believe that what the therapist does should primarily be guided by what works rather than by a theoretical perspective. Perhaps the most well-known advocates of the technical eclectic approach to psychotherapy integration have been Arnold Lazarus, Larry Beutler, and John Norcross (Lazarus, Beutler, & Norcross, 1992). In general, they hold that the therapist should assess what the client's problem is and choose whatever intervention or approach will work best with that problem.

Many therapists who adopt this approach place a strong emphasis on research to discover what approaches work the best with what problems for what types of individuals. For instance, rather than "prescribe" empathy for everyone based on a theoretical perspective such as that of either client-centered therapy or self psychology, Beutler, Crago, and Arizmendi (1986) note that research has found that active provision of empathy with highly suspicious clients may be counterproductive. With this in mind, technically eclectic therapists have argued that even the therapeutic relationship should be tailored to fit with clients (Norcross, 1993). With some clients, the therapist should be more active and directive; with others, the therapist should be more passive and nondirective. With some clients, the therapist might adopt a more informal interactive style; with others, the therapist might need to be more formal and businesslike.

One can be technically eclectic and still adhere to a theory. Arnold Lazarus, for instance, generally adheres to a social learning point of view. There are many cognitive and client-centered therapists who are technically eclectic in the procedures they utilize in therapy, but they ground these procedures in their particular theoretical perspectives. However, for true technically eclectic therapists, theory is secondary to what works.

An example of technical eclecticism is found in a book by Beutler and Harwood (2000) entitled *Prescriptive Psychotherapy: A Practical Guide to Systematic Treatment Selection*. In this book, these authors use research findings to structure therapy. They suggest that prior to therapy, therapists assess such factors as the client's expectations about treatment, level of coping skills, motivation, problem severity, personality style, environmental stressors, and environmental support systems. These plus other factors are taken into account in developing a treatment plan. A series of decisions are made about whether the client is treated in an individual, group, or family therapy format; treatment duration (short- or long-term); how to structure the relationship; and what techniques to use. For instance, one needs to decide whether intense eye contact between therapist and client is either indicated or contraindicated by various client variables (such as the client's personal sense of boundaries or culture).

As examples of how to choose techniques, if the client is dealing with unidentified feelings, the therapist might choose to use client-centered reflection as a technique. If challenging a client's dysfunctional cognitions is important, one may use various cognitive techniques.

A second approach to technical eclecticism is that of Arnold Lazarus (2002). Lazarus assesses clients along the following dimensions: behavior, affect, sensation, imagery, cognition, interpersonal relationships, and drugs and biology (BASIC-ID). He then chooses interventions based on the areas where the assessment has revealed problems.

A third approach is that of Prochaska, Norcross, and DiClemente (1994). They have argued that there are six general stages in the change process. The first stage is the precontemplation stage. Clients in this stage are not generally aware that there is a problem. The second stage is the contemplation stage. Here, the client is aware of the problem, and is engaging in self-examination. However, the client still does not have a good formulation of the problem. The third stage is preparation, which involves getting ready to change and making a commitment to change. The fourth stage is action. Here, the client is aware of the problem and has developed some formulation of it, and is therefore ready to take action. The fifth stage is maintenance, that is, maintenance of change once it has been achieved. This stage can include the awareness of the possibility of relapse and the willingness to recycle through the earlier stages if necessary. The sixth stage is termination, in which the person is totally confident of his ability to maintain the change (this last stage may be an ideal achieved by only a few people).

For Prochaska et al., different therapies appear to be most appropriate at different stages. For instance, when clients are in the precontemplation stage, strategic therapies or psychodynamic therapies might be the treatment of choice. During the contemplation stage, cognitive therapies or existential therapies might be most appropriate. During the action stage, behavior therapy, gestalt therapy, or structural therapy might be most appropriate. Finally, for maintenance, behavior therapy may be most appropriate.

Still another model of the process of therapy is the "assimilation of problematic experience" model of Stiles (2002). Stiles believes that an experience is problematic because it creates emotional disequilibrium until it is productively assimilated. A scale has been developed for modeling this process of assimilation. At the lowest end of the scale (stage 0) a problematic experience is warded off and the client is unaware of it. At the next stage (stage 1), unwanted thoughts about the discomfort begin to break into awareness. Unwanted thoughts may also be associated with various negative feelings, such as anxiety, fear, or anger. In the next stage (stage 2), the client begins to acknowledge the existence of the problematic experience but is unable to formulate the problem clearly. In stage 3, the client is now able to make a clear statement of the problem. In stage 4, some understanding and insight are gained. This leads to stage 5, in which the understanding is used to actively work on the problem. In stage 6, the client achieves some successful resolution of the problem. In stage 7, this resolution is generalized to other problems.

In terms of prescribing treatment, Stiles and his colleagues have suggested that when the problem is warded off or is vague and unclear (e.g., stages 0 to 2), psychodynamic or humanistic approaches are most appropriate because of their exploratory nature. Once a clear problem formulation has been reached (stage 3 and above), a more prescriptive approach to therapy, such as a cognitive-behavioral approach, might be more appropriate. One research study (Stiles, Barkham, Shapiro, & Firth-Cozens, 1992) found that therapy proceeded more smoothly when exploratory approaches preceded prescriptive approaches, rather than vice versa.

Certainly if we take the ideas of multiple realities, constructivism, and cultural diversity seriously, then it may well be that there are a variety of ways to be mentally healthy and that each of the traditional theories is a model of one possible way. Different theories may fit different clients. Perhaps some clients simply live in a psychodynamic reality better than a behavioral reality. Our teaching experience has shown that different students seem to resonate with different theoretical stances. Showing films of therapists of varying persuasions in class reinforces this: No therapist is uniformly liked by all students, and there is usually much diversity in their responses to them. If this is the case, then it may make sense to keep the diverse theoretical models. Each may represent a worldview that is more compatible for some clients than for others. Thus the idea that different approaches may fit different clients, or at different times in the therapy process different approaches might be needed, makes sense.

Common Factors

In our years of teaching, we have often had the experience of students studying the different approaches to psychotherapy and concluding "they're all talking about the same thing!" This observation by students is consistent with the approach to psychotherapy integration called *common factors.* Those who follow this approach believe that there are common factors that appear in the differing therapies. They cite the fact that research has repeatedly failed to find significant differences in effectiveness among the differing approaches as evidence that there could be common underlying factors at work in the different therapies.

Jerome Frank (1982) was one of the first to suggest that there were some common dimensions to therapeutic change. He has suggested that one underlying dimension of all therapies is that they combat demoralization. In addition, they provide an emotionally charged, confiding relationship; a healing setting (such as hospital, clinic, office); a rationale or conceptual scheme to help the client make sense of her experiences; and a ritual to restore health that both client and therapist believe in. These function to provide a therapeutic relationship that combats alienation and demoralization and creates expectations of help, new learning experiences, arousal of emotions, enhancement of the client's sense of self-efficacy or mastery, and opportunities to practice new learning.

Goldfried (1980a) has noted the following common features: a facilitative therapeutic relationship, creation of client expectancy of help, encouragement of reality testing of client ideas and perceptions, provision of corrective experiences through which faulty ideas and behaviors may be modified, and provision of an external or objective perspective.

In an issue of the journal *Cognitive Therapy and Research* (Goldfried, 1980b), therapists of differing orientations were asked for their opinions on the importance of various elements of the therapy experience. Almost all agreed on the importance of a good therapeutic relationship; the provision of new, corrective experiences; the provision of direct feedback on thinking, emotion, and behavior; and the utilization of cognition and awareness. Some research has supported both the use of corrective experience (Drozd & Goldfried, 1996) and facilitation of awareness (Castonguay, Raver, Wiser, & Goldfried, 1995) as therapeutic commonalities.

Bohart and Tallman (1999), synthesizing ideas from a wide range of sources and other writers, have argued that perhaps the most important therapeutic commonality is the active agency of clients themselves. They have argued that the best solution to the question of why all psychotherapies seem to work about equally well, despite wide differences in methods and philosophies, is that clients are the agents of change in therapy, more so than therapists. Clients are able to use widely differing approaches, coming from widely different philosophical bases, to manufacture change for themselves. Further evidence for this thesis comes from studies that have shown that self-help approaches to therapy and activities such as journaling often work as well as professionally provided therapy (Christensen & Jacobson, 1994; Segal & Murray, 1994). Bohart and Tallman suggest that what all therapies have in common is that they provide a safe and supportive "work space" where clients can do the work of thinking through their problems and engaging in self-change and self-healing. Such a work space is not usually available in everyday life, where clients are too stressed and overwhelmed to think clearly and creatively and where friends and relatives are not adept at listening and responding in ways that promote productive thinking, exploring, and self-healing. Therapists facilitate change through (a) providing such a safe work space and (b) providing "tools" (e.g., ideas, suggestions and techniques) that clients can use in manufacturing their own solutions.

Most approaches now recognize the importance of the active agency of the client. Bergin and Garfield have said:

> Another important observation regarding the client variable is that it is the client more than the therapist who implements the change process. . . . Rather than argue over whether or not "therapy works," we could address ourselves to the question of whether or not "the client works." . . . As therapists have depended more on the client's resources, more change seems to occur. (1994, pp. 825–826)

However, what most therapists mean by client agency is that the client is actively involved in the process, exploring her childhood, challenging her dysfunctional cognitions under the tutelage of the therapist, engaging in the exposure exercises, and so on. Psychotherapy is still portrayed as a process of the therapist applying interventions to the client, which fixes the client. Bohart and Tallman (1999) go further to argue that it is not merely clients' active participation, but their active, creative thinking and experiencing that is important. Instead of it being therapists' interventions that operate on clients to fix them, it is clients who operate on therapists' interventions to make them work.

The common factors approach to psychotherapy integration is intuitively appealing, and our approach to psychotherapy integration, presented later in this chapter is based on it. However, different theorists identify different common factors. Furthermore, Mahrer (1989) has argued that many of the common factors proposed are at such a general level of description that they are not very helpful. For instance, the fact that all therapies provide for cognitive learning or for corrective feedback does not tell us very much about the specifics of how these work or don't work in the different therapies. So far, there is only a little research to support the idea of common factors.

Theoretical Integration

Perhaps the most difficult and challenging approach to psychotherapy integration is the attempt to come up with a unifying theoretical view that transcends the traditional views presented in this book. This is difficult, because the assumptions of the major approaches to psychotherapy are so different (Messer, 1986). Below, we consider some incompatibilities among varying perspectives.

Psychoanalysis tends to focus on defense against and avoidance of painful feelings, experiences, and conflicts as a major theoretical construct. If a patient thinks dysfunctionally, a psychoanalyst assumes that such thinking is really a symptom of deeper, underlying avoidance mechanisms. On the other hand, behavior therapy and cognitive therapy focus on learning. Pathological thoughts and behaviors are bad habits that have been learned and can be unlearned. Thus, for a cognitive therapist, a client who thinks dysfunctionally is simply misled. There is no assumption that the dysfunctional thinking is serving purposes of avoidance at deeper personality levels.

Both psychoanalysts and cognitive therapists emphasize rationality as the sine qua non of effective human functioning, and both strive to "strengthen the ego" or the ability to think and behave rationally. Both tend to assume that "nonrational" aspects of the personality, such as emotion and motivation, are "irrational" (not "nonrational"), and can interfere with rational functioning. In contrast, client-centered and gestalt therapists, as well as many family systems therapists whose ideas have been influenced by Milton Erickson, believe that the "nonrational" feeling side of the personality can often be the source of deep creativity. It is often precisely an overdeveloped, exclusive reliance on rational functioning that interferes with the utilization of this more intuitive, organismically wise side of the person. Carrying this further, cognitive therapists see their job as replacing dysfunctional cognitive schemas with functional ones, while client-centered therapists see the job as loosening rigid dysfunctional cognitive aspects so that a person's creativity may operate.

Finally, family systems theorists believe that behavior is heavily influenced by the immediate interpersonal systems of which people are a part. This view is compatible with behavioral and social learning views, which emphasize the importance of immediate situational influences on the person, such as reinforcers. These views tend to de-emphasize internal personality characteristics, in contrast to the typical psychodynamic view of the person, which emphasizes a relatively fixed, set personality structure established in childhood.

The point of all this is that these differences make theoretical convergence difficult. But you might say, "All of these are true! People are influenced by their past, they do have personalities, and their current interpersonal relationships affect them. People do need to become more rational, and they need to learn to trust their more intuitive side. People have often simply learned bad habits, and sometimes people are avoiding things they don't want to face. There! Now, can't we come up with a unifying theory of the human being, and get on with it?"

The problem with this is: how do we weight each of these factors? It is precisely here that theorists of various orientations differ. A psychodynamicist might agree with the above but argue that the most important factors are the tendency to avoid painful experience and the impact of the past. A family systems therapist might agree that personality exists, but believe that the here-and-now family system is the most important factor influencing behavior. A client-centered therapist might agree that humans avoid painful issues, but believe that the most important factor is the human capacity to change and grow creatively.

At the present time, we are a long way from being able to properly assign weights to these different factors. We simply do not know enough about human behavior to do this with any degree of accuracy. As a result, claims that any one theory can be used to integrate all psychotherapy are premature. It is unlikely that any one theory would be able to please individuals who have allegiances to any of the traditional viewpoints (Bohart, 1992).

As a result, theoretical integration is the approach to psychotherapy integration that is most fraught with potential problems. There are those who do not even believe that it is a useful one. Beutler (1989) believes that theories are primarily reflections of individually held values. They are more like philosophical worldviews and have little to do with actual therapy practice. Therefore, it is more fruitful to concentrate on the empirical question of what works best with what problems than on unifying theory. On the other hand, there are those such as Arkowitz (1989, 1992) who believe that theoretical integration is ultimately important because it helps practitioners to frame and understand the use of various techniques, as well as to develop new techniques.

Several approaches we have covered in other chapters are actually attempts at theoretical integration, such as the emotion-focused approach of Elliott, Watson, Goldman, and Greenberg (2004; in chapter 9), and the interpersonal cognitive approach of Safran and Segal (1990; in chapter 11). In addition, there have been several other interesting attempts at theoretical integration. One of the most influential is that of Paul Wachtel (1997), who has tried to integrate behavioral and psychodynamic ideas. Wachtel holds that early childhood experiences set the stage for adult dysfunction. However, he believes that these early childhood experiences create adult dysfunction in "cyclical" unconscious, self-fulfilling prophecy ways. That is, they lead the person to behave in a way that then brings reinforcement from the here-and-now situation for the pattern of behavior carried forward from childhood. Thus, both childhood and here-and-now reinforcement play a role in the maintenance of adult pathological behavior. Suppose a person unconsciously learned to be submissive to her parent as a way of avoiding her anger toward a parent she perceived as mistreating her. Now, as an adult, she acts in a timid, deferential way, all the while repressing her anger. It is likely that she will actually elicit mistreatment from others, thereby reinforcing the dysfunctional behavior pattern. The more mistreated she is, the more deferential she becomes. In psychotherapy the goal is not only to help her gain insight into her unconscious patterns and anger, but also to get her to behave differently in the here and now. Either can break the dysfunctional pattern.

Mahoney (1991) has proposed an integrative developmental cognitive model. Mahoney adopts the constructivist position that reality is relative and that each individual constructs his reality. There is no "one" objective reality that can be said to be the correct one. Therefore, one cannot talk about the rationality or irrationality or the truthfulness or falsity of constructions. One can only talk about whether a person's construction of reality works or is viable. This also implies that ideas about reality are never perfect or finished but continue to be modified with experience. Learning and development involve elaborating, differentiating, and refining ideas about the world. These ideas or constructions exist to a large extent at a tacit or nonconscious level. Some of these constructions may have been developed early in life. People resist rapid change in their core constructs because they strive to protect the integrity and coherence of their worldviews. In contrast to some cognitive theorists, Mahoney emphasizes the importance of affect or emotion. He sees emotions as powerful, knowing processes. He also emphasizes the unity of thought, feeling, and action.

For Mahoney, psychological difficulties represent discrepancies between challenges and capacities. In other words, difficulties arise when coping skills cannot match the challenges of reality. Furthermore, pathological responses often represent behavior patterns that were adaptive in some prior life situations. Therapy for Mahoney includes utilizing cognitive insight, exploring affective responses, utilizing behavioral methods, working with rather than against resistance, and providing a safe, caring therapeutic relationship as a context that facilitates change. Mahoney's approach draws on psychodynamic, humanistic, cognitive, behavioral, and systems perspectives. In this respect, it represents one of the first truly eclectic theoretical attempts at integration.

Bohart (1992) has proposed an integrative theory based on the idea of process. First, he suggests that psychopathology is not primarily a matter of misconstruing, distorting, or misperceiving. Nor is it primarily a matter of behaving inappropriately. In fact, if you think back on your previous week, you will probably be able to remember at least one incident when you misperceived something and one incident when you behaved in a way that was either not very effective or was inappropriate. Bohart suggests that such misperception and misbehavior are a part of life. Psychopathology occurs when the person fails to learn from feedback and therefore fails to modify misperceptions or dysfunctional behavior.

To put it another way, the issue is not "Why am I chronically misperceiving myself as no good," but rather "Why am I not learning from feedback that this misperception is not helping me deal with life effectively?" Put this way, psychopathology becomes a matter of a failure to learn. Life is complex and humans are like explorers, trying things out and learning from feedback. Encountering problems is a part of life. Throughout their lives people are continually challenged to alter perceptions and beliefs so as to cope more comprehensively, adaptively, and flexibly. They are also continually challenged to learn and refine behavior so that it becomes more fine-tuned and adaptive. Failure, frustration, and loss are a part of life, and learning how to learn from them and to move on is the key to effective functioning. Psychopathology is a function of how people cope when they fail, confront loss and despair, or experience blocks and obstacles in their life path.

All therapies operate by helping the client learn how to learn, that is, by helping the client function more intelligently. The therapy process itself models the very skills that are needed to learn creatively. First, in order to master problematic experiences, a person must be able to "stay with" these experiences, which means tolerating and acknowledging the unpleasant emotions, such as anger, anxiety, despair, or fear, that accompany them. Therapists model and encourage this process of tolerating and staying with these emotions in order to learn about the problematic experiences. This is modeled by psychodynamic, humanistic, and cognitive therapists. Even behavior therapists, by encouraging their clients to keep records of when and where they feel negative emotions, implicitly encourage attending to the emotion in order to learn about it rather than avoid it.

Second, therapists model the idea that people must continually check abstractions about self, others, and life in general against data and experience. This allows them to learn and modify abstractions to better fit their experiences of reality.

Third, therapists encourage clients to broaden their range of attention. Clients are often failing to find new solutions to life problems because their attention span is overly constricted. They fail to notice information available either in the environment or in themselves. Both psychodynamic and humanistic therapists encourage clients to track the flow of their inner experience, that is, to pay greater attention to internal information. Cognitive and behavior therapists encourage a broader attention span with respect to external information. Cognitive therapists encourage clients to notice exceptions to the generalized dysfunctional rules and beliefs they are using to guide their lives. Behavior therapists encourage clients to pay attention to when and where problems occur.

Next, most therapies encourage the client to pay more attention to the process of struggling with a problem rather than to the product or outcome. They encourage an exploratory attitude, that is, individuals must try things out, learn and explore. And part of that exploratory process is that there will be stops and starts and setbacks as a person moves toward resolution.

Assimilative Integration

Even if no one had become interested in actively fostering the integration of the differing approaches to psychotherapy, there is ample evidence that a movement toward psychotherapy integration has been happening anyway in the form of ***assimilative integration*** (Messer & Warren,1990; Stricker & Gold, 2003). This means that integration may happen as a given approach begins to assimilate insights from the other approaches.

Assimilative integration appears to be happening on all fronts. In the area of psychodynamic theory, object relations theory is moving toward a rapprochement with cognitive theory, as it begins to focus on the idea that our behavior is driven by internal cognitive representations of our relationships with people. Self psychology is really an integrative theory, comprising aspects of both psychodynamic and humanistic theory (Tobin, 1990). Cognitive approaches (see Alford & Beck 1998) have integrated insights and techniques from both behavioral and humanistic approaches. We have already mentioned that many cognitive theorists are now incorporating ideas from psychodynamic attachment theory. Existential-humanistic approaches have begun to integrate insights from cognitive theory and from psychoanalytic attachment theory (e.g., Greenberg, Rice, & Elliott, 1993; Greenberg, Safran, & Rice, 1989), as well as from self psychology (Tobin, 1990). A recent existential-humanistic integrative model shows how existential therapists can fruitfully use cognitive, behavioral, and psychodynamic approaches within an existential framework (Schneider & May, 1995). Finally, most modern psychodynamic, humanistic, and cognitive theorists take the idea that people are affected by their current interpersonal systems quite seriously. And there have been several attempts to integrate family systems theory itself with ideas from other psychotherapeutic approaches (Allen, 1988; Feldman, 1992; Wachtel, 1994).

In the previous editions of this text we presented our version of a "common factors" approach to psychotherapy integration. We believe there do appear to be a number of factors that are common to differing approaches, particularly an attempt to solve a common underlying problem, that of access.

The Basis of All Therapies: The Problem of Access

In a sense, all therapies exist because people's attempts to control their own or others' behavior and feelings by rational argument, persuasion, command, and analysis frequently fail. Suppose you have a friend named Sue. Sue is involved with Bill, but Bill constantly mistreats her. He goes out on her, is inconsiderate and self-centered, and has even hit her on occasion. All of Sue's friends tell her that Bill is no good for her. She will even say that she knows that he is no good for her. Yet this knowledge seems to have no effect on her feelings. She loves him nevertheless. At the same time, there is Ron. Ron is kind, considerate, faithful, and reliable. Everyone tells Sue that Ron would be perfect for her. Intellectually, Sue believes this also. But knowing that Ron is right for her seems to have no effect on how she feels. She just doesn't feel attracted to him.

We will give one other example. You are about to go on a job interview. You begin to feel anxious. You tell yourself there is nothing to fear. You may even try to argue rationally with yourself: "It is in my better interest to be relaxed at the job interview." Yet, perversely, against your own better interest, you find your pulse racing, you are sweating, and your voice may be quavering as you begin the interview.

People may know intellectually what they should do or what would be best for them but find themselves unable to act or feel accordingly. When they dislike some way they are behaving or feeling, they may try different intellectual means to change. They may self-engineer (Gendlin, 1964), that is, decide how they should behave and command themselves to act accordingly. They may argue rationally with themselves, marshalling evidence for why they ought to change their behavior. Or, they may hunt for reasons why they aren't acting the way they believe they ought—they speculate that there may be underlying reasons for their behavior. They play detective and gather clues for various possibilities. Maybe they are staying in a dysfunctional relationship because they have an underlying need for security. Or perhaps they eat too much because they are compensating for dissatisfaction in their love life. Or maybe they have an underlying need to fail. But such deductions do no good. They still don't change. Thus, it could be said that people try to cognitively control their behavior either through rational argument, command, and persuasion, or through attempts at self-analysis. Underlying these attempts to change behavior are usually expectations of how people think they should be in order to be happy.

People use similar methods to try to control or change others' behavior. Parents say, "Eat your spinach. It's good for you." They warn adolescents of the dangers of drug abuse. They present a friend with rational arguments in favor of leaving a destructive relationship.

If behavior and feeling states could be controlled consistently through conscious, rational means, we would not need therapists. People would simply explain to themselves and others logically why they should act or feel in such and such a way and they would do it. But people come to therapy when such efforts fail. They come when they are unable to persuade themselves not to be depressed or that there is nothing to fear if they go outdoors. They come because they cannot control their drinking or change the pattern of arguing in their marriage. They come because they have physical illnesses that are inexplicable and do not respond to medical treatment. They are sent by parents or the legal system, who have failed to persuade them to comply with society's norms.

We conceive of the person as an organized system of behaviors, thoughts, perceptions, motives, beliefs, and emotions. The problem of access is: Why does direct rational, intellectual information fail to gain access to the system of the person and facilitate change? For instance, why doesn't it work when a person says to herself, "I can control my impulses to eat, if I try," but it does work when a therapist, utilizing Erickson's techniques, says, "Pay attention to what you do this week when you control your urge to eat"? The message "I can control my impulses to eat" is implied in both, but the less direct communication somehow gains access and works, while the more direct communication does not get through.

Put another way, the access problem has to do with the fact that one part of the person can know what is needed to change, but that knowledge somehow does not affect other parts of the person. Different therapies have different theories of why direct, conscious, rational communications do not have an immediate impact on the person. Different therapies also have their own ways of gaining access. In fact, most therapy techniques could be viewed as different methods of communicating or generating information so that it gets through and facilitates change. We will first look at general strategies for facilitating access and then at each major perspective and how it deals both theoretically and practically with this problem.

Strategies for Facilitating Access

Experiential Methods

Cognitive learning and consciousness raising have been postulated as common underlying dimensions in psychotherapy, yet, as we have repeatedly pointed out, no approach relies on cognitive learning alone. All, in one way or another, include an experiential component to increase the effectiveness of cognitive learning (Bohart, 1993). The importance of experiential learning has also been cited as a common dimension by Goldfried (1980a), Gendlin (1996), and Arkowitz and Hannah (1989). However, we wish to point out the interrelatedness of cognitive and experiential learning. That is, sheer cognitive learning alone seems to be ineffective. However, cognitive learning plus an experiential component seems to be one of the ways of gaining access. There are at least three different, but overlapping, ways in which experiential learning is utilized to facilitate access: direct experience, experiential articulation, and experiential evocation.

Direct Experience. Many approaches rely on direct experiential learning. Behavioral approaches are perhaps the best example of this. Behavior modifiers reinforce or extinguish behavior at the moment it is occurring. Meichenbaum and Bandura provide direct modeling of individuals learning how to cope with various problem situations and then encourage practice of the behaviors involved. Social skills training programs involve direct behavior rehearsal. Conditioning techniques, such as systematic desensitization, attempt to modify directly emotional reactions to real or imagined stimuli.

The cognitive-behavioral approaches of Beck and Ellis include homework assignments in which clients are instructed to test their cognitions directly against experience. Beck also believes that the therapeutic relationship itself is an important source of learning. The client can learn how to challenge dysfunctional cognitions from watching the therapist. George Kelly's cognitive approach included having clients act out roles in real life to try out different behaviors that would lead to different experiences and evidence to correct faulty cognitive constructs.

From a client-centered perspective, Gendlin (1967) has argued that direct experiential interaction in the therapeutic relationship is a potent source of learning. Clients learn how to be self-accepting, how to listen to themselves, and how to be genuine through interaction with an accepting, empathic, genuine therapist.

Recent psychoanalytic approaches, such as those of Kohut and object relations theory, see the therapeutic relationship as a situation in which the client can directly experience the distorting aspects of primitive childhood constructions of reality. Change takes place through a corrective emotional experience as much as through cognitive insight.

Strategic therapists also use exercises involving direct experience. For instance, a client may be coached in how to woo his wife (Madanes, 1985). Other techniques encourage the client to engage in certain behaviors in the hopes that they will break up the client's old system. Once the system is broken up, new, more adaptive behaviors may be creatively discovered through action, without the necessity of cognitive learning or insight. Finally, gestalt therapy also relies on direct experiential learning. Rather than talk about conflict resolution, gestalt therapists will have clients role-play the various sides of the conflict to experience direct learning (Greenberg, 1984).

Experiential Articulation. Many approaches value the acquisition of some kind of insight, or the generation of new, useful self-knowledge. In psychoanalysis, insights may be acquired by the client's own processes of introspection or may be given by the therapist. In client-centered therapy, the process of finding just the right words to formulate what is implicitly known or sensed at the experiential level "carries forward" the growth process (Gendlin, 1964). In both cases, the formulation of this new knowledge in words is not therapeutic unless it articulates or matches the client's experiential state.

Psychoanalytic interpretations are effective only if the proper affective context has been established, that is, the relevant concrete memories and feelings must be close to consciousness. It is like discussing a movie: You are most likely to "gain insight" into the movie when it is "fresh" in your mind. Similarly, insights only work when the problem is "hot," "present," or "alive," rather than cold. At that point, an insight can articulate or connect with a host of bodily aspects of the problem: vivid memories, feelings, or bodily reactions. In the words of one of our colleagues, therapy may connect "feelingless words" with the experiential feeling and "wordless feelings" with meanings (Beverly Palmer, 1987, personal communication).

Client-centered reflections or experiential responses are also attempts to articulate what is currently being felt at the experiential level. Gendlin (1964, 1968) says that words are therapeutic if they come from the client's experiential sense of the problem, rather than being cognitively generated and applied to experiential sense. Thus, a client may say, "I feel really bothered by my wife," and a client-centered therapist may articulate that sense of being bothered more fully, "You feel like she never lets you alone."

Something like experiential articulation also plays a role in Beck's cognitive therapy. For instance, a cognitive therapist could say to a depressed client, "You generate your own depression by interpreting events in a negative way." Such an abstract cognitive insight would probably have little effect on the depressive. What Beck has the client do is keep a daily record of dysfunctional thoughts. At the moment the client is experiencing depression associated with some dysfunctional thought, he attempts to capture that thought in words and write it down, along with an objective description of the situation. The abstract cognition that the client generates his own depression through his cognitions is now matched to a vivid, concrete experiential example.

Finally, de Shazer (1985), a strategic therapist, also uses a kind of experiential articulation. A client who is having trouble dieting may say, "I never can control my eating." De Shazer points out that clients often phrase their complaints in terms of "always" or "never," but things are rarely "always" or "never." However, it would be useless to tell the client, "Oh no. It's not true that you never control your eating. Sometimes you do." It is more effective to instruct the client to "pay attention to what you do when you control your urge to eat," because there will almost always be times that the client does control the urge. The client thus learns concretely and experientially that self-control is not a matter of "always" or "never." We will have other occasions to consider this intervention, as there is more to it than the client's matching of cognitive insight to experience.

All this suggests that cognitive articulation can be useful if it is done in relation to the relevant, directly felt experience. While Beck has his clients keep daily records of dysfunctional thoughts primarily for data-gathering purposes for later discussion and evaluation, psychoanalysis and client-centered therapists believe there is an immediate, direct benefit of experiential articulation. For psychoanalysts such articulation is an emotionally experienced insight that leads to change. For client-centered therapists, experiential articulation leads to a directly felt change in the problem, a sense of integration, clarification, and closure.

It is possible that formulation or articulation of an experience at the moment it is "fresh" consolidates or facilitates learning from it. Consider the example of talking over a movie with friends when you have just seen it and it is fresh. As you attempt to put your reactions into words, you clarify, integrate, and consolidate your impressions of it. Another example might be recording your impressions of a situation as you observe it. Your articulation of what you observe will help you to organize and consolidate learning from the observations (see, for instance, Bandura, 1986). Trying to articulate your impressions later when the situation is not fresh is more difficult and will probably have less of an impact on learning.

There is a question as to whether experiential articulation creates change or merely consolidates it. Psychoanalysis assumes that gaining insight causes change. Gendlin (1964) has argued that insight actually follows change. For example, by the time a person can articulate her anger toward her father, a change has already taken place to make that anger consciously available. Repression has already been overcome. The formulation of the anger in words may serve only to consolidate and integrate this change into the personality structure.

Other models (e.g., Bucci, 1995; Martin, Paivio, & Labadie, 1990) of why verbal knowing does not necessarily create change at the bodily, nonverbal level have proposed that there are two fundamentally different *knowing systems*, a verbal one and a nonverbal one (Paivio, 1986). These models have argued that therapy must work to build "bridges" connecting verbal knowing to knowing that has been achieved through primarily nonverbal, imagistic means. Only when such bridges are built will full therapeutic change take place.

Experiential Evocation in Therapy. In order for new meanings to be developed and learned in an experiential context, therapy may have to evoke the relevant experiential reactions. This can be done through the use of words, images, or exercises. Techniques may be used to evoke vivid memories, images, relevant feelings, "felt meanings" (Gendlin, 1964), or other whole body experiences associated with a problem situation. Or there may be a specific focus on the evocation of strong emotional reactions.

There are various ways therapists attempt to evoke experiential reactions in therapy. One way is to use vivid, everyday language. Concrete language is more likely to evoke an experiential reaction than abstract jargon. Most therapy orientations advocate the use of concrete, vivid language.

To make information vivid and concrete, therapists of many schools attempt to get clients to "flesh out" vague, abstract characterizations of their problems with concrete details.

Fleshing out abstractions partially allows hypothesis testing. The client is able to see if generalizations such as "I can never control my hunger" or "I always fail" are accurate. In addition, however, recalling a concrete example of when the client failed or when he had difficulty controlling his hunger will be more likely to evoke the bodily feelings and experiences associated with the abstract statement. This is an explicit part of the problematic reaction point procedure in emotion-focused therapy (Elliott et al., 2004). The client is asked to imagine himself in the specific situation in which he experienced the problem. Then exploration takes place with that specific situation as a constant referent. The gestalt role-playing technique also re-evokes the concrete experiential components of a problem.

Imagery is also used in the cognitive therapies of Beck and Ellis, and therapy approaches based on Erickson's work, such as strategic therapy, often use stories or metaphors. Such stories probably work both because they convey the meaning in an experientially evocative context and because their indirect nature bypasses the "negative self-monitor" (discussed below).

Arousal of Emotion. Some approaches to therapy focus explicitly on the arousal of strong emotion. The belief is that certain emotions, usually anger or sadness, are so repressed by society, and thus by the individual, that they "build up" like fluids inside the person, causing psychological problems. This is often called the "hydraulic model" of emotions. These approaches attempt to evoke these emotions and to cause them to be discharged through expression, called "emotional catharsis."

While catharsis therapies and techniques may be effective, the idea that emotions are like fluids that need to be vented and discharged is debatable. Gendlin (1984b), for instance, has pointed out that merely "feeling the feeling" is not, by itself, therapeutic. People often fully experience and express their anger without undergoing any change or resolution of their problems. Beck (Beck, Rush, Shaw, & Emery, 1979) has noted that crying and the expression of sadness in cognitive therapy sometimes make clients feel better, but often do not.

Summaries of research on anger have concluded that the hydraulic model of emotions does not fit the data and that catharsis or expression of feelings alone is not therapeutic (Bohart, 1980; Kennedy-Moore & Watson, 1999). Sometimes anger expression makes people feel more angry rather than less, and again, though crying sometimes makes people feel better, frequently, it does not. What is therapeutic about approaches that stress emotional arousal and expression is that such approaches provide experiential opportunities for cognitive insight or working through. Without such an insight or working-through process, the sheer expression of feelings will not be therapeutic. In other words, to relate it to our current topic, it is likely that emotional arousal and expression evoke the whole range of bodily experiences and memories associated with a conflict situation. It is not merely the emotional expression itself that happens. In addition, the whole experiential context of the problem is made available for cognitive reworking.

Beck (1987) has said that cognitive therapy works better when affect is aroused. It is easier to work on a client's anxiety or depression when the client is experiencing these feelings. However, this is not because the emotions are being expressed and drained off, but because when the client is feeling anxious or depressed, the associated dysfunctional cognitions are more available and more readily modified.

Experiential Components in Therapy

All these various uses of an experiential component in therapy suggest that therapy must ultimately have an impact at the bodily or experiential level. Sheer cognitive insight, especially if couched in abstract terms, seems to have little impact at the bodily or experiential level. Therefore, some therapists attempt to work directly at that level. They reinforce behavior changes. These behavior changes presumably include the bodily cues and schemas that direct and control the behavior. Or they attempt to teach new behavior schemes or to directly condition emotional responses.

Other approaches attempt to modify these bodily reactions and schemes through cognitive reconstruction. They may help the client to gain insight, or they may convey a new way of looking at something in a story. In either case, such cognitive insights are useless unless the relevant bodily, experiential cues are present. There must be a match between bodily experience and cognition for the cognition to influence or consolidate behavior change. Experiential evocation, then, may make bodily cues available for reworking and reprocessing. Cognitively talking about and articulating one's experience as one is experiencing it may create change at the bodily level. In a similar manner, observing someone do something is a direct visual experience, and learning may be facilitated if one articulates to oneself the relevant factors being demonstrated.

This would explain why abstract, cognitive insight is frequently useless. Such abstract cognitive insights by themselves do not evoke the relevant concrete bodily reactions. If they are to be useful at all, they need to be timed to when such cues are present.

We should also point out that the relevant variable is the presence of experiential cues, not necessarily emotional cues. Many therapies have focused on emotion or affect. But emotion is actually a subset, or one kind, of experience. It is likely that emotional focus in therapy is helpful because it evokes experiential reactions. When a client gets in touch with her childhood anger toward her father, this usually also evokes vivid visual memories and other bodily reactions. The therapeutic learning probably involves all the bodily components of the experiential reaction, not just the emotional ones, just as learning to drive a car evokes and involves experiential reactions that are not necessarily emotional.

We will conclude this section with a relevant story of a friend. When this friend was a young woman she was in a play. Her role was of a pregnant woman considering an abortion. Until our friend played this role she had never really "worked out" her own feelings about abortion. Oh, sure, she had heard pro and con arguments. But, as we have seen, most such arguments tend to be abstract, and they often do not have an impact on people because they are not "meaningful" or "relevant" at the time. How often do you hear people say: "They were just words until it happened to me"? In terms of what we have been saying, the arguments do not have an impact, they are "just words" because the person is not having the relevant bodily experience. For our friend, arguments for and against abortion had been just words until she played the role of someone struggling with the issue. She found that through playing this role, the issue became much more concrete and real to her, and she had to work through her own feelings about it. When, sometime later, she accidentally became pregnant and had to face the issue for herself, she found that her prior experience in the play had helped her clarify her choices. She was able to decide fairly confidently on the right thing to do for her.

Practice and Habit

Practice to develop new habits also plays a role in creating experiential change. There are at least two reasons for this. The first is evidential, that is, people are not going to give up a belief system simply because of one or two disconfirmations of it. Even though Beck could demonstrate that a client's failure at wallpapering wasn't really a failure (see chapter 11), the client will need repeated demonstrations before he is willing to give up his general belief that he is incompetent. People want good, stable evidence (i.e., repeated experience) before they are willing to change their beliefs.

Second, it is through practice and experience that people often come to understand what abstract formulations really mean. Suppose you are learning to drive and your instructor gives you directions: "Let out the clutch slowly as you step on the accelerator." While this may seem fairly specific, it is actually an imprecise, abstract description of what you are to do. How slowly? How much do you step on the accelerator? When do you coordinate the two events? You jarringly find out that the instruction is only a rough guide to what you are to do as you lurch forward wildly or stall the car. The words of the instruction are abstract because they do not precisely tell you (nor could they) the specific bodily movements and events involved. You have to use the words as a rough guide and then practice. Eventually, you learn at the bodily level the specific reactions and movements involved and no longer need to guide yourself with the imprecise words. When you finally get it right, you may even find that the vague and abstract words now make concrete bodily sense. "Oh, I see! Let the clutch out as I step on the accelerator!" Practice with any cognitive abstraction may eventually cause bodily change. The abstract generalizations guide the learning of specific bodily skills. Suppose I challenge myself every time I catastrophize: "It's not awful that I didn't get an A on the test, although I would have preferred an A." I may eventually change the bodily schemas associated with the catastrophizing in a manner similar to my learning to work a clutch. Eventually I may no longer need to verbalize to myself. Suddenly I may find that the words make more sense to me: "Oh, I see! I would have preferred to get an A, but it isn't awful that I didn't!"

We have given examples of habit as a method of creating access for certain cognitive insights. Of course, habit is also a key component of behavioral approaches, in which repeated practice facilitates direct experiential learning.

Neutralizing the Effects of Negative Self-Monitoring

One of the most important abilities that human beings have is to monitor their own actions, thoughts, and feelings. They not only respond to stimuli, perform behaviors, think, and feel, but watch themselves do these things and use their observations to change if they are not responding adaptively. It has been argued that virtually all dysfunctional behavior involves dysfunctions in self-monitoring (Bohart, 1992). An integrative approach to psychotherapy by Ryle (1982) is based on a similar idea. All of us have mistaken ideas about reality from time to time and occasionally behave in ways that are not adaptive. However, most of the time, we are able to correct this behavior, while in cases of dysfunctional behavior, the person fails to correct or modify mistaken ideas or maladaptive responses.

In psychotherapy, we suggest that there are various ways clients have of monitoring themselves and others that contribute to the access problem. Information can result in change only if it is fully and accurately heard. However, this does not always occur in therapy because people tend not to listen to the information being given but instead evaluate it in ways that seem to interfere with its therapeutic function. We call this *negative self-monitoring*. For instance, clients may find ways of discounting or misusing the information they receive. They may hear feedback as criticism and use it to further devalue themselves. Clients may discount positive feedback because they believe the therapist is being paid to "say nice things," or they may resist input because they perceive it as a threat to their autonomy or to unconscious maintenance of repression. Or, as part of how they monitor themselves, they may use their perceptions of what is wrong to implement dysfunctional methods of fixing things. For example, they may try to fix a sexual arousal problem by trying to become aroused, which may instead make matters worse.

Similarly, if clients' existing ways of interpreting the world are inadequate, then any self-analysis they engage in will reflect these inadequacies and will merely perpetuate the problem. Depressive thinking is a good example. Even information that most people see as positive fails to change a depressive because it is evaluated in terms of the depressive's existing negative conceptions. Similarly, a depressive critically monitors her own behavior and sees it as inappropriate, bad, or maladaptive. She does not merely receive information, but interprets it to conform to her view of the world and herself. Because of this monitoring, any internal or external communication loses its therapeutic potential.

Critical self-monitoring may interfere with information processing because it mobilizes resistance. Many people resist being influenced by others, even if resisting is to their disadvantage. People also resist internal behavioral and emotional prescriptions. If I critically tell myself I ought to diet, I may experience my freedom as being restricted and rebel. This may be particularly true if I perceive dieting as a demand internalized from my parents and society. It is for this reason that gestalt and client-centered approaches are so interested in getting clients to choose their shoulds and oughts as their own or discard them.

There are other reasons for resistance. The critical monitor may evaluate information as a threat to repression and therefore distort or deny it. Similarly, information that is evaluated as a threat to existing ways of viewing the world and the self may be interpreted and modified to be compatible with the existing schemes. The information's potential for causing change is therefore neutralized. Resistance may also be generated by internal conflict (Arkowitz, 1991)—one part of the self wants to change and another doesn't. In this case, information will once again not be utilized therapeutically.

Phenomenological Attitude. The phenomenological method was originally a philosophical approach developed by Edmund Husserl (1964). The goal of the phenomenological method is to "get back to pure experience" by suspending preconceptions. Therapeutically, this means the client should try to simply observe something without attempting to figure out what it "means" at an underlying level, or without judging it or evaluating it as good, bad, adaptive, maladaptive, appropriate, or inappropriate. This also means that the client suspends the way he already views and interprets the world and his experience. Only by doing this can new learning occur.

Many therapies attempt to get the client to suspend critical evaluation; for example, psychoanalysis encourages the client to free-associate. In normal social conversation, a person evaluates the thoughts that pop into his mind. Those that are seen as irrelevant or morally or socially inappropriate are censored by the person and not verbalized. With free association the client is to report whatever comes to mind. Psychoanalysts believe there is an unconscious censor that critically evaluates both internal and external information. It screens out of consciousness forbidden wishes, impulses, and thoughts. It also leads the person to distort, deny, or otherwise misuse information from outside, such as communications by the therapist. Getting the client to consciously suspend the censor and simply listen nonevaluatively to whatever comes to mind gradually allows forbidden material to appear. As this happens more frequently, the client's conscious "observing" ego becomes strengthened, and the client has less and less need to evaluate and screen out or distort information. In some sense, the goal of psychoanalysis is to enable the client to listen nonevaluatively to all his thoughts, feelings, and fantasies, no matter how primitive.

Client-centered therapists similarly encourage a nonevaluative attitude. They do this through their own nonjudgmental acceptance of the client and through attempts to intuit a human, understandable motive behind behavior, even if the behavior is dysfunctional or repugnant. Gendlin (1964) emphasizes that attempts at self-monitoring and self-regulation "from above" are untherapeutic and that the client needs instead to wait and listen to her experiential self. A person cannot therapeutically hear what is in her experiencing if she is critically evaluating what ought to be there.

Gestalt therapists have argued that "pure awareness" is therapeutic. They encourage attempts to observe and be aware of what is, without analyzing what it means or judging how it ought to be or whether it is good or bad, appropriate or inappropriate, adaptive or maladaptive.

The phenomenological method is used in its purest form in meditation. Martin (1997), similar to our argument here, has suggested that the meditational attitude is a therapeutic common factor. Washburn describes receptive meditation as "the practice of open, nonreactive attention. Experience is witnessed nonselectively and without interference or interpretation" (1978, p. 46). Meditation itself has become an important part of both cognitive and behavior therapy (Segal, Williams, & Teasdale, 2001). In addition, behavioral approaches to habit control include having clients keep a diary of when and where they engage in the habitual behavior. Keeping such a record makes clients observe their own behavior and reactions and the situations that seem to elicit them. Reinforcement procedures can be utilized to modify the behavior. However, simply keeping the diary itself is often helpful, perhaps because it increases clients' awareness.

Beck's (1987) cognitive treatment for depression includes keeping records of when and where depression occurs and the dysfunctional cognitions present. This employs the phenomenological method because the client is learning to separate the situation itself from his analysis and evaluations of it. Beck has clients practice writing alternative interpretations of the situation. This further reinforces the client's learning to perceive a situation independently of his preconceptions. Ellis's A-B-C model, in which A is the situation, B the interpretation, and C the emotional or behavioral reaction, also encourages the client to observe nonevaluatively (Ellis, 1973).

Finally, de Shazer (1985) also uses a variant of the phenomenological method. As we have shown, a client with a dieting problem may be encouraged to pay attention to what she does when she resists the urge to eat. The intervention is to simply pay attention to these things, not to try to make them happen.

Adopting the phenomenological attitude encourages the client's "gaining distance" from the problem. Mahoney lists "distanced manifestation" as one method of problem resolution. He says it "entails a joint effort to allow the problem to manifest itself fully while one simultaneously disidentifies from it" (1985, p. 30). This can be seen to operate in various therapeutic approaches. For instance, psychoanalytic free association allows parts of the problem to become "fully manifest" and the client learns to "disidentify" with the unconscious impulses: "I am not identical to my primitive incestuous desires. There is more to me than that."

From a client-centered perspective, Gendlin has described what happens as clients learn to listen nonevaluatively and focus on felt meanings: "In learning to put problems down one learns a specific relation to problems: sensing them but not being in them. . . . That distance enables one to relate to the problem as a whole, *from a spot a little outside it*" (1982, p. 27, italics Gendlin's). From a cognitive perspective, Beck et al. say, "As situations and cognitions are recorded, the patient gains some distance from their effect. The therapist's goal is to increase the patient's objectivity about his cognitions" (1979, p. 164). Gaining distance and learning that "I am not my problem" is a key part of narrative therapy (White, 2004).

Indirect Circumvention. These techniques are used primarily by therapists who have been influenced by Milton Erickson. They include indirect suggestion, communication through metaphorical stories, reframing, and paradoxical interventions (see chapter 13). The intervention we have considered several times previously is an example of indirect suggestion: a client who wants to diet is not directly told "You can control your eating." Instead, the message is indirectly suggested: "Pay attention to what you do when you control your urge to eat."

Paradoxical interventions and reframing apparently encourage the persistence of symptoms and problem behaviors. A contentious client may be told to deliberately get in arguments. A couple who continually fight may be told that their fighting is a sign of how much they love one another. They may even be told that to stop fighting would be disastrous for their marriage. How do such paradoxical interventions work?

There are a variety of theories as to why they do work. We suggest that one reason is they circumvent or turn off critical self-monitoring. The activity of criticizing themselves for problem behavior such as arguing is disrupted if people are told to do it, or if they are told that it would be disastrous if they stopped. Similarly, the activity of trying to self-engineer, control, and demand that they act differently is also disrupted.

Therapeutic Value of Suspending Self-Monitoring

Why is it therapeutic to cease self-criticism, conscious intellectual self-analysis, and self-engineering? Why is it therapeutic to observe and listen nonevaluatively, that is, to receptively self-monitor? One positive result of suspending critical, analytic, and evaluative monitoring is that new information can get through and facilitate change. For instance, if you continually evaluate your behavior and feelings in terms of shoulds and oughts, you may distort them. If you think you should not be behaving in a certain way, you may either deny the existence of this behavior or misrepresent it. You may "repress," "deny," or "split off" your feelings or other parts of yourself. You may also misrepresent or distort messages from outside. Information then fails to have an impact and facilitate change.

Another way that reducing self-monitoring may help is that there appear to be times when a person is more likely to change if she does not try. Perhaps the best example is modifying sexual behavior. If clients are busy trying to change behavior, they are less available to experiencing the pleasurable, self-corrective aspects of the activity. In this case, monitoring behavior and trying to self-engineer become part of the problem and interfere with natural self-regulatory processes. De Shazer (1985) and Watzlawick (1987) point out that a person's attempts at solution often perpetuate or magnify the problem. This is particularly true if these attempts grow out of the person's way of viewing the problem and the world, and these views are dysfunctional.

For instance, suppose a husband and wife both believe that "If you love me, you will make no demands on me. You will be sensitive to my needs." The husband comes home from work and does not want to talk. The wife, who has been at home with only a 3-year-old to talk to all day, wishes to talk. She interprets the husband's wish not to talk as a sign that he doesn't care about her. Her solution to this is to criticize and accuse him of not caring about her. Similarly, he feels that if she cared about him, she would not demand that he talk. His solution is to criticize her. Then they both see the arguing as a further sign of the other's lack of caring. So both become increasingly guarded and defensive, looking for further signs of lack of caring and responding with further criticism. In other words, they try to solve the problem by criticizing each other, but the attempt at solution itself becomes a part of the problem.

Disrupting the clients' attempts to try to solve the problem, then, may facilitate solution ("Don't just do something. Stand there!"). If arguments are reframed as "showing love," then people will not worry so much if an argument occurs. They will not interpret the argument as a sign of difficulty. They will then not get so defensive and be so vigilant for further signs of lack of caring or "insensitivity" or whatever. And the relationship will become less of a battleground.

Paradoxical interventions also suspend negative self-monitoring. Suppose the couple is assigned the task of noticing and responding to anything that appears to be a slight. They have been assigned to try to do what they have apparently already been doing. But actually, what they had previously been trying to do was fix up the marriage by noticing apparent slights and challenging them. Now they have been assigned to try to be critical and defensive, rather than to try to save the marriage. Thus, the paradoxical intervention suspends their attempts to save the marriage. This may interfere with their interpreting apparent slights as threats to the marriage. If they are busily on the lookout for slights because they are supposed to notice them and defend themselves, they are less likely to be thinking that a slight means "My spouse doesn't love me." As they no longer worry so much about whether they love each other, the tension may ease. Put another way, the paradoxical intervention may disconnect the occurrence of an argument from the interpretation that "This means that you don't love me."

Finally, we believe that methods of dealing with negative self-monitoring partially work by shifting the client's attentional focus; that is, by either defocusing or refocusing the client's attention. Clients partly create their problems by dysfunctionally focusing attention on aspects of their own behavior and the environment, which feed back and maintain their problematic reactions. For instance, according to Beck's cognitive theory, depressives overfocus on aspects of their experience that are negative. At the same time, they neglect positive aspects. All that a person might see in a particular situation is its potential for failure, rather than noticing the potential available for success. Psychoanalytically, someone who has failed to develop a stable sense of separation and individuation as a child will overfocus on aspects of relationships that involve autonomy or dependency. Such a person might focus only on a prospective romantic partner's apparent ability to provide a merging experience, and therefore may neglect to focus on other things relevant to a good relationship. Encouraging clients to adopt the phenomenological attitude encourages them to defocus or decenter their attention (Safran & Segal, 1990). Instead of paying attention to only selected aspects of their experience, they are encouraged to "stand back." This may lead to their noticing previously neglected aspects and may by itself cause a shift in the way they view things.

Indirect methods appear to work in part by shifting attentional focus. For instance, reframings shift the focus of the client's attention away from the failure aspects of an experience to more positive ones. If the client is not overfocusing on failure aspects, she may now be free to notice aspects of the situation that can lead to new, positive behavior or to solutions. Paradoxes may also do this. Suppose a husband and wife who argue are ordered to argue at 5:00 PM every day. Knowing they are going to argue at that time, they may find their attention free to flow to other aspects of their relationship at other times, rather than continually looking out for potential conflicts between them. They may begin to focus on positive aspects and find ways of compromising so that by 5:00 PM they have nothing to argue about.

Theoretical Reasons for the Access Problem

Now that we have considered the various ways therapies attempt to deal with the access problem, we will briefly look at some theoretical explanations for its existence. In one way or another, they all involve a lack of conscious awareness.

Our whole consideration of the problem of access was based on the observation that people frequently cannot change problem behavior or feeling through abstract, cognitive self-commands or self-analysis. Nor are such commands and information from others necessarily useful by themselves. In considering different therapeutic solutions to this problem we have encountered a variety of therapeutic techniques in which cognitive formulation of insight is irrelevant. Behavioral approaches may work whether or not the client formulates a cognitive, verbal insight about what is going on. Metaphorical stories may convey meaning and initiate change even though the individual cannot consciously state how she has been changed. Similarly, paradoxical techniques may instigate change without the client's being consciously aware of how the change has occurred. Watzlawick (1987) has said that change occurs all the time in everyday life without insight.

Thus, it is not certain that in order to change, the client needs to be able to formulate the problem or its presumed cause or what needs to be done. Yet the issue of awareness or its lack is involved in each theoretical perspective on the access problem. These theories either assume that conscious, rational self-direction doesn't work because of a lack of awareness of the relevant factors involved or that the human is built in such a way that cognition is simply impotent to modify behavior.

For psychoanalysis, conscious, rational self-control is normally impotent because the real causes of behavior have been repressed and are unconscious. In therapy, conscious insights work only if they are timed to coincide with the availability to awareness of the relevant previously repressed concrete memories and affects. For client-centered therapy, conscious, rational self-control often does not work because it consists of shoulds and oughts learned from society and directed at the person. The result is that the individual's experiential organismic wisdom is ignored or denied. In therapy, verbally formulated self-knowledge can be therapeutic if it arises from listening to the experiential, organismically wise bodily level, rather than simply being cognitively derived. For gestalt, conscious, rational self-control frequently fails because it has been split off from ongoing organismic awareness. Words and symbolizations can create behavior change if they arise from the ongoing stream of organismic awareness. Cognitive-behavioral approaches assume that behavior is often controlled by automatic thoughts of which the client is unaware or by cognitions that are conscious but that are not recognized as dysfunctional or irrational.

Each of the above approaches assumes that lack of awareness—of repressed material, experiential bodily wisdom, automatic thoughts, or dysfunctional cognitions—

plays a role in dysfunctional behavior and is why people cannot consciously control such behavior. In various ways they suggest that increasing awareness, under the proper circumstances, can effect change. Other approaches also see a lack of awareness as important in causing dysfunctional behavior but are skeptical that cognitive awareness under any conditions is therapeutic. Behavior therapy is one example. Most problem responses are seen as being learned at a subcortical level and are therefore simply not modifiable by conscious, cognitive activity. Many family systems theorists believe that problems arise from the dynamics of the family system, and family members are not aware of these dynamics. Even family therapists may not have direct knowledge of these dynamics, but may have to infer them. Furthermore, many such therapists do not believe that increasing awareness of these dynamics is particularly therapeutic. They believe that therapeutic interventions must work to change the system directly. Increased awareness is irrelevant.

What is common to practically all the theoretical perspectives is the suggestion that behavior is at least partially controlled by factors that lie outside of conscious awareness.

Other Commonalities in Psychotherapy

The Importance of Self-Acceptance

In previous chapters and in the discussion of negative self-monitoring, we pointed out some negative effects of low self-evaluation. Individuals with feelings of low self-efficacy may pay so much attention to evaluating themselves that they pay less attention to the demands of the task and, as a result, perform less well than they could have. Similarly, focusing on the self may magnify negative feelings and lead to attributing negative character traits to the self.

Theorists such as Ellis, Rogers, and Beck have pointed out the dysfunctional aspects of making negative self-attributions. They suggest that while it may be functional to make process evaluations of how one is performing on a task ("Is this behavior that I am engaging in working or not?"), it is not functional to generalize from specific behavioral failures to one's whole self. It is one thing to say, "I am not understanding this material" and another to conclude, "Therefore I am stupid and no good."

Self-acceptance, however, does not necessarily mean having a positive view of oneself. We have already seen that Ellis, Rogers, Beck, and others believe that attributing global positive traits to oneself may be as dysfunctional as attributing global negative traits. Ellis and Beck suggest that nonevaluative acceptance is healthier than either positive or negative self-evaluation. Ellis has perhaps been most forceful of all in arguing that one would simply be better off never making generalizations about one's whole self from one's behavior. It is better to focus on evaluating one's behaviors and actions.

A common goal of psychoanalytic, humanistic, and cognitive approaches is to facilitate client self-acceptance. Each attempts to get the client to believe that "I am not an overall bad person because I have primitive incestuous wishes and fantasies" (psychoanalysis); "I have certain thoughts, feelings, or perspectives that do not agree with the 'shoulds' I have been taught" (humanistic); or "I have not behaved perfectly or my life does not match my perfectionistic, rigid either/or schemas" (cognitive approaches).

Recently, acceptance in a broader sense has become a major variable in radical behavioral approaches (Hayes, Follette, & Follette, 1995; Linehan, 1997). For instance, in couples therapy, it has been recognized that it is as important to promote partners' acceptance of one another as it is to try to change each partner's behavior so that it pleases the other partner (Christensen, Jacobson, & Babcock, 1995). Linehan (1997) notes the essential paradox between the necessity of accepting clients as they are (and thereby promoting self-acceptance), while encouraging them to change. She argues that it is precisely the therapist's ability in negotiating a continual balance between these two contradictory demands that is involved in the promotion of change.

Rigid Schemas as a Major Cause of Psychopathology

The idea that it is people's interpretations of events that cause problems, rather than the events themselves, is a common theme in psychoanalytic, humanistic, and cognitive therapies. More particularly, these diverse theoretical approaches see psychopathology as the result of rigid, repetitive constructions or worldviews that are imposed on reality. Psychoanalysis holds that the diversity of the real world is reduced by the client to a repetitive reliving of perceptions and interpretations developed in early childhood. Humanistic therapies address how the client boxes reality into rigid shoulds and oughts learned in childhood. Feelings that do not fit the boxes may be disowned or ignored. Gestalt suggests that the client splits experience into rigid categories, such as "good and evil," "mind and body," and then treats these rigid categories as more real than the reality they were meant to describe. Beck's cognitive therapy is based on the assumption that both depression and anxiety are in part the result of dysfunctional cognitive interpretations of reality. These interpretations are based on schemas learned in early childhood and are held rigidly by the client.

Many family systems therapists (Watzlawick, 1987; de Shazer, 1985) hold that problems are caused by the individual's perception and construction of events. They argue that therefore what is needed in therapy is a second-order change, in which the individual's way of construing the world is fundamentally reorganized. Solving a problem from within an established way of construing the world is a first-order change. Second-order changes involve reorganizing clients' basic premises for dealing with the world and would seem to be the goal of most therapies. For instance, psychoanalysis is not interested in helping clients cope from within their rigid childhood-based way of construing the world. Instead, it hopes to cause a fundamental reorganization in this system, so that new, more flexible and accurate solutions to their problems appear.

Rigid schemas have a primitive either/or quality. De Shazer (1985) has said that construing problems in either/or terms is itself part of the problem. For psychoanalysis, the primitive construct systems developed in early childhood include a number of simplistic, either/or ways of construing reality: "Mommy loves either me or daddy, but not both"; "Mommy is either all good or all bad." Some constructions are so primitive that, according to object relations theory, the child does not separate himself from the mother.

Common Therapeutic Goals

Development of a Hypothesis-Testing Attitude

If psychopathology is based on the rigid application of a primitive interpretation of reality, then therapy must involve an attempt to change this interpretation. But most therapists are not interested in merely changing the client's existing way of interpreting reality. They are also interested in developing a hypothesis-testing attitude toward reality. In other words, they do not want the client to recognize her interpretation as limited and simply replace it with another interpretation that is applied the same way. They want the client to realize that any interpretation of the world is a construction, or hypothesis, and that it should be subjected to continual and lifelong evaluation. Carl Rogers said a goal of therapy is to get the client to "hold his constructs tentatively." Beck teaches his clients the method of empirically testing and evaluating cognitions. Similarly, Ellis wants his clients to dispute their irrational cognitions. Finally, Schafer has argued that a key event in psychoanalytic therapy is not merely learning that one has been interpreting the world through primitive childhood constructions, but that such interpretations are constructions and are therefore modifiable.

Reorganization of Personal Meaning

Therapy, therefore, is the reorganization of the client's personal meaning system (Mahoney, 1985). In particular, therapy can be seen as including the differentiation and integration of meaning. A good example would be object relations theory. Object relations theory holds that borderline personalities construe people in rigid ways as either "all good" or "all bad." Part of therapy is learning to develop a more integrated view of people, that there are gradations of good and evil and that a person may be a combination of both. Then, if someone does something "bad," the client does not see him as "all bad." Client-centered, gestalt, and cognitive therapies similarly attempt to create more differentiated and integrated ways of construing the world.

Mahoney (1985) has argued that therapy often works not by eliminating a problem behavior, but by consolidating it into the personality in a more functional way. Something that is currently maladaptive is integrated into the personality in such a way that it loses its destructive qualities and may even come to possess functional qualities. For instance, rebelliousness that may be causing a person difficulty at a job may be "tamed" or integrated into the personality in such a way that it comes to have adaptive uses. When the person learns when, where, and how to express her rebelliousness, it may become useful in fighting injustice or in challenging rigid, conformist ways of doing things.

Similarly, a client who is "oversensitive" to signs of rejection may not eliminate that oversensitivity, that is, he may still notice the subtle cues that he previously interpreted as rejection. But he may learn that his interpretations are not necessarily correct and become able to engage in reality testing. His oversensitivity may become adaptive in that he notices subtle cues others don't, and this quality may make him more effective with other people.

Reframing may work in part by facilitating consolidation and integration (see chapter 13). The ultimate in reframing is R. D. Laing's (1967) view of schizophrenia as a growth process instead of a disease. Regardless of whether or not schizophrenia is a disease, reframing it as a growth experience may be therapeutic. First of all, it will encourage the schizophrenic to no longer view part of herself as bad or socially undesirable. Therefore, it should raise her self-esteem. This should lead to a reduction in anxiety and an increase in effective functioning. In addition, it should encourage the schizophrenic to "use" her schizophrenic experiences in adaptive, prosocial ways. For instance, she may learn to "tame" them and use them artistically. Reframing the experience of being paralyzed in an automobile accident in such a way as to find some meaning may help patients cope. This has been called the use of ***interpretive secondary control*** (Fiske & Taylor, 1984), in which a person "controls" an event by extracting meaning from it. The person may then reorganize the priorities in his life.

Insights into the past also are ultimately therapeutic only if they can be consolidated and reframed. To know that you are the way you are because your father mistreated you may be of little help if all that does is leave you feeling angry. However, if you can reframe the experience and learn to forgive him or see him as an imperfect human being who made mistakes, then the experience can be consolidated into your personality. As you forgive him, you forgive yourself and others, so you take a more flexible, differentiated view of others. You may even be able to use your own experience of being mistreated to empathize with others or to gain a sense that you can triumph over tragedy.

Self-Empowerment

Another common theme among the various therapy approaches is that they all try to give the client a sense of control or "empowerment," a sense of "I can . . ." or "I am able. . . ." (Hubble, Duncan, & Miller, 1999). We have chosen the term empowerment as an umbrella term for several related concepts: overcoming a sense of helplessness, gaining a sense of self-efficacy, taking responsibility for oneself, becoming able to choose, and becoming autonomous. While empowerment is a goal of several approaches, they differ somewhat in how it is to be achieved.

In psychoanalytic theory, a sense of empowerment develops as a result of reclaiming disowned parts of the self. As people are able to acknowledge what has been repressed, they become able to control, coordinate, and integrate their own functioning. In social learning theory and social skills training, the goal is expressed as increasing feelings of self-efficacy. Self-efficacy is the perception that one is able to enact certain behaviors, and it usually increases as one learns effective skills. One of Ellis's goals of therapy is for the client to take responsibility for choices. This occurs as the client learns to challenge her rigid, absolute, musturbatory tendencies.

Research has shown that having a sense of personal control is generally adaptive (Thompson, 2002). Frank (1982) argues that one of the main things therapy does is help clients to overcome feelings of demoralization. And Bandura (1996) thinks that the ultimate outcome of all therapies is to increase feelings of self-efficacy. Both overcoming demoralization and increasing feelings of self-efficacy lead to a sense of hope. And the mobilization of hope may be one of the major ways therapy helps (Snyder, Michael, & Cheavens, 1999).

We have also noted that trying to control oneself is, at times, counterproductive. There are times when receptive acceptance seems to be more therapeutic than attempts at control. However, this may be because active attempts at control do not work and receptive acceptance is the best way to control the situation. Giving up attempts at control is sometimes more adaptive than continuing attempts to control. Beck, Emery, and Greenberg (1985) prescribe acceptance of anxiety as part of their treatment program for anxiety disorders. The old maxim that wisdom is controlling what can be controlled, accepting what cannot be controlled, and knowing the difference may be the essence of self-empowerment.

The Interpersonal Nature of the Human Being

An important, emerging common factor across different approaches is an increasing emphasis on the interpersonal nature of the human being. Psychological problems are increasingly coming to be viewed as primarily interpersonal in nature by all theorists from the systems, humanistic, cognitive-behavioral, and psychodynamic camps. Systems theory, of course, always held this view. Some humanistic theorists, and client-centered theorists also held that psychological problems developed primarily in an interpersonal matrix and could be cured in an interpersonal matrix (e.g., through the provision of warmth, empathy, and genuineness). Some early psychodynamic theorists such as Harry Stack Sullivan emphasized the interpersonal nature of psychopathology and psychotherapy. However, it is only recently that all approaches have come to place the interpersonal in the forefront. Now in the psychodynamic area, object relations theory, attachment theory, and self psychology hold that psychological problems are primarily a matter of disturbed relationships with other people, and therapy is primarily a matter of repairing such relationships. Cognitive therapists see personality disorders as dysfunctional interpersonal strategies that have been learned in an interpersonal matrix. And in the humanistic camp, gestalt theory has moved away from Fritz Perls's highly individualistic emphasis to a more interpersonal focus.

Carrying this further, there are signs of a "paradigm revolution" occurring in how we view the nature of the human being. In chapter 15, we note that the Western view of the self as separate, autonomous, bounded, and directed from within is both masculine and culture-specific and does not fit the experience of many other groups of people in the world. For many other cultures, as well as for women, the self is a "self-in-relation." That is, self exists and has meaning in terms of its relationships, rather than by virtue of its separateness and autonomy.

The emphasis on a view of the self as a self-in-relation has been most forcefully promulgated by feminist and multicultural theorists. However, it fits with new developments in client-centered therapy (Bohart, 2003), gestalt therapy (Wheeler, 1991), and self psychology (Stolorow, 1992). Stolorow, for instance, holds that the person does not exist apart from an interpersonal matrix. One cannot understand an individual's experience in a given moment without reference to the "intersubjective field" of which the person is a member. This is a fundamentally radical shift in how we view human beings, suggesting that our subjective experience, far from being something entirely within us, is fundamentally, in some sense, between ourselves and another person or persons.

From a cognitive perspective, Martin Seligman (1990) has argued that our culture's overemphasis on individuality has left the individual all alone, a fragile, separate, tiny speck in the universe. He argues that to ultimately overcome our culture's current high rate of depression, people must begin to identify with causes larger than themselves. In sum, there may be a paradigm revolution occurring in how we view the nature of the human being—a shift from seeing the human as fundamentally separate to seeing the human as fundamentally interconnected. On the other hand, there are those who disagree with this trend. Anspach (1991) argues that there are many cultures in the world that are aspiring toward the individualistic model of the self in Western societies. Therefore, it is too early to know the outcome of this possible paradigm revolution: It is unclear whether this new, emerging view of the human being will ultimately replace the old, individualistic view.

A Focus on Strength

A focus on strength is emerging as a commonality across at least some forms of psychotherapy. This is compatible with the larger *positive psychology* movement (Snyder & Lopez, 2002). Positive psychologists hold that psychology has excessively focused on pathology and weakness. Replacing this, they study such topics as hope, optimism, courage, creativity, empathy, forgiveness, and wisdom. Recently, they have called for the development of a positive counterpart to DSM (Maddux, 2002). And others (Luborsky et al., 2002) have argued that one reason that all approaches to therapy work approximately equally well may be that they all rely on strength-building positive elements such as the relationship, hope, and other factors.

The emphasis on strength can be traced back at least as far as Carl Rogers. Rogers's method was to listen to and follow the client no matter what the client talked about, whether it was positive or negative. The underlying agenda was to support the client's positive, self-actualizing, self-healing process. Although psychoanalysis was not as overtly strength-focused, even psychoanalysis had its strength-focused aspects. For instance, the analyst was to side with the "healthy" part of the client's ego, and it was that healthy part that actually made therapy work. Solution-focused therapy is particularly strength-based. Therapists do not even dwell on the negative. Instead they resolutely help clients focus on and expand the positive in their lives. Finally, cognitive-behavioral approaches are increasingly becoming focused on using clients' strengths to effect change. For instance, building social skills is a strength-based approach. Fostering forgiveness is another strength-based strategy used by some therapists.

The idea of focusing on strength is a radical shift from the idea that therapy "cures pathology." Instead, the idea is that psychotherapy promotes the positive in people. By promoting strength, clients are able to expand their positive capabilities to deal with life. Negative aspects of behavior (depression, anxiety, and so on) shrink as clients become increasingly adept at joining with life in positive ways.

We shall briefly review three integrative approaches to psychotherapy that grow out of a strength-based approach. They are Bohart and Tallman's (1999) approach emphasizing "the client as active self-healer," a closely related "client-directed" approach developed by Barry Duncan, Scott Miller, and Mark Hubble (Duncan & Miller, 2000; Hubble, Duncan & Miller, 1999), and motivational interviewing (Miller & Rollnick, 2002).

The Client as Active Self-Healer

We have previously reviewed Bohart and Tallman's (1999) contention that the client as active self-healer is the agent who makes therapy work. Expanding on this idea, Bohart and Tallman have proposed an integrative model of therapy. Instead of the doctor–patient hierarchical model that characterizes how many therapists practice (diagnosing clients' problems and development treatment plans for them), they propose a collaborative model, a "meeting of minds," where the therapist's intelligence and knowledge creatively joins with the client's intelligence and knowledge. Different therapy approaches are all valued as different "learning opportunities" that therapist and client can employ together to foster client creativity and resilience. For instance, gestalt techniques, such as the empty chair technique are essentially exercises in creativity. They give the client the opportunity to learn through creative improvisation and discovery. Cognitive-behavioral therapy is more like a tutorial approach. The therapist "coaches" the client by teaching him skills or by supporting him as he confronts fears (exposure). Different clients will be able to utilize these different tools or "learning opportunities" at different times. The goal of the therapist is to collaborate with the client in choosing which learning opportunities will be most beneficial for a client at any given time. Ultimately it is the client's creative application of whatever the therapist offers that fosters change.

The Client-Directed Approach

The approach of Barry Duncan and his colleagues also relies on clients' strengths. Their approach emphasizes the importance of the therapist respecting the client's ideas and working within the client's frame of reference rather than deciding for the client what the problem is and what needs to be done. Duncan, Hubble, and Miller (1997) report the case of Molly, a young girl who has night terrors. She has been taken to various therapists, each of whom decides for her what her problem is and imposes treatment. Nothing works. When she sees Barry Duncan, he asks her what she thinks will work. She comes up with a strategy and within a few weeks the problem is solved. In a subsequent interview with Barry Duncan, she talks about how little other mental health professionals had treated her like she had any ideas at all. For Duncan and his colleagues the key is to work with the client's view of the problem and the client's ideas for how to solve it. In a collaborative dialogue, therapist and client join together to forge the solutions used.

Motivational Interviewing

Motivational Interviewing (Miller & Rollnick, 2002) is an empirically supported approach for working with addictive behavior. More deeply, it is a method for working with resistant clients in general. It is difficult to classify this approach. In one advanced textbook it is listed under the behavior therapies. This is probably because William Miller originally worked within a cognitive-behavioral framework. However, after an early study found that the cognitive-behavioral techniques used did not correlate with abstinence from drinking in alcoholics, but that the empathy of the therapist did (at a very high level; the correlation coefficient was 0.81) (Miller, Taylor, and West, 1980), Miller and his colleague Stephen Rollnick developed Motivational Interviewing as an approach that was heavily based in Rogerian empathy. In contrast to typical weakness-focused treatments for alcohol, in which alcoholics are confronted with their failings, such as denial, Motivational Interviewing works by mobilizing the alcoholic's strengths—namely the alcoholic's own positive reasons for stopping drinking.

How do Miller and Rollnick do this? First, they use a good deal of Rogerian empathic reflection and empathic listening. In contrast to the idea that you have to confront and break through alcoholics' denial, it is surprising how empathic listening actually facilitates alcoholics dropping their defenses and beginning to open up. Then action-oriented questioning strategies are used to further help the client develop her own "change talk"—her own reasons for changing. Miller and Rollnick point out that it is not very useful for the therapist to try to convince the client that she needs to change. What happens when the therapist does this is that the client is liable to move into a position of defending herself and arguing against change. It is better to help the client do the self-convincing. We shall not review all the strategies here. but one is to first ask the client to explore all the reasons for *not* giving up the bad habit, whatever it is, and then reasons for giving it up. Having the reasons for drinking, smoking, or whatever the bad habit is taken seriously seems to help clients then move to the other side and take more seriously reasons for changing.

In Conclusion

When we were completing the 1994 version of this text, we were convinced that psychotherapy integration would be the wave of the future. We expected that most practitioners would be eclectic, borrowing from different approaches and using whatever worked. We envisioned the particular clinical psychologist choosing what would work best with a particular client from a host of possible procedures and philosophical ideas. Based on this, we even contemplated doing away with or significantly shortening our discussion of the major traditional theoretical approaches. However, these expectations were premature. The influence of managed health care on the field of psychotherapy is changing its face (see our discussion in chapter 16). There have been renewed demands for research showing that specific treatments work for specific disorders. This has led to a shift away from the study of common elements in psychotherapy to a renewed focus on so-called "pure-form" psychotherapies (e.g., cognitive-behavioral, psychodynamic, humanistic) and how they can be specifically designed to be used to treat depression, panic, generalized anxiety disorder, eating disorders, and so on. Under managed care, it is as possible that the individual clinician may be required in the future to use a manualized (see chapter 16) version of a pure-form psychotherapy for a client with a particular disorder as it is that the therapist would be allowed to eclectically choose what might work best for that client from a host of procedures and ideas. In accord with this, many psychologists are devoting their attention to developing treatment manuals for psychodynamic, cognitive-behavioral, and experiential-humanistic therapies in order to subject them to empirical test. Correspondingly, energy is being diverted away from psychotherapy integration.

Nonetheless, the psychotherapy integration movement remains vigorous and alive (Norcross, 2005). Researchers and theoreticians continue to work on studying eclectic therapeutic practice, common factors, and theoretical integration. In keeping with the push for therapy practice to be based on empirical evidence, evidence-based approaches are being developed that are integrative in nature (e.g., Beutler & Harwood, 2000; Grawe, 1997). Additionally, we believe that what is going to happen (and what is already happening) is that efforts to empirically validate specific therapies for specific disorders will ultimately lead the field to the same place it has been in the past—toward psychotherapy integration.

POSTMODERNISM, DIVERSITY, AND CONTEMPORARY THERAPY APPROACHES

The "social revolution" of the 1960s was more than just people protesting the war in Vietnam, wearing flowers in their hair, and listening to the Beatles. In psychology, it marked the beginnings of an important change from an exclusive focus on the individual psyche to a greater awareness of the human in society. A general consciousness that individual psychological problems and their treatment were intimately and intricately bound up with society as a whole arose. Feminists began to assert that many problems suffered by women reflected society's sexist attitudes rather than individual flaws in a woman's character. Ethnic minority groups began to argue that many of the mental health problems they suffered were caused or exacerbated by such factors as racism and poverty. Gays and lesbians similarly began to challenge society's labeling of them as "deviant." The advent of the community psychology movement in the 1960s argued that *all* psychological problems are embedded in social factors.

About the same time, a revolution in scientific thinking was also beginning, and it became the postmodern view. In the modern view, science was objective and trying to discover the truth about biology, chemistry, physics—in essence, the truth about reality. It was assumed that there was one true reality that could be *discovered*. The postmodern view in science is that there is no one truth, no one discoverable reality. Scientific findings are *constructed* by scientists in their cultural, historical, psychosocial context. We shall see how the postmodern view is being applied to professional psychology and psychotherapy.

Traditional models of psychological treatment were challenged. It was argued that individual psychotherapy too often laid the blame for the client's problems at the client's doorstep and ignored the role of important social factors. It was also argued that therapists tended to impose a model of mental health on the client that reflected an implicit Western, white male view of what constitutes healthy functioning, while ignoring the unique experiential backgrounds of women, people from other cultures, and gays and lesbians.

Multicultural and feminist psychology challenges professional psychology and society to change their fundamental thinking, which often emphasizes individualism, relationships based on hierarchical differences in power, and linear logic. Feminist and multicultural psychology offer a view that values community, egalitarian relationships, and holistic thinking. The benefit of this challenge is that it encourages psychologists to analyze their therapies and their relationships with clients in terms of what they may be doing to replicate and reinforce the very social structures that are causing the clients' problems. This analysis will lead to new types of therapy, more effective psychotherapy, and improved services to clients.

Besides diversity, professional psychology has responded to many other social issues. Due to consumer and third-party payer demands for quick, low-cost help, psychology has developed new treatment modalities that emphasize brief therapy and self-help. Diversity and social change have profoundly influenced psychology, and we now turn to a detailed examination of these effects.

Postmodernism

Modernism held that there is a fixed objective reality. Through appropriate scientific and intellectual methods, one can come to know the one objective truth about the world. Modernism led psychology to the belief that there are universal laws and truths about human beings. Modernism also led to the belief that there are objectively "right" and "correct" ways to be. Modernist ideas in psychology have typically privileged the values and beliefs of dominant groups, such as those of Western, white, heterosexual males.

Postmodernists, in contrast, hold that the experience of different groups of people constitutes different personal realities, and there is no one objective truth about human nature (O'Hara & Anderson, 1991). Each culture creates its own way of viewing and experiencing reality, as do individuals. Typically, postmodernists argue that people must be understood in their own terms, rather than compared to a dominant group's "objective" standards. Therapy, then, must be conducted in terms of the perspectives and values of the individual client and the client's cultural background. Furthermore, contemporary treatment approaches must consider psychology's place in the power structure of the larger society. It is possible that the modernist approach of considering the dominant group's view to be "objective truth" replicates that power structure and thereby exacerbates the client's problems. Of course, groups privileged by the modern view oppose the postmodern view.

In response to these views and to several social forces, professional psychology has developed a number of treatment alternatives to traditional psychotherapy. All of these approaches challenge professional psychology and society, because they involve shifts in fundamental assumptions about reality and the nature of psychological problems. For example, seeing problems as existing objectively in individuals must change to placing the problems in the constructed reality of the situation or social context. (Perhaps you can see the postmodern thinking in the radical behavior therapies described in chapter 10.)

Constructivism

Constructivists hold that at the individual level, each of us constructs our own reality. It is impossible to say what is the "truth" about objective reality, because no one can ever know objective reality. We always know reality through the lens of our cognitive structures and mental representations of reality. This view does not mean that we can make the world anything we want, simply that our ideas about the world are always constructions and therefore limited and incomplete. Furthermore, our ideas about the world cannot be judged by any criteria of "objective validity," but they can be judged by their capacity to afford adaptation and development.

Constructivist therapies (Mahoney, 1991; Neimeyer & Mahoney, 1995) work with clients when their ways of dealing with the world are not working and do not lead to adaptation and development, and they help clients develop new, more viable constructions of the world. (Note the similarity of these ideas to the earlier views of George Kelly, discussed in chapter 11.) Therapy becomes the process not of "correcting" the client's distorted views but of helping the client evolve her own unique views of the world in ways that make them more functional. The therapist is therefore not the "expert" on the client but rather an expert on helping clients "make new meaning" and use their already existing beliefs and experiences to develop new and more helpful ways of dealing with the world. For instance, instead of eliminating "shoulds" as a traditional cognitive therapist might, the constructivist therapist helps clients consider how such thinking functions in their lives and then helps them to evolve ways of using "shoulds" so that they promote rather than interfere with coping.

Constructivist therapists may use any number of procedures borrowed from cognitive, humanistic, family systems, or psychodynamic approaches. It is not what the therapist does so much as how the therapist does it that matters. Techniques from other approaches are used to help clients explore and create meaningful new perspectives and ways of viewing the world.

Narrative Psychotherapies

Narrative therapies (White, 1993, 2004; Freedman & Combs, 1996; Angus & McLeod, 2004) are a form of constructivist therapy. ***Narrative perspectives*** hold that we live our lives as if they were embodied stories (Howard, 1991). People have told stories since ancient times; stories are all around us like the air we breathe. We organize our lives along storylike lines. Therapy becomes the restorying of one's life so that new possibilities are opened up. From a narrative perspective, the past is never fixed. The past's impact on the present is determined by the story we are currently telling about our past. We can "restory" our past and then it will have a different impact on our present. To quote Keen and Fox (1973, p. 42) "What happened to you in the past has yet to be determined."

But what about someone who was sexually abused as a child? Isn't that historical fact? Yes. At the same time, the person's story about the abuse may be contributing to his present problems. For instance, the person's story about the abuse may include "I am a helpless child and I have been irreparably damaged" and even "I am responsible for what happened." This story leaves the client feeling helpless and depressed. Therapy alters these interpretations of the fact of abuse and makes a new story: "I am not responsible, I am no longer a helpless child, and I can recover from this experience and grow strong because of it." Narrative therapies help clients construct more viable and workable "life stories" that help them see new possibilities in their lives. Michael White (2004) is one of the most well-known narrative therapists. White views the problem as an "it" so that the person can gain some distance from it and realize that "I am not my problem." This alone is therapeutic and helps counter paralyzing self-criticism.

Like constructivist therapists, narrative therapists may incorporate traditional approaches such as psychodynamic, cognitive, or family systems methods. In fact, any traditional therapy can be seen as providing a new story for the client, a new view of the past, one that contributes to better functioning. For example, a troubled man who constantly feels guilty because he is not perfect can, in psychoanalysis, tell himself a new story about how he unconsciously developed a severe super-ego and now that it is conscious, it will not plague him any more.

Narrative therapists, as with other postmodern therapists, do not portray themselves as the experts on their clients' problems. They adopt a stance of "not knowing" in therapy. From that stance they are able to ask questions in a curious and open way, helping the clients discover how to resolve their problems. The therapist does not start with a preplanned goal about what the client needs to change in order to get well. Nor does the therapist apply a specific standardized set of treatment procedures to correct the client's "disorder." Instead, constructivist and narrative therapists try to remain open to the emerging process between themselves and their clients and to facilitate the client's own creative "story repair and elaboration" processes spontaneously. In so doing, narrative therapists are particularly sensitive to political issues that might affect their clients, such as social oppression through gender discrimination and racism.

The Challenge of Diversity

Many have argued that most of the theories we have considered in this book—psychoanalysis, object relations theory, humanistic and existential theories, cognitive and behavioral theories, and systems theories—have largely been the product of white males and reflect Western cultural values. Most of these theories emphasize an individualistic perspective. That is, the healthy individual is self-sufficient, separate, controls and is in charge of him- or herself, takes responsibility, is not enmeshed with others, has good boundaries, has a clear, solid sense of self and identity, and so on. Psychological dysfunction is seen as some deficit in the ability to be an individual, and a general goal of most therapies is to increase individuation. Therapists do not want to tell the client what to do, for instance, because that will foster or perpetuate dependency rather than encourage self-sufficiency and autonomy.

But are the theories that value individuation *universal* theories of human nature? What if they are culture-specific and reflect distinct cultural biases? What happens when these theories, and the therapists who practice using these theories, encounter people who do not share these values?

Initially, therapists tried to be aware of and empathic to differences by taking the client's cultural backgrounds into account, but only as a *treatment strategy.* Empathy for cultural values would be used as a strategy to create a context in which the therapist's interventions could be utilized. With an Asian American client or family, for example, the therapist would respect the client's need for a therapist who was directive. While respecting these differences, however, the goals of therapy remained basically the same: to enhance autonomy, to "de-enmesh" families, and so on. The therapist simply "blended" his techniques with the client's cultural background so that the same old therapy goals could be achieved.

However, this way of dealing with diversity in therapy has been challenged. It is argued that multicultural therapy is not merely modifying our therapeutic procedures in order to take ethnic differences into account so that traditional therapy goals, which would effectively reduce ethnic differences, can be achieved. Rather, we need to be truly open to the meaning of cultural differences and fundamentally reexamine the very bases of our theories and views of healthy functioning. We need to accept that our cultural assumptions are just that, cultural assumptions, and not objective truth, and that it has been assumptions not facts that have determined our goals and how we practice therapy. We need new theories, new goals, and new ways of achieving them (Hays, 2001).

The Self

One of the most fundamental assumptions of Western culture and modern psychotherapy is that each of us knows our separate identity as a "self." The healthy self in most Western psychological theories is a separate, autonomous self. It is a self that has its own separate, private universe of its own values, beliefs, goals, and desires. Having a firm, stable sense of identity is important. From this perspective, individuals who are not self-sufficient, who are dependent on others, who do not have clearly defined and articulated stable senses of themselves, or who have difficulty separating their own wishes, values, and desires from those of others around them, are seen as pathological. Borderline personality disorder is one of the best examples. A person who feels identityless and abandoned unless she is in a relationship is seen by object relations theory as suffering from a major defect in ego structure going back to the most formative period of early childhood.

Having a separate and autonomous self is related to having self-control. The healthy self controls itself. It is not swept away by its emotions or passions. Its intellect is in charge of itself. It manages its own emotions, solves its own problems, sets its own goals, and directs its own life. It does not blame its problems on external forces. It does not see itself as externally controlled. It accepts responsibility for itself. The ability to take care of itself and self-manage are therefore also healthy qualities of this self. This emphasis on self-control may be so extensive that individuals may believe they can control virtually anything if they only adopt the right psychological attitudes and take responsibility for themselves. Recently, this idea has even extended into the area of physical health, as discussed in chapter 12, and some may assert that people are responsible for contracting illnesses.

All of these models of healthy and pathological behavior are based on a particular view of the nature of the self. This can be called the Western self, and it is also more particularly a *masculine* self. In this view of the self, there is a clear and unequivocal distinction between the self and the not-self. The boundaries of the self end at the skin of the individual. It is important to have clear boundaries. The self is separate and is controlled from within. Ideally, it is free of all contexts and is self-sufficient. It is an autonomous entity so it has rights, such as the right to privacy. Development is the process of moving this self, which is initially dependent, toward self-sufficiency and autonomy.

These ideas are advocated not only by psychoanalytic and humanistic points of view; cognitive and behavioral perspectives have also advocated many of the same ideas. Healthy individuals, according to Beck and Ellis, do not need relationships in order to be happy. Effective people regulate their own lives through rational thinking. Behaviorism has similarly emphasized the development of various self-management techniques, including strategies of self-reinforcement. In family systems theories, one of the major ideas is that psychopathology is due to such factors as "lack of differentiation," "enmeshment," and so on. These concepts all imply that healthy families promote individuality and independence. Having diffuse or poor boundaries in a family is seen as pathological. It is healthy to have good, solid (but not too rigid) boundaries.

The Self Across Cultures

The model of the separate, autonomous self is highly culture-specific. In other cultures, the boundaries of the self are extended to include one's family and even one's social group. The belief in a separate, context-free self is simply not held. For instance, in our culture, because we believe in a context-free self, we have the concept of *personality trait*, that the self has characteristics independent of contexts. We describe individuals as "shy," or "friendly," as if these traits exist within them, independent of different social contexts. In contrast, in other cultures, individuals are described in terms of their relationship to their contexts. An individual may be described as "friendly at social gatherings," instead of "friendly." Similarly, individuals are often identified in terms of their relationships. In many cultures, an individual may be called by a name that means the "son of X" or the "mother of Y," rather than having a separate unique name.

For these cultures, the self is truly a "self-in-relation." *Interdependence* is stressed, rather than *independence.* Duty and obligation to one's social group are valued over individual self-actualization. One "actualizes" *through* strengthening one's bonds with others, rather than by breaking free from those bonds. For women, the self is also primarily a self-in-relation. Theorists at the Stone Center in Wellesley, Massachusetts, have published a book entitled *Women's Growth in Connection* (Jordan, Kaplan, Miller, Stiver, & Surrey, 1991). The title suggests the radically different perspective being advocated by feminists and multiculturists.

Contributions of Diverse Views of the Self

Adopting such a different view of the self has important implications for doing psychotherapy. Clients' experiences are viewed differently. As an example, a colleague of ours was seeing a woman who was devoting herself to her ill mother in a way that was interfering with her own life. Rather than seeing this as "codependent" or "pathological," the therapist validated the value of interpersonal connectedness. This was vastly relieving to the client, who had experienced a good deal of shame from other therapists who had told her that she was "enmeshed," "dependent," and so on. In our culture, it is pathological to sacrifice oneself for another. But validating the positive thrust in this client's behavior paradoxically gave her life meaning and purpose.

Similarly, Linehan (1989) has argued that many borderline women define themselves in terms of their relationships and to try to get them to be independent is to work against their deepest sense of identity. Thus Linehan's strategy is to teach them to be more "healthily" dependent, that is, to learn how to be dependent without destroying the very relationships they are dependent on. She goes on to argue that our society needs to provide more vehicles for healthy dependency rather than trying to force everyone to conform to the cultural model of independence.

In the self-in-relation view, the therapist must respect the individual experience of the client. That is, the therapist must be willing to listen to this client's experience *as this client's experience*, rather than seeing the client through the lenses of the therapist's own cultural biases. Therapy must be *particularized*, and therapists cannot apply a generalized model to a client. Therapy is the specific "meeting of persons." The therapist and the client establish an egalitarian relationship, a hierarchical therapeutic relationship in which the therapist has power and is the expert is eschewed, and share a *mutual* relationship, in which the therapist as well as the client is willing to be open and self-disclosing. Empathy is highly valued and prized, and the *relationship* is the primary source of growth. Problems are understood as being matters of relationship; growth is seen as learning how to be more effectively in relationship, and therefore, the therapeutic relationship itself is the "learning laboratory" for growth. As therapist and client deal with ruptures and difficulties in the therapeutic relationship itself, the client learns how to be in and grow through relationships. The therapist is as much changed by the therapy process as the client is.

Multicultural Counseling

In doing therapy with members of diverse cultural groups, the same general principles as are discussed above in working from a self-in-relation perspective are advocated. Multicultural therapists avoid stereotyping and encourage clients to explore their full potential; at the same time, they realistically acknowledge social barriers to their client's aspirations. They recognize ethnicity and culture as significant parameters. They are respectful of the roles of family members, community structures, values and beliefs, religious and spiritual beliefs, and so on.

Therapists must be aware that many of the assumptions of Western culture we have previously considered may not be held by members of other cultures. For instance, members of other cultural groups may not share the emphasis on internalized control shared by Western civilization. They may emphasize the role played by destiny or fate in their lives and assume that individuals cannot control everything, but only a portion of the events in their lives. Furthermore, many members of other cultures place a greater emphasis on religion and spirituality than do Western psychotherapeutic cultural values. Psychological problems are often seen as an imbalance between the spirit and the body, and the neglect of one's spirit is seen as unhealthy. The result is that spiritual beliefs and practices are often valued as an important part of life and of change. Other values may be different as well.

As an example of these points, Heide (1989) described the treatment of a young Asian American female college student who was suicidal because she was not doing well in school. A typical cognitive intervention with such a client would be to challenge her dysfunctional thoughts that she is "no good" because she is not doing well in school. However, this intervention failed to help her, because it did not take account of her cultural background, in which to do poorly in school is shameful to the family. Modifying the intervention to get her to consider which would be more shameful, doing poorly in school or killing herself, was effective when she realized that suicide would be even more shameful.

Treatment Issues in Multicultural Counseling

Two related and particularly important issues in working with multicultural clients are the formation of a positive ethnic identity and *acculturation* versus *biculturation*. There appear to be stages in ethnic identity development, of which there are several models (Bustamente, 1992). In a typical model, individuals begin with their original cultural identity, and they may have to struggle to accept themselves when the larger society demeans them. They have often internalized the negative evaluations of the dominant culture and may be trying to assimilate into that culture. As they mature, they may go through a stage of embracing their original culture and angrily rejecting the majority culture that rejects them. Finally, they integrate aspects of both cultures into their unique positive ethnic identity. The process of forming a positive ethnic identity is similar to a ***dialectical process*** in which a thesis (original devalued cultural identity) leads to an antithesis (new aggressively valued cultural identity), which leads to a new synthesis (integrated, accepting cultural identity).

Acculturation is defined as the degree to which the ethnic individual attempts to assimilate to the dominant culture. For instance, does a Latino attempt to become like the larger Anglo culture in terms of values, beliefs, and behaviors? Basically, many models of the development of ethnic identity see either acculturation, in which the individual relinquishes his or her cultural identity to assimilate, or the opposite, when the individual refuses to acculturate at all, as stages along the way to developing a fully integrated cultural identity. In bicultural models of ethnic identity formation, the individual develops an integrated bicultural identity, which involves building a bridge between her cultural background and the larger culture, while relinquishing neither. Biculturalism involves realizing that there are good and bad things in both cultures and helping clients sort out their own stance on acculturation and biculturation.

A Theory of Multicultural Therapy

Derald Wing Sue and his colleagues (D. W. Sue, 2004; D. W. Sue, Ivey, & Pedersen, 1996; D. W. Sue & D. Sue, 1999) have developed a theory of Multicultural Counseling and Therapy (MCT), based on six assumptions: (a) MCT is a metatheory, or a theory about theories, that offers an organizational framework for understanding all helping approaches, including the worldviews of Western psychotherapy and non-Western helping models. (b) Treatment must focus on the multiple levels of experiences (individual, group, and universal) and contexts (individual, family, and cultural) that affect the identities of both counselor and client. (c) The identity development of both counselor and client is a major determinant of their attitudes and behaviors, and the level or stage of ethnic or cultural identity of each will determine what they believe to be appropriate counseling goals and processes. For example, a bicultural therapist should be sensitive to the different treatment strategies that would be necessary for a culturally different client whose identity involves assimilation to the majority culture as opposed to one whose identity development seems to be in the stage that completely rejects the majority culture. (d) No one helping approach is effective for all populations. The effectiveness of MCT is enhanced when the therapist intervenes in ways that are consistent with the life experiences and cultural values of the client. (e) MCT stresses multiple helping roles, including systems interventions and prevention. For example, an African American student referred for fighting in school may be the victim of racist comments from other students. In this case, the therapist will have a better understanding of how to help by visiting the student's environment and observing it directly. The therapist may have to play the roles of advisor, advocate, environmental change agent, and educator, as well as counselor, in order to help this student. (f) MCT emphasizes the liberation of consciousness of both therapist and client. Competent multicultural counselors must constantly develop attitudes, knowledge, and skills related to an awareness of their own values and biases and an understanding of the worldviews of culturally different clients. Competent multicultural therapists, if they are white, must work to become aware of something that they unconsciously take for granted—they are white and therefore privileged. MCT especially challenges white therapists, and ideally, the research and theories of professional psychology will also change and grow as a result of MCT.

Another model for multicultural therapy, developed at the University of Hawaii at Manoa, focuses on training specific skills and strategies to guide culturally appropriate therapy interventions. Skill clusters, such as becoming aware of one's own worldview and facilitating cultural identity development, are being developed, tested, and taught. In addition, the model specifies adaptations of traditional interventions and practices so they are more culture-centered and effective. The development of this model can be observed on the Internet, and training in multicultural key strategies (MKS) may be obtained there as well (www.multiculturalskills.com).

Trying to take a multicultural approach with pets.

The Need for Multicultural Therapists

There is a great need for multicultural therapists, given the population shifts in the United States, and until enough nonwhite individuals become trained as psychologists, the need for multicultural Caucasian therapists remains. There is also a great need for bilingual therapists, including therapists who can use sign language with the deaf. When therapists are unable to learn the needed language, it is possible to use interpreters or to collaborate with bilingual and bicultural nonprofessional counselors. Some therapists encourage the use of indigenous healers or other community authorities as adjuncts to therapy.

Landrine (1992) proposes a *cultural triage model* of intervention for those working in different cultures. In this approach, a Western clinician, an indigenous healer or other community authority from the culture, and the family of the individual with a psychological problem consult and agree on several conceptualizations of the problem and attempt a multicultural/multilevel treatment by the Western clinician, the indigenous healer, and the family. For example, when Southeast Asian children in Stockton refused to return to school after their classmates were shot by a sniper in 1990, therapy failed until an indigenous healer removed the spirits of their murdered friends through a culturally appropriate ritual.

The ethnic distributions of therapists and the population mean that for the foreseeable future, many Caucasian therapists will have to attempt multicultural therapy. Because cultural beliefs are unconscious and feel "right," white therapists must work hard to increase their awareness of their own cultural assumptions, in addition to educating themselves about the values of other cultural groups. In fact, D. W. Sue and D. Sue (1999) urge Caucasian therapists to become aware of the formation of white identity, especially as it overprivileges them. At a minimum, they must be careful not to impose their cultural beliefs on others, and ideally, they should remain open to the value of others' beliefs even for their own lives. They must try not to replicate the power structure of dominance over other ethnic groups by Caucasians. In fact, perhaps they should work to change that power structure through advocacy and social action.

Afrocentric Psychotherapy

Afrocentrism, also known as the African-centered view, is a worldview developed over decades in various academic fields, including history, literature, and art. In this view, the basis of analysis is the life experiences, history, and traditions of people of African ancestry. This view also criticizes traditional academic subjects for being Eurocentric and privileging the white, European worldview. In a typical American history course, for example, the focus is on the actions of white men descended from Europeans, as if their behavior is naturally of great importance and justified by that history. Sometimes, mention is made of Native Americans or African Americans, but it is within the context of the values and beliefs of white men and how they affected or were affected by other groups. Other groups are just that—"other." African-centered subjects focus on the cultural image and interests of people of African descent and emphasize such concepts as "beingness" and "becoming." Within the intellectual tradition of Afrocentrism there is a great deal of controversy, such as which part of Africa was most important, whether Egyptians were black, and whether Afrocentrism helps or hinders present-day African Americans. This chapter cannot do justice to these issues, and the discussion of Afrocentrism here is necessarily greatly simplified.

Afrocentric psychology developed because of an interest in defining mental health for African Americans. This exploration furthered the critique that within academic and professional psychology, as with other disciplines, the white, Eurocentric, male view has been privileged. White male behavior is "normal" and the focus of most research, while women and ethnic groups are "other" and judged by white male values and beliefs. Mostly white male therapists treat females and "others" with methods developed for and by white men. The main problem with the Eurocentric view in therapy is that in the context of white male behavior, the behavior of other groups appears to be "abnormal," and they are then "treated" so they better fit in to a society that underprivileges them.

Afrocentric psychotherapy posits that Westernized theory and practice are insufficient to understand and treat people of African descent. For example, Afrocentric therapy embraces the values of connectedness and spirituality, rather than those of individuation and self-determination. It explains and treats the behavior of African Americans in a context that values their behavior and beliefs, that makes their worldview of central importance, and that instills esteem and confidence. It begins with trying to understand the core values and worldview of African Americans, and then clarifies the negative effects of an environment that does not value the core belief system of people of African descent. Their "abnormal" behavior is recognized as damage caused by the experience of slavery in the past and racism in the present.

The African history of black people is considered a unique and inescapable element of their lives, and one cause of their problems is that they lack knowledge of it. Afrocentric therapy teaches this history as a way to help African Americans recognize and understand their experiences and oppression and to stop their negative effects on their feelings and behavior. The survival of African Americans and their accomplishments are points of special pride given their history.

Like multicultural therapy, Afrocentric methods have been developed for use in most of the traditional therapies. As a few examples, there are Afrocentric Reality Therapy for substance abuse (Moore, 2001), Radical Black Behaviorism for African-American children (Neal-Barnett & Smith, 1996), and African-Centered Support Groups for men (Elligan & Utsey, 1999). Often such therapies recommend that therapists increase their awareness of and sensitivity to the unique problems, issues, values, and experiences of African American clients. Like multicultural therapy, Afrocentric therapy has been criticized by feminists for ignoring the worldview of women, and an Afrocentric-feminist, or "womanist," therapy has been proposed (Taylor, 1999). Afrocentrism provides a legacy of theory and research rich with potential for developing and improving professional psychology.

Feminist Therapy

As with multicultural counseling, feminist therapy presents the challenge of a fundamentally different way of thinking to professional psychology and society. To a society that emphasizes individualism, relationships based on hierarchical differences in power (with Caucasian men in the dominant position), and "masculine" linear logic, feminist psychology offers a view that values community and connectedness, egalitarian relationships based on sharing power, and holistic thinking. The early feminist slogan, "The personal is political," is at the heart of the feminist critique of traditional therapy in that it decontextualizes people's problems. A therapy that emphasizes individual problems and individual solutions fails to recognize the degree to which women's limited gender role, devalued status, and lack of power contributes to their frustration, depression, low self-esteem, and other problems such as unassertiveness. Feminist therapy challenges psychologists to analyze their therapies and their relationships with female clients in terms of what they may be doing to replicate and reinforce the very social structures that are causing the women's problems. The following case history illustrates these points.

Mildred came to see one of us in therapy (the *male* of us, by the way). Mildred was a 48-year-old woman, in a program in nursing. Mildred was divorced. She recounted that she had been married to a businessman for many years and had had several children, all of whom were now adults. This businessman had neglected her emotionally and kept her in a subservient role. He had controlled all the finances in the marriage. As her children grew older, she wanted to go back to school, but her husband was opposed to this and put considerable pressure on her to stay at home, telling her that that was her place, and so on. Because he controlled the family purse strings, she was dependent on his cooperation to go back to school. In the face of this resistance, she soon gave up her plans and subsequently lapsed into a depression.

Her husband arranged to have her treated by a traditional psychiatrist who assumed that her depression reflected both a biochemical flaw in her brain and psychological ego weaknesses based on early childhood experience. She was hospitalized, pumped full of medication, and told that her problems were due to unconscious anger toward men based on early childhood experiences, which she was turning inward on herself as depression.

This went on for several years, and she was repeatedly told that her depression reflected exclusively her own inadequacies. Finally, by some miracle (and we are often amazed at the resiliency of the human spirit), she dragged herself out of this situation. She mustered enough strength to initiate a divorce, even though both her husband and psychiatrist continued to label her as the problem. After Mildred started back to school, her depression began to lift. However, the divorce had left its mark: She continued to worry that she was indeed "flawed." This continual fear was undermining her ability to utilize her full capabilities.

Therapy was brief and consisted primarily of allowing Mildred to recount in detail the horrors of this experience. The therapist encouraged Mildred to evaluate for herself her husband's and the psychiatrist's claims that the problem was in her, and in the supportive atmosphere provided, she was able to begin to see how oppressed she had been. The therapist himself also validated her point of view, helping her to see how her problems reflected a social issue rather than an individual, intrapsychic deficit.

Early Roots of Feminist Therapy

Although the beginnings of feminist thought can be traced back to ancient times, as in the Greek play *Lysistrata*, the modern women's movement in the United States began in the last century with the struggle for women's suffrage. After American women won the right to vote in 1920, feminist activism died down until the general political activism of the 1960s. The lessons of the civil rights movement led women to reconsider their own unequal status in society. Women formed consciousness-raising groups to discuss and analyze their common problems and the social and political contexts of them. Such meetings were often therapeutic, and there was a fruitful exchange of ideas between feminists and therapists so that by the late 1970s, feminist versions of most of the traditional schools of therapy had been developed.

Between these two waves of feminist activism, female psychoanalysts, such as Helene Deutsch, Marie Bonapart, Jeanne Lampl-de-Groot, Joan Riviere, and Frieda Fromm-Reichmann, struggled with issues of female sexuality and feminine identity. Karen Horney and Clara Thompson developed theories that most differed from Freudian theory. Horney pointed out that women did not envy men's penises, but rather, their greater social and economic power. She also theorized that male envy of women's childbearing ability was at the root of their devaluation of women. Thompson and Horney both examined the role of women's economic dependence and restricted opportunities on their development. Although later feminists objected strongly to psychoanalysis for devaluing, restricting, and pathologizing women, it was women psychoanalysts who began and continued feminist theorizing during the 1930s, 1940s, and 1950s.

Because its egalitarian philosophy eschews identified leaders or authority figures, there is no one precise feminist therapy. Nevertheless, there is a professional identity for the field of feminist therapy, as seen in a number of journals, such as *Women and Therapy*, *Journal of Feminist Family Therapy*, and others, as well as a number of organizations, such as Division 35 (Psychology of Women) of the APA and the Association for Women in Psychology.

Types of Feminist Therapy

As already noted, there are feminist versions of most types of therapy, although most of these focus on deconstructing and reducing the sexism inherent in them. Sometimes a distinction is made between therapies that are nonsexist but still focus on the individual and radical feminism, which holds that social change and political action are necessary for the healing of the individual.

Feminist psychoanalysis (an oxymoron to some) has developed out of the work of Nancy Chodorow (1978), who drew on object relations theory and Marxist social theory to place analytic ideas about the family into its sociocultural context. Therapists and researchers at the Stone Center continue to develop feminist-based psychodynamic theories and methods (Jordan et al., 1991). Feminist psychoanalysis rewrites the account of feminine development in an affirmative, woman-centered way, with the emphasis on early experience leading to an identity rooted in relationships and other strengths.

Feminist behavior therapy, like other behavior therapies, asserts that dysfunctional behavior is learned from and maintained by the environment, but in addition, it identifies sex role training and factors in the environment that affect women differentially. For example, assertion training may work well to help men attain their goals, but when women engage in the same assertive behavior, it is often met by hostility and rejection from others. Behavior therapists are urged to set goals and utilize methods that are appropriate for women.

Feminist family therapy agrees with traditional family therapy that the individuals in a family cannot be taken out of context, but they add the importance of the context of the power structure outside the family, which is replicated in the traditional family. The strengths and needs of the women in the family, the right of women to extrafamilial life, the forces within and without the family that impede women's movement outside the family, and nontraditional families, such as single mothers or lesbian families, are emphasized in feminist family therapy.

Core Principles of Feminist Therapy

Although diverse, feminist therapies share certain core principles, which have been listed by Brown and Brodsky (1992). Feminist therapy: (a) values the diverse and complex experiences of women from all racial, class, religious, age, and sexual orientation groups and reconstructs reality so that the values and experiences of women are seen as normal and equal in value to those of white, heterosexual men; (b) attends to the power dynamics in the therapy relationship, with the goal of developing egalitarian relationships and empowering the less powerful; (c) attends to both individual variables and the social context, especially the effects of assigned gender roles on identity, development, and mental health; (d) relies on the empirical database arising from feminist scholarship that studies disorders of high prevalence in women, such as depression, eating disorders, and the effects of abuse; (e) values a balance of both healthy autonomy and relational competence for all adults, rather than seeing only males as independent and only females as socially skilled; (f) focuses on the empowerment of the individual, with the possible need to change society and not the person.

There are other commonalities in the feminist therapies. As with multicultural therapy, feminist therapy differs from traditional therapies in its insistence on a nonhierarchical therapeutic relationship. Therapy goals are developed cooperatively between client and therapist. Although the client and therapist have different roles to play, one exploring her life and the other offering assistance, therapy is seen as a cooperative relationship between the two. The myth of value-free psychotherapy is rejected, and feminist therapists attempt to make their own biases and values explicit so that client and therapist can deal with them. In fact, many argue that white feminist therapists, like multicultural therapists, have the obligation to deconstruct their own white privilege as part of therapy (Pewewardy, 2004).

Current Issues in Feminist Therapy

A goal for feminist therapy is to articulate a comprehensive theory that can encompass all the variations and to integrate with multicultural therapy. The ultimate goal of feminist therapy is to become widely accepted in all of psychology and to influence the direction of the entire field. In the meantime, there is a demonstrated need for more training in feminist multicultural therapy and research and for more therapists so trained (Fassinger, 2004).

Earlier feminist thought rejected the possibility of any real difference between women and men with the idea that all differences were due to cultural training and oppression of women. In recent decades, there has been a renewed emphasis on research demonstrating biological differences between the sexes, such as differences in brain organization of language, in the hypothalamus, and in the corpus callosum. As Marecek and Hare-Mustin (1991) have observed, the focus on male–female differences has pushed the question of male dominance and female subordination to the periphery.

The current emphasis on biological sex differences is dangerous, as earlier feminists realized when they rejected such differences, because it is easy for differences to become differentially valued in favor of the dominant group. How the dominant group differs is seen as superior, and then the difference is used to substantiate their dominant position. For example, in the nineteenth century boys were believed to be superior to girls because they learned to read faster. When empirical research in the early twentieth century demonstrated that in fact girls learned to read faster than boys, then slowly learning to read showed that boys were superior to girls since they were slowed down by their more complex minds. "Different but equal" is apparently a difficult concept, especially for groups that value hierarchical organization and are privileged by it. Feminist therapists must once again force attention to be paid to questions of gender, power, and equality and to how differences in power affect the construction of reality to the detriment of the less valued group.

Therapy with Lesbians, Gay Men, and Bisexual People

Many of the same principles that apply to treating members of different cultural groups and female clients apply also to treating gay men, lesbians, and bisexuals, and the APA Guidelines for working them are shown in box 15.1 (page 413). The therapist must be aware of her biases, be empathic with the experience of the client, and understand the special issues and needs facing a gay or lesbian client. It is also important for therapists to be knowledgeable about resources in the lesbian and gay communities. Many support groups and workshops are available, and often a referral to these resources in addition to or instead of therapy is helpful.

In our Western, predominantly Christian cultural tradition, homosexuality has generally been looked on negatively as a "sin." This bias was reflected in psychological theories, particularly psychoanalytic theories, in which homosexuality was seen as a developmentally more immature form of sexual expression. For a long time, homosexuality was seen as a psychological disorder. It was only in 1974 that the American Psychiatric Association decided to remove homosexuality from the list of mental disorders. This followed a number of research studies showing that gay men and lesbians were no more psychologically disturbed than heterosexual men and women and that the problems they did have stemmed in part from negative stereotyping, prejudice, and discrimination.

Despite a lack of evidence to support their position, a small number of mental health professionals still consider homosexuality to be a psychological disorder, and they practice "conversion therapy" aimed at helping people with same-sex attractions change their sexual orientation. Advocates of this position argue that therapists have abandoned people who are unhappy with their sexual orientation by blaming their unhappiness on homophobia. The professional organizations of the mental health professions have issued statements criticizing conversion therapy and questioning whether it is ethical to offer "therapy" that has no evidence of being effective to treat something with no evidence of being a disorder (Jenkins & Johnson, 2004).

The decision by the American Psychiatric Association to destigmatize homosexuality has not eliminated negative stereotypes in the culture at large, not even in the mental health profession itself as evidenced by the "conversion therapy" advocates discussed above. Gay men and lesbians still face considerable societal discrimination.

For therapists working with gays and lesbians, it is particularly important to be aware of the fact that the client's problems may well have a real basis in the client's life context and of the psychological and physical dangers the client may face. It is important for therapists to disentangle problematic behavior and personal difficulties from problems engendered by being gay or lesbian in a hostile society.

Two of the most important issues faced by gays and lesbians are the connected issues of developing a positive gay or lesbian identity and "coming out." Coming out (of the closet) involves gay men and lesbians revealing their identity to the community at large, including sharing this information with their families and with people at work.

Similar to the dialectical process of developing a positive ethnic identity, the development of a positive gay or lesbian identity takes place in stages. There are several models of gay and lesbian identity development. In general, in these models, individuals start out struggling with the idea and perhaps denying that they might be gay. They may have their own internalized homophobia, and the therapist particularly needs to be sensitive to this. Persons who are just beginning to confront the possibility of their gayness may be uncomfortable and unwilling to bring the issue up to a therapist. If the therapist does not ask, "Could you perhaps be gay?" or if the therapist does not support fledgling attempts to open the issue, the client's own conflicts may block its being explored. As gays and lesbians begin to assimilate their sexuality into their identities, they may go through a period where they are angry at or deny the larger society, identifying exclusively as gay or lesbian and rejecting heterosexual society. Later, they will move into an integrated stage, accepting of the good and bad in both worlds.

Coming out can be a difficult, emotionally challenging, and sometimes dangerous process. Gay men and lesbians need help in assessing the real dangers involved and to decide who to come out to and how. Coming out, for instance to one's family, may or may not be productive, and gay men and lesbians sometimes need to face the issue of emotionally "cutting off" from their families. Along with this may come the issue of loss, and an important part of counseling with gay men and lesbians may be to deal with the grief over such loss. On the other hand, coming out can also be a courageous act of love and self-affirmation, and ways of making it a positive experience have been developed (Eichberg, 1990; Tanner & Lyness, 2003).

Therapists must be aware of many other issues confronted by gays and lesbians. For example, gays and lesbians have few role models for establishing relationships and family structures, and many of them, alienated from their families of origin, form "surrogate families" with all the conflicts and complexities of other families. While bisexuals have similar issues, therapists must be aware of issues unique to gays and lesbians. For example, they may face disapproval from both homosexuals and heterosexuals, as well as from their families, and they and others may think it should be easy for them to "go straight" and so face a great deal of pressure to do so. As with other groups, therapists have an obligation to educate themselves about the unique life experiences and views of lesbians, gays, and bisexuals, as described in the APA Guidelines in box 15.1.

Religion and Psychotherapy

Religion is very important in many cultural groups, including among the majority of the population in the United States. Yet psychotherapists in general have tended to

Box 15.1 APA Guidelines for Psychotherapy with Lesbian, Gay, and Bisexual Clients

Attitudes Toward Homosexuality and Bisexuality

Guideline 1. Psychologists understand that homosexuality and bisexuality are not indicative of mental illness.

Guideline 2. Psychologists are encouraged to recognize how their attitudes and knowledge about lesbian, gay, and bisexual issues may be relevant to assessment and treatment and seek consultation or make appropriate referrals when indicated.

Guideline 3. Psychologists strive to understand the ways in which social stigmatization (i.e., prejudice, discrimination, and violence) poses risks to the mental health and well-being of lesbian, gay, and bisexual clients.

Guideline 4. Psychologists strive to understand how inaccurate or prejudicial views of homosexuality or bisexuality may affect the client's presentation in treatment and the therapeutic process.

Relationships and Families

Guideline 5. Psychologists strive to be knowledgeable about and respect the importance of lesbian, gay, and bisexual relationships.

Guideline 6. Psychologists strive to understand the particular circumstances and challenges facing lesbian, gay, and bisexual parents.

Guideline 7. Psychologists recognize that the families of lesbian, gay, and bisexual people may include people who are not legally or biologically related.

Guideline 8. Psychologists strive to understand how a person's homosexual or bisexual orientation may have an impact on his or her family of origin and the relationship to that family of origin.

Issues of Diversity

Guideline 9. Psychologists are encouraged to recognize the particular life issues or challenges experienced by lesbian, gay, and bisexual members of racial and ethnic minorities that are related to multiple and often conflicting cultural norms, values, and beliefs.

Guideline 10. Psychologists are encouraged to recognize the particular challenges experienced by bisexual individuals.

Guideline 11. Psychologists strive to understand the special problems and risks that exist for lesbian, gay, and bisexual youth.

Guideline 12. Psychologists consider generational differences within lesbian, gay, and bisexual populations, and the particular challenges that may be experienced by lesbian, gay, and bisexual older adults.

Guideline 13. Psychologists are encouraged to recognize the particular challenges experienced by lesbian, gay, and bisexual individuals with physical, sensory, and/or cognitive/emotional disabilities.

Education

Guideline 14. Psychologists support the provision of professional education and training on lesbian, gay, and bisexual issues.

Guideline 15. Psychologists are encouraged to increase their knowledge and understanding of homosexuality and bisexuality through continuing education, training, supervision, and consultation.

Guideline 16. Psychologists make reasonable efforts to familiarize themselves with relevant mental health, educational, and community resources for lesbian, gay, and bisexual people.

Source: American Psychological Association. (2005). Public Interest. www.apa.org/pi/lgbc/guidelines.html

minimize or ignore the influence of religion in people's lives, and the population of mental health professionals is, on the average, less religious than the average client. This has led to a state of affairs in which many religious clients are suspicious of mental health professionals, whom they expect will not be empathic with their views. As a result, many religious clients seek help from their pastors and ministers rather than from mental health professionals. Some psychologists are increasingly emphasizing the importance of therapists' understanding the role of religion in personal functioning. In addition, some have argued that therapy must go beyond normal psychological functioning and deal with the spiritual in order to be fully effective. Below, we consider two different approaches to psychotherapy that include a religious element: approaches that utilize Eastern mysticism and Christian counseling.

Transpersonal Counseling

Transpersonal approaches generally hold that full personal growth cannot be achieved through a psychological approach alone. They emphasize the necessity for a spiritual or transpersonal transformation as well. While there has always been a tradition of Christian counseling, the transpersonal view was dominated in the late 1960s and 1970s by Eastern mystical traditions. Mystical experience, meditation, and altered states of consciousness were important topics.

Eastern mystical thought tends to see the subject–object dichotomy as an illusion. In other words, the idea that the self observing the world is somehow separate from the world that is observed is an illusion. Further, the idea that the world consists of separate things, which have fixed identities, is also an illusion. Actually, the world is an ever-changing "flux" or "dance" (Zukav, 1979). Eastern mystical approaches hope to get the individual to suspend these illusory concepts about the world.

The main tool of attaining such realizations for many transpersonal psychologists is meditation. There are two kinds of meditation: concentrative and receptive. In concentrative meditation, the person attempts to keep attention focused on one object, usually a word, image, or phrase. In receptive meditation the person attempts to do what appears to be the opposite: to allow consciousness to flow freely and uninterruptedly, to let go and become a pure observer of experience. Washburn (1978) has argued that the seemingly different types of meditation ultimately have similar effects. As internal chatter is suspended, the individual becomes able to become aware of herself as the constructor of her own conscious activity. She becomes aware of the unconscious, automatic thoughts and schemas that she uses to shape and form concepts and perceptions. As these are suspended, she moves toward clearer perceptions and better functioning. As with hypnosis, there is controversy over whether meditation involves an altered state of consciousness or not.

Christian Approaches

Christian approaches to psychotherapy hold that accepting Christ and trying to lead a Christian way of life are the ultimate healing acts. Christian approaches stress human finiteness and imperfection in comparison to God. Being finite and imperfect, people should be tolerant and forgiving of themselves and others. We may ask for God's forgiveness. Forgiveness leads to a kind of living in the here and now. Instead of ruminating over past sins, the Christian focuses on how he can improve now. Instead of judging himself, since he and all other human beings are imperfect and will occasionally err, he focuses on what he can do in the future to live a better life. Christianity also values selflessness and doing away with pride. If people are able to do away with pride, then they will not need to be defensive and protect their self-esteem. They will be able to accept their failings and drawbacks with humility.

There is no one specifically Christian way of practicing psychotherapy. All the traditional psychotherapies have been utilized in Christian approaches. Existential-humanistic concepts may easily interface with Christian ideas, but Christian therapists can utilize cognitive techniques, behavioral techniques, and the like. For instance, Propst, Olstrom, Watkins, Dean, & Mashburn (1992) gave an example of combining Christian imagery with a cognitive-behavioral therapy technique. They had a client visualize an image of his imperfections and then visualize Christ overlooking these imperfections and refusing to condemn the client. These authors found that a cognitive-behavioral approach modified to deal with religious themes in such a manner was more effective with religious clients than was a standard cognitive-behavioral format. Among some of the other techniques utilized are prayer and meditation, religious imagery, and the encouragement of forgiveness.

Contemporary Treatment Modalities: Faster and Cheaper

It is ironic that at the same time the above treatment approaches were developed, there was also an emphasis on short, problem-solving, practical therapies. Narrative, multicultural, and feminist therapies focus on the process of self-exploration in the context of the relationship between client and therapist and in the context of society. This process may take quite a while to deal with all the issues of culture and identity. At the same time that demographic and political changes led to this type of therapy, there were strong economic forces encouraging the development of short-term, practical therapies focused on immediate, concrete problems.

The reduced level of funding for mental health care from all sources has impacted theories and methods of psychotherapy. Many consumers have always been interested in quick, effective help. Health care companies have always been interested in cutting costs. Reduced funding along with new technology and research findings have increased the pressure for the development and acceptance of new treatment modalities, or ways of delivering therapy. Psychological services no longer have to occur within a context of face-to-face talking with a professional over several weeks, months, or years. Instead, therapy can be delivered in a short period of time, in groups, with technological assistance, or through self-help.

Brief Therapy

Most of the therapies covered in previous chapters are considered time unlimited, in that clients are allowed, even encouraged, to attend therapy for as long as necessary, however long that is. Throughout the history of professional psychology, beginning with Freud, who complained about "interminable analysis," there have been those who have argued in favor of brief therapy, variously called "short-term therapy," "time-limited therapy," "time-sensitive treatment," even "single-session therapy."

There has been the moral argument that therapists have "the social responsibility to provide needed services to the many rather than many services to the privileged few" (Hoyt, 1995). There has been the theoretical argument that the prospect of a short time limit benefited therapy because it heightened its intensity and impact (Davanloo, 1980; Strupp & Binder, 1984). In recent decades, reduced funding for mental health services and the cost cutting of managed care organizations has added a pragmatic argument in favor of brief therapy.

What is "brief"? Traditional psychoanalysis can last for years, so some psychodynamic therapists consider a year of therapy to be brief. Many health plans pay for 10 sessions, with 20 possible if necessary, and that may be considered brief therapy. The brief therapy called crisis intervention, developed by community psychology, is traditionally no more than six sessions. Some psychologists have presented a model for single-session therapy. They argue that since we can never be certain that a client will come back, all therapy sessions should be treated as single-session interventions.

Although the issue may have been forced by economics, brief therapies are effective, worthwhile types of interventions with a solid theoretical and empirical basis. Reviews of the research (Bloom, 1992b; Elliott, 2001b; Hoyt, 1995; Rosenbaum, 1994; Rosenbaum, Hoyt, & Talmon, 1990) repeatedly find that short-term psychotherapy is as effective as time-unlimited therapy, regardless of diagnosis or duration of treatment. Psychologists should find this conclusion comforting, because in fact about 20% to 50% of people who consult a therapist come for only one session and the overall average number of sessions per client is about eight.

Theoretical Bases of Brief Therapy

Although all brief therapies share certain assumptions, the theory is largely eclectic. Since the therapy must necessarily be focused and specific to the particular client's goals, it is argued that brief therapists must have the knowledge, skill, and flexibility to use a wide range of intervention methods that may be appropriate for a particular problem. Even brief therapists who prefer a certain theory can be technically eclectic.

Some of the assumptions of long-term therapy are that change is difficult, that a "cure" or "deep" change in basic character must be sought, that presenting problems is not as important as the "basic" pathology, that change occurs mainly in therapy and not in everyday life, that client resistance is inevitable and must be carefully worked through, and that therapy is good and more therapy is better. The assumptions of brief therapy challenge all of these. In line with a connectionistic philosophy and with the strategic and family systems therapies, brief therapy emphasizes the interconnectedness of life, and it assumes that a small intervention or small change can have far-reaching ripple effects. Brief therapy also assumes that change occurs all the time in everyday life. Thus, in a sense, change is easy, and the therapist needs to make just one well-timed, precise intervention to have a profound effect. A well-designed intervention need not take a long time, and the therapist is viewed as a catalyst or change-agent in the ever-changing process called life.

Rather than attending to pathology, brief therapy focuses on client strengths and resources. By believing in the client's resources, brief therapists accept the client's definition of the presenting problem as well as the client's goals, thus avoiding the problem of resistance. Brief therapy assumes that therapy may not always be good, that less is more, and that change should occur outside therapy, perhaps long after the initial intervention. In a way, brief therapies see the therapist's job as rather like nudging the client on to a more adaptive developmental path.

Although the research suggests that brief therapy is as effective as time-unlimited therapy for all diagnoses, most brief therapists believe that it is unsuitable for certain individuals, such as those with psychotic symptoms, suicidal intentions, alcohol or drug addictions, a propensity to violence, or severe character disorders. (It might be noted, however, that long-term therapy has not been demonstrated to be very effective with these problems, either.) The ideal candidate for brief therapy is suffering from anxiety, depression, other symptoms, or a situational problem, and has sought therapy or otherwise shown evidence of attempts to change. Such clients may well agree more with the assumptions of brief therapy than with those of long-term therapy, because most people who are seeking help want and expect immediate change. Brief therapists assume it is possible, and they focus their work to help bring it about.

Brief Therapy Methods

What the therapist actually does in brief therapy reflects these underlying assumptions. Brief therapies, whether for one session or six or more, share certain characteristics and elements. The brief therapies are pragmatic, structured, directive, goal-oriented, and focused on problem solving. The time-limited nature of the contact is made clear, sometimes through an explicit contract between client and therapist. Although brief therapies may be as varied as traditional therapies, most contain at least the following steps.

First, the therapist and client together identify a focal problem, and the therapist actively keeps the therapy focused on that. Because it is assumed that everything is connected to everything else, focusing on almost any problem and bringing about a change in it will have ripple effects on other difficulties, including possibly the "basic" pathology, whatever that may be. Throughout the session, the therapist attends to the relationship with the client, assessing what kind of relationship the client wants and trying to create trust and a sense of safety. Client affect about the focal issue is explored and expressed, possibly as a result of therapist empathy and reflection. Then the therapist actively begins a problem-solving process, by emphasizing client resources and skills and searching for information, such as past client successes, that would help the client change. At this point, the therapist may use interpretation, suggestion, reframing, hypnosis, metaphor, or specific behavioral or cognitive methods to help the client begin to organize her or his own resources and act on the problem. Often, specific homework is assigned, in line with the assumption that change occurs outside of therapy. A fitting end to the session includes summarizing what has been accomplished in the session, client plans for further problem solving and change, and leaving open the possibility of returning for further assistance if desired. The client may be asked to describe what was accomplished to encourage memory and recall of a useful lesson.

This brief description of brief therapy cannot convey the variety of methods incorporated into the short-term or single-session structure. An example case may convey what it is like. Michael Hoyt reported the following single session (reported in Rosenbaum, Hoyt, & Talmon, 1990, p. 168):

> A young married couple sought consultation, complaining of "communication problems." He referred to stresses at work, financial frustrations, and sexual dissatisfaction with the marriage. She felt depressed and unable to connect with her husband, worried he would abandon her, and wondered if she should return to her parents' house. They looked reasonably healthy, and neither had any previous psychiatric contact, but both now sat avoiding the other's eyes and appeared depressed. The room grew unpleasantly quiet.
>
> "You look like someone died," the therapist observed aloud. "What happened?"
>
> Previously unmentioned, a painful story was told: A midtrimester pregnancy had miscarried the year before. The couple had tried to bury their grief with the unborn child and had pulled back from one another to avoid the sadness that closeness brought. . . . An hour spent talking, crying, and hugging "unstuck" the grieving/healing process. No further professional psychotherapeutic intervention was needed.

Types of Brief Therapy

All of the therapies we have already covered have brief versions. Behavior and cognitive-behavioral therapies are short-term to begin with, and they are highly goal-directed and offer specific remedies for specific problems. Perhaps the most contrary to stereotype are the brief forms of psychoanalysis, which psychoanalysts prefer to call short-term psychodynamic psychotherapy to distinguish it from "real" psychoanalysis.

The time-limited dynamic psychotherapy focuses on dysfunctional interpersonal relationship patterns, as opposed to early childhood sexual and aggressive wishes. It is assumed that earlier difficulties with significant others have given rise to patterns of interpersonal relating that originally served a self-protective function but are now self-defeating and maladaptive. These central relationship issues will manifest themselves in the therapeutic relationship, and reexperiencing them in the transference relationship will be therapeutic. While transference involves bringing past relationships into the current, therapeutic relationship, the client's feelings toward the therapist also include some real aspects of the here-and-now relationship. The therapist uses her own feelings as signals of how the client is attempting to structure their relationship. Empathic listening is important, and the therapist is encouraged to engage in honest self-disclosure, if necessary and appropriate. Compared to the acquisition of insight, the relationship may be the more potent therapeutic factor.

There are types of brief therapy that are not based on traditional therapies. The Task-Centered Model of Epstein and Brown (2002) is an example. Although sharing similarities with other brief therapies, this model emphasizes that most problems have two components; the client lacks the resources to solve the problem or the client lacks the skills to solve the problem (or both). Clients are assessed on these components and a plan for dealing with them is developed. The brief treatment focuses on client and therapist accomplishing the tasks that develop resources and skills. Epstein and Brown describe their procedures and how they are used with surgical patients, HIV/AIDs patients, and homeless families and individuals.

Single-Session Therapy

Many have noted that there is a parallel between the structure of each individual therapy session and that of the overall course of treatment (Hoyt, 1995). It seems entirely possible that a precise, well-timed intervention could have a profound effect in one session. In fact, Rosenbaum (1994) argues that psychology should study single-session therapies for a picture of therapy in miniature in order to research what really works in therapy and to achieve theory integration. He also argues that the 20% to 50% of clients who attend only once should not be considered therapy dropouts, but rather, examples of single-session therapy attendees. His research and that of others indicate that people who come to therapy once rate its effectiveness just as high as those who come for several sessions and do not differ from them on any outcome measure (Rosenbaum, 1994).

Like other brief therapies, single-session therapy is focused and goal-oriented, assumes that change can occur in the moment and outside of therapy, emphasizes client strengths, accepts the client's definition of the problem, and is eclectic. The single-session therapist is active and directive, taking responsibility for keeping the session focused on the agreed-upon issue and goal. However, the choice of a single session is usually left to the client, and the therapist should be ready to work for as long as two hours or more. It is also left open that the client can return at any time, so in this sense, single-session therapy is not time limited.

Similar to the structure of other brief therapies, the single session generally covers the following steps. First, the therapist engages the client and establishes rapport. Second, therapist and client define the purpose of the meeting and agree on realistic and attainable therapeutic goal(s). The therapist creates an opportunity for the client to express thoughts, feelings, and behavior, all the while assessing the client's strengths, resources, and motivations. Third, the therapist then makes the treatment intervention(s), assesses its effects, and adjusts her behavior accordingly. Homework may be assigned or practiced right in the session. Finally, client changes are reviewed, summarized, and rehearsed to consolidate learning.

Brief therapy has a long future. As discussed above, research demonstrates that it is as effective as long-term therapy, and it is probably more cost-effective. Psychologists would do well to seek training in the brief therapy methods.

Group Therapy

Early on, it occurred to psychotherapists that they could help more people by treating them in groups, instead of individually. Now group therapy is used extensively in the United States, and it may be the most important method of providing mental health care in the future, especially in managed care settings (MacKenzie, 1994). Furthermore, research generally favors the conclusion that group approaches are at least as effective as individual approaches (Vinogradov & Yalom, 2003).

One of the advantages of group therapy is that it is cost-effective compared to individual therapy. Groups also provide a context for interpersonal learning. Since most individuals' problems involve interpersonal relationships, at least to some degree, individuals can directly experience these problems in the presence of others in a group, and therefore have an "alive" context within which to work them out. Group experiences are more likely to approximate the day-to-day reality of clients than individual therapy. Groups, therefore, provide greater opportunities for interpersonal interaction and experimentation, as well as for feedback. In that sense, they offer opportunities for learning that either may not exist or may exist to a lesser extent in individual therapy. For some clients, groups may be the treatment of choice instead of individual therapy.

A great deal of research in social psychology demonstrates the power of a group of people to influence the behavior of any one individual. These group forces may be used to bring about therapeutic changes in individuals. For instance, in highly cohesive groups, pressure in the form of positive attention and support may encourage clients to open up and confront their problems. Thus, a highly cohesive group may be able to bring a positive kind of "pressure" to bear on clients who are resistant to confront and explore their problems. Pressure here need not be thought of as something coercive. Rather, the pressure is positive in that it provides rewards through support, interest, and acceptance for conforming to ***norms*** such as those of self-disclosure, exploring one's feelings, confronting one's problems, trying out new behaviors, and so on.

Group dynamics occur in all groups of people, and it is the job of a mental health professional leading a therapy group to ensure that these dynamics support positive change in the group members. (The presence of one or more professional leaders distinguishes group therapy from self-help and mutual support groups.) What the group therapist does to create group dynamics that bring about therapeutic change varies according to the theoretical beliefs of the therapist.

Most group therapists see the group as a system in its own right, rather than as merely the setting in which they work with individuals. The therapist learns from interactions among the members and the therapist helps the group understand how various forces and pressures in the group itself influence behavior. Furthermore, all problems outside the group, such as with bosses, spouses, and family, can be dealt with inside the group by focusing on how the group member interacts with other group members.

Despite theoretical differences, group therapies share certain features. Most groups meet once a week, sometimes twice a week in the case of group psychoanalysis. Group sessions tend to be an hour and a half to two hours long. There are 6 to 12 group members, with 8 to 10 generally considered an ideal number. Some group therapists believe a carefully constructed group of equal numbers of men and women with different but complementary problems is best, while others prefer groups composed of people all with the same problem or characteristics. Some therapy groups are very structured, with active therapists following planned agendas, while others are not. Although traditionally time unlimited, group therapy is now often time limited (MacKenzie, 1997).

Almost every form of individual psychotherapy has its parallel group approach. We will examine a few in detail. There have been approaches that began in the group format, and we will discuss one example below.

Psychoanalytic Groups

Group psychotherapy as we know it today actually began in the psychoanalytic tradition. Since the disturbance in the individual's internal functioning leads to difficulties relating to others, analysis in groups may foster more or faster insights. Psychoanalysts assume that groups develop a parent transference relationship with the therapist and a sibling transference with group members. The therapist interprets both transference relationships. Clients free-associate to each other and report dreams, and both therapist and group members interpret the dreams and the resistances. Group members reinforce the analyst's interpretations of individuals by agreeing with the interpretation and citing examples of it from the group's interactions.

The group symbolically becomes each individual client's "family" psychologically, and transference relationships get played out with vivid emotional intensity. For instance, one group member may begin to feel jealous of the attention the therapist is giving another group member, and that may vividly evoke childhood experiences of having been the unfavored child. Thus, insight is attained in an emotionally "alive" context.

The Tavistock Institute in London, England, founded by Freud's daughter, Anna, is an internationally recognized training center for psychoanalytic therapy. Analysts there developed the first theory and methods for psychoanalytic group therapy, and they continue to develop and train therapists in innovative group formats. Tavistock groups range from the traditional small group of 6 to 10 people meeting weekly with one or two analysts to large groups of 50 to 100 people meeting with two to six or more analysts for weekly sessions, intensive weekends, or two- or four-week workshops. With these very large groups, the analysts also meet with smaller subgroups for developing issues to bring to the entire group. At the risk of simplifying the analytic rationale for the Tavistock group method, it can be said that the emphasis in all Tavistock groups, regardless of size or format, is on group interpretations. While the analysts leading these groups occasionally make individual interpretations and process comments, the leaders are supposed to intervene as little as possible, so that the group must learn to rely on its own resources and to make only group interpretations. The group therapists point out group behavior and how individual behavior is part of group behavior, and they interpret this group behavior as reflecting group transference, group resistance, group defensiveness, unconscious group emotions, group wishes to depose the leaders, and the like. Disagreements within the group may be interpreted as transferred sibling conflict, as splitting, as aspects of group ambivalence, or as reflecting internal conflict or different parts of conscious or unconscious functioning. The Tavistock group believes its methods can bring the benefits of genuine psychoanalysis to large numbers of people.

Client-Centered Group Therapy

The goal of a client-centered group is to provide a warm, supportive, and empathic emotional context within which individuals can explore their relationships with themselves and with each other. A greater emphasis is placed on the process of interpersonal relating in client-centered groups than in psychoanalytic groups. Individuals are thought to learn through the process of opening up to others, confronting each other's misperceptions, and learning to trust themselves in the context of others. For instance, person A may perceive person B as "a bully." Through the process of the two talking to one another (and through the process of other members offering their feedback), these two members directly experience the process of opening up to one another, listening, being misunderstood, struggling with being misunderstood, learning how to communicate better in order to be understood, learning how to communicate in a more open, prizing way, and learning how to solve an interpersonal problem. The client-centered therapist helps this process by tuning in to each party and empathically helping them "say" their personally felt meanings in ways that become more "hearable" both by themselves and by others.

The therapist tries to empathically understand each group member and tries to effectively be genuine himself. The therapist tries to relate as an equal in the group,

Using group therapy with pets.

self-disclosing and sharing his own feelings and reactions but always trying to do so in a facilitative, effectively communicative way. Client-centered therapists believe there is a "wisdom of the group" just as there is a wisdom of each individual. Therefore, client-centered groups are democratic in that members may suggest exercises or activities for the group to do, and the process of deciding on the direction the group takes is democratic. However, the leader's main task is to provide the therapeutic conditions of warmth, empathy, and genuineness. The leader hopes that by modeling these conditions through his activity, he can help group members learn to respond to one another with the same therapeutic conditions.

Gestalt Groups

As run by Fritz Perls, gestalt groups could not be said to be "proper groups" at all. Perls's groups did not really work with the interaction between members of the group. Perls's primary method was to work with individuals—only in a group format. Perls would have an individual come up and sit on the "hot seat" and work in front of the group. The rest of the group functioned as a kind of Greek chorus and Perls utilized them as a part of working with that individual. For instance, if a person felt like all others in the group were critical of him, Perls might have that person go around the group and stare at each individual member. This exercise of staring at others would have the goal of the person "taking back" his own ability to make judgments himself.

Other gestalt therapists stress the interaction among group members more so than did Perls. The goal of a gestalt group is to help individuals be fully present in the moment; to be able to make full, open contact with the self and with others; and to take responsibility for themselves. How a person is presently feeling is stressed as that person interacts with others. A gestalt group could therefore be seen as a "learning laboratory" in that people learn to be fully aware of their own experience *as they live it* in interaction with others in the group.

Gestalt therapists tend to be relatively active in groups, compared to both psychoanalytic and client-centered leaders. They are more likely to actively structure interactions, create experiments, or interrupt interactions that are taking place if they feel that doing so will lead to learning and awareness. Similar to client-centered therapists, gestalt therapists will attempt to "be real" themselves in the group and will self-disclose their own reactions.

Behavioral and Cognitive-Behavioral Groups

The goal of behavior therapy conducted in groups is the learning of new skills and the unlearning of old, dysfunctional behavior. Behavioral techniques such as exposure methods, skills training, parent training, stress inoculation, and coping can all be utilized in group formats. The therapist's role is more like that of a teacher in a behavioral group. The therapist provides structured activities for learning, conducts discussions to foster that learning, gives feedback, may engage in role playing, gives lectures and demonstrations, and so on.

Cognitive groups typically include the use of behavioral techniques as well. However, they focus on confronting and dealing with clients' dysfunctional cognitions. Cognitive therapists give homework assignments and then explore clients' reactions to those homework assignments in terms of their dysfunctional cognitions. The therapist models the skills of challenging dysfunctional thinking, facilitates individuals' confronting their own dysfunctional thinking, and encourages other members of the group to learn how to challenge dysfunctional thinking. The therapist may also have guest speakers come in, assign homework, or provide structured exercises.

Group-Based Forms of Group Therapy

Some forms of group therapy began in the group format and developed somewhat differently from those based on the individual therapy approaches. In psychodrama, for example, the group is essential, and it is difficult to imagine an individual form of this approach. ***Psychodrama*** was developed by J. L. Moreno (1934), and it stresses insight and catharsis through the acting process. Clients act out scenes of conflict from their childhood or present life. Group members help each other by acting the necessary parts in an individual's scene. If a depressed client has had trouble with his mother, another member of the group plays his mother. Coaches or "alter egos" stand behind the actors and suggest what to say and do. The members may switch roles, or the alter egos may play out a scene. As in gestalt, the client may be asked to play the role of the person with whom he had the conflict. However, in contrast to gestalt, the client's role would often then be taken by another group member. This way, the client can gain insight into how she appears to others. The therapist plays the role of "director." He structures the action, assigns roles, and decides at various points if other members of the group are to be called in to play new roles. In this sense, the leader is highly active and directive.

Uses of Group Therapy

Groups are used for many different kinds of problems, in many different settings. Groups are used extensively in hospitals, clinics, correctional institutions, student counseling centers at universities, and so on. Group therapy is often combined with other approaches, as in a client seeing a therapist both in a group and individually. Another example is group therapy as part of in-patient treatment, which may include medication, individual therapy, occupational therapy, and so on. Groups have been developed for people with specific disorders, such as eating disorders or depression, to deal with certain issues all the clients have. We shall consider one example of the use of group therapy in treating a specific type of problem, that of substance and alcohol abuse.

Group therapy is one of the most important vehicles for working with substance abuse problems, and virtually all treatment programs for substance abuse include group therapy. This is not merely because it is more cost-effective than working with individuals alone, it is also because of the powerful learning effects in groups. For instance, overcoming denial is more likely to "stick" when done in front of a group of other substance abusers than when done in front of one therapist. There is something about publicly admitting one's problems in front of a group that seems to be a particularly important part of the process of coping with a substance abuse problem.

Because substance abuse appears to be a problem in which the impairment of self-awareness is particularly involved, feedback from a group of people is especially useful. Various reasons have been offered for this impairment in self-awareness. Perhaps the most common is that of denial. That is, substance abusers deny the existence of a problem. They will blame circumstances; they will say that they can manage the problem on their own; they will say they can "cut down." Another possible reason for the impairment in self-awareness is the effects of the substance itself. Over time, this may lead to a chronic impairment in cognitive functioning. A third possible reason for lack of self-awareness is that when abusers are "high," they are especially unaware of how they are acting. It is for these reasons, among others, that group procedures with alcohol and substance abusers appear to be helpful.

Another advantage of using groups is that it is often easier to see things in *others* before one sees them in oneself. Therefore, the group situation provides a particularly powerful learning environment for the substance abuser. The group will be able to identify patterns of denial and self-evasion in a given patient and provide feedback to that effect. At the same time, as the members notice these patterns in others, a context is prepared in which they can come to notice them in themselves.

Groups for substance abusers have similar goals and procedures to many of the other groups we have discussed. First, the major goal is to become aware of one's problem and to accept its existence. Second, efforts are made to explore the feelings that underlie the problem. Through that, feelings of low self-worth are often accessed, and the group situation is utilized to help abusers come to prize themselves more. In some groups, childhood roots of the problem may be explored and discussed (especially, for instance, experiences of child abuse). Third, such groups help abusers develop and identify more positive values and goals. Fourth, they help substance abusers begin to develop better coping skills. This may include helping them develop good communication skills, better problem-solving skills, and better skills for dealing with their feelings.

Self-Help and Mutual Support Groups

As members of a largely individualistic culture, Americans have always liked self-help. The forms of psychological self-help are many and range from books and self-administered computer programs to mutual support groups such as Alcoholics Anonymous and Recovery Inc. Some believe that self-help should be called "psychoeducational methods" or "self-administered treatment" in order to distinguish it from psychotherapy and counseling. Professional psychologists are involved in designing, marketing, supervising, consulting, and referring clients to self-help methods.

The bookstore shelves devoted to psychology and self-help books are always loaded. Some therapists recommend such books to their clients and discuss them with them, and it is possible that many people use such "bibliotherapy" alone without ever seeing a therapist. With the development and marketing of computerized programs for skills training, behavior change, and treatment of specific problems, the self-help shelves of the CD-ROM and DVD sections of book and media stores will soon be comparable to the self-help bookshelves. People can buy all sorts of CDs and DVDs to self-administer treatments to change a number of behaviors or to change the behavior of others, such as their children. For example, a special videotape has been developed to train children with attention deficit disorder to focus and pay attention to the cues needed for reading and learning.

Mutual support groups are based on the premise that people with similar problems can help others and in turn be helped by that process. Members of mutual support groups run the meetings, and often the groups are volunteer based or part of nonprofit organizations. They do not rely on professionals to run the groups but may use them as consultants from time to time. A particular benefit of self-help groups is the sense of empowerment that comes from the fact that the members are getting help on their own. They are not being "helped" or "fixed" by a professional.

Different groups have different philosophies or theoretical bases, but all assume that people with similar difficulties can exchange useful information, learn coping methods from each other, provide each other with emotional support, and reduce feelings of isolation and being "the only one" with that problem. Besides group meetings, mutual support encompasses other consumer-operated programs, such as drop-in centers, outreach and referral services, employment and housing programs, crisis intervention, and even advocacy and social or political action.

People participate in all sorts of support groups, either informally in hospital waiting rooms and the like or formally by joining Alcoholics Anonymous or other groups. In fact, more Americans use self-help to change their behavior than use professional treatment or programs (Davison, Pennebaker, & Dickerson, 2000). Furthermore, there is a great deal of evidence, reviewed in the 1999 Surgeon General's Report (U.S. Department of Health and Human Services, 1999), that self-help and support groups are effective in helping their members in a number of ways, including reducing symptoms, improving coping ability, increasing self-esteem and social cohesion, reducing hospital admissions, and that they are as effective as traditional therapy. Other research (Kyrouz, Humphreys, & Loomis, 2002) has substantiated the helpfulness of mutual support groups.

One of the most important functions of a self-help group is to provide a support network for individuals who are struggling with some kind of problem. A good deal of research by community psychologists has supported the idea that a good social support network reduces the likelihood of individuals developing problems such as depression and anxiety. One of the biggest differences between many self-help groups and formal, professional therapy groups is that they are available on an as needed basis and therefore serve as a part of a person's support network. For instance, with Alcoholics Anonymous, members may attend meetings every night of the week if they wish. In fact, during initial stages of recovery, alcoholics are encouraged to attend virtually every day for several months. In the sense that they may provide an ongoing source of social support, self-help groups may offer benefits and advantages that professional groups do not.

The development of the Internet has increased the opportunities for self-help and mutual support groups. Some chat rooms and Web logs have probably served functions similar to mutual support groups all along. Now therapists, agencies, and self-help organizations have designed and set up Web sites for the specific purpose of providing online mutual support groups for people with certain disorders. People can exchange useful information, share coping strategies, and support each other emotionally online, perhaps as effectively as they can in face-to-face groups.

Although challenged by the possibility that self-help may equal professional help, psychologists can participate in self-help in several ways. "Giving psychology away" includes, after all, teaching the public how to help themselves. Some self-help books, CDs, method manuals, or Internet sites are more effective than others for certain people and for certain goals. For example, one study found that members of conservative mutual support groups felt empowered through greater self-expression, while radical groups inspired increased optimism and feelings of control over one's life (Hatzidimitriadou, 2002). With enough appropriate research, psychologists can refer people to the Internet sites and mutual support groups that best meet their specific needs. Psychologists can both design and research the various self-help methods and make appropriate recommendations with the goal of educating consumers as to how to make the best use of the helping alternatives available. Self-help is popular, and professional psychologists should work to make it as effective as possible.

Technology-Mediated Methods

Many professional psychologists, like many Americans, have fallen in love with modern technology. The possibilities for utilizing technology in all aspects of psychological services are being explored in research and practice. However, it must be pointed out that Freud was the first, as he was in many areas, to attempt to deliver psychological help through means other than face-to-face contact. He was a voluminous letter writer and sometimes delivered psychological advice and interpretations by mail, including a short dream analysis for an American woman who wrote to him for help in 1927 (Benjamin & Dixon, 1996).

Since Freud, technology has developed and expanded rapidly, and the use of technology in the helping professions has also grown, enough that there are now several journals, such as the *Journal of Telemedicine and Telecare, Computers in Human Behavior, Journal of Technology and Human Services*, and *Cyberpsychology and Behavior*, as well as professional organizations, such as the International Society for Mental Health Online. However, growth is so rapid that whatever we say about technology-mediated helping methods in this section will likely be out of date by the time you read this.

Telephones

Telephones have been incorporated into attempts to help people since their invention. "Hotlines" for people suffering suicidal or other crises are well known, and some clinics offer "warmlines" for people with less serious problems, such as parenting or health issues. Some private therapists offer counseling and brief therapy over the telephone for a fee. Individuals can call a 900 number anytime and speak with a therapist trained in this type of work. The therapy offered is, of course, brief, and it shares the assumptions and methods of brief and single-session therapies. Telephone mediated therapy is also called "telehealth," and the APA offers a continuously updated list of telehealth resources (www.apa.org/practice/telehealth.html). In one study, depressed patients were randomly assigned to a group receiving antidepressant medication with ordinary follow-up or to a group receiving medication plus eight sessions of telephone therapy. Telephone therapy with medication was more effective in reducing depression than medication without it (Simon et al., 2004).

Mass Media

Some people use call-in radio and television programs in a way similar to telephone counseling. While most talk show, radio, and television psychologists see themselves as performing an educational function, sometimes they also do brief therapy on the air and make appropriate referrals off the air. With the popularity of reality TV, there are now television shows explicitly doing therapy and counseling to accomplish behavior change on air. One example is "Intervention" in which drug addicts are confronted by their families with the goal of getting them into recovery programs (Elber, 2005).

Computers

With the development of powerful computers, the potential uses of technology have expanded. Computer-like machines were first used in psychological assessment to score personality questionnaires. Since then, computer programs have been developed that administer, score, and interpret many types of psychological tests, including the Rorschach inkblot test. Computers are also used to compose assessment reports, bill clients, keep client records, and the like. Computerized databases, many available on the Internet, can also be used to make referrals and organize services.

The most challenging and intriguing use of computer technology is in the delivery of psychological treatment. An early computer program attempted to replicate traditional psychotherapy and counseling with a computer serving as the therapist. The client typed what he wanted to say directly into the computer, which was programmed to ask questions, make comments, and even give reflections or interpretations. There was some evidence that some people found this type of "therapy" helpful (Christensen & Jacobson, 1994). This early program was called ELIZA, and it can now be found on the Internet. Just Google ELIZA and try it out. It's fun to see ELIZA mimic therapy.

Newer computerized treatment programs involve administering specific types of therapy for specific problems, such as cognitive-behavioral interventions for phobias, incorporating educational video, interactive exercises, and other CD-ROM technology. For example, Bloom (1992a) reviewed computer-assisted interventions, and Christensen and Jacobson (1994) reviewed published computerized treatments for obesity, phobias, and depression, all of which were reported to be as effective as therapist-administered treatments. Furthermore, creative professional psychologists are developing and marketing CD-ROM and Internet programs to help people with daily living skills such as parenting and communication and to change many other behaviors.

The Internet

Self-help is available on the Internet, as already mentioned. "Bibliotherapy" can be done on the Internet; see www.helping.apa.org for psychological assistance or Google any disease or disorder to get all sorts of information on it. There are Web sites for self-help and mutual support for every possible disease and mental health problem, such as the site of the Anxiety Disorders Association of America (www.adaa.org/public/selfhelp.cfm), which helps people with anxiety disorders. And there are sites for the family members of the people with the various problems. There are clearinghouse sites that refer people to support groups in their area, such as the American Self-Help Group Clearinghouse (www.mentalhelp.net/selfhelp/). There are sites with detailed instructions on starting self-help groups, such as the National Mental Health Consumers' Self-Help Clearinghouse (www.mhselfhelp.org). Research on the effectiveness of self-help Web sites has just begun, but one review found that evidence for the effectiveness of Internet-based self-help for panic disorder was "promising" and that there was no evidence that it was harmful (Andersson, Bergstrom, Carlbring, & Lindefors, 2005). Studies have found that Internet support was helpful for eating disorders (DeAngelis, 1997), recurrent headache (Strom, Pettersson, & Andersson, 2000), and weight loss (Tate, Wing, & Winett, 2001), among other problems.

As with the telephone, professional therapy through the Internet is offered to individuals either alone or in conjunction with face-to-face therapy. Such therapy and other Internet-delivered help may be called e-therapy, Web counseling, cybertherapy, or online therapy. E-mail and other online methods are used to provide therapy. Family and couples therapy are available, and group therapy is done in chat rooms and on message boards. By the time you read this, group therapy may be conducted over the Internet with live streaming video. Psychological tests are on the Internet, as we mentioned in chapter 4, and it is possible for online therapists to develop professionally managed testing sites to help with online therapy by, for example, assessing the best e-therapy methods for a particular client. Online therapists also make use of and refer clients to all the self-help and education resources online. For those interested in learning about recent developments in e-therapy, consult the following Web sites:

www.rider.edu/~suler/psycyber/psycyber.html
www.fenichel.com/OnlineTherapy.shtml
www.metanoia.org/imhs/
www.ismho.org/
www.grohol.com/best/

The Internet may be a good way to "give psychology away," that is, to publicize psychological findings and methods so that people can help themselves, live effectively, and prevent the development of problems. For example, there are psychologists who produce weekly podcasts on mental health issues in order to educate people and create positive attitudes towards therapy as well as to attract clients. The use of the Internet in prevention has not been studied much, but the potential is great.

The Internet may even be used to *train* professional psychologists. Courses on the Internet are now offered by almost every college and university. Some may be found for programs in clinical psychology, social work, and other mental health professions. The use of the Internet in training therapists in multicultural skills has already been mentioned (www.multiiculturalskills.com), and some continuing education courses for therapists are delivered through the Internet. Training in appropriate online counseling skills and supervision of e-therapy cases are available online.

A final note on the use of computer technology in mental health services must include mention of Internet-based case management programs. The ethical and political issues involved in managed care and case management will be discussed in the next chapter, but there are computer programs that allow case managers to track all of each client's data, treatment program, referrals, contacts, and services through the Internet in order to ensure appropriate care and assess treatment effectiveness. Besides the case manager, other permitted providers and clients can log on to a client's account and see what else has been done and what needs to be done. A case manager or parent can check, for example, whether an adolescent went to therapy and if not, find out why not. Communication between service providers and between providers and clients can be constant and completely up to date. The potential for more efficient and more effective case management is obvious. An example of a well-designed Internet-based case management program can be found at www.caregiveralliance.com.

Issues in Technology-Mediated Therapy

Critics of technological psychological services charge that telephone, computerized, CD-ROM, or Internet-based therapists miss vital information supplied by the in-person encounter and therefore may make ineffective or harmful interventions. Internet sites labeled as self-help or mutual support have the potential to misinform or exploit vulnerable people who go to them for help, since the Internet is largely unregulated (Finn & Banach, 2000). Technology-mediated treatments are criticized as unethical for a number of reasons, including the potential for hackers to destroy confidentiality. Another criticism is that it can help only people who are comfortable writing expressively. Technology-mediated treatments are so new that specific ethical requirements have not been enacted, as of this writing, although ethics have been proposed (Bloom, 1998; www.ismho.org). The APA has issued a continuously updated statement on ethics in e-therapy as a guideline for therapists (ISMHO, 2000). The ethics of televising therapy, which can be emotionally painful for those going through it, for the purposes of entertainment are especially questioned.

As a new field, online therapy must address many legal and ethical issues. Some people who offer online therapy explicitly state that they are not doing psychotherapy or counseling but simply conversing, clarifying, encouraging, educating, and advising. Others are licensed professionals and do offer therapy services for a fee. Is online therapy even legal? Can a professional psychologist licensed in one state legally do online therapy with an individual living in another state? How can potential clients judge their online therapist's competence? Who should regulate online therapy and how? If a state tried to outlaw e-therapy, would people simply get it in other states?

The resolution of these issues includes the necessity for more research, educating consumers, instituting professional evaluation of Internet helping sites, and developing guidelines for ethical, professional e-therapy. Perhaps online therapists will organize and regulate themselves. Technological developments may solve some problems. For example, live streaming video of clients and therapists can make Internet therapy almost exactly like face-to-face therapy, and there are technological solutions to confidentiality and privacy problems. Technology changes so rapidly that these steps may be completed by the time you read this and new problems probably will have developed.

It must be asked whether the benefits of technology-mediated therapy outweigh the risks. The benefits of technology-mediated treatments are that therapy is made available to large numbers of people and that it can be quick, convenient, and relatively inexpensive. It may reach people who would not otherwise consider therapy because of the cost or stigma or because of living far from services. Some online therapists believe that e-therapy has advantages over traditional in-person therapy in that people must consider their words carefully when composing written descriptions of problems or giving advice, people have time to think about what they are writing and saying, and a written record can be kept so clients can review advice or encouragement any time they feel the need. Although research so far indicates that technological psychological treatments are as effective as face-to-face therapy for some important behaviors (Finn & Holden, 2000; Maheu & Gordon, 2000), much more research is needed in this area as new technology develops. Research is also needed on the effects of conducting therapy on television. It is possible that such programs educate the public, assist in prevention, and even help the participants.

The use of technology in psychological services will not cease, nor will it stop changing and growing. Professional psychologists may have an ethical obligation to work with technology-mediated treatments and services to make them as safe and effective as they can be.

In Conclusion

Diversity and other social issues have challenged professional psychology and presented it with the opportunity to develop new psychotherapy theories, new treatment modalities, and in essence, a new worldview. This challenge has not always been welcome, because these changes deal with our most profound assumptions, beliefs, and values. The change from time-unlimited to brief therapy, forced by economics, contradicts many of the basic assumptions of traditional therapy and those of postmodern therapies as well. A worldview in which reality is constructed rather than objective, in which truth is relative rather than absolute, is both difficult to grasp and not universally accepted. In addition, the change from an individualistic, hierarchical view to a connectionistic, egalitarian one is difficult for many people in our culture to make, especially for those privileged by the hierarchical view. In dialectical terms, the thesis of individualism is being challenged by the antithesis of connectionism, and we trust that psychology will be part of the resulting synthesis, preserving the best of both views. The development of self-administered and technology-mediated treatments delivered through the global electronic community may be part of this synthesis.

PROFESSIONAL, ETHICAL, LEGAL, AND SOCIAL ISSUES

> In the inevitable specialization of modern society, there will become increasing need of those who can be paid for expert psychological advice . . . [and] in the end there will be not only a science but also a profession of psychology.
>
> —R. Cattell, *The Fight for Our National Intelligence*

Despite this early prediction, psychologists have to ask, does professional psychology *have* a future? George Albee was saying it was uncertain at best as early as 1970. Social forces, changes in the health care system, and shifts in the economy guarantee that all the mental health professions will change dramatically in the next few years. In this chapter, we will examine some of these forces and attempt to predict how psychology will change.

First, however, we will examine professional issues that have concerned psychology since its beginning and that will undoubtedly continue to be important in the future. Some of these issues reflect clinical psychology's attempt to establish itself as an independent profession. Others reflect its response to the forces of social change. Most of these issues show how professional psychology and the other mental health professions interact with society as they try to define and solve social problems.

Professional Issues

This section examines issues relevant to psychology as a profession that offers helping services to the public. These issues are relevant to other helping professions as well. The present and future practice of professional psychology reflects its past efforts to define itself as an independent profession in the face of opposition and competition from medicine, psychiatry, and other groups. Past controversies over ethical and legal issues and the definition and diagnosis of mental disorder, discussed in this chapter, mask economic and political struggles over professional territory and the right to practice. Often, these conflicts are couched in "scientific" terms or posed as efforts to "protect clients" in order to avoid facing the underlying political issues of territoriality. The ability of professional psychologists to practice as they believe is best has been and will continue to be under threat from a number of sources.

At present many professional psychologists work in private practice or in separate departments of psychology within mental health institutions. They have achieved recognition from the public as independent professionals, and this status is at present substantiated in the law. However, professional psychology's status as an independent mental health profession is historically recent and remains tenuous. Some psychologists' plans to make psychology a health profession, not just a mental health profession, may well lead to additional conflict.

Competition with Medicine

Until World War II, only psychiatrists were allowed to perform psychotherapy with adults. In spite of the pressure of the need for therapists to treat the returning veterans, the American Medical Association continued into the 1950s to claim that psychotherapy was a medical procedure to be done only by medical doctors. The increased number of trained clinical psychologists and the increased funding for mental health in the 1960s allowed clinical psychology to establish itself as an independent profession. However, in recent years competition for mental health business has increased, and there have been several attempts once again to constrain the practice of clinical psychology and other mental health professions.

Chapter 1 noted that psychoanalytic training used to require a medical degree. Psychologists argued that this requirement was unnecessary except for the purpose of restricting who may become psychoanalysts. In the 1980s they sued certain psychoanalytic institutes over this requirement as constituting restraint of trade, that is, restraint of their right to practice their profession. While psychologists (and social workers) won the lawsuits, they still have great difficulty being accepted in psychoanalytic training programs.

Relations between psychology and medicine remain uneasy. The AMA pays for staff to help state medical societies resist new legislation that expands the independent practice of psychologists and others and also to support amendments to current law in order to restrict that expansion. With its tremendous economic resources, the AMA may succeed in reversing some of the gains psychology and others have made as independent professions.

Defining and "Diagnosing" Mental Disorders

Originally formulated as an attempt to reduce the stigma of mental disorder (it seemed better to be ill than wicked or possessed), the definition of psychological disorders as "mental illness" can also be viewed as a way to establish professional territoriality. If psychological problems are viewed as biological illnesses, then they should be treated by medical doctors in clinics and hospitals with medication and prescribed treatments. By this definition, psychologists are not qualified to treat the mentally ill. However, if mental disorders were defined as psychological or behavioral in nature, then psychologists and other therapists would be qualified to treat them. The problem, of course, is that mental disorders are both physical and psychological.

The Biological Model

The view that the cause of mental illness is to be found in a disorder of the physical body is an old one, but it showed a resurgence in the 1980s as the model of choice in psychiatry. The biological view represents a challenge to professional psychology, which has long emphasized psychological, familial, and social causes of disorder. The challenge is not only to psychology's theoretical stance, but also to its right and competence to treat psychological problems.

Since the 1980s many drugs have been developed to modify disordered thoughts, feelings, and behaviors. It is not certain how these drugs work, but they have been observed to have varied benefits, such as reducing anxiety, depression, or thought disorder, as well as some negative side effects. Although the ideal is to be able to prescribe a specific drug, for a specific symptom in specific types of individuals, at present, such precision is not possible. In addition, it has not been demonstrated that medication is actually more effective than psychotherapy.

Years ago, electroconvulsive shock therapy (ECT), another biologically based treatment, was found to be useful in the treatment of severe depression. It was rarely used for many years after the development of antidepressant medication, partly because it resulted in injuries and some degree of brain impairment, but it may be regaining popularity. The technology has improved so that injuries are much less likely, and proponents argue that it works much more quickly than antidepressants and that in some resistant cases it is more effective. Critics might argue that it is still barbaric to administer shocks to the brain even though it is a quick and cheap method of protecting someone until a combination of antidepressants and intensive psychotherapy can begin to work.

Biologically based therapies have been the domain of psychiatry, but as neuropsychological research on the brain and behavior advances, psychologists may also include biological interventions in their treatment plans, as discussed in chapter 12 on prescription privileges for psychologists. It may be that a holistic model emphasizing the unity of biological and psychological processes can be embraced by both psychology and psychiatry. Under this model, interventions can be made through either psychological or biological points, with similar effectiveness, since mind and body are one. Thus, psychologists can be primary health care providers.

DSM

The *Diagnostic and Statistical Manual of Mental Disorders* (DSM) was largely written by medical doctors, although other mental health professionals were consulted for later revisions. In spite of its careful avoidance of the term *mental illness*, the words *diagnosis, prognosis, illness*, and *disease* appear throughout the DSM-IV, reflecting its medical assumptions. Since health insurance companies and managed care providers require DSM diagnoses, all mental health professionals must use it, reinforcing the medical definitions of psychological disorders.

Professional Competence

As part of their attempt to attain professional parity with psychiatry, clinical psychology determined in 1949 that the Ph.D. degree was a necessary part of training, as were so many hours of supervised practice. Later the Psy.D. degree was developed, and the role of master's level psychologists remains an issue in the field of professional psychology. A doctorate in clinical psychology may take more years to complete than medical school, and the amount of training in treatment and psychopathology is probably greater than that for psychiatrists. Nevertheless, psychiatry still argues that psychologists are not competent to treat certain groups of people, because they are not trained in medicine and pharmacology.

Certification

Certification in specific skills is offered by many training programs. Different from state certification, these certificates are available in alcoholism counseling, hypnotherapy, hospital practice, marriage counseling, and other proficiency areas. Some consumers and health care companies are demanding certification of specialized therapists, and some psychologists have complained that certificates have become more important than doctoral degrees in psychology. Because of the demand for certification, the APA began offering certificates itself in 1992 as part of its continuing education programs in order to prevent control of certification from devolving to other groups. In 1995, the APA College of Professional Psychology was established to serve as a certificate granting body. In the future, psychologists may find they need both a license and certification in a proficiency or specialty.

Continuing Education

Ethical therapists maintain their competence and keep their skills up to date by taking continuing education courses. Some believe that specific continuing education should be required by law for the maintenance of the license. For example, California requires that all therapists take courses in child abuse, human sexuality, and alcohol and drug abuse, as well as complete a certain number of hours in approved continuing education courses per year in order to maintain their licenses.

Hospital Privileges

Until 1984, only psychiatrists and medical doctors were allowed hospital privileges and the right to hospitalize their clients. The Joint Commission on Accreditation of Hospitals (JCAH) accredited only hospitals that allowed only psychiatrists and medical doctors to admit their private patients and to treat hospitalized patients. Due to pressure in the form of a lawsuit brought by the psychological community (*Capp v. Rank*) in 1984, the JCAH agreed to accredit hospitals that extend hospital privileges to licensed psychologists, although physicians would still determine patient care. However, it was entirely up to individual hospitals whether to include psychologists, and since hospitals are governed almost exclusively by medical doctors, few hospitals have extended staff privileges to psychologists.

Prescription Privileges

Because some believe that biologically based interventions or the biopsychosocial model is the wave of the future, since about 1985 some psychologists have been fighting for the legal right to prescribe medication (as discussed in chapter 12). Prescription privileges enhance psychologists' ability to address certain societal needs, such as making appropriate medication adjustments for the elderly, to provide quality care for the chronically mentally ill, and to serve rural and other underserved populations. Psychologists need prescription privileges because of their increasing identification as practitioners in a health discipline and to increase the breadth of available treatment options. Unfortunately, the process of obtaining prescription privileges includes a divisive, potentially expensive legal battle that may alienate consumers. Furthermore, some believe that what distinguishes psychologists from doctors is their ability to treat problems without "resorting" to medication. They argue that prescription privileges would buy into and reinforce biological and medical views of mental illness (DeNelsky, 1991).

It seems clear that psychologists *can* be trained to prescribe medication and that they are perfectly capable of doing so competently and to the benefit of patients. It is possible that in the future, health care systems may prefer to contract with psychologists to dispense medication for psychological disorders rather than with the more expensive psychiatrists.

Corporate Control of the Health Care System

A profound threat to psychology as an independent profession (and to medicine and all the mental health professions) has been the shift in the U.S. health care system to control by corporations. In the United States today few people pay directly for their own medical care, only the very poor or the very rich. By 1990, about 85% of all American health care was covered by some form of government insurance, private insurance, health maintenance organizations, or other corporate health care systems (Flanigan, 1991). Thus, corporate-owned health care systems and insurance companies wield tremendous power in determining the nature of health care in the United States and the practice of the mental health professions. Furthermore, the failure of the U.S. government to reform the health care system in the early 1990s solidified corporate power over the system.

The potential for conflict between the interests of for-profit corporations and those of consumers and citizens is great. Corporations are interested in profits, and not all forms of health care are profitable but are still needed. It is argued that the corporate health care system is not responsive to the special characteristics of people needing psychological help and prefers an approach like treatment manuals. The corporate system is not responsive to the mental health professions, other than psychiatry with its emphasis on biological causes and drug treatments.

Accountability and Peer Review

Corporations and states demand accountability from their health service providers. As a result of increasing costs, procedures to make the mental health professions more accountable for their claims and services have been introduced into all health care delivery systems. In order to continue to receive funding, providers of psychotherapy must now demonstrate that their services accomplish what they claim.

Peer review was seen as a way for clinical psychology to become accountable while retaining the professional independence to judge its own performance. Peer review is the examination of an individual psychologist's cases by other psychologists to see if the treatment provided is appropriate, competent, and necessary. Many mental health agencies instituted their own peer review programs in the 1970s before it was required by their funding sources. Now, many health care companies require peer review of certain cases before they pay for the costs of the treatment, and some require it of all cases after as few as four to ten sessions.

Insurance companies and managed care health organizations may insist on evidence based practice. Clinical psychology has always combined research and practice, so their methods are already evidence based. However, insistence from those outside the profession on evidence for best practices, defined their way, may disguise another way psychological practice may be controlled by corporate health care delivery.

Cost-Effectiveness

Along with general accountability, there have been increased demands that psychology demonstrate that its services are cost-effective, that its services or solutions to problems both work *and* cost less than other methods of treatment or doing nothing. Many studies demonstrate that psychological services can be very cost-effective. Providing certain patients with psychotherapy can reduce overall health costs by decreasing utilization of other, more expensive medical services. Alcoholism treatment programs save companies more money than they cost by reducing lost workdays and the costs of training new employees. Relatively inexpensive stop-smoking programs save enormous amounts of money that would otherwise be spent on expensive cancer treatments or wasted on lost workdays and reduced productivity due to illness. People must be convinced that psychotherapy is worth it. Forceful and persuasive education and marketing is needed, including empirical demonstrations of cost savings.

On the other hand, an emphasis on cost-effectiveness may cause psychology and society at large to lose touch with other worthwhile goals. For example, a study by O'Farrell et al. (1996) compared the cost-benefit of behavioral marital therapy with or without 15 additional relapse prevention sessions in the treatment of alcoholism. For both treatments, the cost savings in reduced health and legal system utilization were greater than the costs of delivering the therapy. Adding the relapse prevention sessions led to less drinking and better marital adjustment than behavioral marital therapy without them, but it did not lead to greater cost savings. Nevertheless, reduced drinking and improved marital adjustment are worthwhile goals, whether we can put a monetary value on them or not. It is important for psychology to persuade the public that cost-effectiveness is not the only measure of the value of psychological services.

Managed Care

In order to cut costs, corporations have turned to ***managed care***, a system that essentially restricts the way consumers may utilize medical services. Managed care includes such strategies as reimbursing fees of only certain low-cost physicians, contracting in advance for specific services at a fixed price, negotiating the price, and controlling how services are utilized. Corporations both contain costs and ration health care through managed care. Another way to cut costs is to eliminate coverage for certain types of practitioners or certain types of treatment. In fact, health care corporations may begin to *demand* certain kinds of treatment, such as using only specific treatment manuals. Many consider this outcome to be one of the dangers of the APA

Task Force on Empirically Validated Treatments, as discussed below. In addition, state governments have been trying to cut public health costs for years. Whether to increase corporate profit or to reduce state spending, managing and rationing health care to reduce costs affects everyone, including psychology and the mental health professions.

Another strategy for containing costs and managing care, started by Medicare and some prepaid medical plans, is the use of prospective payment systems (PPS) and ***diagnosis-related groups (DRGs)***. Hospitals and health care professionals are paid a flat fee based on the average cost of care for a patient's diagnosis, whether that actual patient's case is treated quickly or develops complications. If treatment costs are less than the set fee, the savings go to the provider as profit, but if the costs are more, then the provider takes the loss. It is especially difficult to predict the course of a mental disorder, and the use of DRGs may lead to inappropriate discharge of patients and financial risks to those who treat more severe cases.

Some question whether psychologists have a future in managed care, and others question whether it is ethical to participate in managed care and whether they even want to. If managed care precludes certain kinds of long-term but needed treatments, then there is a question of whether it is better to provide a little bit of help and do an inadequate job of treating people or to refuse to participate. On the other hand, managed care challenges psychology to develop effective short-term treatments, such as brief therapy and single session therapy discussed in chapter 15 (Austad, 1996a, b). These issues about the future of psychology in managed care programs are far from settled.

The survival of professional psychology will depend on demonstrating and convincing the public of the importance and cost-effectiveness of psychological services. Working within this framework is based on the assumption that resources are always going to be limited and we must learn how to ration them, rather than working to direct and increase resources to mental health. All of this sounds terribly money grubbing. Whatever happened to helping people in distress, to the sense of community responsibility for the less fortunate members of society, to the desire to enhance human functioning and improve our society? These American ideals can probably be elicited, especially if it is shown that it saves money to act on them.

Treatment Manuals and Empirically Supported Treatments

The development of treatment manuals and the APA Task Force on Empirically Validated Treatments (also called empirically supported treatments) were described in chapter 5. Many see the reduction of psychotherapy to standardized methods that can be described (and prescribed) in a manual as imposing the medical model and increasing corporate control of health care. Therapy comes to resemble how a physician proceeds. The client comes in and the doctor conducts an intake interview to gather information for the purpose of making an accurate diagnosis of the person's problems. Then, based on that diagnosis, a treatment plan is taken from a manual to alleviate this client's specific symptoms. The treatment is then applied to the client. Such treatments are highly symptom-focused and do not deal with issues of meaning in an individual's life. For example, anxiety problems are seen as reflecting problems of internal overattention to physiological signals, and clients are taught to use relaxation when they notice these internal signals, rather than addressing whether their anxiety has any meaning in terms of how they are conducting their lives.

Health insurance and managed care companies like the idea of treatment manuals. As discussed in chapter 5, many psychologists object to them. First, there is the issue of the reliability and validity of diagnosis, especially diagnosis based on DSM. Diagnoses may not be of much value in deciding what to do with a unique individual in a unique social context. Second, there is a body of research that indicates that these types of treatments do not work for everyone and that a substantial number of people are helped only by long-term, exploratory psychotherapy (Roth & Fonagy, 1996). Third, some people desire traditional psychotherapy. We know of a head of a major health maintenance organization who paid out of pocket for exploratory humanistic therapy rather than try any of the therapies in the HMO. Research should be directed to determining the types of people for whom long-term and intensive psychotherapy services are indicated, in addition to developing treatment manuals for specific symptoms.

In terms of professional psychology, the advent of treatment manuals has several implications. The right of psychologists to practice their profession is circumscribed by whether health corporations will pay for anything other than manual treatments. It is possible that there will be a major split in the profession. Some psychologists may remain involved in the implementation of the manualized approach. Others may choose to practice outside the health care establishment so they can practice the kinds of therapy they and some clients prefer. Some psychologists who favor the use of empirically supported treatment manuals have suggested that those who do not use them could be subject to malpractice suits (Austad, 1996b). The threat of malpractice suits unless such manuals are used is clearly designed to restrict the practice of professional psychology.

Ethical Issues

As an independent profession, psychology, like medicine and law, developed a set of ethical principles to guide its own practice and internal methods to police and discipline its members, rather than being regulated by the government or any other external agency. These professions argue that only fellow professionals understand the field well enough to judge the correctness of other professionals' practices.

Ethical principles are supposed to protect the welfare of the public. The need for protection rests on the assumption that there is a disparity in power and expertise between psychologists and consumers. People seeking psychotherapy are assumed to be vulnerable and liable to be harmed by improper practices. Therapists are assumed to be more knowledgeable than clients and to hold a position of authority over them. Clients, then, must have additional protection.

Early in the development of psychology, the APA established a set of ethical principles to guide psychologists, including professors, researchers, and clinical and counseling psychologists. The principles are all based on a concern for human rights and human welfare. The welfare of the consumer of psychological services is paramount, and the principles, such as confidentiality and competence, are designed to ensure that welfare. "Consumers" include students and research subjects (including animals) as well as therapy clients. The APA ethical principles, as most recently revised, can be reviewed on the APA Web site (www.apa.org).

The APA ethical principles undergo constant revision in response to professional and social problems. The APA Ethics Committee periodically publishes proposed revisions for discussion by the profession. For example, the problem of dual relationships has come up in different forms over the years. While the ethical principles have always considered it unethical for therapists to have other types of relationships, such as friend or supervisor, with clients, early versions of the ethical principles did not explicitly prohibit sex with clients, but assumed that as a dual relationship, it would be unethical. As sex between therapists and clients became recognized as a serious social problem, the ethical principles explicitly prohibited it. In the 1992 revision, the APA attempted to address sex between therapists and *former* clients, but this issue has remained controversial.

Recent developments in technology have presented ethical questions for psychologists. Psychological tests are now freely available on the Internet, and there is concern about how this will affect reliability and validity of the tests (Naglieri et al., 2004). Additional concerns with Internet tests include the fact that people have no way of knowing if a test on the Web is a good one or not and they may be upset by their results. The use of the Internet to provide therapy services has led to discussion of whether it is ethical to do so and of criteria for making it ethical, safe, and effective (as discussed in chapter 15). There are ethical guidelines for professional psychologists appearing on television and radio, but none yet for any participating in real-life, real-time therapeutic interventions televised for entertainment.

Every mental health profession has a code of ethics, and they are all quite similar in their emphasis on protecting the welfare of clients, keeping confidentiality, and the like. The ethics codes of specific groups can be seen on their Web sites.

Confidentiality and Privilege

Confidentiality is the *ethical* responsibility of psychologists to safeguard information they receive in the course of their practice (including teaching and research, as well as therapy). ***Privilege*** is a *legal* right of consumers of medical, legal, and therapy services to control information about themselves. Both the ethic of confidentiality and the legislated right of privilege are based on two assumptions: (1) that successful treatment of consumers of medical or therapy services rests on the full disclosure by the client of potentially embarrassing or harmful information and (2) that consumers will not disclose this important information unless they are assured it will not be revealed. Both of these assumptions are open to empirical verification, which has not been done, and are not necessarily true. However, they guide ethical practice and legislation.

Privilege is a legal right that has evolved over the centuries for people who consult priests, lawyers, and doctors. The holder of the privilege chooses whether information is revealed to others, such as the court or other professionals. The therapist may release information only with the written permission of the holder of the privilege. In the case of children or incompetents, privilege is a legal right held by their parents or guardians, although in some cases, it devolves to the therapist.

Privilege is legislated in the evidence codes of most states to apply to the people who consult mental health professionals, as well as lawyers and doctors. In 1996, the Supreme Court ruled in *Jaffe v. Redmond* that licensed therapists cannot be forced to testify about confidential communications between them and their clients, so the right of privilege for clients of therapists now has national recognition.

There are several exceptions to confidentiality and privilege. In most states, privilege does not apply in certain cases, such as a child who is a victim of a crime (such as physical or sexual abuse) or a person who seeks counseling in order to commit a crime. Another important exception to confidentiality is embodied in the 1971 ***Tarasoff*** decision of the California Supreme Court. The court ruled in favor of parents who sought damages against a psychologist for failing to warn them that the psychologist's client was intending to (and did) kill their daughter. In its famous alliterative statement, the court said that "Private privilege ends where public peril begins." This ruling has been interpreted to mean that therapists of homicidal patients are obliged to break confidentiality and inform the police and the intended victim(s) of their patients' intentions.

Some have argued that the *Tarasoff* case and similar court rulings place an unreasonable burden on therapists in terms of assessing and predicting dangerousness. The best predictor of dangerousness is past dangerous acts, yet the police and prisons are not usually held liable when they release dangerous individuals without warning the public. Other critics of these court rulings argue that any breach of confidentiality threatens the therapeutic process and that dangerous people will be deterred from seeking the treatment they need, thus increasing the danger to the public.

The ethical obligations of therapists with suicidal clients are not clear-cut. *Tarasoff* and the ethical obligation to prevent suicide would appear to indicate that confidentiality may be broken when a client expresses suicidal intentions. Family members or close friends (if there are no family members nearby) should be informed so that they can provide extra support to the client and be alert to indications of suicidal behavior. The suicidal client should be informed of the therapist's intention to so inform others. Some argue that breaking confidentiality may heighten the possibility of suicide by reducing the effectiveness of therapy or making the client less trusting of the therapist. Others respond that preventing the suicide takes precedence over all other considerations.

In 1996 Congress passed the Health Insurance Portability and Accountability Act, known as HIPAA. That act coupled with the Homeland Security Act has led to many regulations that changed the procedures for ensuring confidentiality, so in a way this discussion belongs in the section on legal issues. For organizations and practitioners to comply with HIPAA, they must also modify their informed consent procedures, so perhaps this discussion belongs in the section on informed consent. However, professional discussions about HIPAA usually focus on privacy and security issues, so we will discuss it here.

HIPAA had two objectives: To protect employees' health insurance coverage when they change jobs and to establish standards and requirements about health information. The health care corporations "traded" health insurance portability for regulations that make it easier for them to share client information, especially electronically. HIPAA regulations are also supposed to protect patients' privacy and confidentiality, but Homeland Security regulations come into conflict with this goal. The steps for health care providers to become "HIPAA compliant" are complex, and many groups hire consultants to help. The regulations require providers to assign responsibility for security of information to a person or organization, to assess risks and determine the major threats to privacy of health information, to establish a security management program, to certify the effectiveness of security controls, and to take several other steps. Few providers have the expertise or resources to do all of this, and some argue that HIPAA regulations and requirements for electronic data storage and sharing conflict with ethical obligations about client confidentiality. Although the consequences of HIPAA regulations on the confidentiality of client information remains to be seen, professional psychologists must be aware of this law and how it affects their practice.

Informed Consent

The appropriate use of ***informed consent*** in psychology has been debated. It is argued that people cannot really consent to something unless they have been fully informed as to exactly what they are consenting to. It is well established that patients submitting to a medical procedure must be fully informed of what is to be done and all the possible side effects before they consent to it. Psychologists have worked toward developing a good informed consent procedure for psychotherapy. Most agree that before clients consent to psychotherapy, they should be informed of the limits of confidentiality, how much it will cost, their rights as clients, and the qualifications and competence of the therapist. Some psychologists believe that clients should also be informed of the type of therapy being offered, including a brief description of what is expected of the client and what the therapist will do. Some state that this should include the possible risks and benefits of therapy. Some believe that clients should be told how likely the form of therapy is to work (based on empirical studies of similar cases) and how long it will take to work. Everyone agrees that the process of informed consent must be documented.

One important aspect of informed consent includes telling clients of the limits of confidentiality. Therapists who do not inform clients of the limits and who later, because of *Tarasoff*, disclose a client's dangerous intentions are liable to be sued for malpractice (if they don't break confidentiality, of course, they are liable to be sued for negligence). However, it may be frightening to clients to hear right away that confidentiality does not hold if they become homicidal or suicidal, or it may lead them to be distrustful of the therapist. A full disclosure of the limits of confidentiality may deter the very people who need therapy from obtaining it. Some recommend making informed consent an ongoing process and raising the limits of confidentiality after two or three meetings when some degree of trust has been established. HIPAA regulations add another set of issues about how best to obtain informed consent. These issues have not been resolved, so informed consent procedures for psychotherapy still vary greatly from one therapist or agency to another.

Legal Issues

Professional psychology becomes embroiled in legal issues in several ways. First, legislation is passed that directly or indirectly affects the practice of psychology, as HIPAA does. Licensing laws directly regulate the profession, and a variety of laws regulating health care affect professional practice. Second, psychologists may be sued for malpractice or negligence, and court decisions in such lawsuits affect the profession. The example of the *Tarasoff* court decision has already been discussed. Psychologists may also be involved in legal issues as expert witnesses and forensic psychologists, but we will not discuss these examples.

Licensing of Professional Psychologists

Licensing and certification of psychologists and other therapists were established amid controversy in the 1950s and 1960s, as noted in chapter 1. Both the desire to protect the public from untrained and incompetent practitioners and the need to establish an independent professional identity prompted organized psychology to pressure state legislatures to pass laws to license psychologists.

A *license* is issued by a state to professionals who have demonstrated competence in their field by academic achievement and by passing certain kinds of tests or requirements set by the licensing board. The license is supposed to protect the public by ensuring that only qualified and competent persons may offer their services to the public. *Certification* by the state is generally seen as a weaker form of control than licensure. The state merely certifies that: the professional has completed the education or experience requirements for that profession. The certificate does not imply competence, while the license supposedly does. *Registration* of therapists is the minimum way to regulate the mental health professions, in that therapists merely inform the state that they are practicing. In California, for example, psychological assistants and psychologists who are not yet licensed must register with the state.

Sunset Legislation

The practice of licensing psychologists and other therapists came under attack in the 1970s as failing to protect the public and instead as merely serving a guild function to protect the professions. Critics argued that licensing keeps the cost of psychological services high by limiting the number of practitioners and reducing competition. Some states threatened to pass "sunset laws" that would abolish licensing boards automatically every five years unless they were evaluated and specifically reenacted. In the late 1970s in Alaska, Florida, and South Dakota, the practice of psychology was unlicensed and unregulated for a period of time. The APA and state psychological organizations lobbied these states, and psychology was once again regulated in all states. However, with the movement in the 1990s to cut government regulation, sunset legislation was reintroduced in several states and passed in California in 1994. It can be seen from these events that the professional status of psychology is still tenuous, for no one has ever seriously suggested abolishing the licensing of physicians.

National Register of Health Service Providers in Psychology

The National Register was established in the 1970s partly in response to sunset legislation. If licensing were abolished, membership in the National Register could substitute. The National Register also serves as a guide to health care companies as to who is a licensed psychologist, that is, whose fees to pay.

Health Care Regulation

Health care corporations and government regulation of them are important factors in determining the nature of psychology as a profession. What types of disorders are covered by health insurance, what types of therapy health companies will pay for, how many sessions are covered, and what types of therapists will be reimbursed are issues that have had a tremendous impact on all the mental health professions. To counter the control of health care corporations, consumers and mental health professionals have both brought lawsuits against the companies and lobbied for legislation to regulate them.

Psychologists struggled for years to force health insurance programs to cover or reimburse their fees. They argued that because there is no evidence that psychiatrists are any more effective than psychologists (see chapter 5 for this research), the policy of insurers to cover only the fees of medical doctors constituted illegal restraint of trade. This issue was supposed to have been settled in the case of the "Virginia Blues." For years, Blue Cross and Blue Shield of Virginia required psychologists to bill for services through a physician. Assisted by the APA, the Virginia Academy of Clinical Psychologists brought an antitrust suit against the insurance companies in 1978, and won on appeal in 1984.

Many states passed ***freedom of choice (FOC)*** legislation as a result of lobbying by both consumer groups and mental health professionals. FOC laws are supposed to guarantee patients the right to choose their own therapists by requiring health insurance programs to provide equal coverage of psychotherapy services by psychologists and psychiatrists (and sometimes social workers and other therapists as well). These laws were supposed to reduce consumer costs by increasing competition. However, under managed care, this point may be moot.

Legal threats to the practice of psychology appear in unexpected places, as seen in the example of ERISA, the Employee Retirement Income Security Act (1980). This federal act was designed to improve all employee benefits, but it did not require health insurance to cover mental health benefits or to provide employees freedom of choice of doctors, contrary to most state laws. Chrysler Corporation announced in late 1984 that it would no longer pay for the services of a psychologist for any of its employees nationwide, citing ERISA as the reason. However, in 1985, the U.S. Supreme Court ruled against Chrysler.

Psychologists and other mental health professionals protect their right to practice by suing insurance companies and corporations. For example, a class action lawsuit against CIGNA was tentatively settled in December 2004, although details were still being worked out at the end of 2005. A group of nonphysician providers alleged that "managed-care companies conspired to reduce and delay payments to providers" (Holloway, 2005). The court found in favor of the plaintiffs, and CIGNA agreed to a number of changes in their procedures that would make dealing with the company faster and easier for psychologists. CIGNA created a settlement fund to reimburse professionals and consumers who were harmed by their prior practices, but they plan to appeal the court decision against them. For recent details on this legal method of defending psychologists' right to practice, see www.cignaprovidersettlement.com or www.apapractice.org.

These issues are far from settled, however, because of constant changes in the health care system. The legislative and court battles of previous decades are being replayed in relation to corporate systems of health care and proposed government controls on them. For example, in 1996 and 1997, the federal government attempted to pass laws mandating equal coverage of mental and physical disorders, as well as minimum maternity stays and other requirements. The process of corporations regulating health care and the government then regulating the corporations will remain of extreme interest to professional psychologists.

Malpractice

Even the best therapists are human, and humans make mistakes. Therapists carry malpractice insurance so that if they make a mistake, the victims of that mistake will be adequately compensated for the harm they have suffered. Malpractice insurance also protects clients if therapists knowingly do something wrong, such as practicing outside of their area of competence. In general, malpractice of therapists is difficult to prove, partly because there may be disagreement as to what constitutes "good practice" and partly because malpractice suits come down to the word of a supposedly mentally disturbed patient against that of a professional therapist.

Corporations sell malpractice insurance, and they typically try various ways to reduce costs and increase profits. For example, in 1985, the malpractice insurance carriers for both the American Psychiatric Association and the American Psychological Association announced that they would not cover therapists who had sexual relations with their clients. Some people saw this announcement as progress, in that the insurance companies seemed to be taking a strong stand against therapist–client sexual relations. However, others saw it as a way for the insurance companies to cut costs at the expense of victims. Certainly, a therapist's having sex with a client is malpractice—it is unethical, it is a mistake, it harms the client. Yet the insurance companies singled out this particular type of malpractice as not covered. Under this regulation, if a client sues a therapist over the malpractice of sexual contact and if the therapist is found not guilty, then the insurance companies will pay the legal expenses of defending the case. If, however, the therapist is found guilty (did have sex with the client, did harm the client), then the companies will not pay the therapist's legal fees or compensate the victim! Corporate control of malpractice insurance indirectly controls the practice of professional psychology and other mental health professions.

Social Issues and Psychology

What is the relation between psychology and society at large? What should that relation be? Psychologists and other therapists are citizens and members of their society, and their professions exist in a certain historical and social context. Should professional psychology try to remain neutral, accept society as it exists, encourage society to change, or work actively to bring about social change? If being an agent of change is an acceptable role, what social changes should be worked toward?

Clinical psychology is in the business of changing people, yet it is often accused of preserving the status quo. Like any established profession or interest group, it tends to resist change and to see its self-interest in keeping the advantages it has. If psychologists are comfortable in private practice, they will resist the drastic changes in the health care system. If professionals make their living by "treating" certain types of people, they will resist anything that redefines those people or reduces their numbers such as prevention. And, like any science, psychology must view the world through its own cultural values.

Change versus Adjustment

Continuing controversy occurs over the issue of whether people should change to adjust to society, as in medicating a psychotic person, or society should change to fit the needs of individuals, as in multicultural and feminist therapy. Many critics have argued that the goal of most psychotherapy is to make people fit into what exists, so they don't rock the boat. We even refer to how "adjusted" people are. These critics contend that it is the situation (the way society is organized) that is the problem, not the "maladjusted" individuals (Albee, 1996). If society is organized in an unhealthy or inhumane way, then people will naturally become disturbed. It is both immoral and futile to help these people adjust without changing the conditions that lead to maladjustment. Otherwise, helping people "adjust" is just another way of shoring up the status quo that harms them.

Many writers have recognized the social control functions of the mental health professions and criticized them for serving as the "soft police." Some behaviors have been defined differently over the years, so that different social control agents have been brought to bear on them. Excessive drinking behavior was once a sin, railed against by preachers and temperance organizations. Then for a few years it was a crime, and alcohol drinkers were arrested and imprisoned. Now excessive drinking behavior has become a disease, treated by doctors and therapeutic programs. In this sense, alcoholism doctors and counselors are now the soft police—the social control agents for excessive drinking behavior.

Feminist critics regard much of the practice of psychotherapy as incorporating the sexism and stereotypes of the current society. Mostly male therapists try to get mostly female clients to "adjust" to their gender role, their stereotype, their oppression. A woman who dislikes the female role and its lack of power may not be suffering from "penis envy" or a gender identity disturbance. On the other hand, she may simply be realistic about her role in society. By helping women "adjust" to unjust conditions, therapists are both preserving the status quo and perpetuating the oppression of women. Psychology has been responsive to these criticisms, for the American Psychological Association has established guidelines for therapy with women that encourage therapists to locate the cause of women's distress in their situation, not as something wrong with them. The same principles would apply to those treating other oppressed groups, such as gays and lesbians and certain ethnic groups.

Some see a growing tendency for our society to "medicalize" intractable social problems such as drug abuse. Since physicians and therapists are not likely to resist new categories of patients and potential income, this trend will probably continue. Medicalization of social problems is also supported by citizens and taxpayers, because it may be a way to avoid the harder task of dealing with the conflicting values and socioeconomic factors that underlie these problems and to avoid the necessity for difficult social change.

Misuses of Mental Health Concepts

The most widely criticized misuse of mental health concepts is the so-called insanity defense. John Hinckley's attempt to assassinate President Reagan and his subsequent acquittal due to insanity enraged many people and brought the issue to the public's attention. Arguing against the insanity defense for decades, Szasz (1961) documented that the insanity defense once resulted in miscarriages of justice in the sense that those judged "innocent by reason of insanity" served longer periods of incarceration in mental hospitals than they would have if sentenced to prison (this is no longer the case since prison sentences were lengthened during the 1980s). Szasz argued that since "mental illness" is a myth and professionals often disagree on whether a defendant was insane at the time of the offense, trials should be conducted solely on the basis of whether the person committed the alleged criminal act or not. Defenders of the insanity defense contend that abolishing it would also result in grave injustice, for each case must be assessed individually and the accused's state of mind, intentions, and capability of making rational decisions must be taken into account.

Other misuses of mental health concepts are not as apparent, although certainly just as debatable, as the insanity defense. Two examples come to mind. Once, a stress management program for blue-collar workers was being advertised in Oakland. The billboard shouted, "Stress at work? Powerlessness is bad for your health." Was this an innovative program showing workers how to organize themselves to gain power at work? No, it was a call for workers to seek counseling. Through stress management, workers would be taught to adjust to aversive working conditions, rather than organizing and demanding that their working conditions be improved (this criticism holds for stress management programs for executives as well).

Our second example has to do with a study once funded by the Department of Energy. The DOE paid a psychiatrist to determine the causes and cures of "nuclear phobia." Several psychologists attacked this study because of its methodological flaws and because of its obvious pronuclear bias. The critics claimed the study was a political use of mental illness jargon to label concerned citizens as having a phobia. Concerned citizens who disagree with the government's pronuclear energy stand and who may engage in political activities against nuclear power and nuclear weapons are just "crazy"—they've got "nuclear phobia"! Potentially, the DOE could next fund a study to "cure" nuclear phobia. Psychological methods could be used to manipulate the public for pronuclear purposes under the guise of "treating" a "mental illness" (Cunningham, 1985). Regardless of the merits of nuclear power, most people would agree that introducing a "mental disorder" such as "nuclear phobia" into the controversy confuses the issue and renders reasonable discussion difficult. And many would agree that it is a misuse of mental health concepts.

It is not only the politically conservative who use mental health concepts to further political aims. Some liberal therapists used to argue that all anxiety and mental disorders were due to the ever-present threat of nuclear war and that the only way to treat them was to eliminate that threat. The point we are trying to make is that in our present society, social values get "medicalized." People can then argue about the nature of "treatment," rather than confronting fundamental differences in values. Psychology must guard against misuse of its concepts while still engaging itself in the solution of our social problems.

Psychological Intervention in Social Problems

How can professional psychology address social problems? In the past, psychology has lobbied for laws, such as the passage of licensing laws and laws regulating health care businesses. In addition, psychology has often used its research findings to try to affect social policy, as when psychologists testify in Congress about child development and many other areas of research that relate to proposed legislation. The APA files "friend of the court" briefings in legal cases that can be clarified by psychological research findings, such as when the U.S. Supreme Court ruled on confidentiality between therapist and client. These same interventions will be useful in the future, and many psychologists urge the field to include strong public education campaigns whenever such issues arise in order to increase public understanding and gain public support.

Where do corporations and insurance companies get their money? Directly and indirectly from almost every citizen. Most health care in the United States is covered by some form of government or corporate health insurance. Taxpayers pay for government insurance. And taxpayers pay for the private insurance, too. They pay premiums or their employers pay premiums and pay them less (an indirect cost to the employee). Any people without health insurance utilize emergency rooms, which pass the costs on to their insured patients. So virtually every citizen pays for the health care system in the United States. However, in the United States, private companies provide this service rather than the citizens through their government, as in countries with "socialized medicine" such as Canada and Great Britain. Thus, the citizens have little power to determine how the health care system is run, and much of their health care money goes for profit. Decisions about the health care system, which affect all of us and which all of us pay for, are made by the corporations. It seems inevitable that health care must be rationed, but the question is who will make the difficult decisions.

It is possible that interested parties must intervene at the corporate level. Consumers and professionals alike have vested interests in the health care corporations, and they can lobby, vote as investors, work for legislative control, and persuade and educate in relation to them. The strength of psychology is its empirical basis, and a research focus on the ways to save money and increase profits by meeting human needs may be a way to bring about needed social change.

The Future

Many social, economic, political, and demographic trends will affect the future of professional psychology. While predicting the future is always subject to uncertainty, broad patterns of change can already be discerned. The growing emphasis on cost containment and biological bases of disorder means that growth in psychological services will be in the areas of brief and short-term therapy, specialties that combine psychology and biology such as neuropsychology and self-help. Although control of health care has shifted to corporations and their systems of managed care, both consumers and professional providers must become active in trying to determine the future availability and types of psychological services in the United States.

One important trend is the decreased availability of government money to pay for training, research, and services in mental health. The tremendous deficit spending by the federal government in the 2000s coupled with tax cuts guarantee reduced spending by government for mental health and other programs for decades to come. The power of the corporate world to determine the nature of both medical and psychological practice will increase. The potential for conflict between the goals of the corporate world and the goals of mental health professionals and consumers is great. However, it is possible that improving the quality of life for all Americans can be shown to contribute to profits, especially in the long run.

Other changes with implications for psychology are easily discerned from the daily news. Since 2001, terrorism and fear of terrorist acts have affected the lives of all Americans. The population of the United States is shifting, and all ethnic groups are increasing their proportion of the population. The aged are also increasing their percentage of the population, and this trend will continue for some decades, since the baby boomers are hitting middle age. The toll of numerous problems, such as AIDS and alcohol and drug abuse, must be addressed. The use of technology in all areas of life is increasing. Although no one seems certain of the direction, it is apparent that the socioeconomic organization of the United States is in the throes of profound change, shifting from production to services and information. Such drastic social changes increase people's stress and, consequently, the demand for psychological, medical, and psychiatric services.

What does all of this augur? Traditional employment opportunities for psychologists in government-funded mental hospitals, mental health agencies, and private practice will decrease, and employment will be available in business and industry and the corporate systems of health care delivery. To say that therapists should consider alternatives to traditional private practice and individual psychotherapy is an understatement. It is imperative that the mental health professions develop new roles and services. It is probably equally imperative that they empirically demonstrate the effectiveness and the cost-effectiveness of these new roles and services, and then learn to market them as well.

Changes in Professional Practice

What changes can be expected in the practice of psychology? It is easy to guess that there will be increasing use of group therapy, brief therapy, self-help, medication, technology, and less expensive forms of treatment. The demand for bilingual, including signing for the deaf, and multicultural therapists will increase. More neuropsychologists and specialists in aging, disability, and handicaps will be needed. With the increase in AIDS, experts in immunocompetence, death and dying, and grief counseling will be needed, too, as will psychologists with expertise in the detection, prevention, and effects of terrorism.

It is likely that psychological treatment will become largely short-term, present-centered, structured, and directive, with an increase in the use of self-change techniques, problem solving, homework assignments, communication skills, cognitive restructuring, and social skills training. Therapists will increasingly utilize technology, as in computerized behavior change programs and Internet mediated treatments. Long-term, psychodynamic, person-centered, humanistic, and existential therapies are likely to be used less. On the other hand, it is possible that the emphasis on short-term, problem-solving therapy will ultimately stimulate a demand for humanistic therapy that addresses issues of emptiness and lack of personal meaning. Undoubtedly, however, people will have to pay for therapy that addresses such needs themselves, but there may be private practice opportunities in helping people deal with their hunger for meaning and personal growth.

Many psychologists agree that psychology as a profession must give up its traditional role of treating psychologically disordered individuals. Not only are corporations and taxpayers disenchanted with that role, but it can also be said that clinical psychologists are wasting their behavioral and research skills in that role. Their skills would be of greater benefit to society if used in dramatically different contexts, including public education and social action. So let us turn to an examination of some of the new roles proposed for professional psychology.

Future Roles for Professional Psychologists

In order for psychology to move into new roles, training and education of psychologists must change, and new definitions of the competencies required of psychologists must be developed, such as knowledge and skills in multicultural therapy, psychopharmacology, neuroscience, and the brief therapy methods.

The emphasis on accountability and cost-effectiveness means that clinical psychologists interested in research may turn to evaluation research. They have been and will be involved in the assessment of the effectiveness of mental health and social programs. Private foundations and government agencies that grant money to groups to carry out various treatment programs demand that an evaluation research component be built into the program. Corporate health care systems also demand empirical demonstration of the effectiveness of treatments before they pay for them. Clinical psychologists are qualified with their research skills and clinical experience to conduct such evaluation studies.

George Albee (1968, 1970, 1982) has long argued that professional psychology should be working to "put itself out of business" by focusing on the prevention of psychological disorders. He believes psychologists should stop providing inefficient and costly psychotherapy to a few individuals. Furthermore, prevention should include competence promotion and social equality for disadvantaged groups, not just the reduction of risk factors for mental disorders (Albee, 1996). Prevention has been demonstrated to be more cost-effective than treatment, and further studies on this point should be done (Reiss & Price, 1996). In addition, psychology should forcefully make the case for prevention to the public and the corporations. If the cost-effectiveness of prevention can be gotten across, then many new roles for psychologists would open up, including psychoeducation, community programs, and social action.

Part of prevention may involve the increasing use of master's level therapists and nonprofessional counselors. The use of peer counselors increases the number of counselors available and decreases costs, in addition to providing counselors similar to the clients. Leaving individual therapy to nonprofessionals, professional psychologists may become involved in the provision of the training and supervision of the nonprofessional counselors. Psychologists will also be involved in innovations in the delivery of services, including electronic counseling and other uses of technology. Education and prevention may involve psychologists in all the mass media.

Many individual behaviors lead to problems that are costly to all of us. Often, these behaviors appear to be matters of individual choice and personal freedom, and the fact that they constitute social problems that cost us all lots of money is not obvious. People cannot be forced to alter these behaviors, but the application of psychological principles can help alter them without threatening individual freedom. AIDS and alcohol and drug abuse are examples of such social problems. Smoking is another. It is not just the individual smoker's business when he gets cancer, emphysema, or heart disease. Each and every one of us pays directly and indirectly for the expensive treatments for these diseases, which are largely preventable. As experts in behavior change, psychologists may be called on to help alter or prevent such "individualistic" behaviors.

There are many other possible future roles for psychologists, depending on the direction that the changes in health care delivery take. In one possible scenario, psychologists (and physicians) end up as the poorly paid employees of corporations, with little independence. A two-tiered system of health care may well develop, with cheap managed care for most people and private care for the rich. The development of so-called "boutique medical practices," in which patients pay out of pocket for special service, suggests that the two-tiered system is on its way. In this case, a few psychologists may still engage in private practice, as psychotherapists helping to provide meaning or perhaps as psychological personal trainers, such as "executive coaches" and the like. Either way, the need for an entrepreneurial attitude and clever marketing is obvious.

On the other hand, some (Ewart, 1991; Galavotti et al., 1997; Gatchel & Oordt, 2003; Resnick, 1997) argue that psychologists should strive for a bigger role in the health care delivery system, that of primary health care provider. The biopsychosocial model implies that behavioral interventions will be as effective as medical ones, and psychologists could easily be the first person ill people would like to see. Prescription privileges would clearly expand the role of psychologists in health care.

Although the possibilities for future roles for psychologists seem numerous, it is incumbent on psychologists to demonstrate that their methods of dealing with these social problems are cost-effective, humane, and good for society and to lobby politically for recognition and payment for their professional skills. Just as the profession successfully fought to achieve the right to practice in earlier decades, psychology will handle the corporatization of health care with negotiation, regulation, litigation, and even clever marketing. Marketing psychological skills to corporations may be preferable to the costly and potentially divisive process of political and legal action. By dropping their old roles and creatively developing new ones, psychologists will both improve society and enhance the prospects for the profession.

The need for care of the physically ill and mentally disordered is universal to all times and cultures. What is less clear is which professions will provide the needed services and who will control the institutions that profit by their delivery. Only by carefully attending to the changes in the health care system and responding promptly and creatively to them will psychology remain a viable, if very different profession.

Employment Prospects in Psychology

Students who wish to pursue a career in professional psychology may be either overwhelmed or encouraged by what we have said about the future. In fact, the services provided by the mental health professions have been and always will be needed and valuable. At present, psychology is a fluid field in a rapidly changing society. The traditional advantage of clinical psychology for someone entering the field was its diversity. The psychologist could go into research, teach at colleges and universities, do private practice, or obtain employment in a variety of clinical settings. Professional psychology will increase in diversity and provide even more different career opportunities. However, it will probably become the student's responsibility to seek out a variety of education and training experiences. Students will have to seek out the special education, supervisory, and training experiences they decide they need on their own.

Students, as well as professional psychologists needing to expand their practice, should explore several options and develop a special skill. As we have already noted, therapy will emphasize short-term and problem-oriented approaches; clients will be increasingly diverse; services will be delivered in corporate health care systems; and technology and potential uses of it in the field constantly change. Specialties that seem to be growing at present include neuropsychology, health psychology, and treatment of AIDS and alcohol and drug abuse. In addition, expertise in evaluation research, a second language, multicultural counseling, aging, and, of course, computers will enhance employment prospects. Grant writing, marketing, and business administration skills are also valuable. If psychologists gain prescription privileges, then training in psychopharmacology will be important for those interested. Patrick DeLeon (2003), past president of the APA, describes "exciting opportunities for the twenty-first century," including training and roles for psychologists as primary care providers in community health centers for the poor and underserved. There are career possibilities in the design, evaluation, and marketing of prevention programs for health care systems (Johnson & Millstein, 2003). Some believe that biologically based assessment will be a highly important skill in the future (Matarazzo, 1992), and if so, special training in neuropsychology and assessment methods such as MRI would be useful.

An advantage of psychology as a profession is that many of the psychologist's skills are "content-free," in that they can be applied in many settings. For example, methodological skills are valuable in many jobs. In surveying psychology alumni of Claremont Graduate School, Oskamp (1988) found applied psychologists working in such areas as health research, planning, and management; organization development; consumer and media research and marketing; computer consulting, planning, and management; educational research and curriculum planning; energy and resource use management; environmental design; legal and criminal justice research; aging research and consultation; and legislative, regulatory, and policy staff positions. The diversity of work roles for professional psychologists is even greater today.

Even if all "care" gets "managed," there will still be possibilities for independent practice for psychologists with business savvy, an entrepreneurial spirit, a willingness to diversify, and an ability to market creatively, such as with podcasts and Web sites. Although we cannot know or cover all future roles, a few examples should suggest the range of possibilities. A practice could include evaluation for workers' compensation programs, consultation to employee assistance programs, and retraining employees slated for termination from their jobs. Globalization may provide the opportunity for psychologists to develop practices devoted to conflict management for people whose behaviors, beliefs, and values are extremely different (Mays, et al., 1997). The potential of the Internet for psychology is just being explored.

Just as professional psychology must become proactive in determining the future of the field, so must individuals contemplating entering the field take responsibility for creating a future career for themselves. They must explore options, seek special training, and consider what contributions they can make and how best to participate in psychology and society in the twenty-first century.

In Conclusion

Professional psychology is exciting precisely because it is a changing field. As it always has, it is responding to important social forces in the midst of social change. Psychology interacts at many levels with individuals and society to attempt to address the crucial issues of our time and place. Thus, it is involved with determining our future, both as individuals and as a society. That makes it a fascinating field and a rewarding career.

Box 16.1 How to Choose a Therapist

After learning about the many types of therapies and therapists available, you may wish for some more practical information about how to choose a therapist for a family member, a friend, or yourself. The plethora of possibilities is perhaps confusing. However, there are two basic pieces of advice: ask others and pay attention to what your own feelings tell you about any therapist you see.

Asking friends, relatives, and other health care professionals to recommend a therapist is a good strategy. You may already have an idea of what type of therapist is needed. If someone is depressed, possibly suicidal, and possibly in need of hospitalization, a psychiatrist would be best. You may already know whether a sex therapist, hypnotist, psychoanalyst, feminist, or behaviorist is needed or preferred. In that case, you can ask state and local professional organizations for therapist referrals. For example, you may telephone the county mental health association, the state psychological association, a psychoanalytic institute in a large city, the United Way, or other groups. Get enough recommendations so you have several therapists from which to choose.

The next step is to call the therapists to ask about their services and perhaps to make an appointment. Do not hesitate to ask questions about fees, therapist training and qualifications, and therapeutic methods over the telephone. A concerned and ethical therapist will be willing to talk about such issues. Furthermore, therapists should be willing to discuss your problem and to make some statement about whether it is within their area of expertise. If you wish to know that the therapist is licensed, you may call the appropriate state licensing board. (You would also call it if you ever wanted to make a complaint against a therapist.)

After getting an idea of the therapists available and getting some information from them, you may decide to make an appointment with one or two. An initial appointment does not mean a commitment to that therapist. Many therapists encourage people who are in the process of deciding to begin therapy to "shop around," to visit other therapists, and to be sure they are comfortable with one before they decide to go into therapy. Again, you should feel free to ask the therapist anything you need to know in order to make your decision. The therapist will also ask you questions in order to assess the nature of your problem and what sort of treatment it requires.

Your own reactions to the therapist and to the therapy hour are your best guides to choosing a therapist. Did you feel comfortable? Do you now feel hopeful? Did the therapist seem competent? Do you feel some degree of trust and confidence in the therapist? Do the methods the therapist intends to use appeal to you? While it is likely that a person trying to choose a therapist feels vulnerable and confused, and while that person's problem may be inability to trust or judge others, nevertheless, a person should be able to give some thought to these sorts of questions. And certainly any strongly negative reactions would indicate that another therapist should be chosen.

You may not develop clear feelings about a therapist until you have seen her or him several times. If, after an initially positive reaction, you begin to have doubts or negative feelings, you should raise these feelings for discussion in therapy. Admittedly, this may be difficult. It is possible that these feelings are important for your therapy and they can be worked on. It is also possible that you may decide to change therapists. Most likely, however, if you have obtained several referrals from good sources and paid attention to your feelings while you interviewed several therapists, you will feel comfortable with your therapist and benefit greatly from therapy.

GLOSSARY

American Board of Professional Psychology (ABPP) awards special diploma to experienced, qualified professional psychologists.

anorexia nervosa an eating disorder in which the individual eats very little or not at all, to the point that weight loss can become life-endangering.

apperception term used in some projective tests, such as the Thematic Apperception Test, referring to the final, clear phase of perception when there is recognition, identification, or comprehension of what has been perceived.

assimilative integration different approaches to psychotherapy become more integrative by incorporating ideas and strategies from other approaches.

attachment theory John Bowlby's psychodynamic theory of development. Healthy development is based on children forming secure bonds or attachments with their caretakers. This allows the development of good working models of reality.

attribution theory a theory in social psychology that in order for people to predict and control events, they will attribute causes to those events. It is the attribution that determines their response, not the event.

automatic thoughts in Beck's cognitive therapy, habitual dysfunctional thoughts that occur rapidly and automatically, often without much awareness.

aversion therapy pairing an aversive stimulus with a previously attractive stimulus in order to create an avoidance response or to suppress undesirable behavior.

behaviorism school of scientific psychology that emphasizes observable behavior over innate or internal variables.

biofeedback technique that allows people to monitor and control their own internal bodily functions by making these functions observable.

Boulder model the scientist-practitioner model for clinical psychology developed by the 1949 APA training conference held in Boulder, CO.

bruxism habit of grinding teeth.

bulimia an eating disorder characterized by uncontrolled binges. May also involve efforts made by the person to regurgitate food so he/she does not gain weight.

caring days in behavioral marital therapy, one spouse tries to maximize the positive experience of the other for a specific day.

certification a way of regulating professional psychology. The state certifies that the psychologist has the claimed training.

classical conditioning a learning procedure developed by Pavlov in which a neutral stimulus and an unconditioned stimulus are paired until the neutral stimulus evokes the same response as the unconditioned stimulus.

classical psychoanalysis Freud's approach to psychoanalysis as opposed to modern theories such as object relations theory and self psychology.

cognitive constructs in George Kelly's theory, the categories people develop to guide their actions. How they categorize events (not the events themselves) determines their behavior.

cognitive rehearsal a cognitive-behavioral technique used when homework is given. The client imagines every step needed to do the homework to anticipate possible glitches.

cognitive triad the three basic components of thinking in depressives, including a negative view of themselves, their personal future, and their current experiences.

common factors approach an approach to psychotherapy theory integration involving the investigation of what all therapies share.

compensation dealing with frustration and inadequacy in one area by investing in another area.

conditioned response a learned response that is made to a conditioned stimulus (in classical conditioning) or as a result of reward or punishment (in operant conditioning).

conditioned stimulus a neutral stimulus that acquires the capacity to evoke a response after association with an unconditioned stimulus (in classical conditioning).

conditions of worth in client-centered theory, parents impose "conditions of worth" on their children, that is, they make their children feel worthwhile only if they act in accord with certain parental expectations or conditions.

confidentiality the ethical obligation of professionals to keep information obtained from a client confidential.

congruence in client-centered theory, to be aware of one's own inner experiencing and to act so that behavior matches that experiencing.

constructivism the philosophy that reality is a construct of each individual. There is no one true, objective reality.

contingency contracting (also called behavioral contracting) contractual behavior therapy in which the client is fully involved in formulating a contingency management plan.

contingency management behavior modification technique that involves setting up a system of rewards for desired behaviors and loss of rewards for undesired behaviors.

control group in scientific research, the group of participants who do not receive the treatment under study.

conversion disorders a psychological disorder involving one or more physical symptoms that mimic physical illness.

coping strategies skills taught in self-management behavior therapy.

covert modeling in behavior therapy, learning by imagining someone else performing the behavior one wishes to learn.

covert practice in behavior therapy, rehearsing positive skills in imagination.

covert sensitization in behavior therapy, pairing some aversive stimulus or negative consequence with some unwanted behavior in imagination.

decentering the ability to step outside of one's own perspective, guessing through imagination or logic how things would look from another person's perspective.

defense mechanisms habitual and unconscious psychological devices used to reduce or avoid anxiety.

defensive pessimism catastrophizing about the possibility of failing in order to motivate oneself to work hard.

demonology early system of belief in demons, spirits, and possession.

denial a defense mechanism involving the refusal to recognize the real nature of one's behavior.

diagnosis related groups (DRGs) groupings of similar disorders for which third-party payers pay a flat fee based on the average cost of care for patients with such diagnoses.

dialectical process the philosophical view that considers social or personal change to be a process of forming a thesis (one view of things), which produces an antithesis (the opposite of the original view), which produces a new synthesis (a combination of the two positions).

differential diagnosis the process of distinguishing between similar disorders.

differentiation the ability to have a clear sense of one's own values, beliefs, and reactions, separate from those of others.

discovery-oriented research research approaches to psychotherapy in which the researcher attempts to identify significant moments or events and explore how they actually function in therapy.

discrimination a type of learning in which different responses are conditioned to different but similar stimuli.

disengaged family family whose boundaries are rigid and in which communication is restricted or avoided between family members.

displacement a defense mechanism involving the deflection of feelings onto a less threatening target.

disputing central technique of rational-emotive therapy. The therapist directly challenges a client's irrational beliefs.

DSM *The Diagnostic and Statistical Manual of Mental Disorders* of the American Psychiatric Association.

ego in psychoanalysis, the part of the personality that is reality oriented.

ego psychology a form of Freudian psychoanalysis that sees the ego as having its own autonomous existence, rather than being an outgrowth of the id.

emotion-focused psychotherapy technique for helping clients to access their emotions and emotional meanings.

empirically supported treatments psychotherapies and treatments that have been found useful according to specified research which includes treatment manuals, specific disorders, and control groups.

enmeshed family family in which boundaries are weak or nonexistent so that roles are unclear and responsibilities are confused.

evocative unfolding technique utilized in process-experiential psychotherapy when the therapist helps the client vividly remember a situation in which the client did something he or she feels uncomfortable with or doesn't understand.

expectancies awareness that a stimulus predicts an event.

experiencing the bodily, "felt" way of knowing at the visceral or "gut level," as opposed to intellectual, verbal, conceptual knowledge.

experiential articulation a formulation of a client's self-knowledge into words that match the client's experiential state.

experiential psychotherapy (1) a generic name for a group of therapies, usually from the existential-humanistic approach, that rely on emotion and experiencing to facilitate change; (2) Gendlin's person-centered experiential psychotherapy, which emphasizes tuning into one's felt or experienced meanings; (3) Mahrer's experiential psychotherapy, which relies on the activation of strong feeling to access inner experiencing potential.

extinction a type of learning that occurs when rewards are no longer delivered and the response ceases.

family of origin the family from which each spouse in the present family originally came.

first order change trying to solve a problem from the same old assumptions, with the same old methods.

focusing in Gendlin's person-centered experiential psychotherapy, the ability to tune in to one's felt or experienced meanings. Also, the name of a specific technique developed by Gendlin to facilitate such tuning in.

free association in psychoanalysis, the patient is asked to say whatever comes to mind without censorship.

freedom of choice (FOC) state laws requiring health insurance companies to allow patients the freedom to choose their own health care providers and treatments.

functional analysis behaviorists analyze the context of a behavior and the function(s) it serves with that context. Functional analysis identifies the conditions that elicit a behavior and the consequences that maintain it.

functional diagnosis identifying types and severity of a client's strengths and weaknesses to determine an appropriate treatment strategy, not just assigning a label.

functionalism early school of academic psychology that studied what the mind does, rather than the contents of the mind.

fused a description of people who are emotionally entangled, and who have a difficult time distinguishing their own feelings and values from those of others.

generalization a type of learning in which a response that has been conditioned to one stimulus occurs with other, similar stimuli.

genogram diagram that shows the relationships of the husband and wife to their families of origin.

gestalt an organized whole.

good moments Alvin Mahrer's list of the kinds of events in psychotherapy that have been theorized to be associated with the facilitation of change, such as a moment of insight or heavy emotion.

hot cognition cognitions associated with emotions.

hysteria early psychological disorder characterized by emotional excitability, excessive anxiety, sensory and motor disturbances, and the simulation of organic disorder.

id in psychoanalysis, the part of the personality that consists of instincts and reflexes.

idealizing need the need to have someone to idealize in order to develop the self's own set of values and ideals.

identified patient the person identified as the patient, the person "having" the problem, even though the "real" problem lies in the entire family, or couple.

implosive therapy also known as flooding, a behavioral technique in which the therapist attempts to heighten or exaggerate the client's fears in hopes that they will be extinguished.

incomplete gestalts uncompleted experiences.

individuation the process of developing a unique sense of self.

inferiority complex the set of cognitions and emotions that maintain a sense of inferiority or insecurity.

informed consent informing clients of all the pros and cons of therapy so they can agree to it with full knowledge.

instrumental conditioning See operant conditioning

intellectualization a defense mechanism in which repressed impulses are allowed into awareness only in an intellectual way, to avoid experiencing them.

interpretive secondary control gaining control by giving up control or by accepting that one does not have control over certain things in one's life.

***in vivo* desensitization** a behavior therapy technique in which desensitization is done with real-life stimuli rather than with imagery.

Larry P. important California Supreme Court ruling in the case of *Larry P. v. Wilson Riles and the Board of Education.* The court ruled that intelligence tests were biased against non-white children.

learned helplessness a hypothesized cause of depression based on research on dogs subjected to inescapable electric shocks who became passive and helpless even when escape became possible.

license a way of regulating professional psychology. The state issues a license to professionals who demonstrate the required education and competence.

managed care attempt by third-party payers to reduce costs of health care by negotiating prices and rationing care.

markers behavior signs that the client is struggling with a certain kind of emotional processing problem in a certain way. Can be used to signal what kind of therapeutic intervention should be used at that moment to help the client process the problem.

meaning protest a therapeutic marker that occurs when a client expresses emotional upset or confusion when a cherished belief is violated.

mental status examination formal part of an interview that assesses the client's current mental functioning.

meta-analysis a statistical procedure that allows results from a variety of studies to be combined so that overall trends can be observed.

metapsychology the implicit, underlying assumptions of a psychological theory.

mirroring in object relations theory, the response of the mother or the therapist that reflects the child's or client's experience; in couples therapy, a technique in which one spouse is asked to repeat as precisely as possible what the other said.

modeling learning by observing another person perform the desired behavior. Also called observational learning.

multiaxial model basis for the DSM-III and DSM-IV. It takes a diagnosis on five separate scales, or axes, to make a complete diagnosis.

multigenerational transmission process from Bowen's family systems approach, the belief that a lack of personal differentiation is passed down from one generation to another.

multiple realities the concept that reality is relative to each person's point of view and, therefore, there is no possible way for any human to determine one "correct" view of reality.

musturbatory thinking in rational-emotive therapy, thinking in terms of "musts" and "shoulds."

narrative perspectives perspectives on human behavior that argue that people live their lives in terms of the "stories" they construct about themselves and events.

narrative truth in hermeneutics, the concept of helping clients develop good "working stories" about their lives.

National Register of Health Service Providers in Psychology listing of licensed professional psychologists that can be used by third-party payers to determine fee reimbursement.

negative reinforcement in learning theory, a reward that involves the removal of an aversive stimulus, such as turning off a painfully loud noise.

negative self-monitoring ways in which clients watch themselves and their own behavior and evaluate them negatively.

neurotic paradox the fact that a learned fear does not extinguish even though the original conditions for its learning have long since passed.

nomothetic research methodology a research methodology that looks at how groups of individuals differ along certain dimensions, in contrast to studying particular individuals.

nonpossessive warmth in client-centered therapy, a set of therapist qualities called, variously, unconditional positive regard, acceptance, prizing, respect, caring, nonpossessive love.

norms (in group therapy) explicit or implicit rules or standards of behavior that guide the behavior of group members.

norms (in psychological testing) the distribution of scores of a large number of representative, typical people. A particular individual's score on a test can be compared to the nouns for an idea as to the meaning of that score.

objective test a pencil-and-paper personality test with a structured set of limited answers.

object relations theory modern psychoanalytic theory emphasizing relationships between people.

observational learning in social learning theory, learning through imitation.

operant conditioning a learning procedure developed by Skinner in which voluntary behavior is rewarded and strengthened.

organismic valuing process Carl Rogers's idea that humans have an inborn capacity to experience what is good for them.

outcome research research that deals with the outcome of psychotherapy and its relative effectiveness.

paradoxical intervention a therapeutic technique that involves prescribing the symptom.

personal constructs beliefs and concepts people develop in order to make sense out of their experiences.

person-centered Rogers's most recent name for his theory.

phenomenological method in Husserl's philosophy, the therapeutic goal is to suspend judgments and preconceptions.

phobia an exaggerated or unrealistic fear of a specific stimulus or situation.

placebo in psychotherapy research, a treatment that is designed to actually be neutral. Then, if the real psychotherapy treatment is more effective than the placebo, it suggests that the effectiveness is not merely due to the client's having an expectation that he or she will get better but, rather, is due to actual components of the real psychotherapy treatment itself.

positive psychology an academic and therapeutic approach that emphasizes positive human characteristics such as empathy, love, and creativity.

positive reinforcement in learning theory, a reward that involves the delivery of a positive stimulus, such as giving a rat food for pressing a bar.

privilege the legal right of the clients of psychologists (and other professionals) to control information about them.

problem-solving training a behavioral method for teaching people how to deal with problems by defining the problem, generating alternatives, evaluating them, acting on one, and assessing the effect of the attempted solution.

problematic reaction point a therapeutic marker in which a client reports being self-critical or puzzled about something he/she has done. In process-experiential psychotherapy, the technique of evocative unfolding is used to help the client process the problem.

process-experiential psychotherapy person-centered approach developed by Leslie Greenberg, Laura Rice, and Robert Elliot. Includes the systematic use of both client-centered and gestalt psychotherapy techniques applied at specific points in therapy when clients exhibit certain therapeutic markers.

process-oriented to see life and the self as an ongoing, changing process and, therefore, to be open to experience in order to continually learn and grow.

process research research that deals with the processes that actually occur in psychotherapy, rather than outcomes.

professional model established the Psy.D. degree and training in practice, not research, for clinical psychology. Also called the Vail model.

projection a defense mechanism in which unacceptable motives or feelings are attributed to others.

projective test a personality test that involves presenting ambiguous stimuli in order to elicit responses from an individual.

psychic determinism the belief that nothing psychological happens by chance.

psychodrama a form of group therapy in which clients act out scenes of conflict from their childhood or present life.

qualitative research research based on description of phenomena in words and concepts rather than numbers. Qualitative research asks, "What kids of things are these?"

quantitative research research based on quantification of the variables studied so that numerical data can be statistically analyzed. Quantitative research asks, "How much?"

rationalization a defense mechanism in which plausible and acceptable reasons for one's behavior and feelings are created in order to hide one's real motives.

reaction formation a defense mechanism in which one behaves in a way that is diametrically opposite to what one unconsciously wants.

reciprocal determinism the holistic view that causation is not unidirectional, but that events influence each other.

reciprocal inhibition in systematic desensitization, the pairing of incompatible responses in order to suppress one response.

reflection of feeling in client-centered therapy, the therapeutic response of accurately mirroring the client's experience.

reframing the therapeutic technique of reinterpreting a behavior that a client sees as pathological in a positive way.

registration a way to regulate the practice of psychology in which psychologists merely register their practice with the state.

reliability the "trustworthiness" of a psychological test.

repression the primary defense mechanism that involves removing from awareness all unwanted or threatening memories, impulses, or feelings.

respondent conditioning see classical conditioning.

response cost behavior modification method involving the removal of positive reinforcers to suppress unwanted behavior.

role playing a technique used in many therapies, including behavior therapy, psychodrama, cognitive-behavior therapy. Client or therapist or both act out a situation that is problematic for the client so that new behaviors can be tried and learned.

scientist-practitioner model established the Ph.D. and training in both research and practice for clinical psychology. Also called the Boulder model.

second order change a shift in fundamental premises so that the problem is framed in an entirely new way, frequently leading to a creative solution.

self-efficacy Bandura's theory that one's self-perceptions of one's competence determine behavior.

self-empowerment therapeutic goal of giving clients the feeling that they have the power to affect their own lives.

self-objects in object relations theory, another person who supports one's developing sense of self by providing certain functions until the self can develop those capacities.

shame-attacking exercises a therapeutic technique in which clients are instructed to do something that creates shame so they can find out that nothing objectively bad happens.

shaping in learning theory, rewarding closer and closer approximations of the desired response.

shouldism see musturbatory thinking.

social learning theory based on Albert Bandura's work, social learning theory adds learning through imitation and interaction with others to traditional learning theory.

split in both gestalt therapy and process-experiential therapy, when clients experience a split between what they want to do and what they think they should do. The gestalt two-chair technique is utilized to help clients resolve the split.

splitting in object relations theory, the idea that the very young child splits positive and negative feelings and perceptions about the mother and about the self off from one another, because it is too uncomfortable to perceive mother or self as having both good and bad qualities.

spontaneous recovery rate the rate at which people appear to spontaneously recover without undergoing psychotherapy. There is much controversy over whether there is a "real" spontaneous recovery rate that applies to everyone.

standardization group in the development of psychological tests, the group of people on which the test is standardized, the group of people whose scores serve as the norms of the test.

stress inoculation a behavioral treatment for managing stressful events and preventing stress responses. Practicing responses to (imaged) stressful events is assumed to inoculate or prepare clients for future stress.

structural family therapy Minuchin's approach in which the family is viewed as a hierarchically organized system.

structuralism an early school of academic psychology that emphasized the structure of the mind, rather than its contents or functions.

sublimation the process of channeling repressed desires and conflicts into socially acceptable outlets.

sunset legislation laws passed in the 1970s that allowed the regulation of professional psychology to cease.

superego in psychoanalysis, the part of the personality that contains the conscience as well as the ideals to which the person aspires.

system in a family approach to counseling, a system is a pattern of interrelationships among elements, such that each element of the system both determines and is determined by the other elements in the system.

systematic desensitization a behavior therapy method in which relaxation is paired with vivid images of phobic situations or objects in order to reduce fear.

Tarasoff 1971 California Supreme Court ruling which set limits to therapist-client confidentiality and privilege. The court ruled that therapists must warn potential victims of dangerous clients.

task analysis research strategy developed by Laura Rice and Leslie Greenberg in which therapy is looked on as a series of emotional processing tasks for the client to engage in. The researcher defines what a given task is and studies the process by which therapist and client strive to resolve the task.

teaching stories stories that convey a therapeutic message metaphorically.

technical eclecticism in psychotherapy theory integration, an approach that emphasizes the pragmatic use of techniques from different therapies, although one theoretical outlook may be maintained.

theoretical integration in psychotherapy integration, the attempt to develop an integrative theory that includes ideas from differing approaches.

therapeutic alliance the general quality of the relationship between therapist and client.

therapeutic marker see marker.

time-out in behavior therapy with children, an extinction procedure in which the child is briefly removed from a situation in which undesired behaviors are being rewarded.

token economy in mental hospitals and other institutions, a reinforcement system in which patients are given tokens as reinforcers for specific desired behaviors.

transference the process in which the client projects attitudes and emotions that apply to other people in his/her past onto the therapist.

treatment manuals for purposes of research and treatment, explicit steps in doing a particular treatment for a particular diagnosis are described in a book or manual.

triangulation in order to deal with tension and instability, or conflict between oneself and another, a two-person system draws a third person into the system in order to deflect or deal with the tension or instability.

unconditioned response in classical conditioning, the response that "naturally" occurs to the unconditioned stimulus.

unconditioned stimulus a stimulus innately capable of eliciting a response. In classical conditioning, it is paired with the conditioned stimulus until both elicit the response.

unfinished business in gestalt therapy and process-experiential psychotherapy, the client is struggling with an issue from the past that is "unfinished."

Vail model the professional model for clinical psychology developed at the 1973 APA training conference held in Vail, CO.

validation technique used in dialectical behavior therapy that emphasizes the validity of the client's experience.

validity the appropriateness of the interpretations of test results.

vertical interpretation a therapeutic response designed to increase client insight into the connection between current behavior and past childhood determinants.

vicarious learning learning through watching others; also called modeling and observational learning.

working model in object relations theory and Bowlby's psychodynamic attachment theory, the idea that a child develops a working model of interpersonal relationships and of reality in general from interactions with the caretaker. This becomes the model for later interactions with the world.

References

AABT (2001). Guidelines for choosing a behavior therapist. http://www.aabt.org/091101%20Folder/091101/public/guideline.html

Abramson, L., Seligman, M., & Teasdale, J. (1978). Learned helplessness in humans: Critique and reformulation. *Journal of Abnormal Psychology, 87*, 49–74.

Accordino, M., & Guerney, Jr., B. (2002). The empirical validation of relationship enhancement couple and family therapy. In D. J. Cain & J. Seeman (Eds.), *Humanistic psychotherapies: Handbook of research and practice* (pp. 403–442). Washington, DC: American Psychological Association.

Achenbach, T., & Ruffle, T. (2000). The Child Behavior Checklist and related forms for assessing behavioral/emotional problems and competencies. *Pediatric Review, 21*, 265–271.

Adelson, J., & Doehrman, M. (1980). The psychodynamic approach to adolescence. In J. Adelson (Ed.), *Handbook of adolescent psychology.* New York: Wiley.

Ader, R., & Cohen, N. (1985). CSN-immune system interactions: Conditioning phenomena. *Behavioral and Brain Sciences, 8*, 378–395.

Adler, A. (1930). *Guiding the child on the principles of individual psychology.* New York: Greenberg.

Adler, A. (1964). *Social interest: A challenge to mankind.* New York: Capricorn Books. (Original work published 1929).

Albee, G. (1968). Conceptual models and manpower requirements in psychology. *American Psychologist, 23*, 317–320.

Albee, G. (1970). The uncertain future of clinical psychology. *American Psychologist, 25*, 1071–1080.

Albee, G. (1982). Preventing psychopathology and promoting human potential. *American Psychologist, 37*, 1043–1050.

Albee, G. (1985, February). The answer is prevention. *Psychology Today*, 60–64.

Albee, G. (1996). Revolutions and counterrevolutions in prevention. *American Psychologist, 51*, 1130–1133.

Alexander, F. (1950). *Psychosomatic medicine.* New York: Norton.

Alexander, J., Robbins, M., & Sexton, T. (2001). The developmental evolution of family therapy. In H. A. Liddle, D. Santisteban, R. Levant, & J. Bray (Eds.), *Family psychology intervention science.* Washington, DC: American Psychological Association.

Alford, B., & Beck, A. (1998). *The integrative power of cognitive therapy.* New York: Guilford.
Alford, B., & Norcross, J. (1991). Cognitive therapy as integrative therapy. *Journal of Psychotherapy Integration, 1*, 175–190.
Allen, D. (1988). *Unifying individual and family therapies.* San Francisco: Jossey-Bass.
Allen, J. (2001). *Treating patients with neuropsychological disorders: A clinician's guide to assessment and referral.* Washington, DC: American Psychological Association.
American Psychological Association Division 12. (1992). *Clinical psychology.* Oklahoma City: Division of Clinical Psychology Central Office.
American Psychological Association. (1987, February). *Model act for state licensure of psychologists.* Washington, DC: Author.
American Psychological Association. (2002). Criteria for evaluating treatment guidelines. *American Psychologist, 57*, 1052–1059.
American Psychological Association. (2005). Health Psychology, Division 38. Mission Statement. Retrieved June 23, 2005, from www.health-psych.org/mission.htm
Andersson, G., Bergstrom, J., Carlbring, P., & Lindefors, N. (2005). The use of the Internet in the treatment of anxiety disorders. *Current Opinion in Psychiatry, 18*, 73–77.
Angus, L., & McLeod, J. (Eds.). (2004). *The handbook of narrative and psychotherapy: Practice, theory, and research.* Thousand Oaks, CA: Sage.
Anspach, M. (1991). Is a change in the theory of the person necessary? A note on Sampson's discussion of individuality in the post-modern era. *Theoretical and Philosophical Psychology, 11*, 111–115.
APA Commission on Psychotherapies. (1982). *Psychotherapy research: Methodological and efficacy issues.* Washington, DC: America Psychiatric Association.
APA Committee on Women in Psychology. (1985, October). *Statement on proposed diagnostic categories for DSM-III-R.* Washington, DC: American Psychological Association.
Applied Psychophysiology & Biofeedback. (2005). Biofeedback and Psychophysiology. Retrieved June 23, 2005, from www.aapd.org/i4a/pages/index.cfm?pageid=1
Arkowitz, H. (1989). The role of theory in psychotherapy integration. *Journal of Integrative and Eclectic Psychotherapy, 8*, 8–16.
Arkowitz, H. (1991, August). *Psychotherapy integration: Bringing psychotherapy back to psychology.* Invited address at the Convention of the American Psychological Association, San Francisco, CA.
Arkowitz, H. (1992). Integrative theories of therapy. In D. Freedheim (Ed.), *History of psychotherapy: A century of change* (pp. 261–303). Washington, DC: American Psychological Association.
Arkowitz, H., & Hannah, M. (1989). Cognitive, behavioral, and psychodynamic therapies: Converging or diverging pathways to change? In A. Freeman, K. Simon, L. Beutler, & H. Arkowitz (Eds.), *Comprehensive handbook of cognitive therapy* (pp. 143–168). New York: Plenum.
Austad, C. (1996a). Can psychotherapy be conducted effectively in managed care settings? In E. Lazarus (Ed.), *Controversies in managed mental health care.* Washington, DC: American Psychiatric Association.
Austad, C. (1996b). *Is long-term therapy ethical? Toward a social ethic in an era of managed care.* San Francisco: Jossey-Bass.
Axline, V. (1947a). Non-directive therapy for poor readers. *Journal of Consulting Psychology, 11*, 68–75.
Axline, V. (1947b). *Play therapy: The inner dynamics of childhood.* Boston: Houghton Mifflin.
Ayllon, T., & Azrin, N. H. (1968). *The token economy: A motivational system for therapy and rehabilitation.* New York: Appleton-Century-Crofts.
Banaji, M., & Hardin, C. (1996). Automatic stereotyping. *Psychological Science, 7*, 136–141.
Bandura, A. (1969). *Principles of behavior modification.* New York: Holt, Rinehart & Winston.
Bandura, A. (1977). *Social learning theory.* Englewood Cliffs, NJ: Prentice-Hall.

Bandura, A. (1986). *Social foundations of thought and action: A social cognitive theory.* Englewood Cliffs, NJ: Prentice-Hall.

Bandura, A. (1996). *Self-efficacy: The exercise of control.* New York: W. H. Freeman.

Bandura, A., & Walters, R. H. (1959). *Adolescent aggression.* New York: Ronald.

Barkham, M., & Mellor-Clark, J. (2000). Rigor and relevance: The role of practice-based evidence in the psychological therapies. In N. Rowland & S. Goss (Eds.), *Evidence-based counseling and psychological therapies* (pp. 127–144). London: Routledge.

Barlow, D. (1988). *Anxiety and its disorders.* New York: Guilford.

Barlow, D. (2004). Psychological treatments. *American Psychologist, 59,* 869–878.

Barlow, D., Craske, M., Cerny, J., & Klosko, J. (1989). Behavioral treatment of panic disorder. *Behavior Therapy, 20,* 261–282.

Baxter, L., Schwartz, J., Bergman, K., Szuba, M., Guze, B., Mazziotta, J., et al. (1992). Caudate glucose metabolic rate changes with both drug and behavior therapy for obsessive-compulsive disorder. *Archives of General Psychiatry, 49,* 681–689.

Beck, A. (1972). *Depression: Causes and treatment.* Philadelphia: University of Pennsylvania Press.

Beck, A. (1979). *Cognitive therapy of depression* (Live demonstration of interview procedures). New York: BMA Audio Cassettes, Guilford.

Beck, A. (1986). Cognitive psychotherapy. In E. L. Shostrom (Producer), *Three approaches to psychotherapy: II* (film). Corona Del Mar, CA: Psychological and Educational Films.

Beck, A. (1987). Cognitive therapy. In J. Zeig (Ed.), *The evolution of psychotherapy* (pp. 149–163). New York: Brunner/Mazel.

Beck, A. (1995). Cognitive therapy: Past, present, and future. In M. J. Mahoney (Ed.), *Cognitive and constructive psychotherapies* (pp. 29–40). New York: Springer.

Beck, A., Emery, G., & Greenberg, R. (1985). *Anxiety disorders and phobias: A cognitive perspective.* New York: Basic Books.

Beck, A., Freeman, A., & Associates. (1990). *Cognitive therapy of personality disorders.* New York: Guilford.

Beck, A., Rush, A., Shaw, B., & Emery, G. (1979). *Cognitive therapy of depression.* New York: Guilford.

Beck, S. (1945). *Rorschach's test.* New York: Grune & Stratton.

Bender, L. (1938). A visual motor gestalt test and its clinical use. *American Orthopsychiatric Association, Research Monographs,* (3).

Benjamin, L., & Dixon, D. (1996). Dream analysis by mail: An American woman seeks Freud's advice. *American Psychologist, 51,* 461–468.

Bergin, A. (1971). The evaluation of therapeutic outcomes. In A. E. Bergin & S. L. Garfield (Eds.), *Handbook of psychotherapy and behavior change.* New York: Wiley.

Bergin, A., & Garfield, S. (1994). Overview, trends, and future issues. In A. E. Bergin & S. L. Garfield (Eds.), *Handbook of psychotherapy and behavior change* (4th ed., pp. 821–830). New York: Wiley.

Bergin, A., & Garfield, S. (1994). Overview, trends, and future issues. In A. E. Bergin & S. L. Garfield (Eds.), *Handbook and psychotherapy and behavior change* (pp. 821–830). New York: Wiley.

Bergin, A., & Lambert, M. (1978). The evaluation of therapeutic outcomes. In S. L. Garfield & A. E. Bergin (Eds.), *Handbook of psychotherapy and behavior change: An empirical analysis* (2nd ed.). New York: Wiley.

Bettelheim, B. (1982). *Freud and man's soul.* New York: Vintage.

Beutler, L. (1989). The misplaced role of theory in psychotherapy integration. *Journal of Integrative and Eclectic Psychotherapy, 8,* 17–22.

Beutler, L., Crago, M., & Arizmendi, T. (1986). Research on therapist variables in psychotherapy. *Handbook of psychotherapy and behavior change* (3rd ed., pp. 257–310). New York: Wiley.

Beutler, L., & Harwood, T. (2000). *Prescriptive psychotherapy: A practical guide to systematic treatment selection.* New York: Oxford.

Beutler, L, Harwood, T., Alimohamed, S., & Malik, M. (2002). Functional impairment and coping style. In J. C. Norcross (Ed.), *Psychotherapy relationships that work* (pp. 145–174). New York: Oxford University Press.

Beutler, L., & Johannsen, B. (in press). Principles of change. In J. C. Norcross, L. E. Beutler, & R. Levant (Eds.), *Evidence-based practices in mental health: Debate and dialogue on the fundamental questions.* Washington, DC: American Psychological Association.

Bickman, L., & Ellis, H. (Eds.). (1990). *Preparing psychologists for the 21st century: Proceedings of the National Conference on Graduate Education in Psychology.* Hillsdale, NJ: Erlbaum.

Binet, A., & Simon, T. (1905). Méthodes nouvelles pour le diagnostic du niveau intellectuel des anormaux. *L'Anée Psychologique, 11,* 191–244.

Binswanger, L. (1963). *Being-in-the-world: Selected papers of Ludwig Binswanger.* New York: Basic Books.

Blatt, S., & Ford, R. (1994). *Therapeutic change: An object relations perspective.* New York: Plenum.

Blatt, S., & Ritzler, B. (1974). Thought disorder and boundary disturbances in psychosis. *Journal of Consulting and Clinical Psychology, 42,* 370–381.

Blatt, S. J., & Wild, C. (1976). *Schizophrenia: A developmental analysis.* New York: Academic Press.

Blatt, S., & Ford, R. (1994). *Therapeutic change: An object relations perspective.* New York: Plenum.

Block, J., & Block, J. (1980). The role of ego-control and ego-resiliency in the organization of behavior. In W. A. Collins (Ed.), *Minnesota Symposium on Child Development* (Vol. 13). Hillsdale, NJ: Erlbaum.

Block, J., Block, J., & Keyes, S. (1988). Longitudinally foretelling drug usage in adolescence: Early childhood personality and environmental precursors. *Child Development, 59,* 336–355.

Bloom, B. (1984). *Community mental health: A general introduction* (2nd ed.). Monterey, CA: Brooks/Cole.

Bloom, B. (1992a). Computer-assisted intervention: A review and commentary. *Clinical Psychology Review, 128,* 169–198.

Bloom, B. (1992b). *Planned short-term psychotherapy: A clinical handbook.* Boston: Allyn and Bacon.

Bloom, W. (1998). The ethical practice of webcounseling. *British Journal of Guidance and Counseling, 26,* 53–59.

Bogdan, J. (1986). Do families really need problems? *The Family Therapy Networker, 10,* 30–35, 67–69.

Bohart, A. (1979). *Personal paradigms, resistance, and change in psychotherapy.* Paper presented at the Western Psychological Association Convention, San Diego, CA.

Bohart, A. (1980). Toward a cognitive theory of catharsis. *Psychotherapy: Theory, Research and Practice, 17,* 192–201.

Bohart, A. (1992). Un modelo integrador de proceso para la sicopatología y la psicoterapia. *Revista de Psicoterapia, 3,* 49–74.

Bohart, A. (1993). Experiencing: The basis of psychotherapy. *Journal of Psychotherapy Integration, 3,* 51–67.

Bohart, A. (2003). Person-centered psychotherapy and related experiential approaches. In A. Gurman & S. Messer (Eds.), *Essential psychotherapies* (2nd ed., pp. 107–148). New York: Guilford.

Bohart, A. (2005). Evidence-based psychotherapy means evidence-informed, not evidence-driven. *Journal of Contemporary Psychotherapy, 35,* 39–53.

Bohart, A. (in press). The active client. In J. C. Norcross, L. E. Beutler, & R. Levant (Eds.), *Evidence-based practices in mental health: Debate and dialogue on the fundamental questions.* Washington, DC: American Psychological Association.

Bohart, A., Elliott, R., Greenberg, L., & Watson, J. (2002). Empathy. In J. C. Norcross (Ed.), *Psychotherapy relationships that work* (pp. 89–108). New York: Oxford University Press.

Bohart, A. & Greenberg, L. (1997). *Empathy reconsidered.* Washington, DC: American Psychological Association.

Bohart, A., O'Hara, M., & Leitner, L. (1998). Empirically violated treatments: Disenfranchisement of humanistic and other approaches. *Psychotherapy Research, 8,* 141–157.

Bohart, A., & Tallman, K. (1999). *How clients make therapy work: The process of active self-healing.* Washington, DC: American Psychological Association.

Borkovec, T., & Costello, E. (1993). Efficacy of applied relaxation and cognitive-behavioral therapy in the treatment of generalized anxiety disorder. *Journal of Consulting and Clinical Psychology, 61,* 611–619.

Boss, M. (1963). *Psychoanalysis and Daseinanalysis.* New York: Basic Books.

Bowen, M. (1978). *Family therapy in clinical practice.* New York: Aronson.

Bower, G. (1981). Emotional mood and memory. *American Psychologist, 36,* 129–148.

Bowlby, J. (1988). *A secure base.* London: Routledge.

Bratton, S., & Ray, D. (2002). Humanistic play therapy. In D. J. Cain & J. Seeman (Eds.), *Humanistic psychotherapies: Handbook of research and practice* (pp. 369–402). Washington, DC: American Psychological Association.

Breuer, J., & Freud, S. (Eds.). (1937). *Studies in hysteria.* Boston: Beacon Press. (Original work published in 1895)

Brewin, C. (1988). *Cognitive foundations of clinical psychology.* Hillsdale, NJ: Erlbaum.

Briere, J. (1989). *Therapy for adults molested as children.* New York: Springer.

Brodley, B. (1988a, May). *Does early-in-therapy experiencing level predict outcome?* Paper presented at the Second Annual Meeting of the Association for the Development of the Person-Centered Approach, New York.

Brodley, B. (1988b). Responses to person-centered versus client-centered therapists. *Renaissance, 5,* 1–2.

Brophy, J. (1977). *Child development and socialization.* Chicago: Science Research Associates.

Brown, G., & Harris, T. (1978). *Social origins of depression.* New York: Free Press.

Brown, G., Harris, T., & Bifulco, A. (1986). Long-term effects of early loss of parent. In M. Rutter, C. E. Izard, & P. B. Read (Eds.), *Depression in young people: Developmental and clinical perspectives* (pp. 251–296). New York: Guilford.

Brown, L., & Brodsky, A. (1992). The future of feminist therapy. *Psychotherapy, 29,* 39–43.

Bruner, J. (1986). *Actual minds, possible worlds.* Cambridge, MA: Harvard University Press.

Brunnink, S., & Schroeder, H. (1979). Verbal therapeutic behavior of expert psychoanalytically oriented, Gestalt and behavior therapists. *Journal of Consulting and Clinical Psychology, 47,* 567–574.

Bucci, W. (1995). The power of the narrative: A multiple code account. In J. W. Pennebaker (Ed.), *Emotion, disclosure, & health* (pp. 93–124). Washington, DC: American Psychological Association.

Bugental, J. (1976). *The search for existential identity.* San Francisco: Jossey-Bass.

Burisch, M. (1984). Approaches to personality inventory construction: A comparison of merits. *American Psychologist, 39,* 214–227.

Buss, A. (1980). *Self-consciousness and social anxiety.* San Francisco: Freeman.

Bustamente, A. (1992, April). Beyond the DSM-III: The role of the therapist in affirming the development of a positive gay identity in lesbian and gay clients. Symposium presented at the Annual Convention of the Society for the Exploration of Psychotherapy Integration, San Diego, CA.

Camera, W., Nathan, J., & Puente, A. (2000). Psychological test usage: Implications in professional psychology. *Professional Psychology: Research and Practice, 31,* 141–154.

Cameron, N., & Rychlak, J. F. (1985). *Personality development and psychopathology* (2nd ed.). Boston: Houghton Mifflin.

Cameron-Bandler, L. (1978). *They lived happily ever after.* Cupertino, CA: Meta.
Camic, P., Rhodes, J., & Yardley, L. (2003). *Qualitative Research in Psychology: Expanding Perspectives in Methodology and Design.* Washington, DC: American Psychological Association.
Campbell, D. (1966). Occupations ten years later of high school seniors with high scores on the SVIB life insurance salesman scale. *Journal of Applied Psychology, 50,* 369–372.
Campbell, D., & Hansen, J. (1981). *Manual for the SVIB-SCII* (3rd ed.). Palo Alto, CA: Stanford University Press.
Caplan, P. (1987). The name game: Psychiatry, misogyny, and taxonomy. *Women and Therapy, 6,* 187–202.
Caplan, P. (1991). How do they decide who is normal? The bizarre, but true, tale of the DSM process. *Canadian Psychology, 32,* 162–170.
Casey, R., & Berman, J. (1985). The outcome of psychotherapy with children. *Psychological Bulletin, 98,* 388–400.
Cashdan, S. (1988). *Object relations therapy.* New York: Norton.
Cass, L., & Thomas, C. (1979). *Childhood psychopathology and later adjustment: The question of prediction.* New York: Wiley.
Castonguay, L., Raver, P., Wiser, S., & Goldfried, M. (1995, April). *Challenging client's view: Similarities and differences between cognitive-behavioral and psychodynamic-interpersonal therapies.* Paper presented at the Convention of the Society for the Exploration of Psychotherapy Integration, Washington, DC.
Cattell, R. (1937). *The fight for our national intelligence.* London: P.S. King and Sons.
Ceci, S., & Williams, W. (1997). Schooling, intelligence, and income. *American Psychologist, 52,* 1051–1058.
Chambless, D., Baker, M., Baucom, D., Beutler, L., Calhoun, K., Crits-Christoph, P., et al. (1998). Update on empirically validated therapies, II. *The Clinical Psychologist, 51,* 3–16.
Chertok, L. (1981). *Sense and nonsense in psychotherapy: The challenge of hypnosis.* New York: Pergamon Press.
Chess, S. (1979). Developmental theory revisited. Findings of longitudinal study. *Canadian Journal of Psychiatry, 24,* 101–112.
Chess, S., & Thomas, A. (1984). *Origins and evolution of behavior disorders.* New York: Brunner/Mazel.
Chodorow, N. (1978). *The reproduction of mothering: Psychoanalysis and the sociology of gender.* Berkeley: University of California Press.
Christensen, A. (1983). Intervention. In H. H. Kelley, E. Berscheid, A. Christensen, J. H. Harvey, T. L. Huston, G. Levinger, et al. (Eds.), *Close relationships.* New York: Freeman.
Christensen, A., & Jacobson, N. (1994). Who (or what) can do psychotherapy: The status and challenge of nonprofessional therapies. *Psychological Science, 5,* 8–14.
Christensen, A., Jacobson, N., & Babcock, J. (1995). Integrative behavioral couple therapy. In N. Jacobson & A. Gurman (Eds.), *Clinical handbook of couple therapy* (pp. 31–64). New York: Guilford.
Clarke, K. (1996). Change processes in a creation of meaning event. *Journal of Consulting and Clinical Psychology, 64,* 465–470.
Clay, R. (2004). Primary-care paths: Psychologists collaborate with primary care providers in an effort to bolster front-line services. *Monitor on Psychology, 35,* 42.
Cohen, S. (2004). Social relationships and health. *American Psychologist, 59,* 673–675.
Coleman, J. (1972). *Abnormal psychology and modern life* (4th ed., p. 33). Glenview, IL: Scott Foresman.
Costa, P., & McCrae, R. (1992). *Revised NEO Personality Inventory (NEO PI-R) and NEO Five-Factor Inventory (NEO-FFI): Professional manual.* Odessa, FL: Psychological Assessment Resources.
Cowan, P. (1978). *Piaget: With feeling.* New York: Holt, Rinehart and Winston.

Crits-Christoph, P. (1992). The efficacy of brief dynamic psychotherapy: A meta-analysis. *The American Journal of Psychiatry, 149*, 151–158.

Crowell, J., Treboux, D., & Waters, E. (2002). Stability of attachment representations: The transition to marriage. *Developmental Psychology, 38*, 467–479.

Cunningham, S. (1985, January). The public and nuclear power: Scientists attack DOE attempt to reduce "phobia." *APA Monitor*, 18.

Dammann, C. (1980). Family therapy: Erickson's contribution. In J. Zeig (Ed.), *Ericksonian approaches to hypnosis and psychotherapy.* New York: Brunner/Mazel.

Dattilio, F., & Padesky, C. (1990). *Cognitive therapy with couples.* Sarasota, FL: Professional Resource Exchange.

Davanloo, H. (1980). *Basic principles and technique in short-term dynamic psychotherapy.* New York: Aronson.

Davison, K., Pennebaker, J., & Dickerson, S. (2000). Who talks? The social psychology of illness support groups. *American Psychologist, 55*, 205–217.

DeAngelis, T. (1997, March). Do online support groups help for eating disorders? *APA Monitor,* 43.

DeLeon, P. (2003). Community health centers: Exciting opportunities for the 21st century. *Professional Psychology: Research and Practice, 34*, 579–585.

DeNelsky, G. (1991). Prescription privileges for psychologists: The case against. *Professional Psychology: Research & Practice, 22*, 188–193.

de Shazer, S. (1985). *Keys to solution in brief therapy.* New York: Norton.

Dohrenwend, B., Dohrenwend, B., Gould, M., Link, B., Neugebauer, R., & Wunsch-Hitzig, R. (1980). *Mental illness in the United States.* New York: Praeger.

Dollard, J., & Miller, N. (1950). *Personality and psychotherapy.* New York: McGraw-Hill.

Dowd, E., & Milne, C. (1986). Paradoxical interventions in counseling psychology. *The Counseling Psychologist, 4*, 237–282.

Drozd, J., & Goldfried, M. (1996). A critical evaluation of the state-of-the-art in psychotherapy outcome. *Psychotherapy, 33*, 171–180.

Dubbert, P. (1992). Exercise in behavioral medicine. *Journal of Consulting and Clinical Psychology, 60,* 613–618.

Dulany, D. (1968). Awareness, rules, and propositional control: A confrontation with S-R behavior theory. In T. R. Dixon & D. L. Horton (Eds.), *Verbal behavior and general behavior theory.* Englewood Cliffs, NJ: Erlbaum.

Duncan, B., Hubble, M., & Miller, S. (1997). *Psychotherapy of "impossible cases."* New York: Norton.

Duncan, B., & Miller, S. (2000). *The heroic client*. San Francisco: Jossey-Bass.

Duncan, B., & Miller, S. (in press). Treatment manuals do not improve outcomes. In J. C. Norcross, R. Levant, & L. E. Beutler (Eds.), *Evidence based practices in mental health: Debate and dialogue on the fundamental questions.* Washington, DC: American Psychological Association.

Dykman, B., & Abramson, L. (1990). Contributions of basic research to cognitive theories of depression. *Personality and Social Psychology Bulletin, 16*, 23–41.

Eagle, M. (1984). *Recent developments in psychoanalysis: A critical evaluation.* New York: McGraw-Hill.

Eckert, J., & Biermann-Ratjen, E. (1990). Client-centered therapy versus psychoanalytic psychotherapy. Reflections following a comparative study. In G. Lietaer, J. Rombauts, & R. Van Balen (Eds.), *Client-centered and experiential psychotherapy in the nineties* (pp. 457–468). Leuven, Belgium: Leuven University Press.

Eckman, T., Wirshing, W., Marder, S., & Liberman, R. (1992). Technique for teaching schizophrenic patients in illness self-management: A controlled trial. *American Journal of Psychiatry, 149*, 1549–1555.

Eichberg, R. (1990). *Coming out: An act of love.* New York: Dutton.

Ekstein, R. (1974). Psychoanalytic theory: Sigmund Freud. In A. Burton (Ed.), *Operational theories of personality.* New York: Brunner/Mazel.
Elber, L. (2005). TV therapy shows turn pain into gain. Retrieved March 9, 2005, from www.sfgate.com/cgi-bin/article.cgi?file/=/n/a/2005/03/09/entertainment/e122620S68.DTL
Elkin, L., Shea, M., Watkins, J., Imber, S., Sotsky, S., Collins, J., et al. (1989). National Institute of Mental Health Treatment of Depression Collaborative Research Program: General effectiveness of treatments. *Archives of General Psychiatry, 46,* 971–983.
Ellenberger, H. (1970). *The discovery of the unconscious.* New York: Basic Books.
Elligan, D., & Utsey, S. (1999). Utility of an African-centered support group for African American men confronting societal racism and oppression. *Cultural Diversity and Ethnic Minority Psychology, 5,* 156–165.
Elliott, R. (1984). A discovery-oriented approach to significant change events in psychotherapy: Interpersonal process recall and comprehensive process analysis. In L. N. Rice & L. S. Greenberg (Eds.), *Patterns of change* (pp. 249–286). New York: Guilford.
Elliott, R. (2001a). Contemporary brief experiential psychotherapy. *Clinical Psychology: Science and Practice, 8,* 38–50.
Elliott, R. (2001b). Hermeneutic single-case efficacy design: An overview. In K. J. Schneider, J. F. T. Bugental, & J. F. Pierson (Eds.), *The handbook of humanistic psychology* (pp. 315–326). Thousand Oaks, CA: Sage.
Elliott, R. (2002). The effectiveness of humanistic therapies: A meta-analysis. In D. J. Cain & J. Seeman (Eds.), *Humanistic psychotherapies: Handbook of research and practice.*(pp. 55–82). Washington, DC: American Psychological Association.
Elliott, R., Greenberg, L. S., & Lietaer, G. (2004). Research on experiential psychotherapies. In M. J. Lambert (Ed.), *Bergin and Garfield's handbook of psychotherapy and behavior change* (5th ed., pp. 493–540). New York: Wiley.
Elliott, R., Watson, J. C., Goldman, R. N., & Greenberg, L. S. (2004). *Learning emotion-focused therapy: The process-experiential approach to change.* Washington, DC: American Psychological Association.
Ellis, A. (1973). Rational-emotive therapy. In R. Corsini (Ed.), *Current psychotherapies.* Itasca, IL: Peacock.
Ellis, A. (1979a). The practice of rational-emotive therapy. In A. Ellis & J. M. Whiteley (Eds.), *Theoretical and empirical foundations of rational-emotive therapy.* Monterey, CA: Brooks/Cole.
Ellis, A. (1979b). Rational-emotive therapy as a new theory of personality and therapy. In A. Ellis & J. M. Whiteley (Eds.), *Theoretical and empirical foundations of rational-emotive therapy.* Monterey, CA: Brooks/Cole.
Ellis, A. (1979c). Toward a new theory of personality. In A. Ellis & J. M. Whiteley (Eds.), *Theoretical and empirical foundations of rational-emotive therapy.* Monterey, CA: Brooks/Cole.
Ellis, A. (1979d). The theory of rational-emotive therapy. In A. Ellis & J. M. Whiteley (Eds.), *Theoretical and empirical foundations of rational-emotive therapy.* Monterey, CA: Brooks/Cole.
Ellis, A. (1984). Rational-emotive therapy. In R. Corsini (Ed.), *Current psychotherapies* (3rd ed.). Itasca, IL: Peacock.
Ellis, H. (1992). Graduate education in psychology: Past, present, and future. *American Psychologist, 47,* 570–576.
Eme, R. (1979). Sex differences in childhood psychopathology: A review. *Psychological Bulletin, 86,* 574–595.
Emmelkamp, P. (2004). Behavior therapy with adults. In M. J. Lambert (Ed.), *Bergin and Garfield's handbook of psychotherapy and behavior change* (5th ed., pp. 393–446). New York: Wiley.
Ends, E., & Page, C. (1957). A study of three types of group psychotherapy with hospitalized male inebriates. *Quarterly Journal of Studies in Alcoholism, 18,* 263–277.

Epstein, L., & Brown, L. (2002). *Brief treatment and a new look at the task centered approach* (4th ed.). Boston: Allyn and Bacon.

Erdberg, P., & Exner, J. (1984). Rorschach assessment. In G. Goldstein & M. Hersen (Eds.), *Handbook of psychological assessment* (pp. 227–298). New York: Pergamon Press.

Erickson, M., & Rossi, E. (1979). *Hypnotherapy: An exploratory casebook.* New York: Irvington.

Erikson, E. (1968). *Identity: Youth and crisis.* New York: Norton.

Ewart, C. (1991). Social action theory for a public health psychology. *American Psychologist, 46,* 931–946.

Exner, J. (1991). *The Rorschach: A comprehensive system: Vol. 2. Interpretation* (2nd ed.). New York: Wiley.

Exner, J. (2003). *The Rorschach: A comprehensive system* (4th ed.). New York: Wiley.

Eysenck, H. (1952). The effects of psychotherapy: An evaluation. *Journal of Consulting Psychology, 16,* 319–324.

Eysenck, H. (1967). *The biological basis of personality.* Springfield, IL: Thomas.

Farber, B., & Lane, J. (2002). Positive regard. In J. C. Norcross (Ed.), *Psychotherapy relationships that work* (pp. 175–194). New York: Oxford University Press.

Farberow, N., & Schneidman, E. (1961). *The cry for help.* New York: McGraw-Hill.

Fassinger, R. (2004). Centralizing feminism and multiculturalism in counseling: Introduction to the special section. *Journal and Multicultural Counseling and Development, 32,* 344–345.

Feixas, G. (1990). Personal construct theory and systemic therapies: Parallel or convergent trends? *Journal of Marital and Family Therapy, 16,* 1–20.

Feldman, J. (1985). The work of Milton Erickson: A multisystem model of eclectic therapy. *Psychotherapy, 22,* 154–162.

Feldman, L. (1992). *Integrating individual and family therapy.* New York: Brunner/Mazel.

Feldman, M. & Christensen, J. (Eds.). (2003). *Behavioral medicine in primary care: A practical guide.* New York: Lange/McGraw-Hill.

Feshbach, N. (1997). Empathy: The formative years, implications for clinical practice. In A. Bohart & L. Greenberg (Eds.), *Empathy reconsidered* (pp. 33–59). Washington DC: American Psychological Association.

Feshbach, S., Weiner, B., & Bohart, A. (1996). *Personality.* Lexington, MA: Heath.

Fingarette, H. (1963). *The self in transformation.* New York: Harper & Row.

Finn, J., & Banach, M. (2000). Victimization online: The downside of seeking services for women on the Internet. *Cyberpsychology and Behavior, 3,* 785–796.

Finn, J., & Holden, G. (Eds.). (2000). *Human services online: A new arena for service delivery.* New York: Haworth.

Fischer, C., Hout, M., Jankowski, M., Lucas, S., Swindler, A., & Voss, K. (1996). *Inequality by design: Cracking The Bell Curve myth.* Princeton, NJ: Princeton University Press.

Fiske, S., & Taylor, S. (1984). *Social cognition.* Reading, MA: Addison-Wesley.

Flammer, E., & Bongartz, W. (2003). On the efficacy of hypnosis: A meta-analytic study. *Contemporary Hypnosis, 20,* 179–197.

Flanigan, J. (1991, September 29). U.S. health-care system getting a dose of reality. *Los Angeles Times,* Part D, pp. 1, 16.

Fonagy, P., Leigh, T., Steele, H., Kennedy, R., Mattoon, G., Target, M., & Gerber, A. (1996). The relation of attachment status, psychiatric classification, and response to psychotherapy. *Journal of Consulting and Clinical Psychology, 64,* 22–31.

Frank, J. (1961). *Persuasion and healing.* Baltimore, MD: Johns Hopkins University Press.

Frank, J. (1974). Psychotherapy: The restoration of morale. *American Journal of Psychiatry, 131,* 271–274.

Frank, J. (1982). Therapeutic components shared by all psychotherapies. In J. H. Harvey & M. M. Parks (Eds.), *Psychotherapy research and behavior change.* Washington, DC: American Psychological Association.

Frankl, V. (1963). *Man's search for meaning: An introduction to logotherapy.* New York: Washington Square Press.
Freedman, J., & Combs, G. (1996). *Narrative therapy: The social construction of preferred realities.* New York: Norton.
Freud, A. (1928). *Technique of child analysis.* New York: Nervous and Mental Disease Publishing Company.
Freud, A. (1946). *The psychoanalytic treatment of children.* New York: International Universities Press.
Freud, S. (1937). Psychotherapy of hysteria. In J. Breuer & S. Freud (Eds.), *Studies in hysteria.* Boston: Beacon Press. (Original work published 1895)
Freud, S. (1955). Lines of advance in psycho-analytic theory. In J. Strachey (Ed.), *The standard edition of the complete psychological works of Sigmund Freud* (Vol. 17). London: Hogarth Press. (Original work published 1918)
Freud, S. (1961). Some psychical consequences of the anatomical distinction between the sexes. In J. Strachey (Ed.), *The standard edition of the complete psychological works of Sigmund Freud* (Vol. 19). London: Hogarth Press. (Original work published 1925)
Freud, S. (1963). Analysis terminable and interminable. In P. Rieff (Ed.), *Sigmund Freud: Therapy and technique.* New York: Crowell-Collier. (Original work published 1937)
Freud, S. (1963). Observations on "wild" psychoanalysis. In P. Rieff (Ed.), *Sigmund Freud: Therapy and technique.* New York: Crowell-Collier. (Original work published 1910)
Freud, S. (1964). The dissection of the psychical personality. In J. Strachey (Ed.), *The standard edition of the complete psychological works of Sigmund Freud* (Vol. 22). London: Hogarth Press. (Original work published 1924).
Frings, Manfred S. (Ed.). (1968). *Heidegger and the quest for truth.* Chicago: Quadrangle.
Gaensbauer, T. J., & Harmon, R. J. (1982). Attachment behavior in abused/neglected and premature infants. In R. R. Emde & R. J. Harmon (Eds.), *The development of attachment and affiliative systems.* New York: Plenum Press.
Galavotti, C., Saltzman, L., Sauter, S., & Sumartojo, E. (1997). Behavioral science activities at the Centers for Disease Control and Prevention: A selected overview of exemplary programs. *American Psychologist, 52*, 154–166.
Gardner, H. (1983). *Frames of mind: The theory of multiple intelligences.* New York: Basic Books.
Garfield, S. (1996). Some problems associated with "validated" forms of psychotherapy. *Clinical Psychology: Science and Practice, 3*, 218–229.
Garmazy, N. (1986). Developmental aspects of children's responses to the stress of separation and loss. In M. Rutter, C. E. Izard, & P. B. Read (Eds.), *Depression in young people: Developmental and clinical perspectives* (pp. 297–324). New York: Guilford.
Gatchel, R., & Oordt, M. (2003). *Clinical health psychology and primary care: Practice advice and clinical guidance for successful collaboration.* Washington, DC: American Psychological Association.
Gendlin, E. (1964). A theory of personality change. In P. Worchel & D. Byrne (Eds.), *Personality change.* New York: Wiley.
Gendlin, E. (1967). Therapeutic procedures in dealing with schizophrenics. In R. Rogers, E. Gendlin, D. Kiesler, & C. Truax (Eds.), *The therapeutic relationship and its impact: A study of psychotherapy with schizophrenics* (pp. 369–400). Madison: University of Wisconsin Press.
Gendlin, E. (1968). The experiential response. In E. Hammer (Ed.), *Use of interpretation in treatment.* New York: Grune & Stratton.
Gendlin, E. (1969). Focusing. *Psychotherapy: Theory, Research and Practice, 6*, 4–15.
Gendlin, E. (1981). *Focusing.* New York: Bantam Books.
Gendlin, E. (1982). An introduction to the new developments in focusing. *The Focusing Folio, 2*, 24–35.
Gendlin, E. (1984a). The politics of giving therapy away: Listening and focusing. In D. Larson (Ed.), *Teaching psychological skills: Models for giving psychology away* (pp. 287–305). Monterey, CA: Brooks/Cole.

Gendlin, E. (1984b). The client's client: The edge of awareness. In R. Levant & J. Shlien (Eds.), *Client-centered therapy and the person-centered approach: New directions in theory, research, and practice.* New York: Praeger.

Gendlin, E. (1996). *Focusing-oriented psychotherapy: A manual of the experiential method.* New York: Guilford.

Gendlin, E., Beebe, J., Cassens, J., Klein, M., & Oberlander, M. (1968). Focusing ability in psychotherapy, personality, and creativity. In J. M. Shlien (Ed.), *Research in psychotherapy* (Vol. 3). Washington, DC: American Psychological Association.

Gewirtz, J., & Baer, D. (1958). Deprivation and satiation of social reinforcers as drive conditions. *Journal of Abnormal and Social Psychology, 57,* 165–172.

Glynn, S. (1990). Token economy approaches for psychiatric patients. *Behavior Modification, 14,* 383–407.

Gold, J. (1994). When the patient does the integrating: Lessons for theory and practice. *Journal of Psychotherapy Integration, 4,* 133–158.

Goldfried, M. (Ed.). (1980a). Special issue: Psychotherapy process. *Cognitive Therapy and Research, 4,* 271–306.

Goldfried, M. (1980b). Toward the delineation of therapeutic change principles. *American Psychologist, 35,* 991–999.

Goldfried, M. (1995). *From cognitive-behavior therapy to psychotherapy integration: An evolving view.* New York: Springer Publishing Company.

Goldfried, M. (1997, April). *Cognitive-behavioral theory and technique for psychodynamic/non-behavioral therapists.* Workshop presented at the Convention of the Society for the Exploration of Psychotherapy Integration, Toronto, Canada.

Goldfried, M., & Wolfe, B. (1996). Psychotherapy practice and research: Repairing a strained alliance. *American Psychologist, 51,* 1007–1016.

Goldstein, G. (1997). Comprehensive neuropsychological assessment batteries. In G. Goldstein & M. Hersen (Eds.), *Handbook of psychological assessment* (pp. 141–178). New York: Pergamon Press.

Goleman, D. (1996). *Emotional intelligence.* New York: Bantam.

Goss, S., & Rose, S. (2002). Evidence based practice: A guide for counselors and psychotherapists. *Counseling and Psychotherapy Research, 2,* 147–151.

Gottlib, I., & Schraedley, P. (2000). Interpersonal psychotherapy. In C. R. Snyder, & R. E. Ingram (Eds.), *Handbook of psychological change* (pp. 258–279). New York: Wiley

Grawe, K. (1997). Research-informed psychotherapy. *Psychotherapy Research, 7,* 1–20.

Grawe, K., Caspar, F., & Ambuhl, H. (1990). Differentielle psychotherapieforschung: Vier Therapieformen im Vergleich. *Zeirschrift für Klinische Psychologie, 19,* 287–376.

Greenberg, L. (1984). A task analysis of intrapersonal conflict resolution. In L. N. Rice & L. S. Greenberg (Eds.), *Patterns of change* (pp. 124–149). New York: Guilford.

Greenberg, L., Elliott, R., & Lietaer, G. (1994). Research on humanistic and experiential psychotherapies. In A. Bergin & S. Garfield (Eds.), *Handbook of psychotherapy and behavior change* (4th ed.). New York: Wiley.

Greenberg, L., & Johnson, S. (1988). *Emotionally focused therapy for couples.* New York: Guilford.

Greenberg, L., Rice, L., & Elliot, R. (1993a). *Facilitating emotional change: The moment-by-moment process.* New York: Guilford

Greenberg, L., Rice, L., & Elliott, R. (1993b). *Process-experiential psychotherapy: Facilitating emotional change.* New York: Guilford.

Greenberg, L., & Safran, J. D. (1987). *Emotion in psychotherapy.* New York: Guilford.

Greenberg, L., Safran, J., & Rice, L. (1989). Experiential therapy: Its relation to cognitive therapy. In A. Freeman, K. Simon, L. Beutler, & H. Arkowitz (Eds.), *Comprehensive handbook of cognitive therapy* (pp. 169–187). New York: Plenum.

Greenberg, L., & Watson, J. (1998). Experiential therapy of depression: Differential effects of client-centered relationship conditions and process experiential interventions. *Psychotherapy Research, 8*, 210–224.

Greenfield, P. (1997). You can't take it with you: Why ability assessments don't cross cultures. *American Psychologist, 52*, 1115–1124.

Greif, G. (1992). Alice Miller's revision of psychoanalysis. *Psychotherapy, 29*, 310–317.

Guerney, B. (1984). Relationship enhancement therapy and training. In D. Larson (Ed.), *Teaching psychological skills: Models for giving psychology away* (pp. 171–206). Monterey, CA: Brooks/Cole.

Guntrip, H. (1973). *Psychoanalytic theory, therapy, and the self.* New York: Basic Books.

Gurman, A. (2003). Marital therapies. In A. S. Gurman & S. B. Messer (Eds.), *Essential psychotherapies* (2nd ed., pp. 463–514).

Gurman, A., & Fraenkel, P. (2002). The history of couple therapy: A millennial review. *Family Process, 41*, 199–260.

Hager, P. (1991, October 29). Court bars psychological tests in hiring. *Los Angeles Times*, p. A20.

Haley, J. (1976). *Problem-solving therapy: New strategies for effective family therapy.* San Francisco: Jossey-Bass.

Haley, J. (1985, December 11). *Strategic family therapy* (Video and discussion). Presented at the Evolution of Psychotherapy Conference, Phoenix, AZ.

Hamilton, N. (1988). *Self and others: Object relations theory in practice.* New York: Aaronson.

Hammen, C. (1985). Predicting depression: A cognitive-behavioral perspective. *Advances in cognitive-behavioral research and therapy* (Vol. 4). New York: Academic Press.

Haney, C., Banks, C., & Zimbardo, P. (1973). Interpersonal dynamics in a simulated prison. *International Journal of Criminology and Penology, 1*, 69–97.

Hansen, J., & Swanson, J. (1983). Stability of interests and the predictive and concurrent validity of the 1981 Strong-Campbell Interest Inventory. *Journal of Consulting Psychology, 30*, 194–201.

Harris, B. (1979). Whatever happened to Little Albert? *American Psychologist, 34*, 151–160.

Hart, J. (1970). The development of client-centered therapy. In J. T. Hart & T. M. Tomlinson (Eds.), *New directions in client-centered therapy* (pp. 3–22). New York: Houghton Mifflin.

Hartmann, H. (1964). *Essays on ego psychology.* New York: International Universities Press.

Hathaway, S., & McKinley, J. (1943). *The Minnesota Multiphasic Personality Inventory.* New York: Psychological Corporation.

Hatzidimitriadou, E. (2002). Political ideology, helping mechanisms and empowerment of mental health self-help/mutual aid groups. *Journal of Community and Applied Social Psychology, 12*, 271–285.

Havens, R. (1985). *The wisdom of Milton H. Erickson.* New York: Irvington.

Hayes, S., Follette, W., & Follette, V. (1995). Behavior therapy: A contextual approach. In A. S. Gurman & S. B. Messer (Eds.), *Essential psychotherapies: Theory and practice* (pp. 182–225). New York: Guilford Press.

Hayes, S., Follette, V., & Linehan, M. (2004). *Mindfulness and acceptance: Expanding the cognitive-behavioral tradition.* New York: Guilford.

Hayes, S., Strosahl, K., & Wilson, K. (1999). *Acceptance and commitment therapy: An experiential approach to behavior change.* New York: Guilford.

Hays, P. (2001). *Addressing cultural complexities in practice: A framework for clinicians and counselors.* Washington, DC: American Psychological Association.

Hazleton, L. (1984). *The right to feel bad.* New York: Ballantine.

Heide, F. (1989, April). Negative outcome in psychotherapy. Symposium presented at the Annual Convention of the Society for the Exploration of Psychotherapy Integration, Berkeley, CA.

Helms, J. (1997). The triple quandary of race, culture, and social class in standardized cognitive ability testing. In D. Flanagan, J. Genshaft, & P. Harrison (Eds.), *Contemporary intellectual assessment.* New York: Guilford Press.

Henggeler, S., Pickrel, S., & Brondino, M. (1999). Multisystemic treatment of substance abusing and dependent delinquents: Outcomes, treatment fidelity, and transportability. *Mental Health Services Research, 1,* 171–184.

Henry, W., Schacht, T., & Strupp, H. (1986). Structural analysis of social behavior: Application to a study of interpersonal process in differential psychotherapeutic outcome. *Journal of Consulting and Clinical Psychology, 54,* 27–31.

Henry, W., Strupp, H., Schacht, T., & Gaston, L. (1994). Psychodynamic approaches. In A. E. Bergin & S. L. Garfield (Eds.), *Handbook and psychotherapy and behavior change* (pp. 467–508). New York: Wiley.

Henschel, D., & Bohart, A. (1984). Egocentric versus decentered empathy (Summary of paper presentation). In G. I. Lubin & M. K. Poulsen (Eds.), *Piagetian theory and its implications for mental health. Proceedings: Ninth through twelfth Interdisciplinary Conference.* (Vol. 2). Los Angeles: University of Southern California.

Herrnstein, R., & Murray, C. (1994). *The bell curve: Intelligence and class structure in American life.* New York: Free Press.

Hill, K. (1987). Meta-analysis of paradoxical interventions. *Psychotherapy, 24,* 266–270.

Hobbs, N. (1968). Sources of gain in psychotherapy. In E. Hammer (Ed.), *Use of interpretation in treatment.* New York: Grune & Stratton.

Hobfall, S. (1989). Conservation of resources: A new attempt at conceptualizing stress. *American Psychologist, 44,* 513–524.

Holdstock, T. (1990). Can client-centered therapy transcend its monocultural roots? In G. Lietaer, J. Rombauts, & R. Van Balen (Eds.), *Client-centered and experiential psychotherapy in the nineties* (pp. 109–121). Leuven, Belgium: Leuven University Press.

Hollon, S., & Beck, A. (1994). Cognitive and cognitive-behavioral therapies. In A. E. Bergin & S. L. Garfield (Eds.), *Handbook and psychotherapy and behavior change* (pp. 428–466). New York: Wiley.

Hollon, S., & Beck, A. (2004). Cognitive and cognitive behavioral therapies. In M. J. Lambert (Ed.), *Bergin and Garfield's handbook of psychotherapy and behavior change* (5th ed., pp. 447–492). New York: Wiley.

Holloway, J. (2005). Managed-care suit brings concessions. *Monitor on Psychology, 36,* 32.

Horney, K. (1945). *Our inner conflicts.* New York: Norton.

Horowitz, M. (1987). *States of mind* (2nd ed., p. 26). New York: Plenum.

Horvath, A. (1995). The therapeutic relationship: From transference to alliance. *In Session, 1,* 7–17.

Howard, G. (1991). Culture tales: A narrative approach to thinking, cross-cultural psychology, and psychotherapy. *American Psychologist, 46,* 187–197.

Howard, K., Kopta, S., Krause, M., & Orlinsky, D. (1986). The dose-effect relationship in psychotherapy. *American Psychologist, 41,* 159–164.

Hoyt, M. (1995). Brief psychotherapies. In A. S. Gurman & S. B. Messer (Eds.), *Essential psychotherapies: Theory and practice.* New York: Guilford.

Hubble, M., Duncan, B., & Miller, S. (Eds.). (1999). *The heart and soul of change.* Washington, DC: American Psychological Association.

Husserl, E. (1964). *Cartesian meditations: An introduction to phenomenology.* The Hague, Netherlands: Martinus Nijhoff.

Ilhe-Helledy, K., Zytowski, D., & Fouada, N. (2004). Kuder Career Search: Test-retest reliability and consequential validity. *Journal of Career Assessment, 12,* 285–297.

ISMHO (International Society for Mental Health & Psychiatric Society for Informatics). (2000). Suggested principles for the online provision of mental health services. www.ismho.org/suggestions.html.

Jackson, L., & Panyan, M. (2002). *Positive behavioral support in the classroom: Principles and practices.* Baltimore, MD: Brookes.

Jacobson, E. (1938). *Progressive relaxation.* Chicago: University of Chicago Press.

Jacobson, N. (1994). Behavior therapy and psychotherapy integration. *Journal of Psychotherapy Integration, 4,* 105–119.

Jacobson, N., & Margolin, G. (1979). *Marital therapy: Strategies based on social learning and behavior exchange principles.* New York: Brunner/hazel.

Jacobson, N., & Christensen, A. (1996). Studying the effectiveness of psychotherapy: How well can clinical trials do the job? *American Psychologist, 51,* 1031–1039.

James, L. & Folen, R. (Eds.). (2005). *The primary care consultant: The next frontier for psychologists in hospitals and clinics.* Washington, DC: American Psychological Association.

Janov, A. (1970). *The primal scream.* New York: Dell.

Jenkins, D., & Johnson, L. (2004). Unethical treatment of gay and lesbian people with conversion therapy. *Families in Society, 85,* 557–561.

Johnson, S., & Millstein, S. (2003). Prevention opportunities in health care settings. *American Psychologist, 58,* 475–481.

Jones, M. (1924). The elimination of children's fears. *Journal of Experimental Psychology, 7,* 383–390.

Jordan, J., Kaplan, A., Miller, J., Stiver, I., & Surrey, J. (Eds.). (1991). *Women's growth in connection: Writings from the Stone Center.* New York: Guilford.

Jung, C. (1933). *Modern man in search of a soul.* New York: Harcourt Brace Jovanovich.

Jung, C. (1956). *Two essays on analytical psychology.* New York: New American Library (Meridian Books).

Kagan, J. (1984). *The nature of the child.* New York: Basic Books.

Kagan, J. (1996). Three pleasing ideas. *American Psychologist, 51,* 901–908.

Kagan, N. (1984). Interpersonal process recall: Basic methods and recent research. In D. Larson (Ed.), *Teaching psychological skills: Models for giving psychology away* (pp. 229–244). Monterey, CA: Brooks/Cole.

Kahn, E. (1985). Heinz Kohut and Carl Rogers: A timely comparison. *American Psychologist, 40,* 893–904.

Kaplan, M. (1983). A woman's view of DSM-III. *American Psychologist, 38,* 786–792.

Kaplan, M., & Kaplan, N. (1985). The linearity issue and gestalt therapy's theory of experiential organization. *Psychotherapy, 22,* 5–15.

Kazdin, A. (1994). Psychotherapy for children and adolescents. In M. J. Lambert (Ed.), *Bergin and Garfield's Handbook of psychotherapy and behavior change* (5th ed., pp. 543–589). New York: Wiley.

Kazdin, A. (2004). Evidence-based treatments: Challenges and priorities for practice and research. *Child and Adolescent Psychiatric Clinics of North America, 13,* 923–940.

Keen, S., & Fox, A. (1973). *Telling your story.* New York: Doubleday.

Keiser, R., & Prather, E. (1990). What is the TAT?: A review often years of research. *Journal of Personality Assessment, 55,* 800–803.

Kelly, G. (1955). *The psychology of personal constructs: A theory of personality* (2 vols.). New York: Norton.

Kelly, G. (1963). *A theory of personality.* New York: Norton.

Kennedy-Moore, E., & Watson, J. (1999). *Expressing emotion: Myths, realities, and therapeutic strategies.* New York: Guilford.

Kernberg, O., Burstein, E., Coyne, L., Appelbaum, A., Horwitz, L., & Voth, H. (1972). Psychotherapy and psychoanalysis: Final report of the Menninger Foundation's psychotherapy research project. *Bulletin of the Menninger Clinic, 36,* 1–276.

Kiraly, J., & McKinnon, A. (1984). *Pupil behavior, self-control, and social skills in the classroom.* Springfield, IL: C. C. Thomas.

Kirsch, L., & Lynn, S. J. (1995). The altered state of hypnosis: Changes in the theoretical landscape. *American Psychologist, 50,* 846–858.

Klein, M. (1955). The psychoanalytic play technique. *Journal of Orthopsychiatry, 25,* 223–237.

Klein, M. (1975). *The psycho-analysis of children.* New York: Delta. (Original work published 1932)

Klein, M., Kolden, G., Michels, J., & Chisholm-Stockard, S. (2002). Congruence. In J. C. Norcross (Ed.), *Psychotherapy relationships that work* (pp. 195–216). New York: Oxford University Press.

Klein, M., Mathieu-Coughlan, P., & Kiesler, D. (1986). The experiencing scales. In L. S. Greenberg & W. Pinsof (Eds.), *The psychotherapeutic process: A research handbook* (pp. 21–72). New York: Guilford.

Kleinman, A. (1988). *Rethinking psychiatry.* New York: Free Press.

Klopfer, B., & Kelley, D. (1942). *The Rorschach technique.* Yonkers, NY: World Book.

Klosko, J., Barlow, D., Toussinari, R., & Cerny, J. (1990). A comparison of alprazolam and behavior therapy in the treatment of panic disorder. *Journal of Consulting and Clinical Psychology, 58,* 805–810.

Kobasa, S., & Maddi, S. (1983). Existential personality theory. In R. J. Corsini & A. J. Marsella (Eds.), *Personality theories, research, and assessment.* Itasca, IL: Peacock.

Kohlenberg, R., & Tsai, M. (1991). *Functional analytic psychotherapy: Creating intense and curative therapeutic relationships.* New York: Plenum Press.

Kohlenberg, R., & Tsai, M. (1994). Functional analytic psychotherapy: A radical behavioral approach to treatment and integration. *Journal of Psychotherapy Integration, 4,* 175–201.

Kohlenberg, R., & Tsai, M. (2000). Radical behavioral help for Katrina. *Cognitive and Behavioral Practice, 7,* 500–505.

Kohut, H. (1971). *The analysis of the self.* New York: International Universities Press.

Kohut, H. (1977). *The restoration of the self.* New York: International Universities Press.

Kohut, H. (1984). *How does analysis cure?* Chicago: University of Chicago Press.

Kostandov, E., & Arzumanov, Y. (1977). Averaged cortical evoked potentials to recognized and non-recognized verbal stimuli. *Acta Neurobiologiae Experimentalis, 37,* 311–324.

Kroll, J. (1988). *The challenge of the borderline patient.* New York: Norton.

Kruglanski, A., & Jaffe, Y. (1988). Curing by knowing: The epistemic approach to cognitive therapy. In L. Y. Abramson (Ed.), *Social cognition and clinical psychology: A synthesis* (pp. 254–294). New York: Guilford.

Krupnick, J., Sotsky, S., Simmens, S., Moyher, J., Elkin, L., Watkins, J., & Pilkonis, P. (1996). The role of the therapeutic alliance in psychotherapy and pharmacotherapy outcome: Findings in the National Institute of Mental Health Treatment of Depression Collaborative Research Project. *Journal of Consulting and Clinical Psychology, 64,* 532–539.

Kyrouz, E., Humphreys, K., & Loomis, C. (2002). A review of research on the effectiveness of self-help mutual aid groups. In J. White & E. Madara (Eds.), *American Self-Help Clearinghouse self-help group sourcebook* (7th ed.). Danville, NJ: American Self-Help Clearinghouse.

Laing, R. (1967). *The politics of experience.* New York: Pantheon Books.

Lambert, M. (1992). Psychotherapy outcome research. In J. C. Norcross & M. R. Goldfried (Eds.), *Handbook of psychotherapy integration* (pp. 94–129). New York: Basic Books.

Lambert, M., & Barley, D. (2002). Research summary on the therapeutic relationship and psychotherapy outcome. In J. C. Norcross (Ed.), *Psychotherapy relationships that work* (pp. 17–36). New York: Oxford.

Lambert, M., & Bergin, A. (1994). The effectiveness of psychotherapy. In A. E. Bergin & S. L. Garfield (Eds.), *Handbook of psychotherapy and behavior change* (4th ed., pp. 143–189). New York: Wiley.

Lambert, M., & Hawkins, E. (2004). Measuring outcome in professional practice. *Professional Psychology: Research & Practice, 35,* 492–499.

Lambert, M., & Ogles, B. (2004). The efficacy and effectiveness of psychotherapy. In M. J. Lambert (Ed.), *Bergin and Garfield's Handbook of psychotherapy and behavior change* (5th ed., pp. 139–193). New York: Wiley.

Lambert, M., Shapiro, D., & Bergin, A. (1986). The effectiveness of psychotherapy. In S. L. Garfield & A. E. Bergin (Eds.), *Handbook of psychotherapy and behavior change* (3rd ed., pp. 157–212). New York: Wiley.

Lambert, N. (1981). Psychological evidence in *Larry P. v. Wilson Riles*: An evaluation of the evidence by a witness for the defense. *American Psychologist, 36*, 937–952.

Lampropoulos, G. (2000). A reexamination of the empirically supported treatments critiques. *Psychotherapy Research, 10,* 474–87.

Landrine, H. (1992). Clinical implications of cultural differences: The referential versus indexical self. *Clinical Psychology Review, 12*, 401–415.

Lang, P., Lazovik, A., & Reynolds, D. (1965). Desensitization, suggestibility, and pseudotherapy. *Journal of Abnormal Psychology, 70*, 395–402.

Larson, D. (Ed.). (1984). *Teaching psychological skills: Models for giving psychology away.* Monterey, CA: Brooks/Cole.

Lazarus, A. (1981). *The practice of multimodal therapy.* New York: McGraw-Hill.

Lazarus, A. (2002). The multimodal assessment treatment method. In J. Lebow (Ed.), *Comprehensive handbook of psychotherapy: Vol. 4. Integrative-eclectic* (pp. 241–254). New York: Wiley.

Lazarus, A., Beutler, L., & Norcross, J. (1992). The future of technical eclecticism. *Psychotherapy, 29*, 11–20.

Levant, R. (2005). Graduate education in clinical psychology for the twenty-first century: Educating psychological health care providers. *Journal of Clinical Psychology, 61*, 1087–1090.

Levy, D. (1939). Release therapy in young children. *Child Study, 16*, 141–143.

Lietaer, G. (1990). The client-centered approach after the Wisconsin project: A personal view on its evolution. In G. Lietaer, J. Rombauts, & R. Van Balen (Eds.), *Client-centered and experiential psychotherapy in the nineties* (pp. 19–46). Leuven, Belgium: Leuven University Press.

Lilienfeld S., Wood, J., & Garb H. (2000). The scientific status of projective techniques. *Psychological Science in the Public Interest, 1,* 27–66.

Linehan, M. (1987). Dialectical behavior therapy: A cognitive behavioral approach to parasuicide. *Journal of Personality Disorders, 1*, 328–333.

Linehan, M. (1989, April). What is support in psychotherapy and is it good or bad? Symposium presented at the Annual Convention of the Society for the Exploration of Psychotherapy Integration, Berkeley, CA.

Linehan, M. (1993). *Cognitive-behavioral treatment of borderline personality disorder.* New York: Guilford.

Linehan, M. (1997). Validation and psychotherapy. In A. Bohart & L. Greenberg (Eds.), *Empathy reconsidered* (pp. 354–392). Washington, DC: American Psychological Association.

Linehan, M., Armstrong, H., Suarez, A., Allmon, D., & Heard, H. (1991). Cognitive-behavioral treatment of chronically parasuicidal borderline patients. *Archives of General Psychiatry, 48*, 1060–1064.

Linehan, M., Cochran, R., & Kehrer, C. (2001). Dialectical behavior therapy for borderline personality disorder. In D. Barlow (Ed.). *Clinical handbook of psychological disorder.* New York: Guilford.

Links, P. (1992). Family environment and family psychopathology in the etiology of borderline personality disorder. In J. F. Clarkin, E. Marziali, & H. Munroe-Blum (Eds.), *Borderline personality disorder: Clinical and empirical perspectives* (pp. 45–66). New York: Guilford.

Liotti, G. (2004). Trauma, dissociation, and disorganized attachment: Three strands of a single braid. *Psychotherapy: Theory, Research, Practice, Training, 41*, 472–486.

Livson, N., & Peskin, H. (1980). Perspectives on adolescence from longitudinal research. In J. Adelson (Ed.), *Handbook of adolescent psychology.* New York: Wiley.

Loftus, E. (1993). The reality of repressed memories. *American Psychologist, 48*, 518–537.

Lovaas, O., & Simmons, J. (1969). Manipulation of self-destruction in three retarded children. *Journal of Applied Behavioral Analysis, 2*, 143–157.

Lubin, B., Larsen, R., & Matarazzo, J. (1984). Patterns of psychological test usage in the United States: 1935–1982. *American Psychologist, 39*, 451–454.

Luborsky, L. (1984). *Principles of psychoanalytic psychotherapy: A manual for supportive-expressive treatment.* New York: Basic Books.

Luborsky, L., Crits-Christoph, P., & Barger, J. (1991). University of Pennsylvania: The Penn Psychotherapy Research Projects. In L. E. Beutler & M. Crago (Eds.), *Psychotherapy research: An international review of programmatic studies* (pp. 133–141). Washington, DC: American Psychological Association.

Luborsky, L., Crits-Christoph, P., & Mellon, J. (1986). Advent of objective measures of the transference concept. *Journal of Consulting and Clinical Psychology, 54*, 39–47.

Luborsky, L., Diguer, L., Seligman, D. A., Rosenthal, R., Krause, E. D., Johnson, S., et al. (1999). The researcher's own therapy allegiances: A "wild card" in comparisons of treatment efficacy. *Clinical Psychology: Science and Practice, 6*, 95–106.

Luborsky, L., McLellan, A. T., & Woody, G. E. (1985). Therapist success and its determinants. *Archives of General Psychiatry, 42*, 602–611.

Luborsky, L., Rosenthal, R., Diguer, L., Andrusyna, T., Berman, J., Levitt, J., et al. (2002). The dodo bird verdict is alive and well—mostly. *Clinical Psychology: science and Practice, 9*, 2–12.

Luborsky, L., Singer, B., & Luborsky, L. (1975). Comparative studies of psychotherapies. *Archives of General Psychiatry, 29*, 719–729.

Lyons, L., & Woods, P. (1991). The efficacy of rational-emotive therapy: A quantitative review of the outcome research. *Clinical Psychology Review, 11*, 357–369.

Machover, K. (1949). *Personality projection in the drawing of the human figure: A method of personality investigation.* Springfield, IL: C. C. Thomas.

MacKenzie, K. (Ed.). (1994). *Effective use of group therapy in managed care.* Washington, DC: American Psychiatric Association.

MacKenzie, K. (1997). Time-managed group psychotherapy: Effective clinical applications. Washington, DC: American Psychiatric Association.

Madanes, C. (1984). *Behind the one-way mirror: Advances in the practice of strategic therapy.* San Francisco: Jossey-Bass.

Madanes, C. (1985, December 12). *Advances in strategic family therapy.* Paper presented at the Evolution of Psychotherapy Conference, Phoenix, AZ.

Madanes, C. (1985, December 13). *Strategic therapy* (Video and discussion). Presented at the Evolution of Psychotherapy Conference, Phoenix, AZ.

Madanes, C. (1987). Advances in strategic family therapy. In J. Zeig (Ed.), *The evolution of psychotherapy* (pp. 47–54). New York: Brunner/Mazel.

Maddux, J. (2002). Stopping the "madness": Positive psychology and the deconstruction of the illness ideology and the DSM. In C. Snyder & S. Lopez (Eds.), *Handbook of positive psychology* (pp. 13–25). New York: Oxford.

Maheu, M., & Gordon, B. (2000). Counseling and therapy on the Internet. *Professional Psychology: Research and Practice, 31*, 484–489.

Mahler, M. (1968). *On human symbiosis and the vicissitudes of individuation: Vol. 1. Infantile psychosis.* New York: International Universities Press.

Mahler, M. (1971). A study of the separation-individuation process and its possible application to borderline phenomena in the psychoanalytic situation. *Psychoanalytic Study of the Child, 26*, 403–424.

Mahler, M., Pine, F., & Bergman, A. (1975). *The psychological birth of the human infant.* New York: Basic Books.

Mahoney, M. (1985). Psychotherapy and human change processes. In M. Mahoney & A. Freeman (Eds.), *Cognition and psychotherapy* (pp. 3–48). New York: Plenum.

Mahoney, M. (1991). *Human change processes.* New York: Basic Books.

Mahrer, A. (1989). *How to do experiential psychotherapy: A manual* for *practitioners.* Ottawa: University of Ottawa Press.

Mahrer, A. (1989). *The integration of the psychotherapies.* New York: Human Sciences Press.

Mahrer, A. (1993). What is "experiencing"?: A critical review of meanings and applications in psychotherapy. *The Humanistic Psychologist, 21*, 2–25.

Mahrer, A. (1996). *The complete guide to experiential psychotherapy.* New York: Wiley.

Mahrer, A. (2004). *Why do research in psychotherapy? Introduction to a revolution.* London, UK: Whurr.

Mahrer, A., Gagnon, R., Fairweather, D., & Cote, P. (1992). How to determine if a session is a very good one. *Journal of Integrative and Eclectic Psychotherapy, 11*, 8–23.

Mahrer, A., & Nadler, W. (1986). Good moments in psychotherapy: A preliminary review, a list, and some promising research avenues. *Journal of Consulting and Clinical Psychology, 54*, 10–15.

Mahrer, A., White, M., Souliere, M., Macphee, D., & Boulet, D. (1991). Intensive process analysis of significant in-session client change events and antecedent therapist methods. *Journal of Integrative and Eclectic Psychotherapy, 10*, 38–55.

Main, M. (1996). Introduction to the special section on attachment and psychopathology: 2. Overview of the field of attachment. *Journal of Consulting and clinical Psychology, 64,* 237–243.

Malcolm, J. (1981). *Psychoanalysis: The impossible profession.* New York: Vintage.

Marecek, J., & Hare-Mustin, R. (1991). A short history of the future: Feminism and clinical psychology. *Psychology of Women Quarterly, 15*, 521–536.

Marra, T. (2005). *Dialectical behavior therapy in practice: A practical and comprehensive guide.* Oakland: New Harbinger Press.

Martin, J. (1997). Mindfulness: A proposed common factor. *Journal of Psychotherapy Integration, 7*, 291–312.

Martin, J., Paivio, S., Labadie, D. (1990). Memory-enhancing characteristics of client-recalled important events in cognitive and experiential therapy: Integrating cognitive experimental and therapeutic psychology. *Counseling Psychology Quarterly, 3*, 239–256.

Marziali, E. (1992). The etiology of borderline personality disorder: Developmental factors. In J. F. Clarkin, E. Marziali, & H. Munroe-Blum (Eds.), *Borderline personality disorder: Clinical and empirical perspectives* (pp. 27–44). New York: Guilford.

Masson, J. (1984). *The assault on truth: Freud's suppression of the seduction theory.* New York: Farrar, Straus & Giroux.

Masson, J. (Ed.). (1985). *The complete letters of Sigmund Freud to Wilhelm Fliess 1887–1904.* Cambridge, MA: Harvard University Press.

Masterson, J. (1981). *The narcissistic and borderline disorders: An integrated developmental approach.* New York: Brunner/Mazel.

Masterson, J. (1985). *The real self: A developmental, self and object relations approach.* New York: Brunner/Mazel.

Matarazzo, J. (1986). Computerized clinical psychological test interpretations: Unvalidated plus all mean and no sigma. *American Psychologist, 41*, 14–24.

Matarazzo, J. (1992). Psychological testing and assessment in the 21st century. *American Psychologist, 47*, 1007–1018.

Maultsby, M. (1975). *Help yourself to happiness.* New York: Institute for Rational-Emotive Therapy.

May, R. (1981). *Freedom and destiny.* New York: Norton.

May, R., Angel, E., & Ellenberger, H. F. (Eds.). (1958). *Existence: A new dimension in psychiatry and psychology.* New York: Basic Books.

May, R., & Yalom, I. (1984). Existential psychotherapy. In R. J. Corsini (Ed.), *Current psychotherapies* (3rd ed.). Itasca, IL: Peacock.

Mays, V., Rubin, J., Sabourin, M., & Walker, L. (1997). Moving toward a global psychology: Changing theories and practice to meet the needs of a changing world. *American Psychologist, 52,* 485–487.

McCrae, R., & Costa, P. (1990). *Personality in adulthood.* New York: Guilford.

Meehl, P. (1954). *Clinical versus statistical prediction: A theoretical analysis and review of the evidence.* Minneapolis: University of Minnesota Press.

Meehl, P. (1956). Wanted—A good cookbook. *American Psychologist, 11,* 263–272.

Meehl, P. (1965). Seer over sign: The first good example. *Journal of Experimental Research in Personality, 1,* 27–32.

Meichenbaum, D. (1977). *Cognitive behavior modification: An integrative approach.* New York: Plenum.

Meichenbaum, D. (1986). Cognitive behavior modification. In E. L. Shostrom (Producer), *Three approaches to psychotherapy: III* (film). Corona Del Mar, CA: Psychological and Educational Films.

Meichenbaum, D. (1995). Changing conceptions of cognitive behavior modification: Retrospect and prospect. In M. J. Mahoney (Ed.), *Cognitive and constructive psychotherapies* (pp. 20–26). New York: Springer.

Meichenbaum, D., & Gilmore, J. B. (1984). The nature of unconscious processes: A cognitive-behavioral perspective. In K. S. Bowers & D. Meichenbaum (Eds.), *The unconscious reconsidered* (pp. 273–298). New York: Wiley.

Messer, S. (1986). Eclecticism in psychotherapy: Underlying assumptions, problems, and tradeoffs. In J. C. Norcross (Ed.), *Handbook of eclectic psychotherapy* (pp. 379–397). New York: Brunner/Mazel.

Messer, S. (1994). Adapting psychotherapy outcome research to clinical reality: A response to Wolfe. *Journal of Psychotherapy Integration (Newsletter Section), 4,* 280–282.

Messer, S., & Warren, S. (1990). Personality change and psychotherapy. In L. Pervin (Ed.), *Handbook of personality* (pp. 371–398). New York: Guilford.

Messick, S. (1995). Validity of psychological assessment: Validation of inferences from persons' responses and performances as scientific inquiry into score meaning. *American Psychologist, 50,* 741–749.

Miller, I. (1996). Time-limited brief therapy has gone too far: The result is invisible rationing. *Professional Psychology: Research and Practice, 27,* 567–576.

Miller, S., Duncan, B., & Hubble, M. (1996). *Escape from babel.* New York: Norton.

Miller, W. (2000). Rediscovering fire: Small interventions, large effects. *Psychology of Addictive Behaviors, 14,* 6–18.

Miller, W., & Rollnick, S. (2002). *Motivational interviewing* (2nd ed.). New York: Guilford.

Miller, W., Taylor, C., & West, J. (1980). Focused versus broad spectrum behavior therapy for problem drinkers. *Journal of Consulting and Clinical Psychology, 48,* 590–601.

Millon, T., Davis, R., Millon, C., Escovar, L., & Meagher, S. (2000). *Personality disorders in modern life.* New York: Wiley.

Minuchin, S. (1974). *Families and family therapy.* Cambridge, MA: Harvard University Press.

Mitchell, S. (1988). *Relational concepts in psychoanalysis.* Cambridge, MA: Harvard University Press.

Mitchell, S. (1997). *Hope and dread in psychoanalysis.* New York: Basic Books.

Moore, S. (2001). Substance abuse treatment with adolescent African American males: Reality therapy with an Afrocentric approach. *Journal of Social Work Practice in the Addictions, 1,* 21–32.

Moreno, J. (1934). *Who shall survive?* New York: Nervous and Mental Disease Publishing.

Morey, L., Gunderson, J., Quigley, B., Shea, T., Skodol, A., McGlashan, T., et al. (2002). The representation of borderline, avoidant, obsessive-compulsive, and schizotypal personality disorders by the Five-Factor Model. *Journal of Personality Disorders, 16,* 215–234.

Morokoff, P. (1985). Effects of sex guilt, repression, sexual "arousibility," and sexual experience on female sexual arousal during erotica and fantasy. *Journal of Personality and Social Psychology, 49,* 177–187.

Moser, D. (1965, May 7). Screams, slaps, and love. *Life,* pp. 90a–101.
Mosher, L. (2001). Treating madness without hospitals: Soteria and its successors. In K. J. Schneider, J. F. T. Bugental, & J. Fraser Pierson (Eds.), *The handbook of humanistic psychology* (pp. 389–402). Thousand Oaks, CA: Sage.
Moss, E., & St.-Laurent, D. (2001). Attachment at school age and academic performance. *Developmental Psychology, 37,* 863–874.
Mowrer, O. (1947). On the dual nature of learning—A reinterpretation of "conditioning" and "problem-solving." *Harvard Educational Review, 17,* 102–148.
Mowrer, O., & Lamoreaux, R. (1946). Fear as an intervening variable in avoidance conditioning. *Journal of Comparative Psychology, 39,* 29–50.
Mowrer, O., & Solomon, L. (1954). Contiguity vs. drive-reduction in conditioned fear: The proximity and abruptness of drive-reduction. *American Journal of Psychology, 67,* 15–25.
Mullahy, P. (1952). *The contributions of Harry Stack Sullivan.* New York: Hermitage Press.
Murray, H. (1938). *Explorations in personality.* New York: Oxford University Press.
Myers, I. (1962). *Manual: The Myers-Briggs Indicator.* Palo Alto, CA: Consulting Psychologists Press.
Myers, I. (1977). *Supplementary Manual: The Myers-Briggs Type Indicator.* Palo Alto, CA: Consulting Psychologists Press.
Naglieri, J., Drasgow, F., Schmit, M., Handler, L., Prifitera, A., Margolis, A., & Velasquez, R. (2004). Psychological testing on the Internet: New problems, old issues. *American Psychologist, 59,* 150–162.
Neal-Barnett, A., & Smith, J. (1996). African American children and behavior therapy: Considering the Afrocentric approach. *Cognitive and Behavioral Practice, 3,* 351–369.
Neimeyer, R. (1988). Integrative directions in personal construct therapy. *International Journal of Personal Construct Psychology, 1,* 283–298.
Neimeyer, R., & Mahoney, M. (1995). *Constructivism in psychotherapy.* Washington, DC: American Psychological Association.
Neisser, U. (1988). Five kinds of self-knowledge. *Philosophical Psychology, 1,* 35–59.
Neisser, U., Boodoo, G., Bouchard, T. J., Boykin, A. W., Brody, N., Ceci, S. J., et al. (1996). Intelligence: Knowns and unknowns. *American Psychologist, 51,* 77–101.
Nicholson, R., & Berman, J. (1983). Is follow-up necessary in evaluating psychotherapy? *Psychological Bulletin, 93,* 261–278.
Nisbett, R., & Ross, L. (1980). *Human inference: Strategies and shortcomings of social judgment.* Englewood Cliffs, NJ: Prentice-Hall.
Nobins, L., & Helzer, J. (1986). Diagnosis and clinical assessment: The current state of psychiatric diagnosis. In M. R. Rosenzweig & L. W. Porter (Eds.), *Annual review of psychology* (pp. 55–69). Palo Alto, CA: Annual Reviews.
Norcross, J. (Ed.). (1993). The relationship of choice: Matching the therapist's interpersonal stance to individual clients (Special Section). *Psychotherapy, 30,* 402–426.
Norcross, J. (Ed.). (2002). *Psychotherapy relationships that work.* New York: Oxford.
Norcross, J. (2005). A primer on psychotherapy integration. In J. Norcross & M. Goldfried (Eds.), *Handbook of psychotherapy integration* (2nd ed.). New York: Oxford.
Norcross, J., Beutler, L., & Levant, R. (Eds.) (in press). *Evidence-based practices in mental health: Debate and dialogue on the fundamental questions.* Washington, DC: American Psychological Association.
Norem, J. (1989). Cognitive strategies as personality: Effectiveness, specificity, flexibility, and change. In D. M. Buss & N. Cantor (Eds.), *Personality psychology: Recent trends and emerging directions* (pp. 45–60). New York: Springer-Verlag.
Norem, J. (2002). Defensive self-deception and social adaptation among optimists. *Journal of Research in Personality, 36,* 549–555.

O'Farrell, T., Choquette, K., Cutter, H., Brown, E., et al. (1996). Cost-benefit and cost-effectiveness analyses of behavioral marital therapy with and without relapse prevention sessions for alcoholics and their spouses. *Behavior Therapy, 27*, 7–24.

O'Hanlon, W., & Weiner-Davis, M. (1989). *In search of solutions: A new direction in psychotherapy.* New York: Norton.

O'Hara, M. (1992, April). *Selves-in-context: The challenge for psychotherapy in a postmodern world,* Invited Address at the Conference of the Society for the Exploration of Psychotherapy Integration, San Diego, CA.

O'Hara, M., & Anderson, W. (1991, September/October). Welcome to the postmodern world. *The Family Therapist Networker,* 19–25.

Ogrodniczuk, J., Piper, W., Joyce, A., McCallum, M., & Rosie, J. (2003). NEO-Five Factor personality traits as predictors of response to two forms of group psychotherapy. *International Journal of Group Therapy, 53*, 417–442.

Ollendick, T., & King, N. (in press). Empirically supported therapies (ESTs) typically produce outcomes superior to non-EST therapies. In J. C. Norcross, L. E. Beutler, & R. Levant (Eds.), *Evidence-based practices in mental health: Debate and dialogue on the fundamental questions.* Washington, DC: American Psychological Association.

Orlinsky, D., Grawe, K., & Parks, B. (1994). Process and outcome in psychotherapy. In A. E. Bergin & S. L. Garfield (Eds.), *Handbook of psychotherapy and behavior change* (pp. 270–378). New York: Wiley

Orne, M. (1962). On the social psychology of the psychological experiment with particular reference to demand characteristics and their implications. *American Psychologist, 17*, 776–783.

Oskamp, S. (1988). Nontraditional employment opportunities for applied psychologists. *American Psychologist, 43*, 484–485.

Osler, W. (1892). *Lectures on angina pectoris and allied states.* New York: Appleton.

Osterrieth, P. (1944). Le test de copie d'une figure complexe. *Archives de psychologie, 30*, 206–356.

Paivio, A. (1986). *Mental representations: A dual coding approach.* New York: Oxford University Press.

Paivio, S., & Greenberg, L. (1995). Resolving unfinished business: Experiential therapy using empty chair dialogue. *Journal of Consulting & Clinical Psychology, 63*, 419–425.

Palmatier, J., & Bornstein, P. (1980). The effects of subliminal stimulation of symbiotic merging fantasies on behavioral treatment of smokers. *Journal of Nervous and Mental Disease, 168*, 715–720.

Patterson, D. (2004). Treating pain with hypnosis. *Current Directions in Psychological Science, 13*, 252–255.

Patterson, G. (1982). *Coercive family process.* Eugene, OR: Castalia.

Patterson, G., & Chamberlain, P. (1994). A functional analysis of resistance during parent training therapy. *Clinical Psychology, 1*, 53–70.

Pedersen, P. (1983). Asian personality theory. In R. J. Corsim & A. J. Marsella (Eds.), *Personality theories, research, and assessment.* Itasca, IL: Peacock.

Pewewardy, N. (2004). The political is personal: The essential obligation of white feminist family therapists to deconstruct white privilege. *Journal of Feminist Family Therapy, 16*, 53–67.

Philadelphia Inquirer. (2005, April 4). Cognitive therapy as effective as drug in treating depression. Section A, p. 1.

Piper, W., Joyce, A., McCallum, M., & Azim, H. (1998). Interpretive and supportive forms of psychotherapy and patient personality variables. *Journal of Consulting and Clinical Psychology, 66*, 558–567.

Practice Directorate Staff. (2005). Prescription for success. *Monitor on Psychology, 36*, 25.

Prigogine, I., & Stengers, I. (1984). *Order out of chaos: Man's new dialogue with nature.* New York: Bantam.

Prochaska, J. (1984). *Systems of psychotherapy.* Homewood, IL: Dorsey Press.

Prochaska, J. (2004). Population treatment for addictions. *Current Directions in Psychological Science, 13,* 242–246.

Prochaska, J., Norcross, J., & DiClemente, C. (1994). *Changing for good.* New York: Morrow.

Propst, L., Olstrom, R., Watkins, P., Dean, T., & Mashburn, D. (1992). Comparative efficacy of religious and non-religious cognitive-behavior therapy for the treatment of clinical depression in religious individuals. *Journal of Consulting and Clinical Psychology, 60,* 94–103.

Pyszczynski, T., Greenberg, J., Solomon, S., Arndt, J., & Schimel, J. (2004). Why do people need self-esteem? A theoretical and empirical review. *Psychological Bulletin, 130,* 435–468.

Ramsay, M., Reynolds, C., & Kamphaus, R. (2002). *Essentials of behavioral assessment.* New York: Wiley.

Reid, J., Patterson, G., & Snyder, J. (2002). *Antisocial behavior in children and adolescents: A developmental analysis and the Oregon model for intervention.* Washington, DC: American Psychological Association.

Reiss, D., & Price, R. (1996). National research agenda for prevention research: The National Institute of Mental Health Report. *American Psychologist, 51,* 1109–1115.

Reitan, R., & Davison, L. (1974). *Clinical neuropsychology: Current status and applications.* Washington, DC: Winston.

Reitan, R., & Wolfson, D. (2004). Use of the Progressive Figures Test in evaluating brain-damaged children, children with academic problems, and normal controls. *Archives of Clinical Neuropsychology, 19,* 305–312.

Rennie, D. (2002). Experiencing psychotherapy: Grounded theory studies. In D. J. Cain & J. Seeman (Eds.), *Humanistic psychotherapies: Handbook of research and practice* (pp. 117–144). Washington, DC: American Psychological Association.

Resnick, R. (1997). A brief history of practice—expanded. *American Psychologist, 52,* 463–468.

Rice, L., & Greenberg, L. (Eds.). (1984). *Patterns of change.* New York: Guilford.

Rice, L., & Saperia, E. (1984). Task analysis of the resolution of problematic reactions. In L. N. Rice & L. S. Greenberg, (Eds.), *Patterns of change: Intensive analysis of psychotherapy process.* (pp. 29–66). New York: Guilford.

Ricker, J. (2004) *Differential diagnosis in adult neuropsychological assessment.* New York: Springer.

Rizvi, S., & Linehan, M. (2001). Dialectical behavior therapy for personality disorders. *Current Psychiatry Reports, 3,* 64–69.

Roberts, A. (1985). Biofeedback: Research, training, and clinical roles. *American Psychologist, 40,* 938–941.

Rogers, C. (1942). *Counseling and psychotherapy.* Boston: Houghton Mifflin.

Rogers, C. (1957). The necessary and sufficient conditions of therapeutic personality change. *Journal of Consulting Psychology, 21,* 95–103.

Rogers, C. (1961). *On becoming a person.* Boston: Houghton Mifflin.

Rogers, C. (1965). *Client-centered therapy* (Film No. 1). In E. Shostrom (Ed.), *Three approaches to psychotherapy* (Three 16-mm color motion pictures). Santa Ana, CA: Psychological Films.

Rogers, C. (1967). Toward a modern approach to values: The valuing process in the mature person. In C. R. Rogers & B. Stevens (Eds.), *Person to person: The problem of being human.* New York: Pocket Books.

Rogers, C. (1977). *Carl Rogers on personal power.* New York: Delacorte.

Rogers, C. (1980). Do we need "a" reality? In C. R. Rogers (Ed.), *A way of being.* Boston: Houghton Mifflin.

Rogers, C., Gendlin, E., Kiesler, D., & Truax, C. (1967). *The therapeutic relationship and its impact: A study of psychotherapy with schizophrenics.* Madison: University of Wisconsin Press.

Rogers, C., & Sanford, R. (1985). Client-centered psychotherapy. In H. I. Kaplan & B. J. Sadock (Eds.), *Comprehensive textbook of psychiatry* (Vol. 4). New York: Praeger.

Rohde, A. (1957). *The sentence completion method.* New York: Ronald Press.

Rorschach, H. (1921). *Psychodiagnostik.* Bern: Bircher.

Rosenbaum, R. (1994). Single-session therapies: Intrinsic integration? *Journal of Psychotherapy Integration, 4,* 229–252.

Rosenbaum, R., Hoyt, M., & Talmon, M. (1990). The challenge of single-session therapies. In R. A. Wells & V. J. Giannetti (Eds.), *Handbook of the brief psychotherapies* (pp. 165–189). New York: Basic Books.

Rosenhan, D. (1973). On being sane in insane places. *Science, 179,* 180, 250–258, 365–369.

Rosman, B., Minuchin, S., Liebman, R., & Baker, L. (1978, November). *Family therapy for psychosomatic children.* Paper presented at the annual meeting of the American Academy of Psychosomatic Medicine, Atlanta, GA.

Ross, L., Lepper, M., Strack, F., & Steinmetz, J. (1977). Social explanation and social expectation: The effects of real and hypothetical explanations upon subjective likelihood. *Journal of Personality and Social Psychology, 35,* 817–829.

Rossi, E. (Ed.). (1980). *The collected papers of Milton H. Erickson on hypnosis: Volume III. Hypnotic investigation of psychodynamic processes.* New York: Irvington.

Roth, A., & Fonagy, P. (1996). *What works for whom? A critical review of psychotherapy research.* New York: Guilford Press.

Rotter, J., & Rafferty, J. (1950). *The Rotter Incomplete Sentences Blank.* New York: Psychological Corporation.

Rowe, C., & Mac Isaac, D. (1991). *Empathic attunement: The technique of psychoanalytic self psychology.* Northvale, NJ: Jason Aronson.

Rozin, P. (2001). Social psychology and science: Some lessons from Solomon Asch. *Personality and Social Psychology Review, 5,* 2–14.

Rutter, M. (1986). The developmental psychopathology of depression: Issues and perspectives. In M. Rutter, C. E. Izard, & P. B. Read (Eds.), *Depression in young children: Developmental and clinical perspectives* (pp. 3–32). New York: Guilford.

Ryle, A. (1982). *Psychotherapy: A cognitive integration of theory and practice.* New York: Grune & Stratton.

Safran, J., & Greenberg, L. (1982). Eliciting "hot cognitions" in cognitive therapy. *Canadian Psychology, 23,* 83–87.

Safran, J., & Segal, Z. (1990). *Interpersonal process in cognitive therapy.* New York: Basic Books.

Sampson, E. E. (1981). Cognitive psychology as ideology. *American Psychologist, 36,* 730–743.

Sandell, R., Blomberg, J., Lazar, A., Carlsswon, J., Broberg, J., & Schubert, J. (2000). Varieties of long-term outcome among patients in psychoanalysis and long-term psychotherapy: A review of findings in the Stockholm Outcome of Psychoanalysis and Psychotherapy Project (STOPP). *International Journal of Psychoanalysis, 81,* 921–942.

Sarbin, T. (1950). Contributions to role-taking theory: I. Hypnotic behavior. *Psychological Review, 57,* 255–270.

Sartre, J. (1956). *Being and nothingness.* New York: Philosophical Library.

Satir, V. (1967). *Conjoint family therapy.* Palo Alto, CA: Science and Behavior Books.

Schafer, R. (1978). *Language and insight.* New Haven, CT: Yale University Press.

Schafer, R. (1992). *Retelling a life.* New York: Basic Books.

Schmitt, R. (1969). *Martin Heidegger on being human: An introduction to Zein and Zeit.* New York: Random House.

Schneider, B., Atkinson, L, & Tardif, C. (2001). Child-parent attachment and children's peer relations: A quantitative review. *Developmental Psychology, 37,* 86–100.

Schneider, K. (2003). Existential-humanistic psychotherapies. In A. Gurman & S. Messer (Eds.), *Essential psychotherapies* (2nd ed., pp. 149–181). New York: Guilford.

Schneider, K., & May, R. (1995). *The psychology of existence: An integrative, clinical perspective.* New York: McGraw-Hill.

Schneiderman, N. (2004). Psychosocial, behavioral, and biological aspects of chronic diseases. *Current Directions in Psychological Science, 13,* 247–251.

Segal, D., & Murray, E. (1994). Emotional processing in cognitive therapy and vocal expression of feeling. *Journal of Social and Clinical Psychology, 13,* 189–206.

Segal, Z., Williams, M., &Teasdale, J. (2001). *Mindfulness-based cognitive therapy for depression.* New York: Guilford.

Seligman, M. (1990). *Learned optimism.* New York: Knopf.

Seligman, M. (1995). The effectiveness of psychotherapy: The *Consumer Reports* study. *American Psychologist, 50,* 965–974.

Seligman, M. (2002). Positive psychology, positive prevention, and positive therapy. In C. R. Snyder & S. J. Lopez (Eds.), *Handbook of positive psychology* (pp. 3–12). New York: Oxford.

Selvini Palazzoli, M., Cecchin, G., Prata, G., & Boscola, L. (1978). *Paradox and counterparadox.* New York: Aronson.

Sexton, T., & Alexander, J. (1999). *Functional family therapy: Principles of clinical intervention, assessment, and implementation.* Henderson, NV: FFT.

Sexton, T., Alexander, J., & Mease, A. (2004). Levels of evidence for the models and mechanisms of therapeutic change in family and couple therapy. In M. J. Lambert (Ed.), *Bergin and Garfield's handbook of psychotherapy and behavior change* (5th ed., pp. 590–646). New York: Wiley.

Shadish, W., Ragsdale, K., Glaser, R., & Montgomery, L. (1995). The efficacy and effectiveness of marital and family therapy: A perspective from meta-analysis. *Journal of Marital and Family Therapy, 21,* 345–360.

Shakow, D. (1949). *Report of the commission on clinical training.* Washington, DC: American Psychological Association.

Shapiro, D. (1995). Finding out how psychotherapies help people change. *Psychotherapy Research, 5,* 1–21.

Shapiro, F. (1995). *Eye movement desensitization and reprocessing.* New York: Guilford Press.

Shapiro, F., (2002a) EMDR 12 years after its introduction: Past and future research. *Journal of Clinical Psychology, 58,* 1–22.

Shapiro, F. (Ed.). (2002b) EMDR as an integrative psychotherapy approach: Experts of diverse orientations explore the paradigm prism. Washington, DC: American Psychological Association.

Shepard, M. (1975). *Fritz.* New York: Bantam Books.

Shevrin, H. (1973). Brain wave correlates of subliminal stimulation, unconscious attention, primary- and secondary-process thinking, and repressiveness (Monograph 30). *Psychological Issues, 8,* 56–87.

Shlien, J. (1988, September). *The future is more important than the past in determining present behavior.* Paper presented at the 1st International Conference on Client-centered and Experiential Psychotherapy, Leuven, Belgium.

Silverman, L., & Weinberger, J. (1985). Mommy and I are one: Implications for psychotherapy. *American Psychologist, 40,* 1296–1308.

Silverman, W. (1996). Cookbooks, manuals, and paint-by-numbers: Psychotherapy in the 90's. *Psychotherapy, 33,* 207–215.

Silverman, W., & Treffers, P. (Eds.). (2001). *Anxiety disorders in children and adolescents: Research, assessment and intervention.* Cambridge, UK: Cambridge University Press.

Simkin, J., & Yontef, G. (1984). Gestalt therapy. In R. J. Corsini (Ed.), *Current psychotherapies* (3rd ed., pp. 279–319). Itasca, IL: Peacock.

Simon, G., Evette, M., Ludman, J., Tutty, S., Operskalski, B., & Von Korff, M. (2004). Telephone psychotherapy and telephone care management for primary care patients starting antidepressant treatment: A randomized controlled trial. *Journal of the American Medical Association, 292,* 935–942.

Skinner, B. F. (1938). *The behavior of organisms.* New York: Appleton-Century.

Skinner, B. F. (1971). *Beyond freedom and dignity.* New York: Knopf.

Skinner, B. F. (1987). Whatever happened to psychology as the science of behavior? *American Psychologist, 42,* 780–786.

Sloane, R., Staples, F., Cristol, A., Yorkston, N., & Whipple, K. (1975). *Psychotherapy versus behavior therapy.* Cambridge, MA: Harvard University Press.

Smith, D. (1982). Trends in counseling and psychotherapy. *American Psychologist, 37,* 802–809.

Smith, M., Glass, G., & Miller, T. (1980). *The benefits of psychotherapy.* Baltimore, MD: Johns Hopkins University Press.

Smith, T., Kendall, P., and Keefe, F. (2002). Behavioral medicine and clinical health psychology: Introduction to the special issue, a view from the decade of behavior. *Journal of Consulting and Clinical Psychology, 70,* special edition.

Snyder, C., & Lopez, S. (Eds.). (2002). *Handbook of positive psychology.* New York: Oxford.

Snyder, C., Michael, S., & Cheavens, J. (1999). Hope as a psychotherapeutic foundation of common factors, placebos, and expectancies. In M. A. Hubble, B. Duncan, & S. Miller (Eds). *The heart and soul of change* (pp. 179–200). Washington, DC: American Psychological Association.

Society of Psychological Hypnosis. (2005). Division 30—Psychological Hypnosis. Retrieved June 23, 2005, from www.apa.org/divisions/div30/

Solomon, A., & Haaga, D. (2003). Cognitive theory and therapy of depression. In M. A. Reinecke & D. Clark (Eds.), *Cognitive therapy across the lifespan* (pp. 12–39). Cambridge, UK: Cambridge University Press.

Spanos, N. (1991). A sociocognitive approach to hypnosis. In S. J. Lynn & J. W. Rhue (Eds.), *Theories of hypnosis: Current models and perspectives.* New York: Guilford Press.

Spanos, N., & Chaves, J. (Eds.). (1989). *Hypnosis: The cognitive-behavioral perspective.* Buffalo, NY: Prometheus Books.

Sparrow, S., & Davis, S. (2000). Recent advances in the assessment of intelligence and cognition. *Journal of Child Psychology and Psychiatry, 41,* 117–123.

Spearman, C. (1904). "General intelligence," objectively determined and measured. *American Journal of Psychology, 15,* 201–293.

Spence, D. (1982). *Narrative truth and historical truth: Meaning and interpretation in psychoanalysis.* New York: Norton.

Spokane, A. (1979). Occupational preferences and the validity of the Strong-Campbell Interest inventory for college women and men. *Journal of Counseling Psychology, 26,* 312–318.

St. Clair, M. (1986). *Object relations and self psychology: An introduction.* Monterey, CA: Brooks/Cole.

Stampfl, T., & Levis, D. (1973). *Implosive therapy: Theory and technique.* Morristown, NJ: General Learning Press.

Steele, H., Steele, M., & Fonagy, P. (1996). Associations among attachment classifications of mothers, fathers, and their infants. *Child Development, 67,* 541–555.

Stefanek, M., Hess, S., & Nelson, W. (2005). Behavioral and social science research at the National Institutes of Health: Is the mission being fulfilled? *Observer, 18,* 11–17.

Stern, D. (1985). *The interpersonal world of the infant: A view from psychoanalysis and developmental psychology.* New York: Basic Books.

Sternberg, R., (2000*). Handbook of intelligence.* New York: Cambridge University Press.

Stiles, W. (1993). Quality control in qualitative research. *Clinical Psychology Review, 13,* 593–618.

Stiles, W. (2002). Assimilation of problematic experiences. In J. Norcross (Ed.), *Psychotherapy relationships that work* (pp. 357–366). New York: Oxford.

Stiles, W., Barkham, M., Shapiro, D., & Firth-Cozens, J. (1992). Treatment order and thematic continuity between contrasting psychotherapies: Exploring an implication of the assimilation model. *Psychotherapy Research, 2,* 112–124.

Stiles, W., Shapiro, D., & Elliott, R. (1986). Are all psychotherapies equivalent? *American Psychologist, 41*, 65–180.
Stolorow, R. (1992). Closing the gap between theory and practice with better psychoanalytic theory. *Psychotherapy, 29*, 159–166.
Stolorow, R., & Atwood, G. (1979). *Faces in a cloud: Subjectivity in personality theory.* New York: Aronson.
Stolorow, R., Brandchaft, B., & Atwood, G. (1987). *Psychoanalytic treatment: An intersubjective approach.* Hillsdale, NJ: Analytic Press.
Stricker, G., & Gold, J. (2003). Integrative approaches to psychotherapy. In A. Gurman & S. Messer (Eds.), *Essential psychotherapies* (2nd ed., pp. 317–349). New York: Guilford.
Strom, L., Pettersson, R., & Andersson, G. (2000). A controlled trial of self-help treatment of recurrent headache conducted via the Internet. *Journal of Consulting and Clinical Psychology, 68*, 722–727.
Strupp, H., & Binder, J. (1984). *Psychotherapy in a new key: A guide to time-limited dynamic psychotherapy.* New York: Basic Books.
Strupp, H., Horowitz, L., & Lambert, M. (Eds.). (1997). *Measuring patient changes.* Washington, DC: American Psychological Association.
Sue, D. (2004). Whiteness and ethnocentric monoculturalism: Making the "invisible" visible. *American Psychologist, 59,* 761–769.
Sue, D., Ivey, A., & Pedersen, P. (Eds.). (1996). *A theory of multicultural counseling and therapy.* Belmont, CA: Brooks/Cole.
Sue, D., & Sue, D. (1999). *Counseling the culturally different: Theory and practice.* New York: Wiley.
Summit, R. (1987, January 16). *Introduction to the problem of child abuse.* Paper presented at the Child Abuse Reporting Course, Harbor-UCLA Medical Center, Torrance, CA.
Super, D. (1955). Transition: From vocational guidance to counseling psychology. *Journal of Counseling Psychology, 2*, 3–9.
Szasz, T. (1961). *The myth of mental illness: Foundations of a theory of personal conduct.* New York: Harper & Row.
Tallman, K. (1996). *The state of mind theory: Goal orientation concepts applied to clinical psychology.* Unpublished Master's thesis, California State University Dominguez Hills.
Tanner, L., & Lyness, K. (2003). Out of the closet, still in the home: Providing queer affirmative therapy for youth and their families. *Journal of Feminist Family Therapy, 15*, 21–34.
Task Force on Promotion and Dissemination of Psychological Procedures, Division of Clinical Psychology of the American Psychological Association (1995). Training and dissemination of empirically validated psychological treatments: Report and recommendations. *The Clinical Psychologist, 48*, 3–23.
Task Force on Psychological Intervention Guidelines. (1995). *Template for developing guidelines: Interventions for mental disorders and psychosocial aspects of physical disorders.* Washington DC: American Psychological Association.
Tate, D., Wing, R., & Winett, R. (2001). Using Internet-based technology to deliver a behavioral weight loss program. *Journal of the American Medical Association, 285*, 1172–1177.
Taub, E. (2004). Harnessing brain plasticity through behavioral techniques to produce new treatments in neurorehabilitation. *American Psychologist, 59*, 692–706.
Taylor, M. (1999). Changing what has gone before: The enhancement of an inadequate psychology through the use of an Afrocentric-feminist perspective with African American women in therapy. *Psychotherapy: Theory, Research, Practice, and Training, 36*, 170–179.
Taylor, S., & Brown, J. (1988). Illusion and well-being: A social-psychological perspective on mental health. *Psychological Bulletin, 103*, 193–210.
Tedeschi, R., Park, C., & Calhoun, L. (Eds.). (1998). *Posttraumatic growth.* Mahwah, NJ: Erlbaum.
Terman, L. (1916). *The measurement of intelligence.* Boston: Houghton Mifflin.

Thompson, S. (2002). The role of personal control in adaptive functioning. In C. Snyder & S. Lopez (Eds.), *Handbook of positive psychology* (pp. 202–213). New York: Oxford.

Tillich, P. (1952). *The courage to be.* New Haven, CT: Yale University Press.

Tobin, S. (1990). Self psychology as a bridge between existential humanistic psychology and psychoanalysis. *Journal of Humanistic Psychology, 30,* 14–63.

Truax, C., & Carkhuff, R. (1967). *Toward effective counseling and psychotherapy: Training and practice.* Chicago: Aldine.

Turner, J., Herron, L., & Weiner, P. (1986). Utility of the MMPI Pain Assessment Index in predicting outcome after lumbar surgery. *Journal of Clinical Psychology, 42,* 764–769.

U.S. Department of Health and Human Services. (1999). *Mental health: A report of the surgeon general—Executive summary* (pp. 289–291). www.surgeongeneral.gov/library/mentalhealth/summary.html

U.S. Surgeon General. (1979). *Healthy people: The surgeon general's report on health promotion and disease prevention.* Washington, DC: U.S. Government Printing Office (Publication No. 79-55071).

Vaillant, G. (1995). *Adaptation to life.* Cambridge, MA: Harvard University Press.

Van Balen, R. (1990). The therapeutic relationship according to Carl Rogers: Only a climate? A dialogue? Or both? In G. Lietaer, J. Rombauts, & R. Van Balen (Ed.), *Client-centered and experiential psychotherapy in the nineties* (pp. 65–86). Leuven, Belgium: Leuven University Press.

Vernberg, E., Routh, D., & Koocher, G. (1992). The future of psychotherapy with children: Developmental psychotherapy. *Psychotherapy, 29,* 72–80.

Vinogradov, S., & Yalom, I. (2003) *Group therapy.* Washington, DC: American Psychiatric Association.

Wachtel, E. (1994). *Treating troubled children and their families.* New York: Guilford.

Wachtel, P. (1997). *Psychoanalysis, behavior therapy, and the relational world.* Washington, DC: American Psychological Association.

Wampold, B. (1997). Methodological problems in identifying efficacious psychotherapies. *Psychotherapy Research, 7,* 21–43.

Wampold, B. (2001). *The great psychotherapy debate: Models, methods, and findings.* Mahwah, NJ: Erlbaum.

Wampold, B. (in press a). The therapist. In J. C. Norcross, L. E. Beutler, & R. Levant (Eds.), *Evidence-based practices in mental health: Debate and dialogue on the fundamental questions.* Washington, DC: American Psychological Association.

Wampold, B. (in press b). Not a scintilla of evidence to support ESTs as more effective than other treatments. In J. C. Norcross, L. E. Beutler, & R. Levant (Eds.), *Evidence-based practices in mental health: Debate and dialogue on the fundamental questions.* Washington, DC: American Psychological Association.

Wampold, B., Mondin, G., Moody, M., Stich, F., Benson, K., & Ahn, H. (1997). A meta-analysis of outcome studies comparing bona fide psychotherapies: Empirically, "All must have prizes." *Psychological Bulletin, 122,* 203–215.

Washburn, M. (1978). Observations relevant to a unified theory of meditation. *Journal of Transpersonal Psychology, 10,* 45–65.

Watkins, C., Campbell, V., Nieberding, R., & Hallmark, R. (1995). Contemporary practice of psychological assessment by clinical psychologists. *Professional Psychology: Research and Practice, 26,* 54–60.

Watson, J. and Rayner, R. (1920). Conditioned emotional reactions. *Journal of Experimental Psychology, 3,* 1–14.

Watson, J., & Rennie, D. (1994). Qualitative analysis of clients' subjective experience of significant moments during the exploration of problematic reactions. *Journal of Counseling Psychology, 41,* 500–509.

Watzlawick, P. (1978). *The language of change: Elements of therapeutic communication.* New York: Basic Books.

Watzlawick, P. (Ed.). (1984). *The invented reality: How do we know what we believe we know?* New York: Norton.

Watzlawick, P. (1985, December 13). *Brief therapeutic interventions.* Paper presented at the Evolution of Psychotherapy Conference, Phoenix, AZ.

Watzlawick, P. (1987). If you desire to see, learn how to act. In J. Zeig (Ed.), *The evolution of psychotherapy* (pp. 91–99). New York: Brunner/Mazel.

Watzlawick, P., Weakland, J., & Fisch, R. (1974). *Change: Principles of problem formation and problem resolution.* New York: Norton.

Weakland J., Fisch, R., Watzlawick, P., & Bodin, A. (1974). Brief therapy: Focused problem resolution. *Family Process, 13,* 141–168.

Weiner, B. (1980). *Human motivation.* New York: Holt, Rinehart, and Winston.

Weiner, B. (1982). The emotional consequences of causal attributions. In M. S. Clark & S. T. Fiske (Eds.), *Affect and cognition: The Seventeenth Annual Carnegie Symposium on Cognition.* Hillsdale, NJ: Erlbaum.

Weintraub, S., Winters, K., & Neale, J. (1986). Competence and vulnerability in children with an affectively disordered parent. In M. Rutter, C. E. Izard, & P. B. Read (Eds.), *Depression in young people: Developmental and clinical perspectives* (pp. 205–222). New York: Guilford.

Weiss, J., Sampson, H., & The Mount Zion Psychotherapy Research Group. (Eds.). (1986). *The psychoanalytic process.* New York: Guilford.

Weisz, J., Weiss, B., Alicke, M., & Klotz, M. (1987). Effectiveness of psychotherapy with children and adolescents: A meta-analysis for clinicians. *Journal of Consulting and Clinical Psychology, 55,* 542–549.

Weisz, J., Weiss, B., & Donenberg, G. (1992). The lab versus the clinic: Effects of child and adolescent psychotherapy. *American Psychologist, 47,* 1578–1585.

Werner, E., & Smith, R. (1982). *Vulnerable but invincible.* New York: McGraw-Hill.

Westen, D. (1998). The scientific legacy of Sigmund Freud: Toward a psychodynamically informed psychological science. *Psychological Bulletin, 124,* 333–371.

Westen, D., Lohr, N., Silk, K., Gold, L., & Kerber, K. (1990). Object relations and social cognition in borderlines, major depressives, and normals: A TAT analysis. *Psychological Assessment. A Journal of Consulting and Clinical Psychology, 2,* 355–364.

Westen, D., Ludolph, P., Block, M., Wixom, J., & Wiss, F. (1990). Developmental history and object relations in psychiatrically disturbed adolescent females. *American Journal of Psychiatry, 147,* 1061–1068.

Westen, D., Novotny, C., & Thompson-Brenner, H. (2004). The empirical status of empirically supported psychotherapies: Assumptions, findings, and reporting in controlled clinical trials. *Psychological Bulletin, 130,* 631–663.

Westen, D., & Weinberger, J. (2004). When clinical description becomes statistical description. *American Psychologist, 59,* 595–613.

Wexler, D., & Rice, L. (1974). *Innovations in client-centered therapy.* New York: Wiley.

Wheeler, G. (1991). *Gestalt reconsidered.* New York: Gardner.

White, M. (1993). Deconstruction and therapy. In S. Gilligan & R. Price (Eds.), *Therapeutic conversations.* New York: Norton.

White, M. (2004). Folk psychology and narrative practices. In L. Angus & J. McLeod (Eds.), *The handbook of narrative and psychotherapy: Practice, theory, and research* (pp. 15–52). Thousand Oaks, CA: Sage.

Wierzbicki, M. (1993). *Issues in clinical psychology.* Boston: Allyn & Bacon.

Wile, D. (2002). Collaborative couple therapy. In A. S. Gurman & N. S. Jacobson (Eds.), *Clinical handbook of couple therapy* (3rd ed., pp. 281–307). New York: Guilford.

Williams, L. (1992). Adult memories of childhood abuse: Preliminary findings from a longitudinal study. *The Advisor: American Professional Society on the Abuse of Children, 5*, 19–21.

Wilson, T. (2002). *Strangers to ourselves: Discovering the adaptive unconscious.* Cambridge, MA: Belknap Press of Harvard University Press.

Winnicot, D. (1965). *The maturational processes and the facilitating environment.* New York: International Universities Press.

Wolf, E. (1983). Concluding statement. In A. Goldberg (Ed.), *The future of psychoanalysis: Essays in honor of Heinz Kohut.* New York: International Universities Press.

Wolpe, J. (1958). *Psychotherapy by reciprocal inhibition.* Stanford, CA: Stanford University Press.

Wolpe, J. (1982). *The practice of behavior therapy* (3rd ed.). New York: Pergamon. www.aabt.org

Yalom, I. (1981). *Existential psychotherapy.* New York: Basic Books.

Zimring, F. (1990). Cognitive processes as a cause of psychotherapeutic change: Self-initiated processes. In G. Lietaer, J. Rombauts, & R. Van Balen (Eds.), *Client-centered and experiential psychotherapy in the nineties* (pp. 361–380). Leuven, Belgium: Leuven University Press.

Zirpoli, T., & Melloy, K. (2001). *Behavior management: Applications for teachers.* Upper Saddle River, NJ: Merrill.

Zukav, G. (1979). *The dancing Wu Li masters.* New York: Bantam Books.

Zytowski, D. (1976). Predictive validity of the Kuder Occupational Interest Survey: A 12-to 19-year follow-up. *Journal of Counseling Psychology, 3*, 221–233.

Web Sites Cited

www.apa.org
www.nationalregister.com
www.abpp.org
www.naswdc.org
www.aamft.org
www.aphsa.org
www.naadac.org
www.asch.net
www.sceh.us
www.apa.org/apags/profdev/prespriv.html
www.multiculturalskills.com
www.apa.org/practice/telehealth.html
www.helping.apa.org
www.adaa.org/public/selfhelp.cfm
www.mentalhelp.net/selfhelp/
www.mhselfhelp.org
www.rider.edu/~suler/psycyber/psycyber.html
www.fenichel.com/OnlineTherapy.shtml
www.metanoia.org/imhs/
www.ismho.org/
www.grohol.com/best/
www.caregiveralliance.com
www.cignaprovidersettlement.com
www.apapractice.org

INDEX